Rupert D.H. B

RUPERT BURSELL
GUILDHALL CHAMBERS
BROAD STREET
BRISTOL

A HISTORY OF THE ENGLISH BAR AND *ATTORNATUS* TO 1450

BY

HERMAN COHEN,
Of the Inner Temple, Barrister-at-Law.

Art thou made of the King's Counsel?—2 Chronicles xxv, 16.

Unum imperatorem in exercitu providere et consulere quid agendum sit debere; nunc per se, nunc cum iis quos advocaverit in consilium: qui non sint advocati, eos nec palam nec secreto jactare consilia sua.—*L. Æm. Paullus*, Livy xliv, 34.

LONDON:

SWEET & MAXWELL, LIMITED,
Law Publishers,
2 & 3 CHANCERY LANE, W.C. 2.

TORONTO:	SYDNEY, MELBOURNE & BRISBANE:
THE CARSWELL COMPANY, LIMITED.	THE LAW BOOK COMPANY OF AUSTRALASIA, LIMITED.

1929.

(Printed in England.)

REPRINTED 1967
WILDY & SONS LIMITED, LONDON.
PRINTED BY EXPRESS LITHO SERVICE (OXFORD)

DEDICATED

TO

THE MEMORY OF

SIR HARRY POLAND,

"FATHER" OF THE BAR.

PREFACE.

IN making this compilation I have often been conscious that it called for a historian and a scholar (and sometimes, to supply a *calculus* of money values at relevant dates, an economist) but as there is no other book devoted to this subject I hope that some such writer will make better use of the materials here collected.

Of these materials much has not apparently been appreciated by editors of old chronicles, records and MSS., who have not recognised that the profession of the law is a substantive interest to which it is worth calling attention. Perhaps that learned class will, *inter alia*, indicate and even index forensic details more copiously.

These pages are not intended to be a law book, but a contribution to the history of professional life in the Middle Ages.

H. C.

P.S.—After these pages had gone to press, my attention was called to valuable *data* (especially on the origins of the Inns) in Mr. E. Williams's "Early Holborn," (2 vols.; Sweet & Maxwell: 1927).

CONTENTS.

	PAGE
The Anglo-Saxon Period	1
Roman Influence	19
Edward the Confessor	29
Continental Europe	32
The Norman Conquest	37
Sacol, Godric, and Alfwyn	45
Lanfranc	49
William Rufus	57
Placitum, Placitatores	59
Trials with and without Counsel	62
Ranulf de Glanville	84
Legal Education	86
Bologna	94
Ricardus Anglicus	99
William of Drogheda	101
The Development of the Legal Representative	112
The *Attornatus*	126
(a) Beginnings	126
(b) Non-Professional Development	134
(c) The Rise of the Profession	137
The Clergy as *Advocati*	143
The Unpopularity of the " Advocate "	160
The Notary	167
The *Narratores*	169
The *Servientes*	182
The City of London	223
The Provinces	262
Ireland	272
The Attorney	277
Apprenticii	306
Attorneys, *Narratores, Servientes*	322
Language	341
Costume	355
Remuneration	371
Foreign Countries	383
Les Assises de Jérusalem	383
France	398
Normandy	411
Germany	414
Spain	418

CONTENTS.

		PAGE
i.	Students	423
ii.	*Clerici*	428
iii.	Inmates of the Inns	446
	Legislation	456
	Literature	474
	Gower	474
	Lydgate	484
	Chaucer	486
	John Fortescue	497
	1450	519

Appendices.

		PAGE
I.	Vouching to Warranty: Anglo-Saxon	527
II.	Stolen Property: Anglo-Saxon	528
III.	*Leges Henrici Primi:*	
	Advocatus	531
	Consilium	532
	Advocatio and *Consilium*	537
	Defensor	538
	Professional Lawyers	540
	Prolocutor	542
IV.	*Patronus* and *Cliens*	544
V.	*Cancellarii*	546
VI.	*Monumenta Historica Germaniae*	547
VII.	The Abingdon Writ	554
VIII.	John of Salisbury: *Policraticus*	556
IX.	Peter of Blois	560
X.	Essoins	561
XI.	Ricardus Anglicus	563
XII.	William of Drogheda on *Advocatus*	566
	Procurator	579
XIII.	*Les Assises de Jérusalem*	583
XIV.	*Les Établissements*	587
XV.	The *Hospitia*	589

SOME ABBREVIATIONS.

Bl.	Blackstone.
Br.	H. Brunner.
Bra.	Bracton.
D. N. B.	Dictionary of National Biography.
F., Fl.	Fleta.
Fr.	Freeman.
L.	Dr. Liebermann.
L. H. P.	*Leges Henrici Primi.*
N. E. D.	New English Dictionary.
P. & M.	Pollock and Maitland.
P. L.	Paston Letters.
Q.	*Quadripartitus.*
R.	Rolls Series.
St.	Bishop Stubbs.
St. R.	Statutes of the Realm.
Th.	B. Thorpe.
Y. B.	Year Book.

ADDENDA.

Page 494 (*y*).—Mr. *Williams* (2 *Early Holborn*, p. 1398: [1927. Sweet & Maxwell]) refers to [*Cal.*] *Pat. Rolls* [1354-8, p. 377] of 1356 for " an apprentice of the Common Bench " who caused the death of a servant of " the manciple (*mancipii*) of the New Temple ": [evidently there was then only one]: he also prints *ib.* from *K.B. Ancient Indictments*, File 174, *m*. 2. of 1395 a reference to " Robert Maunsipul del Temple " whom he identifies with great probability with the Robert, p. 592 below: if so, by 1404, the two Temples were distinct.

Page 540, five lines from bottom.—*Add* :—L. later conjectured *talia* professum : omit bracket; the passage ceases to be relevant.

Page 515 (*r*).—*Add* :—Probably this was true of cases under *Modus levandi fines* (1 St. R. 214: 1290 ?) where it is assumed that a " countour " would be employed and his *formulae* are prescribed " because a Fine is so high a Bar: " the parties would be wealthy.

A HISTORY OF THE BAR.

THERE is no period in English history so little known, perhaps we may say so obscure, as that from 400 to 600 A.D. Yet it is important (and might, if we knew more, be decisive) for our subject. For soon we must consider the possible influence of some Roman institutions on some early English usages and laws which may have led, or led the way, to what we now call the Bar. This tentative suggestion of hypothesis will, perhaps, be found to justify deferring an attempt at a more positive treatment until we have some likely material. In fact, we must go a little forward in order to work backward. "Along one path or another," says Maitland (a), "we can trace back the footprints which have their starting-place in some settlement of wild Germans who are invading the soil of Roman provinces and coming in contact with the civilisation of the old world. Here the trail stops: the dim twilight becomes darkness: we pass from an age in which men seldom write their laws to one in which they cannot write at all. Beyond lies the realm of guesswork."

We will start at a "footprint" in

The Anglo-Saxon Period (b).

"Hlothære and Eadric, Kings of Kent, made additions to the laws . . . which principally relate to the singular

---

(a) 2 *Coll. Papers*, 418.
(b) All citations from Liebermann (" L.") are from *Die Gesetze der Angelsachsen*; Halle, 1903—16, 3 vols.

system of pledges and warranty (c) intended for the purpose of preventing theft and larceny, an institution holding a conspicuous place in the Anglo-Saxon policy " (d). Liebermann says of this little code, which he dates 685-6 (III, 18) : " Advance in legal material. In court procedure, calling in to warranty, suretyship for tenants' offences, slander, we have here met England's earliest laws." This institution—for the origin of which see Appendix I—seems to have developed later in two directions :—

(a) One is concerned with the recovery of stolen property and is sufficiently relevant to be touched on in Appendix II. We there meet the term *advocatio*, etc., for the first time (e); something may hinge on this; the choice of the word by early Latin translators may be significant.

(b) Following the other direction we get not only the the same word but, perhaps, the thing—the first gleam of representation in formal legal matters.

In the so-called Treaty of Edward the Elder (or I) with Guthrum assigned by L. to 921-38, § 12 (as translated by L. in German from Q.'s Latin, I, 135) runs : " If anyone seriously injures one in holy orders or a foreigner then the King (or in Daneland the Count (*comes*)) or the bishop of the diocese shall be to him as a kinsman, and protector

---

(c) Called by Thorpe and others "vouching to warranty," of course not in the exact sense of later English law (*e.g.*, in Blackstone)—though there is a general similarity and even identity in the "calling into court."

(d) Palgrave, 1 *English Commonwealth*, 1832, c. 2, p. 45, and 34 *Quarterly Review* 259, July, 1826.

(e) Hence, though we are not concerned with classical usage, we may remember "An advocate was not necessarily a trained lawyer. Cic. Orat. i, 15 § 56; 58 §§ 249, 250, etc.; *Top.* 17 § 65." Roby, 2 *Roman Private Law*, 409 n.

The fundamental difference between the classical and modern view is expressed by Jebb : " the real error both of Greece and Rome (until, at some time before Justinian, Trajan's renewal of the *Lex Cincia* was repealed) lay in their refusal to recognise advocacy as a profession " : 1 *Attic Orators*, p. cxxxi.

(*pro cognatione et advocato* (*f*)), unless he has one already . . ."

The Anglo-Saxon word for *advocate* was *forespeca* (*g*); a letter written " after 900 " apparently to King Edward the Elder runs : " When Helmstan committed the crime of stealing Æthered's belt, Higa at once began to bring charges against him among other accusers and wanted to litigate the land from him. Then he sought me [unknown] and prayed me to be his intercessor (= *forespeca*) because I had received him formerly from the bishop's hand before he committed the crime. Then I spoke on his behalf (*spaec ic him fore*) and interceded for him with King Alfred . . . so he allowed him to be lawworthy at my intercession (*for mire forspaece*) and plead against Æthelm, about the land. Then he [Alfred] ordered an arbitration. . . ."

Earle (*h*) translates *forspeca* " advocate " in a document of 997 : the " advocates " of Æthelric's widow were Abp. Ælfric and Æthelmær; the court was the King's and he was the judge. It would seem (*i*) that the word had a tinge of formal advocacy. It is not surprising that these two actual cases come from a high social class.

In the dearth of certain information, we may cite what Brunner (*k*) says incidentally : " Name and thing," *i.e.*, attorneyship, " are alike unknown in Anglo-Saxon law.

(*f*) See App. III, *advocatus*. Lambarde, *Arch.* 44 here has : " loco cognatorum et patroni sunto "; Th. 74 " in the place of a kinsman and of a protector." L. (III, 92) says of his translation here —" Vogt, gerichtlicher Schutzherr "—that it (*adv.*) is common in Franko-Norm. Latin.

(*g*) *Select cases in Anglo-Saxon Law*, No. 17, p. 338, App. to *Essays in Ang.-S. Law*, Boston, 1876; from *Cod. Dip.* cccxxviii [2 Kemble 131]; cited by L. II, 726, as " after 907; Birch 591."

(*h*) *Handbook, etc., Saxonic Documents*, 217 (1888).

(*i*) Index, *Ib*.

(*k*) *Forschungen zur Geschichte des deut u. fran. Rechts*, p. 422, 1894 (originally 1878); pp. 389—443 relating to England are translated by Prof. J. H. Wigmore, 3 *Illinois Law Rev.* 257 (at 267), Dec., 1908; L., 2 *Gesetze*, " Vorsprech," accepts this view. The office goes back to the Frankish period : Br.

4   A HISTORY OF THE BAR.

How far the Anglo-Saxon law permitted a party to be represented in court is not clear. But it is noteworthy that the word *forspeca, forspreca* (of rare occurrence) does not signify, unlike our ' Vorsprecher,' a helper restricted to representation in speech, but a plenipotentiary or (a guardian or) trustee (*Vormund*) who speaks his own word— a phenomenon which points to the fact that Anglo-Saxon law did not (as the Anglo-Norman did) treat the profession of ' Vorsprecher ' and attorney (*Anwalt*) as incompatible with one another."

These are meagre gleanings from the Anglo-Saxon period. But there is a much more fruitful source known as Q. or *Quadripartitus*, that is, some Latin writings, the editing of which is one of the greatest feats of Dr. Liebermann's great work *Die Gesetze der Angelsachsen*. The most important and greatest part of Q.'s work is known as *Leges Henrici Primi* (*l*).

It is generally accepted as the best authority on pre-Norman law and procedure. Obviously if the author has

---

(*l*) Pollock & Maitland, v. I, B. I, c. 3 (in 1895) expressly adopting L.'s work (up to that date) say : " In the reign of Henry I some one sets himself to translate the old dooms [*laga Eadwardi*, etc.] into Latin . . . what he has left as a monument of English law is in the main a laborious but not very successful translation of the old dooms. He translated after his fashion most of the dooms that have come down to us, except the very ancient Kentish laws, and he translated a few which have not come down to us save through his hands. He translated for the more part without note or comment what he found, transcribed honestly if unintelligently. But he aspired to be more than a mere translator. He put Cnut's code in the forefront; this was the latest and most authoritative statement of English law. . . ."

L. himself says, III, 310 : " The merit of *Quadripartitus* as a collection of Anglo-Saxon Law is very great. It is by far the fullest known to us, surpassing its five contemporaries of the same class in wealth of matter. . . . For tone, law and custom (*Sitte*) of the last century before 1114 Q. supplies a source of the first rank." He thinks the author was born between 1050—70, was probably a Frenchman, perhaps a judge, and that the whole was written about 1114—8; " that this queer being striving to make himself understood, is not only professionally engaged in the work of the law, but sits among King Henry's Justices . . . the evidence is not easily resistible " : Maitland, 3 *Coll. Pap.* 471; *Q. R.* July, 1904.

lived over from *pre-* to *post*-Conquest times and was a man of even ordinary powers of observation he would be a good witness of the transition of *régimes*. "He wrote," says Thorpe (268), "for the benefit of his own profession ... the object of his work was to make a collection of the laws and customs that prevailed in England under the Confessor."

Liebermann, who was the first to identify the author of *Quadripartitus* with that of the *Leges* points out that but for these writings many institutions (or arrangements) of Anglo-Saxons and Normans would be lost without a trace, and that he, making his work centre on Canute, tried systematically to reconcile the two systems, but that he never obtained official recognition and influenced neither literature nor practice: the *Leges*, he thinks, was meant for the eye of Henry I (I, xliii; III, 309, 314).

In Appendix III will be found passages from *L. H. P.* under (1) *Advocatus*; (2) *Consilium*; (3) *Advocatio and Consilium*; (4) *Defensor*; (5) *Professional Lawyers*; (6) *Prolocutor*.

Now there can be little doubt that when Q. wrote there was some kind, however rudimentary, of help, whether professional or not, for parties in the law courts; there is more evidence of this still to be produced. Is there, then, any significance in his use of the same word *advocatus* for the two kinds of relationship (a and b above)? He could not have been ignorant of the original meaning of the word (nor so conscious of its special mediæval ecclesiastical use as to have forgotten that original). Our earliest quotations come from a time when it is evidently assumed that an honest man will have no difficulty in "vouching his warranty," in pointing to the person with whom he dealt, for it was a time when a man, short of running away, could not get far—transport was too difficult; he could easily "call" the other "in" or "to" him. When there were comparatively few unfree men the system would work easily, but we know (and should expect) that as material progress was made, the class of the landless and dependent, the poor, would grow : Q. often refers to the " headless " men (*m*); foreigners would come in. Who was to be surety for such abnormal people? The King, we are told, *i.e.*, theoretically there must be someone responsible for every underling, at any rate (*i.e.*, not a lord or " notable "—a question about him could hardly arise).

In a society in which the common expedient of warranty had lasted for two or three hundred years, it is natural that the warranted should be a dependent of the warrantor and that a comparatively late writer or translator should use the same Latin word for the superior of the two whether he held this theory or not. The theory is well borne out by the historians, but it seems that so far no one has actually applied it to the origins of forensic life in this country. The net result of the historians' theories about the society of these ages is stated by Bishop Stubbs (*n*). " The Anglo-Saxon laws recognised ... a class of serfs or theows, who were the mere chattels of their master. The landless man, on the contrary, was free in all personal relations, although he must have a surety or a patron to answer for his forthcoming or to assert his rights in all matters of which the law took cognisance. The landless man might settle on the land of another or take service in his household; he might act as a hired labourer or as a small rent-paying tenant; he might be attached hereditarily to his master or to the land that his master owned. And the lowest class of landowner, that is, the ceorl who possessed a little alod of his own, had often, perhaps generally, found it necessary

---

(*m*) L. H. P. 21; " acephalos et pauperes " : Herrenloser, Unbeschützter ; L.

(*n*) 1 *Const. Hist.*, 485, c. 11, § 132; p. 179, § 65.

to put himself under the protection of his powerful neighbour, who would defend his rights and discharge his public services in consideration of a rent paid or labour given or an acknowledgment of dependence. . . . The *villani* of Domesday are no doubt the ceorls of the preceding period, the men of the township, the settled cultivators of the land who, in a perfectly free state of society, were the owners of the soil they tilled, but under the complicated system of rights and duties which marked the close of the Anglo-Saxon period had become dependent on a lord and now under the prevalence of the feudal idea were regarded as his customary tenants . . ."

In Frank vassalage . . . " the act of commendation placed the freeman and his land under the protection of the lord to whom he adhered. . . . Each of these practices had its parallel in England. . . . The choice of a lord by the landless man for his surety and protector and even the extension of the practice to the free landowner who required such a protection was less liable in England than on the Continent to be confounded with feudal dependence and in fact created no indissoluble relation."

Maitland on " Commendation and Protection " (o) helps us even more. " Certainly Domesday Book seems to assume that in general every owner or holder of land must have had a lord. This assumption is very worthy of notice. A law of Æthelstan (II 2) had said that landless men ' of whom no right could be had ' were to have lords, but this command seems aimed at the landless folk, not at those whose land is a sufficient surety for their good behaviour. The law had not directly commanded the landed men to commend themselves, but it had supplied them with motives for so doing. (Also it had declared that every man must have a pledge, and probably the easiest way of fulfilling this command was to place

---

(o) *Domesday Book* (1897), pp. 70, 71, 86.

oneself under a lord who would put one into a tithing.) What did a man gain by this act of submission? Of advantages that might be called 'extra-legal' we will say nothing, though in the wild days of Æthelred the Unready, and even during the Confessor's reign, there was lawlessness enough to make the small proprietor wish that he had a mightier friend than the law could be. But there were distinct legal advantages to be had by commendation. In the first place, the life of the great man's man was protected not only by a *Wer-gild* but by a *man-bot*—a *man-bot* due to one who had the power to exact it; and if, as one of our authorities assures us, the amount of the *man-bot* was varied with the rank of the lord (*Leg. Edw. Conf.* 12 § 5: but this is contradicted by *Leg. Henr.* 87 § 4) this would help to account for a remarkable fact disclosed by Domesday Book, namely, that the chosen lord was usually a person of the very highest rank, an earl, an archbishop, the King (p). There, again, if the man got into a scrape, his lord might be of service to him. Suppose the man accused of theft: in certain cases he might escape with a single instead of a double ordeal, if he had a lord who would swear to his good character (*Æthelr.* I, 1 § 2; cf. III 3 § 4). In yet other cases his lord would come forward as his compurgator; perhaps he was morally bound to do so: and being a man of high rank, would swear a crushing oath. And within certain limits that we cannot well define, the lord might warrant the doings of his man, might take upon himself the task of defending an action (q) to which his man was subjected (1 *L. H. P.* 82 § 6; 85 § 2); what

---

(p) Cf. App. III : rex debet esse pro cognato.
(q) Is not " Glanville's " Case in B. III, c. 6, an instance of this? *Demandant* v. *Tenant*: to which dominus does the fee belong? " Both *domini* must be summoned; and trial must proceed *ex debito modo* "; after his three essoins *dominus* " ipse ad curiam veniat vel *responsalem* mittat "; if he does neither, *tenens ipse respondeat* et defensionem *suscipiat*; for *responsalis* see Index.

the man has sought by his submission is *defensio, tuitio* : the lord is his *defensor, tutor, protector, advocatus*, in a word, his warrantor " (citing *inter alia* D. B. 227b *et dicit regem suum advocatum esse*) (r); " . . . to all appearance in the eleventh century it is rather as lord than as giver, seller or lender that the vouchee comes to the defence of his man . . . ' I will defend any action that is brought against you for this land ' : as yet men see no reason why such a promise as this, if made with due ceremony, should not be enforced. A certain amount of ' maintenance ' is desirable in their eyes and laudable." " If we look back far enough in the Anglo-Saxon dooms there is indeed much to make us think that the act of seeking a lord and placing oneself under his protection and the consequences of that act, the relation between man and lord, the fealty promised by the one, the warranty due from the other, have been known as *socn*. If so, there may have been a time when commendation and soke were all one. But this time must be already ancient . . ."

The " texts of an earlier age . . . at times seem to speak of the lord as ' doing justice ' when a charge is brought against any of his men. . . . The state demands that the lordless man of whom no right can be had shall have a lord. It makes the lord responsible for the appearance of his men in court to answer accusations (Æthelstan, ii, 2). It is not unlikely that the whole system of frankpledge grows out of this requirement. In some instances the state may go further; it may treat the lord not merely as bound to produce his man but as responsible for his man's evil deeds. But, at all events, anyone who has a charge to make against a lord's man must in the first instance demand justice of the lord. . . . Originally a lord ' does right ' to the demandant by producing in a public court the man against whom the

---

(r) See on *L. H. P.* 43 [3], App. III.

claim is urged; or he does it by satisfying the claim. . . . Probably we ought to distinguish between a laxer and a stricter measure of responsibility, between the lord's responsibility for his men in general and his responsibility for such of his men as form his *familia*, in the language of later days his *mainpast*; but our texts do not lay much stress on this distinction and, as a matter of remote history, the relation between lord and man may grow out of the relation between the head of a household and the members of it.

" At any rate, in numberless cases, the law begins to interpose a third person, namely, the wrongdoer's lord, between the wrongdoer and the wronged; it is to this lord that the claimant should, in the first instance, address himself. . . . Then, on the other hand, he has the right and duty of ' warranting ' his men. If, as will often happen, the bond between a lord and his man is complicated with the bond between landlord and tenant, then, as in later days, he will vouch his lord to warranty and the lord will defend the action. But besides this, within limits which are not well defined, the lord is the man's *defensor* or *tutor*. It is expected of him by morality, if not by law, that he will take upon himself the responsibility for his man's acts, if they be not open crimes. He must stand by his men and see them through all trouble " (s) (*ib.* 284). Earlier Maitland had expressed this in terms absolutely modern : " The landless man is *represented* in the courts by his lord : his lord begins to answer for him " (*t*).

In view of this doctrine, and looking at the passages in Appendix III it is an easy suggestion that Q. threw back

---

(*s*) Citing *L. H. P.* 57, 8; 82, 4, 5, 6; [App. III].
(*t*) And continues : " he is losing his right to attend on his own behalf, to sit there as judge and declare the law. Probably he finds this very convenient. Attendance at the courts is a sore burden for the poorer men . . . as to their private rights the lord will look after these for they are much implicated with his own rights " : *Const. Hist.* 149.

the *advocatus* (−*io*) of his own day or, at any rate, its terminology to an earlier one, when the same *sort* of responsibility rested on the surety for a party—it is tempting to write—on *patronus* for *cliens* (*u*); we shall see. At any rate, in Q.'s *advocatus* we have the rudimentary germ of legal representation in this country.

We will attempt to sum up Q.'s evidence. Now, it is clear that Q. had in his mind the picture of a trial in court. *Consilium* is a very common Latin word and is often used by Q. and all other writers in its most homely sense. But can it be doubted that it is sometimes (*x*) used in a special, even a technical sense (which it has kept ever since)? *Placitum, consilium, perorator, emendatio,* all become technical terms. With whatever object he wrote—and however inaccurately—it is obvious that it had become an important practical matter whether the party had *consilium* or not (*y*); there is too much discussion " up and down " whether and at what stage he should get it to doubt this. See, for instance, the Bishop of Durham's trial in 1088. And likely litigants even bargained for it. About 1100 Abbot Faritius got judgment against Nigel d'Oyly, and part of the terms he made with

---

(*u*) From *cluere*=to hear, listen to; Mommsen : others, from *colonus*, a man on one's estate; it is not always=client but sometimes, " retainer," *e.g.*, " si aliquis reprobet communem clientem " (of Beverley, 1405)=Common Serjeant; 14 *Seld. Soc.*, 16.

(*x*) *E.g.*, § 46, 5.

(*y*) Cf. the speech of Demetrius, during his altercation with his brother, to his father Philip of Macedon, about 180 B.C. : sine advocatis, sine patronis ipse pro me dicere cogor. Si pro alio dicendum esset tempus ad meditandam et componendam orationem sumpsissem, quum quid aliud quam ingenii fama periclitarer? . . . [he pleads surprise]. *Livy* xl, 15. Livy was justified in transferring to another country (and language) the emotions and the incidents of a Roman tribunal, for their august legal system has impressed (perhaps more than any other memory of their past) every civilised nation since their time.

On the other side—the value (and the origin) of the *consilium*—Livy tells us of Publius Scipio's trial (about) 185 B.C. : Citatus reus, magno agmine amicorum clientiumque per mediam concionem ad Rostra subiit; xxxviii, 51.

him was that "if at any time the abbot should have business (*placitum*) in the *curia regis* (obviously when it sat in Berkshire or Oxon only) Nigel should be there on his side unless indeed he was litigating with the King and, moreover, he must put the Abbot up" (z).

Here, too, we see the origin of the time-honoured rule that in the gravest charges "counsel" cannot plead for the accused; the matter was too serious; he must answer for himself; whenever the usage sprang up of the cohort of kinsmen or friends "backing up" a man in peril the authorities were not going to allow such an innovation, say, in treason. No doubt at first technical advice was not wanted and, if it was, would not have been forthcoming; the great bulk of trials would be simple affairs; a man's friends would be few and would go out of curiosity. But if a ritual or "formulary" system grew up gradually —into which we must look—a larger number of parties might want simultaneous advice on the spot, especially if they were not of the lowest social class. And note the touch of the expert practitioner or pleader in the hint (a) to the man in danger to consider whether it "pays" (*inpresentiarum*) to go to trial at once or not, according as his friends are there and his opponents absent or *vice versa*. Q. is here, at any rate, as Liebermann says, acting as the defendant's counsel. If such deliberations were common the rise of a class of professional advisers might have been foretold. Green remarks: "A yet weightier obstacle to efficient justice was often found in the course of procedure itself. Accuser and accused brought kinsmen and friends in their train to the folkmoot whether to sway its doom or to enforce it or to guard against vengeance without law. With such a crowd of adherents at the moot it must have been hard for meaner men to get

---

(z) Bigelow *Pl. A.-N.*, 77, from 2 *Hist. Abingdon*, 132; Rolls.
(a) 49 § 2.

justice against King's thegn or country thegn " (*b*). And we notice that it is mostly in criminal (*c*) proceedings that Q. contemplates the organisation of *consilium*—" if," as Maitland put it, a " man got into a scrape."

But, it may be asked, has he forgotten his own *advocatus*? Certainly he nowhere says, as we should like, the *advocatus* slowly merged into the *consilium*—he went to the *placitum* with the rest of the party and he did what he could. But Q. is not a philosophical historian and that process may have gone on from a more primitive to a less primitive time. But looking at some passages (*d*) we learn that sometimes the lord can intervene to save the man from giving security (other than the lord himself?); sometimes he cannot; sometimes, if he is *legaliter* summoned, he must make some answer, whether his lord, *i.e.*, his guarantor, is there or not—that is, in other circumstances he can wait till that personage comes; indeed, in less grave cases he can insist on an adjournment to secure his presence (61). And we do almost get the two capacities combined in *consilio pariter et auxilio* (*e*); when the man is in trouble, which is always illustrated by his being a defendant, the lord must help him with word and act, with the proper legal exceptions (*f*); moreover, this proposition is derived directly from a law of Alfred's, when the lord could literally fight for his man, whose *advocatus* he was; *consilium* as an institution has come in since.

That the *consilium* was mostly wanted by an accused or sued person is borne out by the instances of *defendere*, etc. (*g*). This line of words, no doubt, is often general,

---

(*b*) *Conquest of England*, c. 1: " The England of Ecgberht."
(*c*) *I.e.*, what had matured into criminal by Q.'s time.
(*d*) § 52.
(*e*) § 82, 4.
(*f*) Non omnes cause omnibus suo possunt *interventu* suffragari : § 85, App. III.
(*g*) § 78, 2 b.

but the *defensor* of children under fifteen is certainly a representative, perhaps a Crown official, perhaps (as in the same section) a *tutor*.

It will be admitted that as soon as there are technicalities in a trial some kind of expert will be wanted by the parties. At what exact point technicality creeps into the administration of justice is not ascertainable in any system; that it had got into that which our author knew is certain—if only from one passage (*h*)—it was a " toss-up " whether you succeeded (*i*). Q. refers here, *inter alia*, to the general formality of court procedure (*k*) which, like that specifically of the oath, threatened many a fall; the result of the trial thus seemed dangerously incalculable; the man who was caught seemed to be punished by God for the injustice of his cause (*l*). " Hence, partly, the ordeal or duel was preferred as proof " : Liebermann (*m*).

Now, later on, we know that nicety in pleading was literally required. And it cannot be doubted that Q. knew and deplored *some* excessive technicality. We cannot always be sure what it was exactly, nor are we certain whether he noticed its existence before Norman influence

---

(*h*) Tot denique sunt et tantis occupata solicitudinibus tot circumduccionibus involuta sunt infortunia seculorum [=torments of the secular courts : L.] ut vitande pocius videantur exacciones [plaints, charges, writs, etc.] et incerta penitus alea placitorum : § 6, 6.

(*i*) Cf. J. F. Stephen, 1 *Hist. Cr. L.* c. ix : " . . . from the earliest times to our own days [1883] the law relating to indictments was much as if some small proportion of the prisoners convicted had been allowed to toss up for their liberty."

(*k*) Cf. Maitland : " The natural man's " law . . . is " a law of procedure. The right words must be said without slip or trip, the due ceremonial must be punctiliously performed or the whole transaction will go for naught. This is the main theme of the wise-man's jurisprudence. One suspects that sometimes the man who in the estimate of his neighbours has become very wise indeed, has it in his power to amplify tradition by devices of his own " : 2 *Coll. Papers*, 426.

(*l*) Brunner, *Forschungen*, 287.

(*m*) II, 585 : *Missesprechen*. Another important reference to the pitfalls of procedure is in § 22.

made itself felt or after. But it seems probable that he believed that it was known in the Anglo-Saxon courts. It is unlikely that if the Normans had brought it with them he would have invented *miscravatio*—a purely Anglo-Saxon root—or the hybrid (*n*) *mis*locutio—words which express the technical forensic errors about which we know most. It would seem that the latter was of such a nature that it is precisely exemplified by Sir Henry Maine thus: " If, says Gaius, you sued by *Legis actio* for injury to your vines, and called them vines, you would fail; you must call them trees, because the text of the Twelve Tables spoke only of trees. The ancient collection of Teutonic legal formulas known as the Malberg Gloss (*o*) contains provisions of precisely the same character. If you sue for a bull you will miscarry if you describe him as a bull; you must give him his ancient juridical designation of ' a leader of the herd.' You must call the forefinger the ' arrow '-finger, the goat ' the browser upon leeks.' There are lawyers alive [1875] who can recollect when the English system of Special Pleading, now just expiring, was applied upon principles not remotely akin to these and historically descended from them " (*p*). " So great is the ascendancy of the Law of Actions in the infancy of Courts of Justice that substantive law has at first the look of being gradually secreted in the interstices of procedure; and the early lawyer can only see the law through the envelope of its technical forms . . . [in England] for many years the practical questions at issue were altogether thrown into obscurity by questions of the proper mode of stating them to the Courts. It was the very state of things which existed when the ancient

---

(*n*) Cf. "*insilia*," p. 30 *n*.
(*o*) " The remains of a vernacular Salic Law " : *Salic Law* : *Encyc. Brit.*; the date is, at any rate, long before our period; see App. VI.
(*p*) *Early Hist. of Institutions*, c. ix, p. 255; *Early Law and Custom*, c. xi.

Hundred Courts of the Germans were administering the rude Salic law." As late as Bracton and Britton a plea " is a formal statement bristling with sacramental words, an omission of which would be fatal. . . . In a civil action begun by writ the plaintiff's count must not depart by a hair's breadth from the writ or there will be a ' variance ' of which the defendant will take advantage " (*q*).

Nevertheless, it would be surprising if in the jurisprudence of a primitive people a party in a suit could lose his case by using a wrong word. We must suppose that Q. was not thinking of primitive—but of later, about 1000 A.D.—Anglo-Saxon procedure, if he was thinking of Anglo-Saxon times at all, when he talks of *emendatio* and *mislocutio*. Here the Malberg Glosses, as being Germanic and early, certainly confirm him. And perhaps we may *conjecture* that while in the earliest native courts in this country there was nothing of the sort, as they grew to what we know them before the Conquest, formality gradually crept in. This we should expect as written laws multiplied and the art of writing spread. A bench more and more bound by legislation and less and less like an oriental *cadi* under his palm tree, and confronted by its own precedents, might very well say : " If you are going to use *formulæ* or technical terms, you must use correct ones." We get the hint about the progress of writing from Livy's famous story of Cn. Flavius. " The publication," says **Mommsen** (*r*), " of the *legis actiones*

(*q*) 2 P. & M. II, c. ix, § 4, p. 603, giving an instance.
(*r*) *Hist.* v. 1, Appx.; Cn. Flavius *civile jus repositum in penetralibus pontificum evulgavit, fastosque circa forum in albo proposuit ut quando lege agi posset sciretur* : Livy (ix, 46). Cf. the man in Iceland " so uniquely wise that though he had made himself liable to an action of a particular kind, no one could bring that action against him, for he and he only knew the appropriate words of summons; to trick him into a disclosure of this precious formula is a feat worthy of a hero " : Maitland, 2 *Coll. Papers*, 426. Cf. Cic. *de Orat.* I, 41 : Veteres illi qui huic scientiae [juris] praefuerunt obtinendae atque augendae potentiae

... was virtually the publication of a revised and enlarged code. The Twelve Tables, indeed, were in substance a regulation of civil procedure, and the object in both cases, as in all similar instances, was to emancipate the common citizen from dependence on the caprice of the noble magistrate and on the advice of the no less noble men of lore [law?] by means of a written code accessible to all "; " ... the obtaining of a written body of law was in itself a severe defeat of the nobility." The courts Q. contemplates are certainly patrician and certainly, as we shall see, partly, if not wholly, ecclesiastical, " pontificum "; the latter element makes it easier to understand the supernatural explanation cited above of the offence of forensic mistake. Compare Maine (s) : " All through the Middle Ages the lawyer who was avowedly a priest held his own against the lawyer who professed to be a layman."

There is a little more evidence about Saxon trials (t). The anonymous monk-historian of the Abbey of Ramsey writing about 1165 gives us a picture of Earl or Alderman Ailwin and Sheriff Edric presiding over a suit at Wendlesbury in (about) 1000. The Abbey sent some brethren as representatives; while the case was proceeding and after both sides had been heard, by the advice of the magnates present, thirty-six *barones* were chosen equally from the friends [*consilium*?] of each party to decide the cause *judiciali sententia* (u). Earl Ailwin, previously called (x) *advocatus noster*, wins the case for the Abbey by a timely protest against monks taking an

---

suae causa, pervulgari artem suam noluerunt; and *De bell. Gall.* VI, 13 : neque fas esse existimant [the Druids] ea [jura] litteris mandare.

(s) *Early Law & C.*, c. 2.

(t) Those reported seem all to be about land or real property; mostly with ecclesiastical plaintiffs.

(u) Gale, *Hist. Script.* XV; Oxon, 1691, p. 415; *Chron. Abbat. Rames.* 79; Rolls.

(x) Gale, 393; Rolls, 26.

oath (*juramentum praestare* : " appearing," Twiss) before a civil tribunal and asserting that he was the *advocatus* of the church of Ramsey and *tutor* of its possessions, and was " in duty bound to defend them and to be their surety in any cause in which an appearance on their behalf was required by any lay court " (*y*). *Barones* and *magnati* look like a translation of *thegns* (*z*), and we know that the writer had a good contemporary authority, of which his sketch may be an accurate version. At any rate, it includes an excellent example of the *advocatus* Q. conceived.

Bishop Hickes generalises thus (*a*) : " We may reasonably infer from what I have said above that causes were habitually brought, heard, argued and decided summarily among the Anglo-Saxons, in a simple plain way, such as would be natural to men among whom law had not yet matured into an art or a discipline, when everyone without any technical pleading either conducted his own case or called in a *causidicus* or a *patronus* (*b*), someone whom friendship or kinship or sympathy or even chance, it might be, offered him." The picture of the litigant surrounded by friends and chance acquaintances reminds us of Q.'s *consilium* before trial. It may turn out that they played a part in procedure (and perhaps led in time to the special jury).

If, then, we may assume that Q. is writing of Anglo-Saxon courts, we shall have no difficulty in believing that, at any rate, shortly before the Conquest, their condition was such that the parties would need some sort of profes-

---

(*y*) So Twiss, 4 *Bracton* XI, paraphrases *huiusmodi juratoriae cautionis exhibitionem*.

(*z*) See L. on *Baro*.

(*a*) In the *Dissertatio Epistolaris* to Bartholomew Shower (1703), p. 8; cited Stephen, *Pleading* (1823), App. XXIII.

(*b*) We must not take these words too literally; they do " not necessarily mean a professional lawyer. Hickes's reputation entitles him to the benefit of the doubt " : Sir F. Pollock, 30 *L. Q. R.*, 465 (1914).

sional help and advice; *emendatio, mislocutio,* etc., offered a good soil for the growth of the *consilium* and the *perorator*. It is too early to speak of *narratores,* but we may suggest legal aid (*c*).

Roman Influence.

It would be easier to come to a conclusion in favour of the existence of, at any rate, a rudimentary legal profession, if we could accept the view that Roman law had persisted for centuries after the Roman occupation has ceased. There is a very obvious analogy between the *advocatus* or *dominus + homo* or *subjectus,* and *patronus + cliens*—though historians do not seem to have drawn it. Whether the analogy is good or bad, it is certain that the English institution was not descended from the Roman, for the latter had been dead for centuries : there was certainly no *patronus + cliens* in Roman Britain.

But it is quite likely that similar circumstances produced similar effects. If the circumstances of lord and man were similar in Anglo-Saxon England to those of *patronus* and *cliens* at Rome, what Forsyth says (*d*) is very much to the point : " In proportion as the state of society became less simple and transactions more complicated the necessity for these applications to the patron became more frequent, and it is not difficult to see how in the case of a patron who had numerous clients, when a habit of answering legal questions arose, others who did not stand in that relation to him, would seek to avail themselves of the benefit of his knowledge and experience " (*e*).

(*c*) No inference can be drawn from *L. H. P.* § 7, 2—*Intersint episcopi* . . . (St. *Lec.* 166), where there is an enumeration of all classes who ought to attend the shire and hundred moot. But they are all bidden to keep a sharp eye on the *gravionum pravitas* or *judicum subversio*; the time was ripe for suitors to be represented.

(*d*) *Hortensius* c. iv, p. 96.

(*e*) See further App. IV.

Far more important is the question whether Roman law had any effect on Saxon institutions. The protagonist of the view that there was Roman continuity between 400—600 A.D. was Mr. Coote (*f*), but his conclusions have not been generally accepted (and in any case hardly touch our quest), a friendly critic (*g*) remarking " he who attempts to build a bridge across the gulf of the Teutonic conquests between Roman and English institutions still builds it somewhat at a venture." The extreme opposite view is expressed by Mr. Laughlin who, dealing with a charter of 844, says (*h*) : " There is certainly no evidence to prove its existence [*i.e.*, of prescription] in Anglo-Saxon law, but every reason to believe the contrary. Admittedly of Roman origin, it existed in those German codes which had been exposed to Roman influence; yet, even though issue must be taken with historians of reputation on this point, it is certain that no effect whatever of any Roman influence can be found in Anglo-Saxon polity." But Maitland puts this more accurately : " As yet [before the Conquest] our Germanic law had not been exposed to the assaults of Roman jurisprudence, but still it had been slowly assuming and assimilating the civilisation of the old world. This distinction we must draw. On the one hand there has been no borrowing from the Roman legal texts. We have no proof whatever that during the five centuries which preceded the Norman Conquest any one copy of a Roman law-book existed in England. We hear faint and vague tidings of law being taught in some of the schools, but may safely believe that little is meant thereby (*i*).

(*f*) *The Romans of Britain* : 1878.
(*g*) Seebohm, *The English Village Community* (1883), xiii.
(*h*) See App. I; p. 253 of book cited.
(*i*) Bp. Aldhelm (d. 709) writes to the Bp. of Worcester " earnestly desirous as I am of being intimately acquainted with all the secrets of the Roman jurisprudence." Henry, *Hist. Engl.* (1774), ii, 320. Theodore, Abp. of Canterbury (d. 690) " brought with him from Rome a valuable collection of books," *ib.*, 319.

The written dooms of our kings have been searched over and over again by men skilled in detecting the least shred of Roman law under the most barbaric disguise and they have found nothing worthy of mention. That these dooms are the purest specimens of pure Germanic law has been the verdict of one scholar after another. Even the English Church, though its independence may often have been exaggerated, became very English. On the other hand . . . to become Christian was in a certain sense to become Roman. . . . From the days of Ethelbert [600] onwards English law was under the influence of so much Roman law as had worked itself into the tradition of the Catholic Church " (k).

In the History (l), Pollock and Maitland say: " It is worth while to bear in mind when we are thinking of any possible influence of Roman forms and institutions in England before the Norman Conquest that there can be no question of Justinian's Corpus Juris. For the legislation of Justinian was still a new thing in the Eastern Empire itself at the date of Augustine's mission to the Kingdom of Kent [597]. Æthelbirht had ruled the men of Kent some five years in 565 when Justinian died."

J. R. Green points the same way: " The Roman tongue became again one of the tongues of Britain, the language of its worship, its correspondence, its literature. But more than the tongue of Rome returned with Augustine. Practically his landing renewed the union with the western world which the landing of Hengest had all but destroyed. The new England was admitted into the older commonwealth of nations. The civilisation, arts, letters which had fled before the sword of the English conquest (m) returned with the Christian faith. The fabric

---

(k) *Outlines of Eng. Leg. Hist.*, 2 Coll. Papers, 428.
(l) I, i, 2; see also II, ii, 5, p. 436 and pp. xxxii—iii, Introdn. So Stubbs *Lec.* 161.
(m) Cf. Mr. Collingwood, *Roman Britain* (1923), p. 100 : " The facts probably are that the Romanised part of Britain was harried to

of the Roman law indeed never took root in England, but it is impossible not to recognise the result of the influence of the Roman missionaries in the fact that the codes of customary English law began to be put into writing soon after their arrival " (*n*).

It is through the Church, then, that we must look for traces of Roman usage in pre-Norman England. Stubbs writes (*o*):

"Where the Roman courts existed they became the model of the Church courts, and where they did not the ecclesiastical procedure followed the lines of the national and customary tribunals. Hence, wherever the Theodosian code spread, it carried the Roman procedure as a part of Church administration; where, as in England, only faint *scintillae* of the civil law were to be found, the Church courts must have proceeded on much the same lines as the popular courts. And this is a matter to be seriously noted as we reach the critical point of the Norman Conquest. It is true, we know very little about ecclesiastical procedure before this date, and what we do know is not very clear; we may, however, affirm pretty confidently that there was over and above the strictly private discipline of the Confessional a system of Church judicature with properly designated judges and a recognised though not well defined area of subject-matter in persons and things. . . . There was a territorial episcopate, and the bishops exercised their judicial powers with the help of archdeacons and deans. But, it would appear, these judicial matters were transacted in the ordinary *gemots*

---

such an extent that its civilisation was clean wiped out . . . a direct continuity between Roman Britain and Anglo-Saxon England must not be looked for."

"Between Roman Britain and Saxon England there is a great gulf fixed ": *The Roman Occupation of Britain* (1924), Haverfield (and Macdonald), p. 268; there had been *juridici prov. Brit., ib.,* 264.

(*n*) *Hist. Eng. People,* c. I, s. 3.

(*o*) *Lec. Med. & Mod. Hist.* (1890), c. 13, p. 344, or *Lec. Early Eng. Hist,* 92—4.

of the hundred and the shire. Just as the court baron, court leet, and court customary of a manor are held together, so the court spiritual and the hundred or county court were held together, and the proceedings were probably in strict analogy—just as *suretyship was the rule in the hundred court*, it was in the bishop's court; so also compurgation and ordeal, the law of witness, and the claim of the *mundborh* over the person of the litigant. I am not prepared to say that through intercourse with the French Church some portions of the Roman procedure may not already have crept in, but, so far as I can see, I am inclined to the belief that whilst there was a customary canonical law and a substantially canonical judicature, the character of the procedure was customary and primitive and differed in nothing materially from the lay procedure. The bishop declared the ecclesiastical law as the ealdorman did the secular . . ."

That the bishops sat in the secular courts we have seen above: Q.'s " intersint episcopi." As Stubbs says, we know very little about the procedure of those courts, but the bishops must have known the procedure at Rome. On the effect of Christianity on Anglo-Saxon England Milman (*p*) says: " There was a constant flow of missionaries across the British Channel who possessed all the knowledge which still remained in Europe. All the earlier metropolitans of Canterbury and the bishops of most of the southern sees were foreigners; they were commissioned at least by Rome, if not consecrated there; they travelled backwards and forwards in person or were in constant communication with the great city in which were found all the culture, the letters, the arts and sciences which had survived the general wreck. . . . They [the native clergy] were in general the admiring pupils of the Roman clergy. . . . Little more than half a century after the landing of

---

(*p*) *Hist. Lat. Christy.* v. ii, B. 4, c. 3, c. 4 (1854); D. N. B., *Alchfrith*.

Augustine, Alchfrid [650-60], the son of the King of Northumbria, had determined to visit the eternal city." Of the effects of this intercourse, he adds, the life of Wilfrid, the teacher of Alchfrid, who [W.] had visited Rome once at least and whose friend Benedict Biscop had been there several times, is a singular illustration. " In less than a century and a half from the landing of Augustine to the death of Bede . . . Christianity became the law of the land, the law underwent the influence of Christianity."

The significance of this relationship lies in the reasonable inference that one class of the Anglo-Saxon bench knew a system of advocacy. Later on this recognition becomes much more important, but we may deal with it here.

There can be no doubt that the *advocati* in the Roman courts (*q*) sprang from the *defensores ecclesiae* and the *defensores pauperum* (*r*) of the early Church. Perhaps at first they were not differentiated—" the business of the ancient defensors was not to do the office of judges but that of advocates at law to defend the rights of the poor and the liberties of the Church against all aggressors and invaders " (*s*). Galletti (*t*) cites a Giovanni Diacono (*u*),

---

(*q*) And in the churches and monasteries whose *advocati* are constantly mentioned; in time the word in this connection came to mean chiefly a church official (and so gave us " advowson "); so much so that we even get *advocata*; Alfwara was *advocata* of the church of Ellesworth : *Chron.* or *Hist. Rames*, 418; c. 53, Gale; 84, Rolls. This use of the word is not in essence different from that so frequently employed by Q. (above). There is an interesting instance in 1026 : *signum Gerbodonis advocati* of St. Bertin, Thérouanne; " the *avoué* of this house " : J. Stapleton, 3 *Arch. Journ.*, 17, 1846.

(*r*) The Church, adopting Isaiah i, 17 : " do *justice* to the fatherless, *plead* for the widow " (where the Hebrew is technical), permitted representation for *miserabiles personae* from the earliest times, and in a very long *catena* of subsequent ordinances. Thus, in 1252 the University of Oxford decreed : si quis sit laesus compareat ipse querimoniam suam [*queri*, a gloss?] coram cancellario cum doctore suo [si velit] cum advocato si indigeat . . .": 1 *Mun. Acad. Ox.* 20—1; ed. Anstey (Rolls, 50); *ib.*, 76 (1300?); cf. pp. iii, 260.

(*s*) Bingham, *The Antiquities of the Christian Church* (1843), B. III, c. 11, § 7. (*t*) Pp. 20, 26.

(*u*) From *de ecclesia lateranensi*. But in *Mon. H. Germ. Legum*,

possibly a writer of the ninth century, as saying that the original *sextus primicerius defensor*, " who is the head of the *defensores* whom we call *advocati*," was in his day only known as *primo defensore*. The title *defensor* was taken from imperial Roman law. But the papal writers are not clear whether these officials were always *clerici*. It seems to emerge from these authorities (*x*) that these two classes of *difensori*—which, perhaps, came to mean judge (*y*)— were at first one and ultimately became the *avvocati concistoriali* who have continued to our own day (*z*). Under this heading Moroni says that the special business of this corporation (*Collegio*) was to take up trials of all sorts and to defend or protect others, and that in 598 Gregory the Great " among the many *difensori* and *advocati* (*a*) who

---

ed. Perz (1868), v. iv, p. 664, the editor includes the passage from Giovanni under *Leges Langobard* and dates before 1059. Galletti observes that though the book may be a forgery, it preserves old matter.

(*x*) Piazza, Εὐσεβολόγιον, Rome, 1698, v. i, p. 137; D. Bernino, *Il tribunale della S. Rota*, Rome, 1717, p. 122; and especially G. Moroni, *Dizionario*, etc., Venice, 1840; *avvocati, Difensori, Placitum, Povero* : the Catholic Dictionary. For an actual instance at Rome, see p. 33.

(*y*) Bernino.

(*z*) It would seem that they are now thoroughly clericalised. " A l'ordre des *défenseurs* ou avocats *régionnaires* on substitua, en 1141, le collège des *avocats consistoriaux* ainsi appelés dans l'origine, parcequ'ils étaient les rapporteurs des affaires que le pape et les cardinaux traitaient en consistoire. Leur nombre et leurs fonctions ont varié avec le temps : ils sont aujourd'hui au nombre de sept; leur attribution principale consiste à plaider dans les consistoires publics les causes des saints, etc., etc."; they examine in the Roman university in civil and canon law : Larousse, *Grand Dict. Avocat* (1081), 1866; " L'autorité pontificale prit de tels développements à partir du XIII siècle que les papes durent confier l'examen et la décision d'un grand nombre de questions à des fonctionnaires, juges délégués ou agents dont l'ensemble constitua ce qu'un appellera désormais la *curia romana*." A Tardif, *Histoire des sources du droit canonique*, 230; Paris, 1887. By 1641 " and for some time previously the *curia Romana* had come to signify what we should call ' the bar,' practising in the Papal courts of justice . . . the proper present ecclesiastical sense of the term is most accurately rendered in English by ' the Roman bar '—the body of those privileged to practise in the different pontifical courts of justice," *Encyc. Brit.* (1878), *Curia*.

(*a*) It must always be borne in mind that in mediaeval documents, unless the context proves the contrary, *advocatus* may be the cleric in

were in Rome chose seven, one for each district of the city and called them *regionarii* "; he gives the Latin formula appointing them : it assumes that each was a *clericus*. Elsewhere (*difensori*) he tells us that the condition of these officials was not everywhere the same; those whom the African churches got from the Emperors were " laici " who appeared [normally?] before the judges; from an Epistle (I) of Pope Zosimus in 416 it may be inferred that in his day even in the Roman Church the *difensori* were " secolari." " Hence it was not strange to see *laici* among the *difensori* " (Moroni). In other churches, he says, the sovereigns insisted on other officials [than clerics] : " these were called *avoves* [*sic*, *avoués*?], avvocati, tutori who were laymen only and had to defend the churches not only in court but even with arms . . ."; he cites Du Cange, *Advocatus* and *Vice-dominus*. In 1141 under Innocent II " the order of *avvocati concistoriali* or *referendarii* " took the place of the *difensori*. Piazza has preserved the oath of " all the judges and advocates *della Corte Romana* " at that date and, as it almost certainly preserves earlier elements, it is here set out :—

" Ego (*b*) N. N. advocatus juro quod ab hac hora in

---

an ecclesiastical court (in, probably, an ecclesiastical matter), but there are instances where he must be a layman before a secular tribunal; *e.g.*, in the instances in the Index in M. Thévenin's *Institutions privées, etc., aux époques mérovingienne et carolingienne* (Collection of *Textes pour servir* : Paris, 1887), p. 120; No. 89 is *Procédure séculière*; see especially App. VI B.

(*b*) It is noteworthy that though this oath is stated to be taken by the judges as well, it is put into the mouth of an *advocatus;* yet at the end occurs " nobis advocatis et judicibus." It looks very much as if, as with us, a man might be a defender in one capacity and an inferior judge in another—see an instance of this in 998 (p. 34); perhaps, too, it points to promotion from bar to bench. This is what Bernino above seems to mean, and so Du Cange, *Advocati Ecclesiarum*, I, 107, col. i; Paris, 1840 : Postmodum vero advocati qui ad hoc primo instituti erant, ut in Comitum placitis ac mallis jura Ecclesiarum tanquam Patroni tuerentur, ipsimet judicia exercuere jusque dixere Ecclesiarum suarum vassallis; and *ib.*, 111, col. 2 : Advocati qui, comitibus inferiores, de minoribus causis judicarent inde a Caroli Magni temporibus memorantur—citing a Capitulary of 805 A.D. Some

ROMAN INFLUENCE. 27

antea [for the future] placita vel negotia Romanorum in quibus Advocatus ero vel Patronus Romanos malitiose non impugnabo vel defendam sed pro conscientia a Deo mihi praestita secundum Constitutiones et leges ac bonos mores ea tractabo; et postquam justitia de iisdem causis a me cognita fuerit, si requisitus fuero judicibus patefaciam; et eis in ipso judicio assensum meum adhibebo : pretium exinde non accipiam nec per me nec per interpositam personam suscipi permittam; et si susceptum fuerit postquam scivero infra quindecim dies illud reddi faciam; et patrocinium meum alicui habenti causam si ab eo rogatus fuero malo studio non negabo, salvis beneficiis quae habemus ab ecclesiis vel aliis; et exceptis sententiis (c) valentibus duodecim denarios quae gratis et sine exceptione nobis offeruntur; haec omnia observabo bona fide sine fraude et malo ingenio quamdiu Papa Innocentius vel Successores sui centum libras valentem (d) denariorum Papalium nobis advocatis et judicibus annis singulis solvere perseverabunt."

What Moroni says about the lay *defensores* is confirmed by Bingham (e) : " learned men," he says, " are not agreed about this. Petavius [*i.e.*, Petau, d. 1652] says they were always laymen [' Fuit Defensor non ordinis sed officii nomen, quod laici gerebant, qui ecclesiae jura in civili foro propugnabant '], but Morinus and Gothofred with much better reason assert the contrary, that at first they were generally chosen out of the clergy, till for some particular reasons it was thought most proper to have advocates at law to discharge this office in the African

---

writers speak of a " College " of *Defensores* and *Advocati* at Rome. The highest court of law, the " Ruota," was, in the 12th century, of European acceptance : Gregorovius, *Gesch. der St. Rom*, V, 585.

(c) Emoluments from awards of 12 *denarii*, *i.e.*, petty. *Sententiae*= judgments which included the adv's. fee.

(d) *Valens* is a coin (at any rate later : Du Cange)=*denarius* : so perhaps here it is a gloss (got into text); or read *valentium*?

(e) V. 1, B. 3, c. 11, § 4, p. 405.

Churches. This change was made about the year 407, when the African fathers in the Council of Carthage petitioned Honorius that he would given them leave to choose their defensors out of the *Scholastici* or advocates at law who were actually concerned in pleading of causes." Bingham cites his favourable answer (*f*) : " he decreed that whatever privileges were specially obtained of the emperor, relating to the church should be intimated to the judges and executed, ' non per Coronatos,' not by clergymen . . . but by advocates at law (*ab advocatis, eorum arbitratu*)." Bingham quotes the Epistle of Zosimus mentioned by Moroni; it certainly implies that some *defensores Ecclesiæ* were *laici*. Bingham (*g*) deals with the early laws prohibiting the clergy (not only, § 9, to do secular business but even) from being tutors and guardians and, § 11, " By other laws they were prohibited from taking upon them the office of pleaders at the bar in any civil contest, though it were in their own case or the concerns of the Church."

Perhaps, then, we may safely assume that the English bishops before the Conquest were well aware of the existence of ecclesiastical advocates in ecclesiastical courts and almost certainly of lay advocates in secular courts, at any rate, as representatives of poor suitors—widows, orphans, *furiosi*, etc., and of propertied persons under age.

Thus one class, at least, on the bench would be familiar with the *consilium*, and would be no obstacle to its expansion in the way which has been suggested above. But in England they could have no experience of a " bar " such as they had seen or heard of in Rome. " As yet," says Maitland (*h*), speaking generally of pre-Norman times, " there is no class of professional lawyers, but the work of

---

(*f*) From Cod. Theod. lib. xvi, tit. ii de Episcop. leg. xxxviii, vol. vi, p. 76.
(*g*) Antiquities, v. 2, B. vi, c. 4, § 10.
(*h*) 2 *Coll. Paps.* 426 (1893).

attending the courts is discharged chiefly by men of substance, men of thegnly rank; the small folk are glad to stay at home," like the modern juryman. And he goes on: " Also, some men acquire a great reputation for legal learning "—mostly on the bench—" and there was much to be learnt . . ." and immediately after the Conquest these *jurisperiti* become very important. It is much too soon to speak of the advocate as belonging to a profession or order in England, but, perhaps, at the Conquest, he is semi-detached. " In England," says P. & M. (*i*), " there was no definite legal profession till more than a century after the Norman Conquest." But there is an indefinite suggestion of one.

Thus, in republican Rome, the Roman Church, and Anglo-Saxon England, legal representation springs from the needs of humble or unprotected persons. Much the same is the descent of our vocabulary; the Church adopts the terms of Roman law (themselves often classical) and supplies models for the later lay lawyers, who translate them into the vernacular (*k*).

Edward the Confessor, 1042-66.

It seems to be agreed that a Chancellor first appears in this reign. " Regenbald . . . was the first Chancellor of England . . . it is well established that he was " Edward the Confessor's " Chancellor " (" not counting Leofric, styled *regis cancellarius* by Florence in 1046 ") (*l*); he was a priest. Freeman (*m*) speaks of " an officer now beginning to creep into a little importance, his Norman Chancellor." Mr. Round does not admit that he was Norman (*n*).

(*i*) Introdn. xxxiii.
(*k*) *E.g.*, the retainer in *Form. Senon. Rec.*, about 800; App. VI.
(*l*) Round, *Feudal England*, 421, 1895.
(*m*) 2 *N. C.* c. ix, 359.
(*n*) At any rate in 1052 the unpopularity of the Normans at court, which led to their expulsion, was partly due to their interference with

Where there was a Chancellor there was a Chancery, which became in time a great nursery of the bar (*o*). " It is only by the supposition of the existence of a trained and organized body of royal clerks corresponding to the chancery of the continent that we can account for the highly technical way in which an old English royal charter is drawn up. From at least the time of Æthelstan these royal clerks possessed an elaborate system of formulae slightly more elastic, it may be, than that of the Frankish Chancery—but still a system that argues the presence of specially trained clerks." Here he follows Palgrave (*p*), who says of the King's " clerks or chaplains "—" the official predecessors of the Masters in Chancery "—that " a situation was thus given in the supreme tribunal to a small and select body of the clergy . . . solely for their skill in these acquirements which were required for the administration of justice. The art of writing was almost wholly confined to the Priesthood and the King's Clerks therefore naturally became his scribes. The Royal Charters and Muniments . . . were intrusted to their care; and upon them also devolved the task of composing the Writs or Mandates which emanated from the King's Court. Hence arose the Chancery, the ' Officina Brevium ' "—of great importance for our theme later.

We may well be using the stuff of those writs now, for Maitland thinks (*q*) that the clerks of Henry II's chancery used formulae then of high antiquity.

---

law; " . . . omni populo rectam legem promiserunt [*sc.* the Assembly] et omnes Normannos qui leges iniquas adinvenerant et injusta judicia judicaverant multaque regi insilia [*in*=Teutonic negative, *i.e.*, ' *consilia* no *consilia* ' : Freeman, 2 *N. C.* c. 9, 336] adversus Anglos dederant, exlegaverunt " : 1 Flor. Worc. 210, ed. Thorpe; copied 1 Roger Hoveden, p. 100, ed. Stubbs, who says " insilia " is correct [cf. *mis*locutio, p. 15].

(*o*) W. H. Stevenson, 11 *E. H. R.* 731 (1896).

(*p*) *Eng. Commonwealth* (1832), c. v, 178—9; II, *ib.*, p. cccxlv; in n. 2 *ib.*, there is a wrong reference.

(*q*) 2 *Coll. Papers*, 126; *Harvard L. R.*, Oct., 1889.

Who, then, was the Chancellor? For our purpose we may at the moment consider him as the King's chief secretary. Originally, apparently, he was one of the *Cancellarii,* our interest in whom justifies a short Appendix (V), especially as there is some authority for believing that some of the " mixed multitude " that may be said to " hang about " all courts developed in practice into lawyers. Spelman (*r*) says " this *magistratus* passed finally into the courts of all European princes, but at first on the model of the French rather than on that of the Imperial Chancellor." The modern historians cited above support this view in respect of the Confessor, whose reign we may regard as the end of the Anglo-Saxon period; the growth of the Chancellorship of the Chancery under the Normans is one of the commonplaces of legal history.

The following passage was written soon after the event in (or about) 1060 to which it refers—and certainly at latest under Henry I; the author of *De Inventione Sanctæ Crucis Walthamensis* (*s*) says (c. xiv) of Earl Godwin: " he had succeeded Thoni [= Tofig (*t*) : Freeman] in the government of the whole of England after the King, by reason of his counsel, statecraft (*astutia*) and skill in the laws of the land." The writer evidently thought that in 1060 there were students of the law. In Chap. xv he adds that Harold in his (re)foundation of Waltham " added eleven discreet men, scholars (*literatos*) carefully selected at large from the best people (*precipuos*) in the land "; and among them was Adelard from Liège, " a man of Utrecht well versed by severe study in the laws customs and constitutions—not only in ecclesiastical affairs but in secular, too—of the churches in which he had been

---

(*r*) Glossary : *Canc.*
(*s*) F. Michel, 2 *Chroniques Anglo-Normandes,* 228 (1836); Stubbs, *Foundation of Waltham Abbey,* 14 (1861).
(*t*) 2 *N. C.* 440.

educated." It is possible that the writer thought of an ecclesiastic dealing with non-ecclesiastical law in non-ecclesiastical courts.

At any rate we know that in this reign there was material to exercise lawyers' minds in codes and enactments, even if some of these put forth by previous kings had fallen into desuetude. Indeed, the existing *corpus* was later idealised as " The Laws of Edward," and as such then played a part which has a bearing on our subject. Freeman (*u*), citing from William of Malmesbury (*x*), explains, referring to " the often promised and often evaded renewal of the Laws of Eadward in the days of the Norman Kings of England," that Eadgar and Cnut had " certainly some claim " to the title of lawgiver, but " Eadward certainly had none." In short, these are cries for " the good old times," like the conservative views of the laws of Lycurgus and Solon. Liebermann (*y*) and Thorpe have been quoted on this point. The latter says : " The general clamor in England for the Saxon laws of the Confessor under the three Norman Kings makes it probable that this compilation [*L. H. P.*] was made by some private person at the time when the restoration of these laws was called for by, and repeatedly promised to, the nation."

Continental Europe.

The gradual growth of intercourse between England and the rest of Europe has already been incidentally mentioned.

(*u*) 1 *N. C.* 463.
(*x*) II § 183, *Gesta Regum*, finished in 1125, ed. Stubbs, p. 224 : omnes enim leges ab antiquis regibus et maxime ab antecessore suo Ethelredo latas sub interminatione regiæ mulctae perpetuis temporibus observari praecepit [Cnuto] : in quarum custodiam etiam nunc tempore bonorum sub nomine Regis Edward juratur, non quod ille statuerit sed quod observârit. L. I, xliii, cites this and i, § 35.
(*y*) Lagam Eadwardi nobis reddit—say, wittily, 1 P. & M. 75 n. For the work *Leges Edwardi Confessoris*, see P. & M. *ib.*, 81 and L., p. 48 *a*, about 1130—5.

CONTINENTAL EUROPE.

The eve of the Norman Conquest is a very convenient point to glance at the facts which may concern us.

That the Church had courts of law and a definite procedure is certain. Galletti (z) cites an "important text" from Anastasius, (probably) the Librarian of the Vatican, who died in 879. "Hic [St. Julius, Pope, 337] constitutum fecit ut nullus clericus causam quamlibet in publico ageret nisi in ecclesia tantum." This is probably aimed at the clergy pleading in secular courts for secular persons (a); in any case, it implies the importance of the legal representative.

Hence a picture of an actual trial in a Papal Court is instructive in itself and significant of what was soon to come in this country. In 998 there was a *placitum* at St. Peter's—*Ugo, Abbot of Farfa* v. *the Priests of St. Eustachio at Rome*, "in the presence of Gregory V and Otto III" (b).

The development of procedure and argument about 1000 A.D. is graphically illustrated : " At the moment there was living in the court (*judicio*) *domnus Leo Archidiaconus* of the sacred Imperial Palace, representing the Emperor, with John, Prefect of the City, and the Roman judges, Gregory, *primus defensor* and others being appointed (*dativi*) by the Pope." Ugo is summoned in person; the cause of action is stated and the following dialogue ensues : Ugo : I beg for an adjournment because I am not yet ready

---

(z) *Del Primicero della Santa Sede Apostolica* : Rome (1776), p. 3.

(a) The following passage is borne out by many of the passages in App. VI. "Originally the clergy had a special preference for speaking (*Plaidiren*) for others in court. Later, however, ecclesiastical authority took objection and only allowed them to appear for their church or monastery." Lass, *Die Anwaltschaft im Zeitalter der Volksrechte u. Kapitularien* in O. Gierke's *Untersuchungen* : Heft, 39, Breslau, 1891—a short and clear account, much used with its authorities in these pages.

(b) Galletti, *ib.* p. 219; doct. no. 21; reprinted (abbreviated) and annotated by v. Bethmann-Hollweg, 5 *Civil-Prozess*, p. 440 (1871); "in the presence" apparently=they were in the building and could be consulted.

with my law and I have neither my judges nor an *advocatus*.

Leo : No. I will give you an *advocatus* who will plead (*respondeat*) for you.

U. : A Roman or a Lombardian *advocatus*?

L : Roman.

U. : God forbid that my monastery should ever be under any but Lombardian law; no Roman *advocatus* for me.

L. : Whether you like it or not you must have Roman law.

But Ugo prevails, goes to his monastery, and comes back with his *advocatus* and *judices*. The former was Hubert, *dativus judex et advocatus ipsius monasterii*; he claims the right to be tried by Lombard law. Leo goes off and consults the Emperor, who decrees that the point shall be settled on the same documents. Hubert also demands to prove " per pugnam (*c*) et per testimonia." The priests object, but Leo reminds them that he must be impartial " qui ex parte Imperatoris sum." Then they ask for an *advocatus* to argue for them, and one is assigned by the court. A strictly legal argument follows and there is an adjournment. The court sits again : " . . . the *advocatus* of the priests made the same objection as before. That being so, the priests objected to Leo that the *advocatus* of the monks was misleading him [on the law]." Leo took time to consider and having taken good advice, as there were no other Lombardian lawyers there to be *judices* except that *advocatus* himself, so that he might get at the true (Lombardian) law, he made him swear on the four Gospels that from that moment he would act as a judge; and thereupon he made him sit in the judgment-seat and pronounce on the issue according to his law (*d*). Where-

---

(*c*) Apparently=*lis* as in § 12.

(*d*) On this v. B.-H. remarks, *ib*. 238 : " A lucrative subsidiary business was that of the ' Fürsprecher ' in court (causidici, advocati) which, though no special privilege of the royal judge, was especially carried on by them as legal experts. Thus a party's ' fürsprecher '

upon the Abbot, displeased, said : " Why, my lord, have you done this? You have taken away my *advocatus*; who is to plead for me? " " I will give you another instead " was the reply, and Leo bade Peter . . . who was on the side of the monastery (*e*), to be the *advocatus*. " But," said the Abbot, " he does not know how to plead." L. : " I authorise your former *advocatus* to instruct (*instruat*) him how to plead [this cause]."

We must note the stress laid on having an expert in a particular code on the bench to do justice—in an emergency he is even taken from the bar—something like a Commissioner of Assize trying cases in default of a judge; he would not try a case in which he had been counsel, but he would instruct his successor on the conduct of the case so far.

Strict procedure is observed on both sides; judgment is finally for the Abbot; it is signed by the president, the *judices*, the *advocati* and other officials.

Advocatus has obviously been the most persistent word in legal nomenclature. But there were others. Lass enumerates the following titles of persons (in some way) legal representatives in the " sources of law in the Frankish period " : (1) Mandatarius. (2) Procurator, dominus, auctor. (3) Causidicus. [*Clamatores*, he says = the parties in court, not *causidici*; perhaps *causidicus*, too, in some of the passages he cites, *e.g.*, from *Lex Wisigoth*, about 500 A.D. = a party.] (4) Assertor, practically = causidicus.

---

when a *judex* of that particular race was wanted could be sworn as an assessor (*Schöffe*) without more ado and put on the bench." Leo consults the assessors of both sides. Cf. A. Weiszler, *Gesch. der Rechtsanwaltschaft*, 20, Leipzig, 1905. " In Italy from the second half of the eleventh century *legis doctores, juris periti, causidici, patroni causarum*, to whom not only *orare* or *patrocinari* is assigned, but also a part in the judgment (*Urteilfindung*) are also constantly called *judices* [citing Ficker, *Forschungen* . . . *Italiens* III, 96, 102] . . . Now, these names which partly point to regular advocacy, reach very far back," he cites from v. B.-H., p. 108 [n. 44] a document of 783 about an Archbishop's " assertor vel causidicus et mandatarius."

(*e*) " Hence a Lombard but not a learned Fürsprecher " : v. B.-H.

(5) Defensor, often = defendant. (6) Patrocinator, patronus. (7) Advocatus (*f*) primarily = " Immunitätsbeamten," officials of privileged institutions, " peculiars." (8) Qui rationem aliorum reddat, or teneat, or pro eis loquatur (*g*); qui praesumat causam alterius agere, causare; qui in placito pro alio rationat. (He declines to include *prosecutor* as it = the manager of the litigation.)

Other titles (*h*) occur here and there, literary rather than technical—which points to occasional usage rather than to settled practice.

The era of Charlemagne—800 A.D.—seems to mark an epoch in the history of the Frankish *advocatus*; at any rate, in his day (and for some time afterwards) he is often regulated, which implies that he was much in evidence.

We are constantly enjoined by the authorities not to think of the *advocati* as a professional class, but it is very much a matter of degree. The Church had had a series of *advocati* for centuries always doing much the same kind of work, and had certainly developed a convenient procedure. But, no doubt, every *advocatus*—especially if he was a layman appointed *ad hoc*—was not a trained lawyer or even a student of any law except that relevant to his case. A bar springs imperceptibly out of those who, to the opportunity of frequenting the courts, add a taste for scientific system which may be gradually encouraged by the prospect

---

(*f*) " In a trial at canon law the *advocati* and *procuratores* were sharply distinguished. The former pleaded in court; on the latter lay the rest of the conduct of the trial for other persons " : *ib*.

(*g*) Cf. pp. 547—9.

(*h*) For instances, see App. VI. In *Officialités au moyen âge* (Paris, 1889), M. P. Fournier mentions also *togati, scholastici*, etc., as corporations in the " Bas-Empire." Pt. I, c. iv, p. 32. In the Bamberg MS., p. 96 x, v. Schulte reads in c. 8 *togati* (for MS. *rogati*) = name of *advv*. " Amongst the Franks or Saliques certain Lawyers were called Sachibarones : because they were (say the Glossarists) Sacharum, *i.e.*, causarum periti . . . Wendelin : *Glossar. Salicum*, p. 175. Saech = Caussa de qua collitigatur " : Madox, 2 *Exch*. 198, c. 5.

of fees. A Capitulary (*i*) of 803 is generally supposed (*k*) to have replaced the tribunals of the *comtes*; c. 3 is: " Our *missi* shall appoint the *scabinii, advocati, notarii* in each place and bring back their names (*l*) with them," as our judges still do those of possible High Sheriffs. Before that we are told, " There exists no regulation or even tradition relating to the French bar in the 6th, 7th, and 8th centuries. . . . From Charlemagne to St. Louis [1270] the bar is lost in the obscurity which envelopes this period of French history " (*m*).

This vague indefiniteness seems to be borne out by French historians (*n*). Thus a greater authority, Luchaire, says : " The same indefinite division (*confusion*) which then existed everywhere between the spiritual and temporal domains was naturally reproduced in judicial institutions. Ivo of Chartres pressed by Philip I to come to his court in 1093 to answer certain charges against him, declares that he is ready to justify himself *vel in ecclesia si ecclesiastica sunt negotia, vel in curia si sunt curialia* (*o*). He would no doubt have been hard put to it to define exactly and in detail these two classes of business " (*p*). In this important work there is no reference to a bar ; the *advocatus* is not as much as mentioned.

The Norman Conquest.

Often as this story has been told our especial interest has been neglected. " It is believed by some," said Dug-

---

(*i*) App. VI; M. H. G. Legum Sec. II, vol. 1, 115; ed. Pertz I, 115.

(*k*) Bataillard, *Les Origines des Avoués*, 27.

(*l*) Not that they were all publicly appointed, but that they were appointed by royal authority : Lass.

(*m*) R. Jones, *History of the French Bar* (1855), p. 112.

(*n*) For the passage from the Roman to the Gallic bar and from that to the Frankish *advocati* see Gaudry, *Hist. du barreau de Paris* (1864), v. 1, cc. 2—4, and La Rousse, *Gr. Dict., Avocat* (1866).

(*o*) Citing *Histor. de France*, v. 15, p. 78.

(*p*) *Hist. des inst. monarc.*, 987—1180, p. 294 : Paris, 1891.

dale (*q*) in 1666, " that we had not many persons in this Realm, other than the Clergy, who were learned in the Laws, before the Norman Conquest." " Not many," perhaps, but that there were some we have endeavoured to show, and for a hundred years there were very few (except on the bench). But when they do appear they are indigenous. Ultimately—when we have surveyed the kindred classes in foreign countries—we may conclude that the individuality—or insularity—of all English social institutions is manifestly visible in this. Coke was not a great legal historian, but modern research has, perhaps, justified his belief—" nec vana fides " (*r*)—that Normandy got much of her law from England.

Sir Francis Palgrave pathetically narrates (*s*) how he was brought up in " the firm belief that the germs of our English constitution could assuredly be recovered in antient Normandy. . . . I searched the historians and the scanty memorials of Norman policy and jurisprudence for proofs in favour of this " opinion, " but I have found none." It is not the fact, as has been supposed (*t*), that the bar " came over with the Conqueror."

(*q*) *Orig. Jud.* c. 8 : Of Lawyers.

(*r*) " . . . it is verily thought (*nec vana fides*) that William the Conqueror finding the excellency and equity of the laws of England did transport some of them into Normandy and taught the former laws written as they say in Greek, Latin, British and Saxon tongues (for the better use of Normans) in the Norman language and which are at this day (though in process of time much altered) called the customs of Normandy." Probably the *Grand Coutumier de N.* is a good instance of this. Cf. Palgrave, 3 *Hist. Normandy*, 626 : " On the whole the most probable hypothesis is that England borrowed less than England gave."

(*s*) 2 *Hist. Normandy*, 258 (1857); and see v. 3, p. 601 : there is " cogent proof that a great revolution was effected not by William but by Henry Plantagenet," and *ib.*, p. 626.

(*t*) By, amongst others, the present writer : 30 *L. Q. R.*, 465. Gervase of Canterbury knew the exact date when " lawyers were first called into England " : see p. 65. (The theory may perhaps be called Normania.)

The extreme " Chauvinist " view is perhaps expressed by E. Glasson, *Hist. du droit, etc.*, . . . *de l'Angleterre comparés au droit, etc.*, . . . *de la France*, Paris, 1882 : v. II, 14, 19, Till John's reign " les

THE NORMAN CONQUEST. 39

We get the scientific view from Stubbs (*u*). " The effect of the Norman Conquest on the character and constitution of the English was threefold. The Norman rule invigorated the whole national system, it stimulated the growth of freedom and the sense of unity and it supplied partly from its own stock of jurisprudence and partly under the pressure of the circumstances in which the conquerors found themselves, a formative power which helped to develope and concentrate the wasted energies of the native race . . . the Norman polity had very little substantial organization of its own; and what it brought with it to England was soon worn out or merged in that of the nation with which it united."

The fact is that when the Normans swept the board such Anglo-Saxon lawyers as there were had almost a *tabula rasa* to work upon. For if the conquerors had any lawyers at all, they had no forensic lawyers. They had become Frenchmen (*x*), and if it was not still " the very midnight of the legal history of France " as it was when they invaded that country, the dawn had not yet come. To the cumulative evidence (*y*) of the Frenchness of the Normans " at least half a century before the battle of Hastings " may we not add their religion? And, as it will be relevant, we may add here that it is equally " wonder-

---

rapports entre le duché et le royaume sont incessants et par la force même des choses l'esprit normand domine partout. Les mœurs, les institutions, la langue, la littérature, le droit, la justice tout devient normand, c'est à dire, français. . . L'influence des Normands sur le développement de la législation anglaise fut immense ; il s'opéra une véritable révolution dans la procédure et dans la jurisprudence. Quelque graves que soient les défauts des Normands au point de vue juridique on ne peut cependant nier qu'ils ont les premiers implanté en Angleterre la science du droit." French writers are apt to forget the 150 years of Anglicisation. See p. 411.

(*u*) 1 *Hist.* c. 9, § 91.
(*x*) 1 P. & M. B. I, c. 2, 42—3.
(*y*) *Ib.* At p. xxxiii these authorities suggest that if any " Romanic " element percolated through from Frankish sources it was in the shape of " procedure," but they can hardly mean to include advocacy.

ful in how short a time the Normans in England became good Englishmen. This was partly perhaps because Normans and English were, after all, near kinsfolk " (z).

Their adaptibility is thus guaranteed. A great Frenchman looking at the facts from a different angle, confirms it. " To what extent," asks Michelet (a), " were the men and the race modified by the French element (*mélange*)? The warrior and tricky (*chicaneur*) spirit, foreign to the Anglo-Saxons, which made of England after the Conquest a nation of soldiers and scribes, is just the Norman spirit pure and simple. This acrid strain is the same on both sides of the Channel. Caen, *la ville de sapience*, preserves the great monument of Anglo-Norman fiscality,—William I's Exchequer."

For the moment we are only concerned with " le mélange français." In one respect the Normans of 1066 are even *plus français que les Français*—they have little law or procedure; fiscality is one of their " strong points."

Our historians seem to be agreed that the Normans brought no written law or jurisprudence with them. Of the great authorities (b) we will only quote a few lines (c). " Even in later days, after the duke of the Normans had

---

(z) Freeman, *General Sketch*, c. ix, 4, who emphasises the point—significant in view of the early jural blend—1 *N. C.* c. 4, p. 166, and 4 *N. C.* c. 17, p. 17.

(a) *Hist. de Fr.* II, 102 (1835). Larousse, *Grand Dict.* (1874), *Normands*, says that they were very fond of litigation and tribunals, for a long period; in fact, it was proverbial; they were
" connus dans notre France.
Par la chicane et la potence."
—merely, perhaps, a tradition (it is suggested) of their predatory origin.

(b) Palgrave, 2 *Hist. Norm.* 257, 451; v. III, 33; Freeman, 1 *N. C.* c. iv, p. 194; 5 *N. C.* c. 24, p. 396; Stubbs, 1 *Hist. Const.* c. vii, § 81, p. 247; c. ix, § 91 (above); Maitland, *Const. Hist.* 122—3; W. H. Stevenson, 11 *E. H. R.* 731 (1896), who deals emphatically with the many *assumptions* of Norman origin: *e.g.*, " It would be difficult to prove from pre-Conquest sources that the dukes of Normandy had any organization worthy of the name of ' chancery,' yet it is tacitly taken for granted that they had a chancery almost as well organized and equipped as that of the empire."

(c) 1 P. & M. B. I, c. 2, pp. 41, 54.

become King of the English, the duchy was slow to follow the Kingdom in the production of abiding memorials of its law." But they had individual men who were learned lawyers : Herlwin, Abbot of Bec, " who had spent most of his life ·as layman and knight, was deeply learned in the law of the land and when he had become an Abbot he still gave opinions in temporal causes; but not until he was near forty years of age did he learn the first rudiments of letters. His legal knowledge was probably the same in kind as that attributed . . . to the English bishop Æthelric and the monks of Abingdon, a knowledge of the law to be evoked by concrete cases, not a body of doctrine to be taught or written in a book."

Another witness is Ordericus Vitalis, half a Frenchman (not a Norman), half an Englishman, born in England in 1075, who lived mostly in Normandy but visited England, and says of Lanfranc in 1069 (*d*) : " It was under this master that the Normans for the first time paid any attention to literary art and from his school at Bec eloquent teachers (*sophistae*) of divine and secular things went forth. For, before, under the six Dukes of Neustria, hardly any Norman cared about liberal studies, nor was a learned man to be found till " God sent Lanfranc. A little before he remarks that the Normans found the English " rustic and almost illiterate," though previously the Roman pontiffs had taken great pains to instruct them (*e*).

But most conclusive of all is a witness who says nothing ; in *Norman Institutions* (*f*) Professor Haskins has not a

---

(*d*) *History*, B. iv.
(*e*) Stubbs, in the passage just cited, after "turning the tables " of culture on the Normans (" The domestic civilisation of England, with all its drawbacks, was far beyond that of France "), cites from Ordericus (B. IV, c. 13) the disparaging opinion of two contemporary earls " Anglorum " (though practically Normans) about *Angli*, obviously given in anger.
(*f*) Cambridge, Harvard University Press, 1918, p. 4, see p. 131. In a private letter (1922) the professor is not aware " of any trace of a bar in N. before the Conquest."

syllable about a Norman " bar " or legal representation of any kind. On the positive side he bears out the English writers quoted. " Normandy has no Domesday and no dooms. Its earliest law-book, the older part of the *Très Ancien Coutumier*, dates from the very end of the twelfth century."

We have, therefore, to account for the fact that from 1066 law and lawyers are ever increasingly in evidence and that we soon get to know—for the first time—the names of some not on the bench.

Historians are unanimous that the two peoples were a mechanical mixture before they became a chemical combination. Freeman says : " What the constitution was under Eadgar that it remained under William . . . the law with a few changes in detail, remained the same. . . . I cannot too often repeat . . . that the Norman Conquest was not the wiping out of the constitution, the laws, the language, the national life of Englishmen " (*g*). " In the department of law, the direct changes introduced by the Conquest were not great. . . . The organization of jurisdiction required and underwent no great change " : Stubbs (*h*). Professor Bigelow is even more precise : " In the *popular* courts . . . of the pre-Norman period . . . the ancient procedure ran its course with little interruption —certainly with no sudden change—during the Norman period. During the time of the Conqueror and of his sons . . . , at all events, the Anglo-Saxon sources are safe guides to follow; safer far, certainly, than any other. The modification of the ancient procedure had been next to nothing in the 11th century, and it was but slight during the reign of Henry I " (*i*). " If," say Pollock and Maitland, " we read our history year by year onwards from 1066 it will seem for a long time doubtful whether in the sphere of

---

(*g*) 1 *N. C.* c. iii, p. 72.
(*h*) 1 *Hist.* c. ix, p. 313—4.
(*i*) *Hist. Proc. in Engl.*, p. 1; 1880.

THE NORMAN CONQUEST. 43

law the Conquest is going to produce any very large permanent changes. The Normans in England are not numerous " (*k*).

On this view the evidence of Q. or the author of the *Leges Henrici Primi* on the working of the Anglo-Saxon courts, which he may have seen with his own eyes, has an unique value. In this state of things it is an easy metaphor that the nascent legal profession was one of the sparks from the hammer on the anvil; " in the local courts confusion has been confounded by the influx of conquering Frenchmen " (*l*), and we may crave in aid the figure of " the collision of the two races " (*l*), or that of Stubbs—the Normans " forced out the new growth of life . . . so far as they continued Norman they provoked and stimulated by opposition and oppression the latent energies of the English " (*m*). One historian has explicitly deduced what is implicit in these literary similes; " during William's reign," says Mr. C. H. Pearson (*n*), " when there were no central courts except the King's Council and no trained advocates, justice was administered by men unacquainted with the vernacular and Latin became the language of official use (*o*). No doubt there was always a steward or clerk of the court who interpreted for the people and with whom the real management of business lay. But it was not the less an evil to the nation that its laws and their science were treated in a foreign idiom and that the assistance of professional men began to be needed by those who

---

(*k*) V. I, Bk. I, c. 3.
(*l*) 1 P. & M. I, iii, 82.
(*m*) 1 *Hist.* c. ix, § 91. The whole of § 91 on these formative effects greatly supports the thesis of the text.
(*n*) *Hist. Engl. Early and Mid. Ages*, 1867, I, c. 23.
(*o*) *I.e.*, of the *records*; " the story that William . . . forbade the use of the native tongue in the courts of law . . . is no doubt a fabrication; the popular courts transacted their business in English and the Kings issued their charters in English as well as Latin. Richard I is the first King of whom no English document is preserved " : 1 Stubbs, § 134. To the same effect, 1 P. & M., B. I, c. iii, 60.

sought justice." In common parlance, the "reaction" tended to produce the profession.

The position, then, was as Freeman (*p*) puts it, that "according to a crowd of earlier precedents in the case of two nations dwelling in the same land, the Norman settlers in England were for some purposes allowed to keep their customary law." "The two races appear on terms of legal equality"—theoretically, surely—"but as in the settlement of the Teutonic tribes within the Roman Empire, each race was, for some purposes, allowed to retain the use of its own Law."

The parallel of India appeals to us more. In the early stage of the transient state of the East India Company from an emporium to an Empire it was often necessary to apply the principles of British justice to the common law of the land. In the charter of 1687 "There is to be a recorder [of Madras] who must be a discreet person, skilful in the laws and constitutions of the place. And there is to be a town clerk and clerk of the peace . . . an Englishman born but well skilled in the language of East India and who is to be esteemed a notary public" (*q*). In 1773 an Act of Parliament regulated the judicature of Bengal and provided civil remedies for British subjects against the natives of specified territories *with the defendant's consent*, but "is silent as to jurisdiction in civil suits by 'inhabitants' against British subjects or against other 'inhabitants.'" Later on, as the result of British legislation "the natives of the country are, so far as is compatible with regard to principles of humanity, left in enjoyment of their own laws and customs." Thus the impact of the two civilisations on each other in time produced the Indian bar.

(*p*) 5 N. C. c. 24, p. 397; v. 4, c. 21, p. 624.
(*q*) *The Government of India*, by Sir Courtenay Ilbert, 1898; c. 1, pp. 24, 50, 54. For native assessors (1772) in court, see p. 46.

Sacol, Godric, and Alfwyn.

Soon after the Norman occupation, then, we should expect to find a struggle between natives and foreigners, especially about private property, and to see it reflected in litigation. For once we can enjoy the method of physical science and, like Leverrier and Adams, fix with our telescope the body we seek. It is the monastery.

That the monasteries were the refuge of the humanities in the dark ages is well known. "The monks were the great teachers and instructors of antiquity, not so much perhaps spiritually as in secular arts and learning" (r).

"As some of the best libraries were formed within the walls of the Benedictine houses, so naturally among their inmates were to be found the foremost scholars and writers of the day, whether theologians or historians," says Dean Stephens (s); "there were often exciting disputes or lawsuits either with the bishop about his right of visitation or with the burghers of the town . . . about tolls dues and rights. . . ."

"The bishop in his palace, the monk in his monastery," says Mr. Stevenson (t), "and the parish priest in his parsonage, each contributed to the great work of education. . . . Persons of different ranks of life were instructed in secular and religious learning, who might afterwards marry and enter the world as laymen (u) . . . the bishop and the parish priest . . . could help the Saxon serf and the Norman villein in various ways. . . . They stood between

---

(r) Brewer, *Chronicon Monasterii de Bello*, xi, 1846; Anglia-Christiana Society.

(s) *The English Church*, 1066—72, c. 14, p. 250; *ib.* p. 270 (1909).

(t) 2 *Chronicon Monast. de Abingdon*, lxv—vii, §§ 71, 72 (1858); Rolls, p. 1.

(u) Cf. " in the early days of the English Church a monk was not necessarily in orders and it was not until the time of Clement V [1311] that all monks were compelled to be ordained ": W. Hunt, *The English Church*, 597-1066, c. 10, p. 175 (1912).

him and the oppression of his feudal superior. . . . They were his advocates in the courts of law. . . ."

The first document in the second volume of the *Abingdon Chronicon* is a writ of William I, and therefore issued not later than 1087. The merits of the case do not concern us, but this document and its sequel (*x*) are so important that they will be found in Appendix VII and are translated here :—

William, King of the English, to Archbishop Lanfranc, Robert d'Oyly, and Roger de Pistri and to all other his lieges of all the Kingdom of England, greeting. Know ye that I have granted to St. Mary of Abingdon and to Athellelm, the Abbot thereof, all the customary revenues of their lands, whichever are situated in the [possession of the] said Church, wherever it has them in the town or without the town, according as the said Abbot can prove by writ or charter that the said Church and his predecessor had those customary dues by grant from King Edward. [The sequel in the Chronicle may be contemporaneous (and probably is), but cannot be much later than 1189, the date of the latest document it gives] :—

The public reading of which letters in the County Court of Berkshire was of great benefit to the Abbot and the Church. For at that time the royal officials were in the habit of inflicting many wrongs on the tenants of the Church in possession at various places : sometimes insisting on one kind of customary dues very burdensome to the tenants and sometimes on another. But when the aforesaid royal order was produced, by which the dues of the Church under the charter of King Edward and the witness of the county in that very court were publicly promulgated, then those officials had to put up with a rebuff and a gain for the Church : my lord Abbot manfully doing his best. To him,

---

(*x*) 2 *Chron.* 1 (above) and in Bigelow's *Placita Anglo-Normannica*, 30 (1879), as "Abbot Athelellm *v.* Officers of the King."

two monks of this Church, brothers, gave much assistance all the time, the elder of whom was called Sacol and the younger Godric with whom was also Alfwin a priest, then rector of the neighbouring royal vill of Suttune [Courtney] —men who had such an extraordinary facility in secular matters and such a knowledge of history that everyone in those parts accepted without demur any opinion they expressed. And there were many other pleaders (*causidici*) too, among the English at that time in that abbey whom, when they agreed, no wise man contradicted. Hence, whenever they took up the defence of the Church's interests, its aggressors were silenced.

Here we have references to a *placitum* in the County Court of Berkshire, the names of two English lay lawyers, and of one clerical one—probably the *advocatus*—and the statement that in that single foundation there were at one time several English lawyers of repute. We may safely assume that Sacol and Godric were laymen, because we are distinctly told that Alfwyn was a cleric; and of the other *causidici* some were probably laymen. The *causidici*, too, are expressly so called; they not only sat in their chambers and gave opinions, but they appeared in court for their clients and fairly silenced the other side. The last words of the context rather suggest such a scene than that their opinion generally prevailed.

If this be so, Sacol (*y*) and Godric are the first known lay English lawyers in the modern sense.

Selden's comment (*z*) puts an even more modern face on this passage: The Conqueror " in his fourth year by the advice of his baronage summoned to London *omnes nobiles sapientes et lege sua eruditos ut eorum leges et*

(*y*) " Saecolf " and " Saecol " occur in W. G. Searle's *Onomasticon Anglo-Saxonicum* : 1897. The monks in England " were with scarcely an exception of Anglo-Saxon origin " : Brewer, above, p. xi.

(*z*) 3 Works (1726), 1334 in a *Review* (*i.e.*, supplement to c. viii) of the *History of Tythes*.

consuetudines audiret (*a*), as the words of the book of Litchfield (*b*) and afterwards confirmed them as is further also related in Roger of Hoveden : those *lege sua eruditi* were common lawyers of that time as Godric and Alfwin were then also who are spoken of in the book of Abingdon to be (*c*) *legibus patriæ optime instituti* (*c*) *quibus tanta approbarent . . . quorum collationi . . . fiebant* [exactly as in App. VII, 2]. And these two and divers other common lawyers then lived in the Abbey of Abingdon. You must know that in those days every monk here in England, that would, might remain so secular that he might get money for himself, purchase or receive by descent to his own use. And therefore it was fit enough for practising lawyers to live in monasteries. But what had those *praeteritorum memoria eventorum* (that is, reports and adjudged cases of the Saxon times) availed in their skill, if the former laws had not continued ? More obvious testimonies to this purpose are had out of Gervase of Tilbury [*fl.* 1211], Ingulphus [d. 1109] and others and we here omit them." If by "get money" Selden refers to remuneration—in this instance, board and lodging—the only element of our modern professional system missing is that of instruction by the solicitor; perhaps the *advocatus* supplied his place.

Selden co-ordinates these two individuals with certain expert lawyers in 1070—which is a reminder that we have already met such persons in 1060; it is quite possible that Sacol and Godric were called in on both occasions.

(*a*) The latest text in full is L.'s, I, 627, as Prologue to *Leges Edw. Conf.*, Roger's (*fl.* 1174) at II, 218; Rolls, ed. Stubbs, who (1 *Hist.* 315, c. ix and 305) attributes R.'s story to " what seems to be the highest legal authority of the next century," *viz.*, Glanville. R.'s text varies a little from that of L., but note R's *consulatus Angliae* for *patrie comitatus :cons.*=a shire as in II Domesday 14, 91 : L.

(*b*) MS. in B. M., Cleopatra D IX; Stubbs.

(*c*) Selden's paraphrase used again in his *Diss. ad Flet.* VII, 7, p. 518, where he cites *Tabularium Vetus* (MS. in Biblioth. Cott. f. 21) : our text all but *verbatim*.

The passage referred to by Selden is so famous that it is set out in App. VII, 2.

Of the famous story of this synod—the framework of which alone concerns us here—Freeman wrote (*e*) : " No one who fully takes in the history and the legal formulae of this age can accept this story as it stands," but he quite believes that " in this passing moment of peace, when William was for the first time undisputed master of England," he should undertake the kind of legislation which the alleged Convention passed, with the object of reconciling the natives by the character of the enactments and the nationality of the members. Liebermann, the latest inquirer, dates (*f*) the composition of this passage as 1130-50; at any rate, at this date it was accepted that the Conqueror found Englishmen learned in the laws.

Lanfranc.

Again, there is *Archbishop Lanfranc* v. *Bishop Odo*, about 1071, " perhaps the best reported trial of the reign " (*g*). Of all that has been written on this case we shall only extract what especially interests us, *viz.*, the plaintiff.

Lanfranc is the best illustration at the moment of the existence of the legal profession on the Continent and of its advance in this country; also, of the notorious fact that the Norman connection at once brought England into closer relations with other countries and with the Papacy.

Ordericus (*h*) pointedly refers to his legal training in

(*e*) 4 *N. C.* 324, c. xix.
(*f*) III, 341.
(*g*) St. 1 *Hist.* 315, c. 9. The report in Bigelow's *Pl. A.-N.* 5—9, is from Textus Roffensis of Ernulf Bp. of Rochester, written about 1120; also printed Selden's *Eadmer*, 197; Wharton's *Anglia Sacra* I, 334; Wilkins's *Concilia*, I, 328. For the story see these writers and *Eadmer* (who died 1124), *ib.* 9, and Freeman 4 *N. C.* 365.
(*h*) " Lanfranco Cadomensium [= of Caen] abbati [1066]. . . . Hic ex nobili parentela ortus, Papiae [Pavia] . . . civibus, ab annis infantiae in scholis liberalium artium studuit et saecularium legum

words which fairly mean that he was designed for the bar; he studied secular law expressly for lay purposes, perhaps at Bologna (*i*); he practised in court, outdid his seniors by his eloquence, and his opinions were highly esteemed by lawyers of standing and by statesmen. Moreover, the practice of law was in the family, for his father was high up in the legal hierarchy of Pavia and enjoyed " a sort of civic nobility " (*k*). Lanfranc was born about 1005 and became Archbishop of Canterbury in 1070. He must then have been well acquainted with the best equipped tribunals in the world—the Pope's. And he was very soon a litigant in person at a " Gemot " (*l*) against the Archbishop of York, whom he " beat "—as the *Anglo-Saxon Chronicle* evidently thinks—partly by his able pleading. Soon, too, he was engaged in another more famous suit; he discovered that Odo Bishop of Bayeux had appropriated lands and revenues in Kent belonging to the Church. He sued him in the County Court of Kent or, apparently, the King referred his petition to that tribunal (*m*). About 1071 the

---

peritiam ad patriae suae morem intentione laica fervidus edidicit. Adolescentulus orator veteranos adversantes in actionibus causarum frequenter precipitavit, torrente facundia apposite dicendo senes superavit. In ipsa aetate sententias promere sapuit quas gratanter juresperiti aut judices aut praetores civitatis acceptabant." B. 8, p. 209, v. 2, ed. Le Prevost, *sub* 1070.

Cf. with this " Merlin's Prophecy, 1100—1200. From Alexander Neckham [d. 1217] *De Naturis*, etc.: Rolls: p. 311, c. 173. De locis in quibus artes floruerunt liberales. . . . *Civilis juris peritiam vendicat sibi Italia*," 2 *Collect.* 185 : Oxf. Hist. Soc. 1890. For the study of law in Italy before and at this time see Rashdall, *Universities*, v. I, c. iv, p. 99, and v. II, pt. 2, App. III, but there is little about a bar. But, I, 118, he says of Irnerius " his name first occurs among the *causidici* in a *placitum* . . . in 1113 "; he teaches, 1100—30; incorporation of the faculty about 1158.

(*i*) Macdonald, *Lanfranc* (1926), p. 4.

(*k*) 2 *N. C.* 223 n. 3 : from a biographer who says he was *de ordine illorum qui jura et leges civitatis asservabant* where *ordo* may be significant; Dean Hook's *Lives* ii, 74, from Milo Crispinus, 282, c. 1.

(*l*) 4 *N. C.* 357, c. 19 : *A.-S. Chron.* ii, 175; Rolls, ed. Thorpe, for a hearing by Pope Alexander II.

(*m*) What appears to have been the writ is set out, Brady's *Hist. of Engl. Introdn.* 191—2, and *Hist.* 54 B.C.—1273 A.D.; Appendix,

Court met " in the ancient meeting-place of the shire on Penenden Heath " and sat three days. The King had ordered not only all the Frenchmen (*n*) in the county, but especially, too, the Englishmen versed in the old laws and customs, to be present. The plaintiff appeared in person and argued (*o*)—so apparently did another Archbishop in this suit—" ipse "—of Mortlach (*p*) for lands in Surrey. Very notable was one English lawyer, Ægelric, ex-Bishop of Chichester (or Selsey : Freeman), " a very old man, well versed in the law of the land, who had been brought thither in a carriage, by the express command of the King, to discuss and to declare those ancient laws and customs "; *i.e.*, " a specially summoned member of the court, which was an extraordinary and re-inforced one " (*q*). Evidence (*r*) was heard and arguments on both sides. Judgment for the plaintiff, which the King confirmed. " Here we have probably a good instance of the principle universally adopted; all the lower machinery of the court was retained entire, but the presence of the Norman justiciar [Bishop of Coutances, lord of Mowbray] and barons gave it an additional authority, a more direct connection with the King and the appearance at least of a joint tribunal " (*s*).

Eadmer has (*t*) yet another story of Lanfranc's advocacy.

pp. 3—4, where it is correctly called a " general " writ, and Bigelow, *Pl. A.-N.* 4—5. The (future) plaintiff's name is in the commission.

(*n*) *Francigenas.* Commissions to *Francigenae* and *Angli* jointly are common in this reign, perhaps with the object here in view; sometimes, however, they are *milites* (perhaps *literati* as well, *i.e.*, experts).

(*o*) *Diratiocinavit* = stated his claim; a technical term. So *ib.* L. *placitavit et totum diratiocinavit.* For a parallel to the Archbishop *in person*, see *R.* v. *Abp. of York* (1888), 20 Q. B. D. 740.

(*p*) " Ipse archiep. Murtelache . . . diratiocinavit, favente rege "; the see was later transferred to Aberdeen.

(*q*) Sir F. Pollock, 30 *L. Q. R.* 469 n. Eadmer, p. 9, expressly says that competent men were summoned from other counties.

(*r*) *Multi testes* : not, probably, oral; or, rarely.

(*s*) St. 1 *Hist.* 315, c. 9.

(*t*) Ed. Selden, p. 9; Rolls edn. 17; Bigelow *A.-N.* 10. The latter's view that this case was an appeal from the former seems untenable; there seems to be no connection between them whatever.

Odo (who died in 1097) began another action against the Church of Canterbury, " and deliberately caused to come thither its guardian (*tutorem*) father Lanfranc and all whom he knew to be most skilled in the laws and usages of the English Kingdom. So when the case came on for hearing all those who had come to give evidence for the churches in the first trial were so exposed (*convicti*) that they lost what they were protecting. For Lanfranc was not there; it was not his habit to be present on such occasions unless there was the most urgent necessity." The news is brought to him; he says at once there is something wrong in the other side's evidence (*dicta adversariorum non recte processisse*, " detects an error in the pleadings " : Bigelow) and orders an adjournment to the morrow. At night St. Dunstan appears to him and bids him " go in and win " in person, which he does. He spoke so well that " he demolished and reduced to nonsense all the evidence of the previous day " and silenced those claimants for ever.

Whatever the exact facts of this case were, Eadmer (*u*), whose authority is high, and who was a contemporary of Odo's, meant to testify to the brilliancy of the Italian ex-lawyer's pleading. He recognises that there is an art in conducting a case—you may lose if you plead a wrong plea. Indeed, Bigelow says (*x*) that this is an instance of *miskenning*—of which actual examples are rare. It is, at any rate, a great confirmation of Q.

Not all litigants are archbishops or ministers, but we may make the usual presumption *omnia rite esse acta* of Lanfranc and gather how a model trial proceeded in his day. So we may look at another in which he was concerned— that of the Bishop of Durham for treason, at Salisbury in 1088 (*y*). " I am ready to answer in your court," says the

---

(*u*) Who, however, " is less of an historian than a hagiographer " : Rolls, cxii. (*x*) *Ib.* p. 328; the *word* is not in Eadmer.
(*y*) 1 *Monast. Angl.* 244—50, ed. 1817, not Dugdale and Dodsworth's, 1655; 1 St. *Hist.* c. 11, p. 498; Fr. 1 *W. Rufus*, 29, 94; II, 469; 1 P. & M. B. II, c. 2, § 5, p. 434.

Bishop to the King, " if you will give me a safe-conduct "; that shows that we are not in the county court. The King gives his word (*bene affidavit eum*); he has audience and again offers to submit to the jurisdiction " secundum ordinem meum " (z). For our purpose this only matters as showing that there is an ecclesiastical procedure and a civil procedure—an important development—for the King replies, " Well and good, provided he takes his trial like a layman, but if he refuses this, he must go back to his diocese." He is not allowed a *consilium* with the prelates there and then present, and it soon appears that they are *prohibited* from taking part; for normally the King could not prevent consultations before or after; hence this feature throws a little light on the ordinary *consilium*—it was generally held as the case proceeded; here *consilium* = moratorium; no delay, said the King. The Bishop insists, no doubt rightly, that his Archbishop owes him this duty, and the prelates all took this view—but in vain. Then the Bishop writes in effect : If I must defend myself, *laico more*, I will, but only on condition that I may reply to any charge " secundum recta judicia mei ordinis in eo loco ubi canonice judicatum fuerit," which seems to mean—anywhere you can try a bishop by canon law; later, he says explicitly, as the canons and *decreta* direct. This Rufus would not accept. At last three barons as " arbiters " (as Freeman well puts it) come to terms—which are not very clear—with the Bishop; apparently they concede the right of appeal (*a*), to either party, thus satisfying the defendant's demand for clerical privilege; the ordinary layman would have no appeal

---

(z) Deprecatus est eum [the King] ut rectitudinem sibi consentiret sicut episcopo suo. Rex autem respondit ei quod, si laicaliter placitare vellet et extra pacem quam rex ei dederat se mitteret, hoc modo rectitudinem sibi consentiret; but—si hoc modo placitare rescusaret—he would have him escorted back to Durham; *i.e.*, surrender your privilege and I will treat you ceremonially as a bishop (?). Later, p. 247, the Bishop complains : in laicali conventu causam meam dicere compellor.

(*a*) To Rome " ubi contentiosa pontificum judicia juste debent terminari."

in the *curia regis*. If this is correct it confirms Stubbs's view (*b*) that here we have that tribunal in a state of transition. We get another glimpse of ordinary procedure in certain interlocutory procedure, which unless settled by consent must go before *judices legales dictis causis*. There was consent and the trial took place at Salisbury in November. " We have, from the Bishop's side only, it must be remembered—a minute and lifelike account of two days' debate in the Assembly . . . we are met at the threshold by . . . the terrible Sheriff of Worcestershire, Urse of Abetot " (Fr.); *unus ex servientibus regis* (*c*) : Again, the accused is denied *consilium* with his brethren; evidently they had by order kept out of his way in the interval, for there had been plenty of time to advise with them. *Consilium* is evidently a privilege legally. The first thing he asks the court is whether he ought not to be robed, for he was clear that canonical custom—and he would only act canonically—required that the trial should be before robed judges and a party in person should be robed. Whether this was a protest against the bench not being robed does not appear; we can get on very well without robes, replied Lanfranc, implying that as the judges had none, the defendant need not have his. But this early reference to a forensic uniform—for it is the *King's* court— is valuable.

We have not heard of Lanfranc in this connection before; it is assumed that in the *curia regis* the Archbishop is in his proper place. No doubt the writ or summons on which the proceedings were founded was read. The defendant wishes to raise a preliminary point of substance, but the lawyer Primate insists that he shall *first* admit the jurisdiction of the court. Then the Bishop asks him : " My lord, is that a *consilium* or a judgment ?" *i.e.*, I am not a lawyer, do you mean to offer this for the counsel

---

(*b*) 1 *Hist.* 498.
(*c*) The same *phrase, H. L. P.* 61, 4, & 68, 2.

of which I have been deprived or is it the judgment of the Court? " It is not," was the answer with the significant addition, " but I am quite prepared that you should have judgment, and that at once." Then the " laici " spoke up (d) and concurred so heartily with Lanfranc that the defendant turns to them for the first time and addresses them " domini barones et laici "—" these last seem to act in close concert with the Primate " (Fr.). Then in the plainest language the Bishop tells the lay members that he does not recognise their jurisdiction; he does that of the King and the bishops—*laicale judicium et quicquid est contra canones prorsus respuo*. A point of *ecclesiastical* law arising, Lanfranc holds that the judges—" tam clerici quam laici "—will decide it *in camera*, which is taken to mean that the defendant *et homines sui* (e) should go out of court, that is, rather, an adjournment *ad avisandum* (f). The court is against the defendant on the point. Then, he says, " you tell me I must accept this decision or appeal (? *contradicere*). I must take advice with my brethren." " But," says Lanfranc, meeting him " as a lawyer " (Fr.) " they are your judges now, not your advisers." " I beg the King to waive the point." " Take advice with your own men," says the King. " The odds against me are too great," was the rejoinder; " my seven followers against the learning of the whole realm." The whole dialogue is a recognition of technical law and pleading.

Ultimately he announces a formal appeal to Rome on all the points he had taken. No objection is taken to this,

---

(d) There is probably some confusion here for the *laici* throughout behave in an unseemly manner, *i.e.*, those in the audience; no doubt those on the bench were orderly.

(e) Cf. the *King* v. *Robert Belisme* in 1102 (Big. Pl. A.-N. 83, from 4 Ord. Vit. 169, ed. Le Prevost): Cumque Rodbertus licentiam, *ut moris est*, eundi ad consilium cum suis postulasset, eademque accepta, egressus . . . : the *cons*. advise him to plead guilty.

(f) For a considered opinion: cf. " C.a.v." It is not like sending a jury out while law and fact are discussed, for there was no jury. Probably the King, the president, had to be consulted.

but Hugh Beaumont, not a cleric (g), tells him : "We, my *compares* and I, are prepared to confirm our own judgment in this court" (h). In the end the defendant loses (subject to his appeal). Then there is a new point of procedure. Before he leaves the court, someone seeks to charge him—*implacitare*—for a private tort : the King calls on Lanfranc, who rules that there is no jurisdiction (at that moment?). Undoubtedly this *placitum* was in several ways, including that of form, exceptional, but the framework of the trial was normal. The proceedings confirm the view that Lanfranc was a master of procedure. The significance of the case is well gauged by Freeman. "We see the forms and the spirit of the jurisprudence of England in the days immediately following the Norman Conquest; a jurisprudence which both in its form and its spirit has become strongly technical, but which still has not yet become the exclusive possession of a professional class. Bishops, earls, sheriffs are still, as of old, learned in the law and are fully able to carry on a legal discussion in their own persons. And we see that a legal discussion in those days could be carried out with a good deal of freedom of speech on both sides." Perhaps it may be pointed out that one bishop is a professional (foreign) lawyer, and the other categorically complains that he cannot get competent legal advice for his purpose—but incidentally that complaint registers the recognition that lay procedure and secular law must henceforth be reckoned with (otherwise William and Lanfranc had been fairly matched in a purely Papal Court). Nor again do the earls

---

(g) It was very significant—and Freeman so deals with it—that earlier Hugh had said to the defendant : "If I may not to-day judge you and your order you and your order shall never afterwards judge me." But we are not concerned with the breach between ecclesiastical and lay, as such.

(h) It looks as if some sort of appeal was recognised from the court to itself but perhaps there were no definite rules. Lanfranc says : " quotiens in curia sua [regis] judicium agitur ibidem necesse est ut concedatur et contradicatur."

here show much learning. But that the sheriffs—and other officials connected with the administration of justice—are beginning to *appear* in Court marks the rise of a tributary stream to the bar. From Lanfranc's *régime*, in fact, we hear more and more of practising lawyers.

Another famous trial about a foundation with which Lanfranc had dealings took place in 1081.

In 1076-9 occurred between the Abbot of St. Edmund's (Bury) and the Bishop of Thetford, Herfast or Arfast, the common case of a dispute about episcopal jurisdiction over the Abbey (*i*). Incidentally we get our first concrete instance of regular legal *placita* being held : *etiam* [=as well as the monks] *accitis illuc ab abbate quibusdam regis primoribus qui dictante justitia in eadem villa regia tenebant placita*, says Herman, " who wrote from personal knowledge " (R.). Lanfranc is sent down to make inquiries. At last in 1081 there is a public inquiry. " The King orders a regular trial " (editor). Herman gives an account of it *con amore* : besides great ecclesiastics there sat *ecclesiae causarum ventilatores*, *i.e.*, the regular people who moved in such matters, perhaps *advocati*, perhaps not but secular experts—and, *non desunt abbates vel docti causis forensibus comites*—no lack of lay lawyers, if they were wanted. And he recognises an art of public speaking : " Every speaker aimed at attaining Ciceronian rhetoric, passing by the two classes of which, the demonstrative and the deliberative, they planted themselves on the third, the judicial style." The abbot won.

William Rufus, 1087—1100.

If Lanfranc gave an impetus to the practice of law or it got one in his time we should expect its development in this reign, which lies practically beyond his lifetime.

(*i*) Round, *Feudal England*, 329; Herman's *de miraculis D. Ead.* . . . *Mem. St. Ed. Ab.* v. 1, p. xxxii, and p. 63 : Rolls.

The conventional disparagement which besets in turn all the professions, seems to take its rise in the case of the legal with just that touch of prophecy that fulfils itself, from Ranulf Flambard. His " exact formal position . . . under William Rufus has in some measure to be guessed at " : Freeman (*k*), who also tells us " under the Conqueror we see the first beginnings of that class of clerks of the King's chapel or chancery who had so large a share in the administration of the kingdom and who even under the Conqueror had often been rewarded with bishopricks. Under William Rufus the chancery became the nursery of clever and unscrupulous Churchmen " (*l*). Of all that has been written about Flambard only his forensic activity or influence concerns us. The net result seems to be that he was Rufus's willing cat's-paw (*m*) to extract money and that that member was as long as the arm of the law; whether he was a lawyer or not he " would have the law " of anyone he could victimise (*n*). In fact, his importance for us is the recognition of the forms of law and of their abuse by an unscrupulous advocate. There might be good common lawyers up and down the country, but there were not yet revenue lawyers, and part, perhaps, of Flambard's unpopularity was due to his finance. " As the annals of the Conqueror's reign furnish the names of no great lawyers or financiers, as Ranulf was employed at court during the latter years of it, and as his subsequent career proves him to have possessed great ability, if not a systematic policy of administration, it is not unnatural to suppose that he

---

(*k*) *W. R.* I, 333; II, note 1; 5 *N. C.* 135, s. 23. Palgrave 4 *Hist. Norm.* 54—5, calls Fl. " a Clerk of the Chancery."

(*l*) Cf. 1 *W. R.* 342, c. iv.

(*m*) Like Empson and Dudley under Henry VII, or Mr. Riah's relation to Mr. Fledgeby.

(*n*) There is an anticipation of the " pettifogging attorney " of modern fiction in his method : audita morte cujuslibet eposcopi vel abbatis *confestim clericus regis* eo mittebatur qui omnia inventa scripto exciperet omnesque in posterum redditus fisco regio inferret : he kept " within the law."

rendered himself useful in the compilation of the great rate-book of the Kingdom " (o). Two or three famous remarks about him do not help us greatly. His contemporary, Florence of Worcester, says of him in 1100 that his ingenuity was such that the King made him dun and prosecute the whole Kingdom (p). Yet a little later (about 1110) William of Malmesbury called him *invictus causidicus* (q), and goes on to tell us that at that time there was no rich man who was not a money-grubber, no " clerk " who was not a *causidicus*, and no priest who was not a farmer (*firmarius* (r)). The use of " causidicus " in both passages *may* be meant to suggest the greedy ecclesiastic who either threatened the law or who put it in motion—or even invented it—or it may be simply the familiar classical word for one who knew or practised the law; in either case there is a hint that people in the position of Ranulf—a great cleric—could both prosecute and give judgment. But there is, unfortunately, no suggestion in the term of counsel normally pleading in the courts in 1100. What is meant is that the laity had no chance against the clergy in politics, " placita " generally; the absence of lay champions in public life is in fact emphasised : there were no Hampdens, Somers, Erskines or Broughams.

Placitum—Placitatores.

In the person of this minister we get an early, if not the earliest, trace in the popular mind of the identification of the party with his pleader; writers seem to regard him

---

(o) St. 1 *Hist.* 394, c. 11.

(p) Placitatorem ac totius regni exactorem . . . constitueret : v. 2, p. 46, ed. Thorpe : the second epithet repeated from p. 44, of 1099 : Henry of Huntingdon a little later improves on the assonance : placitatori sed perversori, exactori sed exustori : Rolls, ed. vii, § 21, p. 232.

(q) Et tum verbis tum rebus immodicus juxta in supplices ut in rebelles furens : 4 *Gesta Regum Anglorum*, 314. Several chroniclers call him William's *procurator*; Selden adds *primarius*.

(r) (Originally) a dealer in church lands (as bursar, steward, etc.).

as the *placitator, par excellence* : the great public man always *at placita,* sometimes trials, sometimes actually a party " in person " (s), sometimes arguing for the Crown. Thus, in *The King* v. *Abbot of Tavistock* (t) (1096), the King sends commissioners including *Randulphum regalem capellanum* [supposed to be our man] . . . *ad investiganda regalia placita* and they are called *regales supradicti placitatores.* We get very near a similar mission when on the day of Anselm's enthronement, September 25, 1093, " there arrived at Canterbury a certain Ranulph, the chief instrument of the royal will, and began proceedings against the archbishop " (u). We have already seen what Henry of Huntingdon thought of this man; he probably had him in his mind when under the first days of William Rufus he wrote (x) : " Those who were called justices (*justitiarii*) were the ringleaders (*caput*) of all injustice. The officers of the law (*vicecomites et praepositi*), whose special charge was justice and good law, were fiercer than thieves and robbers and desperate oppressors." Though he happily ignores pleaders in this context, he thereby deprives us of

---

(s) Big. *Pl. A.-N.* 131, 324; *Ermenold* v. *Abb. Faritius,* time of H. I, from 2 *Mon. Abingd.* Rolls, 139 : *dies postea statutus venit nec placitor* . . . *affuit* : pl.=*placitator*=a party.

(t) Big. *ib.* 69, from 2 *Monasticon,* 497.

(u) A rege missus quidam nomine Ranulphus, regiae voluntatis maximus executor qui, spreta consideratione pietatis ac modestiae, placitum contra eum ipsa die instituit; et ferus ac tumens . . . : Eadmer, ed. Seld. *Hist.* 20; Rolls, p. 41; Freeman, 1 *W. R.* 427.

It is at this time, too, that in § 2 of the London Charter (dated by L. I, 524, III, 303, " probably " 1131) " the citizens shall not plead (*placitabunt*) outside the walls of the city for any plea (*placita*)." (St. *Lec.* 124.) So in § 3 *de placitis corone implacitatus.* This and other instances (Q. 5, 4) L. (II, 173) explains of the *party*; III, 305, he mentions a similar privilege—*placitare*—for Breteuil and Rouen in the 11th century. For Newcastle-on-Tyne under Henry I, see St. *Sel. Ch.* (1st ed.), p. 107.

Placitum seems to be derived from the formal resolution of a meeting or assize, *placet, placitum est; placitator* always has a technical tinge =a party in some capacity or other at a trial. A derivation from Germ. *platz*=place, has been suggested.

(x) VI, s. 38, p. 209, Rolls.

light. His learned editor cites (*y*) the case of one Bricstan, about 1115, who had taken sanctuary in a religious house— and that with a view of becoming a novice—and had been torn thence by the *placitatores regis* (*z*) for a debt and put in prison in London. By the way, Ordericus, in his account of his trial, does not mention legal aid of any kind. It cannot be said that the writers of this period distinguished sharply between *causidici* and *placitatores*, but they seem rather to imply that the former, as one would expect from their name, had less personal interest in the matter at issue. As we are trying to catch the process from Anglo-Saxon to Anglo-Norman institutions we may relevantly note here " an invaluable link between the Norman and Anglo-Saxon treatment of the most characteristic of our early institutions, the county court and the hundredmoot " (*a*).

Stubbs translates a writ (*b*) of (about) 1111, part of which runs : " If henceforth there arise a plea touching the division of lands, if it is between my own barons, it shall be treated in my court, and if it is between the vassals (*vavasores*) of two lords it shall be treated in the county court [the only alternative before itinerant justices] and that shall be done by trial by combat unless there be some obstacle to such proceeding in the parties themselves " (*c*).

(*y*) Rolls xxv from B. ix (unprinted); see Big. *Pl. A.-N.* 111.

(*z*) Here they look like menial officers of the law, perhaps purposely identified with their superiors, who had set them in motion. Ordericus, *Hist. Eccl.* vi, p. 123, gives the name of the agent Robert Malarteis, certainly a layman, " nullum penitus officium habebat nisi insidiari " cleric and lay alike : a reminiscence of Flambard.

(*a*) St. *Lec.* 129.

(*b*) Text, *Sel. Chart.* (1st ed.), p. 99; L. I, 524; St. *Lec.* 129.

(*c*) " Et hoc duello fiat, nisi in eis remanserit." " Here trial by battle is prescribed as the regular practice, recourse to other methods being exceptional. . . ." : St. *Lec.* 133 (rest, as above). L., too, III, 300, points out that both parties, if agreed, could compromise on other procedure than duel. In 1200 the King ordered the justices " in banco " that two " duella . . . de roberia " should take place before himself, as he wishes to see them : 1 *Cur. R. Rolls*, 278-9. In 1313, in *A Lady* v. *The Abbot of Fountains* (right to a common of pasture),

Stubbs did not " think that there is any document in our history containing in twelve lines [of the extant writ to the magnates of Worcestershire] so much valuable information as we have here." It helps us to understand how new laws and habits required new interpreters.

Trials With and Without Counsel (d).

1115. We have already had Bricstan's case where, it seems, there were only lawyers for the prosecution.

1121. *Modbert* v. *Prior and Monks of Bath* (e). The Prior takes advantage of the accidental presence of *viri boni et juris periti* to try before them. And later the bishop who presided says : " You, whom we know to be neither *advocati* nor partisans (*partium fautores*) carefully

---

" the abbot . . . went out of court to imparl. When he returned he advanced to the bar (*bare*) accompanied by his champion . . . and the lady saw that he intended to claim trial by battle (bataille)—we must suppose it was his right." Toudeby Sjt. for the lady " recognising this advised his client to withdraw "; so " she left the bar " and was nonsuited. Mr. Turner does not understand Toudeby's advice : 43 *Seld. Soc.* 134, ix, xl. Actual instances of duel occur as late as 1249-69 : 2 *Chron.* . . . *de Melsa*, 98, 100, xvii, xviii; Rolls, contemporary; suit between *Meaux Abbey and W. de Lasceles* v. *Abbot of St. Mary's, York, in cur. regis*, about a fishery; they give W. de L. 5 marks to get a writ and begin the cause; " post longam altercationem [in pleading] jus partium utrarumque ad duellum fuerat placitatum quod in curia d.r. *coram justiciariis fuerat vadiatum armatum et percussum*; during its course the parties come to terms. Then the Abbey had another try without W. : ad duellum II hominum est commissum. Quapropter tirones VII cum equis et famulis eorum conductos sumptibus nostris ad magnas expensas *retinebamus*. . . . Tandem commissum est duellum apud Eboracum a mane usque ad vesperum, athleta nostro paulatim succumbente; it was stopped *per cautelam* Roger de Thurkelby J.

(d) See also Index, *Trials*.

(e) Big. *Pl. A.-N.* 114 from 1 Madox, *Hist. Exch.* 110, 2nd. ed.; fol. ed. 75, who gives almost a translation. It is difficult to believe that this was not a " witness action." The issue being what was " the testament . . . the last words " of a deceased, the Prior says : " Praesentes hic etiam quosdam video quos omnibus his interfuisse simul et andisee gratissimum habeo." Whereupon " Surgentes ilico testes quidam legitimi stantes in medio constanter asserebant se modis omnibus probaturos " every syllable the Prior had said. But perhaps nuncupative wills were proved by an exceptional procedure : 1 P. & M. II, 6, 3, p. 335.

perpend judgment." " Then some Persons of the Company who were gravest and most knowing in the law withdrawing from the crowd " considered their verdict. The plain distinction between lawyer-judges and advocates is modern.

1120-30. The possibility rather than the event of trials is supposed in a document thus dated. It is a grant of land by the Abbot of Ramsey to Hervey, a monk, " on condition that he and his heir shall to the best of his ability defend all the land of St. Benedict at trials (*defendat placitis*) and wherever it shall be necessary " (*f*). The foundation was Saxon and evidently knew what litigation was.

1139. " An ecclesiastical synod came together to sit in judgment on the King " (*g*). It has some significance for us, though not so much as Dean Hook thought (*h*) : " in the celebrated action which arose out of Stephen's treatment of the Bishops of Salisbury, Ely and Lincoln the King was induced to employ a counsel or pleader . . . the trial is a memorable one; because from it we date the origin of a learned profession . . . " that " of the law . . ." (The technical correctness of the last statement is on a par with that of the procedure described; no other writer has fixed this date for the alleged origin.) " The King was weak enough . . . to appear before a tribunal of his own subjects; not indeed in person, but by counsel (*i*). Aubrey de Vere, ' a man deeply versed in legal affairs,' argued the cause (*k*) on the King's side with much temper and great skill. Roger, bishop of Salisbury, conducted his

---

(*f*) *Chron. Abb. Rams.* 261; Rolls.
(*g*) 5 *N. C.* 289, c. 23.
(*h*) *Lives*, ii, 334, c. 6.
(*i*) So, too, Fr. *ib.* citing William of Malmesbury *Hist. Nov.* ii, 23 [or § 473, p. 552, Rolls] : " . . . de Ver homo causarum varietatibus exercitatus." It is much more to the point that he calls Albericus *causidicus ib.* 554, § 476; Selden *ad Fletam*, c. 7, s. 7, calls him the King's *procurator primarius*.
(*k*) " This, however, required more of policy than law " : Foss, I, 139.

own defence and threatened that if he could not get justice 'he would seek it in a higher court,' *i.e.*, appeal to Rome.

"... The King's advocate applied for an adjournment of the council. ... Everyone was impatient to hear " the Archbishop of Rouen, " an archbishop (*l*) pleading the King's cause against the hierarchy of England. ... A compromise ensued ... it is clear that notwithstanding the lamentable condition of the country, there was still left some respect for law. The only inn of court for lawyers then existing was to be found in the archbishop's palace " (or other religious houses?).

If Aubrey de Vere was the first King's counsel, it must be remembered that the King was now the subject of a judicial inquiry—we cannot say sued or charged—for the first time. Probably there was then no machinery for making the Crown a defendant, and other trials mentioned above were either held under the sovereign's commission or did not concern him personally.

We are approaching the time of the *serviens ad legem pro domino rege* : Aubrey is merely *serviens*. Here we have a layman pleading before a very high ecclesiastical " court "—a high official, " great chamberlain " (*m*), who as sheriff for more than one county had been a *placitator* in his various causes. He is a good sample of the stuff of which the early bar was made and it is no wonder that he is roundly called *causidicus*.

1142. Estate of Ranulf Peverell (*n*). The Bishop of

(*l*) These two points are well illustrated by better authorities. Liebermann (on Vacarius) says : " The archbishop's [*sc.* of Canterbury] clergy treated legal questions as a matter of professional training " : 11 *Eng. Hist. Rev.* 308 (1896). Round, dealing with this time (1130), remarks that " the very name of 'plea' became a terror to all men ... even to secure one's simplest rights, money had always to be paid " : *Geoffrey Mandeville*, c. iv, p. 105 (1892). He is explaining " sine placito " in many charters, *i.e.*, immunity from process.

(*m*) Round, in *D. N. B.*

(*n*) Bigelow, *Plac. A.-N.* 147, from Madox, *Exch.* 198, 2nd ed. ; 134 fol. ed. (a record).

London's judgment *in audientia et praesentia nostra per barones* [chief tenants : Madox] *nostros et per legales homines ecclesiæ nostræ clericos et laicos.*

1143 (about). Gervase of Canterbury (*o*) tells the story of Theobald, Archbishop of Canterbury (d. 1161), getting Henry of Winchester removed from his Legatine office in England. " Hence began," he says, " serious quarrels, litigation and appeals hitherto unheard of. Then were laws and lawyers first called into England [from abroad] of whom Master Vacarius was the first. He taught law at Oxford . . . " (*p*).

All we can safely get out of this is that in the undoubtedly closer intercourse with the Continent since 1066, Roman law, in both senses, was more and more studied. The ecclesiastic Lanfranc and the layman Vacarius were both well acquainted with the practice and forensic procedure of Italian tribunals, ancient and modern; advocacy would be nothing new to them. Miss Norgate (*pp*) paraphrases Gervase : the quarrels of the prelates " led to more frequent appeals to Rome, to elaborate legal pleadings, to the drawing of subtle legal distinctions unknown to the old customary procedure of the land . . ." This is, in effect, a forecast of the professional lawyer, but we must not understand

---

(*o*) Oxf. Hist. Soc. 2 *Collectanea*, 2nd ser. 168, from *Actus Pont*, ii, 384 ; Rolls ; Gervase, *fl.* 1200.

(*p*) Oriuntur hinc inde discordiae graves lites et appellationes antea inauditae. Tunc leges et causidici in Angliam primo vocati sunt, quorum primus erat magister Vacarius. Hic in Oxonefordia legem docuit. . . ." Possibly the absolute use of *lex* here = [jus] law—its earliest or a very early use—points to familiarity with a growing systematic study (or " Fach "), Selden, 2 *Works*, 1173; *de X. scriptoribus Angl.* seems to accept Gervase and calls attention to the fact that immediately after this date books *utriusque juris* were greatly increased in the English monasteries. Rashdall, *The Universities of Europe*, vol. 2, pt. 2, c. 12, s. 1, p. 336, points out that Gervase is the only writer who puts Vacarius at Oxford at this time—1149; if he (G.) meant *this*, he is wrong; but his words may mean a later date and we know that V. was living in England in 1198; probably his date was wrong and V. did teach at Oxford after 1167 (a date due to John of Salisbury, *Letters*).

(*pp*) *England under the Angevin Kings*, i, 379-80 (1887).

the "pleadings" too technically; and for the subtleties, an educated churchman was at least as good as a trained legist. When the same writer anticipates a little (*q*) she remarks, happily, "the English clerical lawyers in Stephen's time and in Henry's early years found their account in combining the two studies [the canon law and the Theodosian code]; by degrees both together passed out of the hands of the clergy, into those of a new class of lay lawyers; and in later days, while on the Continent the Canon law fell into neglect with its exclusively clerical professors, in England it was being preserved by being linked with the civil law under the care of lay *doctores utriusque juris.*"

1158-63. *Richard de Anesty* v. *Mabel de Francheville* (*r*). In this case we have lay parties, lay judges, lay lawyers as well as ecclesiastical. The plaintiff, "the heroic English litigant" (Maitland), is the narrator. Picking our material—he sends to the King in Normandy to get his writ (*breve*) "whereby I brought the other side into court" (*s*): he pays for it. He knows that the cause will be tried in the Archbishop's court. He delivers another writ which he had got from the Queen (as Regent?) to Richard de Lucy, one of the Justiciars, who fixed the trial (*diem placitandi*) at Northampton. Then he sent his *clericus* Nicholas [is it he who drew up this story?] to get witnesses. Then he went to the trial *cum amicis et auxiliis meis*—*the consilium.* Next the cause is duly—by the King's writ—removed into the Archbishop's court; there are adjournments from day to day and always to a different place—wherever the bench will be; the plaintiff

---

(*q*) *England under the Angevin Kings,* ii, 466.

(*r*) Palgrave, 2 *Commonwealth,* v, lxxv, text and translation; Bigelow, *Pl.* 311; 1 P. & M. 192; I, c. vi; this case might be called the ancient *Jarndyce* v. *Jarndyce.*

(*s*) Per quod posui adversarios meos in placitum.

counts every penny of the cost (*t*). At one point " I went for Master Ambrose, who was then with the Abbot of St. Alban's in Norfolk." Here Maitland has an interesting speculation (*u*) : " Another guess is inviting. If we attribute " the *Summa de Matrimonio* by Vacarius " to the years which closely follow 1156, we give it to a time when England and Rome, Normandy and Gascony, were witnesses to the dogged litigiousness of that immortal plaintiff, Richard of Anesty. . . . He had the professional aid of another Italian lawyer whose name has elsewhere been coupled with that of Vacarius, namely, of Master Ambrose. Is it impossible that if Magister Ambrosius was of counsel for the plaintiff, Magister Vacarius was retained for the defence? Or, again, if in 1159, Vacarius still remained an inmate of Archbishop Theobald's household, we can hardly doubt that he was consulted about a case which raised nice questions of matrimonial law, and tasked the wisdom of the archiepiscopal court to the uttermost?"

Richard goes on : " Having thus got at the aforesaid clerks " [bishops, etc.] " I kept my day with my helpers at London. . . . Then I sent John my brother beyond the seas to the King's court because it was told me that my adversaries had purchased the King's writ exempting them from pleading (*placitaturos*) until the King should return to England; and therefore I sent my brother for another writ lest my pleadings should be stayed on account of " their writ. Then he secures Hilary, Bishop of Chichester, " much celebrated for his knowledge of the Civil law . . . a very favourable witness, and that same

---

(*t*) To this ledgerliness we owe an account of every minute stage. The costliness of law at this time is illustrated by Bigelow, *Pl. A.-N.* 247, " before 1163 "; from *Chron.* Jocelin de Brakelond : Camd. Soc. (1840), p. 51. Someone was to be tried for rape in the court of the monastery of St. Edmunds (bury), but Henry of Essex insisted that as the girl was born " in dominio suo de L." the trial must be in his court, " on which pretext he had the effrontery to harass the court with journeys and innumerable expenses for a long time."
(*u*) 13 *L. Q. R.* 141; 3 *Coll. Papers*, 101.

favourable witness was afterwards appointed by the Pope to decide the case concerning which he had testified " (Palgrave) and—*N.B.*—a written document to the effect that he (H.) had been present at a divorce is evidence (*x*). There is another hearing at London with *clerici, testes, amici,* and *auxilia*—verily the *magnum agmen* of Livy; and for four days he was *placitans.* Then the *adversarii* apparently got an adjournment *sine die,* and he has to go to Gascony and wait thirteen weeks and spend a large sum before he got *praeceptum Regis placitandi.* More *magistri* —possibly clerks, not lawyers—are consulted, and at last Richard falls sick and has to " essoin." Next, he crosses the Channel to get and gets *licentiam appellandi Romam* " though judgment had not been given against him, because he is tired of repeated continuances " (Bigelow, *Pl. A.-N.* 313), *i.e.,* you could appeal on an interlocutory point of procedure. Then a curious incident happens : " I sued for the Archbishop's writ of appeal "; when, at last, he got it, it was " without seal (*y*) in order that I might show the same to my Advocates (*advocatis*=here, canonists) " —so called for the first time—" and obtain their opinion whether it was according to law (*rationabile*)." Amongst those who see it is Master Ambrose; they amend it but the authorities at Canterbury refuse to seal that document —probably it was no longer a fair copy—but they gave him a new parchment : more references, more amendments; at last it is signed. Now the scene shifts to Rome : the plaintiff sends *clericos meos* his chaplain and a *magister* Peter; the Pope commissions the Bishop of Chichester and the Abbot of Westminster (*in eorum curia*); they give him an appointment at Westminster and thither he went with his *advocati, amici, testes* and *auxilia.* Then a witness

---

(*x*) But soon after he gets good " viva voce " (his own words) evidence to the same effect; he brings the witnesses back with him; perhaps he had been told that the first evidence was insufficient.

(*y*) *I.e.,* unsigned and therefore capable of amendment and final settlement.

who was too ill to come sends his son instead—quite possibly to give secondary evidence of his father's knowledge. At last he came to London, *paratus et munitus placitandi*, because he thought judgment would be delivered, *i.e.*, he was ready for the formalities. At this point the other side appealed to Rome—probably they were now beaten on the merits : " so I asked for a form (*scriptum*) of Appeal " ; he got it at Oxford. This document went through the same vicissitudes as the last, but in the end was signed. Then several prelates are asked to and do give Richard *brevia* to the Pope and the Cardinals, *i.e.*, probably they said something in his favour, one is called " de prece " : only his *clerici* go to Rome, and they bring back a certificate (*carta*) for the Archbishop, the chief ecclesiastic judge, one for Richard de Luci, the chief lay judge, and one for the winner, the plaintiff. The King was annoyed that he had not got one (because of a fee attached) and he would not let Richard " make fine " with him till he, too, got one. There are more hearings and adjournments before the plaintiff gets the fruits of his judgment, but, at any rate, he gets rid of his *clerici* and *advocati* (probably the two words mean with him the same persons, for he never speaks of both classes as present together); we only hear of *amici* and *auxilia*—*quotquot habere potui*; law, in a sense, was done with, but now, perhaps for that reason, Ranulf de Glanville is called in (" special," we might say) as a " helper " (Pal.). De Lucy is too busy to take the case himself, but hands it over, after many delays, to two competent commissioners. The other side are duly cited and at long last at Woodstock *gratia d. regis et per judicium curiae adjudicata est mihi terra avunculi mei.*

Then, quite modernly, we are told of the costs; they are called *dona* and, perhaps, in view of the wholly exceptional incidents of the case—especially the pertinacity of the plaintiff—we could hardly call them fees; they are distributed to *placitatores* and *clerici auxiliantes* in the Archbishop's court, to persons not described in one bishop's court, and in the *curia regis* and to some named *magistri*; those *placitatores*—here mentioned for the first time—were no doubt ecclesiastics and intended to be distinguished from other recipients, *ceteri placitatores de amicis meis qui ad placita mea solebant venire,* by which, it seems, are intended lay legal assistants.

This famous suit will hardly serve as a typical instance of the period, but it is easy to discern that the elaborate framework of this litigation was in essence that of humbler tribunals. One absence is noteworthy—especially as the plaintiff spared no expense, indeed ran into debt for sums of which he gives us details of interest in more senses than one—*viz.*, that of the *attornatus* at some point or other (unless, indeed, he be concealed among the *auxilia, amici*, etc.), who is also absent from the other trials we have mentioned; the fact is that it is early for him yet, though we shall see him (by another name) in the next. In all of them the parties have been more or less aristocratic; so far, litigation is hardly a popular right; people only go to law for " big " interests.

    Neque enim levia aut ludicra petuntur
                      Praemia.

On the other hand, it is curious that pictures of a trial at this time often ignore the *advocatus*—the bar, so to say, does not seem to be missed, though there is an ample forensic phraseology (z).

    (z) *E.g.*, in 1169 Arnulf, Bishop of Lisieux, writes to Pope Alexander complaining of a vexatious suit against the Bishop of London : " Tractus est . . . in *causam,* si tamen causa dicenda est, ubi nullum potuit *contradictio* facere *quaestionem,* ubi nullum *litigium,* nulla *judiciarii ordinis* forma *processit* : ubi sine *reo* et *teste* idem *actor* et *judex* solitariam formavit de singulari voluntate *sententiam.* Felicem se iste judicaret si ei *judex* suus *auditorii* communis *aream* impertisset, si *citatus* venire, si *conventus respondere,* si denique dubium experiri potuisset *sententiae* fatalis *eventum.*" (6 *Materials for Hist.* . . . Becket, 635; Let. 529; Rolls.) In 1193 Nigellus *Contra Curiales et Officiales Clericos* (Wright, 1 *Sat. Poets, 12th Century,* 161; Rolls) says of Conscience : " non est amicus qui *consulat* tibi utilius, actor qui

1164. When he does appear we cannot always be sure that he was a *jurisperitus*. In the litigation (*a*) about Lutone Church, William Chamberlain " laicus et uxoratus " had wrongfully seized it " sicut advocatus " and turned it into *servitium officii militaris* (*i.e.*, feudal). The Bishop refused (even the King) to turn him out *nisi judiciario ordine* and so appointed *placitandi tempus et locum*; the defendant did not appear, but sent *nuntios* with a tale; still the Bishop would not determine against an absent man. At last the King appointed a local jury of inquisition and so did the Bishop (the same men?); it was found to be " alms." " So, uncontradicted found (*probaverunt*) with their hands on the Gospels, the *tres electi*."

Anticipating a little, we will deal with some trials mentioned in the *Chronicle of Battel Abbey* (*b*) written before 1200. In Stephen's time " now regal justice was sought and now ecclesiastical, but by reason of abounding iniquity it could not be had at that time "; both sides in the (ecclesiastical) litigation in question appeal to Rome. Under Henry II there is more law. The Abbot appears *non in propria persona sed per procuratorem sufficientem*, the other side *nec per se nec per responsalem*. When the Abbot makes " complaint of . . . interferences, in the royal court " he is heard " *in audentia magnatorum qui in curia regis vices domini regis exsequebantur*," *i.e.*, the King no

---

alleget subtilius, *judex* qui *causam* tuam *judicet aequius*. *Vocetur* ergo *ad diem legitimum* conscientia *tribus edictis* vel *peremptorio* uno, etsi necesse est praestentur et *indutiae legitimae*. Ipsa cum venerit, *pro tribunali* sedeat, ipsa siquid habet *adversa proponat*, ipsa *testes* suos, sciliet seipsum *producat*, ipsa *judicium proferat*, ipsa *sententiam* excipiat. . . ." *Amicus* may include "learned friend." *Ib.* 166 : " Quid autem dicemus de his qui *scienter* pro causa iniqua fovenda et *defendenda* animum exhalarunt cum constet quod quaestus et ambitio fuerint in proposito? "—perhaps a (very early) satire on " leather lunged " and *hireling* advocates.

In John of Salisbury's *ideal* sketch of a trial about this time the " bar " is very prominent; see App. VIII.

(*a*) 1 P. & M. I, v, p. 124, the issue was " Lay fee or alms " ? *ib.* from 1 *Gest. Abb.* 113; Rolls.

(*b*) Lat. text, 113, 116; Engl. transl. by M. A. Lower, 1851, p. 125.

longer always sat in person. Richard de Lucy is spoken of as *procurator* (c) of the Abbey.

1159. " The King's writ to his justices granting permission to the Abbot of Abingdon to plead by Attorney " (d) : permitto quod abbas mittat senescallum suum vel aliquem alium in loco suo ad assisas vestras et ad placita; the judges must receive " quem ad vos miserit loco suo." " Attornatus " is not used.

1176. Another Abbot wanting (e) legal advice against the great Godfrey de Lucy seeks as his " advocate " (f) " one Master Gerard Pucelle," a very learned man and a " clerk " of Richard Archbishop of Canterbury, and asks him to " defend," but he excused himself because " he could not defend any part of it, lest by so doing he might seem to disapprove as unreasonable the acts of his own master." The Bishop of Exeter also declined because Godfrey was a priest of his church, and Master John of Salisbury refused for the same reason; " the common and general excuse of all being that they were unwilling to incur the displeasure of Richard de Lucy," the powerful father of the plaintiff. " The Abbot being in great difficulty someone advised him that he should speak to a certain *clericus*, a good lawyer (*legisperito*) who had come with the Legate from Italy "— characteristic of the times—" and arrange with him to undertake his case at the trial "—mark the reason—" as he was neither a native nor an inhabitant of the King's realms and was under no obligation either of gratitude or friendship to anyone on this side of the Alps, he feared neither King, prince, archbishop, bishop nor any person in the Kingdom, ecclesiastical or secular, in the advocacy of any

---

(c) Commissum sibi procuratoris officium, p. 165 Engl. : 150.

(d) Hence inserted here, though not a trial : from 2 *Chron. Mon. Abing.* 222; Rolls; in Bigelow, *Pl. A.-N.* 206.

(e) *Chron. Bat. Abbey*, and Bigelow, *Procedure*, 358 : *Godfrey de Luci* v. *Odo, Abbot.* The trial is at Westminster, Cardinal (a *latere*) Hugh, Papal Legate, presiding.

(f) Eng. trans. 188; Lat. 172.

cause whatever "—the earliest and most uncompromising declaration of the independence of the bar. It proceeds, however, from the English chronicler and not from the Italian lawyer, who after promptly " taking on " the case for a silver mark—not, indeed, in cash, but on trust (*recepturus*)—declines it " because he was unwilling to incur the displeasure of the King and the great men of the realm." The venerable client is greatly distressed; then a friend says : " If you had afforded me and others enough money to attend the schools (*scolas frequentare*) we should have been expert in law and the *Decreta* (*in lege et decretis*) and could have helped you. As it is we are ignorant of the books (*scripturis*) and cannot judge ourselves (*consilium non habemus*) and are not able to get good advice for love or money." The Abbot replies : " I am beginning to regret that I did not apply my mind to the study of law (*studio legum*) "; this defect is also referred to later on. The next day he goes to the trial, " when the opposite party came attended by a long train of *advocati*." Their chief *procurator et advocatus* was one *magister* Ivo of Cornwall, who tells (*g*) the court that Godfrey de Lucy is abroad " in the schools " (*scolarum studia frequentantem*).

After Ivo's speech the Abbot is hopeless ; again and for the same reason as before the *potestates* decline *ad consilium suum benigne venirent*. At last Master Waleran and Master Gerard Pucelle (*h*), clerics, come to the rescue ; after

---

(*g*) He gives himself a *locus* : " . . . litterasque patentes Godfredi de Luci tunc in transmarinis scholas frequentantis in publicum proferens, commissam sibi manifestavit causae procurationem et Godefridi ratihabitionem "—a very early and accurate mention of *attornatio*. He says to the court : " satis vobis, domini judices, ex patenti testimonio litterarum domini mei G. credimus constare ipsum utpote in remotis extra hoc regnum partibus scholarum studia frequentantem huic causae suae interesse non posse, mihique causam eandem procurandam commisisse, cujus ego, advocatione suscepta, non minorem mihi quam si dominus meus praesens adesset postulo dari audientiam." *Postulo* is from technical Roman law.

(*h*) He lectured in Paris about 1160, where Walter Mapes (*Nugae*, 73; Camd. Soc.) heard him; he was perhaps an Englishman; he died

a short consultation, outside as usual, they return into court (*i*). Gerard according to the chronicler exhibits that independence of speech which the latter had (above) commended; *inter alia*, he says (*k*) : " Subject to His Majesty's rights, we reply that in ecclesiastical affairs the secular power has no rights."

The result is a compromise and the moral is " advocatorum confunderetur multiplicitas." Our moral is that when these pages were written the law school was a recognised institution and advocacy an art.

Here incidentally we meet the " attorney " for the first time in action; he is not yet differentiated from the *procurator* or *advocatus*.

1184. The ecclesiastical element in non-ecclesiastical courts is exemplified by an incident (*l*) in Ranulf de Glanville's career. One Gilbert of Plumpton was charged with forcible abduction and marriage (and of the robbery of the chattels of the father usually alleged on such occasions). Glanville as Justiciar orders a prosecution; the youth pleaded not guilty (*m*) to the felonies, but it is said that Glanville, having designed the heiress for one of his officials, deliberately suborned the itinerant justices at Worcester to pass sentence of death. This they did, and the rope was actually round Gilbert's neck when Baldwin, Bishop of Worcester, who had ridden " post-haste " with a great

---

in 1184; he became bishop of a diocese which had three cathedrals—at Chester, Coventry and Lichfield : 14 *Hist. Littér. de France*, p. 303 (1817). As he was " domestic chaplain of the Archbishop of Canterbury . . . his advocacy [is] the more generous and disinterested " : Lower, 193.

(*i*) Non diu protracto sed maturo expeditoque consilio redeunt pariter ad judicum consessum.

(*k*) Salva pace domini regis respondemus quod in rebus eccl. nihil juris obtinet potestas secularis.

(*l*) Benedict of Peterborough, *Gesta H. II*; I, 314, Rolls; *Glanvill* in *D. N. B.* (Maitland); *Baldwin, ib.*; *Plumpton Correspce.* xvi, Camd. Soc. 1839.

(*m*) " Modis omnibus defendebat et super hoc se juri stare obtulit," *i.e.*, everything was in due form of law. Ultimately he was detained during the King's pleasure, *i.e.*, Gl. kept him in prison till Henry died.

TRIALS WITH AND WITHOUT COUNSEL. 75

mob, forbade—*de jure*, we are told—the *carnifices* to proceed " sub anathemate " because it was Sunday and St. Mary Magdalen's day. The executioners naturally asked by what right " he impeded the King's justice?" However, the prelate so intimidated them that they agreed to leave Gilbert in the custody of the King's *castellanus* for one day, during which the King remitted the sentence of death. The story smacks of its age, not only by its legal ingredients.

1198. " *Abbot of St. Augustine [Canterbury]* v. *Men of Thanet* " (*n*). The defendants came to a court at Westminster (*coram* the Archbishop of Canterbury, the Bishop of London and the King's Justices) and " nominated in their place to win or lose thirty men of a common interest in that suit against . . . the Abbot . . . those thirty came for the other men of Thanet who were not the Abbot's men and they were held to be *in misericordia* for a false claim (defence?) " (*o*).

Note that the word *attornatus* is not used in this and the Battel cases. The number of representatives here alone forbids any theory of professional *attornatio*.

1202-5. Although entirely enveloped in an ecclesiastical atmosphere, the tone and phraseology of *Evesham (Monks of)* v. *Worcester (Bishop of)* conveniently illustrate, indeed richly reveal, contemporary procedure.

Thomas of Marlborough was about 1190 a monk and ultimately Abbot of Evesham, whose *Chronicle* he wrote; he had been a law lecturer at Oxford, and he tells us thrice that he was *jurisperitus* (*p*); that the Abbot liked his

---

(*n*) Bigelow, *A.-N. Plac.* 224, 226 from 2 Twysden's X *Scriptores* (pp. 1842-3); W. Thorne's *Chronica*.

(*o*) " Posuerunt loco suo ad lucrandum vel perdendum XXX homines in ipsa querela socios . . . qui ad abbatem non tenebant . . . pro falso clamore." Had " Glanville " made the phrase *ad. luc. v. p.* common? Cf. for the " thirty " the appearance later of the " Inhabitants of ——shire " by two defendants.

(*p*) 109, 117, 141; 122, 127; 123; 121; 130-1, 150; 120, 139; Rolls. His point is, " I know law, though you would not expect it," for in

elegantes allegationes; at one " interlocutory " (his own term) hearing in London both sides were *copiose muniti advocatis*; the crushing expenses of litigation may be gathered from the recital of the prolonged self-sacrifices of the monks; he exhibits a true lawyer's joy in the other side's grave error of forensic tactics whereby judgment was delivered in the second year of the suit (*p*). The Bishop took advice from the *magister* Will. de Verdun *summus consiliarius ejus*. At last there is an appeal to Rome whither Thomas goes as *procurator totius causae*. There in 1205 he has to pay an *advocatus* to be ready to protect him from his own Abbot's devices. The latter also wanted to get rid of another *jurisperitus* at home, Thomas of Northwich. Incidentally they give sums of money to the Pope Innocent III and cardinals and the court, many of whom would not accept the gifts until they were satisfied that the givers had no cause pending in their courts. Being at Bologna for six months he studies more law there for the benefit of his cause (147, 149). The trial comes on before the Pope, who rules that the argument must be on the principle, not on the details, of the case (151). Then Robert of Clipstone, *procurator* of the Bishop (*q*), " although he was the defendant both in the matter in dispute (since he had been placed in possession of the jurisdiction of the monastery) and also in the actual condition in which he

---

1213 (*ib*. 237) he says to the Legate in court at Evesham : " quia juris periti estis [=a singular] non est necesse mea circa hujusmodi jura allegare . . . quamvis ad excusationem mihi sufficiat quod licet monachis jura ignorare."

(*q*) So the learned editor translates : quum esset reus a re quia in possessione jurisdictionis monasterii erat constitutus, immo a reatu, sicut per sententiam contra eum postea latam est declaratum, actor effectus est. But William of Drogheda says, *Summa Aur*. c. 86 : " Potest dici reus, dupliter vel a re vel a reatu. Reus diciter a reatu cum sententiam reportaverit contra se contrariam. . . . Unde ratione delicti dicitur reus. . . . Et secundum hoc non dicetur reus pendente lite, sed ea finita per sententiam diffinitivam. Dicitur et alia modo reus a re quae petitur ab eo . . . et sic reus praesumptus non autem verus." Cf. Rayner, *Ars Notariae*, c. 69.

stood (as was shown by the sentence afterwards given against him), was nevertheless appointed to open the pleadings as plaintiff." His very learned friend on the other side made, in his ignorance of that court, such a long exordium that His Holiness stopped him and said : " Come to business." Then, says his opponent, he made a very good legal argument. Then (152) addressing Thomas, the Pope says : " All we want from you *procuratores* is to be certified of the facts, for you are both *jurisperiti* [*i.e.*, can do it properly], and when the need arises the *advocati* can make us answer about the law," but not on the facts (162). " For we stood there entrenched in our *advocati*, for both sides had hired four, but mine were the better men "; he had, in fact, collected his *magistri* from " different parts of the world " (*r*), and he not only paid them fees but refreshers, too. His opponent actually complained to the Pope that Thomas had left him nobody. "Nobody," said the Pontiff with a smile, "ever wanted good store of *advocati* in the Court of Rome." In his speech Thomas, mindful of the court's love of brevity, gives us page after page of it. The Pope formally calls on Robert to reply, and in his turn (162) on Thomas—" Procurator, responde." Then (164) the Pope says : " We have heard enough from the *procuratores* about the facts; now for the law—when I sit again." When he does, he stops the subtle and very learned legal arguments in both *jura*, canon and civil, of the *advocati* and says : " Now, *procuratores*, back to the *privilegia* " (164). After the *procuratores* the *advocati* have another turn. " Well, procurator Thomas," says the

---

(*r*) So in 1363 Whitfield, Provost of Queen's College, Oxford, prosecuting a suit in the *curia* at Avignon [1309-77] consults and pays three named English lawyers there; " apparently advocates from all nations pleaded at the *curia* "; " the expenses of legal advice at the court are enormous " : Thorold Rogers (v. 1, p. 137) *Hist. Agric. & Prices*. So the Abbey of Meaux, 1367-72, having an appeal to Rome, paid John of Appleby, " decano Londonio tunc advocato in cur. Rom.," 40s. annually for the rest of his life, for his help, etc. : 3 *Chron*. . . . *Melsa*, 166; Rolls. Appleby was one of Whitfield's *advv.*, each of whom got ten florins.

Pope, " what have you to say to that? " " I think I can deal with it." " I don't think so," says the judge. Thomas makes another speech and craves in aid some " leges " which he had—*non sine pretio*—from dominus Azo, then the lord of law-lords at Bologna. Thereupon his adversary formally withdraws his charges (*allegationes*), and on December 24, 1204, the Pope gives a judgment which makes Thomas faint with joy (170). Next (184) he was in jeopardy of arrest by Roman creditors for the sums he had borrowed to carry on the suit—in fact, they seized his documents as security (198)—he had no money to hire an *advocatus* for the next issue to be heard, so he has to argue himself; in doing so, he admits more than once that he distorted the facts (*s*), " to give colour in pleading." In reply (189) his adversary remarks : " We have learned in the schools and it is the better opinion (*magistrorum nostrorum*) that prescription does not run against episcopal rights." " Then," said His Holiness, " when you and your lawyers learned this you must have drunk a good deal of your English beer." On the point of prescription the Pope makes a remark—indeed, gives evidence about certain facts (190)—which leads Thomas to say : " And though *dominus Papa* spoke this like a just judge, for prescription is odious, yet I regretted that he thus cured (*suppleret*) the defect in my opponent's argument, and not being able to hold my tongue for annoyance, I said : ' Holy Father, you have full authority and therefore may do as you please, but according to the civil law other judges may not supply to *advocati* what is wanted in their facts but only in their law.' ' That,' said the Pope, ' is bad law.' I was silent, though I felt that I was prejudiced, for unless the Pope had supplied the facts ' beyond all doubt we should have won our point about prescription.' " At another hearing (191) Adam Sortes stood nobly by him (*astitit*) *quia in attesta-*

(*s*) Cf. (199) more litigantium audacter at praesumptuose respondi.

tionibus erat valde expeditus. Finally the suit is referred to ecclesiastics in England.

This account, though the merest sketch of the original (from the pen, it must not be forgotten, of one who was at once litigant, pleader and reporter—a rare combination), has been included here because a suit in the " super " court of the world might not only attract attention in all Christian countries, but this did so primarily in England where the exuberance of its rules of procedure and its highly developed technical legal argumentation were sure to lead to imitation. Especially noticeable is the recognition of the abstract difference between law and fact and the actual difficulty—which every practitioner knows—of keeping them apart in practice. Not only is this seen in the incident above (152, 164), but at one point (162) " the Pope had forbidden the *advocati* to address themselves to the facts, they must stick to the law and that when it is wanted, ' for,' said he, ' the *procuratores* know the facts and the law.' " This must refer to the individuals before him at the moment, for the normal distinction is notorious and is insisted on by the Pope himself in several passages (above). The fact is that at that time it depended on the man whether he was a mere mouthpiece or a deputy or an arguer or an agent or a plenipotentiary—despite any theory; it was impossible for a speaker, who knew the ins and outs of a case as Thomas did, to confine himself mathematically to any one capacity.

Between 1235 and 1249. After this view of the great stage at Rome minor local exhibitions at home may appear insignificant, but a trial (*t*)—or rather a series of hearings—about 1240 is here outlined not only because procedure is almost wholly at home, but because it is minute and illustrates as does the last, exactly the kinds and forms of litigation with which William of Drogheda, who is writing at this very

---

(*t*) 2 *Chron. Mon. de Melsa*, xi, 12-22; Rolls, ed. Bond, from whom the outline above is borrowed.

moment, is concerned and especially that dislike of the ecclesiastics of being driven into secular courts with which he made play by his constant reminder of the royal writ of Prohibition (*u*). The nuns [of Swine, E. Riding] claimed the tithes of the monks of Meaux for pasture in Sutcoates and Drypool which they rented of Sir Sayer of Sutton. "They cited us *coram officiali curiae Eboracensis*"; the Abbot, appearing in person, "pleading exemption by virtue of Papal privilege." Stephen, the official, rejected the plea and the Abbot appealed to Rome. Stephen, despite this *legitima appellatio*, not only pronounced sentence of excommunication against " our abbot and monks," but (*x*) condemned them in costs. The clergy generally were against us (*n.b.*, we have only the monks' version). Prosecuting our appeal, we got *litterae apostolicae* sent to the (named) *judices delegati* against Canon Hamo, the Master of the nuns and the nuns and other *litterae papales* to the same against Stephen.

Nothing was done in the former appeal, but that against Stephen was set down; he was cited *abbati responsurus et juri pariturus*; he appears *per procuratorem*; the Abbot has an easy victory, and the judges add the extraordinary injunction, " on pain of excommunication, that Stephen should neither directly nor indirectly do or procure on any pretence whatever that the proceedings of those judges should be delayed or hindered by any lay authority " (*y*). The reversal of the excommunication (and condemnation in costs) was to be publicly recited all over the East Riding—the judges send this order *per litteras praecentori eccl. Eborac.* " on pain of excommunication," and to other local ecclesiastics.

But the ladies were a very different story; they neither

(*u*) *E.g.* 2 *Chron. Melsa*, 77; about 1250-69.

(*x*) *Nihilominus, i.e.*, if excommunicated, they could not be made to pay costs.

(*y*) " Quocunque colore per quod processus eorundem judicum per potestatem laicalem differri posset vel impediri."

appeared in person nor *per proc. legitimum*; nor did their Master; they are naturally (z) condemned in the costs of the day—taxation to be reserved till the last day of the hearing; another hearing is fixed. Then the Abbot appears " personaliter " (as the *officialis* had once done) and the nuns *per quendam Stephanum clericum proc. suum— legitime constitutum* says one MS., unlike Hamo (below); the Abbot claims 500 marks " out of pockets." The judges find it necessary repeatedly to warn the *procurator* to keep to the point (*ut dictas moniales juxta formam mandati defenderet*); he would keep insisting on trumpery points, and at last *contumaciter a judicio recessit*. They excommunicate him; he submits and is pardoned on paying 20s., the costs of the last day; the nuns, for " open contumacy," are fined 20 marks; another hearing is fixed.

This order they treat with contempt, and their Prioress is excommunicated in her own chapel (*a*). Again they fail to appear; the judges give them one more chance, peremptorily denying any future adjournment; and as *crescente contumacia crescere debet et poena*, Merton Chapel is summarily awarded to the monks; Stephen not paying his 20s. is excommunicated and called up for judgment. As for Canon Hamo, " as he would appear (*comparebat*) by *procurator* and not by a *legitimus* "—which was contumacious—he is suspended *ab ingressu ecclesiæ*, and ordered to appear. Still the holy women default; their chief officials are suspended *ab ingressu eccl.* They had resisted (*irreverenter impediverunt*, may we say, like suffragettes?) the handing over of Merton Chapel, and had not paid a sou; the judges deal faithfully with every breach of the law; distress, *e.g.*, is granted. Hamo is brought to submission; before he gets relief he has to give security. After more

---

(z) One MS. says the Court had oral and written evidence that they were properly cited.

(a) " Candelis accensis et pulsatis campanis " (by the *executores*) says one MS.

C.H. 6

feminine contumacy the judges shut up the parish church of Swine and all its chapels, and cited before them six lay brethren (*conversi*) who had been concerned in the Merton affair; Hamo again in default was finally suspended " from everything." The nuns being still *indefensæ*, *i.e.*, not appearing, the whole institution is suspended *a celebratione divinorum*, and further " two canons and seven lay brethren were excommunicated by name because they had resorted to the sub-sheriff for help (*b*) in preventing the distraint of their cattle for payment " of the 20 marks. At last " the judges wrote to Henry of Bath, royal Justiciar, and to the Sheriff of York bidding them in no wise to hinder an ecclesiastical suit which had arisen between ecclesiastical parties." Then Meaux is put in possession of the church of Drypool—" the execution for the 20 marks having been revoked by the royal jurisdiction (*a potestate regia*)," the Archbishop of York now being officially informed of Hamo's degradation and required to give effect to it. And they further suggested to his Grace about the (now) large numbers of people " who, setting at defiance the keys of the Church " (*i.e.*, themselves), " had for more than forty days comfortably submitted to the ban of excommunication," that " according to the laws of the realm in such matters he should put forth the normal [secular] arm of his supremacy against them by writing to the Sheriff of York " (*c*).

(*b*) " Procurando abb. et monach. nostr. *ad forum saeculare* vocari." But, *ib.* p. 111, between 1249-69 " we took the Prior and Monastery of Watton into court before the King's justices " on a point of eccl. patronage; a *finalis concordia* was ultimately reached *per consensum* W. Gray, Abp. of York and the King's Justices. See *ib.* 174, for a purely eccl. cause, 1280-6. Later, however, there are some purely lay trials; the canons of Bridlington made a claim against the Abbey in 1372-96; they got a *breve regium*; the case was settled: *ib.* iii, 198. When a tenant " implacitavit " the Abbot, " we lost " and had to pay 20 marks: *ib.* 199. In that period the monastery, we know, retained lay legal advisers: so, *ib.* iii, 182 and xxvi; n.b., " primus et praecipuus dicti consilii," *i.e.*, the chief of several.

(*c*) " Secundum quod jura regiae majestatis de talibus exigunt, in eos brachium excellentiae suae vicecomiti Eborac. scribendo extenderet consuetum."

Meanwhile, four nuns, three lay brethren and many more *saeculares* broke through the wall of the church and occupied it. More excommunications, suspensions, citations, and another application to the Archbishop for secular support; " the judges could not *durius procedere* " (except to excommunicate all the nuns, paid and unpaid servants, helpers and sympathisers). Through the agency of the Archbishop the royal pleasure was signified, for at last " on a fixed day the said nuns and other excommunicated persons being no longer able to bear the Church's censures and the royal anger at their contumaciousness appeared by a (" sufficient " : one MS.) *procurator*." Terms are arrived at, by the mediation of friends; the nuns withdraw their claims, pay 200 marks damages and the costs. " In which *placitum*," says the chronicler, " we lost in meal and malt 700 marks."

We cannot but notice the alternation of fear of the interference of the secular law and of the actual resort to it, at convenience. The ultimate sanction, force, is obviously in the secular arm. Perhaps the chronicler, practically a party, makes too much of a local dispute; the abbey employs no lawyer (as it does in other suits), the other side sends somebody who is held not to be *sufficiens*, and at the crisis only, a *procurator*, the proper person. The writer is very much interested whether the latter is duly qualified or not.

We may note generally in the above cases that there is no oral evidence (*d*) (and, of course, no jury); there are plenty of admissions and documents, including *attestationes* (= affidavits). In these altitudes there was no room for a professional *attornatus* at this time; it was all " High Court " work, where fees are a very serious consideration.

In the great legal changes which mark the reign of

(*d*) R. de Anesty's *testes* do not depose in court.

Henry II one man, says Maitland (*e*), must have had a hand, *viz.* :—

Ranulf de Glanville,

" the father of the study of English Common law " (*f*). We met him (*g*) about 1160 as a consultant; that is, before he held any office. Whatever his profession (*h*) was, he was not in orders, and that is one reason why he makes an epoch in the history of English law. His secularity is well illustrated by the story in Walter Mapes (*i*), himself an itinerant justice in 1173, who once heard a speedy and just judgment for a poor man against a rich in the Exchequer, and said to Glanville, C.J. : " Considering that a poor man's suit can be put off by many dilatory expedients, you did it, under Heaven, very well." " Yes," said Ranulf, " we certainly do give judgment here quicker than your bishops in their cathedrals." " True," said Walter, " but if our King was as far off from you as the Pope is from the bishops I imagine you would be as slow." He laughed and said nothing (*k*). Here we get the two judicial systems which had exercised so much thought at Clarendon side by side and contrasted. Whoever wrote " our first classical text book " (*l*), we are only concerned with a small part of its

---

(*e*) *D. N. B.*
(*f*) St. *Seventeen Lect.* vii.
(*g*) P. 69.
(*h*) No one says he was a *trained* lawyer; " he writes as a lawyer keenly interested in legal problems and not ashamed to confess that he does not know the answer to all the questions that he raises "; " he writes not as a statesman but a lawyer." W. of Newburgh calls him *regni procurator* : *Hist. Rer. Angl.* B. IV, p. 297; c. iv, p. 302; Rolls, v. 1. Possible authors of " Glanville " are Hubert Walter, R.'s nephew and secretary who *omnia regni novit jura* (*Gerv.* ii, 406) or a clerk of the royal court : Maitland, *D. N. B.*, and 1 P. & M. B. I, c. v.
(*i*) *De Nugis*, 241; Camd. Soc. 1st ser. (50).
(*k*) For another instance of his liberalness, see *ib.* 8. At 242 Walter says : " Non in omnes loquor judices sed in majorem et in insaniorem partem . . . a praedictis inferri potest quod curia locus est poenalis; infernum eam non dico sed fere tantam habet ad ipsum similitudinem quantam equi ferrum ad equae " (a horse's shoe to a mare's).
(*l*) Finished 1187-9; 1 P. & M., B. I, c. v, p. 142.

contents.   But it is all concerned with secular law in a secular court.

Chapter XII of Book I deals with an absent defendant and is evidently the outcome of a routine which had developed with time and, in the interest of justice, required regulating, *e.g.*, in the case of a sick party. It provides for genuine Essoins (*m*), and goes on (*n*) : " If on the third day he neither appear nor essoin himself then let it be ordered that he be forthcoming *in propria persona* on another day; and that he send a fit attorney in his place to win or lose for him " (*o*).

Thus, whoever on the appointed day may appear " in his stead offering to undertake his defence (*defensioni*) whether authorised by his letters or without them, is immaterial; if it be known that he be allied to the absent " one " he shall be received for him in court." Here, then, the principle is that representation normally depends on reasonable absence (*p*), and the tribunal ought to have formal authority for the representative.

Thus we are here, for the first time in England, face to face with a code meant to be authoritative for a legal representative in court.

This is confirmed and expressed by the title and contents

(*m*) App. X. Essoins seem to have died out by (about) 1400; cf. 1 *Lib. Alb.* 202, the Ordinance of 1356, p. 235 (*w*) (where see the date), and the absence of reference to them in later Ordinance (*ib.*).

(*n*) Beames's translation, 1812.

(*o*) Aut pro se sufficientem responsalem mittat ad lucrandum vel perdendum pro eo, !oco suo : so cc. 19 & 21. The famous phrase *lucr. v. perd.* is taken from Tac. *Germania* 24 : aleam sobrii [Germani] inter seria exercent, tanta lucrandi perdendive temeritate ut . . .

Sufficiens resp. is not original in G. John of Salisbury writes to Pope Adrian in 1155-8, of an ecclesiastical court : Quum ergo reus tertio legitimis intervallis citatus esset . . . non faceret copiam sui nec ut oportebat sufficientes excusatores aut responsales misisset . . . Letters (7) p. 8, ed. Giles, 1848, " resp." goes back to at least 535 : *Novel,* 37.

(*p*) So the tenant's lord in a suit, practically a party, may send a *responsalis.*

of Book XI (*q*). Whoever wrote it was familiar with a normal system of legal representation (and an organized judicature (*r*)) not, indeed, that of the Bolognian *advocatus* —a topic which probably he avoided deliberately, for, even in 1180 a jurist could hardly ignore that school; the author " knew something of Roman and of canon law . . . probably his idea of what a law book should be had been derived from some one of the many small manuals of romano-canonical procedure that were becoming current " (*s*), *i.e.*, the influence of Bologna on practice was just beginning. At any rate, " Glanville " practises and lays down secular law in a secular court.

The title of Book XI is *de responsalibus qui loco dominorum ponuntur in curia ad lucrandum vel perdendum pro eis*. We cannot yet speak of a serjeant at law or counsel or attorney, but we are on the traces of the last, for the *responsalis* is a primitive *attornatus*, with whom from this point our quest is concerned.

Legal Education.

We have had references by the way to study of the laws. It has crept in, so to say, since the Conquest. Whether it be wholly or partially due to the revival of learning which took place about 1160, it is certain that when learning revived in England legal education began to be organized, too. " In connecting the sudden rise of Oxford into a *Studium Generale* with the recall of the English scholars from Paris by Henry II in or about the year 1167."—which we get from the Letters of John of Salisbury—" I am

---

(*q*) The relation of this to Book I (if there is any inconsistency) cannot be discussed here: both assume representation.

(*r*) *E.g.*, note the modernity of: magna juris dubitatio et virorum juris regni peritorum disceptatio et contentio super tali casu in curia d. r. *aliquando evenit* vel evenire potest super hoc [a point of law]; or of—Aliquando tamen super hoc casu in curia d. r. de consilio curiae ita ex aequitate consideratum est: B. vii, c. 1.

(*s*) 1 P. & M., B. I, c. 5, p. 144.

far from denying that there were already or had been at an earlier date Schools of considerable importance at Oxford..." (*t*). That a " School " (*u*) may take its rise from the chance presence of a single teacher is well known and happens to be exemplified in the history of our law, namely, by Vacarius (*x*). The contemporary *locus classicus* (*y*) is by John of Salisbury : in Stephen's time " were banished from the kingdom the laws (*leges*) which the house of the reverend father, Theobald, the primate of Britain had sent for to Britain. For, by royal decree it was forbidden to anyone to keep the books and our Vacarius was commanded to hold his peace, but the more profanity (*impietas*) tried to disparage it, the more the value of the law (*legis*) was increased." In the *Chronica* (*z*) of Robert de Monte or de Torrigny, written about 1150-60, we read : " Magister Vacarius (*a*) . . . *jurisperitus* who taught *leges Romanas* in England in 1149 composed nine books of excerpts from the Code of the Digest which suffices, if one knows them thoroughly, for the decision of all legal controversies which are usually mooted in the schools " (*b*).

The chief monograph on this point is Wenck's *Magister*

(*t*) Rashdall above, p. 65*p*. His corresponding date for Cambridge is 1209 : *ib.*, p. 546. But Cambridge does not seem to have taken to the law as readily as Oxford.

(*u*) Cf. under this word Cruden's *Concordance* of the Bible : " The schools or colleges of the prophets are . . . where the children of the prophets, that is, their disciples, lived in the exercise of a retired and austere life, in study and meditation, &c."

(*x*) For exact dates, see p. 65*p*. If he did not live at Pavia and Bologna he " certainly has been influenced by both these schools " : L. 11 *E. H. R.* 306.

(*y*) *Policraticus*, B. viii, c. 22, finished in 1159 : App. VIII.

(*z*) Holland's *Collect*, p. 65*o* above.

(*a*) Liebermann, 11 *E. H. R.* 309 (1896), points out that silencing V. was a *political* move aimed not at the Canon but at the civil law, as being foreign : see I P. & M., I, c. 4.

Magister [sometimes] = clerical teacher, *not* having an university degree : L.

(*b*) Omnes legum lites quae in scholis frequentari solent : " in sc. fr." a technical term (used also by Ivo) quoted here from V.'s own preface.

Vacarius (c). In his Preface Vacarius says : " I picked out from Justinian those topics which are discussed in the schools (cc), and so I excerpted nine books, etc."

" It is certain," says Stubbs (d), " that what Vacarius taught was the *corpus juris* of Justinian " (e). But he could not do that systematically without doing much more, for example, touching on the duties of advocates.

We have had a reference to the birth of a law school in the Archbishop's palace, the conditions for this purpose being similar to those which produced lawyers in the monasteries. Becket grew up in an atmosphere of lawyers and in his day the recognition of the systematic teaching of law becomes marked. His contemporary, Herbert of Bosham, writes (f) : " Among the great intermediaries (*apocrisiarios*) (g) of the *sacred* law I say nothing of that crowd of secular lawyers (*in forensi jure peritorum turbam*) which, to the dislike of the age, he [B.] used always to have with him—not a company of theologians, but men who practised speaking in the courts (*civicam quandam facundiam*) " (h). In 1169 there is a letter which someone at Winchester sent " Cantuariensibus," generally supposed to be the Chapter (i) : " in your schools (*scolis*) like practising lawyers (*causidicorum*) you have deduced your propositions

---

(c) Leipzig, 1820; Pref. p. 68; printed *Collectanea* II, 167; Oxon, 1890.
(cc) See note (b), p. 87.
(d) *Seventeen Lect.* xiii, p. 302 (1886).
(e) *I.e.*, Oxford was not a school of practice, but of principle—the distinction still existing between the Universities and Inns of Court.
(f) *Life*, B. 3, c. 12; 3 *Materials*, etc., 207; Rolls.
(g) They seem to have been high officials, first of the Emperors and then of the Church, who brought the formers' *responsa*; hence *responsales*, p. 8q—later of importance—is a translation of *Apocr.*; *e.g.*, *accitus est dom. Wintoniensis per responsales suos* : Let. 553 (below).
(h) He continues : Nihil modo mihi et illis; nec enim ipsi mensae ipsius [B.'s] commensales; alia potius horum professio et communio alia—an early instance of pitting the Church and the Law against each other.
(i) 7 *Materials*, p. 56; Let. 553; Rolls; Lupi. p. 616; B. 3, Let. 91.

(*themata inde elicueritis*) and in the regular style of oratorical or legal training (*oratoriam vel legitimam institutionem*) you have imitated Quintilian or Papinian in your arguments or pleas (*or* charges = *allegationibus*) " (*k*).

In a preface written by Daniel of Morley or Merlac, " written at any time . . . 1175-1200," he deals with the " prevalence of legal studies " (*l*). The writer arrived in England from Toledo in that period " with a large number of books "; he was grieved to find that liberal studies here " get a miss " (*m*), and that Aristotle and Plato (*sic*) are completely abandoned (*n*) for Titus and Seius (*i.e.*, the John Doe and Richard Roe of Rome); " and so that I might not be the only phil-Hellene (*Graecus*) I ' pulled up ' where I knew that sort of learning flourished." There is general agreement (*o*) that he means Oxford.

We may follow the fortunes of this foundation by simply transcribing some other extracts (*p*). " Emo studies law and copies the work of Vacarius, 1190 "; this Frieslander went to Oxford, at the age of twenty, in 1190, " whence he returned with the title of ' Magister ' and with a great amount of knowledge of the liberal arts and especially of canon and civil law "; his *Chronicum* (*q*) says that his love of justice made him give up the humanities and study law (*disciplinæ juris*). Menko (*r*), his friend who continued the *Chronicon*, tells us that he and his brother copied and

---

(*k*) The writer quotes from a letter from the Bishop of Winchester : " I am not equal to making an appeal to a civil court (*saeculari et forensi app.*)," and he mentions the rule of law, *qui appellat, appellationi prosequendae sese ex necessitate astringit* : exactly = our " binding over to prosecute."
(*l*) II *Collect.* 171.
(*m*) The colloquialism exactly = *silentium habent.*
(*n*) Cf. Peter of Blois's attraction to the law : App. IX.
(*o*) II, *Coll. ib.*; Rashdall, p. 338, n. (2).
(*p*) From 2 *Collectanea.* 175, etc.
(*q*) 23 *M. H. G.* 467 : Pertz.
(*r*) *Ib.* 23 *M. H. G.* 524, 551.

glossed books (s) on which they had heard lectures at Paris, Orleans and Oxford; " for at Oxford they wrote, heard and glossed *Decreta, Decretales, Liber Pauperum*, as well as other books of canon and civil law (*canonici juris et legalis*). . . ."

" *Legal Discussions at Oxford, 1187-1200* " (t).

" This *saltus* or skipping from one science to another " —as in Emo's case above—" before they have hardly made an entry, caused much abruption in literature and a great displeasure in critical and knowing men that lived in these times and especially for this cause, that they, who had spent many years in Arts and had thereupon gained great respect, were now with their doctrine neglected by upstarts. . . . Gyraldus upon his mentioning the incommodiousness of this *saltus* which Scholars took from good letters to the Laws hath this story : ' There was a merry blade called Martin a Clerk of Oxford in our time but had been a student in the Lawes at Bologna. Him in the larg meetinges of Scholars where Causes were bandied to and fro by Advocates before the judges, all were wont to oppose and he also would verie redily oppose them in all things (u). One law or case which seemed to be expressly against him

---

(s) *Et etiam glosses diversas et bursarios retulerunt* : L. kindly suggested " they took home glosses and manuals " or " students' *compendia*," *bursa* being taken = *thesaurus* (often applied to books) and *bursarios* = the guide to the treasures : should we read *thesauros* ?

(t) 2 *Collect*. 176; the passage is in *Speculum Ecclesiae Distinctio* I, *Prooemium* (*Opera*, ed. Brewer, Rolls, iv, p. 3), by Giraldus Cambrensis, who was born in 1146 and after 1176 studied civil and canon law at Paris : Bishop Elect of St. David's, 1176 and 1199; died 1220. The actual text is in Rashdall's *Universities*, App. xix; Antony à Wood's paraphrase, *Hist. et Antiq. Univ. Oxon* : Oxf. 1674, B. I, p. 56, under 1188; his somewhat free translation, Oxf. 1792, i, p. 169, is that above.

(u) Rashdall cites the Latin MS. Both that MS. and à Wood (*ib*.) mention that the point was made against the *jurisperiti* known as *pauperistae* (because they were devoted to " pauperum S. liber ille ") of whom there were many at Oxford.

was objected to him. . . .'" Then follows the " quip," evidently on the " saltus," but we have lost the key to it. Immediately before, à Wood tells us that there was authority, apparently Gerald's, for saying that about this time there were many deserters from polite learning to law; as soon as they had learned *literarum rudimenta* and some grammar they " did in *hopes of lucre* without any farther proceeding run with a free and hasty course to the Imperial Books, that is to say, as well to the Digests and Codes as to the Institutions and Books of Elements " (*x*).

(*x*) So as late as 1254 Innocent IV complains—quod jam fere omnes scole res, intactis grammaticae rudimentis, auctoribus et philosophis, ad leges properant audiendas quas constat non esse de numero artium liberalium : artes enim liberales propter se adquiruntur, leges autem ut salaria adquirantur, &c. . . ." : M. Paris, 5 *Chron. Maj.* 428; Rolls. Innocent's letter to the Bishops of England, Scotland and Wales, etc., on this point, as in 6 *Chron. Maj.* 293; No. 146 " forbidding professors of secular law to hold any ecclesiastical dignities or benefices unless otherwise well educated and of good life "; he repeats the statement above and says that nowadays the *praelati* prefer no one to honours, etc., in the Church *nisi qui vel saecularis scientiae professor vel advocatus existat*—just whom you would expect them to repel; his own *advocati* with their pomp, he says, are a scandal to God and the laity and he decrees *ut nullus de caetero saecularium legum professor seu advocatus, quocunque in legum facultate singularis gaudeat praeeminentiae privilegio speciali*, shall have any preferment unless of liberal education and good repute. Later on, he forbids in those kingdoms the *leges saeculares* to be read, unless the government permits it, for there *causae laicorum non imperatoriis legibus sed laicorum consuetudinibus decidantur.*

More than a hundred years later Bromyard strikingly confirms (or re-echoes) these passages : *Advocatus* 35 A, B; after pointing out that the *advocati causarum terrenarum* are paid dear and become rich, those *animarum* are poor and despised " where the former make 40 *solidi* the latter hardly get 40 halfpence "; he goes on : " hence it is why there is such a crowd of the former and everyone " volunt leges audire *lucrativas*," and so parents, etc., send their youth to the law-schools : " those of the *legistae* have a hundred or two hundred, where those of the *theologi* perhaps have not five "; the bishops promote the lawyers and not the *theologi*; he knew of one bishop who said : " You don't give the dog food for his own sake, but so that he may guard the fold." Just before Bromyard's time, about 1355, Robert of Avesbury says of Oxford : " Quidam in arte dialectica, quidam in theologia, quidam in jure civili, quidam in Canonico et quidam in utroque jure inceperunt " : *de Gest.* E. III, p. 423; Rolls (91).

Again, about 1195, Gerald was present (*y*) at Oxford in " a concourse of Scholars and jurists (*jurisperiti*) "; perhaps a trial as an Archbishop was sitting " pro tribunali." Before 1196 Senatus, a Prior of Worcester, refers to Oxford as abounding in lawyers (*ponderantes verba legis*), yet, he says, you ask me points of law (*z*).

In 1243 Henry III made " an appeal " by the counsel of certain men " learned in the law " and consulted *inter alios* " the masters of Oxford reading in law " (*magistros in jure legentes*) and is prepared to abide by the decision of the masters regent in law " (*m. i. j. ibidem regentes* (*a*)) at Paris (*b*) and " others learned in the law who can be found."

M. Caillemer (*c*) has printed a *Practica Legum et Decretorum* by William Longchamp, Richard I's Chancellor, who died in 1197. As the historian M. Hauréau thought that this fragment was " a treatise on procedure as much civil as canonical," we may note that the only extant reference (*d*) to an *advocatus* is a commonplace from Roman law that a judge who has at an earlier stage acted as counsel in a case may properly be objected to. He is so little technical that he does not use the word *cliens* (but *hi quorum causae aguntur*). William of Drogheda had certainly read this book.

To the development of legal education we must return;

(*y*) 2 *Coll*. 178.

(*z*) *Ib*. 180; 1 Rashdall, pt. 2, p. 348, n. (1).

(*a*) *Legentes?*

(*b*) Cal. Pat. Rolls (1232-47), pp. 438, 440; cited 1 Mallet, *Univy. of Oxf.* 49. Henry explains to the Pope that he by no means distrusted his own English lawyers: it was because he was so certain that he was in the right that he accepted as referees " the masters of that city which he hates above cities as the one which his chief enemies rule and frequent." For the controversy, see *Raleigh, W.*, in *D. N. B.*

(*c*) Le droit civil dans les provinces anglo-normandes au XIIe siècle: Paris, 1883; see 1 P. & M. 100; dated before 1189, not mentioned in *D. N. B.* For M. Hauréau (p. 49 in *Le Droit*, etc.), see *Hist. Litt. de Fr.* v. 28, p. 498 (1881).

(*d*) Section 17: a mere reproduction of a Decretal specified by Caillemer, p. 47; cf. App. XII.

for its state about 1300 an authority (*e*) says : if the Year Books " were not produced for citation in court—and it seems to be well established that they were not—we must seek some other purpose for this organized production. None seems more probable than that they were compiled for the instruction of those who were studying law and legal procedure. The beginner would need something more than *Bracton, Britton,* the *Registrum Brevium* and a few 13th century tracts . . . a student who had mastered the forms of writs and the broad principles of pleading could hardly do better than study reported cases [sc. Year Books]. It is significant that with the appearance of the Year Books the production of brief instructional treatises, such as *Fet a saver, Hengham Magna* and *Hengham Parva,* ceased and, except for Littleton's *Tenures,* new and revised versions of *Noue Narraciones* and *Breuia Placitata,* we have no new works of instruction of any importance in the 14th century."

These few allusions illustrate the development of law-study in England; that it went on almost *pari passu* with that on the Continent may be seen from the work so often quoted, Rashdall's *Universities* (*f*) : " It was from the age of Irnerius, or at least very early in the century ushered in by his teaching, that men of mature age—men of good birth —beneficed and dignified ecclesiastics or sons of nobles— flocked from the remotest parts of Europe to the lecture rooms of Bologna. Connected with this change in the position of the Law-students was the rise of the Law-Doctor in Southern Europe to a position of marked superiority to that of all other Masters. Legal knowledge possessed then, as it still possesses, a political and commercial value to which no purely speculative knowledge can pretend. No teacher perhaps in the whole history of education had hitherto occupied quite so high a position in public estimation as the early Doctors of Bologna; their rise to this

---

(*e*) G. J. Turner, 42 Seld. Soc. xl.
(*f*) Vol. 1, c. iv, § 1 end.

position marks an epoch not only in the evolution of the University system, but in the development of the legal profession."

We must acknowledge our debt to Italy, but, if in the last sentence we substitute Oxford for Bologna, we may adopt this summary for our own country—at any rate, till London competes.

Bologna

was, as one of her sons (*h*) called her, *ipsius juris alumna et fons et origo ejus atque principalis*—containing the oldest University in Italy, and about 1088 beginning to be the greatest house of learning in Europe. Our duty confines us to her influence in England, which culminated in one Englishman (or English subject), William of Drogheda, the second of two through whom, among many others, mostly Bolognians, it can be clearly traced.

It was almost the fashion at Bologna for Professors to write an " Ordo Judiciarius." Indeed v. Bethmaan-Hollweg (*i*) has a section *de ordine judiciorum* composed of (a) Legists, (b) Canonists. It is impossible to cite them all, even those which treat *ex cathedra* of the *advocatus*, but a few of the Englishmen's forerunners (some of whom they simply copied as occasion arose) may be mentioned with some critical dates.

1090. The *Pan(n)ormia* of Ivo of Chartres, pupil of Lanfranc, dies 1116 or 7 : " becomes of importance in English history " (*k*); " he forms a sort of summary encyclopædia of canon law. In his day the rules of the

---

(*h*) Rayner of Perugia, *Ars Notariae*, c. 69, p. 73 (ed. Wahrmund; see p. 99*h*). There is no law school at Rome till 1243, when Innocent III, an ex-professor of Bologna, founded one : Gregorovius, *Gesch. der St. Rom. V.* 585.

(*i*) *Civil-Prozess*, etc., v. 6 (1874); s. 5—(a) § 123, pp. 60—82; (b) §§ 124-6, pp. 82, 147; (b) is divided : (1) General, (2) Of the 12th Century, (3) Of the 13th Century. Section 6 is *de instructione advocatorum*.

(*k*) 1 P. & M. 97, B. I, c. iv.

ecclesiastical tribunals were very simple—containing only the elementary principles of all procedure (*instruction*).
. . . This primitive procedure was only sensibly transformed in the last part of the twelfth century when the Church adopted the Roman procedure for the pleadings (*contestations*) of the public forum (*for extérieur*) . . .
The canonists followed the example of the legists and like them composed " O. J.," in which they traced the rules of ecclesiastic procedure, which derived largely from civil or Roman procedure but, in its turn, re-acted on the latter. Pillius and the other *Legistae* often quote canon law, while maintaining a very clear distinction between the two codes. The canonists on their side only admit the validity of the *Leges* in the ecclesiastical tribunals when they are confirmed by the canons—*canonistae*—or, at any rate, are not contrary to them " (*l*).

1139-48. *Decretum* of Gratian (*m*).

1148, before. Bulgarus (d. 1166) : " the most famous of the Four Doctors " of Bologna : *Summa de Judiciis*, on procedure, including *advocati* (*n*).

1150, after. " Ulpianus de edendo," " so called " an O. J. (*o*) : " about 1160, perhaps by Vacarius, the oldest of the legists " (*p*); probably by one of the school of Vacarius and written in England (*q*); Caillemer, stating that von Schulte dates 1139-42, insists against these views on an Anglo-Norman origin—" was there not in Normandy, too, some school of Law?" (*r*).

(*l*) A. Tardif. *Histoire des sources du Droit Canonique*, 171, 297-8 : Paris, 1887; for *Decretum*, see *ib.* 170.
(*m*) " Grazian, che l'uno e l'altro foro
Aiuto si che piacque in Paradiso."
Parad X, 104.
(*n*) v. B.-H. 6 *C. P.* 9, 62; Tardif, *ib.* 297-8.
(*o*) Published in 1838 as *Incerti auctoris* O. J.
(*p*) Tard. *ib.*
(*q*) v. B.-H. *ib.* 65.
(*r*) *Ib.* p. 41, he asks " Y avait-il une École de Droit a Caen au XIIe siècle?"

1161 or 1171. *O. J.* by an unknown writer : " The most ancient of these manuals of ecclesiastical procedure at present [1887] known is a little commentary (*s*) on Question I of Clause II of " Gratian's *Decretum* (*t*); the date here is von Bethmann-Hollweg's (*u*), who describes the writer as a Canonist, probably Bolognian. This *O. J.* distinguishes very clearly between civil and ecclesiastical trials, and both from criminal : *item dicitur civilis forensis tantum.* When he speaks of the *advocati* he seems to include civilians : " His transactis contestabuntur litem per se ipsos [the parties] cessante adhuc advocatorum opera.—Mox per advocatos causa ventilabitur usque ad testium vel instrumentorum productionem." In criminal trials he mentions *disputatio advocatorum* on points of law.

1181-5. An *O. J.* (*x*) which, the editor and von Bethmann-Hollweg think was written by an Englishman from Oxford : c. 8 *de advocatis* is a clear source of later Ordines ; c. 6 is *de procuratoribus.*

He has worked out a clear scheme for *clerici* in both ecclesiastical and civil jurisdictions (and hence seems to imply a recognition of non-clerical *advv.*). His general principle is (c. 8)—*clerici* must not appear in a civil cause before a secular judge—(common form), except for himself, etc. : " By *clerici* I mean sub-deacons and upwards or those in minor orders if they enjoy benefits from the Church." In a civil cause any *clericus* may appear as *adv.* before an ecclesiastical judge, but in a criminal case they may only appear before a civil judge for the defendant—by no means for the prosecutor ; but " I think that they might

---

(*s*) Ed. Kunstmann in *Kritische Überschau*, München (1854), v. 2, p. 17.
(*t*) *Tard. ib.* 299.
(*u*) *Ib.* 90; cf. *Wahrmund*, p. 99*h*, *Ric. Anglicus*, p. xx, n. (2).
(*x*) From a Cod. *Bambergensis*, ed., 70 *Transactions Vienna Acad.* 285 (1872), by v. Schulte; see v. B.-H. *ib.* 104-5, and *Ric. Anglicus*, xx. *N.B.*—" The *adv.* must not think himself aggrieved if he has not the right of a seat *dum necessitatem eligunt standi.*" " The bench " alone sat.

do so before a clerical judge " [because there was no fear of capital punishment]. He (first) distinguishes *decretistae* from *legistae* (y), and gives " a representation of the purely Church process in the last third of the 12th Century." On this dichotomy (which is not always strict) we must bear in mind some remarks of A. Tardif (z). After the Decretals of Gregory IX " the Romanists who glossed and exhausted the parts of the civil law desert it to some extent for these texts which excited more their curiosity as scholars. Henceforth we find laymen among the most renowned professors of Canon law, and now the *Constitutiones* of the Popes are commented on, as used to be those of the Emperors. Nicholaus Furiosus, Lanfranc were at once Romanists or civilians and canonists." " The 13th century is the great epoch of the Canonists: they dominate the legists who had played the chief part during the 12th century: the latter had studied all their texts which henceforth had no attraction for them as the unknown, while the Decretals of the great Popes of the 13th century were incessantly feeding anew the activity of the Canonists."

Another O. J. is that (a) of *Otto Papiniensis*, who wrote soon after 1181. He has a title on *procuratores* and one on *advocati*, who must take the oath *propter calumniam*.

Placentinus (b) went from Piacenza to Bologna, taught

(y) Mat. Paris, an Englishman (d. 1259) mentions under 1196 a *clericus eorum quos Legistas et Decretistas appellant peritissimus* (Wats 187) who got very rich from the revenues of churches.

At a great Council in Westminster of prelates and *domini temporales* in 1374 " decretistae vero et legistae super tapetia in area sedebant " : 3 *Contin. Eulogii*, 337. (z) *Dr. fr.* 352; *Dr. Can.* 301.

(a) v. B.-H. *ib.* 67, 69, 107; Ric. Angl. (who perhaps copied him) p. xx, n. (2); Tard. *Dr. Cau.* 301.

(b) Tard. *Dr. fr.* 362; v. B.-H. *ib.* 9, 119; the " strange description of the *advv.* of his day " (v. B.-H. 6 *C.-P.* p. 80) printed with P.'s work [Morguntiæ (Mainz), 1530, p. 73; *Tractatus Illustr. Ictm.* . . . Venice, 1584, v. VII, pt. 1, f. 92, *de judiciis* tit. 2] is not by him but by or edited by Nicholas Rhodius Chambergus in 1530 (Tard. *ib.* 364); it may be of interest for that day, but is not for 1190—1200. Benedict, Abbot of Peterborough (d. 1193), had the *Summa* copied: 1 P. & M. pp. 89, 100.

there and elsewhere, and in France, and died in 1192. If he wrote on *advocatio* in his Summa *de varietate actionum* that part is lost.

About 1198 Pillius (c) was writing in Modena, after having lived in Tuscany and elsewhere in Italy. He has little to say about *advocati*. One sentence throws light on the procedure of his day : " a judge may be delegated to try a single cause or, generally, to try many—that is ' delegation ' proper, the sort nowadays common from the ordinary judges to the *advocati* of states and cities *vel castrorum*," *i.e.*, of armies.

1197. Johannes Passianus dies : pupil of Bulgarus; Master of Azo; purely Bolognian (d).

1210-16. Damasus, school of Bologna : founded on Pillius (e).

1214-6. Tancred's *O. J.* (f). It sent all the others to oblivion : " this practical treatise was the most famous and widely known of those of the School of Glossators " (g); it includes *de adv. et eorum officiis* and their salaries;

(c) *Pillii Tancredi, Gratiae libri de j. o.*: Göttingen, 1842, ed. Bergmann; P. is a " legist," v. B.-H. *ib.* 70; Tard. *ib.* 302. Gratia of Arezzo writes *Summa de O. J.* after 1234; v. B.-H. *ib.* 131; Tard. *ib.* 304, 321.

(d) v. B.-H. *ib.* 10, 24, 67 : not according to Tard. *Dr. Can.* 318, *Dr. fr.* 352, the J. B. who was the first *doctor utriusque juris* (civil and canon).

(e) v. B.-H. *ib.* 112; Tard. *Dr. Can.* 301, 320.

(f) v. B.-H. *ib.* 115, *Tractatus*, etc. (above), v. III, pt. 1, f. 47a; *Pilii, Tancredi, Gratiae, etc.*, ed. Bergmann; Göttingen (1842), pp. 111-23; titles 5 and 6 of part 1. He repeats that the old way of paying *advv.* had gone out and adds that then *par distributio adv^m. a judice fiebat*, but now the *adv.* may bargain *sine peccato secundum utriusque placitum consensum*, provided that there is no champerty.

He has an interesting passage on pleading (pt. 3, tit. 3, p. 207, ed. Bergm.) *de interrogationibus faciendis*, § 2 : " Custom which is *maxima legum interpres* makes the *adv.* frame interrogatories or *positiones* (practically=pleadings) in this way . . . "; § 3 : " He must not put two positive statements (*positiones*) in one question, for if the answer to one is yes and to the other no, the respondent might honestly reply no to both."

(g) Tardif, *Dr. Can.* 230, 302.

also *de procuratoribus*, but there is nothing about *attornati*. He was a *canonist* of Bologna, and William of Drogheda evidently follows him. He repeats much from various predecessors (of whom he " imitated " *Ricardus Anglicus* : *D. N. B.*), as, in the orbit of Bologna (that is, practically, Western Europe), all the juniors adopt, so to say, the seniors—often without recognition. This must be borne in mind in reading later writers, and among them

Ricardus Anglicus.

He is a memorable link between Bologna and England, because though he was born in the latter nothing is heard of him except in the former, where at the end of the twelfth century he was a student and then a teacher at the High School; nothing else according to his latest (*i.e.*, his second) editor (*h*) is certain about him. Internal

---

(*h*) Wahrmund, now (1927) Professor at Prague, whose introduction to the *O. J.* (1915) supersedes v. B.-H. (above) p. 105, and, generally, when they cover the same ground. Perhaps R. A. is the *magister ricardus anglicus* who died in 1234 and is commemorated at the Priory of San Salvatore, Bologna; Allaria, 112 *Dublin Review*, 81 (1893); *English Scholars at Bologna*; or *robertus anglicus frater noster*, *ib.* 78, who died 1254. See also *D. N. B.* under Poor, Rich., Bp. of Chichester.

W.'s very useful series of *Quellen zur Geschichte des Römisch-Kanonischen Processes im Mittelatter* appeared at Innsbruck thus :—

Band	Heft			By	At or In
1905	I	1	Summa Libellorum ...	Bernard Dorna	Bologna : 1213-7
		2	Summa Minorum ...	—	Paris : 1250-4
		3	Curialis	--	France : 1251-70
1906		4	Rhetorica Ecclesiastica	—	France? : 1160-80
		5	Ordo Judiciarius ...	Eilbert of Bremen	Passau : 1191-1204
		6	Summa...	Magister Ægidius	Bologna : 1243-54
		7	Ordo judiciorum	Martin of Fano	Arezzo *or* Modena : 1254-64
1907		8	Formularium	Martin of Fano	Fano : 1229
1913	II	1	Ordo Judiciarius : "Scientiam": see p. 405	—	France : 1235-40
			Ordo Judiciorum ...	Dinus Magellanus	Bologna or Rome: 1298-9
1914		2	Summa Aurea ...	William of Drogheda	Oxford : 1239

evidence makes it probable that his *O. J.* was written there, and external, too, that it was written about 1196. He was probably a *clericus* or, at any rate, wrote for clerical

Band	Heft		By	At or In
1915	3	{ Summa de Ordine judiciario }	{ Ricardus Anglicus }	Bologna: 1196
1916	III 1	Ordo Judiciarius	{ Ægidius de Fuscarariis }	Bologna: 1262-6
1917	2	Ars Notariae...	{ Rayner of Perugia }	Bologna: 1224-34

In this series more works come from Italy and Bologna than from any other country or city.

Thus, William of Drogheda's predecessors were the author of *Rhetorica Ecclesiastica*, (on which is based) the O. J. of Eilbert of Bremen, Bernard Dorna, Rayner of Perugia, and Martin of Fano (*Formularium*)—nearly all Italians. Except Rayner they say nothing about the *adv.*, perhaps because he was not within their scopes : with a slight exception for *Rh. Ec.*

The *Rhet. Eccl.* has in a formula (p. 93) : *Ego H. et P. syndici* [=defensores : ed.] *canonicorum sanctae Mariae* . . .

In Martin's *Formularium* we have, c. 45, *de sindico*, a formula appointing *notarium syndicum actorem et defensorem communis* [municipality] *dicti in causa* giving *licentiam agendi, defendendi, replicandi contradicendi et omnia faciendi*; cf. c. XLVII; c. XCIX is *de procuratore*.

In the important Ars Notariae, though all the incidents of a trial are explored—in an *O. J.* (cc. 69, 276)—there is very little about the *adv.* : even in a list (p. 76 : W.) of those who *pro aliis agunt et defendunt*—i.e., tutor, curator, procurator, actor pro curatore vel tutore constitutus ac actor universitatis, yconomus pro episcopo, sindicus pro universitate, pater pro filio, negotiorum gestor—there is no *adv.* He does, however, say (p. 77) : Et his processis actor vel advocatus ejus pro eo simplicem postulationem facit judici and defendant may object to the *judex* because he has been *adv. in eodem negotio.* In c. 209 *de interrogationibus atque positionibus et responsionibus in placito faciendis*, specially important for *advv.* they are not mentioned. In c. 293 de cause indagatione : Ut patroni causarum [=advocati] de jure suorum clientulorum possint in omnibus certi esse . . . ; and c. 294 *de allegationibus advocatorum* : Previsis rationibus sue partis advocatus actoris recitabit seriatim petitionem ejus . . . ; c. 299 among *officiales* in different countries are *procuratores advocati. N.B.* c. 302 : Set judex clericalis faciet resarciri expensas viarum et omnes, suo; tamen, arbitrio, de juramento actoris, ut dictum est, taxandas.

W. well says (pp. XLIII—IV) that legal pleading was the *adv.'s* business and not the notary's : the former was the lawyer learned in the law; the latter, outside the " Juristen-fakultät," a busy, active, " very present " help to the litigant and skilled " in forms "—the manifest forerunner of the solicitor. Rayner seems to have been exceptional in giving a number of precedents, *libelli*.

courts : note, *e.g.*, excommunication as a sentence on the *adv.* by divine law (*i*).

As he was the first Englishman to deal systematically with the duties and the rights of the professional representative in court we set out in an Appendix (XI) some of his most noteworthy *dicta* (*k*). They leave no doubt about the professionalism. Despite his Englishry, his learning and atmosphere are Bolognian. He may be said to transmit both to the far more important

William of Drogheda.

A researcher in our subject feels that about 1230 to 1250 there is some influence at work in this country which is helping to create and form the bar. If any book may be so described it is William's *Summa Aurea de Ordine judiciorum* (*l*), written probably about 1239. Gregory IX was Pope and had issued the Decretals in 1234. *Magister* William was in orders and a teacher of law at Oxford and, there is strong reason to believe, a practising *advocatus* (*m*) in ecclesiastical courts : " half priest, half lawyer " Maitland calls him. . . . The book was printed for the first time in 1914 (*n*), but Maitland had read the MSS. and says (*o*) : " In a certain sense his book is academic, that

---

(*i*) Cf. *sine peccato*, p. 98*f* and App. XI.

(*k*) It must be remembered that the mediæval jurists constantly copy Roman law *verbatim*—some of them without the citation. See, *e.g.*, App. XI, largely copied from *de postulando*, Cod. III, 6 ; as they all copied openly and copiously from the same sources, the Digest, etc., probably this is the reason why ignoring predecessors is almost a rule with the Bolognians.

(*l*) The full title, probably by the author, is " S. a. continens modum advocandi, opponendi, respondendi, consulendi, distinguendi verum a falso "; this by no means exhausts the details of the plan : see App. XII.

(*m*) To a famous ecclesiastical suit, 1241-5, his death—as he was " suus [one party's] diligentissimus advocatus in Anglia " (M. Paris. *Chron. Maj.* iv, 423 : ed. Wats, p. 660)—put an end.

(*n*) See p. 99*h;* hence, owing to the war, it was not known in England till 1918.

(*o*) 12 *E. H. R.* 625, with copious extracts not reproduced in the reprint : c. III of M.'s *Roman Canon Law in the Ch. of Eng.* (1898).

is, it was meant in the first instance for the Oxford law school. On the other hand it is intensely practical. He is going to teach his readers to win causes, and begs that a few of the fees that they (*p*) earn may purchase masses for his soul. His object is to trace an action through all its stages, to solve the questions about procedure which will beset the practitioner, to supply him with useful formulas or models for the various documents which he may have to indite and to offer him sound advice in the shape of *cautelae*. This last word we can hardly translate without condescending to the slang of ' tips ' and ' wrinkles ' and ' dodges ' : and in truth some of William's *cautelae* (*q*) do not deserve very pretty names, for they are none too honest. . . ."

His " procedure is strikingly similar to that which is open to an Englishman who wishes to bring an action in the English King's Court. In either case we begin by ' impetrating ' a writ. In the one case it comes from the English, in the other from the Roman chancery. The same technical term is in use . . . ' the original ' . .
Drogheda knows well enough that England is full of judges ordinary; but he assumes and steadily maintains the assumption that all the big and remunerative litigation, all the litigation in which Oxford doctors are likely to have a professional interest, will be litigation which is brought

---

(*p*) " Ex qualibet sua advocatione *per hunc libellum* ordinata." Pref. " Dr. merely registers the fact that the Pope is the universal ' ordinary ' in order that he may teach his pupils how fame and fees are won " : M.

(*q*) *E.g.*, c. 65 : " The smart (*cautus*) *adv.* may construct three actions out of one wrong, as I did for a pupil of mine against the mayor of Oxford, before the University, arising out of the imprisonment of the pupil's servant : one I framed for the victim (*passi*), a third for the University, and a fourth for myself " (*v. 1.* " and fifth for the University and myself jointly "). See App. XII. This " amusing *cautela* " reminded M. that Oxford was a " privileged society " where the Univy. " seems to have been both plaintiff and judge."

in the first instance to a court constituted for that occasion by a papal *breve*."

This description of his objects at once suggests that this book is the first (and indeed, in one sense, the last (*r*)) of its kind written in England by a subject of the English Crown, *i.e.*, one which *purports* to make a complete study of the art (and we must add the trade) of the *advocatus*, and that with results which justify, perhaps, a somewhat lengthy notice here. No doubt he was in the legitimate Bolognian line, as probably he would himself have asserted, though he ignores his predecessors (and " Glanville," too). Roman Law is one of his Gospels, though the Bible is not his *titular* authority nearly as often as it is of others of his school. His interests are entirely English (*s*).

Indeed, he may have been moved to write—he cannot have been uninfluenced by—the famous Constitutions (*t*) made by Cardinal Otho (to which he often refers) at the

---

(*r*) For a certain similarity of treatment and liveliness, see Charley's *The Legal Profession* (1873); to some extent, *e.g.*, for professional discipline, Marchant's *Barrister-at-Law* (1905) may be compared.

(*s*) The Glossator of Durand (d. 1296), *Speculum* (ed. 1668), B. I, Pt. 4, p. 253, says : " Gul. *Ang.* satis plene tractavit "; cf. *ib.* c. 5, § 14, p. 263.

" The material of this book is *casus de facto*, which happen every day in England." " I intend to give my Oxford pupils points, decisions and ' tips ' (*cautelae*) emerging from the various cases in England " : Preface. He tells the judge a point of procedure, *consuetum usum litigandi in Anglia* : c. 9. (So Bracton, who was obviously influenced by W.; cf. Wahrmund, *Einl.* xxxiii : " sciendum est quod materia est facta et casus qui quotidie emergunt et eveniunt in regno Angliae . . ." " My object is to teach ' qualiter et quo ordine lites et placita decidantur secundum leges et consuetudines Angliae ' " : *De leg.* B. I, c. 2; 2, 3; I Rolls, 4, 6.) There are many references (*e.g.*, cc. 65, 67 : see App. XII) to royal Letters of Prohibition to ecclesiastical courts owing to *maliciis hominum* (baseness of lay objectors?) : " I never saw anything of the sort done in England in my time," c. 169 (apparently referring to pleading a *consuetudo* in a *libellus*). " Certain *positiones* (positive allegations) are not used in England and so I say no more about them," c. 172, though in c. 171 he had given specimen *libelli* from Lombardy, Bologna and Rome : see App. XII. Of Oxford he tells us, c. 116, that St. Mary's was regularly used as a law court.

(*t*) M. Paris, *Chron. Maj.* v. 3, p. 439; Rolls, p. 109; ed. Wats, 455.

Council of London in 1237, about the date of his *Summa*. Those dealing with litigation merely repeat the Italian lawyers on the abuses of ecclesiastical judges (*u*), *advocati* and *procuratores* : they are attested not only by the Cardinal's sanctions, but by the number of William's *libelli* = practically, statements of claim—for various forms of perverting the course of justice (and in the secular courts *aliunde*).

In fact, he is the only Bolognian legist who cares only about England. He is almost patriotic and probably the first scholar (*x*)—in vindicating the rights of the vernacular (*u*) : " *Advocatio* may be in English, French or Latin " (*y*), and the Latin terms of an appeal to Canterbury are, if necessary, to be explained in French or English to the witnesses (*z*).

His religious orthodoxy, too, may be noticed.

Of course, he accepts the Church's tradition that justice is a religious duty, as do Richard Anglicus and others of his predecessors and his imitators. His anxiety about his own soul has already (*a*) been mentioned, but what is significant

---

(*u*) Otto's grievances were mainly the ignorance of the judges, the unscrupulousness of counsel, and their *cavillationes* and *versutiae* and the dilatory tricks of the *procuratores* [wearing out their opponents]—all points that William touches. Note the Const. that no obstacles are to be raised to the settling of law suits and no money to be exacted for compositions.

(*x*) Latin was identified with law and lore : hence Dante's
" Quell' avvocato de' tempi cristiani
Del cui latino Agostin si provvide."
Paradiso X, 119.

(*y*) C. 98 : *Anglicis vel Gallicis acsi Latinis* (citing Dig. B. 45, c. 1, § 6 : eadem an alia lingua respondeatur nihil interest); hence he says, generally, *ib.*, " each *adv.* (or party?) must understand the other's language." The point is incidental to the discussion whether a *laicus* or *idiota* may be admitted to argue (*advocandum*) against a *clericus*? Cf. App. XII.

(*z*) C. 326.

(*a*) Cf. " For if we take thought for our material affairs how much more attention ought we not to pay *pro animarum salute*? I ask my readers to pray for my soul because I fear death and nothing is more certain than death " : " *annuente deo* " : " He knows, who knows everything that I am writing this *Summa* not for the empty applause of this

historically is the juxtaposition of religion and business with which Maitland made play, and to which he returns. If, says William (*b*), an action is brought against a layman, matrimonial and testamentary cases excepted, the *advocatus* must be very careful, in drawing his statement of claim, to use moderate language, to state the facts with art, to make no mention of money, but only of the desire for defendant's reduction to penitence, " lest in England a royal prohibition issue." " He is well aware," says Maitland, " that of some of " his *libelli* " no use can be made in England, any attempt to employ them would at once call down a royal prohibition . . . but [after the words just cited from c. 67] he goes on to explain that practically you can gain your end (*c*) by nominally asking that the defendant may be chastened for his soul's health, since he will be unable to obtain restitution until he restores anything that he is wrongfully withholding."

These and many other passages leave no doubt that Drogheda speaks from full personal experience, even, we may probably say, of the secular courts, in which also he quite possibly practised. At any rate, he must have known their procedure well.

Maitland insists on the similarity of his procedure to that of the *curia regis* of the day, and he adds about his *libelli* : " These are of the most purely temporal kind, that is to say, there is nothing ecclesiastical about them (*d*). He will retain some of the *libelli* which deal with pure temporalities lest anyone should accuse him of ignorance ; also,

---

age, but to blazon the eternal truth and remembrance of God [read *dei* for printed *rei*]. . . . Still the labour of the teacher may be rewarded and ought to be especially by the prince " : Pref. The *libellus* for disobedience to suspension or excommunication charges that the defendant is acting *in grave animae suae periculum* : c. 333 and foll. Cf. *propter periculum animarum*, c. 464.

(*b*) C. 67, a *cautela*.
(*c*) Sic indirecte potest consequi quod non potest directe.
(*d*) Except in a few, *e.g.*, c. 333, etc., cited above : part of the *lib.* is, " unde peto quod canonice puniatur."

by means of a *cautela* which will conceal their temporal character they may be of use to practitioners in the our ecclesiastical courts. Also he seems to think that practitioners in the King's court may find them serviceable, and it is true that some of these *libelli* are not unlike, though they are vaguer and laxer than, the ' counts ' or ' declarations ' to which the royal justices listen. . . ." The royal courts, in fact, must have reflected back, sometimes polarised, the light that had filled them from the church. William was a medium that would absorb a temporal improvement. Thus, in his doctrine of trusts, we see in solution both the clerical and secular jurisdictions of which the latter has survived as " Chancery." The impression of the judges he leaves is that they were not professionals and that their characters and practices varied very much— which is probably truer of the many ecclesiastics on the bench than of the fewer laymen. But that the bulk of his interest and attention (and probably practice) was given to the ecclesiastical courts there can be no doubt. Hence, too, the great prominence of the *procurator* in his pages (while the *attornatus* is not mentioned). " He shirks," says his latest editor, Wahrmund (*e*), " the fundamental question of principle, he avoids a clear and express decision in favour of " Church or State . . . he ranges himself tacitly on the side of the Roman Church, but he is by no means ignorant of the *consuetudines Angliae*.

We have tried to show that English procedure grew gradually out of ecclesiastical practice grafted on an indigenous pre-Conquest system (ecclesiastical and lay). The essence of justice honestly administered must be the same everywhere, and the code of advocacy by one canonist or legist will only vary from that of another in " local colour " or custom; at any rate, the ethics will not vary much. Thus we may be sure that William " dovetailed "

(*e*) *Einleitung*, XXXIII.

the best of both systems that he knew—perhaps the most striking distinction of the English secular system being then the royal prohibition. At any rate, from William's time onwards, his scheme of the advocate in England is that adopted and used, at any rate, theoretically. For a long time there are many lapses from it, but these we know chiefly from the measures provided to maintain William's standard. On this assumption, a short analysis of the *forensia* of the work is warranted; it will be found in Appendix XII; but one or two topics may be selected as specimens of his treatment.

Cc. 54-6 (see App. XII), *de salariis advv.* He full recognises *vendit adv. patrocinium* (see, *e.g.*, c. 46 in App.) and he is well aware that the ancient practice was to pay the *adv.* beforehand (*f*); this is still the proper way; he ought to be on " the right side of the hedge " (*g*) before he moves in the suit—perhaps the earliest and extremest avowal of commercialism in the profession. The defendant's *adv.*, too, ought to see that he gets his fee before the end of the case " or put off the business "; if he cannot get " satisfaction " otherwise, let him keep the papers (*acta et processum judicii*) till he does —a lien (c. 95); still he must not be inconsiderate and must take into account the persons with whom he is dealing and perhaps remit part of his fee; apparently something depends whether he has secured the *acta* of the day, in favour of the defendant : c. 96. But, generally, if a fixed sum has been agreed between *adv.* and client, an action lies for the former—up to the legal limit—100 aurei. If not, the judge must fix the amount " according to the nature of the suit, the eloquence of the *adv.* and the practice of the court." The client has no action against him for the return of the fee, if he is not to blame for

---

(*f*) He cites *Dig.* 19, 2, 38 : Advv., si per eos non steterit quominus causam agant, honoraria reddere non debent.

(*g*) Melius est salario incumbere quam in personam agere.

not appearing [the case being settled or for other reasons beyond his control]. Perhaps, too, the amount of time he has given should be taken into account in his claim. He repeats that the *adv.* may not bargain for an uncertain sum; at any rate, not if it may be unreasonably great (*h*). Again, on demeanour (c. 57) : " Don't," he advises, " be put off by clients' big promises of reward, for they are often merely for show; remember the doctors' axiom : ' get your money while the patient is ill ' " (c. 56).

The next " hint " is simply " de l'audace," etc. : " *audaces* fortuna juvat." The laws do not help the timorous—care for nobody's threats—and stand up to a bad tempered judge.

Another MS. insists on (and cites) the " soft answer," but if this does not soothe his " friend " (*amicum*) retort with interest is permissible.

The litigation contemplated is expensive, one party often being no match for the other, and the jurisdiction, at any rate, of the judges may be bought; hence, partly, the lessons in chicane, as it would now be called. It must be remembered that there was not the same wide chasm between the judicial and the social that there is nowadays; the cynical suggestion of " getting at " the judge's friends privately (not for judgment, but delay) was probably not illicit; it is still not unknown in Latin Countries in some classes of case, where it is defended as merely recommending the suit to the judge's attention. At any rate, William is impartial as between his rival counsel—he " coaches " them equally. The variation in judges' lore and law comes out in his remark (c. 97) that one pleads " otherwise and more effectively before learned judges "; " otherwise " is a true stroke. Broadly it is true that he does not con-

---

(*h*) But not the *procurator* who (at any rate, in Roman law) was not paid (citing Cod. II, 12 (or 13), 15) : c. 54 : see App. XII. The difference is due to the fact—*plus gravatur advocatus quam procurator* (apparently = he has more trouble than the *proc.*) : " so the law helps him more."

template a professional monopoly of audience, but (c. 98) he recognises and perhaps prefers it, at any rate, for the plaintiff in a civil action (*i*). To us with a rigid rule that a party may always (with one exception) appear in person, but that otherwise his representative must be professional, his provision that the *adv.* for a stranger (see c. 98 in App. XII) must know some law (or have some practice) needs no defence; probably all this topic rests not on any legislation, but a mixture of sagacity and of a procedure then in flux.

" As parties often appear by *procuratores* I will now deal with them " (c. 98); to them forty-three (99—141) are devoted. The writer never seems to confuse the two representatives : they are sharply divided in his mind; the *procurator* is known by his *mandatum*. The space he gives him is more than he gives the *advocatus*, in view of his more frequent appearance. A very large number of points of practice are raised, many almost certainly, some expressly, taken from life; the author had doubtless often acted as *procurator*. There is a short analysis in App. XII (*k*). The prime distinction between the two—the provinces of fact and law is made in c. 119—it is a forecast of the future differentiation of solicitor from counsel.

Considerable space is given to the art and precedents of statements of claim, *libelli*; the author's own definition

---

(*i*) But not for *reus* in a criminal case : see c. 144, App. XII.
(*k*) App. XII summarises other cc. For the " Proctors and Advocates " of the purely spiritual courts, see Reichel's 2 *Canon Law*, p. 224 (London : 1896), where much is identical with William of Drogheda's code of the *advocatus*. (*N.B.*—" A person is said to be client to an advocate, but master and mandator to a proctor " : p. 230.) The precise origin of the College of Advocates seems to be unknown; see W. Senior's *Doctors' Commons and the Old Court of Admiralty*, c. iv, p. 59 : London, 1922. In 1293 there is a citation before the " Official " of the Court of Arches (1 *Rot. Parl.* 97 a), and in 1330 a grant to John of Shoreditch, " Advocaet de la Court des Arches," in lieu of the great profits he might have had by his " Advocassie " there for years. Foss, III, 507, says he was a layman and is called " legum doctor " and " juris civilis professor " : 2 *Rot. Parl.* 41 a.

is *brevis cartula petitionem et causam et actionem continens agentis* or *brevis explanatio ejus quod intrinseco est* : c. 168. These precedents naturally reflect or are part of the pleadings, and we can see the art of pleading as it grows; thus costs are very much in the pleader's eye (c. 169). The writer is much exercised whether the *adv.* ought to plead positive statements of fact (*positiones*), and he concludes that he ought not; he must leave that to the *party*, for he cannot vouch for the facts (and so at the trial he might be in an awkward situation). Apparently the writer was puzzled, as he admits that he had no experience of these " positiones " in England. It seems that he considered that what the *adv.* said in open court was sacrosanct, and that was why he was slow to give advice about unfamiliar details (*l*).

Of the long list of *libelli*, we have quoted Maitland. William tells us (c. 281) that they are *editiones* taken from *dominus Remfridus* (or *Rowaldus* (*m*)) " shortly excerpted with additions of my own, which have no *locus* to-day in these parts, except with the qualification of the *cautela* which I have given . . . always remembering that in England it is not essential to name your action in the *libellus*, as dom. R. did, but the *factum* must be set out more fully than R. taught. . . . I have put in the aforesaid *libelli and they are current every day in the royal court*, but never in the ecclesiastical court because of royal prohibitions. Ecclesiastical causes require special forms and to them I turn "—for a good deal of space.

These disjointed passages together with those cited in the appendices will probably satisfy the reader that the writer contemplated a definite and permanent system of judicature in England. That is to say, that he wrote for the benefit of the English variety of forensic Canon law;

(*l*) Hence, perhaps, the obscurity of the pleas suggested.
(*m*) Identified by Wahrmund, *Einl.* XXXIII, as Roffredus Beneventanus, who wrote an *O. J.*

he is well aware that a trial in an English ecclesiastical court is not quite the same process as one in Rome, though the sanction and the fundamental rules must come from the Curia. He knows that side by side with the clerical courts with which he was so familiar there is a purely secular judicature, and it is very hard to believe that in laying down the law of procedure for the ecclesiastical he did not, when it suited his book, borrow practices from the secular courts. Nothing so far had been written in England on the same scale as the *Summa*. " Between Glanville's and Bracton's works," says Wahrmund (*n*), " Drogheda's book inserts itself, a document of a different nature." As that editor says, Bracton put William quite in the shade—which accounts for our so seldom finding any English reference to him.

It is not easy to decide absolutely whether William expected his treatise to be an authority in the secular as he did in the ecclesiastical courts. But it is inconceivable that it should not have had weight in the former appearing as it did when clerics still manned the bench and were not yet excluded from advocacy—though we cannot, again, say precisely when they disappeared from either. At any rate, there was time for the practice inherited from the Canonist-Legists to take root, and, in fact, the secular courts have always maintained a practice which without much qualification may be called that of William. Practically the reasoning of both (perhaps of all) systems rests on a few fundamental principles of " natural " justice. The chief striking superficial difference in method between the two is the absence or the presence of a doctrine of Sin and of the implications of cardinal theological dogmas.

Of the *advocatus*, perhaps, he had no exact view; certainly not of his limitations. His theory is not clear of the distinctions between him, the *procurator*, the

---

(*n*) *Einleit.* XXXII.

responsalis, the *defensor*, etc. But one definite position does emerge : whatever else the *advocatus* may do incidentally or exceptionally, his mark, his ἔργον, is that in court he conducts the legal argument; he discusses the law of the case with the judges. In practice, and as time went on, he might conveniently do much more, as he does to-day, but his gist abides.

The Development of the Legal Representative.

The new system of administration since the Conquest, the dispatch of a large amount of business of a quite new kind, brought about a new method of pleading, or, rather, *placitandi*, and gradually created a new race of pleaders. *A priori* we should expect that a visible increase of verbal formalism would beget in mere spectators the suspicion that the proceedings were a sort of organised tricks (*o*) conventionally played by the actors on both sides, that the words used had more weight with the judge than the facts of the case, and, indeed, very early we find that the lay mind took this view, and from that day to this lawyers' " quibbles " have figured permanently in the stock-in-trade of popular " humour."

We have incidentally noticed the incipient traces of this excrescence in the writer " Q.," who bridges over the Saxon-Norman curialogy. Its progress is more forcibly attested by a jurist, whom we must presently cite again for subject-matter (and not, as now, merely for apt expression), dealing with a similar effect of similar causes. Le Comte Beugnot says (*p*) : " Philip of [Novara (*q*)] gives, at the beginning of his work, full details on procedure (cc. 1—8, 23—6), and elsewhere he deals with this subject

---

(*o*) See, for instances, J. G. Phillimore's pamphlets, 1846-7 (or extracts in the *Spirit of our Laws* (1st ed.), p. 46).

(*p*) *Ass. de Jér* v. I, p. xlii, see p. 382.

(*q*) Beugnot always has " Navarre " : more recent research shows that " Novara " is correct, p. 387.

(cc. 89—92). It seems, too, that in the opinion of his fellow citizens, his work was a guide for parties who were at litigation in the High Court and not a treatise on general jurisprudence. . . . A procedure obscure, complicated, malicious to an extreme, but inflexible and agreeable to the old customs of feudalism, was established in Syria and Cyprus and became the object of studies and researches that carried its importance much too far. In fact, it is not without surprise and pain that we see a man so wise and enlightened as [Novara] teaching with perfect good faith the odious science of *chicane*, showing by what dodges, what sharp practice (*finesses*), what ' counterfeit of reason,' a pleader (*plaideur*) could check or promote the progress of a case and spin according to the needs of his cause, a web of miserable subtleties round the other side, the judges, and the lord (*seigneur*). We bring no charge against Philip nor against all those who came after him and imitated him; we are astonished that in this wholly military society, where loyalty and frankness (*franchise*) should have been common virtues, *chicane* should have been constituted by law and pushed to a height of authority which most happily it has not reached anywhere else. . . (p. lii). In such a system of procedure the words or formulae employed by *les conseils* were of the highest importance, since, on a word (*r*), placed

---

(*r*) Cf. p. 125. A notorious instance is in c. 90 (I, 144, 147), where B. says :
" On retrouve ici l'esprit de chicane dont l'auteur a fait preuve dans plusieurs chapitres précédents. Ibelin conseille au plaignant de mêler l'accusation de meurtre avec celle d'homicide, dans une plainte dont il donne la formule, parce que le meurtre se prouve par gages de bataille, et l'homicide par témoins. Cette confusion étant établie, si l'accusé accepte le gage, l'accusateur reprend son plaidoyer de telle manière, qu'il mette *ou* au lieu d'*et*, là où il est dit qu'il a meurtri *et* donné les coups dont le défunt est mort. Il insinue d'abord l'emploi des conjonctives, parce que les plaideurs sont attentifs au commencement d'un plaidoyer ; mais ensuite et lorsqu'ils se sont échauffés à donner les gages de bataille, il est bon de glisser les disjonctives [the word of the text] : par ce moyen l'accusateur obligera son adversaire à combattre, sans s'exposer lui-même, à être puni comme parjure faute d'avoir prouvé le meurtre dont il l'aurait chargé." This was

well or badly, might depend first the course and then the decision of a case. . . ." Ibelin's " only object was to supply novices among *les conseils* with the arms necessary to sustain with advantage their fight in the closed lists of *la chicane*." This tended, he says, to undermine the authority which was wielded in the bosom of the feudal courts by certain men grown old in the study and practice of juridical frauds. . . . Ibelin teaches the defender the art of giving the plea the go-by (*fuir le plaid*), *i.e.*, to make the plaint useless by means of *chicanes* and evasions; but then with complete impartiality he shows the plaintiff how in his turn he must cast about to catch the defendant in his own nets (cc. 29—51). . . . All this part of Ibelin's book breathes very much the subtle spirit which gave birth to the scholastic philosophy of which in the 13th century the influence on all branches of human knowledge made itself so painfully felt. . . . Feudal procedure as it is described by Ibelin shows only slowness, side issues (*détours*), subtleties and poor chicaneries. It looks as if the object of this legislation is not to secure the victory of honest right, but to embarrass the judges and to make trials last for ever, and we cannot understand how the lords, who in

---

copied into *Stilus Curiae Parlamenti*, about 1330, by G. Du Breuil : " — et ipsum reddere mortuum vel devictum . . . si enim concluserit per copulativam ad utrumque se obligaret . . . " (c. 16, § 8, p. 27, ed. H. Lot, Paris, 1877) *i.e.*, he must kill him. In the *Très ancienne coustume de Bretaigne* (in *Nouveau Coutumier Général*, ed. Bourdot de Richebourg, Paris, 1724, vol. 4, pt. 1, p. 235), about 1330 (or 1456?) : " *gens de basse condition* must not interfere in laws or customs : car une conjonction peut porter une cause de cent livres de rente comme de trois deniers et aussi une disjonction." B. says, *ib.*, that the play of *ou* and *et* had got on to the comic stage.

About 1280 a writ had "Hardlestone" for "Herliston" : on exception taken the court was bound to allow it, for the day before a similar plea had been allowed, but the party was permitted to get another writ " sine hac litera *d* " : *Barnwell Book*, pp. lxiii, 155.

Cf. (about 1690) Holt's hearing argument to arrest judgment for treason on a misspelled Latin word indorsed on an indictment : Macaulay, *Hist.* c. 15, or Gay, *the Mohocks* (1712), A. I, sc. iii : " Justice Scruple : A misspell'd word or a Quibble will baffle the most convincing argument in the world."

one day were apt to pass from the bench of the *conseils* to the seat of the judge, could permit a sort of farce of which soon they themselves would feel the impropriety and the danger. The source of this evil was to be found more in the absence of written documents than in the subtle and punctilious mind of the Latins of the East. When all formalities proceeded *viva voce* with the help of interrogations, answers, declarations, statements, counter-statements, oaths, denials, when there was only the memory of the judges to retain these floods of contradictory speeches, when, finally, there was no written law which could deliver judges, parties, *conseils* and advocates from the labyrinth in which they were lost, how can we imagine that disorder was not the principle and injustice the result of such a system of procedure?" Again (s), " the second part of the Abridgment of the Book *des Bourgeois* is entitled ' Matter and manner of pleading ' (*playdoier*) and treats of civil and criminal procedure. It alleges that in its day, and in spite of all the labours of the jurisconsults, people used to say ' pleading in the *bourgeoisie* [court] is just like the sea, it has no bottom ' (*t*). Indeed no positive law regulated the formalities of procedure, and the subtle mind of the Latins helped to obscure those which custom sanctioned; hence there was ground for maintaining that procedure in the court of the *bourgeois* had no solid base. . . . No. The procedure, despite its gaps, its calculated slowness and its minute formalities, did not deserve to be called a bottomless sea. . . ."

Remembering that these passages did not specifically refer to the first hundred years after the Conquest, perhaps we may say of their tone that " Q." would have expressed himself thus if he could. Undoubtedly, in that period, what disinterested laymen regarded as a game of word-

---

(s) *Ib.* vol. II, *Assises de la Cour des Bourgeois*, p. lxv.
(t) From the *Abrégé* : *ib.* p. 293.

spinning grew to great proportions and tended to bring the advocate into disrepute in their minds.

We have quoted the evidence of an advanced stage of what—it must be remembered—was a process, for an earlier stage, of which, however, we are not left without a witness and that, indeed, an indigenous one. John of Salisbury, Bishop of Chartres, who died in 1180, probably when he was about seventy, was a prominent ecclesiastical member of the secular law-school of Canterbury, from about 1150 to 1176. His writings are an authority for many contemporary events, including the normal doings of the law courts; indeed, sometimes he writes as if he was a practising counsel—he knows exactly " where the shoe pinches " (to use his own expression). He had lived in England, France and Italy, and was acquainted with the courts, canonical and lay, of the three countries (*u*). His *Policraticus* (*x*) seems to have been written in England in 1159; we are more concerned with its sub-title *de nugis curialium* " on the pettinesses of those about the courts." So far as the law is concerned he is certainly aiming primarily at ecclesiastical courts, for the simple reason that in no other was there such a system of *advocati* as would supply the mass of details he knows. But, of course, he is not ignorant of the secular courts and their *causidici* whom he, by no means, exempts from his censure, and he specifically mentions (*y*) English judges (and perhaps practitioners) for the same purpose.

Perhaps we shall conclude that much development which we are apt to think modern, has been theory, if not practice, even before " the profession " existed. He, too,

---

(*u*) He must have known and may have been present at some of the trials mentioned above. R. L. Poole, *Historia Pontificalis* (1927), p. lxxiii, says : " When Eugenius heard a law suit in 1150, probably at Ceprano, he was in attendance."

(*x*) Some very important extracts will be found in App. VIII. There is a French translation : *Des Vanitez*, etc., of 1640.

(*y*) Cc. XV—XVI in App. VIII.

saw the rank and rapid growth of pleadings; if there was a germ or a nucleus or the elements of a school of law it is quite certain that this kind of study or dialectic or disputation is from every point of view the natural and congenial food of academic life, the very " grist to its mill," even without the advantage of active tribunals hard by—and that John was observing that forward movement. But before drawing upon him bodily, so to say, it must be pointed out that, though undoubtedly he had before his eyes and described the practice of his day, yet his moralising and his incessant Roman law often leave it doubtful whether any given passage is due to his philanthropy or his erudition or his observation (z). He is a reformer and in ethics every reformer states what ought to be as what is, but when this method is applied to a working system of law we should like to know which is theory and which is practice. Thus there are innumerable diatribes against venality of all sorts, including that of lawyers; can we conclude that the regulations he lays down about counsel's fees, for instance, were recognised by the practitioners of the time? But, at any rate, the ideas he publishes were " in the air " and were very " catching."

But he was not writing a law book, and it is only when we read the Bolognian writers that we realise that the extraordinary vigour of diction which strikes us so much in John's pages is not always original; they copied law, idiom and style from the Roman lawyers and from one another, and so did John from them. Hence the principles with which he deals generally, William of Drogheda, for instance, later works out specifically, often copying John's very words (or those of their common source), and the

---

(z) In reading books about law which are not text books by lawyers (and in some, especially early ones, which are) we must remember Beugnot's caution (above) *in pari materia* (v. 2, p. LII) : some of the penalties said to be inflicted are so " ridiculous or indecent " that we must put them down to the " false or pretentious science of a legist " who thought that he was entitled to refine on pains and penalties.

former is only quoted here as a valuable witness for his day.

He is never tired of castigating the venality of the underlings of the court, *i.e.*, clerks, bailiffs, etc.—of which we hear from many quarters. Unless you " square " them —more than one—you will find all sorts of formal obstacles —" your style [in the *libellus*] is bad, you don't tell the story properly, this is not the way a notary or a chief clerk (*scrinarius*) would draw it up, it is bad law, etc." Technicalities are the bane of the law.

As for the *causidici*, by whom he clearly means practitioners, he fiercely denounces the greed and extortion —of all of them, from top to bottom.

He denounces, too, barrators, judges and lawyers who foment litigation and all who make capital out of people's quarrels; he has a peculiar horror of judges who do not know the law—*leges et consuetudines quibus nunc vivitur*— (*i.e.*, predominantly common law); incidentally he censures the costliness of law—obviously only the rich can afford to pay for it (the *pretium* of the judge, to which he often alludes, was sometimes only a due fee); he insists so much on *calumpniae*, false charges and oppressive suits, that they must have been very rife; dilatory or illusory defences are an abuse, there must be no " tips " or champerty " except what the law allows to *advocati* or certain other defined persons "—a reminiscence of Roman law and of continental; if of English, it is probably the earliest recognition of professional dues. The advocate may sell *sanum consilium*. On the other hand, constituted legal advisers at a definite point, *a contestatione litis*, *i.e.*, when the writ is issued, are held to the highest good faith and diligence for the *cliens*; they must not protract causes—another " mischief " of the time. We are bidden to be satisfied if a decision is given within two or three years.

The next provision is surely a mere aspiration, often echoed by modern suitors, that the courts will provide the parties with advocates of equal power, so that neither has an accidental advantage. We gather that his ideal advocate had *virtutis meritum, vivacitas ingenii, consilii profunditas, opinio scientiae,* and *nominis auctoritas*—no mean equipment. If the opponents are not equally matched, the judge will see to it to restore the balance — a duty by no means unknown to the bench to-day. There must be no chicanery to discover prematurely the other side's case or to inveigle his adviser. Nor may an advocate asked by the judge to take up a case refuse without good cause—a rule still in force in criminal trials—on pain of never appearing again.

And if he mislead (*praevaricatus*) the court, he must be punished according to the facts; evidently there was no definite tribunal for such an offence. Abuse of an opponent or " bullying " is not permitted.

Then we get an echo of the Frankish distinction between the full authority of the speaker to conduct the whole business and the mere " voicing " of his client's story— between counsel and pleader; if the *dominus* is present and does not disclaim within three days he is bound by his representative's (*patronus*) action. Perhaps the word *dominus* (*a*) is significant here—when John thinks of a litigator his natural example is a lord, not a " small man." The *advocatus* must not mind a beating if he has fought fair.

Clearly, too, he has the picture of a good working law-court in his mind. And he expresses it : " When we get into court where mere empty argumentation is silenced and there is only serious discussion, there can be no mistake in the judgment without danger to the parties or the judge. It is better to delay decision than to run the risk

---

(*a*) Perhaps this use led to the technical *dominus litis*. " Glanville " often assumes a *tenant* as one litigant against a *petens* and he, too, makes *dominus* = the representative's principal.

of error, but delaying judgment may mean damage to the suitors."

Other writers confirm John generally. His friend Peter of Blois, who flourished in England about 1190: wrote: " Nowadays *patroni causarum* serve only for money, and that once respected title and noble profession (*professio advocati*) is sunk to notorious venality, for a low creature sells his tongue, traffics in law suits, breaks up valid marriages, dissolves friendships, rekindles the ashes of dead litigation, tears up contracts, distorts agreements, derogates privileges and to get money turns law upside down by laying traps and nets " (b).

That these critics took the ecclesiastical courts for their special purview is certain; the great St. Bernard of Clairvaux was probably thinking no other (c). He lived 1091—1153 and never was in England. His value for us is that he knows the Church courts of the generation immediately before that of John of Salisbury. C. 10 of B. I of *De Consideratione* (d) addressed to Pope Eugene III is headed " *Abusus Advocatorum, Judicum, Procuratorum, eorumque fraudes graviter perstringit.*" Many, he says, are the trumped-up charges, defenders (*defensores*) are rare, everywhere the stronger oppress the weaker; there must be *legal* justice (*judicium*); unless suits are fought out, and parties are heard, how can justice be done between them? By all means fight out the cases, but as they should be fought. For the present practice is obviously disgraceful— it would disgrace not only the Church but even the *forum*. For I wonder how your sacred ears can bear those

---

(b) App. IX : Ep. 26.
(c) But Michaud, *Histoire des Croisades* (1857), v. 4, p. 284, thinks that in the passage above St. Bernard is not only thinking of the papal *Curia*, but that he saw the same abuses everywhere : " In all the councils of this epoch, the same complaints were repeated. Jacques de Vitri, who lived at the beginning of the 13th century, judges the legists with even greater severity."
(d) V. I, 420 : Paris, 1719.

DEVELOPMENT OF THE LEGAL REPRESENTATIVE

wranglings of the *advocati* and their verbal disputes which make much more for suppressing than expressing the truth. Check this shameful habit, stop (*praecide*) these tattling tongues, and shut those tricky lips. These are the men who have trained themselves to lie, learned against justice, experts (*eruditi*) in falsehood. He advises the Pope, sitting as a judge, to be on his guard against dodging (*venatorius*) delays.

C. 11 is aimed at *Advocati, Procuratores*, who make money out of wrong-doing (*iniquitas*); he seems to hint that a good deal of bargaining for ready cash went on in the papal courts.

It cannot be denied that if our jurisprudence took the ecclesiastical courts as a model for procedure, they also took over some abuses.

We have been gradually led on into the reign of Henry II.

If the legal representative now becomes a more familiar figure, is more talked about, it is natural, for " his reign, it has been truly said, ' initiated the rule of law ' as distinct from the despotism . . . of the Norman Kings " (*e*). Glanvill was in 1180 his Chief Justiciar, " prime minister, we may say, and viceroy " (*f*). " The fabric of our judicial legislation commences with the Assize of Clarendon, the first object of which was to provide for the order of the realm by reviving the old English system of mutual security (*g*) of frankpledge." Now, it was suggested above that the earliest germ of our indigenous lawyer, the *advocatus*, was to be found in this system; if there be any truth in that view we should expect that its restoration would be followed by fresh tendencies of development in that class, and we shall not be disappointed. The first and last innovations mentioned below, p. 144, must have led to an expansion—or a creation—of such a class.

(*e*) Green, *History*, c. II, s. 8.   (*f*) 1 P. & M., B. 1, c. 5.
(*g*) See Stubbs' *Sel. Ch.* : *Ass. of Clar.* § 9 : Introd. III.

Though in the Constitutions (1164) or the Assize (1166) of Clarendon there is not yet a hint of the legal representative, yet his early development is implied in the new jural result of Henry II's reforms.

And here, as we cannot trace his growth as minutely as we should like, we will endeavour to confirm this statement by a glance backward and forward. The following facts present conditions which provide an " atmosphere " for the gradual growth of a class now known as " the legal profession."

1085 (h). The survey for Domesday; representative " jurors " for localities.

1100-35. Rudimentary *Itinera* (i).

1136. Stephen's Charter; laws and customs of Edward and Henry I restored.

1166. The Assize (k) of Clarendon; " the origin of trial by jury "; the jury of presentment : J. R. Green, as cited above.

(h) That in 1070 the laws of the English were declared by twelve men from each shire is now generally discredited : 4 N. C. c. 19, p. 324; St. Lect. 48 : " the fable or tradition preserved in Hoveden." 1 P. & M. c. 3, p. 82.

(i) " Henry I did not invent the system of itinerant justices. . . . The true path of Frankish influence would seem to lie through Normandy," by means of the royal *missi*. " As early as the reign of William the Conqueror the King's *missi* presided in some of the local courts of England " : Prof. Hazeltine in Bolland's *General Eyre*, xiii (1922).

There *itinerantes* are often found to have local *socii* commissioned with them often *milites* (perhaps *literati*). Trivet, the Annalist, describes his father about 1268 as " justiciarium militem quendam qui et justiciarius itineris fuerat ad coronam " (*Ann.* 279 from 2 Foss. 181, 486). This system is recognised by the Oseney Chronicler, 4 *Ann. Monast.*, Rolls, in 1289, p. 320 : " *collegas* quoque suos [Weylond, J.'s] justiciarios qui sibi in banco judiciis exercendis *assidere consueverant, viz.*, J. de Lovetote et R. de Boyland, *milites* W. de Bramtone et P. de Litlebyre *clericos*." See *d'Amory's Case*.

(k) " *Assisa* was originally a court or place where judges, councillors or other assessors met, to hear, to consult or to determine. . . . Hence the following tertiary uses of the term, *viz.* : an ordinance or statute; a trial or series of trials; a tax or other assessment; a power of assessing or of prescribing " : Eyton, *Henry II*, 89, n. (3).

DEVELOPMENT OF THE LEGAL REPRESENTATIVE 123

1170. The Inquest of Sheriffs.
1176. The Assize of Northampton; for itinerant justices.
1178. Five judges selected from the *Curia regis* for ordinary cases; the " King in Council " for appeal.
1181 (about). Special officers, *servientes regis* or *hundredi* to keep (*custodire*) the pleas of the Crown, known after 1194 as *coronatores* (*l*).
1189 (before). The Great Assize; " recognition " by jury; " the term would seem to point to some great ordinance " (*m*); Henry II dies.
1191. The *Commune* of London.
1194. See 1181.
1213. " The first representative assembly on record " (*n*).
1215. The Great Charter; " the vague expressions of the older charter were now exchanged for precise and elaborate provisions . . . the baronage now threw aside . . . the bonds of unwritten custom . . . for the restraints of written law " : Green.
1216 (by). Various towns have charters for their courts (*l*). The Lateran Council abolishes the ordeal.
1220 (about). The coming of the Friars; then " the study of the law was the one source of promotion whether in Church or State " : Green.
1244. Peers, etc., meet in a parliament; control over ministers.
1254. Summons to Parliament, by royal writ, of two knights of the shire " to be chosen by the counties in the county courts " : Stubbs.

As the decades go on the pace of legal growth is

(*l*) Bolland, 24 Seld. Soc. lv (9 Seld. Soc. xv) : the controversy, *ib.* about dates is perhaps helped by the passage from Stow of 1152, p. 182*p*; the word is said to occur first in the Barons' Articles (14) in 1215, but in 1204 per *coronarios comitat' Sumset* is in *Rot. Chart.* 129 b. P. & M. I, 642, speak of " coroners " in an Ipswich Charter of 1200, but the *word* is not there : *Rot. Chart.* 65 b.

(*m*) 1 P. & M. 126.

(*n*) St. 1 *Hist.* c. 12, p. 592; *Sel. Chart.*, under 1213.

manifestly accelerated : the 13th century is faster than the 12th. The literary revival of which Green speaks is going on at the same time (or is a cause of that growth) : " It is in the reign of Henry III that the English Universities begin to exercise a definite influence on the intellectual life of Englishmen." Foreign academies, too, had contributed, as we have seen, to English thought, especially to English legal thought, and were still doing so. Of one class of contributors, Maitland says : " These clerical lawyers [Thomas of Marlborough, etc.] are memorable, for the very rapid development of English law in the first seventy years of the 13th century, was in great measure due to the fact that the *causidici* were also *clerici*, men whose education had been liberal and catholic and who were not ashamed to learn from all quarters " (*o*).

We must not forget when we examine the rise of the English bar the *impetus* from a bench thus nourished to critical or subtle argument; there is not only no impatience of the new curb on judicial omnipotence, there is encouragement of it. Nor is it surprising that the events and institutions mentioned in the above list should generate a body of interpreters and reinforce the ranks (or *cadres*) of men willing to represent other persons. Magna Carta alone was enough to create a race of lawyers and a harvest of litigation. Of a particular sort, indeed. At whatever point we date the rudiments of " Parliament," it is certain that a " talking " body cannot do its work properly without a *posse* of lawyers; our Parliament never has been able to, as the incessant " quips " on the subject prove. And the moment its " acts " are recorded in writing the need of " learned " colleagues is more imperative than ever (*p*).

(*o*) *Pleas of the Crown* (*Glos.*), XII. He continues : " From that time onward the quality of the English lawyer's intellect became steadily worse, and for two centuries after Bracton's death [1268] not a law book was written worthy to be kept in the same room with Bracton's book." The English lawyer was too busy practising.

(*p*) See p. 16.

DEVELOPMENT OF THE LEGAL REPRESENTATIVE 125

In the actual trials cited above we began with a state of things when English law chose its homes in the monasteries and ended (in 1213) with a monk who was proud of his jurisprudence, asserting that *his* order was not expected to know the law (for *another* was).

Of one proximate cause we may be tolerably sure. Historians insist on the immense importance of the " original writ "—" soon [after Henry II] to become the ground-plan of all civil justice " (*q*). Written documents in any affairs may require interpreters, and in important matters expert interpreters. Yet we do not know when written pleadings (*r*) were first introduced; probably they came in gradually, and with them, assuredly, specialist composers. But the writ alone, with its long history, would account for a rise of a specialist class; form was the very essence of a writ (*s*). The Year Books are full of arguments on writs. That they were sacrosanct was natural when even oral pleadings were. Originally drawn by ecclesiastics (*t*), they attached a superstitious importance to every " jot and tittle " which, first applied to Holy Writ, was a tradition from the Rabbis. The sacrosanctity has continued unimpaired in the indictment (which may be traced back (*t*) to our period—about 1200) almost to our

---

(*q*) 1 P. & M. c. v, p. 129.

(*r*) The text books, including Stephen on *Pleading* (1824 : p. 29), refer back to L. C. Baron Gilbert's *Hist.*, *etc.*, *of the K. B.* (1763 : appended to his *Law of Executions*), p. 315, who seems to imply that written pleadings became compulsory owing to 36 Edw. 3, c. 15 (1362), but he gives no authority. Cf. Coke 8 *R.* Pref. xxviii : Thirning C. J. [1396] said that under Edw. III " the law was of the greatest perfection that ever it was and that pleading (the greatest honour and ornament of the law) " was far better than before.

" The earliest recorded plea " is of 1181 : Maitland, 1 *Sel. Pleas of the Crown*, xxvi ; 1 Seld. Soc. : printed, Bigelow's *Procedure*, 400.

(*s*) Bolland, 27 Seld. Soc. xxvi ; Maitland, 20 Seld. Soc. lxvi—lxviii. In Edw. II's time " we are tempted to say that argument precedes [oral] pleading and that pleadings are evolved in the course of argument."

(*t*) P. 30. *The Indictments Act, 1915*, p. 47, London, Stevens & Haynes, 1916.

own day, and in other pleadings nearly as long. Conversely, when there was no writ, a lawyer was not wanted, at any rate, in early stages.

The *Attornatus*.

(a) *Beginnings*.

Responsalis has meant one who answers for me in court by my authority (and, perhaps, one who answers my questions when I consult him), and *respondere* is for a long time the technical term of the *attornatus*'s pleading (even for the plaintiff); *procurator* (*u*) is in " Glanville " a synonym for *responsalis*, which, in fact, it, being by far the more familiar word, drove out, having in its turn to yield to *attornatus*. This word " Glanville " never uses, but in a precedent for a writ (B. 12, c. 19), the King says to the Sheriff : " You have deputed—*attornastis*—others in your place " (explained further down as " transferring it to others ") to do certain things; *attornatus* thus clearly means a deputy or substitute, as it does in the earliest instances known to us, *viz*., in the Pipe Roll (*x*) of 1162-3, 1163-4, 1166, 1168—all in " Glanville's " day. In a document (*y*) dated by Mr. Round before 1180, Paganus is called the *attornatus* of the sheriff of Exeter when he appears in the Exchequer; the word is rarely explained, but this *clericus* is expressly said to be *gerens vices vicecomitis*. In the Cornish Pipe Roll of Michaelmas, 1199 (*z*), it is said " *attornatus est* per justiciarios " to repay £100,

---

(*u*) On the word see Index and App. XII. " A proctor . . . is a sort of monkish attorney " : Steerforth in *David Copperfield*.

(*x*) " De Att^{r}nata q^a debuit Rob." : 6 Pipe Roll Soc. 23; perhaps = a woman substituted to pay a debt to R.; " At^{r}nata Willo. Cade " : *ib*. v. 7, p. 46; " est att^{r}nat' in [de] ad Isaac " : *ib*. v. 9, 18 = instead of paying [it] to the Crown, he has to pay it to I.; " fuerat ei atturnatus de Debito " : *ib*. v. 12, p. 222; for 1166 see p. 127*b*; " Beatricia attornata esset ei " : 3 Br. *N. B.* 190, in 1236-7.

(*y*) *The Commune of London*, p. 86.

(*z*) Eyton, 7 *Antiq. of Shropshire* (1858), 163, n. 22.

i.e., by agreement with another named person he takes the debt over. In 1200 a certain Mabel, who " is said to be " ill, appoints (*attornaverit loco suo*) a deputy (Devon); Adam and Richard, defendants, were not *attornati* loco " of the treasurer of Salisbury, though they were his men," *ad luer* v. *perd.*; and the case was put back for his " warrant " (Wilts); Simon's " *attornatus* comes and says, etc." (Norfolk) (*a*); to take an instance from a chronicler (*b*), certain lands were *attornate*. The term in these cases can hardly be called technical; no one is thinking of a professional person, certainly before 1200 and perhaps for a long time afterwards. Indeed, to fix such a date is one of our problems.

The word is Latinised from the French *atorner* or *atourner*, which is attested by Godefroy as existing in the 11th, and by Littré (and, perhaps, Sainte-Palaye) in the 12th century, and meaning (*c*) to put in order, furnish,

---

(*a*) 1 *Cur. Reg. R.* (1189-1201); 143, 264, 309 (1922); and in the Index are many instances of the office where the word does not occur in the text (as in the case of Ivo of Cornwall, and that of 1201, p. 299); so in that of 1 *Sel. Civ. Pleas* (1200-3); 2 Seld. Soc., where, too, the word is used (add p. 64). Nor does the *word* occur in the Indices to *Rot. Cur. Reg.* (1835), ed. Palgrave, but *ponere loco suo* is frequent in the text, *e.g.*, v. I, p. 138, in 1198. In I Br. *N. B.* (Index of Things, "*att.*") there are many references, the earliest (II, 4) in 1218 from Gloucestershire.

N.B.—In 1 *Cur. Reg. R.* 464, in 1201 " Magister Hospitalis presents his brother R. B. ad esse ballivum eorum in omnibus."

(*b*) *Chron. Joc. de Brakelonda*, 103 & viii, Camd. Soc. 1840: " tempore r. Stephani [1135-54] . . . attornate fuerunt in feodum dimidii militis, cum primo essent socagia S. Æd.," written perhaps as late as 1190. Cf. " Rex Henricus dedit de suo dominio quod Comes attornavit ad servitium milit. scilicet terram R. H. pro feod. I. milit. et terram R. de B. pro feodo dimidii militis." 1 *Lib. Niger Scac.* p. 65, ed. Hearne: from a return in 1166, written in the time of John: Poole, *Exchequer*, p. 13-4; Hearne says " attornavit " here=" vertit " or " commutavit."

In 1284 in the account of the same trial we find defendant (after appearing) making " attornatum quendam canonicum suum ad etc.," and in the Plea Roll " attornavit se eisdem " (plaintiffs): *Barnwell Book*, pp. xlvi, 51.

(*c*) In the poem by Guiot, p. 162*d*, l. 2501, is: *se lor sens estoit atornez; at.*=in order, perhaps from *adornare*. In a French custumal

arrange, equip : " disposé à, préparé à." The French word is said to be from L. *tornare*, to turn (*d*), especially a lathe (and the Latin of Greek origin), but probably *adornare* (*e*) influenced the French non-legal word and its Latin equivalent, coined in England, and gradually (*f*)

---

of London (probably about 1300, but perhaps much earlier) *atourne* of wool=dressed : Bateson, 17 *E. H. R.* 498, 501; so *plicare et attornare (pannos)* = to fold and dress cloth : (1261), Bateson, 1 *Leic. Rec.* 95. Cf. Walter of Henley (*fl.* 1250), " le baillif seit atorne pur deners "= " be appointed money wages for his needs " : p. 92, ed. Lamond (1890); " les terres soient . . . bin atornees e semez "=" well turned over " : *ib.* 98. The only instance (apparently) of *atourner* in Beaumanoir's *Coutumes* (about 1280 : ed. Salmon) in § 560 = *disposer*. In *le Domesday de Gippewyz* [Ipswich], 2 *Black Bk. Admy.* 64, Rolis, dated 1291, " tenauntz ne deyuvent attourner "=transfer their service, but *ib.* 134 *attorne receyvre* or *prendre* is in the legal sense.

The earliest *atorné*=attorney, in Godefroy, is in 1217 from L'Exchiquier de Falaise. The word never took root in France and has now totally disappeared, though it does seem sporadically to have meant *procureur*, with which and *avoué* the French were contented. Thus, in *les bons usages etc. de la commune d'Oleron* about 1314, 2 *Black Bks.* c. xx is devoted to a substitute in court, but neither *at.* nor *proc.* is mentioned; whereas in 1389 in the Petition of the Hansards, 35 Seld. Soc. 77, Conrad of Lübeck is " attourne et procurour " for other Hanseatics in England.

(*d*) " The statement found in the law dictionaries for the last two hundred years that the word means one ' who acts in the turn of another ' is a bad guess " : *N. E. D.*

(*e*) Maitland, *Pleas of Glouc.* 145; see next note.

(*f*) In 1221 a man is *male attornatus*=maltreated, got a " pretty dressing " : Maitl. *Pl. Glouc.* 43, 145; so in 1272 Henry III's *corpus* was *nobiliter attornatum sicut decet reges* : *Lib. de Antiq. Leg.* 153. In 1239 M. Paris (*Chron. Maj. Addit.* VI, 66; Rolls; Add. 150, Wats) has : " per visum VI episcoporum ad hoc specialiter attornatorum "= deputed; in 1273 " aliis civibus . . . per totam communam civitatis attornatis et juratis ad arreragia examinanda " : *Lib. de Ant. Leg.* 241. Under 1286 the Dunstable Chronicler (3 *Ann. Monast.* 335; Rolls) tells how anxious the Prior was that the justices should only try Dunstable cases there; he got a royal writ to that end; they and their *socii* sit there three whole days *at his cost* and only took Dunstable cases : " de forensibus ibidem alias attornatis nihil : sed omnia apud Bedeforde sont remissa "; if we do not read *adjornatis* (for *att.*) this=sent thither from other places.

From *attornare* the English *aturne* (noun or verb) is taken; the earliest instance in *N. E. D.* is in 1303 from Robert of Brunne's *Handlyng of Sinne* (ed. Furnivall, 1901), p. 179; ll. 5501-2 are : " So shulde eche aturne seriaunt. But many one holde no cunnaunt (covenant)." The whole passage deals with unjust men of law, and

monopolised by the law. Thus, the essential meaning is someone prepared, fitted out, equipped, instructed to be a substitute.

It will be noticed that the person got into Anglo-Norman customs or law not direct, so to say, from the French, but from the Latin of Anglo-Norman or English lawyers and writers. In other words, he is not a Norman institution, and if he is Anglo-Norman, he is more Anglo than Norman. This thesis is put forward with diffidence, as there is great authority against it.

The chief is that of Heinrich Brunner (g). In his view the *attornatus* is a purely Norman importation. " In the Anglo-Norman law the *attornatus* was preserved and independently developed. The ' attorney ' of the English common law goes back to this Norman *attornatus*. . . . The *attornatus* or *atourne* (g) meets us in the Norman legal sources as a special type of representative for legal proceedings. . . . The *attornatus*, like many other institutions of Norman law, was transplanted to England, there to receive in its details certain features departing from the original. . . . In the doctrine of legal representation

---

this is addressed to " thou bayle " : " so should every attorney-sergeant act " *sc.* with honesty and mercy; the poet advisedly uses technical language, but can hardly mean the *serviens ad legem; aturne = attornatus* = ballivus as often. The combination " a. s." is unique.

By 1430 (*i.e.*, earlier than any instance in *N. E. D.*) in a strictly legal sense, " to attorn and surrende " occurs in a conveyance to Rich. Newton, Serjt. : H. Flasdieck, *Mittelenglische Original-Urkunden* (1405-30), p. 86 (1926).

In 1445 an Englishman " at Caleys " is described as " factour and attourne " to other Englishmen : petition to H. VI : *Wars of Engl. in Fr.* 465 ; Rolls (No. 22), v. 1.

The sense of a " substitute " persisted long ; in 1484 a suppliant of the King's Council speaks of his " attournes et deputees " : 35 Seld. Soc. 95.

(g) *Forschungen*, see p. 3k, where this text (pp. 261, 267 of translation) is continued. Since Bru. wrote there is much new material; perhaps, too, to the scholars of his day Norman origins of English institutions were a sort of fetish.

(*Anwaltschaft*) also English law has its roots in Norman law " (*h*).

With the general influence of the Norman Conquest we have endeavoured to deal.

With regard to our present theme, it must be submitted with all deference to the master that he has not attempted to deal with the period, say, 1150—1200. He abounds in citations, but, so far as can be traced, everyone is later than 1200, the earliest (*i*) being from *Assisiae Normanniae* (1234-6). Not one of the references *by name* to *attornatio* in England from 1160 onwards, collected above, is mentioned. Maitland, speaking of pre-1066 law in Normandy, remarks (*k*) that it will always be a very difficult study : " unless some great discovery remains to be made," because the law " has left no contemporary memorials of itself. We have at present hardly anything that can be called direct evidence of the legal condition of Normandy between the time when it ceased to be a part of the West Frankish realm and a date long subsequent to " 1066. " It is only about the middle of the 12th century that we begin to get documents, and even then they come sparsely."

In the *Très Ancien Coutumier*, the earliest Norman law book, the oldest part of which dates from the very end of the 12th century, *attornatus* is not so much as mentioned independently, and, like *procurator*, only once in any way (*l*).

(*h*) Yet it "is not exclusively peculiar to Norman law." "The thing is found in German laws : so perhaps the origin is in Frankish law " : transln. p. 262 n. (20).

(*i*) The earliest *atorné* we have cited is of 1217, p. 128*c*.

(*k*) 2 *Sel. Essays in Ang.-Amer. Leg. Hist.* 68 (1908); 4 *Pol. Sc. Q.* 496-518, 628-47 (1889).

(*l*) In c. 82, *de dilationibus et exoniis*, in Part II (which begins at c. 66), dated about 1220 by Tardif (1881), s. 7 : on the appointed day, defendant must come and answer either *per se vel per procuratorem ab ipso in curia attornatum* ; the word is on its way to the ultimate sense ; nor in English documents do we get the combination "proc. att."

THE *ATTORNATUS*.

But most significant of all is the fact that the greatest living authority (*m*) on Norman institutions on whom we have relied for an even wider generalisation, here, too, relevant—does not, in either of his works, so much as mention the *attornatus* (nor, indeed, any of the titles in p. 132, n. (*o*), except *procurator* barely and not in our sense).

We may perhaps conclude, especially from the priority of the documents, that Normandy got the word and the thing from England rather than *vice versa*. We have men doing attorney's work in trials even before Glanville's day. We cannot expect astronomical synchronism, but surely Professor Haskins is using the language of common sense when he remarks : " During nearly a century and a half of personal union with England " Normandy " afforded a constant example of parallel development " (*m*). Spelman asserts roundly that the Normans took their attornatus from " us " (*n*).

Advocatio is still ecclesiastical, c. 73, and *advocet . . . regem ad garantum* : *ib.*

In this book there is implied a system of judicature (*e.g.*, cc. 25-6 *ib.*), but advocacy is still in the stage of the *consilium*; the *senescallus* (the judge) lays it down that an accused person without advice (*accusatus* . . . [sine] *consilio* : sic ed. Tardif, c. 62, § 2, p. 54, *de questione mota* in Part I about 1199-1200; see page 42), who at once denies everything, though he does not traverse (*respondeat*) the charge word for word, may leave his place and seek counsel (*consilium petat de loco suo recedens*), and when he has got it then he ought to meet the charge word for word and reproduce them or be at the court's mercy (*vel in emendatione curie remanebit*), § 3. , An accused who thus traverses word for word and offers to disprove is a [good] *placitor* (*sic*), because in a lay court it is common for traversers thus to exculpate themselves if the accuser has witnesses.

This seems to be the solitary recognition in this code of legal aid. *Placitatores* (cf. *placitor* above) are frequently mentioned—correctly— as officers of the court (*e.g.*, cc. 63-5), but *placitare* is used of the litigants (*e.g.*, 17, 19, 44).

(*m*) *Norman Institutions* (1918), Pref. Similar instances—from similar causes—will occur in the case of the two partners of Great Britain.

(*n*) Gloss. *Atturn.* : Habet item Normannia suos Atturnatos lege et more nostro institutos. Cf. Stubbs, 1 *Hist.* c. 116, p. 500, n. (2) : " There is the strongest probability that Henry II was as great a legal innovator in Normandy as he was in England."

No doubt both before and after the Conquest both races were well acquainted with the *advocatus* and the *procurator* (o) of the Church courts where central unity

---

(o) For a French—St. Bernard's—view, about 1100, see p. 120. In the Battel Abbey trials (Hen. II) the Abbey's *procurator* seems to have been a layman; for " Glanville's " see p. 126.

In 1160-1, we have *procuratori vinee* : 4 Pipe Roll Soc. 42, 51; in 1167-8, in *procurationem liberorum* : *ib.* v. 12, p. 59.

In the *Dial. de Scac.*, finished about 1179, *procuret itaque sibi procuratorem vel responsalem et ipse regiis addictus negociis ad curiam sine simulatione festinet* (I, viii, B. p. 94 : ed. Hughes), the learned editors suggest, p. 189, that *proc.*=agent in an ecclesiastical, *resp.* in a civil court; *sed quaere*; *generalis ejus proc.* (*ib.* p. 123, II, iv, B.)=they say, p. 214, " not an attorney but a representative," but is there any distinction? In 1338 a society has both *g.p.* and *att.* : p. 187*h*. Clearly *Dial.* p. 93, I, viii, B. *experiri per proc.* does not refer to an ecclesiastical matter.

In the story of Thomas of Marlborough we see how easily in 1205 *procurator* and *advocatus* melted into each other in the Papal court; a little later (*Chron.* 231) he tells us how the Abbey sent him as *procurator* to deal with the Roman creditors and how he got a composition from them—implying the very full powers which his unique acquaintance with the case necessitated.

For the canonical view of the *proc.* about 1236 see App. XII— William of Drogheda's code thereon, certainly not confined to ecclesiastical courts. For that of Ric. Anglicus see App. XI (cc. 28, 38). In 1237, in a " Composition between London and French merchants," *attourneez et procuratours des marchantz de Amyens* : 1 *Lib. Alb.* 420, B. 3, Pt. 3, Rolls, is obviously foreign; a French " power of attorney " follows.

Under 1254 M. Paris, 6 *Chron. Maj.* 291 (Rolls), has a letter from the Abbot of Evesham whence it appears that the Abbey retained generally a *magister* W. de Marsilia as *procurator in curia Romana* and sent another specially to London.

In 1280 William of Woodford is *commonachus et procurator religiosorum virorum abbatis et conventus* in an eccles. suit : *Chron. Petrob.* 48, Camd. Soc. 1st ser. No. 47; but in 1276 (*ib.* 128), before the Barons of the Exch. he is the Abbot's *frater* W. de W. *attornatus suus et commonachus suus* and the other party has his *att.* In the *Mirror of Justices pr.* clearly=attorneys. In 1296 the Prior of Dunstable makes his peace with the King *per procuratores saeculares* : *Ann. Dunstap.* 407, Rolls. In 1344 the Commons petition about " Procurators, Attornies, Executors, Notaries and Maintainers," 2 *Rot. P.* 153 b, who, in s. 1 of St. of Provisors, 1353, are the classes who may take the place of the party in person.

For *proc.*=M.P. in a writ of 1404, see p. 463; it is assumed that he is not a *miles*. In fact the word gradually became popular and=man of business; in 1448 Oriel College appoints " nostros veros legittimos et indubitatos procuratores actores factores negociorumque nostrorum

could command uniformity. And as, probably, on this side it came to be convenient to have a word which had not been monopolised by Churchmen, so, perhaps, on the other (*oo*), the existence of the homonymous, but by no means synonymous, *atorne* (or—é) left no room for the vernacular of *attornatus*.

The evidence, then, seems to show that the English *attornatus* owes his origin to the conditions which, we have endeavoured to maintain, gradually produced our general legal system after the Conquest. He was born and bred here, though he may, occasionally, have crossed the Channel.

Thus he begins as a simple messenger, a " mere conduit pipe," with duties almost trifling, *e.g.*, to get a document, to hear a judgment, to fix a date (*p*). Any friend could

---

gestores ac nuncios speciales " : *Dean's Reg. of Oriel* (1446-1661), 84 Oxf. Hist. Soc. (1926), 372; cf. 353 (1446).

In 1437, says H. VI in 1447, " we . . . ordeigned " Andrew Holes " oure procuratoure in the courte of Rome " : *Wars of Engl. in Fr.* (No. 22) Rolls, v. 1, 472.

For a derived sense, see 5 Séld. Soc. 71, xxxvii : a Leet jury of Warwick present three women as " common touters " (*procuratrix*) for the ecclesiastical courts, *i.e.*, they delated offenders.

(*oo*) The French had and have for the collateral of *advocatus*, the *notaire* on a much larger scale than we have. So our " solicitor " who has not been nearly so vigorous in France is displacing " attorney." As the *procureur* flourished in France, a word from *atorné* was not wanted. Indeed, the early French *procurator* stands to the *avocat* very much as the early English *attornatus* (when he emerges) to " counsel " : " Le procureur accomplit les formalités et prépare les pièces qu'exige le procès. Mais c'est l'avocat qui conduit l'affaire. Le procureur c'est le client agissant, répondant aux appels, réclamant les délais, produisant dans les conditions requises les actes nécessaires. L'avocat c'est le client articulant ses griefs, soutenant sa cause oralement et par écrit, se débattant au milieu des objections et cherchant à convaincre le juge. L'avocat c'est le conseil c'est la plume c'est la voix c'est l'éloquence, s'il se peut, du plaideur " : Ducoudray, *Les Origines du Parlement de Paris aux 13° et 14° siècles* (1902), 196—exactly Drogheda's view, p. 579.

(*p*) Brunner's instances from 1 *Rot. Cur. R.* above. John Bacon, Queen Eleanor's *att.*, was also her executor in 1289-90 : *Issues of the Exch.* 98 (1837); but *att.* does not = executor as Foss (III, 220) seems to think. In 1290 her *attornati* and Walter of Wymburn, J., are to be called (as witnesses?) : 1 *Rot. Parl.* 53 d.

go for you to the court, if, for instance, you were ill, like Mabel above, or take a message or an excuse; a well-to-do man like Hubert sends his "private secretary" or *ballivis* (*q*). Your deputy himself might be unable to go and have to send an excuse like Turstan. Originally the job is rather "casual." Even a woman could do it; in 1203 a woman puts her sister in her place and then removes her (*r*), but she is not called *attornata*. But in 1313 a man claims "per Isabellam de Uptone attornatum suum" (*s*). Katherine Bompuz in 1306 was "appointed" attorney (*t*) to receive a gold ring. Thus the word is originally not technical but lay, if not popularly coined, while all the words with which it soon has to compete were by this time—though they, too, had once been of popular origin—stamped with a jural character. Perhaps this is the reason why for some time we do not hear of the *attornatus* being paid, as we do of the man who actually argues in court.

Such are the beginnings of the *attornatus*. "Glanville" meant his work to be a "practice" book, and he fairly works out a consequential code for his *responsales*. His rules have been developing continuously since his day. His stage may perhaps be described as that of

(b) *Non-professional Development*,

which must be shortly noticed as a bridge to the professional.

(*q*) Laurence was *fidelis ac providus supra terras* [of H.] *custos ac seneschallus . . . solatium singulare et immobilis columna veritatis*: M. Paris in 1232; ed. Wats. 381. Cf. W. de Valentia's right-hand man, p. 359.

(*r*) 1 *Sel. Civ. Pleas*, 56 : 3 Seld. Soc. : she wishes to "go on" (*persequi*) for herself.

(*s*) Y. B. 6 Edw. 2; 43 Seld. Soc. 110 : the masculine is official, so to say. The "atturnata" of 1162 and 1163, p. 126*x*, can hardly = *attornatus* in the sense that Isabella is one.

(*t*) Thomas, *Early Mayor's Court Rolls*, 246; but "attorn." only appears in margin; for women "attorning to" others, see p. 126*x*. *The Mirror of J.* B. 2, c. 31, p. 88, distinctly says that women cannot be attornies—an instance of its method of stating as law what it is in favour of.

First, however, we must quote Brunner's remark about *lucrandum vel perdendum* : " It signifies that the representative was given power to act, not merely for a particular step in the proceedings, but for all acts without limitation which the party himself could do in the proceedings; thus the attorney's acts are the party's acts, whether done to his advantage or to his disadvantage. That this formula was intended to cover all procedural doings, without exception, is clearly seen from those entries which do set limits "; the phrase conveys unlimited control. This theory, much insisted upon by German writers, may have been regularly applied on the Continent, but no concrete instance is given in this country (or even there), though, no doubt, there was a stage, well authenticated, when English courts required proof of the *attornatus's* authorisation by the " client." The point is that writers, especially on the Continent, construct *catenæ* of suggestions on this subject which cannot be verified in detail. This is the case, too, with some of " Glanville's " own details—we do not hear of them again; though he cannot be mistaken about the practice of his own day. In view of later documents, a few instances (*u*) may be in place here.

Some civil pleas may be prosecuted by attorney, but his principal ought to be present in court [to vouch him], otherwise the attorney ought not to be received (*x*). But the opponent need not appear in person nor, indeed, the substitute [the *responsalis*], if he be known to the court [he could send a message]; there may be two or more *responsales* either having separate or collective authority (*y*). A plea may proceed to the end just as if the party in person had appeared. [Apparently] in real property the lord could

---

(*u*) From B. XI.
(*x*) As late as 1255 the King says that a Prior who is bound to make suit in the King's Court " cannot by the custom of the realm appoint a proctor or attorney except " by his word of mouth in court : *Cal. Pat. Rolls* (1247-58), p. 437.
(*y*) P. 137.

not send any official he liked to appear for him; he must give him special authority [*mandatum*] for the business and make him attorney for it. And [apparently] whoever has a suit pending in any court can make an attorney to take it into the King's court; a form of writ for doing this is given. The *procurator* effaces his principal to such an extent that we need not trouble about the latter's essoins. But can the latter revoke his authority at his will and substitute another representative? especially if he quarrels with the first (*capitales inimicitiae*)?—which, we may suppose, was the most likely ground of a rupture (and so, a modern touch). Of course he can, for the right of representation is founded on the theory of the non-presence of the party, and therefore it is within his control to withdraw his *mandatum* at any moment. But he must (*distringendus ad tenendum*) abide by the result of the work of the *responsalis*, whether he comes to terms or there is a judgment. On this general rule a notable theory has been founded, thus expressed by Brunner (as above) : " The ' for-speaker ' stands alongside the party in the tribunal's presence, so as to pronounce the words for him (*z*). He is not empowered to say what he thinks is proper; his sole right is to say what the party expressly desires him to say. . . . It is not that his will is substituted for the party's will, but his word for the party's word. . . . Entirely different is the position of the attorney, selected by the party. He stands before the tribunal not with, but *instead of* the party. His acts, within his authority, count as the acts of his principal " (*a*). Maitland states (*b*) the same theory as if it survived to Edward II's day. The triple

---

(*z*) A survival from the days of sacramental *formulæ*.

(*a*) *Per contra*, two of Brunner's "conclusions" (not in Mr. Wigmore's essay) may be usefully noted : (1) In old Norman and English law only special counsel (*Anwälte*) are found : this is borne out by our instances of trials (above); (2) Norman and English *attornatio* has got rid of Frankish symbols : it is a purely oral or verbal act in court.

(*b*) P. 205.

authority of Glanville, Brunner and Maitland are warrants for the principle, but except on the mediæval Continent was it ever put into practice? Is there any definite instance of a court drawing this distinction or insisting by word or deed that the *attornatus* binds his principal but the serjeant does not? Does a court ever say : Your attornatus has committed you and you are estopped? It is notorious that both representatives are from time to time " thrown over."

The *responsalis* [of course], " Glanvill " continues, is not personally liable for damages awarded against his *dominus*.

The last words of this book show how greatly this institution had developed. " When one or more (*c*) have been substituted in court to conduct a suit for another . . . whether the one can delegate his authority to another or whether one of the two can nominate the other or a third in his place or (*d*) in that of his principal (*d*) to win or lose for him in that suit are points at least questionable "— doubts surely suggested by actual practice.

To trace the development of the regulations here laid down or suggested would be to follow

(c) *The Rise of the Profession.*

Great industry might discover an actual instance of every proposition of law and every rule of practice, *e.g.*, about essoins and *responsales*, attested by " Glanvill," but for us the value of his book is that it shows a living code for these persons, such as a flourishing industry would require and, in time, enlarge. This likelihood is fulfilled. We cannot " spot " the process year by year, but a sense

---

(*c*) In 1200 *Willelmus advocatus* [ecclesiastical] " puts in his place L. or P. with the others he had so put, or any one of them if they cannot all be there *ad lucr.* v. *perd.*" : *Cur. Reg. Roll.* 266. So *Hengham Parva*, c. 1, " si duos habuerit attornatos vel plures . . ." See p. 293.

(*d*) The meaning of these words is obscure.

of progress is gathered from a few (of the innumerable) chronological records.

1159. Even in Glanvill's lifetime we have a royal writ giving Abingdon (*e*) leave to send an *attornatus* to assizes and courts generally. Either there was some special reason for seeking this leave or at that date only individuals could be so represented without leave; probably the Abbey thought it well to be on the safe side and practice was yet by no means rigid.

1201. Radulf, defendant, appoints his brother Turstan *ad luc. v. perd.* in a trial at Warwick Assizes, but he goes alone and meets Henry *positus loco* of the plaintiff; a day is fixed—*tunc essoniavit se idem Radulfus et Turstanus attornatus ejus non essoniavit se neque venit*; so Henry argues that his opponent is in default, etc., *petiit defectum Thurstani sibi allocari . . . et tunc tulit attornatus abbatis breve d. r. &c.* (*f*); each is only called " attornatus " after explanation.

1218-40. In Bracton's *Note-Book* (*g*) there are many cases of *attornati*, not yet digested into a system.

1219. A lady in Bedfordshire brings an action *homagii* and sends her named *attornatus*; defendant says if she will come in person he will reply to her claim, *i.e.*, he will not do so to her attorney, for in such a suit she cannot be represented. The attorney answers that he was received as such before the justices of eyre. But it was held—*attornatus non potest huiusmodi placitum sequi*—she must come in person, if she cares to; if the other court had received an *attornatus* it had been misled (*h*).

1221 is perhaps the earliest date of *facere attornatum*; it is in the programme of the London Iter (*i*):

(*e*) P. 72.
(*f*) 1 *Cur. Reg. R.* (1922), 463.
(*g*) Ed. Maitland : more than appears in the Index, *e.g.*, v. I, 189.
(*h*) 2 Br. *N. B.* 39.
(*i*) 1 *Lib. Alb.* 63, B. 1, Pt. 2; Rolls : transln. (1861), p. 56; *Quaestio*, II.

THE *ATTORNATUS*.

" How is an attorney to be admitted at the Hustings?"
" A non-citizen (*forinsecus*) dwelling without the City but holding land there is a defendant in respect of it by the King's writ may *facere attornatum suum* and the *att.* will be admitted; but if a foreigner wants to implead a citizen, he may not *fac. at s.* in any way, for in such case it would be in his power whether justly or unjustly " to embarrass and annoy any citizen. But when this disability was removed in 1268 or 1270 by a charter (*k*)—*tam agendo quam defendendo*—we are expressly told—it was to be *sicut alibi in curia nostra*. An example of this right is recorded (*l*) in 1373-4; J. Wale and Herman Langhe, " merchants of Almaine," name their attorneys to recover a debt from a citizen; Edward III grants a writ to accept and return such names, and the names are returned and recorded.

1223. " An appointment of a proxy to appear in the shiremoot of Staffordshire " (*m*). See 1235-6.

1227. In a MS. *Registrum Brevium* (*n*), *i.e.*, a list of writs sent in that year as precedents to Ireland, two (28, 29) are respectively for sending knights to view an essoinee and to hear a sick man appoint an attorney. Another MS. *Registrum* " of very nearly the same date " as the Irish, has writs (37) " announcing appointment of attorney," one (38) like the 29th Irish, and one (39) like the 28th Irish. A third MS. Register (perhaps 1236-59) has (96) a writ *de attornato faciendo* . . . *sine breve regis*

(*k*) *Lib. de Ant. Leg.* 104.
(*l*) *Letter Bk.* G. 320.
(*m*) St. 2 *Hist.* 224, c. xv, § 203, from 1 *Rot. Lit. Claus.* 537. *D'attornato* : the King tells the sheriff that he has admitted W. de B. to plead (*respondere*) in the place of T. de B. in the County and hundred courts, and " wherever there must be and is wont to be a plea for " T. and orders him to receive W. *tanquam att. suum ad hec* : " tan. att. s." occurs twice.
(*n*) Found by Maitland : 1 *Harvard Law R.*, Oct., 1889; 2 *Coll. Papers*, 110.

founded on c. 10 of Stat. Merton; No. 98 just as 37 above and No. 100 combining 38 and 39 above.

1230. A suit between two Abbots about jurisdiction is heard at Westminster before two bishops and several justices of the King " in Banco "; the defendant is attached and *came, per atornatum suum* [named] *et cognovit* (admitted), whereas the plaintiff only " says *per atorn. s.*," *i.e.*, they both *pleaded* by attorney and one certainly was present (*o*).

1235-6, see 1223. The Statute of Merton sanctions the practice.

1238. Galfrid says in a cause that he had never made A. E. or anyone else his *attornatus* (in certain previous proceedings), but the rolls were searched and it was found that he had made him and others *attornati*, who in fact conducted (*sequebantur*) his *loquela* for him (*p*).

1240. The Abbot of Ramsey in his court on Feb. 23 prohibited his tenants bringing *placitatores* thereinto *ad impediendam vel prorogandam justitiam* of the Abbot *et suorum* : penalty 20s.; and he made the same decree (*q*) word for word on Feb. 26 in a neighbouring court; probably " placitator " is used because *attornatus* was not so familiar. So in

1260. The Abbot of St. Albans will not have *adventitii placitatores* in his halimoots who *partes cum solemnitate* [formality] *sustineant*; all the *bundi* (free heads of families?) are to try *sine calumnia verborum*; " he would not have any verbal quibbles."

These expressions of provincial and ecclesiastical conservatism suggest that an innovation was making its way and the old order is a little impatient of the new. There

---

(*o*) Chron. Petroburg. 11—13; Camden Soc. No. 47 (1849).

(*p*) Bra. 3 *N. B.* 276.

(*q*) 1 *Cart. Rams.* 412, 428; Rolls, cited Maitland, p. 264; later, v. III, *att.* of Abbots (and of the King) occur frequently : 1 *Gest. Ab.* (St. A.) 454; Rolls.

THE *ATTORNATUS*. 141

are stronger grounds for thinking that we can now descry a legal " profession " emerging, and we shall find the *attornatus* among the other co-adventurers, where we shall see him in a larger perspective. Before looking for them we will glance at a text-book writer on the *attornatus*.

Bracton, writing about 1250, naturally knew " Glanville " (r), whose *responsalis* is certainly Bracton's *attornatus*; with this change there is almost word for word agreement (s). Bracton has no idea of a *serviens ad legem*, but he, as we have seen, supplements his doctrine of essoins by that of the *attornatus*, his references (t) to whom show that custom was forming a code for him. But the details are often difficult to understand (u), and the pre-*attornatus* system, which Bracton had in his mind, is not now intelligible.

However, we do get a clear principle when he says " an *attornatus* represents the person of the principal almost in all matters [except an essoin for bed-sickness] . . . and although a person has made his attorney he may proceed

---

(r) Maitland, *Bracton and Azo*, xxiv, n. (4); 8 Seld. Soc.

(s) *E.g.*, de *Essoniis* in a writ " si A. . . . , misit C. . . . ut reponsalem suum ad audiendum vel ad respondendum eidem B. . . . et si ratam habuerit responsionem quam . . . C pro eo fecit in eodem placito et similiter ad audiendum si velit eundem C in pdcto. plto. attornare in pdcto. loco suo ad lucr. v. perd. &c." f. 362, B. 5, Tr. 2, c. 143; 5 Rolls, 348; cf. " Glan." B. 11, c. 2, and cc. 1, 3; see p. 86, and App. X.

(t) *E.g.*, many in Index, 5 Rolls : nearly all, *n.b.* in " Essoins "; see, too, Britton's Index by Nicholls.

(u) *E.g.*, if one duly summoned " can neither come [to the court] nor send nor constitute an attorney because the King is not present he is, perhaps, excused, &c." : f. 337, *de Ess*, B. v, Tr. 2, c. 1; 5 Rolls, 149; apparently it was still necessary to get a royal writ to " make an *att.*"—at any rate, a general *att.* By the " King's presence " is meant a *curia reg.* judge. Or, *ib.* c. 2, p. 156 : " As the essoiner (*essoniator* : for illness) is not the *procurator* of him [the absentee] who made him essoiner, and therefore it is not his business to prove the state and act of another, nor of an *attornatus* to prove the act of the lord his principal (*principalis*), accordingly the lord shall make his law (*faciet legem*) if this can be done conveniently and if the lord has not come the *att.* shall swear on the soul of the *dominus litis*. And he shall promise (*affidabit*) that he will have his lord there on the day."

(*sequi*) in his own person when he wishes " (*x*) (a passage immediately followed by an obscure one on the relations between *attornatus* and essoiner). Again, it is apparently a general rule that an *attornatus* cannot make an *attornatus* for the principal (any more than a *procurator* can a *procurator*) " whether he be *attornatus* in the county or the King's court " (*x*).

The *responsalis* is not unknown to Bracton, but he has little " use " for him; he seems to allow him some sort of authority above that of a *nuntius*, but less than that of an *attornatus* (*y*). The notorious statement that " there is a great difference between a *responsalis* and an *attornatus* " (*z*) has long been expelled as a gloss on Bracton's text. Coke tried to harmonize various passages (by a plausible guess) thus (*a*): *Responsalis* was he that was appointed by the tenant or defendant in case of extremity and necessitie to alledge the cause of the parties absence and to certifie the court upon what tryall he will put himselfe, *viz.*, the combate or the country. So as his power was more than the essoinor which casteth an essoigne only to excuse the absence of the party as an estranger which casteth an exception doth. For by the common law the plaintife or defendant demandant or tenant could not appeare by attornie without the King's special warrant by writ or letters patent, but ought to follow his suite in his own proper person (by reason whereof there were but few suits).... And therefore Bracton saith truly *Attornatus*

(*x*) *Ib.* f. 342 a, p. 190; f. 364, p. 364.
(*y*) *Ib.* f. 349 b, p. 248; f. 361 b, p. 346-7; " sufficiens " *resp.*: f. 362, p. 350; cf. p. 85*o*.
(*z*) *De leg. de Nov. Diss.* f. 212 b, B. 4, c. 32, 2; 3 Rolls, 410: " a *ballivus* [which Twiss, *ib.* lxiv, thought=*responsalis*; no doubt the *ball.* could represent the lord sometimes, p. 127*a*] cannot do everything his lord can: *attornatus tamen haec omnia facere potest. Est igitur differentia magna inter responsalem et attornatum* "; *resp.* is not even mentioned before these words. The interpolation is perhaps from Fleta, iv, 6, 7.
(*a*) *On Littleton*, s. 196: 128 a.

haec omnia facere potest (that is, plead all manner of pleas). *Est igitur* [&c.]. So as the statutes that give the making of attorneyes have worne out *responsales*."

To pursue this figure through the immediate post-Bracton text writers would not be profitable until we have traced some converging clues.

The Clergy as Advocati.

All the evidence converges to show that by the time of Glanvill the secular was displacing the clerical representative; the *attornatus* or *procurator* was by no means always a *clericus*. Here we may fairly ask, what is a *clericus*? The authorities do not altogether agree; for our purpose we will cite one (*b*) of them, Rashdall, on the inadequate appreciation of clericality in the Middle Ages. " Even Savigny treats the term ' clericus ' when used of a mediaeval student as a synonym for ' scolaris ' without any distinctive meaning. The Bishop of Oxford [Stubbs], on the other hand . . . seems to assume that every *clericus* was necessarily in minor orders. The fact is that clericality in the Middle Ages, though it did not necessarily imply even the lowest grade of minor orders, did imply a great deal "; tonsure and dress *plus* celibacy conferred many immunities; . . . " the judges and practitioners of the ecclesiastical courts, at one time many of the secular judges and lawyers, as well as a host of ' clerks ' (*c*) in the service of the Crown or the great nobles, belonged to this class. . . . The relation between clerkship and the minor orders is, however, an obscure subject," but it is just this which concerns us as we advance in our period.

" If we try," say P. & M. (*d*), " to sum up in a few words those results of Henry[II]'s reign, which are to be

---

(*b*) 2 *Universities*, Pt. 2, c. 14, p. 644.
(*c*) For those of Chancery, see Maxwell-Lyte, the Great Seal (1926), p. 280.
(*d*) I, v, p. 117.

the most durable and the most fruitful, we may say that the whole of English law is centralised and unified by the institution of a permanent court of professional judges, by the frequent mission of itinerant judges throughout the land, by the introduction of the ' inquest ' or ' recognition ' and the ' original writ ' as normal parts of the machinery of justice." The upheavals of the reign which brought forth these innovations had " thrown up " the whole position of the clergy for discussion, and we cannot entirely disconnect the fortunes of the clerical bench from those of the clerical " bar." " It ought not to be forgotten," says Stubbs (e), " that the source of the evil [struck at by some of the Constitutions of Clarendon] was in the Conqueror's measures of division," *i.e.*, the distinction of the ecclesiastical and civil jurisdictions introduced into England by William. Under the Anglo-Saxon system in which the bishop and [the] archdeacon sat in the shire-moot and hundred-moot, all offences touching the clergy, except those of a purely spiritual character, which were treated of in special courts or councils, were decided according to the law of the land. . . ." We have met the dyarchy in practice; the Chronicler (f) of Battel Abbey could find justice in neither limb.

The *Dialogus de Scaccario* (before 1179) recognises (f) the system in its Exchequer officials.

In " Glanvill " (IV, 13, and X, ii, 21) there is a writ to ecclesiastical judges prohibiting their hearing in a court Christian suits belonging to the King's court (*mea curia*); in VII, 13, if a question of legitimacy arises there, *i.e.*, whether there was a good marriage, that issue is sent to the local ecclesiastical court, who must return it to the King's court.

(e) *Select Charters*, Pt. IV, p. 129—130; William's undated Charter is in Pt. III, pp. 80, 81.

(f) " Whether who sit by command are of the clergy or the *curia regis*. . . . Whether the judex who presides at the trial is an ecclesiastic or a layman (*forensis* : I, viii, A.)."

THE CLERGY AS *ADVOCATI*. 145

If, then, the forensic rights of clerics in lay tribunals had been considerable, we should expect that they would fight for them, when they were fighting for other privileges. But perhaps such rights were at that time of no great pecuniary value to any class, and for that reason we hear so little about them. At any rate, it is certain that clerics appear less and less for laymen, and that great churchmen discourage them from doing so; John of Salisbury and Peter of Blois—and " Glanvill "—were observers who looked beneath the surface. From Peter of Blois's letter (*g*), it looks very much as if at one time he was allured by the emoluments to desert theology for law (as we saw students at Oxford did) and his words conceivably are aimed at a state of things which he deplored, *i.e.*, there were too many priests trying to make money " at the bar." So Bernard of Morlaix laments (*h*) the degeneracy of the priest. Peter is almost certainly thinking of others besides those in the ecclesiastical courts; when he says the *advocati* of his day *militant avaritiae*, he can hardly mean the officials of the religious houses (technically so called) appearing (*i*) for those societies, for they would not have

---

(*g*) App. IX.
(*h*) Nomine clericus, actibus aulicus esse probatur.
    Aspicias . . . . clerum
    Ad popularia stare negotia resque forenses :
        de contemptu mundi, 2 *Satir. Poets of 12th Cent* , ed. Wright; Rolls, p. 53 (about 1150?).

About a century later Ruteboeuf in France joins the chorus against venal clerical lawyers (*teste* Beugnot, 1 *Assises de Jer*. 39 n.), where B. makes the extraordinary statement : " Lorsque, vers la fin du XIIe siecle *les clercs entrèrent* dans les cours de justice et *s'emparèrent d'une portion du pouvoir judiciaire* ils eurent soin de ne pas négliger les fonctions de conseils, mais alors ces fonctions perdirent leur ancien caractère, et il n'y eut plus rien de féodal ni de militaire dans leur exercice." This may be true of France (for which no authority is vouched), but this is not the order of progression elsewhere.

    (*i*) In 1163 " obiit Henricus primus de Oyli advocatus noster " says the Chronicler of Oseney : Rolls, 4 *Ann. Monast*. 33. The Worcester Chronicler in 1224 means the same post when he says " Cumanus de Crema got from us—literas procurationis ad impetrandum et contradicendum " [imitating *ad lucr. v. perd.*] at specified pay and

C.H.   10

much chance of getting rich, merely in their capacity of *patroni causarum* (*k*); he is speaking, as so many others (*l*) do, of what he saw in the courts generally. He was much too good a churchman not to insist on the old canon that the priest should plead for the orphan or widow; that very reference shows that he was thinking of the specific law of the Church. And the express mention of a reasonable fee (*salarium*) makes it fairly certain that he was thinking of the ordinary lay practitioner, and that by his time the latter was normally paid for his services.

It would seem, then, that the number and partly, therefore, the importance of clerical advocates in lay causes were not sufficient to excite resentment against them as a class—though no doubt there were individual clerics who exploited their abilities commercially—and that the severe criticism we sometimes read comprehended indiscriminately the ecclesiastical bench, whose prelates, if they were venal, had a much more valuable article to sell than the lawyers before them, and whose corruptibility was, rightly or wrongly, a favourite theme with reformers (*m*) throughout the Middle Ages.

But sometimes the clerics were excellent judges and advocates, and the fact, *pro tanto*, retarded their elimination. Stories (*n*) about Abbot Samson of St. Edmund's,

---

one mark per year [retainer] " quibus steterit pro nobis in curia Romana ": *ib.* p. 416.

(*k*) Though in course of time the office was endowed and sometimes passed into secular hands.

(*l*) For instance, the anonymous monastic author of *Gesta Dunelmensia M⁰CCC⁰*, 13 Camden Miscellany, 41 (1924), to whom the editor, Prof. R. K. Richardson, attributes a decidedly legal bent —" the book is full of legal terms "—says : Secundum quod vulgariter dicitur, juriste et advocati non mediocriter lites et contenciones affectant quoniam per lites et discensiones inter divites et magnates *lucrum temporale et comodum consecuntur pocius quam per pacem.* Advocati igitur et clerici [of the Bishop] eundem . . . suis suggestionibus *vernenosis acriter stimulabant.*

(*m*) *E.g.*, Bromyard.

(*n*) In Jocelind of Brakelond's, his chaplain's *Chron.*: Camd. Soc. (1840), pp. 24, 57, 77—78.

elected in 1182, illustrate what was said on one side and the other. Soon after his election Lucius III made him judge *de causis cognoscendis*, in which he was quite inexperienced, though he was deeply versed in liberal arts and Holy Writ, being indeed a literate man, and a *rector scolarum*. So he called in two clerics skilled in law, on whose advice he acted in ecclesiastical matters and studied the Decrees and the Decretal letters, so that soon, what with books and what with trying cases, he came to be a sound judge who observed strictly the form of law. This made someone say : " Hang that Abbot's court! Neither my gold nor my silver helps me to win my case." In time he got some little experience—*n.b.*—in secular cases, having a logical and subtle mind; indeed, Osbert Fitz-Hervey, then sub-sheriff, used to say of him : " That Abbot is a born arguer (*disputator*); if he goes on like this he will cut the whole lot of us [laymen] out." And the Abbot was made an itinerant justice, that is, for secular work, and was very careful. His detractors in his own abbey, impatient of his slowness in his court (there)—due to his view that the " merits of a case " were ascertained by hearing both sides—used to say that he would only do justice to a suitor for money promised or paid, and he was supposed (wrongly) not to lean to mercy's side, for when a party was *in misericordia* for an offence, they said he put justice above mercy, for, when it was a question of getting money, he rarely gave up what could justly be taken (*o*).

When his monks want him to raise the rent of the burghers (who claim to be outside his jurisdiction (*p*)) he privately attends the monks' meeting to protest " as if

---

(*o*) " in misericordiis accipiendis pro aliqua forisfactura dicebatur judicium superexaltare misericordiam [Ep. James, II, 13] quia, sicut visum fuit pluribus, cum perventum erat ad denarios capiendos raro remittebat quod juste accipi potuit "—a combination of the views of his detractors and his apologist.

(*p*) Se esse in assisa regis : p. 57.

he was one of us" and tells them that this can only be done by action in the King's Court and that he must proceed by legal forms : " otherwise he would be at the King's mercy *per assisam regni.*"

We hear, too, how easily his actions in his own court could be misrepresented. " Look," said one of his critics —not a monk—" how, *by the King's writ*, he gets suits and pleas of claimants of lands that are in the fee [and jurisdiction] of the convent, and especially suits in which there is money; where there is none, he sends them to the Cellarer or *Sacrista* or other officials." To this his biographer replied (*q*) : " I have never seen the Abbot appropriate our pleas, except when our proper official was not there, but he has sometimes taken money to ensure, by his own authority, causes proceeding properly on their course. I have, too, seen suits which concern us tried in the Abbot's court; that was because there was no one [else] when the litigation began who could on behalf of the Monastery suggest the proper *forum.*"

In these passages even an admiring (and trustworthy) follower implies that on the bench even a scrupulous judge could profit from the " heavy " cases—presumably from the fees of the parties—and that, if the royal writ could be obtained, cases might be withdrawn from the secular courts and tried by him—with a prospect of fees from both sides— and it is hinted, that when a fine was imposed the sum might not be a matter of indifference to the judge. And it comes out plainly that the Abbot did what he could to keep the Abbey's litigation in his own court. Moreover, we get an object lesson how men in orders are appointed

---

(*q*) " sibi usurpasse placita nostra *nisi pro defectu justitie nostrae* " : p. 78; the last four words are difficult : does the chaplain mean by " just." the bishop? or by *nostr.* (twice) does he mean " of the monks " (or individual monks) as opposed to the Abbot Apparently " there was no one else " means, no monk as against the Abbot, and so *his* court got the case.

THE CLERGY AS *ADVOCATI*. 149

judges in ecclesiastical courts and gradually learn and practise secular law.

And about the same time we get another lesson—how Rome, when it suited it, could insist on old decrees against priests holding secular offices, including judgeships, when the new Pope, Innocent III, insisted in 1198 on the great Hubert Walter, Glanville's nephew, Archbishop of Canterbury and justiciar since 1193, ceasing to be the latter; it is needless to point out that thereafter many clerics sat on the bench.

It is not within our scope to examine the reason why Henry II set up a cohort of " professional judges " (*r*), but it was only natural that as ecclesiastics diminished on the bench (*s*) their clerical brethren should tend to disappear from tribunals whose untonsured atmosphere would no longer be congenial.

But the gradual homogeneity of the bench is so important for our theme that the results of the authorities must be stated. The movement begins about 1178, when Henry II appoints two clerks and three laymen to be " a permanent and central court "; apparently mere noblemen disappear from the bench before the ecclesiastics—very

---

(*r*) It is odd that de Diceto, in the memorable passage (*Ymagines Hist.* v. I, p. 434 (cf. 371 of 1173), Rolls, ed. Stubbs : see v. II, xlviii) in which (under 1179) he attributes Henry's legal changes to a burning love of justice, yet, omits all mention of secular lawyers; the King sought diligently " in variis professionibus amatores justiciae "; the *claustralis professio* and military force have relieved the oppressed—nam abbates modo comites modo, capitaneos modo, domesticos modo, familiarissimos modo, causis audiendis et examinandis praeposuit. He implies the same partiality in judicial officers, especially in the provinces, as so many other writers, but points to some great ecclesiastics who were good judges, though he knows that it is against the Canons for them *se negotiis se immiscere*) : he reports great improvement (not only in the ecclesiastical, but) in the county court " in foro civili . . . in comitiis," with the bishops sitting there.

(*s*) How gradual it was is illustrated by the remark of the monk Wykes when in 1265 Simon de Montfort committed the royal seal to two laymen " militibus," P. de Montforti and Ralph of Sandwich : " such a thing had never been heard of in the world before !" : 4 *Ann. Monast.* 168; Rolls.

naturally. Perhaps Hilary, Bishop of Chichester (d. 1169), was the last English prelate who was a great lawyer (t); R. de Anesty went to consult him, as an able practitioner in court. Laymen preside over the great ecclesiastics in that court during Henry's reign. At first under Henry III there are many such ecclesiastics, but before he dies the lay element (u) among his judges " is beginning to outweigh

---

(t) " Ad ministerium Apostolici translatus, in reddendis et prosequendis causis advocatus disertissimus et jurisconsultus peritus in curia Romana fuit." John of Hexham : Continuator of Symeon of Durham, 2 Rolls, 321 (under 1148); 44 Surtees Soc. 156.

(u) For several reasons the case of Henry de Bathe or Bathonia (d. 1260) is instructive. It is agreed (2 Foss 224 : D. N. B.) that he was a layman (though 2 *Rot. Cl.* 156 has in 1226 " Warin' le Despenser attorn[avit] Henr' de Bathon' clcum.," *i.e.*, a clerk, he was not of course a professional *att.*). He was " brought up to the legal profession " (F.) He was certainly a judge from 1238. In 1251 Matthew Paris (5 Rolls, 213 : ed. Wats. p. 811) calls him " miles literatus, legum terrae peritissimus, d. regis justitiarius et consiliarius specialis." He was charged with various offences and was saved by John Mansel " clericus capitalis d. r. consiliarius," another aristocrat who became a judge. Foss infers from Dugdale (*Chron. Ser.* 15) calling B. only *justiciarius*, but putting him first of three that he was senior, but that " capitalis "=C.J. was not yet used : *cl. cap.* that of Mansel, of course, does not mean C.J. (Foss, *ib.* 153, 395).

Yet another " quidam miles literatus Robertus de la Ho " mentioned in 1252 by M. Paris (5 Rolls, 345 ; 856 Wats.)—but apparently by no one else—had a legal post, *viz.*, " tutela Judaeorum et sigilli " regis " quod ad scaccarium pertinet eorundem . . . R. Judacorum justitiarius " was " bajulus et custos " of the seal; Du Cange (*miles lit.*) citing these words from M. P. explains that it means men of good family who studied law (like the *nobiliores*, p. 450, in this country) to prepare for the high court bench " our *Chevaliers en Loix*," he says, and then called *domini legum*, nearly all his instances coming from France. (So of a trial in Paris in 1422 : " in diversis regni partibus baillivi justitiaeque ministri viri literati et juris consulti constituti sunt " : Titue Livius (contemporary) *Vita Hen. V*, p. 90, ed. Hearne (1716).) The *Chevaliers en Loix* were contrasted, he tells us, with the *Chevaliers en armes* : so in this country were the *servientes ad legem* with those *ad arma*. He equates *miles legalis* with *m. literatus* and mentions even " miles utriusque militiae." In England *m. lit.* (=" noble and learned ") was perhaps used because *leg.* was appropriated to another sense. Murimuth calls his contemporary John of Shordich " dominus J. de S., doctor legum, advocatus et miles de concilio regis existens " in 1345; in 1343 simply " militem " : *Chronica A. M.* Rolls, 171, 143, ed. Thompson; elsewhere " miles sapiens et juris professor " : *ib.* 229; 3 Foss, 507.

Murimuth was himself *juris civilis professor* and was proctor for

the ecclesiastical," " bishops no longer steadily sat in the law courts "; still, even under Edward I, " not a few " judges were clerks (*x*). There is a sort of sensational transition.

" Thomas de Waylond (*fl.* 1272-90) became a clerk and a sub-deacon in early life, but attaining success as a lawyer, he kept his clerical status in the background . . ."; " he was a knight and a married man," and Peckham denied the validity of both of the " ex-sub-deacon's " marriages (*y*). The case of Hervey de Staunton is well known. What is very much to our point is that the growth of " a *class* of advocates under Edward I is part of the same phenomenon " (*z*). And about this time the *Mirror of Justices* is recommending that no *countour* should be " a man of religion nor ordained clerk above the order of sub-deacon nor beneficed clerk with the cure of souls " (*a*).

---

the University of Oxford at Rome in 1312 *versus* the Black Friars, and for some years " found business enough " to keep him there: Stubbs, 1 *Chron. E. I. & E. II*; Rolls, lxi, lxiii, lxviii.

(*x*) 1 P. & M., B. I, c. 6. Dugdale, *O. J.* c. 8, mentions many canons of St. Paul's who were judges, up to 1278; and see G. J. Turner, 22 Seld. Soc. xvii—xviii.

Blackstone, less precisely, says (1 *Comm.* 20) : " the clergy, finding it impossible to root out the municipal law, began to withdraw themselves by degrees from the temporal courts; and to that end very early in the reign of " Henry III " episcopal constitutions were published (Spelman, *Concil.* (A.D.) 1217), 1 Wilkins, 574, 599) forbidding all ecclesiastics to appear as advocates *in foro saeculari*." Hook, 5 *Archbishops*, 173, 175, is well within the mark when he makes the withdrawal complete by 1440 : " legal practice had now become sufficiently lucrative to enable a lawyer to support himself without holding church preferment in addition to any honorarium he might receive from his clients. Many of them were men who were glad to be released from those restraints, which, whether strictly observed or not, were imposed by the Canons upon the Clergy."

(*y*) Tout, *Polit. Eng. Hist.* (1216—1377), p. 172, and D. N. B. No other writer seems to mention his orders and no source is given.

(*z*) 1 P. & M. (1st ed.) 133, 139, 182-4, citing *Gesta Henrici*, ii, 207.

(*a*) Tout, *Edward II*, 336, says that there was nothing to prevent a clerk in minor orders or simply admitted to the first tonsure, who had no cure of souls, from being a pleader. In " Political Songs," at 206, there is a hint of the coming fissure. " Adversatur legibus omne genus cleri / Cujus status hodie pejor est quam heri." " Affluunt

But of Edward III " the lawyers were frankly laymen. . . . There were no longer any Weylands who concealed their clerical beginnings and hid away the sub-deacon under the married knight and justice, the founder of a land-owning family " (*b*).

By the end of Edward I's reign, perhaps, we may say that lay lawyers are solely left in possession of the lay courts. " In 1284-5," says (*c*) Bartholomew of Cotton, " the King ordered an enquiry which *clerici* had sued certain people about their *fief* (*feudo*) or *lay* property (*catallis*) in a Christian court, and about their superiors (*praelatis*) who had severely punished illegalities (*excessus*) of laymen by fines; and the *clerici*, the *praelati* and their servants convicted of this kind of offence he punished (*vinxit*) and imprisoned." The same point emerges in the Barnwell Priory book (*d*) by a monk of the house, written 1295-6. The church had innumerable law-suits and the work " lays stress on litigation," copying many original legal documents from 1092 onwards. Naturally for the early years we hear little of lawyers. But for the contemporary time we see the parallelism of the two judicatures. Thus the Prior mentions a suit between himself and a certain incumbent, about the *vicaria ecclesie* of the latter heard before the Dean of Arches in London, in which, despite his

---

divitiis legistarum sedes / Et modo vadit equis qui solet ire pedes."
" Si forte deliquerit artibus imbutus / Ad legistas fugiet si vult esse tutus : / Quia se defendere nescit plus quam mutus / Graecorum studia nimium diuque sequntus." But when the *legista* arrives " the doors of the aristocrats fly open." It ends " Galen and Law are riches enough."

(*b*) Tout, *Pol. Hist.* 426. Under Edw. II in the C. P. lay were to clerical judges 10 or 11 to 8 or 9; in K. B. 6 to 3; and in Exch. 12 to 13 : from 2 *Holdsworth*, cited by Tout. In *Edw. II* he has much to say on ecclesiastics in the Exchequer, who were rather administrators than judges.

(*c*) *Hist. Anglic.* 166 : Rolls.

(*d*) *Ecclesie de Bernewelle Liber Memorandorum*, Cambridge, 1907, ed. Willis Clark; Introdn. by Maitland, p. 185; p. lxi; pp. 101, 103; pp. lix, 171; p. 138.

THE CLERGY AS *ADVOCATI.*

yearly retainer of 40s., Alan of Freston, the *advocatus* of the House, failed them. When the Chancellor of Cambridge University claimed jurisdiction over the church, the Prior appeared by " clericum suum magistrum H. de M." in St. Mary's there, before the " Official Archdeacon *in pleno consistorio* "; the procedure is purely ecclesiastical, and he gets inhibition from the Official of the Bishop of Ely. But in 1248, when the Prior is defendant before justices, he sends one Seyc " essoniare " for him, and in due course goes in person to warrant the essoin; but at the trial Seyc and another are his " attornati . . . loco suo ad. l. etc." —the common form. And when *advocatus* Alan in 1293 had to sue the House for his retainer, he does it in the King's Bench. The writer says that Alan had worked hard for the Church, but that when he had become Archdeacon of Norfolk he appeared for them no more, and naturally they stopped his *pensio*. The Prior puts in this plea *per attornatum* at Westminster alleging that Alan had actually refused his services (giving the particular above). Alan denies this, saying that it was open to him to send a substitute at the House's expense, if for good reason he could not appear; a mixed London and Cambridge jury is empannelled, but the Prior's *attornatus* thinking that the jury were " against them and especially the Londoners, who had been ' got at ' (*procurati*) by the plaintiff and the *clerici in banco*, etc.," came to terms; he paid £12, five marks of which go to the *clerici*, " pro dampnis "; " the money was soon paid and the receipt is in the hands of the *attornatus*." Then there is a lifelike scene of a provincial assize, in 1286 at Cambridge. " The Prior acted so astutely that he lost only one case, and that by the false verdict of a Cambridge jury. . . . For he had the judges well disposed and the *clerici* friendly and the ushers (*precones*) publicly showing him respect. He retained, too, as his counsel (*de consilio*) from beginning to end of the *Iter* three wise and vigilant serjeants, *viz.*, Gilbert of

Thornton, William of Kellou (*e*) and John of Insula; and he gave each 40s. And he ' gratified ' the judges, too, ' by frequent presents ' so well that when he went away, all of them—judges, *clerici*, sergeants, ushers, thanked him and his monks profusely." But the tone of our literary monk changes when the Prior loses (*f*). Thus, at the same Eyre, he tells us that in a suit by the Chancellor of Cambridge the Prior was " intimidated " (*perterritus*) by W. de Saham, J., who declined to allow him to consult anyone (*quamvis reclamasset consilium suum*), into signing terms. Another *placitum* at Westminster " *ad Bancum* " lasts ten years, 1274-84, and then the parties " go to the country " (*g*).

At any rate, by the time of Dr. John Bromyard, 1380-90, the divorce of the two systems of advocacy is complete. He was Chancellor of Cambridge about 1380; Leland (356) calls him " legum consultissimus." In his *Summa Predicantium* (*h*) he is an uncompromising critic of his times and devotes chapters to the abuse and the abuses of *Advocati* and *Judices*, to say nothing of *Consiliarii* (under *Consilium*). He is well aware that ecclesiastical and secular courts are quite distinct, and castigates impartially *advocati* —" in curia *vocabulo* Christianitatis " he says (*i*) bitterly— and *juridici* or *sergantes in curia regis*. Naturally, he was

---

(*e*) Carleton? Not otherwise known.

(*f*) Pp. 95, l. Monkish writers often, when their house loses, complain of terrorism on the part of their adversary, the court (or the jury, as above, and cf. Bromyard, below); so in 1330 in cross-suits between the Prior of Peterborough and the Earl of Hereford, in a Northampton Eyre the Prior " not daring to go to law with the earl *ibidem infra dominium suum*," and seeing that it would cost him £100, agreed with him for that sum; Henry of Pytchley's *Book of Fees*, 39 (1927); 2 Northampton Rec. Soc.

(*g*) P. 138.

(*h*) For Bromyard, see (D. N. B. or) *Preaching in Mediæval England* by G. R. Owst, Cambridge, 1926. References here are to the Venice edn. of 1586 (a mass of misprints), corrected by that of Nuremberg of 1485.

(*i*) *Adv.* 34 A.

THE CLERGY AS *ADVOCATI*. 155

well acquainted with the professional grades (*k*), and he says distinctly that there was going on a struggle between the priests and the lawyers to capture the *seigneur* (*dominus*)—the well-to-do; consiliarii . . . dicentes confessorem nescire leges terrae (*l*). His careful observation of the behaviour of the petty juries (*m*) of twelve is enough to show that he had the secular courts in his mind, and his ethics of the practitioner in court are enjoined on and directed to both varieties there—their common ground. Some of his morals are derived from John of Salisbury, whose *Policraticus* he cites, and some, perhaps, from William of Drogheda whom he had certainly read. It is true that he does not mention in terms the appearance of *advocati* in secular courts (nor, of course, laymen in ecclesiastical), but the many incidents he mentions *en*

(*k*) Quidam enim vocantur advocati quidam etiam *vulgari nomine* sergantum quidam attornati quidam aprenticii quidam procuratores et sic de aliis : *Adv.* 31 B. So multum delinquunt alii qui *vulgariter* vocantur sergantes : *ib.* 36 A; his insistence on *vulgariter* can hardly mean " (commonly) so called," for in 1380 the title was well known ; probably it=less august, not in the Christian courts.

(*l*) *Consilium*, 140 B.

(*m*) His sidelights on the jury system of his day have perhaps been overlooked by its historians (as indeed have been his little touches of contemporary manners); he very much suspects the *ductores* or *ductores patriae* (who, like the *placitatores*, blackmail simple folk), apparently the foremen, who played into one another's hands from county to county, for a bribe : munera hinc inde judicibus et officialibus de curia et duodenariis dantur ; judges and juries (*falsea duodena*) were " packed " by the lawyers who tell the client " the Court is with us, we've got the judge and the *ductor patriae* " : 34 B; cf. 401 A : *Judices*; *patria*=the modern " country "; the *duodeni* are false, and conspire, for cash : 35 B; the court forces the jury " to slay or acquit " a man when they do not know the facts : 38 A—more fully developed 401 B—402 A (under *Judices*) : in curia laicali . . . ita [as in *Susanna's case*] nunc duodecim assertive testificantur hominem esse dignum vita vel morte sub juramento praestito . . . de quo tamen nulli eorum vel pauci scientiam habent quae ad testificandum requiritur; a conscientious juror is compelled by the judge to agree with the rest by his sending them all back till they are agreed.

When the judge asks the twelve " Are you agreed, gentlemen?" one has been known to say " No, for my *socius* here has got 40 *solidi* and I've only got 20 !" It would appear that in B.'s day the number of the jury was fixed at twelve. Cf. p. 91*x*.

passant leave no doubt that by his time the divorce of the two benches and bars was complete.

No doubt, as Blackstone (*n*) suggests, the decline of clerics from bench and bar went on *pari passu*. Probably the intrusion of laymen into both encouraged their disappearance from each.

It must not, however, be supposed that promotion to the bench could always be described as from the bar. The *system* only begins to emerge about 1250. The most satisfactory available induction must be founded on the laborious statistics collected by Foss in his first two volumes of *The Judges*, for 1066 to 1272. Invaluable as that work is for our subject, it still seems that that scholar tended to infer a legal training from the fact of legal employment (*o*). His own estimate was (III, 1) that within that period he had written 580 (short) lives; as these did not all end when Henry III died, twenty-five overlap into the third volume (1272-1377), making 605 in all; of these he calls 278 Itinerant Justices, 206 Justiciaries (our " puisnes ") and 32 Chief Justiciaries (*plus* 65 " connected with the Chan-

---

(*n*) 1 *Comm.* 20, citing Spelman, *Concil.* (A.D. 1217), and 1 Wilkins, 574, 599. Following Selden, in *Fleta*, 9, 3 : p. 541, he thinks that the ever growing pre-eminence of the Common Law drove them from the bench (except the Chancellorship, which they kept).

(*o*) *E.g.*, II, 469 of St. de Segrave; his " Normanic " theory, I, 160-1, is not that adopted here.

Thus, Osbert Fitz-Hervey, II, 59, *fl.* 1180, was " evidently a lawyer by profession." Hubert Walter, II, 123, *fl.* 1185, " was brought up . . . to the two learned professions of the Church and the law "; W. de Warenne, *fl.* 1190, " like his father he pursued the profession of the law "; Henry de Bathonia, II, 224, *fl.* 1240; Hugh Bigot, II, 240, *fl.* 1240, " it may naturally be presumed from his being selected by the Council . . . at Oxford " to be " Chief Justiciary that he had originally adopted the profession of the law and had gained some eminence in it . . . he is described by M. Paris as . . . *legum terrae peritum* "; John le Breton, Bishop of Hereford, 1269, II, 259, " pursued his father's profession of the law." None of these men are known as legal representatives in the courts. Foss (III, 140) is, perhaps, more successful in applying his method to Gilb. de Preston about 1240.

cery" and 24 Barons of the Exchequer). Disregarding the sixty-five—who were nearly, if not all *clerici* of some sort (p), and most in major orders—Foss holds that of the thirty-two Chiefs, twelve were clerical, seventeen (or perhaps only twelve) " baronial " and three " legal," *viz.*, Glanvill, Geoffrey Fitzpeter and St. de Segrave. But from the details he gives of these men it seems that they served their apprenticeships in public life—as exalted J. P.'s, if it may be so put—rather than that they had a systematic legal training.

Foss distributes the 206 (quite recognising a want of precision) as eighty-one " baronial," " officers of the household," and 125 who " pursued the law as a profession; probably the administration of justice in the *curia regis* was then [H. I] almost wholly confined " to the baronial order. " Under Henry II . . . out of forty-eight justiciers, eighteen may be selected as probably brought up as lawyers "; the other thirty either sat as barons or as officials. Under Richard I there were twelve legal to twenty-four non-legal; under John the figures were six and sixteen. " But in the reign of H. III . . . the proportions were reversed, for out of 100 justiciers I can only find eleven who may not be supposed to have previously practised in some manner in the court." Thus, to date promotion from bar to bench at about 1270 tallies with what has been already said; in short, at the epoch when the Serjeants emerge.

Foss judiciously assumes or implies that training for the bench was rather practical than academic. The few judges who are represented as having studied " law " had very

---

(p) Even here there were laymen; John de Lexinton (*fl.* 1230) was five times Keeper of the Great Seal (but only as custodian), but never had any clerical preferment; Ric. de Middleton, Chancellor, " was certainly a layman ": *fl.* 1260; 2 Foss, 150, 383, 408 (but L. Campbell had " little doubt " that he was not). These instances are inconsistent with F.'s own statement (III, 2) that sixty-three of the sixty-five were certainly ecclesiastics, and the other two probably.

little to read except the Canon law with here and there a glimpse of the Roman imperial codes; the old Saxon *corpus* would only be known to a few scholars; the age of Acts of Parliament has not yet come; recent charters and statutes would be what newspaper knowledge is for us. The differences between an ordinary territorial nobleman and one like Aubrey de Vere would be that the latter, an exceptionally good specimen of his class, would have a taste for any of the old " laws and customs " of the country of which he might hear, and would read such manuscript books as there were—not a gigantic task; while the former—both, indeed—would in his constant contact with public affairs, especially as a sheriff or other *serviens* of the Crown, pick up an aptitude for business. The famous record of Aubrey that he was " a lawyer who has seen all sorts of practice " is amply borne out by what we know of his career as a " public man." The early bench consisted of " Notables." Hence itinerant justices are frequently reinforced locally by *socii*, laymen (*q*).

It is convenient and supplementary to conclude briefly the course of Church legislation on ecclesiastics in *foro saeculari*.

There is authority that a *capitulum* of 819 is really a canon (*r*) of the Council of Mainz in 813, *Ne clerici vel monachi saecularibus negotiis se immisceant* which prohibited churchmen from taking any part in secular suits, except defending orphans and widows. That rule and that exception are often repeated. Thus, in 1179 the Lateran Council made a decree (*s*)—*Clericus in sacris vel minoribus*

(*q*) In 1345 R. de Bury, Bp. of Durham, appointed William Bassett " an additional judge of Assize " : *Fragments of Register*, 89; 119 Surtees Soc. *ib.* p. 115, are *placita* before him and others " *justic. d. episcopi assignatis apud Dunelm.*" W. B. was, perhaps, the permanent judge of that name.

(*r*) *Corpus Juris Canonici*, Pt. II (Leipzig : 1881); *Decr. Greg.* IX, B. III, Tit. 50 : App. VI.

(*s*) *Ib.* B. I, Tit. 37, c. 1, *de postulando* : " . . . before the middle of the 8th Century a stringent reform was demanded and the secular were synodically divided from the monastic clerks " : St. 1 *Hist.* 255.

THE CLERGY AS *ADVOCATI.* 159

beneficiatus in saeculari foro *postulare non debet nisi pro se vel sua ecclesia vel miserabilibus personis*; the poor persons are defined, *quae proprias causas administrare non possunt*. Durand says (*t*) that in the course of the centuries the rules of the Church were infringed and that the defence of lay persons before lay judges had come to be usurped by ecclesiastics, " seculars or regulars indifferently," and had greatly aggrandised them in wealth and lay (*profanes*) honours, and that it was this " indécence " which the Lateran Council was expressly correcting. The encroachment arose, he says, because " in these centuries of ignorance " there were no other defenders in lay courts. Note that these centuries are the 9th, 10th and 11th, *i.e.*, end in our period.

In due course these enactments circulated in England.

In 1217 there was a *Constitutio* by the Bishop of Salisbury, *de bono pacis*, in which it was laid down, " Neither *clerici* nor priests are to appear as *advocati* in a secular tribunal (*foro*) unless in their own cases or in those of poor persons " (*x*). Clearly the latter might and did have a clerical adviser and other persons a secular. This provision " seems to have been observed faithfully " (*y*). It is repeated in the Constitutions (*z*) of Otho in 1237, which, as we have seen, were known to the contemporary William of Drogheda, who was well acquainted with the practice of both systems. From this time onward *advocati* in ecclesiastical causes are often regulated by bodies of ecclesiastics (*a*), though the practitioners sometimes seem

---

(*t*) *Avocats*, in *Dict. of Can. Law* (1776).
(*x*) Spelman, *Concilia*. Selden's date, 1164 (*ad Fletam*, 519), is for a Synodal prohibition, which clearly refers (see *ib.* 509) to monks and lectures, as Manning, *Serviens*, 170-1, says.
(*y*) G. J. Turner, 22 Seld. Soc. xvi.
(*z*) M. Paris, 3 *Chron. Maj.* 440; Rolls.
(*a*) *E.g.*, the Council of London, 1237 (last note); Worcester Synod, 1240; 13 *Concilia*, 1460 (Coleti); Council at London in 1268, *ib.* vol. 14,

to be laymen. It must never be forgotten that there was always in the courts of the Church the model of an organised procedure before the eyes of laymen.

The Unpopularity of the " Advocate."

The incidental glimpses of this sentiment which we have had tend to show the growing prominence of the class, and if only for that reason, the ground of this feeling must be sought.

Perhaps unpopularity is the wrong word, for, so far, certainly, the *populus* has had little to do with the law; our instances have almost all been taken from high life, and the men who dreaded a *placitum* were certainly persons of means and position. Indeed, it is clear that many of them looked upon their adviser in litigation as a feudal retainer in whom it would be like treason in war to go over to the enemy; hence the many naive refusals to appear for a party, lest the other might be offended and show it, and the eulogy of the *magister* who had the courage to risk his material prospect. Of the weaker non-clerical individuals it must not be forgotten that they were as yet a small and fortuitous number without *esprit de corps*; there was no embryo trade union or " powerful profession " (*b*). Though it cannot be said that the moment the avocation is recognised by authority the low standard disappears, yet the more it is organized, the less it is defamed. Neutral observers might naturally regard timorousness as a form of time-serving, and the important neutrals were the chroniclers, verse-writers and satirists who attack the lawyers or

---

427; Canterbury Synod, 1295; *ib.* 1234; other instances in Index (*advocatio*).

The other extreme is reached by 1330, when Sir John Bourne was sent to prison by a secular court for bringing a " Publike Notary of the Pope " thereinto " to make an Instrument of a suit pending therein of purpose to question it in the Spiritual Court *in derogacionem juris nostri regio etc.*" : Prynne, *Animadversiions, &c., Dedicn.* and p. 58.

(*b*) Disraeli in the Queen's Bench : the *Times*, Nov. 23, 1838.

record the attacks upon them—as was illustrated above; the men of letters were often, too, in a sense, persons of means and position; their writings show that they had the power of making themselves heard and were in a position to judge—they could read and write and knew Latin, etc.

William of Drogheda (c) looks with a genial sympathy on the contortions and tricks of the lawyers *inter se*, but no one denounces more fiercely or probes more minutely the " fraus innexa clienti." He could not be expected to celebrate the unpopularity of his own specimens, but he shows his sense of it by his efforts to make them acceptable to laymen. Moreover, the venal practitioner whom the literary men denounce was comparatively a novelty. Like the Hebrew prophets whose place they supply to some extent in English literature, they are always angry.

The sympathy they often express for the humbler classes is not caused by any alleged oppression of the courts, but by the sight of general misgovernment in definite periods which we can date, when, no doubt, suitors before those tribunals, the people " worth powder and shot," suffered from judicial and forensic corruption. Thus " Q " never loses his pity for the common people and the unhappy poor; he attacks the local magistrates and blames

---

(c) In 1300 an University statute (1 *Mun. Acad. Ox.* 76, 77, 306, Rolls) throws light on his conditions at Oxford : the *advocatorum effrenata multitudo*, it says, leave the Masters and Scholars no peace; they (*advv.*) promote litigation for their own profit and do all they can to prevent parties coming to terms; in important suits and appeals, against law and custom, they get unfair delays *to the peril of their own souls*, etc.; therefore the University decrees that " whoever wants to go to law "—*actores, rei, ac etiam procuratores caus. vel negot. grosso modo* [*i.e.*, without technicality : Du C.] *et idiomate quocunque communiter intelligibili factum proponant*. The pious tone of this st. suggests that it was framed by churchmen against lay lawyers—a sort of counterblast to the attacks of laymen on the ecclesiastics in the lay courts. But it may be due to the righteous indignation of the Univ. authorities against excessive litigiousness : n.b.—" *Anyone* wishing *postulare*, or *litigare*," *sc.*, a party. In any case the " *adv. effr. mult.*" is very surprising in a small city in 1300. For the various representatives in the Oxford courts in 1432 see p. 522g.

the noble lords as well as them for oppressing the people (**L., I, 308**).

In this period, no doubt, the actually corrupt lawyers were mostly ecclesiastics (*d*), and the priest, to whom all doors were opened, would, if he were so inclined, have many opportunities in his position as the family adviser, but it has been submitted that these opportunities by not slow degrees diminished after " **Q.**'s " period.

Moreover, not only was there for the *laics* no guild-discipline, but (as is pointed out for France—though later —by Sainte-Palaye (*e*)) " the chief cause of the misconduct (*malversations*) for which the *avocats* were blamed was the ease with which all sorts of persons were admitted to exercise their functions. The reproach was just, provided that it was not general. . . ."

Possibly another inconspicuous tributary of the current may be suggested by the hypothesis that for two centuries

---

(*d*) Apart from the " parallel development " theory, p. 131, it is worth notice that about 1180 Guiot de Provins, troubadour and monk of Cluny, wrote in his *Bible* :—

    (l. 2465) Por morz tieng-je et por periz
                Les fax pledéors lóeis [hirelings]

    (l. 2484) [The lawyers] autant aiment tort comme droit.

and that about 1200 Gautier de Coinsi (or-*cy*), also troubadour and monk, is writing at Soissons about the clergy :—

    (l. 1107) Poi voi Prelat qui à droit doigne
                Por ce vont li Clerc a Boloigne;
                Là devienent fort boléor [treacherous]
                Fort avocat, fort plaidéor.

The prelates—
                Plus tost donent les granz provendes [food, " prebende "]
                As avocaz, as pledéors
                Qu'il ne font as bon préeschors.

(*Fabliaux et Contes, Seinte Léocade*, Barbazan; Paris (1808), v. II, p. 386; v. I, 306.)

Both these writers are undoubtedly thinking of ecclesiastical lawyers at a date when it is difficult to get a glimpse of French lawyers; there seems to be no reference to *attornatus*.

(*e*) *Dict.* (about 1760) : *Advocat*. He adds that in early times the advocate could sue for his fee. " Opinion (*préjugé*) to-day regards such an action as dishonourable." . . . " De là ces plaisanteries qui ont passé en proverbes. . . . Cotgrave eu a rassemblé plusieurs dans son Dict. : *Advocat*."

THE UNPOPULARITY OF THE "ADVOCATE." 163

after the Conquest important litigation, at any rate, had to be carried on in French (*f*). If so, the necessary recourse to a foreigner must certainly have inured to the unpopularity of his office.

We shall hardly find a more representative expression of the traditional literary diatribes against lawyers than in one of the " Political Songs " of the time of Edward I (*g*). One touch—the corruption of the official fringe round the bench—which we shall meet more than once again, is here put in convincingly. The corrupt judges have many a go-between (*nuntius*) (*h*); they come to the suitor and whisper adroitly " Halves ! " The judges' hungry clerks (*i*) sit at their feet and give nothing for nothing; the empty suitor may " hang about " for long. Some there are in the court who extort (*k*) judgment; they are called *relatores* (*l*) and are the worst of the lot. They grab with both hands and cheat those whom they ought to defend (*tutores*). But there is no *express* allusion to either *attornatus* or *narrator*.

(*f*) Vissing, *Anglo-Norman Language and Literature* (Oxford, 1923), insists strongly on the " favouring of French . . . even into the 15th century "—even against Freeman, Horwood and Stubbs; the latter (1 *Hist.* § 134) cites Holkot whom Vissing accepts. Horwood, *Y. B.* 30-1 E. I. xxv : " What the tendencies of Edward the Confessor made a fashion, the Conquest made a necessity," *viz.*, French as the language of " pleaders and judges," but he rejects Holkot's statement.

(*g*) Camden Soc. (1839), 224 : ed. Wright.

(*h*) *Ib*. 226 : "—Amice care / Vis tu placitare? / Sum cum justitiario / Qui te modo vario / possum adjuvare; / si vis impetrare / Per suum subsidium / Da mihi dimidium / Et te volo juvare. / Ad pedes sedent clerici / Qui velut famelici / sunt, donis inhiantes / et pro lege dantes / Quod hii qui nichil dederint / Quamvis cito venerint, / erunt expectantes " : see 3 Foss, 206. For the venality of the Roman *curia* in John's reign see Wright, p. 14, or Camd. Soc. (1841), p. 36, by Walter Mapes : " You needn't fear even Tully against you [if you have bribed] " or " if they quote Justinian or the Canons against you "; " pro Marco marca " = a fee for the advocate.

(*i*) Cf. the regulations of 1280, p. 233, to prevent any " getting at " even the inferior judges.

(*k*) " Express judgment " (Wright) for *exprimunt juditiam*.

(*l*) He cites Du Cange : = querelam ad judices referunt; *i.e.*, *delatores*, which perhaps the word is meant to suggest as = narratores.

"And what about the *janitores*?" They tell the lackpennies boldly "unless you are prepared to give something to everyone here you had better stay outside," *i.e.*, the ushers took "tips"—a thing not unknown at the present day. As for the clerks (*clericos*), they make me laugh, says this bitter songster, when I see the fellows I knew as paupers give themselves airs, and the pomp they make when they get a job (*ballivam capiunt*). Yes, and when they are learned in the law (*m*), they make new laws.

The burden of the judges' clerks is a long story, and those of the Chancery must have a chapter to themselves. The tale was by no means finished when "before 1351" the Prince of Wales writes a "formal" letter (*n*) to "Johan de Stonor et ses compaignons de Comun Banc" about *Prior of Merton* v. *His tenants*, asking them "to be as favourable and yielding in this plea as you reasonably can," and not to allow the tenants "to be vexed by clerks, serjeants or other people of the court," and Henry earl of Lancaster writes to the judges "in the same behalf."

As Maitland put it: "The rather sudden demand for professional pleaders seems to have engendered a great deal of corruption and chicane; there is much evidence that the lawyers of Ed. I's day, great and small, judges, pleaders and attornies, had no very high standard of professional honour" (*o*).

In the next reign we read (*p*):—
(l. 289)—
And justices, shirreves, meires, bailiffs, if I shal rede aricht
   Hii kunnen of the faire day make the derke niht;
Hii gon out of the heie wey, ne leven hii for no sklaundre (*q*)

    (*m*) ? "fiuntque sapientes."
    (*n*) *The Stonor Letters* (1290-1483), v. I, p. 3; Camden Third Series, v. 29 (1919).
      (*o*) 2 Seld. Soc. 136, citing the City Ord. of 1280.
      (*p*) Wright, *ib.* p. 336; cited p. 257 on *countors*.
      (*q*) ? leave out no form of offence.

And maken the mot-halle at hom in here chaumbre
                                  wid wouh [wrong].
For be the hond i-whited ["greased" ?] it shal go god
   i-nouh.

(l. 337)—
And baillifs and bedeles under the shirreve
Everich fondeth [tries] hu he may pore men most greve
The pore men beth aver al somouned on assise (*r*).

This *rhetorum mastix*, unlike his predecessor, does not forget the (pleaders or the) attornies—a telling indication of the growth of the profession from 1300 onwards.

(l. 349)—
Attourneis in cuntré theih geten silver for noht;
Theih maken men biginne that they nevere hadden thouht;
And whan theih comen to the ring, hoppe if hii kunne (*s*).
Al that theih muwen [may] so gete, al thinketh hem i-wonne
                                  wid skile [reason].
Ne triste no man to hem, so false theih beth in the bile
                                  [? bill, beak, face].

As late (perhaps) as Henry V an Ordinance (*t*) of the City prohibits the sheriffs' clerks from being attorney for anyone in these courts or "of counsel (*conseil*) of any party (*parte*) in any cause" there, on pain of losing their office; it is significant, as we shall see, that the same instrument restrains the malpractices of pleaders and attornies at that date.

Gradually, of course, the objects of literary commisseration learn to cry their own grievances, they are taught (by a sort of precursor of the modern "press agitation") that the courts of law are the seats of depravity, and that

---

(*r*) The Ed. I writer took this very point: De Vicecomitibus / Quam duri sunt pauperibus / . . . / Qui nichil potest dare / Huc et illuc trahitur / Et in assisis ponitur / Et cogitur jurare / non ausus murmurare / Quodsi murmuraverit / Ni statim satisfecerit / est totum salsum male.

(*s*) ? Get out of the legal mesh, evidently a metaphor from a game.
(*t*) 1 *Lib. Albus*, 519; Rolls.

the same upper class which does wrong or shows favour to the well-to-do there does wrong to *them* elsewhere; and the wicked lawyer soon becomes a " cant " or a " tag "— and he is still with us. The phenomenon is something like that of the French proletarian Revolution being inaugurated by the destruction of the Bastille, where no one belonging to the besiegers had ever been confined—as French writers are never tired of pointing out (*u*); it was a symbol of lawlessness in high places. But the outcry of the common herd against the lawyers, such as that of Wat Tyler's mob, was not yet raised. So far as lawyers are disliked, the feeling is against the heads of the class, the *potestates*.

An illustration may be given of the sort of chicane which excited the ire of these worthy writers—a state of things which implies a developed technicality. Nígellus Wireker (*x*) about 1190 tells the story of a grasping cleric who, being joint tenant of a church, schemes to oust the other clergyman; he goes to a *causidicus*, who was the son of an important person (*potens*) in the province, York, and pays him to appear as plaintiff in a collusive suit; there is no need to go into the legal details, but clearly all the forms of a trial—apparently before an ecclesiastical tribunal, for leave of some sort has to be got from Rome—are observed. When the documents come from Rome " causidicus ille in jus traxit utrumque "; from this stage it is possible that the dishonest *causidicus* was in a common law court; at any rate, " post . . . inducias legitimas et altercationes varias," his client failed to appear, as was part of the scheme; and apparently the plaintiff got judgment for half the church, but he could not get the other half, and when the prime mover demands his property from the lawyer the latter threatens to publish the illegal compact

---

(*u*) *E.g.*, Larousse. *Dict.* Bastille, p. 336, col. 4.
(*x*) *Contra Curiales et Officiales Clericos*, 175-7; 1 Wright's *Satirical Poets of the 12th Cent.*; Rolls. The author seems to have been an English monk at Canterbury.

THE NOTARY. 167

(which was under seal) between them, and so one rascal blackmails another. The contract, he said, did not operate till he had got the whole church; meanwhile the other cleric was appealing vigorously. The whole point of the story is that to get a dirty job done in form of law, you must go to a *causidicus*—the word is perhaps used contemptuously, like the " attorney " is so much modern fiction.

The Notary.

We are not called upon to indicate this personage's precise place in the hierarchy of the law (*y*), but his work did and does blend in popular notions with the lawyer's. We met him first, (*z*) when Richard de Lucy, who died in 1179, gave orders to his " notaries and sealkeepers." There seems to be no doubt about their origin; they were note-takers and secretaries under the Empire and were " taken on " as such by the Church (*a*). They would be a useful link between the ecclesiastical authorities and the growing municipalities, and so Lass says (*b*) that in Frankish times Roman towns had kept their voluntary jurisdiction, which continued in the keeping of the *codices publici* (*gesta municipalia*) (*c*), while their litigious jurisdiction was

(*y*) The charter, so to say, of the profession was the *Ars Notariae* of Rayner of Perugia about 1220 : see p. 100*h*. Its home was naturally Bologna. In Martin's *Formularium* (1232), *ib.*, there is a section (p. 1) on *Ars N*. To Rayner the *not*. seems to be a " special pleader " : see v. Bethmann-Hollweg, *Civilprozess, etc.* vol. vi, § 128, pp. 159-97 (1874) : *de ar. n. seu tabellionatus*. See generally *les Notaires* in Du Coudray, *Origines de Parl. de Paris*, p. 230.

(*z*) P. 168*g*, but in literature perhaps in John of Salisbury : App. VIII.

(*a*) Bingham, 1 *Christ. Antiq.* 419, B. III. There seems to be little doubt that Rayner's work is intended for ecclesiastical courts, but his editor points out that he constantly reproduces expressly the " civil " practice and statute-law of Bologna (and not that of judges delegated by papal rescript). But it would seem that in 1200 the local municipal courts of Bologna would not be very important and, in any case, their procedure would be that of the papal courts, even if they were not administered by ecclesiastics.

(*b*) P. 32, § 6; above, p. 33*a*.

(*c*) So the serious business of drawing up answers to the *Iter* judges' *capitula* and *objecta* against the City is to be done by clerks *ad universa*

replaced by the Frankish legal organization, and suggests that in course of time the *gesta municipalia* were converted into a kind of Notariate; thus local government law would concern both the Church and the borough; it looks as if they did administrative rather than litigious work; their especial duty was to draw up Forms and Orders. Nigellus (*d*) has some curious passages about them. Some people, he says, will not be doctors—(the clergy were from time to time prohibited from practising medicine)—cannot be *causidici*, and so betake themselves to the *curia*—the Papal Court—become notaries running all over the country; their chief seems to be the *cancellarius* (*e*), through whom, apparently, they, as placemen, did "get at" the great folk (*f*). He seems to be at his favourite occupation of attacking the clergy, as they are by far the chief class who could not openly be *causidici*. The significance of these lines is that to Nigellus the *Notarius* is an important, if not the chief lawyer (*g*); if so, he was soon overshadowed by the other ranks.

. . . *memoriter notanda : ne suo defectu notandi oblivioni tradantur. Et unus illorum sit prothonotator, a cujus nota, etc.:* Lib. Alb. 56 (Rolls). It looks as if the word *notarius* was purposely avoided.

For custody, etc., of documents, see Ric. Anglicus, App. XI, c. 31.

(*d*) p. 166*x* : at 166.

(*e*) At 215. Perhaps this is explained by Spelman (*Cancellarius*) : Transferebatur mox vocabulum *C.* a scribis Imperatoris ad Notarios quosq : publicos.

(*f*) Ermefred of Evesham curiously fulfils all these conditions; in 1202-3 he is sent by his brother monks to represent them before papal delegates—he was *vir discretus, bene literatus et optimus notarius* and he died *in curia Romana: Evesham Chron.* 123 (Rolls); the monks could not trust the Abbot in litigation and *vice versa: ib.* In that suit the Pope in person calls on *Magister Phillipus primus notariorum* to read his judgment (170).

(*g*) So Richard de Lucy the Justiciar (d. 1179) gives directions *notariis suis sigillique sui custodibus:* Battel Abbey, p. 154 (Eng.). Cf. from a satire of the beginning of the 13th century—" a fair specimen of that universally directed against " the nobles in general but particularly . . . the Romish prelates "—*commissus notario munera suffunde, etc.* : Wright, *Political Songs*, 31, Camd. Soc., where *notarius* = generally, judicial underlings to whom the suitor is " commissus " by the Cardinal, the Patriarch and the judges. Rayner of Perugia was such a *judex* or *Schöffe* (Warhm.) = sheriff.

Though he still survives (*h*), he has never taken root in this country (*i*). " John of Bologna, Peckham's [Archbishop's: died in 1278] notary . . . compiled a treatise on the art of drawing up official documents, because, as he says, the archbishop's court and the whole kingdom of England lack persons who are acquainted with the notarial art according to the style of the Roman Court " (*k*). In the movements under Edward III against papal encroachment on patronage the Commons petition in 1344 against " Provisour ou Procuratour Promotour Executour ou Notaire " (*l*); in 1353 the " Procurators, Attornies, Executors Notaries and Maintainers " of certain offenders are to be punished (*l*). In the Chancery Ordinance (*m*) of Henry V two *Notarii* or *Tabelliones* are assigned to deal with the *acta* of a suit in all its different stages, " so that litigants may know with little trouble the state of their case at the moment."

The *Narratores*.

It cannot be said that we have yet—say, in 1150—reached an organic whole; " the law " is hardly a conscious profession. But we have got definite names and places of persons who were conducting cases in English courts and who were sometimes paid for doing so. How the different

---

(*h*) See Brooke's *Notary* (8th ed., 1925) and 1 P. & M., I, vi, p. 172.

(*i*) In 1237 Cardinal Otho says in his *Constitutions of London*: " Angliae, ubi publici Notarii non existunt . . . : tabellionum usus in regno Angliae non habetur " : Mat. Paris, ed. Wats. 454. In the *Chartulary of Winchester Cathedral* (1927) two are appointed in 1306 : p. 223 (Wykeham Press).

(*k*) C. Trice Martin, 1 *Registrum Epist. J. Peckham*, liii (Rolls). In 1 *Black Book of the Admiralty* (Rolls) 371, is a notarial attestation in full of (about) 1410. In 1405 the Abp. of Canterbury in a dispute with Henry IV has a notary ready and calls on him to draw up a *procès-verbal* to send to the Pope : 3 *Cont. Eulog. Hist.* 407 (Rolls).

(*l*) 2 *Rot. Parl.* 153 b; 27 Ed. III, st. 1, c. 1; 1 *Stat. R.* Statutes, 329.

(*m*) See p. 439. " By the 15th century the notaries were in effect registrars of the chancery as a law court " : Tout, *The Household of the Chancery*, 76 (1927).

or isolated embryos, so to say, were welded into the living organism, recognisably the same as and continuous to that which we know, is our immediate sequel. But, unfortunately, an intermediate chapter is missing—material for the evolution of the casual representative (other than the *attornatus*) into the full-grown serjeant-at-law. It is easy to glide uncritically over this interval. Thus Foss says (*n*) : "The natural consequence of the proceedings in the Curia Regis being carried on in a foreign tongue, whether French or Latin, was that the parties who were engaged in the causes before it, were incompetent to conduct them, and were therefore obliged to employ persons who were not only conversant with the law as administered but familiar with the language of the court. These persons were designated ' Contours ' or in Latin ' *Narratores* ' (*o*). They were at first principally imported from the Norman Courts; and none others were allowed to be heard." This simple picture is, perhaps, a composite of various periods; authority is desired for some of its strokes, but that the early second century after the Conquest "threw up" the *Narratores* cannot be denied.

"For a long time, however, we hear very little of professional counsellors; of men who are ready to sell their skill in pleading. This is the more noticeable because Matthew Paris is full of complaints against the pack of bellowing legists whom the King employs and whom he lets slip whenever an episcopal election goes against his wishes" (*p*).

Matthew Paris was born about 1200, became a monk of St. Albans, edited the *Chronica Majora* up to 1235, wrote them from 1235 to 1259, in which year he died; no chronicler

---

(*n*) I, 22.

(*o*) Cf. *Cod. Just.* III, ix : Iis enim tunc videtur contestata cum judex per narrationem* negotii causam audire coeperit.

* Later jurists, *e.g.*, Scientiam, add—*et responsionem* (c. xviii). For *n*. see Greenidge, *Leg. Proc. Cicero* (1901).

(*p*) 1 P. & M., I, vi, p. 193.

is more trustworthy. A famous passage (*q*), rhetorical rather than historical is a good link between what we know and a new fact; it is written in and of 1239.

Henry III brings certain charges against the ex-justiciar Hubert de Burgh; the inquiry, perhaps, was in the King's presence.

Perhaps it was more like an impeachment than a trial in *curia regis*—at any rate, the pleadings or indictments with the *responsiones* of *Magister* Laurence are set out (*r*) with their respective forms and traverses in full. "Laurence did his work so well that in spite of the efforts of the King and the pleaders of the royal court the earl's innocence was thoroughly established " (*s*). There is no express authority for the royal pleaders speaking at the trial; Matthew certainly did not mean that they all spoke (and possibly only implies hyperbolically that if they all (*t*) had spoken, it would have made no difference). But it is clear that Laurence did make a speech, and noteworthy that it was not mere argument in law but an oration to (as it were) a jury.

(*q*) 3 *Chron. Maj.* 619; Rolls; 516, ed. Wats. Ad omnia autem praedicta per fidelem et idoneum responsalem Laurentium scilicet clericum de Sancto Albano qui in omnibus tribulationibus inseparabiliter eidem comiti (Hubert) adhaesit, distincte et articulatim eleganter respondens omnibus auditoribus ibidem congregatis satisfecit suam innocentiam demonstrando et sufficienter probando : licet rex cum omnibus prolocutoribus banci quos narratores vulgariter appellamus in contrarium niteretur.

It is evident that " licet rex, etc.," and so " quos . . . appellamus " is not part of Laurence's speech; it is probably a note on revision, such at Matthew was fond of; he " continually inserts " " explanations of English names " (Luard, 1 *Chron. Maj.* xliv). And in his *Gesta Abbatum* (I, 316, Rolls) after 1235 he tells us that a bad Abbot " shut the mouths *omnium justiciariorum et placitantium advocatorum* (quos Banci narratores appellamus) "; the Abbey have to send their cellarer, *circumspectus et facundus*, as *advocatus* " before the judges, aye, and the King himself and the barons." However, the nomenclature is accurate and contemporary. For Laurence, see p. 134*q*.

(*r*) *Addit.* 6 Rolls, 63-74; ed. Wats. 149-53.

(*s*) D. N. B.

(*t*) He can hardly be thinking of the " dodge " charged against Ed. II, p. 217, that he briefed all counsel whom he did not want against him.

We expect the *responsalis* and are not surprised at the *prolocutores* (*u*), but we meet the *narratores* for the first time (*x*). They had, it seems, displaced from polite diction the *prolocutores*, who had never been much talked about in England.

What Matthew really means by *vulgariter* is that the common folk have given the persons who put their cases for them before the judges a name of their own which he translates *narrator*; he assuredly does not mean that the *vulgus* spoke Latin. Of its popular origin there is good confirmation.

Itinerant judges are traced back to the reign of Henry I definitely, though "not perhaps with the systematic regularity enforced by his grandson" (*y*), and in embryo to "traces of this arrangement as early as the time of Alfred, who may have been acquainted with the system in use under the Frank emperors." Of several instances there given the earliest (*z*) is a trial held before Ralph Basset

---

(*u*) See App. III. Perhaps to avoid confusion with *procurator*, which was fairly common. To Matthew the word was literary = spokesman, rather than legal, for he has *prol. d. r.* in 1254 of one of two commissioners to open Parliament neither of whom was a pleader, they are "speciales d. r. nuntii": 5 Rolls, 243; f. 157 b. As late as 1287 at the Fair Court of St. Ives a chaplain is sued for detaining 18d. (a fee?) from his *prelocutor* in a previous action: 23 Seld. Soc. 30; it may be an ancient *local* word—the Fair began about 1110: *ib.* xxviii. Indeed, Richard of St. Ives, who is called *narrator*, *ib.* 32, in 1287 (another, *ib.* 31) is *prelocutor*, *ib.* 34, in 1288 and in 1293 he is *attornatus*, *ib.* 56. In 1293, *ib.* 65, a count is called *narracio* and *nuntius* and *att.* interchange; probably these names survive locally: see p. 234*w*. In 1275 at that court a named man and three *socii sui narratores* sue for a fee for helping defendant at a fair, evidently as spokesmen—hardly as professionals in such a trivial matter: the official record is *narravit versum J. etc.*: 4 Seld. Soc. 159-60.

(*x*) In *L. H. P.* 33, 2: *judicibus* narraciones *repetere judicii*: too early to suggest the *narrator* except in the Roman sense. L. translates *Prozessrede der Partei*. At any rate, this is our earliest instance.

(*y*) St. 1 *Hist.* c. xi, § 127. The references to those judges by John of Salisbury and the *Dial. de Scac.*: App. viii, may refer to both reigns.

(*z*) Citing Ord. Vital. vi, 10, *i.e.*, *Hist. Eccl.* v. 3, p. 126: Paris, 1845: "sub fidejussoribus missus [defendant] ducitur ad judicium. Radulfo autem Basso, sedente pro tribunali, congregatis etiam provincialibus, universis apud Huntedoniam (*ut mos est in Anglia*). . . .

in the county court of Huntingdon in 1115-6. *Iters* from 1197-8 are enumerated by Hunter (*a*).

Mr. Bolland (*b*) has practically discovered the "bill" system. The justices had power (*c*) "to hear ... all matters of complaint by what was known as a bill instead of in the ordinary way by writ, which was the only procedure open to the justices sitting in the courts at Westminster. ... The King's residual or extraordinary function of causing justice to be done where ordinary means failed lay in their hands, and they were not only entitled but bound to exercise it. In the ordinary way a complainant before the King's justices had to begin by getting a suitable writ from the Chancery in London, and this writ had to be worded in the most scrupulously careful way. It could not be subsequently amended in form, and the smallest error, even a grammatical error in the Latin in which it was written, might be fatal to the plaintiff's case when it came before the Court. A bill in Eyre might be written by anyone; and some of them, many of them, were certainly written by people without any legal training, by people whose general illiteracy is patent not only in their hand-

---

(*a*) 1 *Fines*, xlix.

(*b*) *Eyre of Kent* (1313-4); *Select Bills in Eyre* (1292-1333); Introductions 24, 27, 30 Seld. Doc.; *The Year Books* (1921); *The General Eyre* (1922), Camb. Univ. Press.

(*c*) *General Eyre*, 75. The system is assumed as quite ordinary in the trial by Ed. I's special commissioners, 1289-93, of Solomon of Rochester, accused of being an unjust judge, *i.e.*, of " falso et maliciose ad ... confusionem H. quasdam billas continentes quod ... H. quosdam felones d. regis receptasset, coram se et sociis suis procuravit presentari et ipsum H. per ... Salomonem fecit imprisonari, qui quidem S. manu sua propria tradidit juratoribus ... quandam billam ... contra ... H. et cum juratores super billa illa plane consulissent et H. culpabilem non invenissent ... S. quia ... H. indictare noluerunt totam juratam illam imprisonavit." S. replied : " nunquam talem billam liberavit et dicit quod si ipsam liberasset hoc posset secundum legem et consuetudinem advocare. Quia dicit quod in itinere justiciariorum est consuetudo pro pace observanda quod quicumque de populo hujusmodi billam optulerit cuicumque justiciario majori vel minori idem justiciarius illam billam debet recipere et tradere eam duodenis juratoribus ... " : *State Trials of Ed. I*, p. 68; Camd. Soc. Ser. 3, v. 9.

writing but in the uncouthness of their language and their amazing disregard of the ordinary rules of grammar. . . . They were usually, almost always, written in the Anglo-Norman of the time; many of them in Anglo-Norman of a peculiarly illiterate kind. Some very few of them are in Latin. I have seen none in English. A writ could not be altered or amended. These bills might be freely altered or amended if it were found, when they came before the Court, that they did not correctly or clearly set forth the complainant's case. Slips that would have been immediately fatal in a writ were put straight in a bill without any detriment to the complainant. In many cases, too, a remedy for wrong suffered could be got by means of a bill before the Justices of Eyre, where no remedy at all could be got by a writ. . . . There was no writ to meet the case. A bill would meet any case where hardship or wrong had been suffered. . . . The justices inquired into complaints brought by bill in a very thoroughgoing way. They were bound by none of the ordinary rules of law or procedure. They even interrogated the parties, a thing unknown to common law process. . . . Many of " these bills " are really in the form of narrative of events." And hence the word *narratores*, story-tellers, as they were called by the people (d), as Matthew says, who employed them. Mr. Bolland insists (e) on the poverty and the illiteracy of this folk. His instances may range from Edward I to Edward III, and some of them peculiarly serve our purpose, *e.g.*, " Dear Sir," (*cher sire*, *i.e.*, the justice) " I tell you that I have not a farthing to spend on a pleader (pleyter) " : 1292. " Robert Goodrich and Alice his wife pray a remedy *pur deu e pur lalme la Reyne* because they are so poor

---

(d) Note, too (App. VIII, c. 15), that lay writers refer to the name of the Eyre (" wandering ") as popular—" as we call them," *vulgariter, vulgari nostro*; the upper classes may have dreaded the Eyres, but apparently they were popular.

(e) 27 Seld. Soc. xxiii-vi; 30 *ib*. xix-xx, 57.

they can get neither counter nor pleader " : 1293 (*f*).
" Alan and Alice his mother, for that they are poor folk,
pray you, dear Sir, for God's sake, that you will . . . grant
them a serjeant (*seriant*), so that they lose not their right,
for the sake of the Queen's soul " (*g*) : 1292. " I pray
you, for your soul's sake, that you will give me remedy of
this, for I am so poor that I can pay for no counter " (*h*) :
1293. Possibly these appeals led to the judges' requesting
counsel to appear for poor defendants.

Originally these bills, petitions in fact, would be presented in person; the *attornatus* (*i*) is unheard of, his peculiar " game " was the writ; the colloquial style (*k*) would be the petitioner's own words, or he might employ some (cheap) local scribe, especially if he did not know Anglo-Norman (much as the letter-writer with his ink-horn, in the Oriental bazaar, is employed, or the non-professional scrivener in the Hall of the Palais du Justice at Paris used to be). Such a writer, as the practice grew, would probably appear before the judges with his client; we may be pretty certain that the man who wrote the bills in Latin would do so. Whatever the English called him, the French-speaking folk would call him *conteur* (*l*); *narrator* would translate both the English and the French word. Thus among " Borough Customs " (*m*) was one about 1280 at

---

(*f*) 27 Seld. Soc. xxv, but these words are not in their bill printed 30 Seld. Soc. 45-6, but they do " pray remedy for God's sake."
(*g*) 30 Seld. Soc. 21.
(*h*) *Ib.* 47.
(*i*) But when the practice is established he could take advantage of it; thus in 1310-11, John Soke, attorney of a party, being defeated by a technicality, says : " For God's sake can I have a writ to attaint this fraud? Stanton, J. : Make your bill and you shall have what the Court can allow " : Y. B. 26 Seld. Soc. 21, 23. Soke was probably a professional *att.*, as he appears for two clients.
(*k*) Possibly it was the lesser formality of this procedure which made the Serjeants object to being justiciable by them in their own court.
(*l*) Littré gives one instance of *conter* in the 11th century and several in the 12th, but none of *conteur* till the 13th.
(*m*) Vol. II, 21 Seld. Soc. 12.

Winchester : " none of the 24 chief citizens may maintain one of the parties in the city court or be a countor or undertaker of pleadings (*enpernur de parole*) (*n*) in prejudice of the franchise of the town." It cannot be doubted that the Normans brought such a common word as *conter* with them, and if the absence of *conteur* for another century from written French implies that the word was unknown in Normandy, then we are confirmed in our belief that he was in existence here earlier than there.

What English speakers said we do not know—possibly *counter*; perhaps there was no special word for them except speaker (*o*). At any rate, making counts and telling the tale (*p*) have gone on to this day. In time a party or his *locum tenens* gradually ceases merely to recite *formulae* in court or to put them in writing; he stands up and tells his story. The significance of Matthew's notices are that he recognises these forensic persons as a class; people outside are beginning to talk of them as such and the learned have found a name for them, if only for convenience, and that this state of things comes into existence between 1200 and 1250.

It is surely significant that in the trials described above there was no inkling of *narrator*, though an inquiry is inconceivable without someone narrating the facts; they were not trials by bill, and the reporters only know the solemn *placitator* or *attornatus*, not the homely *narrator*. But from that half-century onwards mention of them and of their art is frequent in all the great writers. But, it

---

(*n*) Literary : there was no separate term for a mere *drawer* of pleas when the *conteur* did not draw them.

(*o*) Or *teller*? *speak* becomes common in the eleventh century, N. E. D.; but *speaker* in literature is later, as *teller* is; P. & M. suggest *forspeaker* (which translates *prae-* and *pro-locutor*), but there is no evidence for this word till 1300.

(*p*) A very experienced clerk of assizes when consulted about the counts or form of an indictment for misdemeanour (in which the pleading was not so strict as that for felony, which has always had some of the sacrosanctity of a writ) used to say " just tell your tale."

seems, unlike the serjeants, they were never appointed by writ.

Of these great writers Bracton (*q*) was the greatest. No one has ventured to date his birth, but his *floruit* is certainly 1250. Thus he helps us a little over our gap in time. The editor of the Rolls edition says (*r*) : " . . . nor does Bracton speak of legal practitioners, but they were well known (*s*) in his time on the continent of Europe." Twice on the same page (*t*) in the same volume *narratio* occurs as a technical term of pleading (which he translates " counting "). Still, perhaps it is too early to expect Bracton to recognise an " order," but in the next volume (*u*) there is a valuable passage, of which the editor's version is : A *justitiarius* " may be refused for good cause, but the only cause for refusal is a suspicion which arises from many causes, as if the judge be a blood-relative of the plaintiff, his vassal or subject, his parent or friend, or an enemy of the tenant [defendant], his kinsman or a member of his household, or a table companion, or he has been his *consiliarius* (*x*) or his pleader (*narrator*), and in any such like capacity." It is barely possible to understand this passage of casual advisers, not of a recognised " order," but it is simpler to read it as implying a system in which the judge had previously been an adviser, and that in one of two contrasted classes, " counsel " or *narrator* (*y*).

(*q*) Bratton, properly : Maitland, 1 B.'s *Note-Book*, 14. *N.B.*—Woodbine's caution, 1 *Bracton*, 50-1 (1915), 14 : "The often repeated assertation that Bracton's book is mainly Roman law in an English dress is utterly without foundation."

(*r*) Vol. v, lxxvii.

(*s*) This may be doubted about 1200.

(*t*) P. 453 : B. V, Tr. 3, c. 6, § 6, *de defaltis*.

(*u*) Vol. vi, Tr. 5, c. 15, § 1, *de exceptionibus*.

(*x*) *I.e.*, a member, sole or not of the old *consilium*. L. suggested that here Br. is opposing the old practice by which in case of need a *cons.* or *narr^r.* was taken from the bench of judgment-finders to help a poor party.

(*y*) So John of Salisbury (App. VIII) had previously said *advocatus* may take pay for conducting a case and *jurisperitus* for an opinion (*consilium*).

But Bracton is still more helpful, for as early as 1218 he preserves a record (z) of parties (who, by the way, have an *attornatus*) saying, etc., *in narracione sua*, and one of them varying from the writ in his *narracio*; in 1229 one party refers to the *narracio* of the other; in 1220 the procedure was *per narracionem narrare et responsum dare* : " by count countant and plea pleadant, *i.e.*, the action was decided on the pleadings . . . without duel, jury or the like," Maitland explained. As the person *narrator* does not (apparently) appear in this voluminous collection of records, but his " job " does, and as they both appear in Bracton's mature work, perhaps we may conclude that the man got his title between 1200 and 1250. The Latin word had the same vicissitude as the English " count," but the latter has literally survived (*a*).

No difficulty need be felt about *narrator* being for a time the chief forensic representative; clerks and chroniclers adopted it, displacing *placitator*, as being the word (and the personage) which common people understood, while the learned did not confuse it with *advocatus, attornatus, causidicus*, etc.—as the layman in course of time undoubtedly did. It is not necessary to prove that *narrator* and *countour* (or counter) were interchangeable, but one instance (*b*) has an interest of its own. R. de Fulham " a justice of the Jews came into the Exchequer " in 1268 " and complained of a violence done to his person in Westminster-hall by R. de Colevill, a Sergeant at Law (*narrator de Banco*) "; he is summoned to appear in the Exchequer, and does so " with a loose girdle and no coif " (*c*) before that tribunal, purposely reinforced by two *justiciarii*, who are like himself *de Banco*, and submits very humbly; " by

---

(*z*) 2 *Note-Book*, pp. 4, 269, III, 345.
(*a*) *Countour* was alive in 1393-4 : see p. 493*u*.
(*b*) Madox, 1 *Exchequer*, 236 (2nd ed.) (1769), from *Ex Memor.* 52 H, 3 Rot. 3 b.
(*c*) " in tunica discinctus, capite discooperto " like de Brewes, *modo felonico* as it is called in 1435 : Palgrave, 2 *Commonwealth*, cxviii.

mediation of the other Sergeants," *sociorum suorum narratorum*, the affair was made up. The last words suggest for the first time a corporate solidarity, which still exists, and before long is more manifest. Indeed in 1275, if not earlier, the Government has to recognise the *socii* as a class; Madox assumes that *narrator* means Sergeant at Law (a title with which we will duly deal), in accordance with the unbroken tradition (*d*); perhaps the facts would be expressed by saying that the latter title gradually absorbed the former, as that in its day had the *advocatus* and the *consiliarius*; it looks as if *narrator* was maturing from 1150 to 1200, and was " the fashion " from, say, 1200 to 1250, when the more permanent *serviens* begins to take shape (*e*);

(*d*) Coke, 9 R. ix; Selden, *Titles of Honor*, Pt. II, c. 5, § 4; v. 3, pp. 661, 102, *Works*, ed. Wilkins.

(*e*) There are not many who are actually called both by their contemporaries.

1281. Gilbert de Thornton and William de Giselham are called by Dugdale (*Chron. Ser.*) *servientes ad legem* from " *Liberate*, 9 E. I, m. 1 " where, however, we only read of each, *servienti nostro*, but in 1282, they are *narratores pro d. r.*: *Abb. Plac.* 274.

1289-93. In the *State Trials* Hugo de Louther is *narrator*, but in 1292 he is *Serjant*: Y. B. 20 E. I, 68, 422; Rolls; not in Dugdale's list at all, but *attornatus R.* (in 1292 *Salop.* Assis. 20 E. I, Rot. 42).

Elias de Bekingham (*serviens* in Dugdale's earliest list in 1276 from " *Liberate*, 3 Ed. I, m. 2," apparently incorrect) gives evidence in a State Trial (above) either as *narrator* or as *justiciarius* in a previous trial.

Nicholas of Warwick and Richard of Gosefeld are *narratores* in the State Trial and were certainly *servientes* in 1292 : Y. B. 20 E. I, 361, and elsewhere, and Y. B. 30-1 Ed. I, 273, in 1302; in 1293 Dugdale, *ib.* (from " *Lib.* 21 E. I, m. 3 ") and in 1300 *Attornatus regis*, Dugdale (from " *Lib.* 32 E. I, m. 4 "). [But in 1309-10, though a " War." argues, 20 Seld. Soc. 136, " we are not sure that Nicholas . . . was still in practice " : Maitland, *ib.* xcv.]

1309-10 : ista fuit oppinio Herle et *omnium servientium pro maiori parte* excepto Passeley . . . Y. B. 20 Seld. Soc. 160; all the names of " counsel " in that volume " have been found on the rolls as those of ' narratores ' . . ." : Maitland, *ib.* xcv; the same of 1307-9 : 17 Seld. Soc. xciv.

1310-11 : " Geoffrey de Hertrepole, Edmund Passelewe [above] and Robert de Malmethorp pleaders (*narratores*) were admitted to serve " the City (*Letter Book*, D. 251); all well-known " counsel " (in 1307 and later : Maitland, above). Dugdale puts P. among the *serv.* in

so " beforetime " prophet was called " seer." The two ultimately meet, so to say, in Thomas le Mareschal, who in 1297 describes himself as *serviens narrator*. In Edward II's reign we know that some of the judges (*f*) had been *narratores* because we have earlier Year Books (and Plea Rolls), but we do not know this in Edward I's reign, because there is no such evidence; the " exhaustive lists " (*g*) of the *narratores* only begin at the end of the thirteenth century; they are always laymen.

Whatever their origin, they were ultimately specially regarded as pleaders (*h*). Before they disappear (*i*) the *narratores* have come to compose the pleas for the *attornati* to enter. Thus in 1278 Juliana de la Blakgreve was about to get judgment from the court for seisin, but did not, because her *narrator* was not there (*k*), or to give her time to consult one, judgment was deferred to the next day; there was evidently some informality, perhaps in the plea, which only a *narrator* could set right. About 1290 one of

---

1310 ("serjeants assignes as Plees le Roy : *Claus.* 3 Ed. 2, *in dorso*, m. 21 ").

Of W. Inge, de Lowther, and N. de Warwick, Miss H. Johnstone (*State Trials*, XXV) only quotes " *qui sequitur pro r.* . . . *circa negocia nostra prosequenda et defendenda*," but Foss (III, 268) boldly calls Inge a " King's Serjeant " in view of passages in *Rot. Parl.* 1290-2, where, however, the words always are *qui seq. p. r.*; Dugd. in 1292 calls him " *serviens* " (from " *Lib.* 20 E. I, m. 3 ").

The absence of " *serviens* " from all the State Trials (above) perhaps points to its not yet being very common.

(*f*) *E.g.*, nearly all those mentioned in the *State Trials* (1289-93).

(*g*) G. J. Turner, 4 Y. B. xv; 22 Seld. Soc. Lists are printed Y. B. 16 E. III, v. 2, xlvii (and see xii), 1342; Rolls; and in several Seld. Soc. vols.

(*h*) Lapsley, *The County Palatine of Durham* (1900), p. 181, refers to two " famosi advocati " of the Bishop's Council and to *expensa* " dom. Stephani et aliorum de consilio et narratorum " in 1307. *N.B.*— Two classes : from *Boldon Book*, App. xxv—xxxvii.

(*i*) The term survives till 1377 at least, or perhaps later.

(*k*) *defecit de judicio suo et seisina quia non habuit narratorem* : 1 *Rot. Parl.* 4 a; this can hardly mean *as a penalty* for not employing a lawyer; it is common to-day to adjourn, to enable a party to obtain legal advice, but was by no means so in 1278 or even in 1302 (p. 328), where the lack of a lawyer is commiserated by the bench.

the charges against Hengham, C.J., is that though the complainant's *narratores* had pleaded correctly (*secundum formam brevis sufficienter narrassent*), yet the judge, to favour his opponent, made them plead something irrelevant to the writ (*ultra formam brevis*) by refusing to hear them till they did, which played havoc with complainant's plea (*placitum . . . taliter confundendo*), as " plainly appears from the tenor of the original writ and the form of the plea " (*l*). It is impossible to get all the facts, but the scribe knows that there is a technical art of pleading and that a false move was a serious matter. So on a criminal trial (rape) in Edward III's reign, because it is a prosecution by the King—the judge is very emphatic (*m*)—there must be no *consilium* (though there may be " comfort "), with the result that defendant's *narratores* are thereupon turned out of court. The development here suggested is very natural; it begins with any friendly person saying what he can for the party to the judges, then someone telling his own or the party's tale formally, then shaping his plea, and finally arguing the law; once get a party's intermediary into court, it is impossible to define his powers too nicely. Henceforward these practitioners—" counsel " we may now fairly call them (*n*)—obtain even greater recognition

---

(*l*) State Trials, E. I; Camd. Soc. 3rd ser. v. 9, p. 49.

(*m*) " Rex est pars in casu isto et sequitur ex officio " : prisoner comes with his *consilium*, " *deducebatur ad barram per*," two named men, one of whom is his *cognatus* : " patresces . . . sed non consules eum " : Y. B. 30 E. I, 529-30, and xliv. " If it was the complainant prosecuting you, you should have *consilium, adversus eam, sed contra regem non* : the law (*jura*) does not permit it " : *Ideo precipimus ex parte regis quod omnes narratores qui sunt de consilio vestro recedant. Quibus remotis*, etc. The judge adds that if he permitted it and the *patria*—the jury (of twelve)—should find for him (as they did), his acquittal would be put down to judicial partiality. " I ask," says the prisoner, " *habere consilium ne subripiar in curia R.* pro defectu consilii "; after claiming clergy, he says, " quia nescio legere peto consilium meum."

(*n*) Thus, in one of the State Trials (1289-93), p. 20, one of Roger's charges against a judge is that when he (R.) himself came into court the judge " forbade all the *narratores* of the court to assist R. et hoc. contra legem et statutum d. r." The judge denies that " subtraxit ei

than their forensic ancestors, and the *narratores* become merely the first edition of the *servientes ad legem.*

The *Servientes.*

Before the trial in 1088 of the Bishop of Durham, Ursus de Habetot, Sheriff of Worcestershire, " unus ex servientibus regis," was sent to summon the right reverend defendant. If Domesday Book was finished in 1086, it is " a near thing " between it and that report which contains the earlier mention of a *serviens regis* (*o*). Again, there is nothing technical in the words; the King might have hundreds of servants; presently he has servants to do his law work (*p*), and " the bar " developes apace.

[R.] consilium suum." The *statutum* is not known (and perhaps the word is rhetorical), but in 1300 the offence was perhaps forbidden by c. 11 of *Articuli super Cartas.*

(*o*) *Serjeant* is obviously from the French *serganz*, in use in France in the eleventh century (Littré). N. E. D. does not give an English form, *sergantes*, till 1200; le Sergent is a proper name in 1209 (*Rot. de Liber.* 134), thereafter fairly common.

(*p*) In 1152 (Stow, *Annales* or *Chron.* (1580)) Norwich got " Coroners and Bayliffes," having before only " a Serjeant for the King that kept Courts " : cited from " the Chronicle of Bromholma " (a MS. : see Tanner, *Not. Mon.* " Bromholm "); the original was probably *Coronator et serviens regis ad placita servanda*; if so, a very early instance of a legal *s. r.* A Binham register (Dugdale, 4 *Monasticon*, 14) referring to his has only *cor.* and *ball.* : see 9 Seld. Soc. XV. It is not always easy to be sure of the class of the *s.*; thus in 1210 " Alanus amouit servientes qui custodiebant pl. cor regis " : Madox I Exch. 442 g (2nd ed.), citing *Mag. Rot.* 11 J. *Rot.* 86 *Cumb.* : almost certainly inferiors. *Annales Lond.* (Rolls, 101), under 1293, has " quemdam serv. d. r. dictum le Bascle," who was active in arresting " two felons of the King "; he might have been a lawyer living in West Cheap, but Fabyan, who also tells the story at the same date (Rastell's edn. v. 2, p. 61), calls him " Rychard Bagle offycer of the Sheryfes of London "; the officer of the Sheriff is called *serv. d. r.*

Serjt. Manning in *Serviens ad Legem* (1840), p. 283, has a long list of " serjeanties," all originally or theoretically for some physical work; they include, *e.g.*, being " land serjeants or keepers of the peace," " carrying writs," " being reeve," *breviandi placita corone versus vicecomitem et faciendi summoniciones, breviandi et faciendi districciones, custodiendi brevia corone*, being marshal ad *placita d. r.*, summoning to the County Court, *pro placitis corone custodiend'* (=perhaps, *ut sit coronator*). These can hardly have been feudal serjeanties in the ordinary sense, as Round, *The King's Serjeants* (1911), does not mention

So far we have not met the Crown as a civil litigant; if it had an interest in a suit it could act through its judges, the earliest of whom were by no means independent. In a " criminal prosecution," as in the Bishop of Durham's case, the King takes part in person. Aubrey de Vere is rather one of Stephen's ambassadors than his counsel, and the whole hearing is anomalous and in the worst of the bad times. As soon as order is restored and administration revives, *attornatio* grows; the Crown has many and increasing civil interests which can be defended legally; there is no need for arbitrary action—" Hoc volo, sic jubeo "; other suitors send an *attornatus* to court, why should not the King? and whom should he send but a *serviens*? Like anyone else, he or the government would begin by sending a man *ad hoc*, as *attornatus*; if he did well like Geoffrey le Scrop, he would be regularly retained and become a *serviens* (*ad legem*); or a *serviens* already in the King's employ might be his representative in court, like many known to us.

them; he does (p. 85) "at least as early as 1250," a deputy or clerk of the Marshal known as " marshal of the household " (*hospicii*), whose Court ultimately became that of the Lord Steward and whose pleas were known as *placita aule*. Round's point is well illustrated 1 *Liber Albus*, 303, B. 3, Pt. 2 : Rolls : in one of those *placita* at the Tower in 1325, *Alanus de Lek* serviens hospitator hospitii d. r. *qui pro eo sequitur, dicit*; the proceedings being in form a trial, quasi-legal language is used, *qui seq.*, etc., being technical. Manning mainly relies on the *Testa de Nevill*, which Round (p. 17) dates about 1250. In St. West. I, c. 30 (1275), there are " les s̄jaunz criurs de feo [fee] " and " serjaunt de fee," translated " officers, cryers of fee " and " officer of fee." *Serviens* was by no means monopolised by the law : see 1 *Rot. Lit. Claus*, xliv (Hardy). Manning was subject to the Norman fallacy, hence Pref. ix : " The fees receivable by the ' countor ' appear to have induced the Conqueror or some of his more immediate successors to treat the office as a serjeanty in gross and to assume if they did not possess it before, the right of appointing to this serjeanty." No authority is vouched for the " serjeanty in gross " and it does not seem to have existed. Of course, the King had the right to appoint his own servants. Vinogradoff, *English Soc. in the 11th Century* (in which lawyers are not mentioned), p. 61, says : " No clear line can be drawn between military sergeanties and services which seem to us to be of a private character."

This is well illustrated in the great suit (*q*) in 1291 between Margery, the wife of T. Weyland J., and Gilbert de Clare, Earl of Gloucester. In order to be certified of the law and the precedents on a point that arose, the King orders *tam justiciarii sui de utroque banco quam ceteri de regno suo, tam* milites *quam servientes, in legibus et consuetudinibus regni experti, mandarentur quod essent coram ipso d. rege et ejus consilio; i.e., milites* who happen to be authorities on this point—perhaps *milites literati* (*r*) —are summoned as well as the ordinary legal employees; as Coke (*s*) says : " Note, the ancient tryall of difficult matters in law." The Earl was represented by " quidam de consilio [suo] ex parte sua missi." The presence of feudal landowners with professional lawyers to decide a point of real property law rather suggests that the profession is not yet a close corporation.

Serjeant Pulling's *The Order of the Coif* (1884) is prefaced by a list of " Serjeants of the Coif with the date of their creation," from which we gather that Geofrey Ridel was the first created in 1117; Reginald de Warenne in 1168; William FitzRalph in 1174; William Basset and Roger Fitz Reinfrid in 1176, etc., etc. On what principle this list was drawn up does not appear (*t*), but no other authority recognises these men as serjeants.

(*q*) 1 *Rot. Parl.* 67 a.   (*r*) P. 150*u*.

(*s*) 1 Inst. 133 a (Co. Litt. B. 2, c. 11, s. 200) : perhaps the *personnel* of the commissioners was affected by the importance of the litigants.

(*t*) Unless the author assumed from the facts in Foss's *Judges*, etc. (1848), that every itinerant justice was a serjeant. Thus John Chaynel (1312) is in his list, but not in Dugdale at all, and not in Foss (III, 246), as a *serviens*. To him and sixteen others, nearly all well-known judges, was addressed in 1311 a writ ordering their attendance in Parliament (Prynne, *Animadversions, etc.* (1669), 40; 2 *Foedera*, Pt. I, 143 (1818); *Cal. Close R.* (1311), p. 437), among whom are Richard of Rodeneye, unknown (except for a bare mention in 1310 : *Cal. Close R.* 333), and John Lovel " of Snotescumbe " (*Foedera* : Prynne, " Faltescumbe "), unknown—the judge of that name (1292, 1294) (Dugdale) was dead—neither of whom certainly were *servientes*. But as they were almost certainly practising lawyers, we may infer that there were others whose names have not come down

THE SERVIENTES. 185

Foss says (*u*) that the first instance " of an advocate being regularly employed in the King's affairs " is in 1253, when Laurence de Brok *sequitur pro rege* (*x*) in a cause, and that there are many such entries for the next fourteen years. He, by the way, " seems to be one of the first men who climb to the judicial bench from the bar " (*y*). He was evidently a servant of the King, but is nowhere, it seems, described as *serviens regis* (*z*). Certainly in 1253— and apparently even in 1291—that title was not established in a technical sense. We have seen that it was common enough in its literal sense (*a*).

1275-6 is, perhaps, the first authentic date (*b*).

---

to us. Thus Weaver, *Funerall Monuments*, 863 (1631), speaks of " that renowned Lawyer, Edmund de Hengrave, who flourished in the raigne of " Edw. I, but there is no other trace of him.

(*u*) II, 200, 267.
(*x*) Abbrev. Plac. 130.
(*y*) 1 P. & M. I, VI, 184, n. (4).
(*z*) But in 1275 he held land *per servitium*. . . . Blount, *Fragmenta Antiquitatis*, 64 (ed. 1679, citing 3 E. I, Mid. Rot. 18).
(*a*) See 120 L. Q. R. 477-8: the word is sometimes misleading; in a document of 1321 (2 *Lib. Custum.* Pt. II, p. 295) *nullus serviens d. r. se intromittat coram justic.* clearly refers to inferior officers or servants : *ib.* pp. 300, 301; more correctly, *serviens ex parte d. r.*; the original of both being a document of 1244; *nullus serviens ex parte d. r.* : *Liber Albus;* Rolls, 77; translation 68.

In 1315 it was charged against the Corporation of Bristol that they had, apparently in a riot, imprisoned " Galfrum Justice " and Lawrence de Kary, driven three named *servientes regis ibidem* out of the town and imprisoned three other named " s. r." " in the town," " whereby the King lost their services "; in their defence they deny this generally, merely calling all the aggrieved persons *ministros regis* : 1 Rot. Parl. 360 a b, 361. Not one of these persons is known and it is difficult to see why there should be so many lawyers in Bristol. In the Index, however (7 Rot. Parl. 807), the six are " King's Sergeants at law "; it seems very improbable that in 1315 they were. But other similar citations in that Index do certainly, from the context, refer to lawyers.

(*b*) In Coke's speech to the Serjeants in 1614 he is reported to have said : " His Antiquitie is longe before He : 3 : Tyme . . . " on the authority of books, etc., all of H. III's time or later; he must have meant that their authors imply a pre-H. III origin.

Whitelocke, *Memorials of English Affairs*, under Nov. 1648, told the Serjeants that there were " such Sergeants " before 9 H. III, 1225, on the authority of " Hoveden and Paris, who lived in R. I and H. III

Dugdale (c) has " Tho. de Weylond, Joh. de Metingham, Joh. de Cobham (d), Elias de Bekingham, Serv. Regis ad Legem," as getting pensions. The first record of one in court, it seems, is in 1292, in the earliest (e) Year Book (at present) printed : " Tiltone said thus : Showeth unto you our Lord the King by Hugh de Louther his serjeant

---

time, and are authors of good credit. They recite the charges of the justices in Eyer, given in R. I and King John's time. One of their Articles is to *enquire of the Sergeants at Law and Attorneys Fees.*" As Manning says (p. 217) : " *Quaere* about this charge." These passages cannot be identified and probably are reminiscences of the well-known passages in M. Paris, p. 171q, and Hoveden ann. (1194), p. 744, ed. 1601, or 3 Rolls, 263 ; but neither serjeants nor attorneys are mentioned ; the reference to " John's time " may be the record of 1210 (p. 182p) : Manning, p. 298. Whitelocke says (*ib.*) that according to " the Book of Entries " [*i.e., Liber Intrationum*, 128 b (1546) : Rastell's edn. 178-9 (1596)] " Serjeants could not be sued by Bill in the Common Pleas, but by writ out of the Chancery ; and this being by Prescription shews that Sergeants were before the time of R. I," on which Manning (p. 73) remarks : " That undoubtedly is a technical argument, but it seems to be legal and sufficient." It would seem that the ground for the serjeants' privilege (if any) is that they were " servants of the King," and that his service would suffer if they were sued so summarily.

Probably they objected to a summary hearing as inconvenient and less dignified. As Serjeants could only (they claimed) be sued in the Common Pleas, so Chancery Clerks (claimed) only in Chancery : Sanders, *Orders in Chancery* (1845), 1027 : Writ of 1386 set out. So the Barons of, and " several of the Residents at," the Exchequer, and " their Clerks and their men " had the privilege of impleading or being impleaded there only : Madox, II, Exch. 12, citing a writ of 1254 allowing " the ancient custom."

(c) He did not mean, it seems, that the words " serv. R. ad 1." were in the MS. (and search shows that if he did, the reference is incorrect, p. 179c), for under 1281 (*ib.*), where he quotes the correct Roll and these four words, the MS. reads *servienti nostro* : *Orig.* 110 ; *Chron. Ser.* 25, citing *Liberate*, 3 E. I, m. 2.

(d) This " entry . . . is difficult to explain, except on the presumption that it was an arrear due to him (J. de C.) in that character before he was raised to the bench " : 3 Foss, 78—because he was raised to the bench in 1270, *teste* Dugdale himself (and itinerant just. in 1268 : *Liberate*, 54 H. 3, m. 6, and *Pat.* 52 H. 3, Surr. m. 6). The two discrepancies (last n.) point perhaps to a confusion of citations.

(e) 20-1 E. I, p. 68 ; Rolls (1866), see p. 195. The earliest extract from a Year Book in Fitzherbert, accepted as genuine, dates from 1283 ; the earliest Y. B. in existence is of 1289-90 : Bolland, *Year Books*, 8.

THE SERVIENTES. 187

who is here (*son serjant ke cy est*), etc." Lowther argues here and in 1293 (*f*).

The fact seems that early employees of the Crown who had no traditional title were spoken of as servants for this or that purpose according to the context of the moment, but as a particular category emerged into importance it became necessary to distinguish, thus—*serviens ad arma, ad clavam, ad feoda,* etc.

If the title *serviens ad legem* was in use in 1253 we should expect Laurence de Brok to be so called in some of the references above. We do not in fact meet " serviens ad legem " till the writ of 1310 below; the full phrase with *regis* not till about 1387 when the Continuator of Knighton, writing then, includes among some lawyers who were consulted " *Joannes Lokton* (*g*) *Serviens dicti d. n. regis ad legem.*" The phrase of 1291 *servientes in legibus et consuetudinibus regni experti* is intermediate between the two extremes (*h*). The fact that the Statute of 1275

(*f*) Y. B. 20-1 E. I, 423.

(*g*) 2 Knighton, 237; Rolls; Twysden, 2694; *ib.* 240 and 2696 respectively, simply *serviens*.

He is described (3 *Rot. Parl.* 169) in 1384 as *assidens* to the judges (with two other *servientes regis*) at the trial of the fishmonger Cavendish. De la Pole, Chancellor, defending himself (*ib.* 168), mentions incidentally that " all the justices and the sergeants of the realm had been present in the chancery " at the former hearing; he does not say whether the parties had had counsel.

L. was the one *serviens* called in with all the judges, as a sort of Royal Commission, and forced to subscribe Richard's unconstitutional demands in 1387—for which they were all sentenced to death in 1388 (but only exiled to Ireland, where they were not allowed to see their families lest they should " put them up " to the law of their case, nor to give legal advice to others) : 2 Knight. 240, 258-9, 295; Twys. 2694, 2706. By 1388 the English " serjeant " is in vogue and so is Latinised; "serjancius " *ad l.* 295.

(*h*) There has been some mistake about "serviens " (alone). On " preceptor inveniet unum fratrem servientem, generalem procuratorem hospitalis et unum clericum [for litigation in the Exchequer] . . . et etiam unum attornatum cum eodem fratre in *aliis* curiis . . . regis " (*Extent of the Knights Hospitallers in England in 1338* : Camd. Soc. no. 65, p. 100 (1857)) Kemble says (p. lxvi) this " shews that the Order had at least one serviens at legem or *serjeant*-at-law. This mentions no other lawyer but " S̄jaunt, Cōtour " perhaps points to the fact that in the vernacular, at any rate, of the French speaking folk, the title was already abbreviated (and may confirm the view that nomenclature and institution were still in a flux).

Coke has preserved from " very ancient registers " (*i*) the writ of appointment by the Crown still used in his day, and he sets out Herle's; he died in 1347 and this document probably dates from about 1310.

Rex &c. Willielmo Herle, salutem : quia de advisamento concilii nostri ordinavimus vos [=plural of " majesty "] ad statum et gradum Servientis ad Legem in quindena Sancti Michaelis proxim' futur' suscipiend', vobis mandamus firmiter injungentes quod vos ad statum et gradum praedictum ad diem illum in forma praedicta suscipiend' ordinetis et praeparetis : et hoc sub poena mille librarum. Teste meipso &c.

Apparently this is earliest known writ (*k*) of the sort; we may, therefore, safely conclude that by (about) 1300 the rank—*gradus*—was ripe for royal recognition—" those writs originally are only *de gratia regis* " (Coke)—and that henceforward every Serjeant is so appointed. To the last (*l*) the Serjeant was a servant of the Crown. Perhaps

---

was their proctor . . . who because he was frater serviens, received no fee. . . . I find it very strange that a frater serviens of the Hospital should have been a lawyer in 1338." He was, of course, *serviens ordinis*; in 1338 a *s. r.* or *s. r. ad l.* would not be a *generalis procurator*, and his allowances (p. 101) in kind make the supposition impossible. *Ib.* p. 100, 8s. 8d. is paid " *serjeantis* of London," see further, p. 376.

(*i*) R. Pt. 10, xxxix; apparently (*ib.* xxiv) he means the *Registrum cancellariae* of St. Westmins. II, c. 24 : " the ancientist book of the law "; Whitelocke, *Memor. Engl. Affairs* (Nov. 1648), said the Register was in manuscript and the writ had never changed.

(*k*) Serjt. Pulling (*The Order*, etc., p. 31) sets out his own of 1864; it is a mere translation of the Latin above (which appears in a slightly different form in Dugdale's *Orig.* 136).

(*l*) The late Lord Lindley, appointed in 1875, was the last survivor. The order still (1927) exists in Ireland. Serjeant Sullivan, K.C., in England, describes himself as " the last Serjeant " in *Old Ireland* : London (1927).

THE SERVIENTES.

we may infer from the fact that the writ does not create Herle a *narrator* that it was not necessary for a Serjeant's privileges; probably it was not in 1300 an official title and was beginning to go out of use. If so, there is an antiquarian touch in David Hanmeare's appointment in 1377 " by the King's will and command to be one of the *servientes* of his laws and a *narrator* for the King in any of his courts whatsoever for any plea of the King's ..." (*m*).

C. 29 of the First Statute of Westminster, 1275, is thus translated (*n*) : " If any Serjeant, Pleader (*sjaunt* '*Cōtour* (*o*)), or other (*p*), do any manner of deceit or

---

(*m*) " David Hanmeare ex voluntate Rs. electus est et per regem ordinatus essendi un' servientum legum suarum et narrator pro rege in curiis suis quibuscunque ad plt̄um. Rs., etc." : *Cal. Rot. Pat.* 197 b; cf. Thomas, p. 80. This, perhaps, is the explanation of " per W. de Bereford narratorem suum [the King's] " in 1311 : 42 Seld. Soc. lxvi-ii (from Plea Roll, 226, Mich.); a Mr. Turner (*ib.*) believes that it refers to the C.J. [since 1309] and not by mistake to any serjeant of that name [*e.g.*, to the contemporary *R*. de B. : III Foss 234]; if it is not a clerical error, it must be a sort of affectation.

(*n*) 1 *St. of Realm* St. 34. Fleta's translation, B. II, c. 37, is almost certainly contemporaneous. It is headed *De Narratoribus* and begins : In curia autem Reg' sunt servientes, narratores, attornati et apprenticii, de quibus constitutum est quod nullus [no noun follows] deceptionem, etc. There is some corruption in Fleta's text, but the version is substantially correct; he modifies (probably correctly) the disqualification of the *narrator* " et ulterius in curia r. pro aliquo narrare non audietur, nisi pro semetipso si narrator fuerit "; he may still appear for himself (which is good law); this makes the French text run better—but " if he be no pleader, etc."; " quod," says F., " dicitur de narratore, intelligatur id dici de quolibet alioqui [alio quantum : Houard] ad imprisonamentum " obviously referring to the *att.* and *appr.* of his first sentence; this is his only equivalent for " or other " of the text. There is, too, a clear echo of the statute in Britton (B. I, c. 23; 1 Nichols, 101) : " and if there was secret malice (*mauvesté*) [or " if he was wittingly guilty " : Kelham] in the act [false pleading] and he [the serjeant] be convicted thereof, then let him be sent to prison and suspended from his office."

Other corroboration (not of much substantive value) is c. 5 of B. II of the *Mirror of Justices* : 7 Seld. Soc. 47 " Des Countours "; *inter alia* it enjoins order in court. There is an express and long criticism of this stat. : *ib.* 184 ff.

(*o*) The question whether the reading is " serjeant-contour " or " Serjeant, Contour " (30 *L. Q. R.* 479; 31 *ib.* 61, 64-5) was probably academic in 1275; it merely reflects the different origins of the two words. (*p*) Pp. 195, 330*b*, and 351.

collusion in the King's Court or consent (unto it) in deceit of the Court (or) to beguile the Court or the Party and thereof be attainted, he shall be imprisoned for a Year and a Day and from thenceforth shall not be heard to plead (*conter*) in (that) Court for any Man; and if he be no Pleader, he shall be imprisoned in like manner by the space of a year and a day at least; and if the Trespass require greater punishment it shall be at the ' King's Pleasure. ' "

With this statute we must read that *de conspiratoribus* (*q*) of 1292 or earlier :—

" Whereas it is openly forbidden by the King, in his Statutes, that anyone of the Court of the King or of any other Court whether Justice, Clerk or Serjeant-Countour (*sic*) attorney or apprentice or any steward of a great man or of any other or bailiff or any other man of the land, shall take in hand or maintain any plea in our Court, or in any other to champerty (*r*); they nevertheless do take to champerty, and upon other bargains, from all persons in all the Courts, whereby the people has been often maltreated, disinherited and ruined through such maintainers and by their doings (*makemenz*) by their works and by their disturbances (*destourbances* : ? exactions), the which such have committed against the people to their great destruction and to their great prejudice : the King at Berwick by assent of the great Lords of the land, and by [advice of] his Council hath ordained and established that

---

(*q*) In I *Stat. of Realm*, 216 : " Cunteurs ne atturnez ne aprentifs seneschaus . . . ne autres "; but transln. above from *Lib. Cust.* 203 (*errata*, v. 2, p. 897), v. II, 577. As the editor of *Lib. Cust. ib.* says the text of *St. of R.* is " very inaccurate "; " Serjeant " does not occur in it. " Makemenz "=" French adaptation " of " make " : *Gloss. ib.*

(*r*) See p. 237*b*. Possibly this legislation caused the vigorous prosecution soon after (1293) of two men who publicly " in Aula Reg' " denounced W. de Bereford, J., " quod partes coram eo placitantes manutenuit et consilium suum eis inpendit in Itinere Staff' et alia ibidem fecit contra sacramentum suum et statum officii." His *socii* in Staff. denied this *per recordum*; as the offenders " had their action against the *Minister* before the King *vel alio modo* " (1 *Rot. Parl.* 95), they were sent to the Tower.

he who shall henceforth be attainted of such emprises suits and bargains shall have imprisonment of three years and then make fine (*seit reint*) at the King's pleasure. . . ."

It follows that the *servientes ad legem* (*s*) existed as a class—and sufficiently large to be the subjects of legislation—some time before 1275. We may suggest approximately 1260 as the date of their appearance, for Bracton, who ceased writing about that year (it is supposed), does not know them, though he knows the *narrator*—who, however, does not figure largely in his pages—whereas Britton, twenty years later, is, as we shall see, quite familiar with the practising serjeant.

A regular system is assumed by c. 11 of *Articuli super Cartas* in 1300—the chapter (*t*) is aimed at champerty and "maintenance" by royal officers : " But it is not to be understood hereby that any one may not have counsel of *countours* or learned men (*sages gents* (*u*)) for a fee (*pur*

(*s*) Bracton, indeed, has a good deal to say about a *serviens d. regis*; false imprisonment is ended by the *s. d. r.* or the King's writ; the victim of a certain crime ought to complain to the *praepositus hundredi*, the *s. d. r.*, the *coronatores*, the *vicecomes*; where there is default in the court of the chief lord, the *vicecomes* is to commission the *s. d. r.* to hear the lord's " proof " (*probationem*), the latter to appear in person or by attorney, seneschal or " other bailiff "; to him, amongst others, a felon may make confession (f. 145b, f. 147; f. 150b. f. 330b; 2 Rolls, 471, 482, 511; 5 Rolls, 93, 95, 99). From these and other passages it would seem that this *s. d. r.* was a superior administrative official—something like a modern Registrar; he has indeed " a record," but so has the *s. hundredi*. In a corresponding passage in Fleta (VI, c. 3, 2) we get *ballivo hundredi vel itineranti vel alteri servienti regis*. In both the *s. d. r.* is sometimes called briefly *serviens*, but he is obviously not the pleading Serjeant known to Britton and Fleta (not *s. legis* but *regis*)—but is excellent material for the future bar.

Bracton recognises the ancient representation of a ward by a guardian, *e.g.*, *de Ass. ult. praesent* (f. 247b; 4 Rolls, 78); a writ goes to him *in cujus manu fuerit* (*sc.* an impeding ward) *et cujus consilio ductus*.

(*t*) It has been doubted whether it refers to civil or criminal proceedings, but for the point above this is immaterial. Previous legislation had been aimed at a few very powerful persons (2 *Inst.* 563), and a large number, mostly clerks about the courts, who took upon themselves to advise suitors for pay; see p. 331.

(*u*) Coke, Pref. Pt. X, xxxvi, thought this term included " appren-

son donant) or of his parents and next friends." The professional adviser is protected as a *matter of course* in his legitimate avocation. It was long before the popular confusion cleared away between the chicane and breedbating of the fringe about the judges, before there was any organisation of the profession at all, and the strenuous zeal, not by any means confined to work in court (*x*), of the genuine advocate. The absolute extra-forensic detachment from the client, of to-day, comes much later. This enactment says in effect : if you are not a practising lawyer, you must not meddle with litigation, and if you are you must be paid in money.

The *servientes* begin and end as *ss. regis*; other people employ them and " regis " is dropped, just as when we say " officer " we mean preferably one who holds the King's commission. For some time we must be content to pick up stray facts about their organisation on the way —even after they emerge historically, so to say, about 1200.

Our material is meagre; perhaps the fact is that the century 1160-1260 was rather the age of the *attornatus*, not indeed always so called. At any rate, there is a period in which representation is casual and social rather than normal or legal, at the end of which if not the chief personage in evidence, at any rate, the most frequent is the *attornatus*. The old *consilium*, which must exist in any society and which may fairly be called an institution in Anglo-Saxon times, still goes on. Anyone can appear for anyone else, anyone can be consulted, probably in court quietly, certainly out of court; it was all very " primitive " as we say. As late as 1233 in the King's (as the lord of the

---

tices "; " but why should app. be included among wise people? " : [L. in *MS*.]

(*x*) Winfield, *Present Law, etc.*, p. 27; Danby, J., in 1454 conceded that a serjeant's duty is to supervise his client's affairs : Y. B. 32 H. 6, f. 24.

manor's) court at Windsor, one Edith sued one William about three stolen pigs; defendant defended in person and his suggestion about the procedure (*y*) apparently troubled the lady. So (the remark is just slipped in) " she went out and sought counsel "—*exiens et peciit consilium*—no doubt by leave of the court, and came back " primed " with a good pleader's answer and formula; evidently she consulted someone who knew, but why he did not come into court and argue does not appear. This little by-play— obviously not invented—suggests the real practical importance of a legal formula in litigation, and as formulae multiplied the fewer would be the persons who knew them, and that formulae multiplied as writs multiplied is certain and natural; that the number of King's writs had been steadily increasing since the Conquest we also know. One of the " abuses " in the *Mirror of Justices* (1285) is that there are so many forms of " pleadable writs " (*z*).

Perhaps the primitive casualness, to which we have referred, accounts for the many scandals of which early clients had to complain. Prosperity and property go hand in hand, and, as we have seen, in the stretches of quiet, wealth—patriarchal, indeed (except for buildings), much land and cattle, a little money, rarely precious stones— was diffused. With such a flowing tide of business there must be mistake, irregularity, carelessness, deceit, chicane " sharp practice," *et plurima fraudis imago* "—not only in the commerce of trade but in that of the litigation which it created, and many an agent called in to advise must have taken advantage of the ignorant or the confiding party. Probably this is why our first *official* notice of the profession

---

(*y*) " Hoc optulit probare per consideracionem curie versus eam " : 2 Bracton's *Note Book*, 633, pl. 824; " on her return counted against W. as against a thief " : 2 P. & M. p. 160, II, iv, § 7. The procedure is by no means easy to understand, but in the end Edith wins and W. is ordered to be hanged.

(*z*) 17 Seld. Soc. X, liv, where Maitland seems to agree.

—that of 1275—is also (as happens with other interests (*a*))
its stern regulation and discipline :

"Showed by one satiric touch
That no nation wanted it so much."

There is a good illustration of the " mischief " of the statute
in Coke's speech (*b*) to the serjeants in 1614 : counsel
" must be faithful and honest not flatter his clyent in a
wrong nor boulster out an untruth; Choke and Littleton
in H. VI's time were entreated to plead a false plea to save
a default in a real action, *viz.*, to plead that the waters
were so great that in 16 days the Clyent could not pass by
any place, which they holding untrue, refused to plead."

In 1275 experience had shown that the unprotected
public suffered from the dishonesty of the legal practitioner.
It is true that the *attornatus* is not mentioned in this connection—though his turn was soon to come—but that is
probably because he was indefinite and ubiquitous, not
concentrated near Westminster like the *serviens*, one of the
crowd of unorganised laymen, whereas the *serviens* who got
his name because till recently he was a *royal* servant, was
a responsible person of social position on whom you could
lay your hand at any moment, he was soon a member of a
recognised body. Another reason why the statutory limelight is turned on him is that the main " mischief " aimed
at is his conduct in court, and hence we have here another
and a strong indication that by this time the lawyer who
appeared in the King's Court at Westminster was looked
upon as the important legal representative; the statute does
not contemplate the *attornatus* arguing in or misleading the
court, though in another section (c. 33) it quite appreciates
his proper activity. And we may safely assume that the
court which would punish the offending *serviens* would not
let the peccant *attornatus* go scot free. In short, the

(*a*) *E.g.*, the licensing of hackney coachmen in 1662.
(*b*) P. 185*b*.

attornatus, the mere man of business, is giving place about 1250 to a man for special business, *viz.*, court work—one who is soon to become a " specialist." The *consilium* outside goes inside.

Sometimes it is puzzling to determine whether a man is *attornatus* or *narrator*; for instance, Tyltone (*c*) probably had some *locus* in the case, for he introduces the *serviens*; unless something has dropped out, why should the reporter merely tell us that he said " I have a *serviens* here ready to argue " ? This a " junior " would hardly do. Was he or had he been *attornatus* in the case and " avows " his serjeant in open court? There seems to be no reason why a man—at any rate, in early days—should not be *attornatus* and *narrator* at once. Or perhaps he was *attornatus* in 1292; he argues *alone* in the two preceding cases (and apparently nowhere else); but he was *narrator* in 1304 and 1310-11. One document (*d*) in 1338 actually includes an " attornatus " (named) among a list of *narratores*.

The fact is that the authors of the Statute of 1275 did not mean to draw a sharp line between the professional and the non-professional representative or to abolish with a stroke the casual substitute for a party (though he was apt to be one of a motley number); the draftsman did not put in " pleader or other " or " if he be no pleader " without more, by accident. He knew that on the fringe of the serjeant or *countor* there were *attornati* and *apprenticii* (as Fleta saw he did), but he was not ignorant that anyone (not under arrest) might " come and say " for anyone else —at any rate, in a civil court—and he has preserved that

---

(*c*) P. 186. Doubtless the same man as Johannes de Tilton in " counsel who are mentioned in this volume," *viz.*, Y. B. 1309-11, 22 Seld. Soc., ed. G. J. Turner, p. xliv, but the name is not in the Index; Mr. Turner adds that his name is " mentioned in the Year Books, but not in the plea rolls of Mich. T. 4 E. II," but in Y. B. 4 E. II, 26 Seld. Soc. ed. by Mr. Turner, the name does not occur. The authority for 1304 (above) is that editor : 22 Seld. Soc. xliv, " de Banco Rolls, No. 161, r. 31."

(*d*) Pp. 187*h*, 376.

privilege for what it is worth, though not so explicitly as the City did for its suitors a few years later. That class did not disappear in a moment. This, perhaps, explains some anomalous advocates from time to time. Thus in 1294, in *T. Cantok* v. *Rob. de Wyche* (*e*), the learned editor says that we have " an advocate who was not a serjeant, but was retained in the Common Bench "; both litigants are called *magister* as a mark of respect, and the editor tells us that the plaintiff became Chancellor of Ireland and Bishop of Emly. He sued under a bond of 1288 for arrears (12 marks) of an annual rent of 40s. to issue from *m.* Robert's *camera* (*f*) during the latter's life, granted for plaintiff's kind service (*obsequium*) in the past—and future. That refers to a case in 1288 in the *curia regis* in which Robert was defendant; he then, he now asserts, over and over again requested Thomas, " who was actually then in the court at Westminster," to advise him (*consulere*), but he refused; the annuity was for " his service " (implying *forensic* service). Thomas admits that he was so asked, but pleads that this was after Robert had put in a forged receipt —so found because of a certain erasure, and he at once told him that as the forgery affected the King as well as the plaintiff, he could not be *de consilio suo* because he was in *obsequio d. regis* (a constant and not unnatural excuse (*g*), due to the prospect of royal disfavour). Robert rejoins that his requisition was before the document was produced, indeed, before the suit was begun, but he asserted that Thomas refused both before and after. In 1294 a jury found that Thomas went, as he said, to court, etc., etc., and only retired from the case because of the forgery—and

---

(*e*) 42 Seld. Soc. lxiv, 199, ed. G. J. Turner; from *de Banco Rolls*, Easter, 22 E. I, No. 104, r. 82, Worc.

(*f*) As plaintiff was seised of it by defendant's " hands " it must be in the nature of a rentcharge.

(*g*) Still technically existing; " K.C.s " must get formal permission to appear against the Crown.

he wins handsomely (*h*). We see here a gentleman of position, a *patronus*, perhaps hesitating between Church and Bar as a profession, but ready to do a turn in court for a friend, not *serviens* or *narrator* or *apprenticius*—for he would have been so called, and it is difficult to understand the learned editor's remark: " This case ... certainly

---

(*h*) He recovers (1) his claim (before writ); (2) 6 marks, writ pending; (3) 20 shillings under the statute of 1278 (of Gloucester, 6 E. I, c. 8—which is followed word for word in the judgment—a rare event) for his costs due to defendant's default, and (4) 60s. costs (*dampna*) taxed at the judge's discretion.

Mr. Turner's *résumé* (p. lxv) seems, with deference, to be inaccurate. Thomas assuredly means that if it had not been for fear of being a party to a fraud, he would have gone on with the case and the jury actually found that on the day of the trial he was there ready, *consilio et auxilio assistere* and did actually do so—*et ei assistebat quousque, etc.*; how then can it be said " nothing is said about T. addressing the court " ? In 1294 there is no line between forensic *auxilium* and " addressing the court."

The words at the end of the record, " dampna—totum clericis," Mr. Turner translates " Damages [=Costs] : All to the Clerks," taxed by the judges at sixty shillings.

Ib. p. lxiii, Mr. Turner cites from the Common Bench plea rolls (Easter, 22 E. I (1294) No. 104, r. 75d) a case where Hugh de Branteston " stetisset hic ad barram ad placitandum cum quodam adversario suo," and one *magister* Antonius, struggling apparently to the same bar, hustled Hugh, coming behind him, Hugh's *valletus*, Thomas, remonstrated with him (perhaps menacingly) and there was a " slanging match." Mr. Turner tells us that Hugh was sometimes a justice to deliver gaols, but " almost certainly not a serjeant." Anthony " may have been an attorney or counsel for the " *adversarius*. " If, however, he were a counsel, he also was not a serjeant, for his name is not in our list of ' narrators,' and he is described as Master, whereas there is reason for thinking that serjeants at this date were never clerks." But there is no reason whatever why they should not both be laymen; *magister* does not, *pace* Mr. Turner, imply " clerk," but roughly = a man with a degree of some sort (or sometimes, merely, a gentleman). Maitland, 8 Seld. Soc. xxi, says of Bracton that it seems " that he had not taken a doctor's or master's degree," for the Chancery habitually calls his fellow-justices of Ass. *Mgr.*, it never so calls him. Foss, II, 84, says : " ' Magister ' began to be adopted *temp.* H. II by the clergy and as some say, by the professors of the civil and canon law, who were generally of that order."

Mr. Turner also infers from " the *juratores* present here in court, who saw what took place," telling the judges the facts on their oaths, " that the incident must have occurred in the trial of an issue "; but it is not said that they were *juratores* in Hugh's case.

cannot be cited as proof that a barrister or any other advocate who was not a serjeant had a right of audience at some particular stage of an action "; it is too early to think of any monopoly; this is by no means the only instance of (so to say) " also ran."

We are not without glimpses of the stages intermediate between casual, unorganised representation and a full-blown system. We shall see in 1201 a little scene in court, an *attornatus* being " disavowed." So in 1228 " John de Planez in pleading for William of Cookham called Henry II the grandfather instead of the father of King John; William disavowed the plea (*deadvocavit . . . narrationem advocati sui*) and the advocate was amerced for his blunder "; William himself then puts the matter right in court—*narrat*—by referring to Henry I, the grandfather of the grandfather of Henry III (*i*). This is one of the few instances where the pleader is actually punished for a mistake, though he is threatened often enough (*k*).

There are other instances (*l*) of *deadvocatio narratoris*, in 1222 and 1234-5. In 1253 a bishop throws over one—a layman, apparently who *narravit pro* [*eo*]—perhaps because he had no authority to plead (*m*). In 1262 a man " desawoa suum narratorem " in a Guild Court (*n*). In 1270 the plaintiff Geoffrey wants to know " whether they have aught else to say and whether their countor (*narrator*) Isaac of Southwark be avowed (*advocatus*). And the said Moses [defendant] says that he has not avowed Isaac at all (*in nullo Isaac advocavit*). . . . And the said Isaac his

---

(*i*) 1 P. & M., I, vi, p. 191, from 2 Bracton's *Note-Book*, 248, pl. 298.

(*k*) *E.g.*, in Dublin and Waterford about 1300 : the disavowed *countour* " shall be sent to prison " or by favour of (mayor and) the bailiffs shall be fined 10s. : Gilbert, *Hist. & Mun. Docts. Ir.*; Rolls, 257; Bateson, 2 *Bor. Custs.* 12; 21 Seld. Soc.; for Ireland see p. 272.

(*l*) 2 Br. *Note-Book*, pl. 131, p. 113 (a " rare notice of the *narrator* " : Maitland); *ib.* vol. 3, pl. 1106, p. 123.

(*m*) P. & M. *ib.* p. 195, citing *Abbrev. Plac.* 137 : " non fuit advocatus : ideo in misericordia."

(*n*) Gross, 2 *Gild Merchant*, 7 (1890).

countor because he is disavowed by the said Moses is in mercy " (*o*). Such scenes are of course rare; they mark a developing system.

These are instances where both the representative and the party have something to say in public, midway between Edith's case where she comes into court and repeats what she has been told to say and the later type of case where the court will hear the party or the representative, but not both. And what the parties say in the above instances— that they no longer require the services of the *narrator*—is, perhaps, a sign that he did not yet belong to an organised or privileged class. He seems in the vague nondescript period to be regarded as Jebb (*p*) tells us the Roman *advocatus* was (and so does the *attornatus*).

Then there is a conference, not like Edith's (above), but between opposing lawyers, while a case is proceeding. In 1292, when Howard and Louther are arguing (*q*), the former says at a point, " We will imparl "—and immediately adds, " Sir, to ease the court we tell you, etc."— very much as if the two counsel had gone aside or outside and agreed upon some point (with or without the consent of the parties).

In 1313-4 Hartlepool says : " With your leave we will imparl (*conceileroms*) with [the counsel of] the twelve of the first assize. . . ." Thereupon defendant " and his counsel consulted with those of the twelve, etc., and they returned into court . . ." (*r*). Again, in that case they went out to imparl and came back. The touch of going

---

(*o*) *Select Pleas of the Jewish Exchequer* : 15 Seld. Soc. 54. Isaac apparently was an officious compatriot; possibly in the Exchequer of the Jews (exceptionally) any Jew could appear for any other, but probably in 1270 it was open for any friend to appear as a *narrator* in any Court. *Advocatus* has come to mean *properly* appointed; the old technical sense is disappearing.
(*p*) P. 2e.
(*q*) Y. B. 20-1 E. I, 51.
(*r*) Y. B. 24 Seld. Soc. lxxix, 165, 175; at p. 175 " *they* went out " probably means counsel.

out to a *consilium* is as old as L. H. P. (*s*). We know that
" imparling " went on much later; parties still " come to
terms."

Now and then, too, it is noticed—a significant fact—
that there was no *advocatus* in the case. Matthew Paris (*t*)
calls attention (*u*) to Richard of Cornwall in 1227 hurrying
off to Henry III and arguing *rationabiliter* and *eloquenter*,
yet *sine advocato*; if the occasion was not a trial, the point
was, as he said, a legal one.

If the *serviens* became known to the public in the gradual
way here suggested, we can understand why we never hear
of the language difficulty (at any rate, since Vacarius's day)
—because it did not exist; the ordinary *serviens regis* would
know some Latin, French and English. A good many lay
litigants would only know English; they would increase as
time went on. Some would only know Anglo-Norman; they
would probably decrease in the same way—we cannot tell
the proportions between the two; not many would know
Latin. At any rate, those who wanted a representative to
address the court must find one who could speak its
language. Thus the *narrator* would only represent his
friend where we knew the tongue of the court. The class
which was tri-lingual was the *clerici*, especially the paid
clerks, who, since the Confessor's day, had been growing
up in the royal palaces and the Chancellery in increasing

(*s*) 48, 1, a, b, c; see App. III. So in the Leicester Borough Court (1277) defendant " if he wishes to take counsel and plead [=*enparler* : so Miss Bateson, 1 *Leic. Rec.* 157, and 21 Seld. Soc. 6, but in old transln. *Leic. Rec.* " emparle "] let him do it by leave and *come back again* to say what he knows may avail him "; the only *legal* consultee would be an *attornatus*, p. 259*p*.

(*t*) *Chron. Maj.* iii, 124; 1 P. & M. ii, p. 191, n. (3).

(*u*) Just as in 1794 a reporter expressed his surprise that the noble defendant in *R.* v. *Ld. Abingdon*, 1 Esp. 226, appeared without any legal assistance. In *Abp. of Canterbury* v. *Bp. of Rochester* (1253), p. 198, the plaintiff argued in person (like his brother of York in 1887 : 20 Q. B. D. 240) and so did the defendant. In 1473 Clarence and Gloucester argued so well against each other *coram rege* that even the lawyers were surprised : Cont. Croyland, 557; Eng. trans. 470.

numbers. It is from that class, that kind of employee, that first the *attornatus* is preferably chosen, and finally the bar is created. " That there was already [say, 1220]," says Maitland (*x*), " a flourishing law school at Oxford is certain; that Bracton may have been of it is not unlikely, but quite unproved; but he may well have got his law, as some of his greatest contemporaries got theirs, namely as a clerk in the King's Court or the King's Chancery. To suppose that he made his fame by ' practising at the bar ' would probably be an anachronism."

Perhaps we can catch a glimpse of the developing publicity of the *serviens*. In the contemporary *Chronicon Petroburgense* (*y*) of 1280 Gilbertus de Torentona (Thornton) *attornatus d. r. dicebat* (*a*); in 1285 and 1286 Gilbert *sequitur pro rege* in trials (*b*). In 1281 and 1282 contemporaries call him and another *narratores* and *servientes* in a trial; "King's Serjeants" Foss (III, 94, 163) calls them. We cannot expect the same technical knowledge in a chronicler-monk as in recording officials, but it is odd that both avoid (*c*) the title *serviens*; apparently about 1280 it was not in universal use. But the title was familiar in some quarters, and one indication of the fact that before 1300 the profession is generally recognised comes from the provinces (*d*), which possibly were not so familiar with it as London. In 1297, in an action (*e*) for conspiracy against Thomas le Mareschal

---

(*x*) 1 *Note-Book*, 17.
(*y*) Camd. Soc. (1849), pp. 42, 125, 141, " Gilbertus etc " (125); etc. = *attornatus* or *narrator* or *serviens*.
(*a*) So Dugdale, *Chron. Scr.* 27, citing *Plac. de quo warr.* 8 E. I, *Rot.* 2 *Nott.*; and *ib.* of W. de Giselham in 1279; both judges in 1289 and so " the first example[s] of ' King's attorney ' being raised to the . . . bench," Gilbert to " the highest place " : 3 Foss, 18.
(*b*) These entries are probably contemporaneous : *ib.* p. vii; Dugd. *Chron. Ser.* 27, makes him " att. r." in 1280 : *Rot.* 2 *Nott.*
(*c*) As the City scribes seem to do, p. 230.
(*d*) P. 262.
(*e*) *Cor. Rege* Trin. 25 E. I, *Rot.* 22; cited in full, Manning, *Serviens*, p. 280, and in part printed *Abb. Plac.* 237a.

and others at Oxford, Thomas is described as *narrator in curia Oxon.* which must mean that he practised locally and was consulted by the local officials—*et frequenter assidens (f) in banco cum ballivis ejusdam ville ad judicia facienda*—and he was sued for maintenance, embracery, champerty and conspiracy, with the other defendants, in respect of an action which had been brought by one John Richardson against one Thomas Thomson at a previous assize. *Narrator* Thomas's answer simply was that he had acted as counsel for John; he " put himself on the country " pleading that " he is *communis serviens narrator* before the justices and elsewhere where he is wanted (*g*); at the aforesaid *assisa* he was with (*stetit cum*) the aforesaid John and was of counsel (*de consilio*). And therein he helped him as much as he could as his (*suus*) *serviens* and as is lawful for such *servientes* to do in such cases . . ." (*h*); *i.e.*, he did not, *e.g.*, offend (*i*) against the practice or the Act of 1275; and he traversed any illegality whatever. It really looks as if in these early days it was not always understood what the function of the *serviens* was, and sometimes he was taken for an officious meddler. There is another instance (*k*) from Lincoln in 1300-1. One William de W. sued two *magistri* (*i.e.*, persons of position (*l*)) William de H. and John of Maldone, in the King's Bench, in much the same way; William de H. brought an action against W. de W. in the King's Court, but defendant had succeeded; then the two " maliciously " had him cited in

---

(*f*) Cf. " assessor," p. 232.
(*g*) " ubi melius ad hoc conduci poterit " perhaps = where he is better hired (paid).
(*h*) " sicut talibus servientibus in hujusmodi casibus bene licet."
(*i*) Coke, 2 *Inst.* 214, gives many instances of such offences.
(*k*) *Abbrev. Plac.* 295b, cited Manning, *Serjeant*, p. 170.
(*l*) This approximate paraphrase is suggested. Manning, *Serjeant*, p. 298, cites Rot. Pat. of 1253 (*Cal. Pat. Rolls* (1247-58), p. 193) "servienti nostro magistro P. de B." etc., and adds, " therefore not *serviens ad arma* but a gownsman, *s. ad legem*," but this is clearly incorrect for de B. was the King's " buyer." *Cal. Pat. R.* 678.

another court (that " of the Archdeacon of the Bishop of Lincoln ") for the same cause. *Magister* John de M., who is not otherwise known, replied that he is a *communis advocatus* and *stetit cum* the other *magister* " pro suo dando " (*m*). The other *magister* lost his case and had to pay William 24 marks, but John was acquitted or *quietus* because he was " a common advocate."

It is odd that he does not call himself either *narrator* or *serviens* and that he is officially described as *magister*. It might be conjectured that he was only an ecclesiastical " advocatus " (and though the epithet *communis* makes this less likely it does not forbid it); in any case, it is strange that William did not recognise that John was privileged to recommend a lawsuit; it looks as if very little was known of the new profession in Lincolnshire in 1300. John himself does not seem to be very conspicuous.

At any rate, here we see the professional lawyer and pleader in full swing, " waiting to be hired," exercising his traditional and titular function of pleading in the old-fashioned way, and conscious that he is subject to authoritative discipline.

That pleading only a very determined specialist (*n*) could understand. Wherever one opens the (printed) Year Books (*o*) one sees literally the intricate interlacing of law and pleas (to say nothing of the facts of the case) and realises that the mystery and the secrecy of the early systems which, we saw, were a legacy from the oracular hieraticism of the ancient world, have been, logically

---

(*m*) So *pur son donant*, p. 191-2.
(*n*) See, *e.g.*, Horwood's pertinent example (Y. B. 30-1 E. I, xxvi-vii), where he refers to Stephen on *Pleading*, which see in 6th (1860) ed. 394, note (25) (ed. 1824, note (38)); 2 P. & M. 613, B. II, c. 9, § 4. For an actual instance of amendment of mistake in court see 29 Seld. Soc. xx, 81 (1313); cf. 17 Seld. Soc. xiv-v (1307-9), and p. 198. The Provisions of Oxford (1257-8) enacted : " les brefs seient pledez solum lei de la tere " : St. *Sel. Ch.* 382.
(*o*) *E.g.*, Y. B. 16 E. III, Pt. 2, p. 78; Rolls, 1342. " Shardelowe. We must know how you plead, etc."

perhaps, but exuberantly developed into a science now lost—some lawyers would say not happily—but whose linear descendants have survived into our own times and included, at only a few remoter stages in the descent, heirs whose full-blooded features harked back to their origin. Moreover we are at present wholly in the realm of oral statements—of claim, defence, etc.—and the traces of that orality are visible in our formulae to-day. Defence especially demanded a mechanical contradiction (*p*). It was a concession when Britton (*q*) suggested that in appeals " it shall be more necessary for the appellor to set forth the words orderly without any omission . . . than for the defendant in his defence, and in every felony we allow the defendant to defend the words of the felony generally, without treating him as undefended, so that for default of a word or syllable he be not adjudged undefended . . ."; but he is encouraged to plead in abatement of the appeal, that it has omitted to name " the year, day or place " or has named " one name instead of another " or set " forth the appeal thus ' This showeth unto you John ' where he ought to say ' John appeals ' or by closing his appeal by these words ' and this I will aver ' instead of saying ' this I offer to prove ' or for variance " (one form used before the justice and another in the coroner's roll).

The following passage by Maitland illustrates graphically the pleader's " job " in court. " In the days of oral pleading, in the days of Ed. II . . . we are tempted to say that argument precedes pleading or that pleadings are evolved in the course of argument. We have at this point

---

(*p*) In 1244 (1 *Lib. Alb.* 115, B. I, Pt. 2, c. 57; Rolls) it was held at an *Iter*—" *si . . . culpatus non defenderit* nominatim *tollagium* [illegal] *quamvis defenderet* de verbo in verbum "—he shall lose. So in 1278 it was argued (*Abb. Plac.* 194b): *quando aliquis solebat implitari in com'vel hundred' baron' vel alibi nisi defensor defendat querelam sui adversarii* de verbo in verbum *statim esset convictus*. Bracton (B. III, Tr. 2 de Cor. c. 27; II Rolls, 480) : *B. defendit totum* de verbo in verbum, etc. . . . *et tunc petet . . . vel se defendat* : so *ib.* p. 488.

(*q*) B. I, c. 23, 7, 8; 1 Nichols, pp. 101-3.

to recall the important fact that the pleader, the *narrator*, does not in any strict sense of the term ' represent ' his client. If a litigant appears by attorney, that attorney does represent his claim. By a solemnly recorded act he has been put in the litigant's place ' to gain or lose ' in that action. But the *narrator* is merely a friend who ' is of counsel with ' the litigant and the record takes no notice of him. [NOTE.—When a fine is levied the *narrator* is named. This we suppose to be a precaution against malpractice in a matter in which the utmost good faith may be required since strangers may be affected by the fine.] Consequently what he says does not bind his client unless and until the client by himself or his attorney ' avows ' it. This gives an opportunity for what we may call tentative pleading. Counsel for the defendant, let us say, experimentally offers a plea. Some little discussion ensues. He discovers that the opinion of the court is against him, or, in other words, that if he definitely pleads that plea, he will be defeated. So he will not ' abide ' (*demorer* (s)) there; he will not let himself be ' avowed ' by his client; he tries some other line of defence . . ." (t).

We may presently be able to illustrate some of the strokes of this picture as it dissolves from *attornatus* through *narrator* to *serviens*.

That process was not complete when in " the stride " of the movement for reform of the bar now—1276 to 1280— becoming more and more tangible, the discipline of pleading was attempted—a recognition that it had become a fine art.

(s) Philologically *demur*, though here the reverse.
(t) 20 Seld. Soc. lxxvi (1309-10). The whole of this passage is of extraordinary interest : *e.g.*, " The introduction of written pleadings is an episode in English history which . . . if we may so say, forced our common law into a prison-house from which escape was difficult."
Mr. Bolland's summary (*The Year Books*, p. 20 (1921)) is instructive. " Pleading . . . had something of the nature of a game of chess between experts, after they came into court. . . . Not even the Serjeants themselves who were fighting the cases in court knew upon what pleas they would finally have to rely "; and see the whole passage.

Accepting as a fact that there was a science of apt words (without being able to trace its descent through every stage), we may note how in due course it tended to specialise the writing or speaking pleader's work and, in his early days, to mark him off more and more from the unprofessional representative. Again, we realise the institution from its abuse; " to plead for " a man has never required any art, but as primitive appeals for justice or mercy became a normal part of litigation, like every other, it had in time to be regulated and that by checking excesses. Of these the chief was *miskenning*.

" Amplius non sit meskenninga in Hustengo neque in Folkesmot neque in aliis placitis infra civitatem " runs the Charter (*u*) of Henry I to the City about 1131 (§ 11 otherwise § 8).

Of this, the oldest extant mention seems to be that in 1114-8. The famous statement that quibbling was at its worst in London (the City?) is not only an indication of the large business done there, but is borne out by many confirmations, after Stephen's formal prohibition (*x*) in 1136, to be found in the *Liber Albus*; the tendency to " pick holes " in an argument or document springs eternal in the forensic breast, and the citizens took occasion from time to time to repeat the unsubtle Stephen's veto, for, apparently, it was not entirely effective even in London.

After that of 1131 (*y*) comes Bristol's in 1188; Thomastown in 1210 (about) (*z*). Who the persons aimed at,

---

(*u*) 1 *Lib. Albus* (Rolls), p. 129; Riley, Transln. p. 115. See for "Q." or *L. H. P.* (1114-8) App. III.

(*x*) *Teste* Richard of Hexham, 314, *fl.* 1141.

(*y*) It is the first of a series of prohibitions down to 1461-83 in Miss Bateson's 2 *Borough Customs*, 1; 21 Seld. Soc.; *ib.* p. cxlix. Stephen used his Coronation Proclamation, *i.e.*, to the whole realm. The instances between 1100 (or 1135) and 1210 are collected 1 *British Borough Charters* (1913), p. 146, by Ballard : " Miskenning and Faulty Defence," *i.e.*, *stulta responsio* (Newcastle). Note that lawyers are not mentioned.

(*z*) " Nullus burgensis trahatur ad placitum per miskenninge. Item liceat omni burgensi piacitare sine mot [ac] ione " : *ib.* p. 2—" without using particular verbal formulas."

when Q. wrote, were we cannot be sure, but that their peccadillos had fallen on the *narratores* in their turn is certain from the comment (*a*) (probably contemporary) of the *Liber de Antiquis Legibus* on the (now) common form in Henry III's charter (1268), *viz.*, " videlicet si bene non omnino narraverint." So that by about 1300, Dublin (*b*) or Waterford spoke with authority thus : " . . . it may be a cause of miskenning if perchance it happens that a man sues at the bar and the other party answers him, the respondent might rise go out and imparl [(*en*)*parler*] once, twice and thrice, and at any time while the bailiffs are on the bench ; And if you wish to know what miskenning is I will tell you.

" If a man has said to the bench something which he ought not to have said, and he perceives that his count is not as good as it ought to be, he who does this can recover his count at any time while the bailiffs are on the bench, but not afterwards " (*c*). In 1221 we get the thing (but not the word) and Maitland's commentary (*d*).

" De villata Bristollie ne occasionentur 15^m," " that occasion may not be taken against them, that the judges will not be extreme to mark what they say or do amiss [they pay 15 marks to the Crown]. This is a fine for beaupleader, *pro pulchre placitando*. These fines became a

---

It is defined about the latter end of the 13th century as " mespris par oir u de fet " : Barth. de Cotton, *Hist. Anglic.* 439, xxi, lxxiv.

Other cities to claim the privilege are Lincoln in 1301, Berwick on Tweed, 1302; St. Peter's York, 1305 (confirming a charter of 1180); St. Mary Bliburgh York, 1319 and 1326 : 3 *Cal. Chart. Rolls*, 8, 28, 57, 414, 484; Drogheda, 1331 : *ib.* v. 4, p. 222. P. 28 of these (Berwick), " si non omnino bene narraverint " is translated " mistelling."

(*a*) Comment because these words are in no other text and are not of command but exposition.

(*b*) Gilbert, *Histor., etc., Documents* : Ireland : 1172-1320 : (Rolls) p. 250.

(*c*) Gilbert, *ib.* p. vii, n., cites from " an ancient hand " appended to John's charter to Dublin (1200) : " Mis-Kenningham—Hoc est quietus de amerciamentis et querelis in curia coram quibuscunque inordinate sive transcriptive prolatis."

(*d*) *Pleas of the Crown* (Gloucestershire), pp. 112, 154.

great popular grievance. At the parliament of Oxford [1257, " Petition of the Barons "] complaint was made against them : ' Justitiarii capiunt finem gravem pro pulchre placitando de quolibet comitatu ne occasione[n]tur.' Probably the fine paid by the burgesses of Gloucester, (case 464, *ib.*) is of the same kind, *viz.*, £5, Bristol £10; see Stat. Marlb. c. 11 " (*e*).

Probably the continuous anxiety of the City of London to protect good pleading was an effect of their equally continuous legislation to protect clients from collusion between their respective lawyers; the two evils sprang together from the novelty and indiscipline of a new profession just beginning to organise itself. Coke (*f*) loyally points out that the stigma is only on inferior courts. No difficulty would be felt about dealing with any abuse of procedure under the statute of 1275. In 1302, in a prosecution (appeal) for rape, counsel for defendant asked for judgment on " a bad count " (apparently the absence of a count). Sergeant Kyng intervenes and says that he had prayed for the benefit of the defect in the county court; Spigurnel, J., then sends the prosecutrix to prison " because

---

(*e*) Next note. The form in the *Annals of Burton* (1259), 1 *Ann. Monast.* 481, Rolls, is : " Provisum est insimul quod in itinere justiciariorum nec in comitatu nec in curia baronis nec libertatis, nec in aliqua alia curia aliquis aliquid capiat propter pulchre placitandum nec propter hoc quod aliquis non occasionetur." The form of 1257 above is repeated in several statutes, including 1 Westminster, c. 8, 1275.

(*f*) 2 *Inst.* 122 on St. Marlborough (1267), c. 11 : " nec in itinere justic', nec in comitat', in hundred', nec in curia baron' " shall fines be taken " pro pulchre placitand' "; " all fines incertain for vicious pleading, and for amendment thereof are wholly taken away "; hitherto justices in eyre, and the suitors in the courts mentioned " did use to set fines at their pleasure upon defendant or plaintife . . . and not upon the councell learned [but cf. note (*j*)] for vicious pleading; and the reason thereof was for that it was in delay of justice, and so a contempt to the court. . . . I have seene and doe know in divers court barons, etc., fines certain for *beaupleder* paid to this day " [1628]. There was no need, he adds, of this sanction in the higher, the King's Court, where the work was well done; it only " extended to pleadings, and not unto counts and pleints," and only to the courts specified.

The theory of Reeves, 1 *Hist. Engl. L.* c. 8, p. 508, that " p.p.p."= for a favourable hearing, is untenable.

of her bad count"; defendant is discharged of her suit, but is ordered then and there to plead " to the King's suit," *i.e.*, an indictment, and as he is now " on the criminal or Crown " side, " Sheriff, put him in irons," says the judge. He pleads not guilty, puts himself on the country and the jury find him not guilty of all charges. " The justice marvelled that they gave their answer in such wide terms " but discharged him (*g*).

In 1310 the following dialogue is reported (*h*). " Hervey [Stanton, J.] to the attorney. Fair friend have you sued a writ? Att. : Yes, sir (*i*). St. : Where is your bill which witnesses it? (*h*) Att. : Sir, I sued no bill for I delivered it (note : perhaps, the writ) to my master (*mestre—dominus*—client). St. : What do you want then? Att. : Sir, I pray a *postea* (perhaps the summons : ed.) St. (to Att.) : You wicked rascal, you shall not have it! But because you, to delay the woman [Plf.] from her dower, have vouched and have not sued a writ to summon your warrantor this Court awards that you go to prison. Att. : Sir, I pray that I may find mainprise. St. : We will have no mainprise, but stay [in gaol] until you are well chastised." This is in the spirit of the judges of 1201 and 1225. We may believe Wilby (*j*), a judge, who said in 1351 :

(*g*) Y. B. 30-1 E. I, 520; the form of report, mere loose notes, is significant of its origin.

(*h*) 22 Seld. Soc. 195, ed. G. J. Turner, who cites from the Com. Bench Rolls of Hil. 1310 : porrexerunt coram justic. quandam billettam *de attorn. admittendo* in hec verba—I de P. et M. uxor ejus ponunt loco suo R, de W. versus E. que fuit uxor R. de R. de placito terre (De Banco Rolls, No. 180r. 18d).

(*i*) *N.B.*, not " my Lord."

(*j*) Coke, Preface, *Booke of Entries* (1614), citing (part of) W.'s speech from Y. B. 24 E. III [Pt. II] f. 48 and " 10 *dors*, Essex de Banco " of 1221 : " R. de Bardfield narravit pro filio J." and was " in misericordia *pro stultiloquio*, which and many other Records doe prove that the fine in those dayes was set upon the councellor and not upon the client . . . who therefore lost his Cause "; see 3 Foss, 537, who (v. 2, 27) gives other instances of fines *pro stultiloquio*, one in 1205, *Rot. de Oblat. et Fin.*, ed. Hardy; but, as he says, there is no certainty that the amerced were lawyers.

" speaking to the Councellours at the barre ' I have seen the time when if you had pleaded an erroneous plea you would have gone to prison [but you hold (*tenes*) us for fools ']."

Though the substantive law of the day is not within our purview, we may ask for what kind of law the *servientes* were wanted. Mostly for points arising out of the feudal tenures of land complicated by the social arrangements (marriages, etc.) springing from the gradual fusion of the races; hence most of the suits in the early Year Books and earlier relate to real property, naturally to a large extent ecclesiastical property—" Rent, Rent, Rent " (*k*). Thus Maitland classified the actions recorded in the early years of Henry III in Bracton's *Note-Book* (*l*) under the following heads (*m*) : " (1) Writs of Right; (2) Dower; (3) Writs of Entry; (4) Assizes of Novel Disseisin and of Nuisance; (5) Assizes of Mort d'Ancestor, Nuper Obiit, Cosinage; (6) Assizes Utrum; (7) Assizes of Darrein Presentment, Quare impedit, &c.; (8) Miscellaneous Proceedings, most of which are reckoned in later days as real or mixed actions, but some of which are closely allied to trespass; (9) Personal actions, including actions on Fines and Warrantia Cartae; (10) Criminal Proceedings; (11) Proceedings of an Appellate Character, including attaint Error, False Judgment, &c.; (12) Prohibition." Under No. 10 are included appeals of felony (*n*), the exact steps in which are not clear. But it is certain that when there was a point of law to be argued lawyers were heard on both sides, *e.g.*, in 1308-9 Herle (or Hartlepool), well-known serjants, and " Asseby " appear in an appeal of homicide (*o*). The substance of the Year Books does not differ much from this material—obviously, for the larger part, the litigation of the well-to-do.

(*k*) *The Age of Bronze*, Byron.
(*l*) V. I, 177, preceded by a Table of the Cases in Fitzherbert.
(*m*) Each duly subdivided *ib*.
(*n*) See esp. 2 P. & M. B. II, c. 9, § 1, p. 570.
(*o*) Y. B. 17 Seld. Soc. 42.

THE SERVIENTES. 211

Thus the chief work of the *Servientes* seems to have been argument (*p*) in court, often on and in the terms of the writ (*q*).

It is likely enough, as Coke said (*r*), that in Edward III's time they " drew their own pleadings " and probably they " opened the pleadings." Something of this sort Coke must have meant when he told the assembled serjeants in 1614 : " Seriants in old Tyme did first plead and after the exceptions thereunto openlye made and the pleading agreed upon the Prothonotary did sett the pleading downe " (*s*).

No doubt written pleadings came in gradually, and it was obviously convenient that the man who had to use them in court should have a hand in composing them; otherwise it would have been pointless to send a bad pleader to prison.

They did not examine (*t*)—still less did they cross-examine—witnesses; into the difficult question of the position of witnesses in, say, 1300, we cannot enter, but whoever took that kind of evidence they did not. If any line can be drawn between civil and criminal, of defence of prisoners there was none—except in a sense, in appeal; misdemeanours are practically trespasses till, apparently, about 1250 (*u*), and of very small account compared to felonies. No doubt the lawyers were spared the trouble of asking questions, because even primitively this was the

---

(*p*) In the records as a rule only the contention is stated, not the argument.

(*q*) Hence probably " brief," *i.e.*, notes or comments on the writ (*breve*). In " Political Songs " (Edw. I, Camd. Soc.), in a satire on the " Consistory Courts," p. 156, there are forty (clerks)—
    " to write (*breven*) my bales (my misdeeds?) . . .
    And sayen y am breved and y-broht yn . . ."
(" I am briefed and brought in of all my fair wealth," transln.). N. E. D. has the word " of uncertain sense " in 1225.

(*r*) *On Littleton*, 304 b.

(*s*) Inderwick, 2 *Cal. I. T.* 348.

(*t*) Even till the Revolution, and perhaps later " cross-examination was hardly understood at all " : Stephen, 1 *Hist. Cr. L.* c. 11, p. 382; cf. p. 431.

(*u*) Maitland, *Equity*, pp. 342-3, 348.

privilege of the judge (x). " The court's habit of interrogating the parties or their attornies, of thus eliciting fatal admissions and saving the trouble and cost of trial may seem very rational to us and perhaps very strange, though Coke (y) has noticed it, and we may be surprised at the ease with which third parties intervene of their own accord or are summoned to declare whether they claim any right " : Maitland (z). It would not be surprising if this sort of interrogation led gradually to cross-examination by counsel, who must have intervened from time to time to correct.

A distinction has been drawn, for which we should like authority before adopting it. Mr. G. J. Turner remarks (a) of the Serjeant of 1311 : " it was " his " business to address the court in certain prescribed forms and to plead and reply to exceptions to the action or the writ. On the other hand, the advocate at the trial of an issue was concerned not with the law but with the facts. *He addressed the jury*, not the Judge. The trial took place in some term subsequent to that in which issue was joined, and in some respects it might almost be regarded as another case. The trial called for none of the special learning of the serjeant-at-law; and it is obvious that the interests of the parties to the trial of an issue in the Bench could have been as efficiently protected by other members of the legal profession as they were at the trial of an issue at *nisi prius* in the country." If this scheme ever prevailed it would seem to be very much later than 1311. No authority, legal or

---

(x) *E.g.*, the City Sheriffs " usent dexaminer les parties en touts accouns (*actions*) personelx," if either demands it, and proceed to judgment, *par examinacoun: Lib. Alb.* p. 217; Rolls, B. III, Pt. 1—apparently before counsel practised in their courts.

(y) Co. *Lit.* 304 a : " The questions moved by the court and the answers by the parties werq also entred into the rolle."

(z) 1 *Note Bk.* 132; 2 P. & M. II, ix, 4, 667-8. He adds : " It will perhaps be doubted whether the history of legal procedure has been the history of an unbroken progress, whether the necessary growth of a class of professional lawyers, if it did much good, did not also some harm."

(a) Y. B. (1311); 42 Seld. Soc. lxiii.

literary, is advanced for the novel theory that the "advocate" addressed the jury, and it would seem that none can be found till long after our period. Records and historians, especially religious ones, *e.g.*, Bromyard, are constantly denouncing the perfidy of juries, and their susceptibility to advocacy, which has gradually become the prize of the forensic orator, would assuredly not have escaped their lash, had it existed, nor their relations *inter se*, had there been any. How these sprang up is not within our scope.

The same learned writer has sketched the forensic relations of serjeant and attorney (*b*). In the Year Books, he tells us, the latter is mute; the former does all the talking, at most and rarely the former avows the latter. But in the Plea Rolls it is the reverse : " whatever is there said is put into the mouths of the actual parties to the actions or, and more frequently, into the mouths of their attorneys (*c*), their personal representatives, with full power to bind them." In a short (imaginary) sham fight which follows the attorney is not mentioned, but he must be behind or near counsel; he must know the facts when he purchased the writ, and to the facts the learned serjeant, after arguments, may be driven. " The mediaeval serjeant very seldom began by relying on the material facts of his case. He would exhaust every possible defence based on points of law before he would take his stand on the facts, no matter how strong they appeared to be; but he was very careful not to carry his objections on points of law to the extreme point of demurring on them, unless he felt pretty sure . . . that the Court was in agreement with him; or else with facts behind him strong enough to win his case he might lose it by an adverse ruling of the Court without ever getting an opportunity of setting up his facts."

(*b*) 43 Seld. Soc. x-xi; such a sketch is valuable as a theory of procedure, but convenience would modify details according to the circumstances—as it does to-day and must in any rational system.

(*c*) Cf. Herle's remark, p. 328.

In 1313 there is an instance of the relationship which is very much like the modern one. *R.* v. *W. Bovill,* says Mr. Turner (*d*), is "unique in giving us a confession by the King's representative of his own helplessness without the serjeants at his elbow." The King is suing in the King's Bench for the right to an advowson; John of Hoo *sequitur pro rege,* defendant has his *attornatus,* John Ward; the two " have it up and down " for a long time; at last John says that he cannot reply to William's (*sic*) arguments without further instructions from the King; there is an adjournment; at the next hearing, John says that John of Westcote and the other *narratores de consilio* of the King are not here because they " are engaged in another court " to wit, that of the Eyre at Canterbury, and that without them he cannot (*nescit*) reply to William; another adjournment; the same thing happens *de novo*; the serjeants never appear, but defendant " throws in his hand." On this Mr. Turner observes : " Obviously John of Hoo must have been allowed the ear of the Court while he made his repeated explanations, though not being a Serjeant, he had no right of audience. Would the attorney of one of the King's subjects have been allowed a like licence? It is, however, perhaps incorrect to liken John to an ordinary attorney (*e*). Anyone fulfilling his functions is very rarely spoken of even in the reports as the King's attorney; is never so spoken of, I think, in the Plea Roll." A little earlier in another case (*f*) in 1313 he infers that any subject of the Crown might intervene in its interests in a trial " if the counsel who was professedly charging himself with " those interests " himself failed to urge them."

(*d*) Y. B. 1313; 43 Seld. Soc. xliii, 131-3.
(*e*) Is not this to put too much weight on " sequitur pro " (instead of " att. pro ")? It may be merely a clerk's variation for so august a client.
(*f*) *Ib.* xxi, on *Ballingham* v. *Burghill,* pp. 78-81.

The report shows that an issue was whether a fine had been levied in the King's court; it is argued " that which is matter of record cannot be annulled by averment of a jury. Bereford, C.J. : In these circumstances we should willingly receive the humblest man of the people to challenge the fine and seek its annulment on behalf of the King." Both these cases, Mr. Turner thinks, show that he *qui sequitur pro rege* " has privileges that an ordinary man has not." That the King's justices leant towards the King was natural enough—in the latter case a writ had actually come ordering them to try it in the K. B.—but these instances hardly show it. Bereford, C.J., does not, in fact, admit a casual listener to intervene; probably we have not all his words in what was a mere " aside," and surely all that the reporter meant to express was that Bereford's sympathies being with one side on the merits, he characteristically (but rhetorically) exclaims that he will not have justice defeated for a technicality. And so of John of Hoo. We cannot admit that in 1313 any one class of men had exclusive audience of the court; John might be an *apprenticius*, a *narrator* (*ad hoc*) or even a serjeant or an *attornatus* (*ad hoc*), *i.e.*, a mere mouthpiece, but he certainly would be heard (especially, no doubt, for the Crown). Evidently the men briefed were not present and there was " a hitch "; perhaps, for that very reason, the court heard him—as in an emergency. Solicitors are sometimes heard to-day where counsel only have audience. But that monopoly certainly did not exist in 1313 and, if it had, the court could still stretch a point (*g*).

Out of court there was the *consilium* in the broad and in the technical sense; in any sense it must give rise to opinions on the case. One from the time of Edward I has

---

(*g*) It is suggested with deference that Mr. Turner ascribes too great rigidity to procedure in his period.

come down and is printed (*h*); it is by A(u)nger of Ripon who appears as counsel (*i*) in 1292 and elsewhere.

Thus about 1310, in the words of Maitland (*k*), " there are about twenty-four counsel in practice. So far as we have gone, a list of the lawyers who are named in the reports for a given year will be almost exactly the same as a list of the ' narratores ' whom the plea rolls will set before us as having levied fines in the same year; in other words . . . we have seen no trace of any class of counsel who have a right to be heard in some but not in all cases, in personal but not in real actions. Some lawyers were much busier than others; still it may be said that, with few exceptions, if a man's name appears once in these Year Books, it soon appears pretty often . . . it is not unusual to see three or four lawyers on the same side of the same case. In a truly important case near half ' the practising bar ' (*l*) may be retained."

The last words remind us that " precise statistics . . . could only be compiled with great labour," but the authority (*m*) who says this adds that some serjeants with large practice in the Common Bench do not appear in the Plea Rolls at all, and, after giving instances, that generally, however, the frequency of a name on those Rolls tends to show practice in the Bench. " Possibly the leading serjeants when overburdened with work declined to undertake such small business as that relating to the levying of fines."

The same words raise a point of interest. Perhaps there is another explanation of the great array in a truly impor-

---

(*h*) Y. B. 20-1 E. I, xviii-ix (Rolls); see 1 P. & M. II, i, § 13, p. 378.
(*i*) Y. B. 363.
(*k*) 20 Seld. Soc. xi.
(*l*) But see p. 220.
(*m*) Mr. G. J. Turner, 42 Seld. Soc. lxvi : he adds (43 Seld. Soc. lxiii) that a Plea Roll Record in 1313 (*ib*. 133) is " unique in giving us the name of a Serjeant retained in the case, the King's leading [n.b.] serjeant John Westcote."

tant case, and in 1300 would " half the bar " be a large number? This extravagance in counsel must have been confined to " heavy " cases (and therefore to wealthy clients). In the articles of complaint of the opposition to Edward II in 1321, read in French by Sir John de Bek, there is a passage (*n*) to the effect that the King now buys up all the lawyers while his ancestors were content with two serjeants only for their cases! We may consider the King a wealthy client, and the device of retaining able advocates merely to deprive the other side of them was an obvious trick (not yet in desuetude), but the general rule still is one client, one serjeant, at any rate, until the existing dual system is established. The " middling " litigant about whom Sir John was so solicitous would, no doubt, be content with one representative (*o*), and, despite Edward II's love of the profession, he would have been able to find him.

Another instance (*p*) of a wealthy client " briefing " on a large scale is the very interesting one of Bishop William of Wykeham. Lord Latimer was impeached in 1377; he " craved counsail and day, to have the articles in writing and withal he desired that he might answer by advisement "; but this William of Wykeham, ex-Chancellor, refused. Soon the tables were turned and that prelate was

---

(*n*) *Chron. Ed. I and II*, Rolls, ed. Stubbs, v. II, pp. 64, xviii, lxxxviii, by a Canon of Bridlington : rex horum consiliatorum instigatione *omnes* legum terrae *retinet defensores* et *peritos* quod si magnates vel *mediocre*s [n.b.] per regem fuerint implacitati consilium non habebunt, cum sui progenitores nisi duos tantum *serjantos* pro suis placitis tenuerunt; the Latin writer only professes to give the gist of this French speech, but these words no doubt were in it; they can hardly be taken literally.

In Y. B. 33 H. VI, 34 (1355), " Serjeants le Roy " appear for the Crown (and the Duke of Norfolk appears *par son attourney*).

(*o*) But Mr. Zane (1 *Sel. Ess. Angl. Am. Leg. Hist.* 659) says of the period (E. I—E. III) : " In almost every case there are two counsel on each side. In some cases there is a great array . . . . No one seems to lead but all speak."

(*p*) From a contemporary fragment appended to *Chronicon Angliae*, lxxii, lxviii : Rolls.

impeached for that (*inter alia*), "While he was chancelor of England, sundry tymes of his owne auctority he caused ye fynes in ye roules of ye chancery to be deminished and ye roules to be rased"; he, too, "craved day and counsell," but Sir W. Skipwith, the new "secundary justice of ye Kinges Common place," refused him on his own precedent in Latimer's case, but Lancaster admitting that that had been done in bad faith granted the application; "also if he wist not how to aunswear for himself, he shold take counsaile of such men of law as were able in his defence to declare his minde . . ."; a day or two later the bishop comes for trial "with the bishop of London to comfort him and some *sixc seriantes of ye lawe of his counsaile*." It is easy to detect their *consilium* in the defendant's answers.

In 1417 and other times there was a public complaint (*q*) that there were not enough serjeants to do the work. But for statistics of this sort perhaps the Year Books have not yet been sufficiently analysed. With this reservation it is interesting to read (*r*): "Sometimes different counsel appear at different times. In a great case of replevin [about 1310] Estrange Scrope and Westcote are for the defendant and Herle and Hertepol for the plaintiff at one time. At the next term Westcote and Huntingdon are for the defendant and Herle and Hertepol for the plaintiff. At the next term Westcote and Huntingdon are for the defendant, while the plaintiff has Kyngesham Warwick and Passeley. The lawyers who are practising at Westminster are also found on the circuit at the assizes."

That by about 1300 the rank of serjeant at law was officially established and generally recognised cannot be doubted. The rise of the *apprenticii* and of their settlements and their title would throw up that of the superior office in bold relief. Two incidents strongly confirm this view. In 1302 " the demandants lost their writ (*bref*) by

---

(*q*) 4 *Rot. Parl.* 107 b; see p. 340.
(*r*) Zane, *ib.* 659.

non-suit; because all the serjeants agreed that the writ could not be supported in this case " (s); there was a solidarity of the bar—they were, as we saw, *socii*.

In 1322 Geoffrey le Scrope, arguing a case, says (t) : " I hear from all the serjeants of England that it has been held, etc."; he tells the bench a point which has been talked about among his fellow-serjeants and, apparently, they approved of the decision; they meet often and discuss points of law. This natural fraternity is the embryo of a trade union.

By this time there was many a *hospitium* in which they (and their *apprenticii*) could meet, after hours, so to say. Fleta (u) tells us that there was a very stringent prohibition against receiving contested *praesentationes Ecclesiarum*. " No Chancellor, Treasurer, Justiciar or any one else of the King's Council or of the Chancery, *de hospitio, scaccario, itinere* [Eyre] or of any bench nor any servant (*minister*) *Clericus* of the King or any layman, etc.," was to have one. Undoubtedly the prohibition would apply to *apprenticii*; indeed, it is possible that by *de hospitio* they only are meant, the *servientes* being *de concilio regis* (and if so, practically, King's counsel). At any rate, here we meet a legal *hospitium* for the first time—1290 or earlier. Previously Fleta had told us that the King has besides those enumerated other *clerici* in his *hospitium* (x), as, for instance, in that of the Treasurer of his wardrobe.

The serjeants are a small wieldy body. " The most striking phenomenon is the smallness of the bar in active practice " (y). Hence, as we have seen, they are easy to consult, and so the Chancellor is very frequently ordered to

---

(s) Y. B. 30 E. I, 107, xxx.
(t) Y. B. E. II (Maynard), p. 464 : so Fitzherbert, *Abridgement*, f. 220a *Corone* 385 (1514) and almost *verbatim*, Coke *on Littl.* 25 b, adding "that is, by all the judges of the coife."
(u) II, 36; II, 14.
(x) P. 430.
(y) Zane (above), p. 655, of (about) 1300-50.

take their opinion (and that of others or of any he chose) about the answers to petitions (z). And this perhaps explains why in so many cases in the Year Books we get a number of them named, jumping up, as it were, and arguing without being told for whom they appear—" no one seems to lead," as Mr. Zane says. Perhaps it may be respectfully suggested that it is not because " half the practising bar is retained," but because so many of them are present and are glad to contribute to the solution of the problem; they are a small " happy family," *amici inter se* and *amici curiae* (a). Perhaps this is what Coke meant when he called the serjeants " judges of the coife "; bench and bar were at first all serjeants, for " if a serjeant appears in large practice he is almost certain to appear later on the bench . . . few great lawyers " (b) do not.

Even earlier we saw that bills in eyre assumed that professional representatives were always to be found for a fee—and that in the provinces the suppliants were not of the class to make fine distinctions between " counters," " pleaders " and " serjeants."

We are not without some indications of their discipline in action, though they are negative. In a case in 1293 counsel " swears by his hood," but this awful profanity was *sotto voce* and at the expense of an unreasonable attorney. The same volume has another instance (c) of counsel, Spigornel, saying to another, Heyham, who was against him, " By St. Nicholas "; but, no doubt, this, too,

---

(z) See the many references in Index to Rot. Parl. *Sergeant-at-law*, *e.g.*, in 1330, 1347, etc., normally to assist the Triers. In the great case of the Petition of Thomas, Earl of Salisbury, in 1414, the errors he assigned were referred by the King *servientibus d. r. a. l. tunc ibidem* [in Parliament] *presentibus* — only — to report on the law to the Chancellor; the King's Attorney is to assist them : 4 *Rot. P.* 189.

(a) The frequency of the *am. cur.* in early days seems to have been overlooked.

(b) Zane, p. 656. He instances Simon de Trewythosa as an exception : from Dugd., in 1335, citing *Lib.* 8 E. III, m. 1.

(c) P. 362; Y. B. 21-2 E. I, 480, xi; 17 Seld. Soc. xv-i.

was an aside. At any rate, this adjuration of the patron saint of lawyers (*d*) seems to be the limit of forensic emphasis. There is an almost total absence of heated altercation (*e*); when the opponent of Mutford Sjt. (*temp.* E. II) got hot and angry, the Serjeant said : " I learned this verse from one of my masters—*Lex vidit* (sic) *iratum*, *iratus non vidit* (sic) *illam* : Selde grendeth (grinds) well the lothe and selde pledeth well the wrothe " (*f*). Such mildness is significant, as the bench did not scruple to express itself forcibly (*g*). We had an instance in Hervey de Stanton (but he, by the way, had never been at the bar). In 1313 Inge J. says to Sutton, counsel : " You will do yourself no good by all this mere talk " (*h*). Horwood (*i*) gives other instances : one says to a bishop in 1371, " alez au grant deable." Bereford J. about 1300 " swore " frequently (*k*). These ejaculations were no doubt " asides "

(*d*) This title is sometimes given to St. Ivonius (Yves-Hélori) of Bretagne (or Ker-Martin), born 1253 A.D. He was really the patron saint of the poor, but the double title is significant of advocacy beginning with the unprotected; " the only advocate ever canonised " : Magnus, *Die Rechtsanw.* (1925), p. 5. His feast is still celebrated at Malta by the Chamber of Advocates there on December 17 : H. P. Macmillan, K.C., *Ethics of Advocacy*, 5 : Oxf. (1927). A hymn says of him,
" Advocatus sed non latro
Res miranda populo."
See Baring Gould, *Lives of the Saints*, v. 5, p. 305.

(*e*) But perhaps in the inferior courts in the City the more pushing lawyers sometimes jostled one another to get a hearing and encroached within the bar; cf. the now obsolete " Bear Garden " outside Judge's Chambers.

(*f*) Bolland, *Year Books*, 76-7.

(*g*) " Both judges and counsel were fond of swearing by God, by St. James or by St. Nicholas " : Holdsworth, II, 548. The reporter " notes, too, the smile with which Paston, J., pointed what he considered to be a mildly humorous illustration [" Mettons que si un home vent defouler votre femme vous justifierez de luy battre en defence de votre tres cher compagnon, *et subridebat* "] (1441) : and the wink by which Stanton J. conveyed to an attorney the best procedure for him to follow " : [1311] *ib.* p. 552.

(*h*) 43 Seld. Soc. 19.

(*i*) Y. B. 30-1 E. I, xxi.

(*k*) Bolland, *Bereford* (1924), 28-9, and see Zane, above, pp. 632—653, 671.

very congenial to student note-takers. Year-Book counsel are always very courteous to the bench (*l*), addressing it as " Sir(e)." But on a proper occasion they can " stand up to " it, too, polite but firm; thus when Toudeby Sjt. humbly disagreed with the law of the bench, he remarked (*m*) : " Not so did we learn pleading "; *i.e.*, I must go to school again. Wilby, perhaps an apprentice, arguing in 1459, speaks (*n*) of " my Master Choke " who was in the case.

Anticipating somewhat, we may trace the *cursus honorum* as it appeared to contemporaries of a *serviens*: " 1407-8. John Hals counsel (' jurisperitus,' ' consiliarius ') and in and after 1413-4 ' sergeaunt ' or ' serviens legis ' . . . appointed a judge of the Common Pleas in 1423 and of the King's Bench in 1424 (Foss) " (*o*).

Perhaps we may notice here a minor form of promotion (and emolument) which seems to be open to the bar, as its growth coincides with the improvement of legal machinery especially in the country. In 1334 a Parliament at York (enacted or) petitioned (*p*) that " in every county be

---

(*l*) Cf. *domini Judices*, pp. 73g, 55, and *Scenes in Court from the Year Books*, 10 L. Q. R. 63 (1924).

(*m*) Y. B. 32-3 E. I, 72 (1304).

(*n*) Y. B. 37 H. VI, f. 22.

(*o*) *Lawyers employed by Winchester College during the 15th century*, by H. Chitty, Bursar, p. 7, privately printed; see also *Notes and Queries*, Dec. 25, 1915; for Hals's fees, see p. 379. Other lawyers employed by the College are "advocatus," 1398-9; later he was in the Consistory Court, Winchester : a " notary " same date, and so an " attorney in the Common Bench," 1399—1400; " attorney in the Exchequer," 1400-1; " consiliarius," 1403-4; " jurisperitus existens de consilio Collegii " : see 4 Foss, 195.

Another instructive career is that of Robert Danvers, of Lincoln's Inn, of which in 1428 he was a Governor; in 1433 he declared before the Council that in 1431 " retentus fuit ad essendum de consilio of one T. S." (35 Seld. Soc. 97, where the edd. say that from 1428 " on he was active as attorney and litigant "; he says that as *unus de consilio T. S.*, etc., *sequebatur*); 1436, J.P. in Oxon and afterwards frequently Commissioner and Judge of Assize; 1442, Recorder of London; 1443, " a serjt. at law; 1444, a King's sergt."; 1445, M.P. for the City; 1450, Justice C.P.; cf. 4 Foss, 428.

(*p*) 2 *Rot. Parl.* 376; English only.

appointed one justice of the Peace learned in the law who shall be Chief " and " all Justices of the Peace may have some certain Fee "; another at Westminster (*q*) in 1344 enacted that " two or three of the best reputation in the counties shall be assigned keepers of the Peace . . . and at what time need shall be, the same with other wise and learned (*sages et apris de la leye*) in the Law shall be assigned to hear . . . Felonies, etc." This seems very natural to us, accustomed to the anxiety of county benches to get professional chairmen, but—as so often happens at this period—we do not find the theoretical system actually at work (*r*). Here and there no doubt it employed those lawyers who appear in the records, but are not heard of again.

Before reviewing the relations of *attornati, narratores* and *servientes* to each other, we will look at the actual state of things in

The City of London,

that great microcosm of our institutions.

All that William Fitz-Stephen (who died in 1190-1) tells us about the law in London is (*s*) " Concerning Causes in question, there are several places and courts (*loca sua, Fora singula*) for causes deliberative, demonstrative and judicial (*t*). Upon their set days also they have their Common-Council and Great Assemblies (*Comitia*)." If Foss (*u*) is right in suggesting that Fitz-Stephen was a

---

(*q*) 1 *St. R.* 301; cf. *ib.* p. 258, *Stat. Northampton*.

(*r*) However in 1341 Essex juries in accusing two local landowners " associated with Henry de Grey as Justices of *oyer* and *terminer* " of judicial malpractices, complain that this was partly due to Henry not being *homo legis* : Dorothy Hughes, *Early Years of E. III*, p. 233 (1915), citing Assize Roll, 258, m. 7.

(*s*) Stow's *Survey*, v. 2, App. C. ii = Strype, p. 679 (1755); 2 Kingsford's edn. (1904), p. 225.

(*t*) " Aristoteles . . . tribus in generibus rerum versari rhetoris officium putavit, demonstrativo, deliberativo, judiciale " : Cic. *de Inventione*, I, 5.

(*u*) I, 371.

Sheriff and often an itinerant Justice, his account of the City courts is oddly meagre. Unfortunately his literary successors (*x*) have not broken his silence. It is at least half a century before we get any more accurate information. We must needs infer what was ripening all this time from the fruit. " The City of London still [1155—1215] furnishes the type of the most advanced privilege and the greatest amount of illustrative detail. Yet even the history of London is obscure. . . . The real importance of London in this region of history is rather that it affords an example of *local independence and close organization,* which serves as a model and standard for other towns, than that it leads the way to the attainment of general liberties or peculiarly English objects " (*y*). Thus it would not be surprising if the City's local bar " gave a lead " to the rest of the forensic world rather than that the converse happened. And we may note that Fitz-Stephen emphasizes the existence of the very conditions which produce a flourishing judicature and bar : " almost all the bishops, abbots and noblemen (*magnates*) of England are, as it were, citizens and freemen of London. There they have fair dwellings and thither they do often resort and lay out a great deal of money; and are called into the City to consultations (*concilia*) and solemn meetings either by the King or their Metropolitan or drawn by their own business." This confirms the general assumption that John's acceptance of " the commune " woke London up. In 1189 under her first Mayor an Ordinance (*z*) was made settling the building rights of next door neighbours (by trial by jury) : litigants

---

(*x*) And predecessors (?) . . . " total darkness . . . covers the history of London in the Anglo-Saxon times and even in the reign of the Conqueror " : St. *Lect.* 123.

(*y*) St. 1 *Hist.* c. 13, pp. 704-7.

(*z*) *De placitato usitato in Civitate quod vocatur . . . assisa* : *Lib. de Antiq. Legg.* 181 (Camden Soc. No. 34); so 207, 210, " dicta provisio et ordinatio vocata est Assisa," as if the word was not yet established. Text also 1 *Lib. Alb.* B. 3, Pt. 2, pp. 319, 330 (Rolls); transln. (1861), pp. 277, 284.

(*litigantes*) are mentioned more than once (*agendo et defendendo*) but there is no suggestion of legal representation—except of minors by the time-honoured means of guardians.

Again, in the Table (*a*) of the City's Charters from Henry III two heads are (105) " as well foreigners as others may make their attorney, both to plead and to defend (agendo . . . defendendo) as elsewhere in the King's Courts. (114) The citizens of London shall have all their liberties and free customs, etc., *tam de forma et modo placitandi quam de aliis quibuscunque casibus*, provided always that such customs be not contrary to justice and rightful laws." It is difficult to conceive that the concession in these Latin words should not engender much legal argument.

No. 140 from Edward I is " the citizens may defend (*disrationare*) themselves against the pleas of the Crown, &c." No doubt if we had the Charters themselves we might find in them distinct references to the normal forensic incidents of litigation — especially as some continuous development of suits is visible (*b*). Yet with the single exception above (105) there are none (unless a bare recognition of the Common Serjeant, in Henry IV's reign be so called : 439) in the 484 *capitula* (a few of which are repeated) from William I to Henry V. Before 1413 no freeman of the City is to be " molested by bill except on those matters which concern Ourselves or Our heirs " (464). This is noteworthy because in 1393 the Crown lawyers are allowed other forensic privileges (*c*)—which at the same

---

(*a*) *Lib. Alb.* 138 (Rolls), B. II; transln. (1861), p. 120.

(*b*) No. 163 : judgments after verdict are not to be deferred unless there is some difficulty, and then not beyond the third court.

(*c*) See p. 235*w*, where the concession to the Crown and City lawyers (in cl. 11) seems so small that perhaps it refers to other clauses besides 11. Prosecution " by bill " (464) and *miskenning, passim*, do not necessarily imply technical advocates : the latter encourages them, but is a legacy from Saxon times.

time, the Corporation reserve to *their* representatives—an advance in its claim since 1280; the City lawyers of 1288 are quite unknown, but by 1310 they are the leaders of the profession.

But that kind of negative evidence may soon after be turned to account. In the *Liber Albus* (*d*) we find the Questions proposed to the citizens at an *Iter* in 1221 at the Tower, with their answers—written, no doubt contemporaneously but perhaps not copied into *L. A.* till 1231. This document is immediately and continuously preceded by a programme for such an *Iter* (though this word is not used) at that place whenever the King shall commission one: it may therefore be safely dated before 1221. Now there is still not the faintest reference to legal representation—and that when there was one opportunity after the other, if the institution had been known there. The City is spoken of as " Barones (*e*) et universitas civium Londoniarum ": the *Barones* are possibly pre-aldermanic (*f*); in any case, the word includes them and other " notables "; it cannot mean Aldermen of Wards exclusively, for they are expressly mentioned in the document (cc. 12, 17 and both in the latter), assuming it to be all of one date. It

---

(*d*) B. I, Pt. 2, 1 Rolls, 62; transln. 2 Rolls, 51, 45, ff. 16 A—19 A; (1861), p 55, f. 19 A. Compiled in 1419 by John Carpenter, a lawyer (or law-student), common clerk of (later M.P. for) the City.

(*e*) Muncipally, not cited by N. E. D. till 1259 (Latin, Mat. Paris); not apparently in *Lib. de Ant. Legg.*; still in use in the Cinque Ports. Of course both " ald." and " bar." are much older words than any date above; in Domesday Book, *barones* = tenants-in-chief; Round, *Feudal England*, 118; in the *Commune of London*, 253, he prints a charter (1189-90), where the *majores barones civitatis* [L.] are mentioned.

(*f*) The earliest mention in London seems to be " Jukelin, Aldermannus " under 1194 in *Lib. de Ant. Legg.* (begun in 1274); cf. under 1216, " factus est Maior Jacobus Aldermannus ": *ib*. 4; elsewhere, of York, 1130; N. E. D., which cites Madox, 1 *Exch.* 562, c. 14, for a long list of Aldermen of Guilds (London) in 1180. Palgrave, 2 *Commonwealth*, clxxxiii, gives a document of Henry II in which several members of a Husting Court are called " Halderman "; one, Peter, Walter's son, was Sheriff, 1174-6: Round, *Commune of London*, 253, whence it appears that there were Aldermen before 1190.

discloses a primitive jurisprudence—the tone is that of the XII Tables—which it is very difficult to attribute to the City at any date after the Conquest, and we are almost driven to the conclusion that the writer deliberately omitted all reference to legal machinery.

Thus " the superior (*magnates*) and more discreet persons of the city ought and of usage are wont to meet together at a certain and fitting place (*ff*) for the allaying of such strifes, rancours and discords, as have before arisen in the city; to the end that peace and friendship being thus renewed among them they may be in will and in deed, as one man and one people in preserving uninjured their persons, their customs and their liberties." A disturber of the peace is to be deemed by his fellows *hostis et inimicus publicus* and he *and his heirs* are to forfeit " the liberties of the city " for ever (*g*). This legislator knows the Common Council (*commune consilium civitatis*) its *Camerarius*, the Sheriffs and their *clerici*, the Common Clerk, a skilful *scriba* to write the rolls each year (which are to be safely preserved with the city's *chartae*). Citizens are to defend themselves *discrete et provise* before the King's Justiciars who try " the pleas of the Crown " and essoins. Three men " discreet and moderate " are to be elected, of whom one primarily is to present (*repraesentet*) the City's Case. Here, if anywhere, we should expect to have expert representation (*h*), especially as we get a line or two lower, almost technical language; when the judges have given the authorities the *capitula* the latter must get a day fixed, *ad se providendos et consulendos* for their reply, and in the interval they are to file carefully (*irrotulare et*

(*ff*) The Guildhall is not mentioned but the Tower is, *passim*: the Constable " Civitatis " perhaps=of the Tower.

(*g*) What he fears is that the King should take these liberties " into his own hand "; is this a voice in the troublous times of Stephen? Cf. Loftie, 1 *London*, 101.

(*h*) " per consilium civitatis ": C. 14, so 19, of an accused person is not technical.

imbreviare) the charges and their replies. And here the Notary is mentioned. Finally, the writer thinks it necessary to explain why there is " no *praesentator* " or " *inventor* "—he means, regular or official—" of felonies or other mishaps . . . as there is outside the City "; the reason is that in such a populous place the common people act at once before the police (*ballivi*) get the information, *i.e.*, private citizens lay the cases before the judges (as above) and not an official (for the *plebs* could not address the court); in other words there is no one public prosecutor (like the Common Serjeant later).

This programme is followed by eighteen " Questions proposed at the *Iter* " of 1221 to the citizens—there is no reason to doubt the date of the title which tells us that they were " also " enrolled at another *Iter* in 1231, with the answers; one pair has already been quoted.

As no record of either of these *Itinera* exists (at any rate, in print) we cannot check the details of this document, but it certainly shows an advance in forensic interests on the last. It frequently assumes the existence of a City court (*curia*), the Hustings—and, indeed of others, for it ends : " in other courts in the City there is no record of such a suit [by a widow], except only in the Hustings." It recognises the *Attornatus* but has very little for him to do whereas the essoiner is more prominent (and more unintelligible than ever), but there is an express statement that legal proceedings may be a very vexatious matter. It is not flattering to the profession, but that seems about the extent to which the City appreciated it in 1220-30.

Nevertheless, the profession must have been thriving in the City. Henry III gave his capital several charters (1 *Lib. Alb.* 134-9), of which many heads are still extant (*i*) in that of 1268. One in 1259, we are distinctly told (*ii*), not only renewed existing rights, but enacted *new* and

---

(*i*) 1 *Lib. Cust.* 251.   (*ii*) *Lib. de Ant. Leg.* 42.

inviolable ones, " namely, that for the future, no one should be obliged (*j*) to have a lawyer (*causidicum*) (*k*) in any plea had in the City whether in Hustings or other City courts, except in pleas of the Crown or in pleas about lands or wrongful seizures. But everyone shall [if he likes] make his complaint with his own lips and the other side, too, without any technical objection (*occasione*) so that the court, advised of the true facts, may do justice in the premisses. Moreover, if any *causidicus* shall stipulate for his remuneration any part of the [real] property involved in the case and is thereof convicted, he shall lose his fee and be suspended from practice (*officio*). Others (*l*), too, thus convicted shall lose their expected gain and be heavily punished."

Now, this entry is probably contemporaneous and, in any case, it seems to recall in its diction the *verbatim* text of the original. Hence, at first sight, it reads as if a lawyers' trade union in the City had attempted (and failed) to force the services of its members on reluctant litigants, but it would be so absurd to suppose that in 1259 there was any such claim to a monopoly, of which there is no trace, that it is simpler to understand the Chronicler, not himself a lawyer, possibly knowing that some such idea had got about and possibly believing it himself, as writing somewhat loosely but meaning that it never was the law that in the City Courts the parties must be represented, though in the named exceptions—the " heavy " cases, so to say—it was usual (and, perhaps, he means, to be recommended); we know that, at any rate, in pleas of the Crown,

---

(*j*) To this day on an application for a *mandamus* a litigant in person is not heard by the High Court : he must appear by counsel—" an inflexible rule," *per* L. Coleridge, C.J., in *Re Eardley* (1885), 49 J. P. 552.

(*k*) Quite possibly the writer means only an *attornatus*, and he may be correct on that point.

(*l*) Clearly not *causidici*; the sanctions against champerty by all sorts of persons at this time are far too common to cause surprise.

it was invariable, and, in some cases open to the defendant to be represented. At any rate, it is only meant to preserve the existing practice in Crown cases. In short, the passage above is a confused reminiscence of the facts and, perhaps, of the royal decree. If ever there was any such idea abroad it was scouted by the great pronouncement of 1280, which saves the right of the lay litigant to appoint a lay (*m*) representative and certainly does not forbid him to appear in person. It is, in any case, significant that the compiler notices these " new " clauses. What makes it almost certain that he was mistaken on the point of compulsion is that in the careful Charter of 1268 it is neither admitted nor prohibited.

The largest and perhaps the best picture of the forensic background (not to say of the whole stage) in 1280 is a remarkable French document in the *Liber Custumarum*, a City Ordinance (*n*) of that year (or very soon after).

But a preliminary word must be said on the nomenclature. Undoubtedly "Countour" and "Serjeant" are used as synonymous terms, but the former is by far the more frequent in City records. We have elsewhere suggested that City scribes tend to avoid the latter because it was intimately associated with *regis* (and they never use *serviens regis*); they had no feeling about it coupled with *civitatis*, expressed or implied; they probably liked to think that appointment on oath taken was as important as that by writ. " The Mirror of Justices " may not be an authority on contemporary law, but the author, in 1285-90, had no reason to invent " Countours are Serjeants wise in the law of the realm who serve the commonalty of the

---

(*m*) But a *Guild* Stat. of Berwick about 1280 forbade anyone to speak *de hoc quod tangat causam* except plaintiff and defendant (*reus*) or their *advocati* : 1 Bor. Custs. 43; 21 Seld. Soc.; *Advv.* may or may not = lawyers.

(*n*) *Munimenta Gildhallae Londoniensis* (1860), v. ii, Pt. I, 280, text : Pt. II, 595, translation (Rolls), ed. Riley; 1 *Liber Albus*, 570; translation, III, 223 (Rolls). Cf. City's *Letter Book*, A 204.

THE CITY OF LONDON. 231

people stating and defending, for hire (*loer*) actions in court (*actions en jugement*) for those who have need of them " (*o*).

The Ordinance of 1280, which we have in its original A* form, is thus translated (*p*)—" because oftentimes there were some who made themselves (*se firent*) countors who did not understand their profession nor had learnt it; as to whom the substantial men (*prodeshommes* : " notables " ?) of the city well perceived that through their ignorance the impleaded and the impleaders lost their pleas and their suits in the Hustings and in the houses [*hostiel* " meaning probably the Counters or Compters "] of the Sheriffs (*Viscountes*) and that some were disinherited through their foolish conduct; seeing that everyone made himself a countor at his own will, such an one sometimes as did not know how to speak in proper language, to the scandal of the Courts aforesaid which allowed (*q*) them so to be, A[1]

(*o*) 7 Seld. Soc. xxiv, 47, ed. Maitland. It is not a City document, but is supposed to have been written by Andrew Horn, Chamberlain of the City.

(*p*) From the French (Rolls). In dealing with City documents it is not always easy to decide—with a view of getting at the date—whether the French is translated from the Latin (to which the authorities generally incline) or *vice versa*. Thus the first French in the *Liber Albus* (1 Rolls, 43, c. 16 of B. 1, Pt. 1) refers to a point in c. 13 " of this First Book "; the reference is correct, but c. 13 is in Latin (and cannot be earlier than 1335); in the " Contents " the titles of both chapters are in Latin. It is improbable that the French writer would cite a Latin passage in *the same* compilation without mentioning the change of language. The learned Editor of *Liber de Antiquis Legibus* (Camden Soc. : 1846), p. i, says that in 1274 the original was written throughout in Latin and the remainder added at different times in French.

* Letters in the margin refer to later parts of this chapter.

(*q*) This looks like a hit by authority (as in the *Mirror of Justices*, 7 Seld. Soc. 48) at the want of dignity and the disorder—see A[2] and A[3]— of *inferior* courts. If so cf. Pliny, practising about 90 A.D. in the centumviral courts : " there are very few counsel with whom I care to argue " : Ep. ii, 14; and the whole letter. Cicero had already criticised in the *Brutus* (68), *fervido et petulanti et furioso genere dicendi*. On the abuses by the lower class of *causidici* about 330 A.D., see (generally, Forsyth's *Hortensius* (1849) and) Gibbon, c. xvii (ii) " advocates who filled the Forum with their turgid and loquacious

as also pleaders (*pledours*) and attorneys and essoiners and sometimes in the Sheriffs' Courts assessors and [thereby] each of them the judge of others (*chescun autri juge* (*r*)) privily or openly : through which, right was intercepted (*desturbe, wrested?*) by them; the Mayor aforesaid with his Aldermen and other substantial men of the City, at the request of the serjeants and countors, who understood their profession (*mestier*) and who therein felt themselves greatly aggrieved, has established that from henceforth such persons shall not be heard as do not reasonably understand their profession and how becomingly to manage the business and the suits of the substantial men; and that such person shall hereafter be admitted (*resceu*) by the Mayor and the substantial men aforesaid ; saving nevertheless unto each reputable man (*prodomme*) such counsel

A¹ (*counseil*) as he shall wish to have either from stranger or from denizen (*prive*) [and] such as he shall think proper to seek for his business. But that this ordinance and establishment shall hold good so far as our serjeants,

B attorneys and essoiners who generally frequent our courts and are constantly dwelling among us. And their will is that each one hold his own estate, that is to say, that no

C countor be an attorney or an essoiner and no essoiner a countor or an attorney.

The duty of a countor is as follows :—standing, to plead
D and to count courts and to make proffers (*profres*) at the bar (*la bare*) without baseness (*vileinie*) and without reproach and foul (*lede*) words and without slandering (*mesdire* : reviling?) any man, so long as the Court lasts.

---

rhetoric." Like Cicero, Pliny, Ammianus, etc., W. S. Gilbert had personal experience of " professional licence carried too far " and of essays " to hoodwink a judge who's not over wise."

(*r*) If the text is not corrupt, it seems to mean that persons who were not so well trained in the law as the countors (sheriffs, assessors, etc.) sometimes sat to determine points (probably small or interlocutory) —as we know the *servientes* themselves did ; their mistakes or perversions, as is obvious in the case of fraudulent essoiners or attorneys, might seriously hamper the progress of a suit.

THE CITY OF LONDON. 233

Nor shall serjeants or attorneys go further in front beyond A² the bar or the seat where their sitting is, nor shall anyone be assessor or sit near (*s*) the bailiff (*t*) for delivering (*rendre*) pleas or judgments, unless it so be that the principal bailiff who is holding the Court shall call him unto him [to consult], and in such case he shall make oath that he will support (*sustendra*) neither side.

Nor shall any countor or any other man counterplead or gainsay the records or the judgments, but if it appear to them that there is some error therein, according to the law and usage of the city, let them make complaint or representation unto the Mayor, who shall redress the error, if there be one, in the matter.

No countor is to undertake a suit (*plai*) to be partner E in such suit, or to take pay (*lower*) from both parties in any action but well and lawfully he shall exercise his profession. No countor or other is to gainsay the judgments of the Hustings or to go about procuring how to defeat (*u*) the acts (*fetz*) and the awards of the community. And F that this they will do the countors shall make oath.

He who shall be near the judge without being invited A³ or who shall counterplead (*contrepledera* : aver against?)

(*s*) See A³. Durand says (B. I, div. 4, cc. 6, 7, cited Horwood, Y. B. 32-3 E. I, xxviii) : " Some say that an advocate should frequently go and whisper to the judge so that he on the other side may fancy that they are talking about him and thus lose his temper," but " Durand does not approve this course." " If the plaintiff appear," says D., " you should sit down, not speak, pretend to be asleep, as cunning advocates often do; and when the judge bids you answer then slowly and wearily rise up as one just waked from sleep and entreat from the judge a favourable hearing," but " Durand does not approve this mode . . ." Durand copies this and other tricks from William of Drogheda. See pp. 161*ff*, and 297.

(*t*) The deputy.

(*u*) Cf. the prohibition to citizens from suing before the justices at St. Martin's-le-Grand (who seem to have been primarily judges of appeal from the City) " who are persons of the Common Law and cannot have full cognisance of the franchises and uses of the City "— which have *in fact* thus been imperilled : 1 *Lib. Alb.* 474; transln. III, 191. Here apparently *appeals* by lawyers are discouraged; the words perhaps include intrigues at court

the records and the judgments [or] who shall slander [revile?] another if [it be] in the Sheriff's Court shall be suspended for eight days, so that he shall count [=appear] for no one or else he shall be amerced by the Sheriff in half a mark. If [it be] in the Hustings he shall be suspended for three Hustings or more, according to the offence. He who takes from both parties and is attainted thereof shall be suspended for three years; where one takes [money] and then leaves his client (*let soun client*) and leagues himself with the other party and where one takes [money] and abandons (*faut a*) his client let such person return twofold and not be heard against the client in that plea. He who goes about procuring how to defeat (*u*) (*defere*) the awards and judgments of the community and is attainted thereof shall be for ever suspended and held as one perjured for ever. And the countor who undertakes a plea to partake (*partenir*) in the demand shall be for ever suspended if he be attainted thereof. The attorneys are to be liable to this same penalty, if they contravene this ordinance and be attainted thereof. If the attorneys by their default or by their negligence lose the actions of those whose attorneys they are they are to have imprisonment according to the Statute of the King (*v*). And no one who is an attorney shall be an essoiner and no essoiner shall be an attorney, under the pain aforesaid."

This enactment—of which there are many echoes (*w*),

(*v*) To which statute this refers is unknown. The mischief, no doubt, was due to the unrestricted right of attorneyship; somewhat later (probably under E. II) attorneys are to be sworn to do their work *sanz nulle manere de lachesse*, etc.: 1 *Lib. Alb.* 473; 3 *ib.* 191; transln. (1861), 407. Some time between E. I and E. III "sureties and mainpernors and attorneys received" in the Sheriffs' courts are to be "held of record" and any Alderman may "enter (*recorder*) attorneys in pleas" in any city court: *ib.* resp. 222; 56: 195.

(*w*) In 1305 it is textually cited *Letter Book*, cc. 147-8: "all Countors, Attorneys and Essoiners wishing to plead at and attend the Courts at the Guildhall" are to be sworn according to this ordinance, and five are so sworn (176).

There is a very loud " echo " " before 1340 " from Norwich showing

some from afar—is clearly not a mere scheme, but shows on the face of it a picture from real life.

With this ordinance we must read the statutes of 1275 and 1292.

Before extracting what we can from these documents, we may consider why from about 1270 the legal profession is so much in evidence both at court and in the City (x). We may suggest that the policy and the influence of two persons, *viz.*, Edward I and his Chancellor Burnell, had much to do with the shape circumstances took. With regard to the King, the following extract seems to express the general view of historians :—

---

that there were *servientes narrantes* (and *socii* against them) in the local court—" locals " apparently, for they (only, it seems) had to take the oath and could not appear *against* the town's franchises : Bateson, 2 *Bor. Cust.* 13; 21 Seld. Soc.

Another ordinance in 1356 is important in itself and as a commentary; " an immense Commonalty " was present : *Letter Book G.* 71. " (3) That plaintiffs (in the Sheriffs' courts) plead in English and may take the advice of counsel. (5) That no plaintiff be bound to pay anything for entering his plaint and that he be ready to prosecute his plaint either himself or by attorney, without having essoin and defendants to have one essoin and no more. (11) That no Pleader (*Countour*), Attorney or Essoiner shall be heard to plead within the Bar of the Sheriffs' Court, but they shall stand without the Bar without making outcry or noise so that the men of law and good folk of the City may be heard in due manner as to their businesses which they have to transact in the said Court. [The learned editor quotes from 1 *Lib. Alb.* 522 where, after an almost literal transcript of cl. 11, it is added " always except those who are appearing (*vullent suire*) for the King or the City "; the editor dates this addition—and presumably the long Ordinance in which it appears—in 1393-4, correctly it would seem : Riley, transl. (1861), p. 447, dates " H. VI."] (12) That no Attorney sit in the Husting among the clerks nor meddle with the rolls or other memoranda. (15) That Pleaders and Attorneys take reasonable fees from their clients and not more than 40 pence. [" A maximum then . . . . It was sometimes a Serjeant's fee—though that on occasion rose to 10s. . . . The attorneys could not expect always so much as 3s. 4d." : Christian, *Solicitors* (1925), 35.] (16) That no Pleader or Attorney advise or compel anyone to make a false prosecution on pain of being suspended for one year."

(x) We might add—and in the provinces—if we happened to know as much about other towns as we do about Leicester or Norwich; the Earl of Leicester's adviser no doubt knew what was going on in London.

"The period at which this chronicle (*y*) commences was one of the most eventful in the annals of history. Through the wars between Henry III and the turbulent barons, London at this time was divided into two parties; the aldermen and the principal citizens were devoted to the King, but the mayor and the populace openly declared for the Barons. . . . False charges were repeatedly made against the citizens for the purpose of exacting money (Fabyan, 7 : Matth. Paris *passim*); exorbitant sums were demanded for purchasing the King's good will and for the granting of charters. . . . It was a government under which, as is justly observed by Hume, ' laws seemed to lose their validity unless often renewed.' On frivolous pretences the liberties of the city were seized upon by the King's ministers and a *custos* appointed. . . . On Edward I's accession to the throne, his first care was to adjust upon a firm basis the shattered constitution and thoroughly to revise the civil administration of the realm; improvements so great that they have justly gained Edward the title of the ' English Justinian.' After depriving the City of its franchises, he ultimately restored them. ' The reign of Edward I, it is said, must be viewed as the transition era, at the close of which we enter on the *second period* of the history of the city ' " (*z*).

Robert Burnell " adopted the church and the law for his profession " (*a*). He became Chancellor in 1274 and remained in office till his death in 1292. His " elevation to the Chancery marks the beginning of Edward's legislative reforms. . . . In 1275 the Statute of Westminster I, a code in itself, began the legislative work which went on as long as Burnell was Chancellor." Thus it is easy to say

---

(*y*) *Croniques de London* (1260—1344), anonymous, p. iii, ed. G. J. Aungier; Camden Soc. No. 28 (1844).

(*z*) *Municipal Report*, p. 8, *i.e.*, Second Report of the Commissioners (Munic. Corp.) (1837), *London and Southwark*.

(*a*) D. N. B.

that the time was ripe for the regulation of the legal profession and that the men were at hand. There was much oppression and corruption, no doubt, throughout the kingdom from 1216, but despite the specially virulent criticism for which they are singled out by literary writers the lawyers as a class (*b*) were not worse than other classes; the mischief most frequently aimed at—notably in the City (*c*)—is champerty, maintenance, etc.—a legacy, perhaps, from the days before organization when a bargain between *causidicus* and client was like any other bargain between two men. Actual instances of this sort of misconduct are rare, but we have had such a case.

Admitting the general chicane, there is still very little evidence of the misconduct of the legal representative *in court*, and we are in the main left to infer it from the laws made against it.

Of these the most remarkable are the Statute of 1275 and the Ordinance of 1280.

E
E[1]

(*b*) Prof. Tout deals with " the scandalous conduct of the judges and royal officials " during E. I's absence from England. " The highest judges of the land forged charters, condoned homicides, sold judgments and practised extortion and violence ": *Pol. Hist. Eng.* (1216—1377), 72. In the many " Political Songs " (1199—1327) (Wright, Camd. Soc.) there is comparatively little attack on " the bar "; most of the passages are quoted in the text.

(*c*) In 1378 there was an Inquisition by the Mayor and Sheriffs " touching " a very large number of named " abettor maintainers [often " common " maintainers] of plaints, conspiracies, champerties, &c." *City Letter Book H.* pp. 112-6 : " many of them are accustomed to frequent the Courts of the Mayors and Sheriffs . . . without cause, to the obstruction of the law." This Inquiry was afterwards looked on as " consule Planco," *e.g.*, in 1 *Lib. Alb.* 522 (and 525), dated as " H. VI " (Riley : transln. 1861), but perhaps more correctly by Sharpe, *Letter Book G.* 74, n. (1), as 1393-4 (accepted, Bateson, 2 *Bor. Custs.* 14). In *Lib. Alb.*, at any rate, the malpractices above are denounced against lawyers and other abettors. " Nulle pledour . . . enfourme *nenforge* "=inform or enforce; " instruct or aid " : Bateson, *ib.*; *instruct* cannot possibly here=its technical sense, probably=put up or inspire like *inform* in later English poetry; *enfourge* is barbarous not found in Fr. then and probably=to put pressure on. In the French oath (p. 249*y*) Dr. Sharpe's " enform nor enforce " no doubt translates these two French words.

A This downright and reiterated exposure of incapable lawyers cannot be merely by way of precaution but, as its authors say, springs from experience. Indeed, it is amply borne out by Britton (*d*), who—as the evil must have grown gradually and Bracton is unaware of it—may be regarded as almost contemporary with this edict. Now his suggestion in so many words is that if an appeal be abated because it is ill drawn " or through other default of the serjeant who ought to understand the art (*e*) or business (*mester*) of pleading " he should be fined 100 shillings " and if there was secret malice " to boot, " let him go to prison and be disbarred," repeated a few lines later *plus* the advice to the client " to get a better lawyer." The dread of treachery is characteristic of the age, but the *gravamen* of the criticism is the mystery of pleading that baffled the ordinary lawyer, honest or dishonest.

In the undifferentiated period, even an unauthorised representative, if he was not too scrupulous, and especially the attorney who controlled the early stages of litigation, might have many opportunities of profit of some sort—and apparently as the two orders of practitioners differentiated, such opportunities grew.

To the intrusion of such persons into the City Courts the preamble of the Ordinance distinctly testifies.

Then we get a characteristic touch from the City of London; it is the leading citizens at the request of the serjeants and countors themselves *who know their business* that measures are taken. Here, again, the City follows the national model. " Who ought to understand the art of pleading " is, surely, in a technical work, a deliberate comment on an actual state of things. Britton, too, throws more light on the " mischiefs " of the City Ordinance, for

---

(*d*) B. I, c. 23; 1 Nichols, 101-2.
(*e*) " The science ": Kelham.

he puts into the mouth of the King (*f*) : " Let inquiry also be made concerning our serjeants, and our attorneys assigned to prosecute and defend our rights, whether through favour or otherwise they have permitted or suffered any great lord of the county or other to continue in seisin of any franchise . . . etc., and let such be punished by fine." Here, no doubt, the Crown is only thinking of its own interest; probably experience had shown that—especially on remote *Itinera*—some of its servants had made bargains with litigants or " let " them " down " too gently in the courts and, it was suspected, not without advantage to themselves. In that case, we may the more readily believe the teeming references of the period to the venality of the Crown lawyers and officials generally in their contact with the public, who certainly would not fare at their hands better than the Crown. The enactments of 1275 preceding and succeeding the chapter above (29) are full of penalties against champertous and extorsive royal officers and others, including clerks of justices, who are forbidden to take anything " for delivering Chapiters [*capitula*] " with the exception—n.b.—of those on Eyre, who may take " deus souz."

We are not, however, informed by what test the incompetent practitioner is to be distinguished from the competent; " the City " will see to that. We are prepared for reforms in legal education soon.

There is evidently no difficulty in getting competent persons—indeed, they have promoted this Ordinance; no man is hindered from getting advice from any other man, learned or not. There are such of all grades " constantly dwelling among us " and " frequenting our " City courts.

These statements are borne out by contemporary

(*f*) P. 93, *i.e.*, he represents " the whole law as statutory " : 1 P. & M. I, vii, p. 155.

evidence. In 1288-9 we have a list (*g*) of four names "admitted and sworn to the office of Pleader (*Narrator*) and sworn to observe the above statutes," *i.e.*, the Ordinance of 1280; on the same day five persons named were "admitted and elected by the above Pleaders and sworn to observe the above statutes" (*ib.*)—presumably as clerks (or pupils) of the said *narratores*.

Probably they were not specially retained by the City, or it would have been mentioned (as below).

In 1305 five persons "were sworn Countors according to the Ordinance" of 1280 (*h*); three of these are quite unknown. Robert de Suttone is called "a serjeant" (presumably *serviens*) in 1304 (*i*) when a "clerk" was bound over before the Mayor and Aldermen for having "abused" him "in their presence, etc."; this, pointing to an offence *in court* coupled with his express admission as a pleader in 1305, makes it probable that he was a *serviens ad legem*. Of the fifth, Robert de Keleseye, afterwards Common *Serjeant*, there is a story characteristic of the times. About 1300 there was a suit for a writ of right, *Thomas le Coffer and others* v. *Adam de la Rose* in a City Court. Thomas "agreed with Robert for 40 pence that R. should be of his counsel (*de consilio*)"; the plaintiff won and "forthwith after dinner R. went to Adam" and counselled him to obtain "a new writ" about the same matter which was now to be heard and in which R. was to appear for Adam; it seemed to T. that R. "ought not to stand against him now in this case" [*Adam* v. *Thomas and others*] "for he knew his counsel" and he "calumniated" [=charged] R. in full court saying that R. "ought to remain with him in

---

(*g*) *Letter Book A*. 205. Not one of these nine persons is otherwise known; William de Marisco might be a son of Geoffrey de M. (d. 1245), Viceroy of Ireland. The first printed Year Book is of 1292.

(*h*) *Letter Bk. C*. 147-8. Riley, *Memorials of London* (1868), 58, n. (3), says that in the margin of this entry there are pen caricatures of (he thinks) these lawyers wearing "to all appearance" the coif.

(*i*) *Letter Bk. C*. 130.

this writ and on that account he had previously paid him 40 pence—to the scandal of R. and to the loss of £100 in damage to him and this he offers, etc."; T. was thereupon attached to answer in a plea of trespass before the Mayor, etc., and he told his story. R.'s answer was that he had acted for T. " at the instance of Gilbert de Toutheby, then ' serviens ' (*k*) of the said T.," but he had never agreed to act for T. (*stare cum*) in *this* case. T. did not deny that R. had " well and faithfully served him in the first writ." With regard to advising Adam, R. " says that although not bound to answer, yet in order to purge his character " he pleads not guilty and " puts himself upon his country, etc., of the *venue* of Fryday Strete & Chepe." T. denied that he had said that R. was " of his counsel " in this writ and appealed to the record of the court. The record was found to be against him and he was convicted of trespass; the matter was then settled on easy terms (*l*).

No doubt justice was done, but we can understand that layman Thomas thought himself aggrieved that his advocate " who knew his counsel " should take a fee from him in one case and advise against him in another arising out of the same facts. He put a high value on his counsel's services when he laid his damages at £100 and the assumption is that de Toutheby's junior or " devil " was a " good man."

In 1310-11 " Geoffrey de Hertrepole, Edmund Passelewe, and Robert de Malmethorp pleaders (*narratores*)," otherwise well known, " were admitted to serve the Mayor, etc. . . . in matters affecting the . . . Commonalty before " the King's justices, *i.e.*, primarily in the *royal* courts—" so that each of them have and receive yearly of the Chamber

---

(*k*) This seems to be the only passage where a *serviens* is so called " of " the party. It is not otherwise known that de T. was a *serviens regis* or *legis* in 1300, though we know he was in 1313 : n. (*m*) below. Probably the record only means that he was a pleader.

(*l*) Letter Bk. C. 185-7.

of the Commonalty 4 marks by the year for his services, etc." (*m*).

This is the earliest general retainer of counsel known; the City can afford to retain (at least) three; we may assume that they took the ordinary oath. The career of John de Waldesshef is instructive and, except his dismissal, typical. In 1318-9 " the freedom (*n*) of the City and on annuity of 100s. [were] granted to " him " for his pains in the late Parliament at York and in divers of the King's courts. And the said John came and pledged himself to serve the City faithfully in the future " (*o*). He " practised in Chancery as an attorney between 1318 and 1322, mainly on behalf of City merchants. He is described as Common Pleader of the City in March 1319 " when the freedom was granted. In 1319 " he was assigned with four others to attend the Parliament at York (6-25 May) and to do therein that which should be ordained by common consent. In neither case is he mentioned in the returns to the writs of Parliamentary Summons. He was probably engaged in legal business before the Council in 1318 and in 1319 he attended in connection with the ordaining of the new City Charter which the King sealed on 8th June. In August, 1322, at which time he is described as *serviens* ('a sworn serjeant of the City'), he was charged with being opposed to granting an aid to the King for the war in Scotland and with disseminating discord. He left the City and in his absence was deprived of the freedom and

---

(*m*) *Letter Bk. D.* 251; at 314 these fees appear in accounts—some years later—not only against these three names, but three others (de Toutheby, Herle, etc.), for the same sum; the whole six are in Maitland's list of " counsel " for 1307 (17 Seld. Soc. xciv) and some in later Year Books; we do not know who were senior. Perhaps by 1311 the other three had resigned (or the City retained more than three). A mark at this time seems to = ⅔ of a £.

(*n*) In 1423 Robt. Blounte was received into "the freedom of the mystery " of the Goldsmiths' Co. " and was retained to be of counsel for the aforesaid mystery " : Herbert, 2 *Hist. 12 Liv. Coys.* 185.

(*o*) *Letter Book E.* 20, in the margin (perhaps contemporary) he is *communis narrator civitatis*.

THE CITY OF LONDON. 243

his annuity, removed from his position as counsel to the City and forbidden to plead for anyone in the City. This is the last mention of him in the City records, and there is no evidence that the City obeyed the King's command to reinstate him " (*p*).

One purpose someone of that rank served which was exceptional. In the rules for holding a Common Council (*q*) " if any matter of great difficulty or doubt shall arise upon which they cannot agree they shall be severally examined by the *serviens legis* (*r*) of the Common Clerk and of the Common Serjeant at Arms " upon the latters' (?) oaths, etc.; the experienced advocate is employed to bring the disputants to terms or to compromise (*s*).

As we saw, the three sworn in 1310-1—as they must have been, like their predecessors—were well known in the King's Courts; they were all raised to the bench. It may well be—probably must be—that in the twenty odd years between the two admittances business had increased (*t*) in the City courts and it had become worth the while of *narratores* living in the City, as many must have done, to seek work in those courts as well as in the King's. In the latter we know that in 1309 " owing to the number of pleas

---

(*p*) Thomas, *Cal. Plea and Mem. R.* 2, n., citing *Cal. Close R.* (1318-23), pp. 47, [95], 106, 328, 432; *Letter Book E.* 20, 32, 103, 104, 139, 161.

(*q*) 1 *Lib. Alb.* 40, Rolls; transln. (1861), 36; later than 1335, as the document refers to the Mayor of that year.

(*r*) *I.e.*, the lawyer who advised these two officials, no doubt the Common Serjeant; the Recorder would have been mentioned and could hardly be thus described.

(*s*) So in 1321 when there was " a very great Commonalty " on some burning question, the Recorder was " put up " to speak to them : *Letter Bk. E.* 147.

(*t*) That business fluctuated we see from the Ordinances of 1388 and Henry V, p. 439, three *clerici* are to be added to the staff " quod negocia in . . . rotulis inserenda indies confluunt multo magis quam solebant : . . . negocia d. Regem tangencia quae indies confluunt." But in the second edition many *clerici* are disallowed " cum multa brevia quae olim fieri solebant ad *pauciora* [conjectured] hodie redigantur," but possibly different departments of the Chancery are meant.

now greater then ever " (*u*) it was " necessary " to have six judges (instead of three) and to make them sit in two divisions; the Chief Clerk got an increase of salary " because he has more to do than before." At any rate, by then, or perhaps earlier, it was worth the Corporation's while to retain the best practising lawyers of all grades in the country; as we shall see, they have their own special *attornatus* as early as 1298, if not before—all just as we should expect from the capital.

The Ordinance of 1280 is further illustrated by the City Recorder. The first known is John de Wengrave, Alderman (Deputy-Mayor (*x*) 1305 and later Mayor), sworn in 1303-4 as " Recordator " (*y*), as clearly appears from the text (*z*). Later we read " The Recorder of the City of London should be and of usage has been (*solebat*) one of the most skilful and upright (*virtuosissimis*) *apprenticii* of the law in the whole kingdom " (*a*). Thus on Jan. 13, 1319-20, Geoffrey de Hertpole (*b*) was elected Alderman of " Candelwitestrate " and on Jan. 22 of the same year he was elected Recorder with the usual emoluments, but

---

(*u*) *Cal. Close R.* 3 E. II, p. 231; Dugd. *Or. Jud.* 39 b.

(*x*) *Letter Book C.* 214.

(*y*) So the margin only. The English word seems to be taken from the French (N. E. D.), not the Latin (which Du Cange barely mentions); if so, there may have been a French original of this document. The word in A. V. = remembrancer, which is a literal translation of the Hebrew.

(*z*) *Ib.* 132 (or " Wangrave "); the " Book of Dignities " (1890), p. 493, gives the earliest name in 1298, but there seems to be no authority for it.

(*a*) 1 *Lib. Alb.* Rolls, 42; transln. (1861), 38; for the date of this (B. I, Pt. I) see p. 231*p*. The word " *appr.*" certainly points to the date being later than the official original recognition (about 1300) of the *serviens r.*—a title which the City tends to avoid—for " appr." implies a teacher.

(*b*) G. de H. was very likely a *serviens r.* at one time, but he is nowhere so called. It looks as if he was one of those who " constantly dwell " in the City and " frequent " its courts; he makes his name as a " pleader," is retained by the City and becomes successively Alderman and Recorder. Perhaps he was removed in 1320 because he was too busy for the Crown in various capacities.

on Dec. 6, 1320, he " was removed from the office of Recorder "—why, we are not told—and his successor Robert de Swalclyve was sworn in (c). In a long suit (cc) in a City case in 1328-9 " the Mayor and citizens " are incidentally summoned to appear " before the King " to defend certain franchises. The various parties appear constantly in different courts by *attornati*, the Crown by Adam de Fyncham (otherwise unknown) *qui sequitur*, etc., before the judges, but the City " appears by Gregory de Nortone, the recorder."

The point of " apprenticii legis " is that the Recorder always has been—(*et solebant: consueverunt Major, etc.*, to employ him : *solent etiam Recordator et . . .* in the same chapter)—a distinguished member of " the bar," though not necessarily a servant of the Crown. At any rate, from the beginning he has been a " learned " person (at least, technically). Thus (though Wengrave's (d) occupation is not known) Geoffrey de Norton was in 1290 " Clerk to the Warden of London " (e).

The Recorder, like every other City official, who took part in the administration of justice had to take the traditional (f) oath and we may gather from it what a sound lawyer was expected to know. The earliest mention (g) of its substance—we can hardly say of its form—is in 1303-4 when Wangrave " was sworn to well and truly render all judgments in the Husting after the Mayor and Aldermen have come from consultation and have arrived at an agreement and also all other judgments [in other

---

(c) *Letter Book E.* 11-2.
(cc) 1 *Lib. Alb.* 437—44, Rolls; a bare note *Let. Bk. E.* 218-9.
(d) He seems to have been an able man : *Letter Books A, B, C*, *passim.*
(e) *Let. Bk. A.* 175.
(f) There are Latin precedents in 1193 (*Commune of London*) and 1205-6 (*xxiv probi homines* of London : Round, *Commune, etc.* 235, 237); and several French in the *Provisions of Oxford*, 1257-8; (the Commons and great officials) : St. *Sel. Ch.* 379.
(g) *Lt. Bk. C.* 132, Latin.

courts?] touching the Commonalty of London, etc. And that he will do justice as well to poor as the rich. And that all pleas in the Husting immediately after the Husting is closed he will survey set in order and cause to be enrolled according as they have been pleaded etc. And that he will come prepared to expedite the business of the City where and when he shall have been lawfully forewarned by the Mayor, etc. . . ." (*h*). As this entry expressly refers to the first (known) Recorder, it is quite likely that no " stereotyped " formula was to hand. But later (*i*) the following (*k*) was in use : " You shall swear that you shall be good and true unto Richard (II, 1377-99) King of England and unto his heirs, kings and unto the City of London, in the office of Recorder; and the franchises and usages of the same City, within the City and without, according to your power you shall maintain and the counsel of the same city you shall not discover; and that well and continually you shall keep and rule the King's Courts (*l*), in the Chamber and the Hustings according to the custom of the City. And that you shall not omit for gift or for favour or for promise or for hate, that equal law and right you shall do unto all manner of people as

---

(*h*) " For which trouble " he is to get " £10 sterling *per annum* . . . and 20 pence for every deed writing and testament enrolled in the Husting, etc. " : *ib*. In 1310 he gets a yearly *bonus* of " 100s. beyond his fee . . . at the pleasure of the Mayor," etc. : *Let. Bk. D.* 233 and 313, where it appears that he was *then* getting a salary of £40 a year.

(*i*) As this is the only one in the large collection of oaths (*Lib. Alb.* B. 3, Pt. 2) which *names* the King its date is very suspicious. The extreme elaboration of the diction of all of them confirms the suspicion as, in this case, does the interpolation below (*m*). Moreover, in the earliest translation " Edward " is read.

(*k*) 1 *Lib. Alb.* 308 (French); II, 120, Rolls; transln. (1861), 268 (above). There is another English translation, *Let. Bk. D.* 33 (after 1326), almost literally the same as above; " the handwriting appears to be of the 15th century " : Ed. and p. 192, and spelling, too; it omits " tenements and forfeitures " (above) and is, therefore, perhaps an earlier version of the French. But it has the (suspected) interpolation; see last note.

(*l*) Is this a mere flourish about the royal charters to the City?

well to poor as rich, to denizens as to strangers who before you shall plead in the Hustings' Pleas and in all other manner of Pleas; and in all pleas which before you shall lawfully be pleaded you shall lawfully record the same and your diligence shall do to see that the said pleas are well and lawfully enrolled and no right you shall disturb; and that no judgment you shall delay, without reasonable cause. And if you shall know the rights or profits (*m*) of the King or (*m*) of the said City be it in lands, rents, tenements or forfeitures to be withdrawn or concealed, you shall show the same unto the Mayor and Aldermen, for the saving of the rights of the said King and the City. And readily you shall come at the warnings of the Mayor and Sheriffs or of their officers for good and wholesome counsel unto them to give; and at all times when need shall be with them you shall go and ride, to keep and maintain the state of the City. And that nothing you shall take from any person, denizen or stranger, who has before you any cause to plead; and no fees or robes shall you take from any one, except only from the Chamber of London, during your office. And that attentive you will be, the rights of orphans to save and maintain according to the laws and usages of the City. And in all other things which unto your office it pertaineth to do, well and lawfully you shall behave yourself—So God you help and the Saints!"

The high tone of this declaration (and of its fellows)—notably of loyalty to a corporation—as well as the wording here and there, recalls that of the *advocati* of the Church, whose relevant *formulae* were certainly not unknown to the composers of adjurations in 1300. It was, of course,

---

(*m*) These four words are omitted in the form in the *Book of Oaths* (1689), p. 241, which coincides literally with a large part of the text above, amplifies the remainder and is certainly taken from the same source as that; these four words are probably an early interpolation (and " the said King and " just below) by a royalist (as above). The MS. *Booke of Othes, Letter Bk. D.* 1 n. (1), is " temp. Elizabeth."

quite normal at that time that the City should exact an oath from its officials.

The model was undoubtedly that of the King's Councillors : " next to the customary oaths of homage and fealty, the earliest official oath of any kind was that required of the itinerant justices on receiving their Commissions " (*n*).

The—traditional—evils, prohibited by this example, testify to the mischiefs which had been detected in the evolving judicature. Of the magic of pleading here celebrated we will speak elsewhere; the eternal anxiety of the City to prevent encroachment on its jurisdiction appears in the first sentence and in the case of one of its officials was, perhaps, needless. Possibly the clause about orphans is meant to suggest that lay lawyers knew their duty to the helpless as well as the ecclesiastical whom the Church had encouraged to appear for " poor persons " in secular courts even when it forbade other forensic activities.

The oaths of the attorneys and of the " Common Countour " have come down to us. We read (*o*) " the pleaders (*Pleidours*) who are commonly residing in the City (*p*) for pleading, shall be sworn that they will not plead or give counsel (*counsel*) against the usages and franchises of the City of London; but that they will maintain the same to the best of their power, within the City and without. Item, that the attorneys shall be sworn in the same manner. And, further, that they will not act (*respounderent*) as attorney for anyone if they are not admitted (*receux*) and set forth (? *retrez*) in the Roll; and

---

(*n*) Baldwin, *The King's Council*, etc. (1913), p. 346, citing *Rot. Lit. Cl.* i, 403, for 1218 and [Roger of] Wendover, iii, 67; Mat. Paris, *Chron. Maj.* iii, 260, for a councillor's in 1233 (and Seagrave's, C.J.'s) and 1237; forms in 1257 and 1307 *ib.* p. 346. Obviously the abuses aimed at are the same as those implied in the City oaths.

(*o*) *Lib. Alb.* I, 473; III, 191; Rolls; transln. (1861), 407. For the Serjeant's oath, see p. 517-8.

(*p*) P. 232.

that they will consult their remembrances (records ?) and make suit unto the Common Clerk of the City that their pleas in the Hustings, touching their employers (*mestres* : ? business) may be well and properly entered without any manner of tardiness; and that well and lawfully they will prosecute the business of their clients (*clyens*) without committing fraud or deception upon the Court or upon them."

No date is given for these formulae, but they are natural developments of the oath mentioned in the Ordinance of 1280 and may well be later than Edward II's reign. A yet later development exists (*q*). It still illustrates the dangers which beset busy courts : " All attorneys of the . . . city who perform the duties (*loffice*) (*r*) in the Guildhall (*s*) and other common pleaders who are resident within the . . . city shall each year be strictly charged and sworn . . . well and lawfully to do their duty (*office*) (*r*) each in his own degree (*t*) and well and lawfully to examine their clients and their complaints [suits] without champerty and without procuring any jurors or embracing any Inquests [" packing " : translator] and that they will wrest no suit from its nature (*u*) . . ."

Finally, they must undertake not to assist in ousting the jurisdiction (*x*) of the City courts in matters where a non-citizen (*forein*) was a party (*y*).

(*q*) *Lib. Alb.* I, 525; III, 217; Rolls; transln. (1861), 449; attributed by Riley (449) to H. VI's time, 1422-61, but on the face of the original (525) there is nothing to show that it is not earlier (E. II?). It may be noticed that in the title and in the text attorneys precede pleaders.
(*r*) Perhaps implying a professional class.
(*s*) As this existed as early as the 12th century no light is thrown by this word on the date of this document.
(*t*) I.e., attorneys or pleaders; hence omitted in the form below (*y*).
(*u*) I.e., not to introduce irrelevant matter, *e.g.*, for prejudice.
(*x*) Often a bone of contention with the royal courts.
(*y*) Another French version is translated *Letter Book D.* 6, undated; it refers only to attorneys and is almost literally the same as in the text (omitting what relates to pleaders; it is drawn, too, in the second pers. pl.), but adds, " ye shall not enform nor enforce [p. 237c] any

The oath of the Common Countor (*communis narratoris*) ran (z). You shall swear that well and lawfully you shall serve the City of London in the office of Common Serjeant (*Sergeant*) and the laws, usages and franchises of the said city shall keep and defend within the City and without according to your wit and power; and the rights of orphans you shall pursue, save and maintain; and good and lawful counsel you shall give in all things touching the common profit of the same city and the Counsel thereof shall conceal (*celerez*); and the common harm (*damage*) of the City you shall not know but to the best of your power you shall prevent the same, or unto the Council of the City shall make it known. And attendant you shall be on the Mayor and Aldermen and Commons, for the causes (*causes*) and needs of the City, at all times when you shall be thereunto required and charged and the same in all places where need shall be you shall lawfully show and declare (*conterez* : ? plead) and shall attentively prosecute and speed (*esploiterez*) for the common profit of the City (a). So

---

man to sue falsely against anyone by false or forged action." The editor (*ib*.) gives another addition from the MS. "Booke of Othes" ("temp. Elizabeth"); both excrescences are clearly later than the text above. "The Oath of an Attorney of the Mayor's Court" (*Book of Oaths* (1689), p. 247, 1st ed., 1649, with fewer precedents) is that of *Letter Bk. D plus* the excrescence just cited.

(z) Text 1 *Lib. Alb*. 310; French; transln. (1862), III, *ib*. 122; Rolls (1861), p. 269; the last dates "Henry V," but it may well be earlier. There is a copy almost word for word of this text in the Collection *Letter Bk. D*. 196, apparently translated from Latin, as the title is "juramentum communis narratoris," which the ed., Dr. Sharpe, observes "strictly means the oath of the Common Pleader," pointing out that to the French (of *Lib. Alb*. above), though also headed "Comm. narratoris," the ed. Riley has put in the margin "Com. Serjeant" and in the transln. "Com. Countor or Pleader." But when Dr. Sharpe adds "the Common Pleader [is] a different official from the Common Serjeant" he is perhaps misleading, for there never was an *official* common pleader in the City; see below on *communis*.

(a) The form in the *Book of Oaths* (1689), 259, up to this point is almost word for word the same; but then follows an avowed addition word for word (except one) the same as that in the Recorder's case above; one is a copy of the other. So the Elizabethan "Booke of Othes": *Letter Bk. D*. 197.

God you help and the Saints!" It is significant that in the long list of grandees who swore allegiance to the new government on the deposition of Edward II were *servientes de curia*, " six noted as " such (*b*) in the City.

This oath (like others in the series) is obviously, *omissis omittendis*, from the same model as that of the Recorder's : hence some of the remarks made thereupon apply to this. The earliest known Common Serjeant seems to be Thomas Juvenal, who in 1291 " was elected by the assent of the " Warden, Aldermen and Sheriffs " to the office of Common Serjeant of London and sworn well and faithfully to perform that office, &c." (*c*). In that capacity he makes " a public proclamation " " throughout the City " in 1304 (*d*). His death about 1309 was an occasion which throws some light on the social position of lawyers in the City at that time. Edward II and Gavestone wanted " the job " for one John Albon (*e*)—" our well-beloved " the former calls him, " our most dear and well-beloved vadlet " (*f*), says the favourite in letters still extant (*g*). The City very politely regret in answers to each, that immediately after Juvenal's death " at the request of the

---

(*b*) Thomas, *Cal. Plea and Mem. R.* 13; they are J. & W. de Denham, G. de Toutheby, J. de Bever, J. de Cauntebreg and Th. Bacoun—all well known except de Bever. As this record can hardly be mistaken on this point, it seems that there were obscure serjeants who are not to be found in the lists; so of *narratores*, p. 376.

(*c*) Let. Bk. A. 123.
(*d*) Let. Bk. C. 138.
(*e*) Let. Bk. D. xxi, 209.

(*f*) = (in effect) esquire : *Glossaire français*; Du Cange, v. 7 : " Nom qu'on donnait aux jeunes gens de la première qualité avant qu'ils eussent été faits chevaliers : Écuyer "; no date. So, in effect, Dict. of French Academy; originally in no disparaging senses : Littré under *Valet* —in 12th century; a diminutive of L.L. *vassus* (from Celtic), English is adapted from L.L. *vadletus* or Anglo-French *vadlet*, probably related to *vassal*; N. E. D. *Valet*; confirmed by Du Cange, v. VI, *valeti* and *val(l)etus*=scutifer, armiger; from a Charter of 1292 in Lobineau's *Hist. of Brittany: v. legum*=a grade of candidate for the Doctorate. Cf. " En cel Ordre [" Fair-Ease "] sunt sanz blame, Esquiers, vadletz e serjauntz " : *Politl. Songs Ed. I*, 137; Camd. Soc. ed. Wright.

(*g*) *Memorls. Lond.* 69-71.

Earl of Lincoln, who was then present, and also by common assent of the good folks of your [the King's] City, the said appointment was given to a vadlet . . . Thomas de Kent . . . who for a long time theretofore had served in your said City in the office of Serjeant-at-Mace . . . " It will be seen from the note below that Thomas de Kent was probably not of ignoble birth—nor was the Court's candidate. He may be the Thomas de Kent (*h*) who acted as a goldsmith's attorney in 1306-76, and is almost certainly the " serjeant of the Mayor and of the Chamber of the Guildhall " when he is one of " the King's Serjeants in the City " (*i*) in 1301. He when " Serjeant to the Mayor " had the patronage of " Sir Edward, Prince of Wales," who in 1306-7 recommended him by letter to a " Husting for Common Pleas " for the custodianship of the gate of " Crepelgate," which he got; his colleagues at other gates were men of substance, including Juvenal, C.S. (*k*). His admission " in full Husting for Common Pleas " in 1309 as " Serjeant of the Mayor and Commonalty of the City of London, *loco* T. Juvenal for life and during good behaviour, &c." is duly noted (*l*). In 1313 as Serjeant he with the Chamberlain has to make a sequestration for non-appearance (*m*). In 1318-9 Gregory de Norton was " elected Common Serjeant and Pleader of the City . . . at 100s. a year " (*n*). This is the only instance in the City of *serviens narrator* or of *communis narrator* (and *c. narrator* is only in the margin). (But the title spread, *e.g.*, in Norwich " before 1340 " (*o*) we have a rule *de*

(*h*) *Let. Bk. B.* 162.
(*i*) *Let. Bk. C.* 100-1. In 1301-2 he is simply " Serjeant of the Chamber " : *ib.* 107; in 1305 " the Mayor's Serjeant " : *ib.* 144; in 1308 he is only " Serjeant," but a colleague of the Sheriff : *ib.* 162.
(*k*) *Ib.* 152, 183.
(*l*) *Let. Bk. D.* 14; *ib.* 89, a friend of his, a surgeon, is admitted to the freedom *gratis* because Thomas was his proposer; 1311-2.
(*m*) *Ib.* 186.
(*n*) *Let. Bk. E.* 20.
(*o*) Bateson, 2 *Bor. Custs.* 13; 21 Seld. Soc.

servientibus narratoribus in civitate.) Robert de Keleseye is stated by Riley (*p*) to have held the office (if so, probably about 1300-1). In the accounts mentioned above (*q*) " the Common Serjeant of the City for the time being "— unnamed, very likely the office changed hands frequently— gets " 1 mark," apparently yearly; and Robert " receives yearly for his service 40s." raised in 1313 to 100s.; these entries are almost certainly contemporary with de Wengrave, so that Robert could not have been Common Serjeant at the moment they were made.

In a document probably (*r*) of the time of Edward III we are told : " The Chamberlain, the Common Sergeant-at-Law (*Sergeaunt de Ley*), who is otherwise called the Common Countour, and the Common Clerk shall be elected by the Common Council of the City and removed at their pleasure. And each of these shall receive for his labour from the Chamber ten pounds *per annum*."

What does *communis* in his title mean? In the City it seems to signify that he is a servant of the *communitas*, as the citizens liked to call themselves, " our Serjeant " *not* the King's, whose trusted legal advisers often lived in their midst; yet it seems that no official City document (*s*) speaks, at any rate, for a long time, of a *serviens regis*. We have had a glimpse of the social position of even an executive official of the City; a Serjeant-at-Mace might hope for promotion to the more or less judicial position of the Common Serjeant. But this probably was an exceptional prospect due to the City's wealth and business. In Leicester, for example, in 1314 the *communis serviens* attaches defendants (*t*), there is no suggestion of judicial

---

(*p*) See *Let. Bk. C.* 185.
(*q*) *Let. Bk. D.* 313-4. In 1345 William de Iford was C. S. : *Lib. Alb.* B. I, Pt. 1, p. 30; Rolls.
(*r*) *Lib. Alb.* B. I, Pt. 1, c. 18, p. 47; Rolls.
(*s*) Galfrid " s. d. r." p. 287, is not an exception, as it is in a royal record.
(*t*) Bateson, 1 *Records of* . . . *Leicester*, 291; *ib.* 290, 227.

work; if he is the same official as the *serviens* there then he distrains and raises the hue.

It seems, then—though there is no direct evidence for it—that *communis* means not only employed by the City but available by it—by the citizens for advice. We had two instances in this sense at Oxford and at Lincoln in 1297 and 1300 respectively. In those cases both the practitioners speak of themselves as *communis*.

And though as soon as we hear of a *communis serviens* in the City he is doing the sort of work the *serviens regis* did for the King and we never hear of his " pleading " for any private person or advising him how he should plead (which is what *communis narrator* means), yet there is nothing to forbid the suggestion that the office of the Common Serjeant grew out of his function of giving legal advice to all and sundry, probably at first without any fee. The *communis narrator* flourished in the City and no doubt was sometimes promoted to that office, but he was essentially " on his own."

In any case it soon became—what it has remained—a second edition of the Recorder's. Possibly from his origin, certainly about 1350, he was the public prosecutor for the City (*u*), and the adviser of the Common Clerk. We can only guess what the *Narratores* of 1288 (and later) and their underlings swore to do, no form has come down. But as the great Ordinance of 1280 enjoins their oath and some of the passages above expressly state that the named persons took it thereunder, we may safely conclude that its substance was derived therefrom and is to be found in the Common Serjeant's form.

It seems that the City alone exacted an affirmation from this class. Otherwise there never seems to have been any sacramental pledge imposed on an unbeneficed practi-

---

(*u*) Riley's *Memorials*, Index; many references under " Common Serjeant."

tioner to do his duty, though in time, oaths of allegiance, supremacy and abjuration were taken by him; these were abolished by the Promissory Oaths Act, 1868 (*x*).

It is in this Ordinance, too, that we find the earliest D reference (*y*) to that great legal chattel, the bar. That document evidently assumes a somewhat cramped court, in which, in early days, a whispered word (*z*) in an official ear might affect a cause—*tenui jugulos aperire susurro*. Soon after—from 1285 to 1290, probably (*a*)—in some famous verses we hear of " apprentices at the bar " or even " bars of the various courts " (*apprenticiis ad barros*) (*b*).

In 1306 a dissatisfied suitor insulted the judge in the Exchequer and " contemptuously got over the bar " (*barram ascendit*) (*c*). In 1313-4 four knights chosen (as a sort of jury) " withdrew themselves from the bar (*barre*) " in an Eyre; others " could not be challenged when they came to the bar to be sworn " (*d*). In 1320 in the accounts (*e*) for constructing the York Courts we hear

---

(*x*) 9 *Best & Smith*, 966 (1868), *per* Lush, J. Cf. Report of the Oaths Commission (1367), p. 32, and Marchant, *Barrister-at-Law*, p. 12. See note, p. 393*g*.

(*y*) There is no such mention in the careful instructions for fitting up the Great Hall of the Tower for a Judges' Iter in c. 17 of B. I, Pt. 2, *Lib. Alb.* (before 1221?).

(*z*) Even at the present day the jury-box is kept well clear of bystanders.

(*a*) Maitland, *Mirror of Justices*; 7 Seld. Soc. xxi, xxiv, liv, 1; *barros* may mean something quite different. In Spelman's day (1626), " to come to the bar " seems to have been a novel expression.

(*b*) Mr. Bolland objects, 28 *L. Q. R.* 235, that there never were any set of people so called and takes " ad B."=the hostels, near Holborn Bars. There were many " bars " (posts, chains, etc.) there and near the present Temple; that of the " New Temple " is mentioned as early as 1301, Loftie : 1 *Hist. of London* (1884), 231; in 1338 and 1339 in records : Thomas, *Cal. Plea and Mem. Rolls*, 109, 189; " the barres in St. John Street " : Kingsford's *Stow*, v. 2, p. 21 (f. 374).

(*c*) *Abb. Plac.* 257 a.

(*d*) 27 Seld. Soc. xviii, 83.

(*e*) Jenkinson and Johnson, *English Courthand* (1815), Text Pt. I, pp. 181-3; plate xxiii, B, where in " ante barram dicti Banci sub pedibus servientum " *serv.* must=bailiffs, etc. (not lawyers).

of *parvam barram inter Barones* [Scac.] *et clericos* . . . and of a *magna*, too (also called *barrera*). In the famous London *Iter* of 1321 the *Justiciarii* order the Sheriffs to come *infra barram et deponere virgas suas albas*, and the Mayor and the citizens stand *ad barram* " according to ancient custom " to apply to the bench (*f*). We know at least one precedent—when a new Mayor was presented at the Exchequer, Westminster, he and his Aldermen and Sheriffs stood at the bar while the Recorder, no doubt, near them, recited the election (*g*).

If the floor of the City Courts required regulation in 1280 it must have required still more in the time of Henry VI (1422-61)—the latest date (the earliest being 1393) (*h*) for the following : " no pleader or attorney shall be heard to plead for their clients within the bar in the sheriffs' court; but let them stand without the bar without making cry or noise that so the people of the law (*les gentz de ley*) and the good folk of the city may be heard in due manner about their affairs in the said courts, except those who are to sue (*suire*) for the King or the City."

As a synonym of the whole profession there seems to be no instance of the word before 1559 and absolutely in our modern sense none till 1695 (*i*).

There are pictures of actual " bars " in the famous four Illuminations in the Inner Temple Library. From the " Observations " of Mr. Corner, F.S.A. (*k*), it appears that they are from a MS. of the time of Henry VI and he thinks that they represent respectively the Courts of

---

(*f*) 2 *Lib. Cust.* Pt. I, 295; Rolls.
(*g*) 1 *Lib. Alb.* 25; Rolls; time of E. I, " astantibus . . . ad barram."
(*h*) 1 *Lib. Alb.* 521; Rolls.
(*i*) N. E. D. " the utter Barr." We shall find that Spelman in 1626 was accurate (*Cancellarius*) : dicuntur etiam *cancelli*, septa curiarum quae *barras* vocant atque inde juris candidati, causas illic agentes : Budaeo [1500] *cancellarii*, ut nobiscum *Barrestarii*.
(*k*) First printed with four plates in 39 *Archaeologia*, 357 (1863-5); reprinted 1865 (Nichols & Sons) and 1909, and cited p. 366.

THE CITY OF LONDON.

Chancery, King's Bench, Common Pleas and Exchequer at Westminster. In all but the last of these he mentions (pp. 2 and 4) a " bar "—which is plainly visible but rather looks like a wooden partition—at the first of which stand serjeants and at the other two a prisoner and a defendant in custody. In the Exchequer appears a similar erection, but it is not mentioned by the writer; he refers, however (p. 7), to one in a picture of the Court of Wards and Liveries (without stating a date) and (*ib.*) to a plate (*l*) of the Court of Exchequer in Ireland where a similar " bar " is seen and mentioned by Mr. Ferguson, the commentator, who attributes the original to the time of Henry IV or V or VI. Finally, in a " Poem on the evil times of Ed. II," the word is vernacular.

l. 342—
> Countours in benche that stondeth at the barre
> Theih wolen bigile the in thin hond, but if [unless] thu
>   be the warre [wary].
> He wole take xl pans [pence] for to do doun his hod
>   [hood]
> And speke for the a word or to, and don the litel god,
>   I trouwe.
> And have he turned the bak, he makketh the a mouwe
>   [mark of contempt] (*m*).

It is impossible to read the extracts cited here and above, especially those from the Ordinance of 1280 and this Poem, without recognising that the author regarded each " branch " (to say nothing of essoiners) as a *professional* class, as did the author of the *Mirror of Justices*. Perhaps in the case of the attorneys it is rather the cumulative evidence which drives us to this conclusion, for even so explicit a decree as that Ordinance does not necessarily imply that there was a class of persons in the

---

(*l*) In the *Gentleman's Magazine*, N.S., vol. 43, p. 37 and p. 43 (1855).
(*m*) Wright, *Political Songs*, 339 (Camd. Soc. 1839).

City whose daily business was to attorn for others (and still less one which spent its whole working time essoining for others—an inconceivable occupation). No doubt the busy City Courts swarmed with individuals who were acting for other people and with other less important persons who brought excuses to the court, and it is easy to understand that any one in one capacity might at any moment be called on to act in the other. The two fold prohibition (*n*) of doubling forensic parts is not easy to understand if it is aimed at the simultaneous representation of the same client; it surely would have been harsh and oppressive if a friend deputed to do one's business in court could not ask for an adjournment or even plead a plea and argue. We are told, indeed (twice), that anyone made himself a Countor at his " sweet will." Perhaps, therefore, the ancient right of " turning " someone " on to your business " *ad hoc* was not invaded, though the mere irresponsible essoiner (who may very well have been a nuisance (*o*)) is discouraged and the professional countor and the professional attorney who were " whole time " advocates are definitely constituted and distinguished—" even unto this day." And we are told that the reputable lawyers approved of this reform.

It would seem that the practical distinction which the framers of the Ordinance drew—which ultimately becomes that between " professional " and " non-professional "— was between lawyers " who generally frequent our courts and are constantly dwelling among us " and those who did not—two classes of whom the criterion was not difficult to the tribunals of the thirteenth century or, indeed, of the present day, for instance, on circuit. This gives the true point of the context—any litigant may have any

---

(*n*) The last sentence adding nothing to the last of the first paragraph (except to extend penalties) may conceivably be a later addition, with that object.

(*o*) ". . . the jurors be often troubled by reason of the essoins of tenants " : Stat. Westm. I, c. 42 (1275).

counsel he likes (*p*) citizen or " foreigner," but if he comes A¹
here, he must abide by the rules which apply to our regular
practitioners who announce themselves as such by taking
the oath—or, at any rate, must do so for the future. We
know that soon after, many did. Perhaps we may infer
that in 1280 there was no such official grade as that of
Serjeant conferred by royal writ, for it is difficult to believe
that the City would have required other credentials in their
courts, whatever its relations to the Court were at the
moment. And we know that about 1300 the Court found
it necessary to regulate its legal " servants," *i.e.*, to create
them by writ—seeing perhaps the successful working of
the Ordinance. But for some time the City did not take
very kindly to the *servientes regis* (*ad legem*).

In the City then, the profession was earlier recognised
than in any other one place (*q*) in England and a fuller
control over it decreed. Still it was long before the
numbers " dwelling " there were large, and in Richard of
Maidstone's long poem (*r*) on the visit of the King and
Queen to the City in 1393, though the processions of
welcome are minutely enumerated by trades, lawyers are
not so much as mentioned nor in the pageant at Temple
Bar nor in the formalities at Westminster. As the verses
are designed solely in the honour of *municipal* London
this may be significant, *viz.*, the lawyers' settlements are
outside the City. So a jury of London was different from

(*p*) So the *Mirror of Justices* (1285-90), p. 47, ed. Maitland : " what plaintiffs and others cannot or know not how to do by themselves they may do by their serjeants proctors (*procuratours*) or friends "; " pr." must mean attornies, so the passage is very near to that from Leicester in 1277, p. 200*s*; in this connection the reference cannot be to the *consilium* out of court, which would be pointless (and could not be prevented).

(*q*) But cf. Leicester, p. 264.

(*r*) Camden Soc. 1838; Rolls, *Polit. Poems*, I, 282 and p. lxxiii—both ed. Wright.

one of Holborn in 1402. But when London received the child Henry VI in 1431

> Than stood also afore the sayd King
> Two jugis withe full hihe noblesse,
> viii sergeauntes . . .

as Lydgate said (*s*)—no doubt, a deputation.

An incident which took place in the City in or about 1389 gives us a glimpse into the working habits of lawyers. William de Beauchamp, says Dugdale (*t*), contemplating (or having) a law suit " invited his Learned Counsel to his House in Pater-noster-row . . . ; amongst whom were Robert Charlton (then a Judge) William Pinchebek (*u*) William Brenchesley and John Catesby (all Learned Lawyers) : and after Dinner, coming out of his Chappel, in an angry mood, threw to each of them a Piece of Gold and said *Sirs I desire you forthwith to tell me whether I have any Right and Title to* Hastings *Lordships and Lands?* Whereupon Pinchbek stood up (the rest being silent, fearing that he suspected them) and said : *No man here nor in England dare say that you have any Right in them except Hastings do quit his Claim therein,*" etc.

Such a scene could not happen to-day. A judge certainly would not attend a meeting of counsel in view of a *contemplated, a fortiori,* a pending suit, but it is quite possible that the date was 1388, not 1389, and if so, Charlton was not then a judge (*x*). In any case we may safely assume that he had advised in the case when

---

(*s*) *Minor Poems*, ed. Halliwell (1840), Percy Soc. The poet opines
"That Kynges princes schuld abouzt them drawe
Folk that be trew and well expert in the lawe,"
and in " comyn custome . . . equité and righte " there *may* be an early contrast of law and equity.

(*t*) 1 *Baronage*, 578-9 (1675); from an old MS. : 4 Foss, 25.

(*u*) Thomas Pinchebeck (who may be meant here : 4 Foss, 77) has been identified as the original of Chaucer's *Man of Law* : J. M. Manly, *Some New Light on Chaucer*, New York (1926); he, as *capitalis baro de scac.*, tried the Meaux case in 1387-8 : pp. 300, 377m, where n.b., the *jurati electi et triati.*

(*x*) Till Jan. 30; Pat. 11 R. II, p. 2, m. 36; Dugd. *O. J. Chron. Ser* he was at the bar (*y*). Indeed, it would seem that at that time it was not uncommon for " justices " to advise clients (especially if, as was frequent, they were only appointed to an Assize—which does not apply to Chief Justices), for by 8 Rich. II, c. 3 (1384), reciting 20 E. III, c. 1 (1346), it is enacted : " Whereas in the time of E. III it was ordained that justices (*z*) as long as they should be in the Office of justices . . . should not give Counsel to any great or small in things or affairs, where the King is a Party or which in any wise touch the King . . . it is " now " ordained that neither they nor the Barons of the Exchequer while in office, shall give Counsel to any great or small [&c. as above] nor be of any Man's Counsel in any Cause Plea, or Quarrel (*querela*) hanging the Plea before them (*z*) or in other of the King's Courts and Places &c." In other words, if the rights of the Crown were not concerned and litigation had not actually begun there was no objection to their advising (*a*).

This is illustrated by the case of Judge W. Paston; an accusation was brought against him—" the Good Judge "—in the Parliament of 1434; the petitioner, reciting the oath of a justice that he will take no fees or rewards " for to be of Counsel with no man but only with . . . the King " alleged that Paston " taketh divers fees and rewards of divers persons within . . . Norfolk and Suffolk and is withhold [retained] with every matter in the said Counties " and charged specifically that he took " X marks against the King for to destroy the right of

---

(*y*) Pulling includes him in the serjeants, but only because he became a judge.

(*z*) As the earlier Act says nothing about judges advising parties (in cases where the Crown was *not* concerned), we may infer that by 1384 there had been such cases; the prohibition probably extends to suits in which the judge had moved before his elevation. *Querela* is technical, not literary.

(*a*) This probably explains " the fees or bribes " (!) which various judges got from the Knights Hospitallers in 1338 : Kemble, *K. H. in Engl.*, xlii; Cam. Soc. No. 65 (1857).

the King . . . "; this was endorsed *falsa billa* but is none the less significant—perhaps of " old annuities " granted to the advocate and " not withdrawn " from the judge (Foss) as, perhaps, in Charlton's case, above.

And note that the statutes contemplate the justices leaving the Bench and going back to the Bar. At any rate, the distinction between the senior Bar and the junior Bench was not as sharp in 1350—1400 as it is now.

Counsel (*b*) meet at the client's house, and though no doubt his high rank procured this indulgence (and could afford such a " team ") it was by no means unique, for there would not be much accommodation for consultations in the Inns. There was not any *attornatus* present, and if there had been, it was not yet his privilege to avert the inconvenient method of payment which the noble lord adopted on this occasion. A fee, it will be noticed, is assumed as normal, and the same amount all round (*c*), but apparently the judge gets and expect none. Why the lawyers should think the bad-tempered client " suspected " them is not clear; it certainly cannot be of thinking he had a bad case, for they told him so to his face by their spokesman. It seems to mean that as they had nothing pleasant to communicate, they left the duty of expressing their common opinion to Pinchbeck, who was no doubt the senior; his juniors, not being called upon to speak, kept silence; the client obviously had an inkling—" suspected "—that they were against him, before he came in. However, that may be, the story carries conviction with it.

The Provinces.

The subject of lawyers not in London has hardly been touched and very little is known about it. The Eyres

---

(*b*) Only Brenchesley is known to have been a *serviens* : Dugd. (1390); the other two are unknown.

(*c*) Perhaps a noble—6s. 8d. : Kenyon, *Gold Coins of England* (1884), p. 35.

THE PROVINCES. 263

naturally yield some material, enough, perhaps, to show that there was some sort of system in the country. The earliest attornacies in England came from the counties and we should expect *a priori* that as that form of representation grew, the dual system which we have seen in the City of London, should grow up, too. We may guess—safely— that when the Itinerant Justice was first seen, say, in Cornwall, the *attornatus* " appeared " (*d*) for parties before the *serviens* did, and in due course there or elsewhere matured into the latter. It was suggested that as early as 1152 Norwich *possibly* had a developed judicature and it seems to have been a " go ahead " town (*e*). There is, at any rate, no difficulty in understanding that *attornati* spring up about the same time in the towns all over the country (*f*), for they were the like effects of like causes.

It is not impossible that in an Inquisition made by the Abbot of St. Ives in 1251 the *placitum servientis aut praepositi* (*g*) may refer to a court presided over by a lawyer. Perhaps, too, the spread (*h*) of the proper name " Le Playdour " (variously spelled) attests the progress of the person.

In 1275 at the court in the Fair of St. Ives (*i*) " William of Bolton complains of John G. . . . that . . . J. . . . came into this court during the present fair and prayed . . . William . . . to be of counsel and aid (*de consilio*

(*d*) *E.g.*, Bracton, *de Esson*; 5 Rolls, *passim*.

(*e*) See *Bor. Custs.* 18 and 21 Seld. Soc., Index to Custumals. Later, it and the whole county were notoriously litigious.

(*f*) For a *conspectus* see Miss Bateson's instances : 2 *Bor. Custs.* 10-16; none from the North till 1574 (Lancaster) and p. 138 on the cases in Bracton's *Note-Book*. The rise of borough courts is not germane to our subject, but for a trace of incipient *procedure* in 1155-65 we might quote : "neque praeposito burgi de Nottingham aliquem burgensium calumpnianti [challenging] respondeatur nisi alius fuerit accusator " [*includes* plaintiff] : *Charters of Nottingham*, 2 *Bor. Cust.* 63.

(*g*) 1 *Cart. Mon. Rams.* 288 (Rolls); so *ib.* 282, 384.

(*h*) *Ib.* 437 and 447 in 1244; in Wilts in 1247 : 2 Seld. Soc. 9.

(*i*) 2 Seld. Soc. 155; Introdn. by Maitland, 135.

et in auxilium) for Simon B. . . . " charged with using a false rod; Simon admitted this, but said he had got it from Thomas, a Rouen merchant, whom he vouched to warranty; William " at the instance of . . . John and for 4s. of silver undertook to defend (k) to the best of his power the estate of . . . Simon that he might have no bodily shame or peril but on the terms that . . . Simon was not to withdraw himself from the plaint but was to press his suit against (*sectam faceret penes*) . . . Thomas " but " John . . . unjustly detains and deforces from . . . William the said 4s. and by his incitement caused . . . Simon to withdraw himself from [his voucher of] the merchant out of whom W. had hoped to get a very large sum of money (*penes quem . . . W. habuisse credidit maximam summam*) (l) to " W.'s damage, 10 marks . . ." Maitland commenting on " the curious and not too creditable proceedings of William " says " we are now in a court where professional pleaders were employed (m) . . . But the Court of a fair could not be so domestic a tribunal [as an Abbot's]: the lawyers invaded it." An *attornatus* appears there in 1275 and in 1258, within the Abbot of Ramsey's jurisdiction (n).

The Leicester Charter of 1277, so often quoted, clearly recognises the attorney in court, but only the attorney not the *narrator* or *serviens*. In a country borough court we could hardly yet expect a reference to the different spheres of *attornatus* and *serviens*, such as London was just now insisting on. But, as we have seen, the representative

---

(k) This circumlocution seems to show unfamiliarity with defences; *defendere* would have been sufficient.

(l) " The sense " of these words " is not very clear. But it would seem that not only does a professional advocate sue for his fees, but he makes it a ground of complaint against his employer that he has been debarred from getting money out of the other side; no one seems to be surprised at this ": M. *ibid*.

(m) But note that *de consilio*, etc., is the only technical term, not *narrator*, etc.

(n) *Ib.* 142, 52, 57. Cf. p. 140.

THE PROVINCES. 265

there must be vouched; no irresponsible meddler may
" butt in." Given enough business and the professional
will soon practise there. Indeed the picture (*o*) of the
Cambridge Eyre of 1286 is almost that of a modern Assize.
It is reasonable to suppose that the great London Ordinance
of 1280, regulating local courts in the City, was kept in
view or copied by other local authorities. Thus " before
1340 " Norwich had *servientes narrantes* in its local
courts (*p*).

By that date, there is no difficulty in understanding the
serjeant's appearance in the provinces.

From time to time the royal courts sit there. In 1278
the King's Bench and Exchequer go to Shrewsbury; in
1393 " the terme was removyd from Westminster unto
Yorke " (*q*).

At the Oxford Eyre (*r*) of 1285 *Robertus le Eyr serviens
d. Regis pro domino R. justiciarius d. regis hic monstravit
etc.* Robert is otherwise unknown. Richard of St. Ives
was certainly " a local " practising in the Fair Court; no
other activity of his is known. In 1297 we had Thomas le
Marischal (*s*) practising as such at Oxford, and in 1300
John de Maldone at Lincoln almost as such (*t*); both, at
any rate, describe themselves as *communis*—in effect, at
any one's service. The Eyres which had now been in
existence for at least a hundred years, easily account for
them and their like, *e.g.*, William Paston (*u*) who, as he

(*o*) P. 153.
(*p*) *Clientulus* (and -i), rather rare words, perhaps mark the Norwich draftsman's sense of the courts being " inferior."
(*q*) 1278 : *Chron. of Engl.* p. 28 (1827), ed. H. Nicolas; 1393, *Chron. Grey Friars, London,* p. 8; Camd. Soc. No. 53 (1852).
(*r*) *Oxf. City Docts.* p. 204 (1891); cited 2 P. & M.
(*s*) Very likely the *Magister* T. M. whose *serviens* John was outlawed by the Eyre of 1285 : *Oxf. City Docts.* p. 202; in 1297 and 1299 T. M. was a *jurator* at coroner's inquests : *ib.* 151, 154.
(*t*) Pp. 201-2; cf. pp. 316, 459 for lawyers in or about Parliament out of London.
(*u*) See p. 261 and D. N. B. *W. Paston*; as counsel he uses in a letter (Gairdner's ed. I, 26) strong language of his lay opponents;

was born in 1378 but does not appear in the Year Books till 1421 when he was made a serjeant, Foss thinks (iv, 350) " confined his practice to his own county [Norfolk] and its neighbourhood."

In early days the *hospitia* in London seem to have found a difficulty in keeping their inmates at harvest and Christmastide, when they dispersed to their homes in the country; the Inns apparently felt the loss of their contributions and, perhaps, of the senior men for discipline. Thus in 1436 Lincoln's Inn got many promises and covenants, including one from " Fortescu," " to contynwe yn harvist a monthe and so euery harvist this iij yere, nowe next comynge, uppon the payn of xxs. to be paijd as ofte as he failith " (x) and others for other periods, which are distinctly called " vacacions."

A chance remark in a letter from Lord Scales to William's son John in August, 1456, shows that this habit developed—indeed it has come down to our own time. " I suppose lerned men wyll not be easy for to gete be cause of this besy tyme of harvest " (y). Thus any given person might not be in town and if he was in the country he would be occupied. But, at any rate, they were to be found there at some seasons.

The need of local practitioners is confirmed by a petition (z) of the Commons in 1364-5; their grievance is that the King's Bench " wandered from county to county throughout the whole Country " so that great numbers of people were detained where the judges were; moreover, owing to the uncertainty of the place [where their case would be tried] litigants could never be sure of " sage conseil," as at some of the places none could be

---

one of them in 1424 " placarded Norwich with bills threatening to murder him " and did him material harm.

(x) 1 *Black Books L.'I.*, 6.

(y) Gairdner's ed. I, 399, No. 292. Said to be the origin of long vacations; cf. 4 *Rot. Parl.* 420 b (1433).

(z) 2 *Rot. Parl.* 286.

found, and they were seriously prejudiced by their absence; they prayed that the court be fixed at Westminster or York, wherever the Common Pleas was, *i.e.*, where one could always get a Serjeant. The Commons petitioned (*a*) again in 1415; the judges, they say—except the two chiefs—have no power to admit attorneys unless the former are on the spot, and as there are "several counties" where the judges do not come (*sic*) the consequences are very grave for a large number of litigants who cannot appear in person and can get no attorney; they ask that the judges *wherever* they are and " every serjeant of the King " should have this power. Whether the flaws in the Eyre system disclosed in these two documents—fifty years apart—were temporary or permanent we cannot discuss, but the latter assumes that serjeants take part in the Eyre and the former implies that they ought to do so. The latter, too, as here set out, and even more in the part not here cited, exhibits an express recognition of the attorney's fuller functions in litigation.

The normal presence of serjeants on circuit led naturally to their becoming " Commissioners of Assize." In 1393-4 it was enacted (*b*) that " in every Commission of the Peace through the realm where need shall be two men of Law of the same County shall be assigned to proceed to the deliverance of thieves and felons " : thus reversing the legislation (*c*) of 1384. Here it is assumed that local legal personages are always to be found.

As time goes on the Serjeants were more and more employed in this way. In 1421 Serjt. Juyn, afterwards

---

(*a*) 4 *Rot. Parl.* 80 a.
(*b*) 17 R. II, c. 10. The reason given is that owing to the long detention before trial prisoners were delivered by " charters and favourable inquests procured," *i.e.*, at headquarters in London; the two extra lawyers would abridge the delay and by their local knowledge defeat more easily extra-judicial favouritism. The judges still have the same Commission of the Peace as local magistrates.
(*c*) P. 261.

a judge, was examined by the Privy Council (*d*) about a case " before him " almost certainly as judge. In 1454 there is a curt record (*e*): " J. Nedeham *serv. r. a. l.* hac vice tantum "; as he was already a serjeant it is difficult to see what the appointment " for once only " can be, except that of judge of Assize or counsel for the Crown; if so, this is an unique reminder that the post was not permanent. In 1422 a clause for those " learned in the law " (*jurisperiti*) elected to the Bristol town council was added to the oath of other members; its gist is naturally that of the City of London lawyers (*f*); and so of that of the Recorder: once they are called *servientes regis*.

The document of 1415 prepares us for the development of the provincial attorney. He must have multiplied apace, for forty years later the state of things in two Eastern Counties (which, though we know they were busy, and from the contemporary Paston letters, litigious, yet, in this respect must have been like other counties) is disclosed by the famous petition (*g*) of 1455, the gist of which was turned *literatim* into the Statute 33 H. VI, c. 7. This legislation may well have been promoted by the powerful pecuniary interests locally threatened, well represented by the barons in Parliament, against weak and unincorporated country practitioners whose mischief-making is no doubt exaggerated, but there can be no doubt about these valuable statistics or that here we have the earliest express statement that men became attornies to get a living. And this we may assume of the whole country—throughout which the natural increase of litigation (*h*) must account

---

(*d*) 2 *P. P. C.* 308.
(*e*) *Cal. Pat. R.* 296 a; 4 Foss, 447.
(*f*) 1 *Little Red Bk. of Br.* 1, 2, 49; cf. 157.
(*g*) 5 *Rot. Parl.* 328; p. 305, which see.
(*h*) " One of the [Paston] Correspondents writing in 1460, said he needed three solicitors during the last term, so much litigation had he then pending. . . . [The 1455 Statute] was not repealed till 1843 by which time there were 82 attornies in Norwich alone ": Christian, *Solicitors* (1925), p. 34.

for these growing numbers and not *vice versa*. We have suggested that the narrator was born on circuit, that while he was growing up there the *serviens regis* was developing at Westminster and living and perhaps practising in London. Whether that was generally his locality of origin is more difficult to determine. If we look through the two earliest Year Books, of 1292 and 1293, almost entirely devoted to trials at Eyre, we find a number of men arguing in court whose names are not otherwise known (*i*), and applicants for legal aid there actually ask for a serjeant. Some of the former must have been " locals." Even the great practitioners at the *Iter*s in the Tower of London were " locals," for they lived within a short distance and the journey thither from Westminster was as much an *Iter* as it was to Staffordshire. But it was natural that those men should be " taken down " to the counties early in the history of the bar, just as it is that " specials " should be at the present day. If we knew more about the pleaders' names, which are not recorded in London, we might find that they were respectively natives in the parts where they are found practising. We get a hint of this probability from those who are training for the bar, who are actually said—if the expression be not mere "padding" —to be drawn from the whole Kingdom (*k*). For instance, in 1377 David Holbecke is " placitator et attornatus regis in Southwall' et Northwall' " (*l*) (South Wales and North Wales?). He was a loyal Welshman and was exempted from the disabilities of his countrymen in England (*m*) by petition of the Commons (*n*); the combination of his

---

(*i*) And so of the Pleas in the Common Bench (same volumes); even there a case may have come up from the country, *e.g.*, 20-1 E. I, 306, from Gloucester; *ib.* 338, Berkeley; *ib.* 348, Herefordshire case sent down to *Iter* there; 21-2 E. I, 47, Salop : 55, Cambridge, etc., etc
(*k*) Pp. 244, 314.
(*l*) *Cal. Rot. Pat.* 197 b.
(*m*) Under 2 H. IV, cc. 12, 20.
(*n*) In 1406 : 3 *Rot. Parl.* 590 b, 600 b.

titles is unique and his position was abnormal; *placitator* probably expresses that he was not a *serviens*.

If it was worth while one could always go to London. Thus in 1300 Leicester paid 8s. 8d. for expenses there in a plea on a writ of false judgment against the *communitas*, and much more at and for parliament (*o*). By the time of Richard II it seems quite normal to go up to town with relevant papers to consult counsel (*son counsaill*); the journey from Bucks and the fee came to more than 40s. (*p*); or perhaps, for a provincial student like young William Paston, to go to an Inn.

But it was not always worth while to go to town, and it is worth while to follow a suit (*q*) fought out almost wholly in the provinces about 1358, typical of the litigation of convents, but interesting, too, as evidence of the state of the secular courts. Serious altercation arose about certain villeins whom the Abbey of Meaux, Yorks, claimed as serfs. One fled to the local king's *eschaetor* who, after inquisition by " natives of the manor " concerned, seized all the insurgents into the king's hand as his; the Abbey petitions the King in Council; a writ is directed to the escheator to account; he with others named is ordered to inquire by the oath of *probi*; the jurors found that the men belonged to the Abbey " in witness of which verdict they put their seals thereunto." It is duly sent to the royal Chancery; then comes a writ to the Sheriff of York to restore the serfs. They then brought an action by bill against the Abbot " for a violation of the Workmen's Act and the rules thereunder promulgated for Yorkshire," and defendant " was suddenly attached [literally] by the horse he was riding to answer the plea." At the hearing

---

(*o*) 1 Bateson, 236, 235.

(*p*) *Wheeler* v. *Huchynden*, 2 *Proceedings in Chancery*, ii (1830 : Record Comm.).

(*q*) 3 *Chron.* . . . *de Melsa*, 127-42, xix, xlix; Rolls, ed. Bond; the monks' version. See p. 377*m*.

at Hedon before royal judges he demurred to the jurisdiction on the ground that his own serfs could not sue him; the plaintiffs admitted their subjection and were at once " non suited," " they took nothing by their bills and were in mercy, etc." They suggested to the King that this decision was *injustum*; the records, etc., were ordered into the Chancery—through " the ill offices of King's counsellors who were no friends of Meaux "; writs go to the Abbot and Sheriff to redeliver the men and the former is summoned to the Chancery " in London." By means of large gifts to the Chancellor, the Bishop of Winchester—*i.e.*, fees for writs—" *despite the opposition of others of the royal council* " he got leave to answer by his attornies and two (named) are admitted. The attorneys " proceed against (*prosequebantur*) the Crown by bill " and upon their personal security, procure restoration of the serfs. One of the ringleaders escapes and gets a writ to the Sheriff of York to try the whole case at the first Assize there before royal judges who were duly assigned and included the well-known W. de Skypwyth, J., and also a Sir Nicholas Damory—otherwise barely known (*r*)—of whose hostility to the Abbey the chronicler bitterly complains, *inter alia*, " that he tried to keep the day fixed for the hearing secret from us," but when he found that the monks were " too many " for him, as they and their friends attended in large numbers, he pretended that there was " a conspiracy " (to overawe defendants—a common party trick) and refused to try the case. In a year there was another writ and another trial at York—Skipwith, J., again sitting. Finally this jury found for the Abbey. But because the matter " would partly touch the King " the judges did not dare " give judgment on that part without his special order "; this the Abbot gets and presents in person to the judges, and he takes care to get the whole proceedings " exempli-

---

(*r*) *Dormant Peerages* (1807), 1 Banks. 280; cf. W. Bassett, p. 158*q*, and for *socii* see p. 122*i*.

fied under royal letters patent"; "every official and courtier was against us," he concludes, "throughout the *placitum* except the Chancellor whom we had to pay." We may be pretty sure that one at least of the *attornati* was a serjeant, but the provincial writer takes no interest in legal technicality; else we might know more of Sir Nicholas.

Ireland affords some gleanings, but her historians have almost ignored the infant (s) bar. John is the acknowledged founder (t) of the English judicial system (u) in Ireland (x), of course, *mutatis mutandis*. Thus in 1220 Henry III writes " to the justiciary of Ireland. The practice in Ireland of having only one justice itinerant differs much from the practice in England where there were always several justices itinerant " (y).

(s) This is true even of Dr. Elrington Ball's *Judges in Ireland*, 1221-1921 (1926), where the introduction of the English system can now be most conveniently read. He does, however, say, v. I, p. 18, of (about) 1300 : " Laymen appear as pleaders for the Crown and for the subject and on attaining to eminence in their profession they are found raised to a judicial seat."

It is startling to read (*ib.* 28) that J. de Grauntsete *while a judge* acted " as the advocate . . . in a suit." Dr. Ball's authorities [Cal.] *Pat. Rolls*, E. III (1329), pp. 471, 475; (1331), p. 97, do not warrant this anomaly; he was deprived and fined, etc., " for unjustly maintaining a certain plea between parties in the King's court before John Darcy 'le cosyn' justiciary of Ireland "; in 1331 it is called " in defence of a plea before J. D. 'le cosyn' justic' etc." Surely this was the offence of maintenance; he took sides in his court and to succeed insisted on certain evidence—which obviously only a judge could do—which ousted the royal and set up " Christian " jurisdiction—his real offence, called twice " contempt " of court to avoid the graver maintenance. Absolutely nothing is known of John Darcy; the records written in England are perhaps mistaken and J. D. was the cousin of a Darcy justice in 1293; in any case, " before J. D. Justic." is mysterious. Or is there confusion with the English Darcy, J., d. 1254? A baron Darcy was created in 1332 : 2 Foss, 210.

(t) Ball, as above, p. 3. On his visit in 1210 nearly all the lawyers with him were laymen.

(u) " The Courts of Chancery, King's Bench, Common Pleas and Exchequer were the same in both countries " : Hallam, *Const. Hist. Eng.* c. 18.

(x) *E.g., Mediaeval Ireland*, 1110-1513, p. 112, E. Curtis (1923).

(y) *Cal. Docts. Ir.*, 1171-1251, p. 151, ed. Sweetman.

IRELAND. 273

Britton assumes the Irish system; in the early pages of his book there are several references to the judiciary and it ends with one. The early Irish bar is a " squeeze " of that of England. The great Dublin Charter of 1192 was, perhaps, modelled on London charters; like them it does not mention forensic lawyers, but makes provisions likely to require legal argument. Similarly the alleged encroachments of the civil on the ecclesiastical courts in Ireland, 1260-70, of which the Popes complain to Henry III and with which Prince Edward deals, suggest litigation, but do not show lawyer's actually at work (z).

The solidarity or rather, perhaps, the parallelism of the two bars (a) was probably promoted by the justice of Ireland (1276-81), Robert de Ufford. His instructions from Edward I were that the *communitas Hyberniae* was —for 8,000 marks—to be under *leges Anglicanae* (b). In

---

(z) Gilbert, *Hist.*, etc., *Docts. Ireland*, 1172-1320, pp. 170-80.

(a) Duhigg, *History of the King's Inns*, Dublin (1806), p. 26, says: " Irish practicers felt the full force of English habits and institutions, and therefore, as early as the reign of Edward I adopted a collegiate connexion, which was extended and confirmed in the time of his illustrious grandson . . . convenience as well as imitation led Irish judges and Practicers to a voluntary association, wherein, with becoming integrity, they adopted as much of the original institution as corresponded with their local station; smallness of number forbad a separation of Judges and Barristers, which was also unnecessary, as no legal degrees were conferred in this country. The whole body still continued a part of the English societies and their conduct as to internal propriety was subject to that inspection with a right of appeal to the prescriptive visitorial authority of the judges at Westminster." The " Irish Inn of Court . . . established in the reign of Edward I for this laudable purpose and subordinate connexion was called *Collett's Inn*. . . ." : *ib.* p. 28.

This literary (and uncritical) account gives no authorities, but is abridged (and therefore probably accepted) by Constantine Smyth, *Law Officers of Ireland* (1839), p. 276. For *Preston's Inn*, see Duhigg, pp. 30, 32.

(b) Rymer, 1 *Foedera*, 540 (1816), old ed. II, 78: "dum tamen in hoc populi, vel saltem praelatorum et magnatum terrae illius qui bonae voluntatis existunt, communis consensus uniformiter intercurrat." The reason given is " pro eo quod leges quibus utuntur Hibernici, Deo detestabiles existunt et omni juri dissonant, adeo quod leges censeri non debeant."

C.H. 18

1278 he writes (c) to the King : " Persons in Ireland frequently bring suits before the justices of the Common Pleas, Dublin, and before the Irish justices itinerant in divers places, and when a decision or final judgment has been given against either party they betake themselves to the King's presence, frequently charge these justices with enormities and demand remedies from the Chancery of England which they might without difficulty have obtained from the Chancery of Ireland. They thus act not on account of an injury done to them but in order that causes which might more quickly and conveniently have been decided in Ireland may be protracted and in order that their adversary may be borne down by labour and expense. Robert therefore prays the K. to enjoin his Chancellor that before he admits these frustrators of causes to plead he enquire whether they had sought a remedy from the justiciary of Ireland and if not that they shall be compelled in shame to do so until the justiciary shall be found wanting in exhibiting justice. Thus their malice will be obviated, suits be more quickly determined, and the K.'s courts which are bound mutually to aid each other will not be disturbed by those frustrations of justice."

The Calendar of the Justiciary Rolls of Ireland (d), 1295-1303, mentions in 1300 " a serjeant pleader, *serviens ejus* [the defendant] *narrator*," *viz.*, Robert de Dalyngho, who " says that he knows the truth of the whole deed "; in a suit in 1302 " William de Berdefeld serjeant pleader of the King (e) shows to the Justiciar [John Wogan] and Council of the King, etc."; David, one of the parties,

---

(c) I.e., thus calendared in *Docts. Ireland*, 1252-84, ed. Sweetman, p. 296; from *Inq. p. m.* 6 E I, No. 92.

(d) Dublin (1905), ed. Mills, pp. 6, 156, 267, 321, 383-4, 427. *Ib.* 325 (1300), parties come " to Will. Alisaundre who is one of the jurors [at a later hearing] seeking counsel." He was a " notable " of importance and probably a lawyer, for later the same parties are " led by another counsel."

(e) In 1309 " nuper narrator Rs." : *Rot. Canc. Hib.* 8 (50).

"joins the King's Serjeants and says for the King"; in that year W. de Berdefeld and Henry de Beuynburgh, and in 1299 John de Horton, are each simply called "pleader" in acknowledgments of debt, a mark to the two latter and half a mark to the former—presumably fees.

In the Treasurer's accounts (*f*) for 1301 we have "Richard Blund the K.'s pleader, his fee of 5 marks for a[nno] r[egis] 30, 0 66s. 8d.; William de Berdefeld, another pleader of the K., his fee of 5 marks for a. r. 30, 0 66s. 8d." And there are later entries to the same effect in this series. But in the three preceding volumes there seem to be no mentions of any pleader, *narratores*, etc., though a John le Pleydour is frequently mentioned from 1290.

The absence of data, apart from ignorance of the economic value of money at the time, makes comparison of these figures with such as we have in England useless. In 1295 a clerk of the King was accused of tampering with a writ; he calls in to his defence "pleaders (*narratores*) and attorneys then being in the Bench" on their oaths. *Narrator* alone occurs as a description in 1297.

Perhaps, indeed probably, we can trace the blossoming of the pleader into the *serviens* as in England. In 1304-5 there was a great Inquisition into the Irish incomes of Roger le Bygod, fifth Earl of Norfolk, before a very strong bench and many illustrious jurors. Among the revenues returned are those from the burgh of Carlow, for judicature, "beyond" that is, apparently, deducting, many enumerated fees to officials, including "sergeants, pleaders and attorneys of the earl of Ireland," which seems to mean that when the Earl was represented in the courts of Carlow, Roger had to pay the fees; at any rate, in this collocation, which is very rare, if not unique, in Irish records about this date, the sergeants must be *ad legem*.

(*f*) *Cal. Docts.* No. 826; p. 380.

Possibly " Johannes le Seriant " about 1304 was a lawyer; he was certainly a *serviens* of the Crown and one of the *two ballivi* of Dublin, and as such he was sued by Galfridus de Morton (*ff*), merchant and sometime Mayor of Dublin; moreover when John's house was burned (with much of Dublin) certain records were there in keeping. Galfrid (who when he loses a case is in *gravi misericordia pro contemptu &c.*, *Et taxatur ad* [sic]) by the way, produces in court a letter under the great seal of Ireland not only allowing him attorney(s) but allowing them or one of them to make attorney(s) in *his* or *their* place *ad lucrandum vel perdendum.*

John de Ponte was " apparently an English lawyer. ... In 1293 he came to Ireland without any definite office " but was " retained in the service of the King. In this volume (*g*) he most often appears as a Crown counsel in cases in which the Royal rights were affected." In 1297 he " prosecutes for the King," the Bishop of Down, and has with him Elyas de Berkeleye. In that year he " puts " four " writs in motion " against the Bishop of Cork and argues for the Crown.

There are singularly few references to attornies (*h*), yet we saw that as early as 1227 a formula for a writ of appointment of attornies had been sent over from England. A suit against a man for " default about " a " plea " (causing a heavy loss) is certainly against an attorney for negligence (*i*).

There is in 1413 striking evidence of the close relations

(*ff*) He is said to be " pluries vocatus ad prosequendum." Gilbert *Hist. Docts. Ireland*, 1172-1320, p. 521; a reminder that this phrase is used of laymen. (*g*) Mills, pp. vi, 29, 87, 103, 142.

(*h*) None in Gilbert's Index (but, p. 204, " attornes "=deputy-guardians—of markets), Ed. I. In *Cal. Just. Rolls*, 6, 104, 211-4, 262, etc., they are mentioned; *Rolls of Attorneys*, 75-6 (1295), 109-11, etc., and see a case (1302), p. 279. In the good Indexes of the three vols. of *Cal. Docts. Ireland*, 1171-1292, there is no entry under this head, but in Vol. 1293-1301 there are a large number. There are many in *Rot. Canc. Hib.*, *e.g.*, 5 (1303). (*i*) Mills, above, p. 92.

between the two bars of England and Ireland, for the Commons in petitioning (*k*) the King to banish certain Irish classes made an exception in favour of Graduates "in the Schools." Serjeants and Apprentices de Ley, etc. In 1429 a Parliament at Dublin instructs (*l*) its emissaries to the English Government to complain generally of the robberies arrests and violence done to Irishmen travelling in England, and specifically that "Irishmen going to England to study law in the inns of the lawyers (*juris consultor*') may no longer be excluded as they are now but may be admitted as they used to be"—a very early and valuable notice of the *hospitia*. When this migration began we do not know. The year mentioned is that in which Fortescue became a serjeant, and we know *aliunde* that the Inns were in their first youth. The Dublin Legislature was, no doubt, correct in saying that these exclusions had been going on for some time; in 1437 "It was ordered" by Lincoln's Inn "that no person born in Ireland should in future be admitted as a Fellow [*i.e.*, member]," and if he is admitted "he shall be expelled . . . so that no Irishman may be held or named as a Fellow, &c." But in 1452-3 "Blonket from the country of Ireland is admitted into the Society, *any act or ordinance to the contrary notwithstanding*, because he has brought many Fellows to the Society (*m*)." Perhaps we may guess that the early English bar thought that the Irish bar had better practise in Ireland.

The Attorney.

By this time the *Attornatus*, as we have met him from time to time, has become, like the *serviens*, a professional man. How did he arrive at this maturity?

(*k*) 4 *Rot. Parl.* 13b.
(*l*) 1 *Rot. Pat. et Claus. Can. Hib. Cal.* Pt I, 248.
(*m*) 1 *Black Books*, L. I, 8, 23; in 1252 Irishmen at Oxford are specially "rowdy": 1 *Mun. Acad. Ox.* 20, 23; Rolls; and from 1300 onwards "a very large number of the earlier culprits" in Oxford courts "are Irishmen": Thor. Rogers, 18 *Ox. Hist. Soc.* 150.

We must go by steps from Bracton onwards.

In Britton (n) (about, say, 1290) the attorney has "come on." In an Assize of Disseisin—only—the defendant may appear by attorney or any other representative, but all such representatives have not equal power; the bailiff has not as wide powers as the attorney; nor he, as his lord, unless he be " general " and not " special " (o). It is perhaps significant that an attorney is expressly forbidden " to be received either for the appellor or for the appellees, or any essoin to be allowed on one side or the other, in any cases of death " (p).

Had any one argued that though, of course, in a capital case, the accused could not have counsel, yet he might have an attorney? and was the appellor really barred from an attorney? C. 10 of Book 6 (2 Nichols, 356) is devoted to Attornies and gives a multitude of details, doubtless derived from experience, like the minutiae of " Glanvill " and very redolent of his atmosphere. But we may notice (section 3) the rule " when any one has been thus (q) made attorney he cannot retire pending the proceedings without the consent of his client " (client).

We should hardly expect, antecedently, to get more out of the *Mirror of Justices* (r) (1285-90), the tone of which is half historic and half hortatory, but it is certain that the former moiety perpetuates early facts and views. *Responsales* are not, it seems, mentioned, but under " Countours " we are told that representatives in court are " serjeants, proctors (*procuratours*) (s) or friends " (n.b. the last—the lawyers, though assumed to be professional,

---

(n) Nichols thinks that he was contemporary with Fleta, but that the latter " wrote first."

(o) B. 2, c. 15, 2,-3, 4; Nichols, 305-6.

(p) B. 1, c. 23, 5; I, p. 100.

(q) Grammatically, one or two special cases just mentioned, but it is hard to see why the rule is confined to them and not general.

(r) 7 Seld. Soc. 47; ed. Maitland.

(s) Only mentioned here, *semble*.

THE ATTORNEY. 279

have not yet the monopoly). Then follows a *mélange* of the pleader's qualifications, some ethical, some ecclesiastical —all creditable, but none probably ever demanded by authority. Some naturally reveal incidentally contemporary mischiefs, *e.g.*, the pleader " will not by blow, contumely, brawl, threat, noise or villian conduct disturb any judge, party, serjeant or other in court nor impede the hearing (*audience*) or the course of justice." Then " there is the salary (*salaire*) "; four points are to be considered—" the amount of the matter in dispute, the labour (*travail*) of the serjeant, his value (*value*) as a pleader (*Contour*) in respect of his [learning] eloquence (*facunde*) and repute (*donur*) and the usage of the court "; here, at any rate, the tradition is unbroken. The author recognises that a pleader guilty of corruption or of contempt of court may be suspended. He has a great deal to say on Essoins (*t*) and a chapter on attorneys (*u*). Note that no attorney is to be removed unless his principal comes into court himself or gives a power of attorney to do so. It is all very reasonable and " cut and dried " till we come to " one who cannot be a pleader " (*countour*) cannot be an attorney and " other dilatory exceptions are against the persons of the pleaders, attorneys, essoiners, for no one may do by attorney what he cannot do in person, and no one can be a pleader, attorney or essoiner who cannot be a plaintiff (*actour*) " (*x*), all of which may have been good law at one time.

Apropos of the warranty of attorneys in open court— once a very practical matter—this is a good instance of the standing difficulty of getting a clear rule from the cases on these agents. In 1302 a case (*y*) was argued at great length " at assizes " in Ireland (where, however, procedure may have been somewhat belated) which illustrates this

---

(*t*) *Ib.* p. 82. See App. X.
(*u*) *Ib.* p. 87.
(*x*) At p. 48 a *pleader* can only be one that may be " accuser or plaintiff."
(*y*) *Cal. Just. Rolls, Ir.* 417.

and several other points, *Nicholas Archbishop of Armagh v. Theobald de Verdoun*. One attorney appears for the plaintiff (z) and two for the defendant; the latter " were essoined of the said plea [the issue] and have a day on this day." But on the said day though plaintiff's attorney appeared Theobald did not, but " Peter Coulok presented himself as his attorney "; the other side challenged his warrant, he declared that he was " general attorney " by royal letters patent : " Where are they?" say the justices; he cannot produce them, but said " they are enrolled in your own bench here "; the opposing attorney " immediately " prays judgment for the default of " Theobald "; the court adjourns on other urgent business; next day the prayer is repeated, but Peter now produces the royal letters to him and another, they are set out *verbatim*.

" Too late," says the opponent : " I insist on the default yesterday," and when put to it by the court he opts for this ground rather than for " the chief plea "—an interesting sidelight on the pleader's art of that day. Peter answers " it is not too late," because judgment was not in fact given, the court having risen *proprio motu*; the reply is, " I stick to my point—you never were legally attorney because your client did not warrant you in court at the outset." *C.a.v.* At the next hearing the plaintiff's only point is made again; but Peter has several new ones. The other side insist that the default has never been cured, and Peter cannot deny it; so " inasmuch as no man ought to be admitted as attorney for any one in any plea before he has proved himself the attorney " the plaintiff wins (a).

(z) Even in a purely ecclesiastical suit before the King in person in 1284, Henry of Eastry, Prior of Christchurch, Canterbury, *attornatos constituit coram rege*; the certificate of the Treasurer and Barons of the Exchequer about a former judgment was read : *attornati ad istud certificatorium respondebant* : *Registr. Epist. J. Peckham, xlv*; Rolls; ed. Trice Martin.

(a) But judgment was afterwards reversed in the " High Court " at Dublin for " error on the record." Hence the point of default was never argued on appeal.

THE ATTORNEY.

There can be no doubt that the City Ordinance of 1280 implies the attorney's profession. But there is another document (*b*) leading *inter alia* to the same conclusion, which, perhaps, has not been adequately appreciated. Its date is 1292 and it is entitled *De Attornatis et Apprenticiis*. It runs :—

His Majesty commanded John of Metingham (*c*) and his brethren (*sociis*) that they should in their discretion look out for and appoint a certain number from every county (*d*) out of those of the best standing and the most willing learners (*melioribus et legalioribus* (*e*) *et libentius addiscentibus*) according as they think it would be good for their courts and the King's subjects; further, that those so chosen shall follow the court (*f*) and deal with the business there and no one else shall. And it appears to the King and his Council that one hundred and forty such persons may be enough. Nevertheless, the said judges may, if they think fit, create more or less (*g*). And of the remainder [of the candidates] it shall be determined according to the discretion of the said judges.

Various questions at once occur. Was the 140 a

(*b*) 1 *Rot. Parl.* 84. The title is accepted by P. & M. (by implication) and by Spelman. A marginal note in the latter's *Gloss*. (*Apprenticii*) is : Videtur non fuisse sub hoc tempore statos in foro regii tribunalis Attornatos : nisi forte Filizarios. *Quaere;* as if the rescript was to provide *att*.

(*c*) He is called *Serv. reg. ad l.* in 1276 by Dugdale, *Chron. Ser.* 25, citing *Liberate*, 3 E. I, m. 2. J. of M. was a judge in 1278 : 3 Foss, 131, and now C.J. of the Common Pleas.

(*d*) So 1 P. & M. 195, 199, perhaps *quol.* = any they choose.

(*e*) For *legalis* see p. 150*u*. " Better class " *appr.* are often mentioned, *e.g.*, p. 318.

(*f*) It was only the Common Pleas which did not follow the court : *Magna Carta*, 17. Pleas of the Crown were in 1292 more diffused over the country than ever before; " royal pleas " *coram rege* subsequently in the King's Bench were not within S. 17, and followed the King till at least 1300; the Exchequer never left Westminster. Even the Common Pleas once sat at York, *temp.* E. III : McKechnie, *Magna Carta*, 308-17, citing 1 Seld. Soc. xiii-vi.

(*g*) *Vel numerum anticipent.* Forcellini (*anticipatus*) cites Ovid, *Metam.* 3, 235 : Anticipata via est =*fu abbreviata*. L. (in MS.) suggested *anticipo* here = praecipio = prescribe.

maximum? And is the decree designed to increase the pupils in question or to decrease them? for, at times, more lawyers are wanted to cope with the business. As that and population grew, we may assume that lawyers increased, but it is difficult to believe that in 1292 the number of any class (*h*) of them was a grievance.

It is impossible to get accurate statistics, but we get a glimpse in 1297. " There are about 142 appointments of attorneys in this term " (*i*) of about fifty-six individuals. " Then as now the bulk of the business . . . was transacted by a few . . . There are several instances of two attorneys being mentioned in the same appointment and it would almost seem, as if we have examples of partnership firms "; one seems to be " the principal member of the firm."

Now it has always been supposed that this document referred to the two classes *attornati* and *apprenticii*, on the strength of the words *de attornatis et apprenticiis* found in the margin of the *placitum*. But *attornati* are not so much as mentioned, whereas *addiscentes* is a synonym for *apprenticii*. And if the two classes are within it, are there to be 140 of each? and if not, in what proportion are they to be appointed? And how could the judges know which of the practising attornies were the likeliest pupils? And were the selected *attornati* to follow the court as, " the other branch " does to-day? Were they to suspend any of them? It was, perhaps, barely possible for the judges to find out who were the most promising, the *libentius addiscentes* among the acting *attornati* or aspirants to attornacy, if they were known, but to make this inquisition systematically seems impossible. There was not even a

---

(*h*) It has been estimated that in 1297 the whole population of England was about 3,800,000 : *Plac. Cur. R.* 1297; ed. Phillimore. Note to Index : Brit. Rec. Soc. 1898.

It is generally assumed that a plethora is aimed at; if so, cf. Spelman's " infesta multitudo " of both *att.* and *advv.* : " to-day [1626] you will find 140 *att.* in one county " : Glossary, *Att.*

(*i*) Phillimore, *ib.* xxiii.

rudimentary corporation of *attornati* as there was of *servientes*, who were, if not yet in name, in prospect the " brethren " of the judges. What seems to have happened is that this attempt at regulation—it seems to have been " a dead letter " (*k*), we never hear of it at work—was designed for the apprentices before they had chosen their " branch," and that the title *de attornatis, &c.*, was added later when the two avocations were definitely differentiated. There is no difficulty in supposing that the title was added by a later hand, perhaps after the Act of 1402, when the judges certainly had not weakened that control over practitioners which we here meet for the first time and which is the forecast of examination for entry. In the circumstances of 1292 that was pertinent and practicable. The " freshman " in early days has not to decide (*l*) whether he will go " to the bar " or the Law Society; he does, indeed, go to an inn, but he takes the same course as the other Apprentices.

This, perhaps, accounts for the story of John Organ; he was an apprentice, his employer, at any rate, thought that he was his *aturne* and " pleader," and no doubt he was for a time; which branch (if either) he followed later, we do not know. Again in 1313-4 suddenly in a very long case (*m*) in the Eyre of Kent, in which many well-known judges and lawyers argue, " Costone attorne " for the

---

(*k*) Like the later analogous attempts to limit the number of lawyers in Parliament.

(*l*) Bromyard, about 1380-90, when the two professions were certainly distinct apparently suggests the youth beginning life choosing between them; he compares the young lawyers to a monkey—animal in juventute sociale et aliqualiter placidum sed in senectute est animal odiosum et damnosum, etc., etc. So young scholars, in jure civili or in their first year (*in banco primo*) or in their second when they leave the school, are affable to everyone, sociable and prettily equipped (*curiose ornati*) and well spoken of by their neighbours, but when they have learned to practise (*placitare*) a little and injure their neighbours and to be *attorneatus & advocatus*, etc.," they begin to show their teeth: *Advocatus*, 33 B.

(*m*) 24 Seld. Soc. 176.

defendant intervenes and puts the court right about what a statute enjoins concerning writs—his special care; being on his legs he goes on to discuss legal principles and ends " we pray a bill of exception or that you will make an entry of our objection in the Roll." The judge replies; neither he nor the reporter is surprised at an " attorne's " addressing the court (despite its rarity or even uniqueness); probably he was an apprentice—and always an obscure lawyer. In 1337 there is a petition to Parliament from " John de Codyngton un Apprentiz de la court nostre seigneur le Roy et Attourne " who complains that though he is not liable he is threatened with military service " to the loss (*desheritson*) of the clients (*cliens*) to whom (*n*) he is attorney and to his own ruin." On evidence " that he is an attorney " he is relieved; the Council disregards his apprenticeship—it confers no *status*.

Thus, whether the rescript of 1292 owed its origin to someone at court who thought that the growth of lawyers was too rapid or too slow, and though, like so many other *placita*, before and after, it disappears (perhaps because the mischief was theoretical and the promoters did not insist upon it or found it unworkable), it assumes that the *apprenticius* is in a chrysalis state and may become a *narrator* or an *attornatus*; at the moment he is undifferentiated, and all that the legislator cares about is that in his pupillage he shall have some sort of education—about which, too, in 1280 the City " fathers " were anxious; both authorities look forward to a future.

Though the famous document in which that paternal disquietude is expressed goes very far to prove our present point we rely equally on that of 1292 because it clinches the argument of the former. It is time, says the City, to regulate all legal practitioners; a dozen years later, the Government with experience of more than one city, but

---

(*n*) 2 *Rot. Parl.* 96.

taking a hint, as it has done so often from the pioneer, essays to insist on some standard of proficiency. The ecclesiastical tribunals had long before either laid down a scheme (at any rate) of examination for its aspirants.

This is the best account we can give of the continuous process of the rise of the profession. In the *catena* of trials there were instances of advisers and representatives who were doing the work later done by the *attornatus* (*o*). The *minutiae* and details, of which a few specimens were given from " Glanvill," are obviously the rudimentary network of the code of etiquette between the two branches of the law with which we are now familiar; into its meshes have evidently been drawn in the centuries, rules and regulations, adjustments, customs and procedure which have been shown by experience, including perhaps some of those trials, to be convenient (though even now the topic, for instance, of what is *intra* or *ultra vires* of a legal adviser is by no means extinct). Perhaps we may say that the modern solicitor (*p*) — and so, by contraposition, the modern counsel — dates from the treatise of " Glanvill."

In Brunner's monograph will be found all the details for this period, which can be inferred from those binding or suggested *later*. Their intrinsic importance is great, but for our immediate purpose it is the process and the fact(s) of development during a given period that we wish to isolate. The nice distinctions between the respective powers of these various agents (or assistants) of the parties and the variations in the terms of appointment of each of them and in the withdrawal or extension thereof and in the multifarious conditions and incidents of multifarious cases rest upon scattered texts and precedents and formulae sometimes quite isolated, but the coherent system, which

---

(*o*) If Richard de Anesty had had one so called, surely he would have mentioned it.

(*p*) Or attorney; the difference was expressed by a wit as that " between a crocodile and an alligator."

they show bit by bit in process, was slow in forming. In short, there was an evolution of the lawyer as we know him, say, in 1300, and in the earliest stages we never can be sure that a variety in the institution here is not counterbalanced by another variety there, and that therefore generalisation may not be premature. Just as the whole legal system was for a time in a flux, so was the lawyer's position in it and—it follows—his nomenclature, as we have seen. So that it may be truer to say that up to 1200 there were several rather than two categories of advocates. The *attornatus* was not, like the attorney to-day (*q*), the broad base of the legal pyramid, but he is the first definite (*r*) character in our forensic *dramatis personae*; hence, to this day the head of the bar bears his name.

For a long time he is often the sole representative mentioned in records of cases, and hence, perhaps, he has been seized, for want of better material by German and other writers, for generalisations with which we have dealt (*s*).

The King, too, *i.e.*, the government, has his *attornatus*, probably when that kind of agent is well established. It is not, it seems, till 1278 that we hear of *attornatus regis* who *persequitur contra* the Bishop of Exeter (*t*), etc.,

---

(*q*) Cf. " the men of the 13th and 14th centuries " who promoted the bills (p. 173) " stood in some degree of professional kinship with " the lawyer of to-day," though the kinship is a distant one in years and distant in essence . . . the men . . . were not lawyers or advocates practising with any kind of public or official authority, but men whose only authority to act was the personal authority of the party, those attorneys whose only modern representatives are the attorneys acting under a power of attorney " : Bolland, 30 Seld. Soc. xliii. Few, he adds, betrayed their clients, " strong testimony to the general honesty of the class of men from which they came."

(*r*) The " essoin," App. X, being an *umbra*. (*s*) Pp. 130, 135.

(*t*) *Abbrev. Plac.* 193 b, because he encroached on the royal prerogative in dealing with lay suits and for other reasons. Perhaps *per*(-sequitur) is a mark of novelty; the invariable *sequitur* (originally from Roman law : Du Cange, *Secta* 4, citing Pliny) soon = to speak in court, even of laymen, *e.g.*, the judges proclaim at an *Iter* in 1321 " si quis pistorium . . . sequi voluerit in hac parte " : 1 *Lib. Cust.* 331; it does not = our " follows."

and "*attornatus regis* hoc non potest dedicere" (*u*). In 1281 W. de Penebrug *sequitur pro r.* (*x*) but called upon for his authority can produce none but his own, neither the chancellor's *preceptum* nor that of any *minister regis* (like Hervi's nominee (*y*)), and is sent to gaol (*z*); another "att. regis allegat contra" (*a*) the defendants (whether orally or graphically is not stated). Gilbert of Thornton appears in a Northampton *iter* against the Abbot of Peterborough (who throughout appears *per att. suum*). In 1325 Galfrus le Scrop " tunc att. r. respondit " (*b*), where *tunc* must refer to an earlier date, for in 1325 Galfrid was certainly a judge after having been a *serviens regis*; he probably is the Scrop who argues (*c*) in 1305, and is certainly the " King's serjeant staying near the person of the King by his order, when journeying through divers parts of England " in 1320-1 and so in 1322 (*d*). Now it happens in his case that the changes are rung on forensic terminology. We meet him as both *orator* and *attornatus* (*e*); in the *Iter* of 1321 he cross-examined (? *interrogavit*) (*f*) the Mayor and Aldermen, " pro r. calumniavit " (*g*) (made a serious claim), " speaks " (*h*) as *serviens d. r.* (when, too, a certain William of Exeter,

---

(*u*) *Abb. Plac.* 194 a.
(*x*) *Ib.* 273 a, rot. 2; as early as 1219 we had *sequi* of attornies : p. 138.
(*y*) P. 298.
(*z*) Exactly as Britton, B. 6, c. 10, 3; 2 Nichols, 358, directs.
(*a*) *Abb. Plac.* 273 a, rot. 35.
(*b*) *Abb. Plac.* 351 a.
(*c*) Y. B. 33-5 E. I, 63.
(*d*) 26 *Archaeologia*, 345, Ward Robe Account; there, too, W. Herle, " King's Serjeant," gets £133 6s. 8d. " in aid of his rank," as he " will shortly receive the order of knighthood," 1321; " the largest fee of that day paid to a lawyer " : Zane, 1 *Sel. Essays*, etc., 655; but was it a fee? And see p. 183.
(*e*) " Orator d. r. pro ipso in illo itinere constitutus " : 2 *Lib. Cust.* Pt. I, 289; *or.* is purely literary by this time.
(*f*) *Lib. Cust.* Pt. I, 305; Rolls.
(*g*) *Ib.* 307-8.
(*h*) *Ib.* 331, 375; *petiit* 368, 375.

not otherwise known, produces an old writ, *venit et dicit quod ipse sequitur pro d. r.* : he is independent of Galfred, so probably he is a mere *attornatus, ad hoc*) : *serviens d. r. qui sequitur pro d. r.* (*i*)—the only instance of this combination; *dicit* simply or *qui sequitur pro r. dicit* (*k*). And on one occasion his junior (or " with him ") John de Denham, who, with G. de Toudeby (who sometimes sat as judge) had appeared with him before now, *loco G. le Scrop serv. d. r. dicit* (*l*). As all these references are from the same *Iter* the writer of the record saw no inconvenience in varying his description of the same counsel, so that perhaps in 1321 phraseology was not very rigid (*m*).

Thus about 1290 (*n*) we are not surprised to find in a record an *attornatus* speaking of his own work in court as *sequi* and *respondere*; still, gradually the formula *sequitur pro* is used only of counsel.

The status of William of Exeter is peculiar. He is a link between the casual *ad hoc attornatus* and the professional, probably called in for the convenience of the moment, owing to local circumstances or knowledge. So in 1313 the name of him " qy suyt pur le roy " (*o*), in a *quare impedit*, is not so much as mentioned throughout the report, though in the Plea Roll he is called William of Langley (*p*). During the trial he asked leave " to vary his title," *i.e.*, amend his plea. After argument Scrope, J. says (*q*) :

(*i*) *Ib.* 336.
(*k*) *Ib.* 401, 405, 421, 422.
(*l*) *Lib. Cust.* 289.
(*m*) *Ib.* 375.
(*n*) P. 297.
(*o*) *The King* v. *Boys* : 39 Seld. Soc. 65, xli; ed. and transld. Bolland.
(*p*) *Ibidem*; in the Patent Rolls of 1315 he is appointed " during pleasure " to do a job exactly of this sort " with a fee of £10 a year " (p. xlii : editor), *i.e.*, as he was wanted, from time to time.
(*q*) " Cryptic remarks " (*ib.* editor), but perhaps the suggestion above solves the difficulty. The reporter would certainly have mentioned Langley had he known his name. It looks as if he appeared just once when counsel for the King were absent, for several are mentioned in the case and one at least may well have been for the Crown. " Except

"He that sueth for the King cannot omit or change aught to the King's possible disadvantage, for he is not in the position of an attorney. Any stranger may appear on behalf of the King and if he make a slip (? *mespryngne*) the King's right ought not to be lost. Inge J. He that sueth for the King will get his punishment but the King's right ought not to be lost by reason of his mistake unless he had changed the count—that is, the right of action &c." William is otherwise unknown and, we may safely assume, only represents the Crown because it was temporarily convenient. When Scrope says that " any stranger " may appear for the King, he might have added " or for any one else," but this does not mean that any unauthorised person could jump up in court and " take on " the case for the Crown. The judge points out, reasonably enough on an application for indulgence, that the casual *attornatus*, is a mere deputy, not like the regular lawyer of a client, on whom it would be hard to suffer for bad pleading and when the client is the Crown, men who are almost literally " the King's judges " constantly avow expressly their duty to protect its rights (until, at any rate, they know its pleasure) and in matters of procedure, to this day, its representatives have privileges, *e.g.*, in the right of reply in certain circumstances. These are not individual concessions, but mere survivals from an original forensic omnipotence. Inge, J., accepting the theory, adds : " Yes, save the client's rights by all means, but the peccant lawyer, even the King's, must take the usual consequences " whatever they were.

Probably before the King wanted a man of business to protect his purse, the great landlords did so even more. This is plain from c. 33 of the great First Statute of

---

for " the Year Book " we should know nothing at all about this incident. The Plea Roll entirely ignores it " : *ib.* xl. As often a Year Book report is capricious. The learned editor's remarks, 41 Seld. Soc. x-xiii, do not seem to carry the matter further; and see *ib.* pp. 75-6.

Westminster (*r*) in 1275; no Sheriff shall suffer any Barretors " to maintain quarrels in their Shires, neither Stewards (*Scneschaus*) of great Lords, nor other unless he be Attorney for his Lord, to make suit nor to give (*rendre*) judgments in the Counties, nor to pronounce (*pronūcier*) the judgments, if he be not specially required and prayed of all the Suitors and Attornies of the Suitors, which shall be at the Court (*Jorneie*) " under pain to Sheriff and usurper. Thus the lord has his attorney—his deputy—just as the suitors have theirs for litigation or other business—but also to sit as his agent or deputy in the Court baron or leet of the manor, as he often does still (*s*).

The King, too, would certainly have no difficulty in finding among his servants an *Attornatus* for his particular business. Now, just at the time when we hear of the King's attorney we find that agent being regulated elsewhere.

Another great corporation which wants an attorney to itself is the City, which often consciously follows the model of Westminster. In May 1298 " William de Grantham " is appointed attorney by the Mayor and Aldermen and " he will receive annually so long as he be attorney 20s."; in August of that year in the presence of the (named) Mayor and Aldermen " the freedom of the City was granted to William de Granham (note : or Graham) (*t*) attorney before the King, *viz*. [before] Sir Roger de Bracbasoun [C.J.] and his fellows, so that however the said William shall remain attorney before the justices aforesaid on behalf of the Commonalty of the City of London from year to year to the end of his life and at the will of the Aldermen aforesaid for 20s. yearly . . . " (*u*). He died in 1317,

---

(*r*) 1 *Stat. Realm; Stat.* 35.
(*s*) 1924.
(*t*) *Letter Bks.* B. 216; *C.* 26. In 1311-2 " William de Graham Serjeant " makes an acknowledgment : if he is the City's attorney above, he may well have become a *serv. ad. l.*
(*u*) *Let. Bk. C.* 26.

having been described in City accounts in respect of this salary as "*generalis attornatus* of the Commonalty before the justices of the King's Bench before the King himself [and] receives yearly for his service 20s." (*x*).

Generalis attornatus means here, there is little doubt, attorney to the Corporation (or Commune); the phrase is probably due to the second Statute of Westminster (*y*), 1285, where and in other contexts, it means, one who has the modern "general power of attorney." Thus in 1295 "Because John . . . is at the King's command, about to cross to him, he may have general attorneys in all his suits" (*z*). This was just the kind of plenipotentiary, like the *generalis procurator*, of whom the City was in need instead of *ad hoc* representatives; hence there may be a hint of two senses in "*generalis*." Possibly "*communis*"

(*x*) *Let. Bk. D.* 314.

(*y*) Of which c. 10 enacted that in certain cases lords "*facere possint attornatum generalem* to sue for them in all Pleas in the Circuit (*itinere*) of Justices moved or to be moved for them or against them, during the Circuit: which Attorney or Attorneys shall have full Power in all Pleas moved during the Circuit until the Plea be determined or that his Master remove him . . . " (*1 Stat. R.* : *Stat.* 80). Again, *ib.* 131; *Ord. de Libertatibus perquirendis*, c. 3 (1299); "People dwelling beyond the sea that have Lands or Rents in England, if they will purchase Letters of Protection or will make general attorneys (*generals attornetz*) they shall be sent unto the Exchequer . . . : c. v. Also such as be not able to travel and People that dwell in far countries from the Chancery which plead or be impleaded shall have a writ (*bref*) out of the Chancery to some sufficient man that shall receive their Attorneys when need is." By 1299 experience had suggested the qualification "sufficient." Then the *Mirror of Justices* (probably 1285-90) has "general attornies can appoint and remove special attornies": 7 Seld. Soc. 87. So Britton, B. VI, c. 7, 3; 2 Nichols, 349 : "Some . . . obtain our letters patent of protection . . . and who nevertheless by virtue of our letters patent do also make general attorneys: and such persons do well and wisely." One of these two cited writers seems to be the first to distinguish expressly between "special" and "general" attorneys: Brit., B. II, c. 15, 4; amplified B. 6, c. 10, 2.

There are many instances of Letters of Protection in *Cal. Docts. Ireland*, ed. Sweetman, 1293—1301, but not before: see *Protection* (Index).

(*z*) *Cal. Just. Rolls Ireland*, 72; at 417 such letters patent are set out: 1302.

att. was not favoured because legislation, royal and civic, had given the other phrase the start.

The passage from *Letter Book* D. 314 quoted above is immediately followed by similar entries about William de Burgh " General Attorney of the Commonalty before the aforesaid justices." Thomas le Palmere " Attorney of the Commonalty before the justices of the Common Bench," Harscolph de Whitewelle " Attorney of the Commonalty before the Barons of the Exchequer "; so exactly Thomas Harold; William de Wyckewan, " Attorney of the Commonalty before the justices of the Bench "—all apparently contemporaneous notes and correct and levelling the attorneys whether " general " or not to the same plane (*a*). Thus de Burgh one of Gra(n)tham's successors, whom the scribe here calls " general " attorney, loses that adjective in the much more full and precise following entry.

In 1310-1 William de Burgo (or Burghley) " clerk came before . . . the Mayor, &c., . . . and was admitted to the freedom of the City and sworn . . . and thereupon the said William became attorney of the Mayor and Commonalty for prosecuting and defending their liberties when challenged before . . . the King and thereupon he took corporal oath. And he will receive yearly . . . so long as he remain in the said office 30s. . . ." (*b*). He acts in that capacity in 1313 (*c*) in the King's courts. The electors choose a " clerk," *i.e.*, a learned person. His salary has been raised above that of his two predecessors to 30s. a year, but his successor goes back to the 20s. In the same accounts (*d*)

(*a*) Unless we suppose the K. B. to warrant a special title. When the learned editor (*ib.*, n. (2)) refers to " J. de Asshebourne as Pleader and Attorney-General for the Mayor, &c. . . . " in 1317 presumably *generalis att.* is in the original.

(*b*) *Letter Bk.* D. 253 " libertas W. . . . et ejus admissio in attornatum " : marg.

(*c*) *Letter Bk.* E. 34, xxvi (1327); 1 *Lib. Alb.* 300 (" Att. Maj. et Communitatis Civitatis Londiniarum "), 434 (1321), 436 (1321); 1321 is the date in Riley's transln. (1861), but (*Lt. Book* D. 14, n. (3)) W. de B. was removed from this office 1317; perhaps he was reinstated.

(*d*) *Ib.* p. 315.

appear named Attorneys of the Commonalty before the justices of " the Common Bench " (*e*) (2 marks), the Barons of the Exchequer (*f*) (one at 40s., another at 20s. (*g*)), " the Justices of the Bench " (2 marks : all yearly). The distribution to the various Royal Courts (*h*) suggests that the City distinguished between its interests in its great constitutional franchises and those in its own courts, where, no doubt, it could at any moment, find plenty of attorneys.

It would seem, then, that—what between the royal and their own courts—the City needed about 1300 A.D. more than one (*i*) *generalis attornatus*. And we may safely assume that these recorded men were eminent in their profession and, it follows, were professional. In the national tribunals, too, at this moment, " the appearance

---

(*e*) Thomas le Palmere " de Cornhulle was sworn, &c., in the King's Bench " very much in the same terms as de Burgo (" and to instruct and inform the serjeant of the City as often as is necessary, &c., for 26s. 8d. *per ann*."): *Lt. Bk. C.* 115-6 (1302-3); *ib.* 145, he is an assessor of damages : 1305. Perhaps he is " T. le P. clerk," who in 1307 acknowledged a debt : *Lt. Bk. B.* 198.

(*f*) *Lt. Bk. C.* 116 (1306).

(*g*) " Thomas Harold," if he=Thomas Harwold, he was one of the City's " Wardens and Attorneys " at Winchester Fair in 1329 : *Letter B. E.* 239.

(*h*) In *Lib. Alb.* B. I, Pt. I, c. 7; Rolls, 25; transln. (1861) 23, where there is an Order of proceedings on presentation of a new Mayor at the Exchequer : The Mayor and Aldermen for the City appointed one attorney of the City for (*or* of) the Exchequer (" unum de scaccario attornatum dict. civ."), " a member of the Exchequer as attorney " (Riley), but what could " member " mean? *Unum* is contrasted with *duos*, below : " ad calumniandas et clamandas suas libertates," similarly in the Common Bench " unum de illa placea att. civ. : in Banco reg. ponere solebant *duos att. conjunctim et divisim* ad. &c." [see below]; *de scac.* is a common phrase.

As this ch. (7) refers quite correctly to a presentation in 1304 " ut patet libro C. fol. cxii° " translated *Lt. Bk. C.* 175-6 (which is f. cxii), it must have been compiled (as probably the whole of *Lib. Alb.* B. I, Pt. I) after 1304; how long after we cannot say.

(*i*) The attorneys cannot be graded according to salary, for the one " before the King himself " earns less than one in the Exchequer.

Private litigants sometimes appointed more than one *att.*, as Joan did—three " conjunctim," of whom two came to court and one did not; of course the point was taken that the two could not be heard " et ita credo " says the reporter : Y. B. 1314; 39 Seld. Soc. 133, see p. 137.

of the same attorneys in a large number of suits term after term shows that they practised professionally," says an authority (*k*), who has counted.

Though it is difficult to believe that London did not regulate its attorneys before a provincial town, at any rate, Leicester did so in 1277. Indeed the references of that year are of especial interest, for the Leicester archives show that in 1257 " attornatus " had not lost its original meaning there but was growing to its legal estate; in February there was a *custos* of the mayoralty, and a few days later Alexander " le deboner " is his deputy (*l*), " attornatus "; in August he and a burgess go to the Earl to get a mayor elected, and in January, 1258, one is appointed; he is himself mayor in 1271.

In the Charter of 1277 we read : " Whereas attornies have not been wont to be taken except in court and in the presence of the parties and that for the plaintiff only, by which many people have lost their other [*sc.* than plaintiff's] business or their pleas, it is provided that the one party or the other, so wishing may make attorney and this as well in the absence of his adversary as in his presence; and that the attorney may be received in his place to do as he himself would, except only in making law [*oath* : 2 *Bor. Custs.* 11] that is to say, in the pleas which may be pleaded by attorney; and that before two jurats who may bear witness to the attorney if need be." The editress points out that it is here implied that " the original custom allowed attorney only to the plaintiff and only in the defendant's presence " (*m*). The attorney's special job is technical; he is to plead the essential plea.

(*k*) Mr. G. J. Turner, 42 Seld. Soc. lxviii, who also says that *temp.* E. II " there already existed a class of professional attorneys specially authorised by the court to act for their clients in each action at law "; they are recorded on the rolls and actually mentioned by name.

(*l*) *Records of L.* (1103—1327), xi, iii, 71-5, 110, 385; *ib.* 161, for the Charter.

(*m*) 2 *Bor. Custs.* clv.

THE ATTORNEY. 295

How did any man get his attorney? Anybody might be an attorney, though he was always liable to be asked for his credentials. We have had traces of a friend taking, as it were, a message to the court (*n*), and from some such simple practice—the lowest terms of *consilium*—selection and specialisation probably sprang. A suggestion has been made (*o*) of a connection with essoins. In that view, by degrees, casual messages of excuse became so frequent—naturally—that at last the court regulated them by a sort of code (*p*) and they got a technical (or adopted a popular)

(*n*) That at first the *att.* was strictly regarded as having a very limited function appears from cases where he was also tendered as a witness (in the sense of the word at the given date); thus in 1224 a man and wife J. & E. *petunt per att.* who *producit sectam* J. S. et *tales*. Robert, defendant, *petit sibi allocari quod J. predictus qui se facit testem est att. J. & E.*: 2 Br. N. B. 719, pl. 941; exactly the same objection taken *ib.* v. 3, p. 8, pl. 953. But Robert (p. 296*s*) is admitted as a " witness " in 1290.   (*o*) P. 85, App. X.

(*p*) That in Hengham Magna, c. VII, *de attornatis faciendis*, is apposite to its time (Ed. I)* *viz.*: " After essoining [App. VIII A] defendant may appear in court and *facere atturnatos*: he may certainly make two if he be seriously ill or the victim of fraud, at whatever stage his suit is. Both defendant and plaintiff may make attorneys by this formula: So-and-So [A] puts So-and-So [B] in his place *versus* So-and-So [C] for his suit about land. [Follows *formula* for removal, p. 299*c*.] Strictly the principal ought to do it in open court, but in proper cases the Chancellor will send one of his *clerici* to him to go through the form. The Chancellor sends a writ to the judges to recognise the *att.* so made. But the King may *ex gratia sua* give anyone [official] the power of accepting attornies so made in any given suit. [Full formula given†: probably a survival from his *exclusive* power to do so]: and so he may if either party is ill [without their essoining?]: formula: 4 *legales milites* of the county to be the Commissioners. The itinerant justices may receive an *att.* and must notify their brethren thereof. But a defendant in a case where imprisonment may follow cannot make an *att.* " for no one ought to be imprisoned for another's *delictum*—a personal matter." [Obviously a survival from the original absolute identification of an *att.* with his principal—probably meant to account for the rule still in force then that an accused of crime could have no *consilium*; but the text may be limited to criminal cases.] For the rest of this c. see App. X.

* It must be earlier than the rescript (p. 281) whether that refers to *att.* or not.

† *dedimus vobis potestatem*, etc.; hence at this date it was not unnecessary, as it is said to have become under the Stat. of Merton, to sue out this writ.

name; an individual who got a reputation for " his way with the court " would in time make a practice of it. There are early indications that unsuitable or designing persons got hold of ignorant clients. Even to-day inferior " officers of the law " about all courts, whether well meaning or not, give legal advice to humble suitors about the conduct of their cases; " foreigners " are naturally apt to fall into menial hands in the early stages of their contact with foreign law. Thus about 1300 Dublin and Waterford decree (*q*) : " Of the catchpole as attorney : if a foreigner brings a writ against a citizen and the catchpole (*seriaunt*; Dublin) of the town undertakes to be attorney for the foreigner against the citizen, he shall lose his mace and go to prison. For it cannot be that he does not know the counsels of the town [which may not be in his client's interest] and if he does anything against any of the city he is perjured. But he can very well be an attorney by leave of the mayor and bailiffs, though not otherwise." This seems to be a " squeeze " of London's provision.

Miss Johnstone well says (*r*) : " There is no hard and fast rule as yet. One imagines that Roger de Thornton [a plaintiff] *e.g.* appointed Henry de la Legh and Nicholas de Cerne [who have their own *attornatus*] his attorneys after watching their successful pleading in their own cause. Certain names, however, recur again and again, as attorneys " (*s*). In fact, she says, " attorneys are practically professional pleaders " : *sc.* in 1290.

We can, indeed, sometimes see the attorney " instructing " counsel; as, for example, in 1293 (says Horwood) (*t*) :

(*q*) Bateson, 2 *Bor. Custs.* 12; 21 Seld. Soc.; Gilbert, *Hist. & Mun. Docts. Ireland*, 264; Rolls.

(*r*) *State Trials, Ed. I* (1289-93); Camd. Soc. 3rd ser. v. 9 : p. xxv.

(*s*) But in the cases in this volume the only named attorney of Roger is Robert Crestyen (as one of several), p. 21; n.b.—he and other witnesses of higher standing are *jurati et examinati*.

(*t*) Y. B. 32-3 E. I, xxxii. See further on the relation of *att.* and serjt. Index.

"In a case in the MS. cited as B the judge asked the attorney if he avowed what his sergeant had said on his behalf, and the attorney said that he did" (*u*).

Again, we find both acting in the same cause, *viz.*, that just cited from the State Trials and clearly with different functions. The question was what had happened in a previous trial; it was charged that W. de Brompton the judge (1) had terrorised Roger's *attornati* to such an extent that they had not dared to plead (*respondere*); (2) had forbidden all the *narratores* in his court to help Roger. To the latter and their relations with the *attornati* we shall refer in the proper place, but here we note that while both classes come forward and deny on oath the respective allegations, Robert Crestyen swears that the judge did not threaten him on the day when " that defence was entered " —*i.e.*, peculiarly the job of the *attornatus*—" nor did or said anything which prevented his going on and pleading for Roger (*bene sequi . . . vel respondisse pro R.*)," but that something else did. Moreover, Robert had evidently appeared in the absence of Roger, but the *narratores* in his presence.

Another case (*x*) in those Trials is illustrative. Complaint is made against one of Ralph de Hengham's, C.J.'s, clerks that in a case pending before him, he, the clerk, had acted (*sustinuit placitum*) for the complainants' adversaries, *et advocavit quemdam J. de B. attornatum in placita ad placitandum H. de A. ubi . . . J. de B. numquam fuit attornatus*. The clerk successfully answered that the complainants had accepted J. as the *attornatus* throughout the proceedings in question. But the implication is clear

---

(*u*) The date of this MS. is not given, but from the implied *deadvocatio* it seems to be of our period.

(*x*) P. 26 : *advocavit*=admitted; literary rather than technical. Fraud of this sort seems to have been notorious, for Britton (B. 6, c. 10, 5; 2 Nichols, 360) says : " people have purchased tenements after the writs have been sued out against their feoffors and have friends in court who put themselves forward as attorneys of the tenants to make a defence against the right of plaintiffs."

that it was possible to represent one's self fraudulently as *attornatus* when one was not really so employed, and that in 1290 it was still essential that there should be a formal appointment *ad hoc*. But the gravest implication in this and other cases (*ib.*) is that a judge's clerk had opportunities for chicane in process. The whole class was castigated by a contemporary satirist (*y*). Even earlier before there was royal or civic organization there was often suspicion that an unscrupulous official would collude with an unscrupulous attorney; thus Walter Hervi, the ex-Mayor of London (1271-2), is said to have vouched (*testificavit*) an attorney, as properly appointed by the King's writ, in the *curia regis*; it was discovered—(the author (*z*) is a bitter enemy of Walter)—that no such writ was ever issued and that Walter had done it to defeat " the other side "; he is charged with suborning citizens to come to the Hustings and make a false accusation against the Mayor by the mouth of a certain *causidicus*; perhaps the attorney above —a very early instance of representation by " counsel " otherwise than in a suit. No doubt it was this sort of abuse which led to the discipline of the 1275 Statute. A later statute (*a*) " de finibus et attornatis " checks in the same spirit encroachments which were even more grievous; no Baron of the Exchequer nor any of " our justices shall admit any Attornies but only in Pleas that pass afore (*coram*) them in the Benches and in Places where they be assigned by Us. And the same Power of admitting Attornies we prohibit and deny to the Clerks (*clīcis*) and servants (*ministris*) of the said Barons and Justices: and do ordain that if any Attornies be admitted hereafter by

---

(*y*) Pp. 163; 118, 239 : Pierre de Langtoft; *Chronicle* (1289) : " Ses (E. I's) Justises e ses clercs attaint de fauseté " : 2 Rolls, 184.

(*z*) *Lib. de Antiq. Leg.* 169, 170.

(*a*) 1 *St. of Realm*, 215, which gives the date variously, the reign being uncertain, but it is not later (*ib.*; *Chron. Tab. V*), then E. II : in 1 Pickering's edn., p. 360, 1322 is given.

any of the Persons aforesaid; their Admission shall be of none effect : Reserved always to the Chancellor for the time being his Authority in admitting Attornies according to whose Discretion they shall be admitted; and to our Chief Justice as heretofore hath been observed in the Admission of Attornies."

Again, the client may formally throw over the *attornatus*; in 1201 he comes into court in person and says that he will himself go on with his suit (*b*). In time avowal is generally assumed as a matter of course, but as early as Edward I's reign there is a formula of dismissal (*c*). In the Leicester Charter (*d*) of 1277 the borough court is reformed and the plaintiff may now " fully state his suit . . . by himself, if he knows how, or if not by another who is avowed (*avoe*)," and exactly the same of the defendant (*d*). As time goes on, too, it sometimes looks as if parties *dishonestly* disavowed their *attornatus* to gain time or to " bluff." Thus in 1299 Ricard de Kerdiff in an action (*e*) for recovery of land against a man and his wife called Thomas del Auney to warrant him; Thomas " essoins according to law," but at the hearing Geoffrey del Auney, probably a kinsman, comes into court, says he is Thomas's attorney " caused the essoin to be annulled and warranted to Ricard and fraudulently against the will of Thomas rendered " one of the properties in dispute to the married pair. Thus they win against Ricard, but he gets [the same quantity of?] Thomas's land " to his [T.'s] great damage, especially as Thomas by the essoin should have had respite

---

(*b*) *1 Cur. R. Rolls*, 421 : [Kent—Comes] de Gines qui posuerat loco suo B. filium suum vel W. de Curton ' versus S. de A. [venit in c]uriam et amovit eos dicens se in propria persona prosequi. *Ib.* 411 a man *amovit* his brother and substitutes two men : 1201.

(*c*) *Hengham Mag.* c. 7. *Talis amovet tales (att.) quos prius (fecerat).* In 1437 the Dean of Lincoln *disallocavit exoneravit et incarcerari petebat* the att. of the Chapter in *communi banco* : *Cathedral Stat.* Pt. 2, p. 424 (1897) : ed. Chr. Wordsworth.

(*d*) *1 Rec. of Leic.* 156; *2 Bor. Custs.* 6.

(*e*) *Cal. Just. Rolls Irel.* 23—31 E. I : 262.

to some day on which he might have said wherefore he ought not to answer " the couple " to that writ." This is, no doubt, Thomas's plea and Geoffrey is promptly " attached " to answer for his " deceit." Geoffrey asserts that all he did was done as attorney by Thomas's own orders and he proves it by witnesses to the satisfaction of a jury; Thomas acknowledges it and is sent to prison (where he may have been) when (and it is perhaps why) he essoined. Later, the *attornatus* had to be guaranteed by some authority. Thus in 1387 Lokton, J., who, at the bar, had been retained by the Abbey of Meaux, formally certified (*f*) their attorney—of whose appointment he would naturally know.

Possibly it is significant that we never meet *deattornatio* (as we do *deadvocatio*) in England and very rarely at all (*g*); the word is in no Latin dictionary. We can only infer that throwing over an *attornatus* was such a frequent occurrence that it never got an official name, whereas *deadvocatio* was a rare and serious business.

Sometimes, again, it is difficult to see why the *attornatus* attends or what is his special function. Thus when in 1313-4 four knights (*chivalers* (*h*)) are chosen for a grand assize " by the assent of the parties and these were then sworn to choose sixteen knights and serjeants (*seriauntz* (*i*)) of themselves and others . . . they then

---

(*f*) " L. . . . cum att. nostrum in eadem placito nostro contra regem in scaccario recordasset et ad bancum regis . . ." : 3 *Chron. Melsa*, 211; the writer is well informed on legal matters and goes into the pleadings and the case at length. The Index states that L. was exiled " for appearing against the Crown " in this case! The reason of his removal is well known and, moreover, he was judge not counsel.

(*g*) Brunner cites from a judgment of the Exch. of Normandy in 1239 (Delisle, *Recueil*, p. 149, No. 671) : " J. . . . non potuit deattornare att. suum . . . est in miser. pro deattornatione." Bracton probably would have used the word, if it had existed, *e.g.*, B. II, c. 35, 14; 1 Rolls, 650 : poterit tenens, si voluerit, illum deadvocare cui fuerat attornatus—before the differentiation of *serviens* and *attornatus*.

(*h*) 27 Seld. Soc. 83, xviii.

(*i*) Obviously not *servv. ad l.*, but who they were is not clear, perhaps merely attendants on the Knights : see p. 182*p*.

withdrew themselves from the bar (*la barre*) and the attornies on both sides were bidden to go along with them and in the presence of those attornies they chose to themselves twelve. . . ." Possibly it was only a matter of arrangement in this case, but it is a reminder that even as late as 1313 practice was not rigid all over the country.

In dealing with statutes, there must be a caution about the Statute of Merton, 1235-6, " the first set of laws " which, in later days, usually bears the name of ' Statute ' (*k*) and the first legislation on attorneys; cl. 10 (*l*) is : " every Freeman which oweth Suit (*sectam*) to the County, Trything, Hundred, Wapentake, or to the Court of his Lord, may freely make his Attorney (*facere att. suum* (*m*)) to do those suits for him." Brunner (*n*) shows that this does not refer to representation in a lawsuit, but to the duty of subjects to attend court as *sectatores* (*o*), citing appositely *Mirror of Justices* (*p*).

By 1275 we get something like the converse of the right of representation in the First Statute of Westminster; c. 29 was, as we have seen, quite wide enough to " hit " a peccant attorney, if necessary. Another chapter (33) is set out p. 289, whence, by this time, it seems, lords as well as tenants were sending deputies to the local courts

---

(*k*) 1 P. & M., I, vi, 158.

(*l*) 1 *St. Realm* : Stats., 4. Twiss, 3 *Bracton*, lvii—viii, lxii, gives reasons for thinking that cl. 10 was not in the original St., but that it dates from E. I. But when in 1270 or 1268 H. III conceded this privilege to suitors in the City courts and included *non*-citizens in the grant—a new concession—he expressly adds *sicut alibi in curia nostra* : Lib. de Antiq. Legg. 104; cf. pp. 138, 225, 229. But Twiss was not aware of Brunner's correction, which, however, does not affect this argument.

(*m*) *Fac. att.* occurs here first in a St. For attornies making their attornies, see p. 276.

(*n*) Cited p. 3*k*; transln. p. 274. Hence the marg. note, " Attornies in County Courts," though in essence and nomenclature good law to-day is misleading for 1235-6.

(*o*) It gives relief " from regular attendance at the ordinary sessions " : St. 3 *Hist.* 437.

(*p*) 7 Seld. Soc. 37-8.

and the sheriff has to be cautious who he allows to sit there; but if the " suitors " are satisfied, he has no further responsibility. In 1278 the Statute of Gloucester reveals apparently an abuse—that of parties appearing by attorney and keeping out of the way if judgment goes against them; c. 8 enacts that while defendants—a concession—may so appear in pleas of trespass, etc., before justices, " if they be attainted in their absence," the sheriff may be asked to take them and " they shall have like Pain as they should have had " if they had been present when judgment was given.

The acquiescence in the view that the rescript of 1292 dealt with practising attorneys has been supposed to prove more than it does. It is suggested (*q*) that as " the precept of 20 Ed. I does not mention the serjeants it is likely that they did not practise before the justices *in itinere* but confined themselves to the more important business before the Court in Banc "; hence " the absence of any mention of serjeants in the earliest reports of cases on circuit. The attorneys would be the ordinary practitioners—those whose business lay chiefly in the local Courts and before the itinerant justices and who possessed that acquaintance with the law which is given by familiarity with business; the apprentices would be those who attended circuit mainly as a means of education, to familiarise themselves with principles and practice that they might hereafter be qualified for the degree of serjeant." But we do actually find, as we have seen, that even common folk ask for a serjeant *in itinere*. Once we recognise (*r*) that this " precept " sets the seal on a legal profession, there is not much

---

(*q*) *A Sketch of the Early History of Legal Practitioners*: 7: J. *Marshall*, Att.-at-Law, Leeds, 1869 : an interesting but uncritical pamphlet. It is admitted (*ib*.) that in Y. B. 21 Ed. I serjeants are twice found *in itinere*—the fact that they appear for the Crown is taken to make a difference; a view apparently taken from Horwood, p. 187*f*.

(*r*) As perhaps Mr. Marshall and Manning (*Serviens*, p. 45) do not.

difficulty in understanding it; it assumes that only professionals will want "to go circuit," *i.e.*, with the royal judges, and is not much concerned who serves the local courts at other times.

The first certain legislation aimed at the rank growth of lawyers is in 1402; 4 Henry IV, c. 18, recites that " owing to the great number of Attorneys ignorant not learned in the Law as they were wont to be before this Time " it enacts that " all " the attornies are to be examined and those of good fame and learning—a point emphatically urged —are to be put " in the Roll " and sworn, " especially that they make no suit in a foreign county "; " and the other attornies shall be put out " and " their Masters," *i.e.*, their employers, be informed thereof; as their places fall vacant they are to be filled by the justices and an admitted man doing anything unprofessional (*e.g.*, " in any default of record ") is to be disqualified. By the next chapter no officer of the lord of a franchise is to be attorney in his court. Control of some sort has existed ever since. For instance, in a passage (*s*) which is valuable for the glimpse it gives us of the actual work of the professional *attornatus*, one of Henry V's Chancellors " warns all attornies that as soon as they receive plaints, answers, replications or rejoinders they must under a penalty, register them " apparently, in the Chancery, where it was the business of two notaries, *inter alia*, to enter the names of the attornies with those of their parties. Moreover, the same document clearly assumes a distinction in the duties of counsel and attorney and, probably, their both being engaged (*t*) in the same action, for on a " summons for directions " which either one (or the party) may ask for, *either* the party *or* his attorney must in person move a Master to settle times for " answers, replies, rejoinders, production of witnesses and their evidence, the hearing of the cause,

---

(*s*) The *Renovacio*, p. 439*a*.   (*t*) P. 332.

and issuing other *brevia*." But only " counsel (*unus consiliariorum*) frequenting the bar of the Chancery " may sign a bill in Chancery. And from the Order of 1388 it seems that a sharp distinction was drawn between the kind of business *attornati* did in the Chancery and in other courts (*u*).

If we want to summarise the near history of the attorney, we can quote two petitions in 1455 side by side (*x*) : the first is from Fountains Abbey who are harassed by " bogus " plaints (" 300 or more ") in local courts " And howe beit " they say " that the commen lawe of Englond will, that every persone enpleted for eny cause in the which he is admittible to wage is (*sic*) lawe, that the same persone so empleted, should wage his lawe be [by] his Attorney, havyng sufficiaunt auctorite yerto," yet, bailiffs and other officers of those courts had refused to receive such attorneys until Parliament had interfered and authorised all " Religious " to appear " be ther Attorneys generallz or generall " (*sic*); to defeat this right, they say, these officials " oftymes for yer singulere lucre and be covyne had betwix them and the seid malicious people " fixed the hearings at different and distant courts on one day. They pray for relief according to the existing law " And that they, yer lawe so [by one or more Attorneys] waged, may doo ye seid lawe or lawes be a Commoyne (*fellow-monk*) of ye same place, with oyer persones with hym, to ye noumbre of vi persones, or elles be another persone assigned and depute . . . with vi persones with him, ye seid lawes to do . . ."; *i.e.*, apparently, the professional attorney pleads technically and the non-professional

---

(*u*) The officials are not to meddle with " *this sort of attornamentum*," *viz.*, in *another* court, but they have very much to do with *att.* in their own; but they might be *generales att.* (*ib.*)—exceptionally but conveniently. Probably the *att.* practising here looked on themselves—as that court did—as superior and exclusive.

(*x*) 5 *Rot. Parl.* 325-7.

deputies give evidence, etc. " Soit fait comme il est desire," says the King.

The second is the famous prayer (*y*) of some citizens of Norwich and, perhaps, of some inhabitants of Norfolk and Suffolk in 1455—all, at any rate, who were interested in preserving neighbouring Courts Baron. It runs :—

" Whereas of late were but vi or viii common Attorneys within " the limits just mentioned, " at ye moost, that resorted unto youre Courts, in which tyme yer was grete quiete and peas " therein " and litell trouble or vexation had by foreyn or wrongfull sewtes; and hit is so nowe that yer be in the said Citee and Countees xx (*a*) ⁄ iiii Attorneys or moo, the most parte of theym not havyng any oyer lyving, but only yer wynnyng by yer seid Attorneyshep, and the moost part also of theym not beyng of sufficient konnyng to be any Attorney, which goo to every Faire, Merkette, and oyer places where congregation of peouple is, and stere (*sic*) procure meve and excite the people to take untreue Seutes, foreyn Seutes and Seutes for lite trespasses, lite offenses and smale sommes of dette, the actions of whome be triable and determinable in Court Baron, * affermyng and promysing the seid people, for to have recovere with grete damages for their costages * : the which causeth many a sewte to be take for evill wille and malice, without reasonable cause : * and also the seid Attorneys, before any recovere or remedie had for their Clientes, sewe ye same Clyentes for their fees, and have theym in Exigents, and often tyme outlawe theym or they be ware ; and than woll the seid Attorneys not ende with their seid Clyentes, but if they have their costes and fees atte yer

---

(*y*) 5 *Rot. Parl.* 326, p. 268.
(*a*) *quatr viginti* in Statute; fourscore, transln.; but surely text = 24?
* * Omitted in Statute.

owen wille, as well for the secunde action, as for the firste,* to ye grete and importable [= ? intolerable] damages manyfold vexation and trouble, of the inhabitauntes of ye seid Citee and Countees, to the perpetuell distruction of all ye Courtees Baron in the seid Countees. . . ."

The remedy prayed is that for the future " ther be but vi common Attorneys " in Norfolk, 6 in Suffolk, 2 in Norwich " to be Attourneys in Court of Record "—the whole 14 to be " electe and admitte be youre too chieff Justices . . . of the moost sufficient and best lerned after her wise discretion." Anyone presuming to be " Attorney in Court of Record " on conviction " by inquisition " may be amerced in £20 for each offence—a half to go to the Crown and a half to the common informer, if he bring the ordinary common law action of debt : " for the love of God and in wey of charitee."

All petitions against abuses exaggerate, and Parliament, while accepting word for word the rest of the petition into an Act, omitted the asterisked passages about costs, but a more vivid " snap-shot " of local conditions is not to be found in our legal annals, and perhaps we may argue that what Norwich was thinking all England was thinking.

Apprenticii.

Of Mr. Bolland's many " finds " none is more valuable than the 1293 Bill in Eyre (*b*) of Lovekin Semon. The translation from Anglo-French runs as printed :—
" Sir Justice, this is a complaint and grievance which Lovekin Semon of Stafford layeth before you against John Organ of Newcastle-under-Lyme, to wit, that whereas the aforesaid Lovekin having provided the aforesaid John with

---

    * * Omitted in Statute.
    (*b*) 30 Seld. Soc. 52, xlv : " the most interesting."

the means (*coustages*) of seeing (*vere*) London for three
years and a half, amounting to a hundred shillings (*souch*)
and more, upon condition that he should assist him if he
had to plead (*pleder*); the aforesaid Lovekin sued one
Harry Miller of Shrewsbury for a messuage (*mes*) together
with the appurtenances, in that same town of Shrewsbury.
The aforesaid John Organ purchased (*purchasa: got?*) the
writ in respect of that messuage in the name of the
aforesaid Lovekin and supported (*empleda*) the writ and
prosecuted the claim (*pursewy le ple*) at Lovekin's charges
and was his attorney (*aturne*) for good three years and a
half. And when the hearing (*ple*) was so far advanced
that the gain or [the] loss of the messuage was the direct
issue this John Organ that was Lovekin's pleader
(*pledour*) went to Harry Miller that was tenant of the
messuage and took ten marks from him to defeat Lovekin's
right; and he forged four pairs of charters for this Harry
Miller, purporting to be the deeds of Lovekin's ancestors,
which ancestors had been dead sixty years and more before
then. And for these ten years past he hath never been able
to recover his estate but all the while hath been a beggar;
and never after did he receive a penny or a halfpenny of the
hundred shillings but only his [? whose] horse in lieu of
twenty shillings which was not worth more than half a
mark, nor of the ten marks hath he ever received ought: to
his damage of twenty pounds and more. And the aforesaid Lovekin prayeth remedy of this, Sir Justice, for God's
sake and the Queen's soul's sake.

Endorsement.
Failed to prosecute."

Leaving other points in this bill, it certainly purports to
tell of a bad apprentice to the law, before that title had
hardened into a technical term. The word is undoubtedly
taken from the French, the first English instance in
N. E. D. being in 1362 from Langland; Littré gives French
instances in the 13th century. We met it earliest in Fleta's

translation of the statute of 1275 in which the word does not occur and the legal apprentice is not referred to (unless perchance " serjeant, pleader or other," includes him). That translation was contemporary with the original, *i.e.*, written not long after it. The writer of the first sentence (and the title?), at any rate, thought that the apprentice was or ought to be included in the sanctions of the statute. But it is very difficult to believe that in—say—1290 legislation was wanted against him.

Yet in 1292-3 John Organ is held up to the judges as having in 1282 betrayed his client to the other side, though from some date in 1278 he had been representing that client apparently without complaint. All the client's charges may be untrue, but it is more likely that the incidents alleged were plausible and probable. If so, Organ must have been " seeing London " at Semon's expense from some time in 1274 at the latest and quite possibly earlier, for the latter does not tell us when " the good $3\frac{1}{2}$ years " of his litigation began. Hence John was in town before, though not much before the statute which we must hope was *post hoc* but not *propter hoc*.

If he was *apprenticius legis*, then we may say that we hear of that undergraduate in 1270 or so—a date most probable in itself. But was he? He has the great authority of his discoverer in favour of his professionalism : " I think that we can see a thirteenth-century Staffordshire law student going up to London to keep his terms and to qualify himself for practice at the bar. If I be right in my interpretation, then we get a glimpse of an organised law school or some sort of an Inn of Court, of very much more ancient date than any of which we have hitherto had knowledge. This prelude tells us that Lovekin Simon of Stafford wanted a pleader and agreed to find John Organ of Newcastle-under-Lyme the means of supporting himself in London—the quaint phrase of the bill is ' seeing London ' —for three years and a half, upon the understanding that

John should act as his pleader when he needed one. A pleader was a very different person from an attorney. Anybody might be an attorney. A pleader was one who had the right of audience before the King's Justices. Organ goes to London for three years and a half and returns [?] a pleader. That is beyond doubt, and I do not see what meaning as a whole this prelude to the bill can have other than that he went to London for the purpose of acquiring the status of a pleader through some recognised course of study maintained during a period of three and a half years, culminating in a formal call to the bar. If it mean this, then it must necessarily mean also that in the latter half of the 13th century there was some organised society in London charged with and performing duties somewhat akin to those of the present Inns of Court."

If this paraphrase is correct the bill is a godsend to the historian; if there was " a formal call to the bar " about 1270 we have got almost all we want for our *apprenticii*. But is not the learned editor much too sanguine? Lovekin does not say that he " wanted a pleader," but that Organ had agree to " assist him [L.] if he had to plead "—which might happen to any man. But, above all, if John was sent to town to be a law student, why is it not said so in the simplest language? No doubt, the bills are " quaint " enough, but they can be expressive, too. Why cannot we be content with what the text says—that John went to " see " London and that Simon, then his friend, helped him with money to go? John's primary purpose was probably to amuse himself, as Shallow did later, when he was not reading at Clement's-inn, and, no doubt, like that eminent justice he heard the chimes at midnight. Like him, too, he may have picked up a little law in the purlieus of Chancery Lane and it may be a good guess that he went through some professional discipline. That he was Semon's " attorney "—apparently *ad hoc*—for $3\frac{1}{2}$ years is likely enough, when, as the editor says, anybody might be an attorney, *i.e.*, a deputy. And probably this is all that is meant when in the same case he is called Lovekin's *pledour*; he further " pursued the *ple* " previously mentioned. For there seems to be no authority for the statement that in 1290 " a pleader was one who had the right of audience before the King's Justices," if it means the only one. In any case, it is not stated that John went before the King's Justices and if it is meant that *only* pleaders had such a right there is authority to the contrary, for in the royal and civic legislation of 1275 and 1280 we saw that the forensic rights of non-professionals were carefully saved and there are instances of *attornatio* in " The High Court." Moreover, if this John Organ was, as Mr. Bolland thinks " the successful complainant " in a suit at the same *Iter* (*ib*. p. 57) it is odd that he is not described there as " le pledour."

Finally, why should this Stafford man want to keep a " tame " lawyer in London or on his premises, so to say? He may have been an usurer, constantly " shot at " by his victims or *vice versa*, but we should expect that he would either be so described or that it would appear in the bill. Again, the learned editor notes " that the cost of a law student's maintenance in London at this time for three years and a half was a hundred shillings (*c*) and more." Nothing is said about " maintenance," and, even if the bill means 100s. odd yearly, as it may do, it is difficult to believe that a young man could live in London even in 1270-90 for a hundred shillings a year.

On the whole, in view of the very serious charges brought against John (but common enough, it must be admitted in that time against legal folk), and of the fact that the bill was dropped (*d*), the most reasonable reading

---

(*c*) *Souch*, otherwise *solz* (French, plural) " Schillinge " L. in *Wörterbuch*.

(*d*) Mr. Bolland has himself lucidly expounded the difference in

of it, perhaps, is that Semon assisted his friend to make the then " grand tour " that the latter did his business in town and when he came back to his native parts with the *prestige* of one who has " seen life " he did assist his benefactor with his knowledge and activity as far as he could and that when he could go no farther, the former fell out with him. Or John may have been a thorough rascal, but if so, it is still less likely that he studied at an inn of court.

Thus being estopped from claiming our first interesting " student " whither shall we turn?

To Maitland. " There is John of Cambridge Justice of the Common Bench . . . Already in 1295 a John of Cambridge represents the borough in Parliament. . . . The surname ' of Cambridge ' was not acquired inside Cambridge. A young man leaves his native town, goes to Westminster, makes a fortune at the bar, is known to his fellows as John of Cambridge and comes back a wealthy man with a new name which adheres to his family " (*e*). As John died in 1335 we may assume that he was at Westminster not later than 1285; Foss tells us that he was continually in judicial commissions for Cambridgeshire from 1311 and was " counsel " in the Year Book of Ed. II, which begins in 1307; in 1330 he became *serviens regis*. In 1329 he is " justic' R." (*f*). Now, the same great authority says of Bracton, who was a judge in 1245, " To suppose that he made his fame by " practising at the bar " would probably be an anachronism." Thus what he thought was an anachronism about 1200 Maitland thought " common form " in 1285, and it is that " common form " that we seek. Happily as well as this particular sketch

---

character between a bill and a writ; bills were much more irresponsible, so to say : see p. 173.

(*e*) *Township & Borough*, 166. Cam. Univ. Press (1898); Foss, III, 415.

(*f*) 2 *Rot. Orig. in Cur. Scac. Abb.* 24 a; cf. 52, 95.

he has left us a general picture (g). " Why, then, were these [Year] Books made? The answer we take to be: Because young men wished to learn the law and to become accomplished pleaders. . . . Outside this small group of practitioners [*narratores*] there stand the ' apprentices ' the learners, and it must occur to us that they had a great deal to learn and few means of learning it. We may indeed suppose that to a young man of this time the law that the justices and serjeants discussed did not seem quite so technical, quite so arbitrary as it appears to us. He could see the social and economic import of rules which we are tempted to regard as perverse displays of ingenuity. Still it is plain that a beginner had a great deal to learn; the mechanism, we might call it, of some thirty forms of action. . . . If then these learners were to learn, it would have to be by attending the court and listening to what was said. Their progress would assuredly be more rapid if they took notes of what they heard, if they borrowed and copied and discussed each other's notes. . . .

This we believe to have been the origin of the Year Books. They or rather the earliest of them (for we would not speak of an age that we have not observed) are students' note-books. . . . Willingness to lend, to borrow, to co-operate, we may take for granted. We are among young Englishmen. Also we are among the founders of those societies, four of which become eminent as ' the inns of Court.' These young men come up to London for term time; there is plenty of good fellowship among them "; —was John Organ a good fellow?—" they club together, perhaps they jointly hire a house. Perhaps they are already devising ' moots ' or other exercises which are destined to become more and more academic, and, at all events, we may believe that they talk a good deal of

---

(g) 20 Seld. Soc. x—xii : *under* 1309-10, but suggesting origins.

'shop.' This is the atmosphere, in which note-books multiply."

Again (*h*), "It does not seem to us in any degree improbable that in the year 1310 four apprentices at law were taking notes in court. Nor does it seem to us in any high degree improbable that the work of all four of them is lying before us in the year 1905." The Master's pronouncement on the Year Books and the Inns of Courts, though not our theme for the moment, will be of great value, especially the latter, in future. In the same one (*i*) "of these precedent books of the apprentice at law" (*k*) he tells us how Bereford, C.J., says in 1310 to Westcote (counsel) in "irony," "Really I am much obliged to you for your challenge, and that for the sake of the young men here, and not for the sake of us who sit on the bench." On another occasion the same judge expressly instructs the "youngsters" in court (*l*). These are the closest glimpses we have so far got of learners actually in court, for we did not find John Organ or John of Cambridge there, in the flesh, so to say. It is consonant with our general view that till about 1270, the profession being inconspicuous, mere aspirants to it were still more inconspicuous and a *status* in court was not thought of; in 1310 the bench is—naturally—favouring them.

We should expect to get an early lead from the City and we do. The Ordinance of 1280 absolutely assumes that the lawyers in court had some means of learning their "business" (*m*); the word "apprentice" is half there. The whole tone of the document is "we must educate our practitioners." And quite consistently we find them soon encouraging the junior branch by appointing Recorders not qualified as seniors.

(*h*) *Ib*. liii.
(*i*) *Ib*. p. 36.
(*k*) *Ib*. xciv.
(*l*) 17 Seld. Soc. xv, n. (2).
(*m*) " qi' lour mestier ne savoient ne ne eurent appris."

But the qualification (*n*) of the Recorder of the City does not carry us back to origins, though perhaps it confirms our dates, for by 1304-5 the City had, it seems, got into the habit of looking for this official in the second (*o*) and not in the first row of practitioners; a junior, so to say, was all they wanted. Without taking *peritissimi et virtuosissimi apprenticii legis totius regni* too literally we can readily believe that the certificate of some superior authority was sought before the appointment—that, probably, of a *serviens*, or of public repute. But the tone of the limitation carries us back to the appropriate atmosphere, that of the *placitum* of 1292, which aimed precisely at the provision of promising learners. Moreover, if we could safely accept Fleta's rubric as contemporary we should have evidence of the apprentice's forensic activity about 1275, exactly the time when John Organ is said to have been one; the hierarchy, too, is punctilious—*servientes, narratores, attornati, apprenticii*: were men just beginning six and a half centuries ago to employ not " devils " but juniors? At any rate, we get one in 1293 as *amicus curiae* or junior or both; Gossefeld Sjt. is arguing in the Common Bench about a writ when one interposed with the remark that " he had seen a case where the assign had brought this writ, &c." (*p*). In 1327 an apprentice puzzled by the procedure in the *coronator's* court in a clerk's case (*q*) boldly asked a question and was answered. In 1292 undoubtedly the government had purported to deal with the *apprenticii*; it was the turn now of " the small fry," as in 1275 it had been of the

---

(*n*) P. 244. Geoffrey de Hertpole seems to be an exception.

(*o*) As late as 1883 he was not a " silk " or a serjeant.

(*p*) Y. B. 21 E. I, 149; Rolls: the interruption in the Anglo-French text is wholly in Latin (except " apprentis "); hence probably it is the note of the actual interlocutor (and reporter?); he uses Latin for differentiation of authority.

(*q*) Y. B. I, E. III, f. 16, pl. 3—the oldest reference in a Y. B. to *app.* which Selden knew: Works III, 1885.

" bigwigs " (if that be not an anachronism). We have
seen " the leaders of the profession " emerging about
1250-75, and naturally a fringe grows around them; how
else could the court work be done? Possibly it was the
idea that the fringe was now under consideration which
inspired the rubric to include the two great classes of
forensic underlings. Before 1292 we hear little of them;
after it a good deal.

Another incident in 1342 is a pleasing touch of nature.
In the course of a trial (*r*) Sharshulle J. says to Pole :
" When you and I were apprentices and Sir W. de Herle (*s*)
and Sir J. Stonore were serjeants I remember a case, &c."
The age of reminiscence has arrived. Shareshulle was
probably born in the time of Edward I; Herle and Stonore
were now both judges, Stonore indeed on the bench here
with Shareshulle. William de la Pole had been a second
baron of the Exchequer in 1339, though never apparently
a serjeant, and never rose higher; his presence at the bar (*t*)
here reminds us of the demotion of some of James II's
judges, Pollexfen, etc. Coke (*u*) cites Wilby and Skipwith
as saying to counsel in court in 1366 : " We never heard
that exception taken, though it's common enough among
the apprentices in the inns," *i.e.*, good enough for novices'
" shop," as Maitland put it. We have not exact dates,
but Shareshulle's recollection carries him back just to the
period when " apprentices " were beginning to attract
public attention. If his story is typical, they were
probably *mutae personae* in his early days.

When they got the right of audience we cannot exactly
say. A case is known (*x*) in which the conduct of one
who " conducted an assize of novel disseisin " in Kent in

(*r*) Y. B. 16 E. III, v. 2, p. 6.
(*s*) When at the bar he, too, had indulged in reminiscence (p. 328).
(*t*) Cf. Coke, p. 188; 10 *R. Pro.* xxxix.
(*u*) *Ib.* xxxix, from 29 E. 3, fol. 47 a.
(*x*) 42 Seld. Soc. lxvi, from *De Banco* Rolls, no. 481, r. 102
London : ed. G. J. Turner.

1381 was considered. Probably as the business of the Courts of the serjeants grew they " got a look in "— especially after the success of the *hospitia*. In 1430 several named argue in one case (*y*), as do several whom, not being called apprentices, we suppose to be serjeants, *e.g.*, Fortescue.

Naturally, too, they attended the consultations of their leaders and even their negotiations with the other side. In 1450 John Paston says (*z*) : " The matier was in trete by th' assent of the Lord Moleyns atwene his counseil and myn, whiche assembled at London xvi dyvers daies and for the more part there was a sergeant and vi or vii thrifty apprentices . . . ." Ld. M.'s " own counseil seide they cowde no further in the matier."

In 1456 in a very " heavy " case (*a*) " Divers Apprentices and all the Serjeants and all the judges were arguing further for two days, &c.," and in 1458 Fortescue C.J. differing from Markham J. on a point of law, spoke to " the apprentices, sergeants and others of his companions " on the point (*b*); apparently he talked it over with them out of court (in an Inn?), an incident, no doubt, frequent at that date.

By this time, too, these juniors had " got into Parliament " or rather, perhaps, being in Parliament, learnt law. Thus in 1400 Owen Glendower, now prominent, had begun as an " *apprenticius* in Westminster " (*c*), and in 1449 " Thomas Yonge of Brystoll (*d*) an apprentice in law (*in lege*) moved in Parliament to nominate an heir apparent—for which he was sent to the Tower " (*e*).

(*y*) Y. B. 8 H. VI, ff. 7—9; n.b. " Hodie Apprentīc junior."
(*z*) Gairdner, 1 *P. L.* 146; no. 108.
(*a*) Y. B. 8 H. 6, 34th year, f. 34 : " arguebant ulterius divers apprentices."
(*b*) Y. B. 36 H. VI, f. 26. (*c*) *Annales H. IV*, 333; Rolls.
(*d*) *I.e.*, of Bristol; in 1 *Members of Parliament* (1878), a Blue Book, p. 341, he is " gentleman "; in earlier Parliaments, *e.g.*, 1436-7, p. 329, etc., a man of the same name is " mercator."
(*e*) W. of Worcester, *Annales*, V. 3, 770 : Rolls.

An even more tangible mark of their being some kind of corporation is the fact that " after the death of Robert de Clifford [2nd son, apparently, of E. I's R. de C.] Isabell his Widdow dimised ' Clifford's Inne ' in 18 E. tertii [1345] to the Students of the Law (*Apprenticiis de Banco* are the words of the Record) for the yearly rent of 10*l*." (*f*). There never was a more memorable lease.

In 1337 we saw (*g*) that the Council declined to regard apprenticeship as exempting from military service. In " How to hold a Wardmote " in the City (*h*) in the same treatise as the reference to the Recorder just mentioned —the whole document *in its present form* not being earlier than the reign of Richard II—absentees from a Wardmote are to pay the Alderman " 4d. unless the absentee be a Knight, Esquire (*miles, armiger*), a woman, apprentice-at-law, or clerk (*clericus*) or some one else who has not here his or her permanent abode (*civitatem*)." It is almost certain that this document reproduces rules and regulations older than 1377-99, and this seems to be one of them; it cannot have been uncommon in 1377, for *apprenticii legis* or any member of the classes enumerated to live in the City, though it may have been common for those who did, not to go to Wardmotes; the exemption of these persons would then be intelligible. But a hundred years earlier the pioneer law students, so to say, were mostly at Westminster, and the City may well have wished to encourage their appearance in the Wards just as it took its Recorders from their ranks. Another mark of antiquity, it would certainly seem, is that almost in the same breath " at such Wardmote also those persons who are not free of the City and who have not been previously sworn there ought to be put on frank pledge (*i*), notwithstanding that

---

(*f*) Dugdale, *O. J.* 187.
(*g*) P. 284.
(*h*) 1 *Lib. Alb.* B. I, Pt. 1, C. XI, p. 38 : Rolls.
(*i*) The exempted classes seem never to have been in frankpledge, at any rate, since 1266, from which date Blackstone, IV, 274, suggests

in other Wards they have been already received therein.' Surely in 1377 frankpledge was all but done with. But be the age of this by-law what it may, under it the *apprenticius legis* has a *status*. They are the "other pleaders" of the great statute of 1362-3 whom Fabyan calls "prentyses of the law."

That *status* is confirmed with time. By 1381 he and his fellows are recognised as "the junior bar." The Commons petition (*k*) the Regents that certain grievances alleged in the administration of justice in the two Benches and other courts (*e.g.*, of "other *seigneurs*") be redressed by the judges and other good and liege men learned in the law (*vaillantz et loialx apris en la Loye*); the Council are asked to get a report on oath from two judges, two serjeants and four *loialx Apprentices*: *inter alia*, how "the law may be better administered" (*l*). It may be that the numerical majority of apprentices suggested by the Commons implies that from *that* order, capable but no so busy as the others, would be drawn the Commissioners on whom the bulk of the work would fall. The Council in response to this (and to petitions on other matters) appoints "the Clerks of the Chancery of the two principal Degrees, the judges, Serjeants, Barons, great Officers of the Exchequer . . . and also certain persons of the better [class] *Apprentices de la Loi*" to report, "each degree by itself." This order of precedence points to the supremacy of the Chancellery whose officials we meet for the first time—though by no means the last—in contact with "the learners."

Even more to the point is the painful review of society in *Richard the Redeles* about 1400; law and justice are dead.

---

its decline. St. 2 *Hist.* 471 speaks of it as in decay in 1376 : 2 *Rot. Parl.* 357, no. 195.

(*k*) 3 *Rot. Parl.* 101 b, 102 a, b.

(*l*) " les Loies et gentz de Loie en chescun pays [Ireland?] puissent mieultz . . . estre governez."

"I could tell of wrongs without number.
For seld were the serjeants sought for to plead
Or any 'prentice of court prayed of his wits (*m*).

That is, the normal bulwark against illegality is the bar and therein first the serjeants and then the apprentices.

And while in the great sumptuary statute of 1363 lawyers as such are not mentioned nor in the similar petition of 1402, yet in that (*n*) of 1406 (evidently modelled on the earlier) while judges and serjeants " du Roy " are only mentioned to be exempted " null Esquier apprentice du Loy " nor the Clerks of the Chancery nor of the Exchequer nor certain others—all evidently of the same social rank—are to wear fur, etc. (*o*). That rank was, as we should expect, generally that of esquire (*p*), as is indicated by the phrase just cited. A hint of social standing may be found in Serjeant Rolf's daughter a "great heiress" marrying " an eminent lawyer " " brought up by her father," *viz.*, John Green of Wydington about 1420.

History has led us on, but Imagination must take us back perhaps a century. The famous verses, the forewords of the *Mirror of Justices* would be a treasure, if we knew their date. It is conceivable that it was all written 1285-90 (*q*); if the inferences that have been drawn from the lines are correct for that date, they are certainly valuable, especially the latest. They run—

Hanc legum summan si quis vult jura tueri
Perlegat et sapiens si vult orator haberi.

(*m*) Skeat, Pass. III, 348 : p. 498.

(*n*) 3 Rot. Parl. 506 a, 593 a.

(*o*) " furrure de grey, cristegrey menyver ou byce " or " perree ou perle, ouches ou bedes ou autre hernoys d'or ou dorrez quelconque "; archaeologists may understand this. The judges and serjeants may use their *chapons* " as it seems best to them for the honour of the King and their estate."

(*p*) In the petition (2 Rot. Parl. 278 a) on which the St. of 1363 is founded the " mischief " of the Esquire's apparel is distinctly stated, see p. 469*s*.

(*q*) See 7 Seld. Soc. xix—xxi, liv, 1.

Hoc apprenticiis ad barros ebore munus
Gratum juridicis (r) utile mittit opus.
Horn mihi cognomen Andreas est mihi nomen (s).

" Dr. Verrall's last line gives the solution. Here for the apprentices at the bar (t) are pleasant visions of the law that are not too true : here for their seniors are profitable things that are not so pretty. Horn is my name but you have Ivory (u) also here."

One rendering (x) drew from Maitland the remark that " the versifier may be speaking of the apprentices at the bars (t) of various courts."

But in 1909 Mr. Bolland propounded a new version (y); he reads " . . . , ad Barros e bora . . . " and translates freely : " The author sends this book from his cell to the hostels near the Bars : a gift that will be welcome to the Apprentices and useful to those already skilled in the law," i.e., primarily their teachers. " The earliest local hostels founded by the Apprentices were in the neighbourhood of Holborn Bars and Temple Bar."

But when were they founded? Clifford's Inn may be so described in 1345 and Lincoln's Inn, we shall see, in 1310. Andrew Horn died in 1328. Thus, whoever wrote the verses, if he meant what Mr. Bolland puts into his mouth, probably wrote from, say 1310 to 1320. If the *Mirror* and the (more or less) metrical poem were written

---

(r) This word is not now in the MS., but is supplied from " a comparatively modern copy," as it is a rare word perhaps the conjecture is wrong.

(s) Translated by Dr. Verrall ap. Maitland : " Read me, whoe'er the substance of the laws/Desires to see or plead with sage applause./ Here Ivory's grace attracts apprentice eyes/While profit for the coif our book supplies/Horn—Andrew Horn—the author is who writes/ (*Aside*) Thus Horn with Ivory—Truth with Grace unites."

(t) The first time we meet *them* there : see p. 232.

(u) I.e., the horn and the ivory gates of dreams (Virgil).

(x) Ib. liv.

(y) 25 L. Q. R. 235. Sir Frederick Pollock does not dissent. The ingenious author's remark that no set of people ever were called " app. ad b." may be met—the equally ingenious poet invented the phrase.

1285-90, then probably the latter do not refer to hostels. We should be surprised to hear that there was any housing question for our professional ancestors before 1300 or thereabout.

We may round off these instances with an encouraging incident of legal research. In 1904 Maitland quoted a MS. of late Ed. I or early E. II (z): " and afterwards it was told in the Cribbe (a) how he [counsel] was received to except " in a case. The learned editor " thought of a part of the court set apart for students " and he called, so to say, for explorers. In 1907 Mr. G. J. Turner (b) " ' happed ' upon a document which goes some way towards explaining . . . ' cribbe.' It is a petition addressed to the King by the apprentices of the Common Bench "— *ses emprentis de sun comun banke*, in the words of the original (c) which he sets out; they ask him to order his Treasurer and Bereford (C.J.) *qe eux puissent faire une Crubbe pur lour esteer* (stand) *a leur aprise* (instruction) *dune part de la dite place autre* [ci] *com il ad de lautre part* " just as (in the Crib) on the other side." Hence it has been called the " rectilineal ancestor " of the students' box from which the defendant's friends heard *Bardell* v. *Pickwick*.

We cannot sum up the situation better than the discoverer of this nursery: " It shows us that in the reign of Ed. II there was a body of men who could be described as the King's apprentices of the Common Bench. It would seem that these *apprenticii*, afterwards to become known as barristers, were originally attached to the same court as that in which the serjeants had an exclusive audience and that they were at this period learners rather than

---

(z) MS. Y. f. 170 d. Brit. Mus. Add. 35116; 19 Seld. Soc. xv-i.
(a) " en le Cribbe," perhaps connected etymologically with a word = basket : N. E. D.
(b) 22 Seld. Soc. xli.
(c) From Ancient Petitions, file 189, No. 9409.

practisers of law." We will not ask what they learned till we have more material.

The time has not yet arrived to narrate the vicissitudes of this word, but they were such that in 1873 a member of the bar " called in 1865 " pointedly described himself on a title-page (*d*) as " apprentice-at-law."

Attorneys, *Narratores, Servientes*.

The City has not given us a generic name for its legal practitioners. An etymologist there writing almost certainly after 1387 says " nowadays we call *legis homo* (*e*) ' jurisperitus ' or better ' legislator '." The term *legis homo* marks the popular need of a general word for all lawyers (and is therefore a sign of their prominence), but despite its obvious convenience it never " caught on " in literature till Chaucer immortalised it—perhaps invented it in English; 1377 is the earliest date for " lawyer " (*f*). We will attempt a harmony of these three titles, but it must not be forgotten that until about 1250-70 they are in a flux.

This, perhaps, is seen within the limits of one book, the *Annals of Dunstable* (*g*), which cover almost exactly 1200—1300. Till 1242 it is written by R. de Morins, the Prior, and thenceforward by an anonymous resident monk. The Abbey was constantly involved in lawsuits, which are carefully enumerated, and at their respective dates must have employed the various grades of lawyers available. Prior Richard took no interest in them or declined to

---

(*d*) *The Legal Profession* by W. T. Charley, D.C.L., Common Sjt. 1878; Q.C. 1880.

(*e*) 1 *Lib. Alb.* 33 : Rolls : B. I, Pt. I, edn. 1861, p. 29; for 1341, see p. 223*r*. P. 235*w* occurs " the men of law " translated from French of 1356. In 1385 we have (8 R. II, c. 2) *nullus homo de lege* and 1393 *homes de la ley* : p. 267. About 1386 is " a lede[man] of the laghe [law]" : *St. Erkenwald*, 1, 200, ed. Gollancz.

(*f*) " legistres and lawyeres," *Piers Plowman*, VII, 59 Skeat.

(*g*) 3 *Ann. Monastici* : Rolls : ed. Luard.

advertise them, but in the very folio in which his death and his successor, Galfrid, are recorded an opponent " Galfridus Dispensarius brought an action against us *per breve d. r.* by R. de Torp his *attornatus*." In 1247, after " our selling land," the buyer died within a month " without heir or *attornatus* (executor?) and so without trouble or suit we got back our land." In 1252 a certain Hawisia de Cateby caused the Abbey a good deal of litigation, but before the royal justices " we beat her (*h*) in argument—*narrando* "—probably a reminiscence of their *narrator*. And the only time they lost against that litigious lady was when they employed Galfrid *serviens noster, i.e.,* one of their officials on the spot (but probably not the new Prior of that name); exactly so the great *servientes regis* began their careers. There is a typical story of 1262. One W. Pyrot brought an action for an advowson against the Abbey before the justices; this he did " per consilium et auxilium Hervici de Borham, qui causidicus erat subtilissimus [afterwards a judge, never apparently a serjeant (*i*)]; whom R. Pyrot had presented against us to a [named] church and by the advice of *Magister* John of Faversham [otherwise unknown] to whom the said William had given himself, his wife [*sic*] and all his lands rents and possessions to hold perpetually." They come to terms and " *pro bono pacis* and in consideration of his being our faithful *consiliarius* we gave Master John 2 shillings a year in perpetuity." In 1288 begins an interminable case against Millicent de Montalt and others " she and others came and denied *vis, injuria* &c. and she replies for herself and others." On one occasion she appears *per ballivum suum* —the most natural type of an *attornatus*. When she wins an early round the chronicler does not hesitate to ascribe it to the " favor " of both judges. He can hardly mean

---

(*h*) *adnullavimus;* twice on same page, prostravimus: *serviens perdidit breve suum—breve* is the object to all four.
(*i*) But in Pulling's list.

(though he says) that the long legal arguments were carried on in person between her and the Prior—once *coram d. r. et concilio* — when one of the most intelligible of the problems debated was whether as she maintained, the issue at the moment could only be tried under a *parvum breve de recto clausum*—the court being first R. de Boyland J., and then our old friends John of Metingham and Elias of Bekyngham. It is simply incredible that the pages of hard argument attributed to these two lay persons did not emanate from a technical legal source. The writer is evidently transcribing what suited his purpose and so an occasional formula sometimes slips out as, in one of the many suits with the Crown about " liberties," *Gilebertus de Thornethone sequitur pro rege* [1286]. The Prior constantly appears in person, *e.g.*, in 1290 " before the justices " in London; he thought he was going to get judgment there and then (*k*), but there was an adjournment, and when it comes on again at Clifton by Nottingham he appears *coram rege per attornatum*.

If there is any truth in the view here expressed, there was a parallel development of the *narrator* and of a legal representative in court, *optimo*, that is *regio, jure*, soon to be known as *serviens regis ad legem* and ultimately as simply *serviens*. But it is not true that *narrator, countour, pleader* are (or is) the same thing as *serviens, serjeant* (*l*), any more than a policeman is the same thing as a constable. The *narrator* is originally a private person (who might or might not be *attornatus*). When the King began to send a *serviens* to the courts who (for this purpose was his *attornatus*, too), he also *narravit* but he gradually—it cannot be put more definitely—began to argue before the judges, as well. This raised the standard of forensic

---

(*k*) The unique *perplacitare* occurs p. 359 (and 335 of the *justices*).

(*l*) The document of 1338 (p. 376) includes among *narratores* one serjeant and three persons who were certainly not serjeants (one is called *attornatus*), but the nature and the origin of the document prevent our regarding it as a conclusive authority on the point.

advocacy and litigants in matters of moment sought the services of a *serviens* or his equivalent, though, being laymen, they continued to think of him as a (re)counter and this habit dissolved into an abiding technicality. As late as 1280 the City while synonymising " countour " and " serjeant " still couples them conjunctively " countour ... and pleaders " : " at the request of the serjeants and countours." And in dealing with nomenclature it is worth recalling that the *advocatus* is the root institution of legal representation, of which *causidicus, responsalis, procurator, attornatus, narrator*, etc., are dim differentiations (*m*) which gradually became more definite. The Attorney-General and (in a less degree) the Solicitor-General, now the extreme of differentiation, testify to the undifferentiated period.

On the point, too, of nomenclature it is difficult to rid our minds of the modern inseparable association (*n*) between attorney and counsel, whereas, so far, there has been the barest hint (*o*) of the former " instructing " the latter. Broadly it has been suggested that for an indefinite period the *attornatus* may do the whole of any one's work in court and, of course, out of it, that in time he overlaps

---

(*m*) Perhaps the following scheme, once suggested by the late Dr. Liebermann, may be of interest:

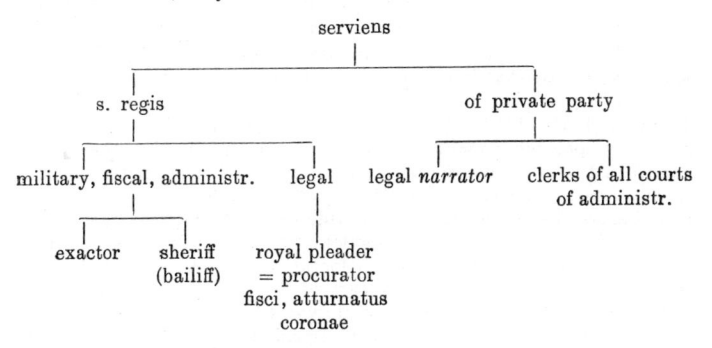

```
                              serviens
              ┌──────────────────┴──────────────────┐
          s. regis                              of private party
              │                                       │
     ┌────────┼────────┐              ┌───────────────┼───────────────┐
military, fiscal, administr.  legal   legal narrator   clerks of all courts
     │                          │                        of administr.
 ┌───┴───┐                      │
exactor  sheriff          royal pleader
         (bailiff)         = procurator
                           fisci, atturnatus
                              coronae
```

(*n*) And dissociation.
(*o*) P. 296, and that unverified.

both the *narrator* and the *serviens*, sometimes doing their work and sometimes working with either of them and that finally he and the *serviens* emerge as two parallel workers (*p*)—the dual system, as we know it. Thus in

---

(*p*) It is not within our scope or period to fix the date of the sharp division between counsel and attorney, but it is to the point to refer to such authority as there is.

An extremely able and erudite argument in favour of the direct access of the client to counsel in the *Law Magazine*, February—May, 1852, p. 25 : " The relation between Counsel, Attorney and Client" (v. 16 New. Ser. v. 47 Old. Ser.) has (p. 26) ". . . the two branches of the profession " existed " distinct in England two hundred years ago." In the next volume of the L. M. (1852), p. 130, on the Ninth Report of the Law Amendment Society (for which see also the *Times*, August 4, 1852) there is a reference to a resolution of the Society in favour of direct access; cf. *ib*. 229. That Society had a Special Committee on the subject, which made a report (apparently that mentioned in the (above) article in the 9th Report, but the Report of the Committee is now unobtainable, as is that of the Society). In 1873, however, Mr. W. T. Charley in the *Legal Profession*, p. 166, quotes from the Committee's report : " even during the last century it [the rule] was not fully established " (another quotation, *ib*., suggests the probability that that report was drawn up by the writer of the article in v. 16 of the *L. M*.). Charley (*ib*.) correctly cites Serjt. Pulling, *Attornies*, p. 12 (1862, 3rd edn.), as stating that " the practice " was gradually introduced " during the last century "; he mentions (*ib*.) that Noy, Charles I's A.-G., actually took a fee in court from a client and " appeared " at once.

In 1854 Sir Patrick Colquhoun wrote : " . . . the very convenient practise of retaining counsel through the intervention of attorneys is of a comparatively modern date—perhaps of not more than one hundred years back " : 3 *Summary of the Roman Civil Law*, 318, § 2009.

On February 2, 1863, Mr. G. Shaw Lefevre, a barrister, read a paper to the Society for Promoting the Law on " The Discipline of the Bar " (the pamphlet is now rare, but is in the Inner Temple Library " I. H. 14 " No. 15). He calls attention at p. 17 to a judgment by L. Campbell in *Bennett* v. *Hale* (1850), 15 Q. B. 171, which while admitting that there was no *rule of law* " to prevent barristers appearing in civil cases uninstructed by attorneys " [though as it was a matter of procedure the judges might have made such a rule] strongly defended the existing practice. " The practice, such as it is," he continues (p. 19), " is comparatively modern, for up to quite a late period of our legal history even the minutest part of the duties connected with it were performed by barristers, and it was not till the year 1557 that we find the rule, already quoted, forbidding barristers to act as attorneys, and it is about that time that we must look for the complete divergence of the two professions; but even much later than this the

1356 " the judge asked the attorney whether he received anything for the purpose of retaining a serjeant, and a clerk of the court testified that he had not; therefore the plea was entered " (*q*). The *attornatus* asserts himself but the *narrator* dies out; he had come into existence for a special purpose and never becomes a mere man of business; how far he shared the work with the *serviens* before the latter absorbed him, we cannot exactly say, probably the merger was gradual, and before it was complete, no doubt, both took advantage of the *attornatus*'s " spade-work "; the *narrator* is midway between the two and ultimately falls on the side of the *servientes*. We have not yet arrived at the line between " counsel " and " attorney." About 1394 " Mathew the Londoner, one of the Attorneys in the Common Bench " recites " that he was of counsel (*de conseil*) in an assize of novel disseisin . . . at Chelmsford " and in that capacity had to complain of a juror in open court. In 1397 a suppliant states that " Thomas Barton, Marshall of the Marshalsea of the Household " of the King had maintained " by force and colour of his office " a third person's suit against suppliant till the latter " put himself in Thomas's grace " (for £12) " to be helpful to him in this case, as well as others " and so Thomas " became of [his] counsel : later " Roger Lynster Clerk of the King's Chancery " was " de Counseille " of

---

attorney was a mere ministerial officer* performing the less important duties of conducting the suit through the forms of the courts, and all the more important duties were undertaken by counsel, who advised personally with their clients. It is quite of late years that the attorneys and solicitors have assumed the important position which they now hold, and that they have become in fact the dispensers of all the business which comes to the Bar."

* Confirmed remarkably by Roger North in *Autobiography*, C. XI (pp. 140—141; cf. 169; ed. Jessop : 1887), about 1730 : " anciently, as I have been informed all conveyancing, court keeping, and even the making of breviats at the assizes, was done by the lawyers. Now the attorneys have the greatest share . . . and men of law expect business to come from their hand . . . "

(*q*) Horwood, Y. B. 32-3 E. I, xxxvi, n. (1).

the suppliant (*r*). Obviously in both these latter cases, " counsel " means " adviser " out of court—the office prohibiting any technical sense.

Under Henry V we saw an official recognition of counsel and attorney in the same case; there was not, as a rule, room for three representatives (*s*) in the same cause; even the dual system is sometimes criticised as uneconomical. The litigant in person was by no means unknown. The learned editor of Y. B. 30-1 E. I (1302) says (p. xxviii); " the cases in this volume show that the principals often appeared and conducted their suits and that the attornies took part even when counsel were employed," and he infers from a case (*ib*. 172) that in Eyre, too, the litigant might appear in person. This hardly requires proof, but when Berrewik J. remarks " The want of a good serjeant makes defendant lose his money " this is strong testimony to the sacrosanctity of pleading or the value of advocacy. In 1303 Herle Sjt. says (*t*) during a trial " we have seen cases where, when the attorney could not explain the matter in dispute, the principal (*le principal*) has been made to appear." In 1302 (*ib*. 151) an infant in court " was examined by the court and adjudged to be of ful! age " (*u*).

An extraordinary case (*x*) in 1305 shows five suitors (*i.e.*, the juror-judges, the tenants) of a lord's court coming as defendants in person to the K. B. to answer for " False Judgment " in their court below; they tell their

---

(*r*) 10 Seld. Soc. 79, 27; the learned editor thinks both acted in a professional capacity; but it is clear that it was Barton's official position only which attracted Mathew; for the services of Clerks in Chancery, see p. 331. Roger L. " a writing clerk in the Chancery " appears again, 1417-24, *ib*. 116, as " of counsel."

(*s*) *Secus*, as an exception, p. 217.

(*t*) Y. B. 30-1 E. I, xxviii, 358.

(*u*) As under the Street Betting Act, 1906, s. 1, sub-s. 3, and the Children Act, 1908, s. 123, sub-s. 2.

(*x*) Y. B. 32-3 E. I, xli, 362 : against the Sheriff of whose personal violence they professed to be so much in fear that they had *all* come together.

story when one Hedon—not otherwise known but probably *attornatus* on one side or the other—thinks he can tell the story better. " You shall not say a word about it " says Bereford J. characteristically, and in the end he says to them " Go aside by yourselves and take a clerk and make him write down such a record of the proceedings as you will avow [their special duty] and let neither R. Hedon nor anyone else come to you "; they did and they won.

We met another dual system in the form of a junior, Gilbert de Toutheby (*y*) (or Toudeby) had in 1315 appeared with G. de Scrop' against Hugh le Dispenser—*sequntur p. Rege coram D. rege*, and in 1320 against the Mayor, etc., of London, both as *servientes d. nostri r.*; in both Toutheby is mentioned first.

Negatively we never hear of anyone constituting himself a *serviens*, as we do of the *countour*, nor do we find an instance of a client disavowing a *serviens* as such, " both strong " in favour of his official origin.

The inveterate habit of centuries has tended to make inquirers reproduce the existing sharp line between counsel and solicitor at a period when, though it existed, it was not sharp, when there was some overlapping. As Mr. G. J. Turner puts it (*z*) : " There are also cases in which a serjeant is named as attorney; but he may in those cases have been acting for persons under disability, by leave of

---

(*y*) 1 *Rot. Parl.* 352, 370; 3 Foss, 532.

(*z*) 42 Seld. Soc. lxviii (1926), after remarking : " The various clerks of the court and perhaps those members of the bar who had not yet become serjeants were qualified to act as attorneys "; see p. 331c.

We may take the proposition in the text as a more mature opinion of the same scholar than that in 22 Seld. Soc. xvii (1907). " Instances of professional attorneys becoming serjeants may be sought in vain "; no explanation of " professional " is offered.

Mr. Turner's researches have not discovered any *attornatus* in his own or other lists of *narratores* of the end of E. II's reign : *ib.* n. He adds (*ib.*) " in the 16th century [*sic*] . . . the lists of ' narratores ' which we may construct from the plea rolls consist solely of serjeants-at-law who had an exclusive right of audience in the Common Bench." By that time the identification was complete.

the court. It seems to be certain that the serjeants never made a practice of acting as attorneys," about 1311; or, of the same date " a study of the rolls makes it plain that it was not normal for those men who had become serjeants to act as attorneys, although here and there in a particular action an exception may perhaps be noticed." *Ex hypothesi* when the two avocations had become distinct there was (and is) little migration from one to the other, but we have seen that great advocates had, in fact, acted as *attornati* and are so called, *e.g.*, Gilbert le Scrop and William de Giselham (*a*), if, as is no doubt the fact, they were paid for their services they ought to be called professional. That there were paid professional attorneys in the City about 1300 is not open to doubt. Finally, in all legislation, royal or civic, when the *serviens* is dealt with, we usually find that the *attornatus*, too, is regulated. And negatively that the *attornati* are not mentioned (*b*) in the *locus classicus*, the statute of 1275, is strong evidence that they did not, at any rate, as such " plead," *i.e.*, argue in court.

There is no reason to doubt that about 1280 when Dugdale mentions the first " attornatus regis," the official now known as the Attorney-General comes into existence, and that from the time of his recognition as a high official of the King's he was taken from the same class as the *servientes*, as we have seen William of Giselham and Gilbert of Thornton were. No doubt there was an indefinite period when the King, like another litigant, sent an *attornatus* into the courts to do his business as his

---

(*a*) W. is *att. r.* in 1201 : *Abbrev. Plac.* 273, rot. 28; Dugdale, *Chron. Ser.* 27, makes him the first " *att. r.*" in 1279 (and Gilbert de Thornton the second in 1280, citing respectively *Plac. Cor. Just. itin. in Com. Suff.* 7 E. I, and *Plac. de Qu. War.* 8 E. I, rot. 2, Notts), but it is almost certain that the words " att. r." do not occur in these records; in *Lib.* 8 E. 1, *m.* 3, which he also cites, the word is *deputavimus*. Dugdale, *ib.* under 1281 makes W. and Gilbert the first *servv. R. a. l.:* " *Liberatae* [sic] 9 E. I, *m.* 1.

(*b*) Unless " or other " includes *attornati*; see p. 195.

deputy without the latter being a " professional " man. The hints taken from Dugdale confirm the conjecture that about 1280-1300 the *attornatus* is beginning to be recognised as a " whole-time " lawyer like the *serviens*, but with differences due chiefly to the particular kind of work which the *attornatus* had in fact been doing for some time and the *serviens* had not, *viz.*, transacting with the clerks and " purchasing " the writ (*c*). At that date, perhaps, no one thought it odd that the " solicitor " was looked upon as a kind of " barrister " who might at any moment become a normal one.

At any rate, by (about) 1340 the two great branches were recognised as distinct. When Richard Rolle of Hampole wants to paint the forlorn condition of the wicked, he says (*d*):

> thai sal than na help gett
> Of sergeaunt ne autourne ne avoket
> Ne of non other for tham to plede,
> Ne tham to counsayle ne to rede.

In 1392-3 the Commons petition (*e*) that " as several clerks of the King's Bench, the Common Bench and Assizes who write the Records and Pleas between party and party are Attorneys of the one party or the other and thus favour them in their documents, to the great mischief, etc.," no such clerk shall be *either* attorney or counsel (*conseill*) in those courts, except for the King. Whether any action was taken on this prayer or not, differentiation of the two branches is here express, though perhaps it was not yet complete. The Chancery clerks, too, had to be warned against irregularities in their office; indeed, their conditions and temptations were not dissimilar from those of their

---

(*c*) As the offices of the courts gradually grew in the early stages the clerks must often have been the most convenient *attornati*, and as the process went on, definitely adopted one or the other branch. Hence the remark quoted p. 329*z* is justified.

(*d*) *The Pricke of Conscience*, 6083; ed. R. Morris, 1863.

(*e*) 3 *Rot. Parl.* 306b.

common law colleagues, and legislation involved them for some time (as the 1st Statute of Westminster in 1275 shows) in a common distrust (*f*). It is difficult to believe that some of the latter did not share in the colonies of the former and drift, as they did, to " the bar."

It is about this time that the government regularly retains and employs an attorney for the King; it would be still premature to call him " Attorney-General," for that title only appears (*g*) about 1585, but he seems to do his work. In 1423 the Privy Council consults among others *servientes r. ad leges* [sic] *et attornat' R'* (*h*). In 1429 there is among a number of legal appointments (*i*) by the Privy Council " in pleno parliamento " that of John Wanpage as *attornatus d. r.* " during the King's pleasure with the usual fees." In 1430 the Council (*k*) orders robes to be

---

(*f*) Cc. 27, 28; 8 R. II, c. 4 (1385), contemplates that both the judge and his clerk may be punished for tampering with process.

(*g*) *N. E. D.*: in 1533 " the King's general attorney and general solicitor "; 25 H. VIII, c. 16, *at. generalis* is analogous only in meaning. Foss (Indexes) and Sir H. Nicolas (*P. P. C.* Introductions and Index in v. 6) often use " Attorney-General " and " Solicitor-General " (5 *P. P. C.* xxv)—the latter title quite without warrant—for " K' sgeantz 't attourney," *ib.* 77 and 35, and the same without " K' ", *ib.* 78, as equivalent to " Att. & Solr. Genl.": *ib.* xvi, xxv; all in 1437. In *Statutes of Realm* " Att. G." is only suggested of 1495; it does not occur in *Abbrev. Plac.* (but in 1282 G. de Thornton and W. de Giselham are *narratores pro d. r.*: 274b). In 1464, 5 *Rot. Parl.* 530a has " oure Attorney General of Duchy of Lancaster . . . and the office of oure Soluciter [sic]." No other " A. G." occurs in *Rot. Parl.*; Foss IV, 398, has " King's Solicitor " in 1461. " Attornati Regine " in 1290 : 1 *Rot. Parl.* 536, and " l'aturne la Royne ": II, *ib.* 410b (E. III, year uncertain) are of ordinary usage.

Roger North (1653-1734) says (*Autobiog.* 140 : ed. Jessop, 1887) : " There used to be two serjeants, called the King's Serjeants, for long time past and these had greater dignity and authority than the Attorney-General "; this is not so now, but " this is the reason that in proclamations for discharge of prisoners in cases of no prosecution the King's Serjeant is named before the Attorney-General which makes me think that of old time the King's Attorney was like a common attorney and not a pleader, and the serjeants pleaded and the attorney prosecuted "; he then suggests the origin of the S.-G.

(*h*) 3 *P. P. C.* 117.

(*i*) 4 *P. P. C.* 4.

(*k*) *Ib.* 71.

given "*s[er]vient'[ibus]* *'t attorn'* *R. ad legē.*" The form "*attorn. ad legem(s)*" is unique and *attornati* never get robes from the Crown. It is therefore an easy suggestion that the donee here (if only one) was both a *serviens* and *attornatus* and so might be described as usual as *ad legem* (or—*es* in P. P. C.). It is true that no name is given (which is rare in P. C. C.) but probably the order is general, "to any one who is both *serv.* and *att.*" and so the abbreviations are of plurals not singulars (*l*). It can hardly be doubted that here we have an early union in the same person of the functions and titles of "the two branches." But it is quite normal for the Crown like other litigants to have both a serjeant and an attorney as it did against Cardinal Beaufort in 1431 (*m*).

In 1432 there was a petition of the Commons and apparently an Act (*n*) to regulate the "Fees and Rewards" of (1) the judges; (2) the serjeants; (3) the Attorney for the time being (les S. et lattourney du Roi pur le temps esteantz : plural (*o*)). Throughout the record this collocation is repeated, so that "for the time being" limits the three kinds of officials and "the attorney" occurs in several other instruments. This terminology seems to point to an official attorney who habitually appeared for the Crown as long as he held office. An English petition (*p*) of 1451 still speaks of "your serjauntes and attorne" and recites an Act evidently founded on the petition of 1439. These

---

(*l*) As must be the case in the grant immediately preceding : "Justic' de banco R'," where also no person is named.

(*m*) " requisic' fact' p. svient' R. et attornat' " : 4 *P. P. C.* 100; why Sir H. Nicolas understands, *ib.* xxxii, " the King's Serjeants and attorney conducted the case " does not appear.

(*n*) Translated as 10 H. VI, st. 2; 2 *St. R.* 277; original also 4 *Rot. Parl.* 394.

(*o*) So in a (French) petition (granted) in 1439 the Latin heading reproduces the original : *Just. serv. et attornatum suos* : 5 *Rot. Parl.* 14. The subject is the same as that of the 1432 Act; it provides for the judges' " Vesture, Pellure et Lynur' " and the " Vesture " of the two other classes.

(*p*) 5 *Rot. Parl.* 214a.

resolutions or Acts suggest that at this period these officials were badly paid (like the clerk Hoccleve), if at all, whereas formerly they " were always paid in Hand " (1432). The gravamen of the complaint was that payment was sometimes made by assignment of debts due to the Crown, which naturally led to partiality; the debtors " do sometimes desire and demand to be rewarded and unreasonably favoured against the oath of the justices, Serjeants and " Attorney "—to say nothing, it is added, of the indignity and out-of-pocket loss in running after defaulters. An *attorney pro hac vice* would probably not be protected by the Commons nor get his arrears paid in this way.

This legislation, the earliest of its kind, has another significance. The time had come to recognise that lawyers practised for their livelihood : throughout the fourteenth century the references to their payment become more frequent, with the inevitable corollary that the clients also regard their engagement as commercial. We saw that about 1300, when a client openly charged his countor with professional misconduct, the latter expressly stated that he was not bound to answer, *viz.*, to anyone (but that he brought the action " to clear his character "). That de Keleseye was here asserting the modern uncompromising legal immunity of counsel seems unlikely *per se*, because, in fact, just when fees are being regarded by law as ordinary contract prices—about 1400—we find a series of cases or *dicta* giving a remedy to a client out of pocket by the *laches* of his lawyer. Somerton's case in 1433 is thus summarised by Manning (*q*) : " if I retain a man of law to be of my counsel to buy me such a manor if he do his endeavour although he procure it not, yet no action lies against him; but if he afterwards become of counsel of my adversary in this matter against me [as Thomas alleged] an action on the case lies; but if there be no retainer and

---

(*q*) *Serviens*, etc., p. 183 : from 11 H. VI, fo. 18, 10; fo. 24, 1; fo. 55, 26; also in 1 Roll. *Abr.* 31.

I shew my evidences to a man of the law, although he after become of counsel to another and discovers the counsel of the said evidence, yet no action lies against him because he was not retained." So in 1436 Paston J. said that if a serjeant undertakes " to plead my plea and do not, or do it in another manner than I told him whereby I have loss, I have an action on the case " (s), and in 1440 one Stokes argued that if my counsel retained does not come to argue for me at the Guildhall on the fixed day " whereby my matter is lost, I have an action of deceit."

Obviously the bar had so far not thought itself privileged in its pecuniary transactions—it was frankly commercial not yet *conscious of itself* as a profession primarily holding a trust for the public (the ground of its modern immunity). As late as 1723 there was printed (t) an indictment of " a councellor for betraying his clients cause and taking fees of the other side "—(about 1667); the allegation was exactly that of 1433 (above)—such a barefaced fraud would perhaps be indictable to-day.

In 1432 there is a singular tribute to the impossibility of carrying on litigation without professional lawyers. In October the Privy Council ordered (u) a *moratorium* of all pending pleas in London because owing to the plague " as we have heard all our serjeants (ad leges) and *attornati* in both benches and other of our courts have left our city of London so that plaintiffs and defendants, cannot get the advice absolutely necessary to their suits."

In 1442 we get a hint of the discipline by that date invoked against attornies. One guilty of a professional irregularity was attached and kept in the Fleet for some months. Newton J. then fined him, ordered his " name to be drawn from the roll of attornies," that he should never

---

(s) 14 H. VI, f. 18, pl. 58; 20 H. VI, f. 34, p. 4. Manning, *ib*.
(t) Tremaine's *Pleas*, 261.
(u) 4 P. C. C. lxxx, 282; *nostri att*. is merely formal; the judges are not mentioned because they are few.

be attorney in that court [C. P.] nor any court of the King nor in any way "meddle in the law therein" and made him swear to abide by this judgment (*x*). Then said the judge "Sir, the King hereafter may pardon you if you have better grace by his letters patent and the Bishop may assoil you of this sin. Then you may return." It would be too much to say that the doctrine of contempt of court grew out of the discipline of the *attornatus* but his ubiquity gave more opportunity for it (*y*).

If the King's attorney was well on the way to becoming "Attorney-General" as yet he is not the primate of the serjeants and is always named after them. Their position is well illuminated by the events of 1460. The Duke of York's claim to the throne engrossed public attention; Parliament referred it to the justices but they in a memorable answer excused themselves. The lords then (*z*) "sent for all the Kynges Sergeauntes and Attourney" and

---

(*x*) Y. B. 20 H. VI, 37; Fox, *Contempt of Court*, 19, 162-3 (1927); he made a *capias* of which there was no original.

(*y*) This appears from Fox, *e.g.*, p. 158 : "the late Mr. Solly-Flood [Q.C.] cites [MS. *Hist.* . . . *of Hab. Corpus* : Royal Histl. Soc.] from the records several cases ' *temp*. H. III—Ed. II ' in which an Attorney was proceeded against by action or information for misconduct and he is of opinion that at that period and for long after there was no power to punish an officer upon a summary proceeding. . . . [He] also cites a case of " 1348 " in which an Attorney was punished under the statute [I Westm.] without an action information or indictment. Being present in court and interrogated the Attorney did not deny the offence which consisted in appearing for the plaintiffs in an action without a warrant and the offence was proved by the record "; sentence—imprisonment for a year and a day and afterwards " to abjure the court : H. *de Brandeston, etc.* v. W. *le Wallsh* : *Cor. Reg. Roll M.* 21 E. III, m. 132." In 1440 an attorney whose warrant is not "entered" (*i.e.*, did not pay for his licence) is to be fined 40s.; by 18 H. VI, c. 9 : *ib.* p. 78.

Their attendance in numbers on the courts is illustrated *ib.* pp. 237, 239; in 1356 a woman was tried in the Exchequer for grossly insulting Seton J. in court, she was tried by "attorneys of the Com. Bench and the Exch." (" *Lib. Assis.* 30 E. III, pl. 19 "); in 1453 twenty-four attorneys " tried " a man for " wrongful detention of an Attorney in the inner palace of the King : Y. B. 32 H. VI, 34, pl. 30 "; they seem rather to have acted as a Grand Jury. In both cases, it seems to have been convenient to employ men already about the courts.

(*z*) 5 *Rot. Parl.* 376a.

strictly bade them carefully " search " for arguments " for the Kynges availe in objection and defetying " of the claim. They replied reciting the judges' answer, " sith that the seid matter was soo high . . . that it ' passed the lernyng ' of the justices [as they had said], it must nedes excede their lernyng and also they durst not entre eny communication in that matier and prayed and besought all the Lordes to have theym excused of yevyng eny avice or Counsaill therein.

To whome it was answered by th' avis of all the Lordes, by the said Chaunceller, that they myght not so be excused, for they were the Kynges particuler Counseillers and therfore they had their fees and wages. And as to that the seid Sergeaunts and Attourney seiden that they were the Kyngs Counseillers in the lawe, in such things as were under his auctorite, or by commission, but this mater was above his auctorite wherin they myght not medle " and again they asked to be excused. This the Chancellor refused but reported the refusals of judges and serjeants to the Lords.

This extraordinary episode has many implications. In the first place, there is the solidarity of the senior bar—the King consults *all* the serjeants—a small wieldy body—as of right, not only his law officers, and they reply as one man. The Chancellor tells them in plain English that that is what they are paid for. This could hardly be true of every individual serjeant, for they could not all be—whatever they might hope—in the King's pay. Probably the retort is general and is meant for the recusant judges as well, whose excuses, we are not told, were specifically " turned down," but must have been even more unwelcome to the Crown. When the Chancellor calls the Serjeants the King's " particuler counseillers " he is perhaps referring to their oath (a).

(a) P. 517.

Most striking is the refusal of the judges and only a little less that of the bar, on supreme points of constitutional law. In both cases—perhaps, by concert of the two ranks—their *apologia* is a palpable subterfuge to avoid taking sides in the inevitable conflict. But, from our point of view, we note that the plea that the duty of advising on such a matter was the bench's and not the bar's may be technically justified and that through the pretext " the mater was so high and touched the Kyngs high estate and regalic *which is above the lawe*, and passed ther lernyng " (as the judges put it) may be descried a sense that all English lawyers were the creatures of the Crown and the common law and that they could not get out of the atmosphere of their origin—at any rate, there is no trace of a conviction that theoretically the English lawyer is competent to advise on any English law (*b*) on which he may be consulted.

The same absorption in the common law may be inferred from Fortescue's account of the bar about this time. There is nothing in it that does not tally with this episode.

In this record and in those of the Privy Council and in others we have met with serjeants with and without the qualification " King's." Of the laborious efforts which have been made (*c*) to distinguish the two, we are content to accept Coke's conclusion (2 *Inst.* 422) : " albeit the King make choice of some serjants to be of his councell and fee yet in a generall sense all be called the Kings serjants because they all be called by the Kings writ." No one has yet pointed out any clear distinction between their respective duties and practice. Possibly it was popular, the fuller title being given to the Commissioners of Assize

---

(*b*) " Namque illos veteres doctores auctoresque dicendi nullum genus disputationis a se alienum putasse accepimus semperque esse in omni orationis ratione versatos " : Cic. *de Oratore*, III, 32.

(*c*) *E.g.*, Foss, III, 370; IV, 138; but cf. III, 94.

ATTORNEYS, *NARRATORES, SERVIENTES.* 339

and those actually appearing for the Crown (*d*). Coke no doubt had in mind two events in their history which emphasized their being creations of the Crown. In 1383 John Cary, E. Clay and another were ordered by a " special writ of summons "—the first of its kind with which Dugdale (*e*) had met—to take the degree of serjeants : presumably the King in Council had nominated them; the penalty for disobedience was £100. Carey did disobey and was duly attached in 1385. He thereupon produced a royal pardon of 1384-5 set out by Manning (*f*). Cary gives no reason for his default but Dugdale surmises that he declined because " the grand Feasts (*g*) made at the reception thereof [serjeants] . . . and the large retinue for attendance they then had was antiently so chargeable," *i.e.*, the junior cannot afford to take silk. But this can hardly be the true reason, for when these burdens were heaviest, according to Fortescue (*h*), the office was most lucrative; probably the shortage was temporary (*i*). There was another better known case in 1415-7 : " several others had the like [sc. special] writs . . . but not at their own seeking "; this was in 1415 (*Claus.* 3 H. 5 m. 20 : Dugdale) and " had a complaint made against them in the Parliament " 1417, " whereupon they were compelled thereto."

(*d*) Thus Dugdale calls Fortescue simply *s. a. l.* when in 1430 his name occurs, Y. B. 8 H. VI, f. 8a, but *s. r. a. l.* in 1441 because Y. B. 19 H. VI, f. 62a, has F. " pur l' Roy," but any serjeant might appear at any moment for the Crown. For another distinction see Sjt. Chauncy's *Hertfordshire*, 75 (1700).

(*e*) *Or. jud.* 110; *Chron. Ser.* 53, citing " Claus. 6 Ric. 2, p. 1, m. 11."

(*f*) *Serviens*, p. 201, the caption is " Devon " (where C. lived) and refers to others " ad hoc ordinati " (*advocati* printed is incorrect): *ad hoc onerati* in recital is correct. An almost exactly similar discharge for Ed[mund] Clay is in " Mich. Recorda 8 R. II Rot. 15 " dors. : " in comitatu Nott " : *Serviens*, Index to Jones's *Memoranda*, v. ii (1795); Manning's document should be cited : " Exch. Lord Treasurer's Remembrancer. Memoranda Roll. 157 Hil. Communia Recorda, m. 4."

(*g*) See *Scrope's Inn*, App. XV.

(*h*) P. 503.

(*i*) For fluctuations in business about this time, see p. 243.

That complaint (*k*) makes the matter clear : the King's subjects could not get such good despatch of their causes, etc., as they were accustomed to, owing to the small number of the serjeants, to the formers' great hurt, etc.; the King to remedy such mischief long ago called up (*l*) certain Apprentices of the Law and straitly enjoined them to take the estate of a Serjeant for the ease, etc., of these who have business in the courts. Six men are named as in default, are summoned before Parliament and ordered by the King to take that estate without delay. Three weeks or so later they returned and asked for a short respite. " Thereupon, after discussion on certain matters put by the Apprentices before " the Council, the Duke of Bedford, who was the King's Commissioner, assented to their prayer on the distinct understanding that they would be at the King's mercy unless they performed their promise, shortly to take that estate. The discussion, we may suppose, bore upon the pecuniary ability of the nominated to accept office; we may surmise that the Crown promised them work.

The most downright expression of what is sometimes heard in modern times—" I cannot afford to go on the bench "—is in a petition of 1440 to Henry VI from William Ayscogh, a justice who recites " that where[as] he late by your commaundement was charged to take upon hym the degree of Sergeaunt of your lawe to his grete expenses and costes. And or he had ben' (*m*) fully two yere in that office at the barre he was called by your " Highness " to the benche and made Justice, by which makyng Justice

---

(*k*) 4 *Rot. Parl.* 107, no. 10 : Dugd. 111.

(*l*) In 1429 there is a minute of the Privy Council " in pleno parliamento," that two named persons should be *s. ad. leges* (sic) *pro. d. r.* and have the customary fees; they replace two *s.* made judges at the same moment : 4 *P. P. C.* 4; for appointment of another *s.* (*ad. l.* ?) in 1437, see *ib.* v, 80.

(*m*) 16 *Archaeologia.* 3 (1812); 4 Foss, 282.

all his Wynnings (*n*) that he sholde have hade in the said office of Sergeant and all the fees that he had in England weere and be cessed and expired fro hym to his grete empov'ysshyng for they weere the grete substance of his lyvelode . . . your besecher is the porest of alle your justices and may noght maynteigne his said degre to your worship as hym ought to do, &c.," and he prays in effect for an increase of £25 12s. 10d. a year. Clearly a serjeant's was a cash business, which a judge's often was not.

But what emerges most notably from the cases of 1383 and 1415 is that from time to time there were not enough serjeants to do the routine business, that practitioners were, at any rate, at times considering whether it would pay them to become " leaders " and that that class was as of course recruited from the Apprentices—all matters which we shall meet again. The insistence of the Government could hardly be due to jealousy for the royal prerogative, for refusal was rare and the rank was generally sought, nor could the crown be much concerned whether any given person became a serjeant at law. It is, therefore, highly probable that now and then more practising lawyers were wanted. If so, the demand of the public for a larger available bar may almost be called a landmark in its history.

Language.

The story ran that William the Conqueror with a view to " Normanification " decreed that no one should conduct a case in the *curia regis* except in French " to make both countries of one speech "; " Anglo-French " is now the usual name. Holkot, a Dominican friar, on whose authority, Selden (1630-40) repeats this (*o*), died in 1349 or 1351;

(*n*) Cf. p. 380.
(*o*) On c. 48 of *de laudibus* citing a Lect. xi, on *Wisdom*; St. 1 *Hist.* c. xi, p. 501. Fortescue's statement (about 1468-70), *ib.*, that after the Conquest the Normans " non permiserunt ipsi eorum [*sc.*

Holkot adds that the order was in force in his day (*p*). The story, says Freeman, is " a dream " (*q*); Stubbs writes to the same effect despite " the high authority " of this " schoolman . . . the popular courts transacted their business in English and the Kings issued their charters in English as well as in Latin. Richard I is the first King of whom no English document is preserved and our first French record belongs to the reign of John." Henry III published a proclamation on the Provisions of Oxford (1258) in Latin, French and English (*r*) : " It is perhaps the first important proclamation issued in English since the coming of the Normans " (*s*).

Moreover, what Ordericus tells us points to the contrary of Holkot's statement; under 1070 he says (*t*) : William's benevolence made him try to learn English in order to do justice to his English subjects when he sat as judge but his age and business prevented his success.

Robert of Gloucester, who *floruit* 1260—1300, " the Ennius of English Literature " wrote (*u*) : " Nor could the Normans speak any but their own tongue. They spake

---

the English] advocatos placitare causas suas nisi in lingua quam ipsi noverunt, qualiter et faciunt [*sc.* 1460-70] omnes advocati in Francia, etiam in curia Parliamenti ibidem " is probably an echo of Holkot and has no independent value. He suggests (*ib.*) that the Normans insisted on all their accounts being in French, to prevent imposition. For the reverse school-process before 1385, see Fr. 5 *N. C.* 536.

(*p*) Evidently he had heard some talk on the subject : it must often have been discussed before 1363.

(*q*) 5 *N. C.* 506. The pseudo-Ingulf (about 1400?) reproduces Holkot : *Scriptores post Bedam*, 512 b : 159 b : Riley, transln. p. 142 : " one of the forger's clumsiest falsehoods " : 1 P. & M., 60, n. (2). Thomas Fuller's story, *Church History*, 133, § 16, of William's " picking a quarrel " with University College, Oxford, in order to forbid English is equally untrustworthy, but his conclusion about his own day —1655—is interesting; French came to " a composition with English mixed together, as they remain."

(*r*) St. *Sel. Ch.* (1258) no. V.

(*s*) Tout, *Pol. Hist. Eng.* (1216-1377) p. 103; English was " looking up " : *ib.* 95.

(*t*) *Hist. Eccl.* iv, c. 7 (p. 215, v. 2 : Paris, 1840 : Fr. trans. v. 2, p. 207).

(*u*) l. 7538 : 2 Rolls, 543, cited by Horwood, below.

French as they did at home and also taught it to their children, so that great men in this land who came of their blood keep to that speech [French] which they took from them [Normans]. For unless a man knows French, people think little of him. But low men stick to English yet and to their own speech. I ween that there are in all the world no countries that hold not to their own speech save England alone." He seems to hint that in his day some of the English upper class also spoke French.

It is of course possible that while William wanted to learn English himself he wanted his native subjects to forget it, but it is improbable. Still Holkot's view is borne out, at any rate, partly, by two of his contemporaries, Higden, writing apparently before 1327, says (*x*) that " to-day (*hodie*) the corruption of the native [English] language proceeds from two causes : one, that schoolchildren since the Norman conquest are compelled to give up their mother tongue and construe (*construere*) in French—contrary to the custom of other nations; another, that the children of gentle-folk (*nobilium*) are from their very cradles instructed in French. Indeed common fellows (*rurales homines*; ' uplondisshe men,' Trevisa) imitate them for the sake of appearances (*spectabiliores videantur*) and ' frenchify ' themselves to the utmost (*francigenare satagunt omni nisu*)." Then Trevisa interpolating a passage (cited by Freeman) definitely dates the restoration of English at or before 1385 and assigns the credit to two named men—that is, as we shall see, twenty-five or thirty years after the law had moved in that direction. Blackstone (3 *Comm.* 318) seems to take Holkot's view, humorously making Juvenal prophesy, " Gallia causidicos docuit facunda Britannos."

There is nothing surprising in a deliberate and concerted

(*x*) *Polychronicon*, B. I, c. 59 : 2 Rolls, 158 : Trevisa *ib.*; translated in 1387. In 1085 the converse was the case with Ordericus; he did not know his French father's language : 4 *N. C.* 496, c. 20.

attempt to popularise the language of the conquerors; applied to the courts it succeeded in the higher for two centuries but not to anything like the same extent in the lower.

An actual relevant instance is recorded by Ordericus in the trial of Bricstan in 1115-6. In a letter from the Bishop of Ely, but written by Abbot Guérin, Bricstan is made to say " *Anglicâ linguâ* That wat min lauert godel mihtin that ic sege soth. . . . *Quod nos* Latini dicimus : Mi domine, scit Deus omnipotens quia veritatem dico " (*y*).

The Abbott (or Ordericus or the Bishop) puts Anglo-Saxon into Bricstan's mouth at this point, while in the remainder of a long narrative he is supposed to speak Latin, to make the exception prove the rule. It is evident however that this ejaculation had " stuck "; probably Bricstan was an Englishman and made his defence in English throughout. Or, as he was a man of means and position possibly he used French and " dropped into " his native tongue only under stress of emotion; the writer who sympathizes with him thus points his natural indignation. But parties under Bricstan's rank must obviously have addressed the county and inferior courts in English : for fifty or sixty years after the Conquest the " High Court " is negligible in this connection; there would be no dearth of interpreters, even if they were wanted.

Vacarius (*z*) about 1150 was writing a law-book, a

(*y*) *Hist. Eccl.* vi, c. 10, p. 127. In the French translation (*Collection des Mémoires* : *Histoire de Normandie*, v. 3, p. 111 : Paris, 1826) the words are : Pat min lauert Godel mihtin hic sege sod; in Freeman's 5 *N. C.* 826 : that min lavert God aelmihtin (eallmihtig) hic sege soth.

(*z*) Wenck, p. 138. If Vacarius himself wrote the note it is important as showing what he thought the rule ought to be (even if it was not so) : it runs—*Argumentum* (sc. hinc sume) (Dig. B. 22, Tit. 6, l. 9, § 3) *contra eum qui litteras citatorias laico lectorem* [=who understood the *litterae*] *non habenti destinavit. Item argum. contra eum qui cum ibi litiget ubi est copia advocatorum petit ut advocatus adversarii sui gallica vel anglica lingua alleget* (sc. argumenta sua) *quasi ipse cum laicus sit latinam linguam non intelligat* : 44 Seld. Soc.

gloss on which possibly by himself but certainly composed in England, is extant; it speaks of advocates (*adv*.) being asked to plead in French or English, at the instance of the other party, being a layman, if he professes ignorance of Latin : " if where the trial takes place there are plenty of advocates," it ought not to be allowed. The suggestion (which seems only to include the arguments and not the pleas) shows that the point early attracted attention. Whatever was the language of any given trial we may be certain that laymen would, like Bricstan, occasionally lapse into their mother tongue. And perhaps we may infer that about 1150—1200 the process is beginning, or is noticeable, which terminates with the triumph of English in colloquy (though it was not complete in the courts), after a bilingual or trilingual period of transition (*a*).

It is probable that as soon as we get into the higher spheres, *viz.*, of the *servientes*, the difficulties of interpretation disappeared; they existed chiefly in the litigation of the less well-to-do including that by " bill." Expanding a hint from Mr. Bolland (*The General Eyre*, p. 9 (*b*)),

---

21 : ed. de Zulueta. Naturally the practical difficulty was felt elsewhere; about 1105-7 in a sentence of the Court of Philip I (Chanoines de . . . *v*. N. : *Textes rélatifs*, etc., 9 : by Ch. V, Langlois : Paris, 1888) : ad hoc mox clerici . . . satis legitime respondentes—causam suam vulgari et latina disseruerunt eloquentia : n.b. *clerici*. About 1280 Beaumanoir (*Coutumes*, c. 6) says that *li clerc* speak Latin very well but the lay folk who have to plead against them in a lay court do not even understand their French, however fine and apt for their cause; because, says Beugnot, the *clercs* were so fond of mixing Latin in their speech.

(*a*) Even in the ecclesiastical courts. See William of Drogheda, p. 104, about 1240; he insists on the *client* understanding what is going on (c. 51).

(*b*) Perhaps he underrates the number of biglots—say, after 1100. Prof. Studer, dealing as a philologer with the records of Southampton about 1300, says : " At the end of the 13th century the English language continued to be spoken at Southampton by a considerable section of the population and was probably understood even by those who usually expressed themselves in French. It seems incredible that these two classes of inhabitants prevalent in all English boroughs, should have lived so long side by side, without finding it needful each

the clerk of the court, who with or without that title, would be found in every tribunal, surely knew something of the three languages (c). The historians seem to be agreed about the facts in the courts. Stubbs has no doubt that their language like that of sermons was " adapted to the understanding of the majority," and hence from 1066 to, say, 1166 English prevailed there and in Charters, and he understands Hallam to mean that the hundred courts were administered in English during the Norman period (d). He certainly does say that " trial by jury (e) must have rendered a knowledge of English almost indispensable to those who administered justice."

It is inconceivable that English folk in the " local " courts after the Conquest spoke anything but English, but it is not only conceivable but certain that when formal pleas were necessary—spoken or written—a point on which we have no exact rules—they were in French (f). Probably immediately after the Conquest, there was a period of utter disturbance in all parts of the country which the tide of invasion touched. When in about a hundred years, order emerges " the practice of pleading in the French tongue was established in the Curia Regis as early as in the reign of Henry II. In the reign of Henry II the French tongue began to find its way over the country. . . . The French

---

to gain some knowledge of the language of the other. It is far more likely that many people of both classes were bilingual and spoke the two languages with equal facility ": *Oak Book*; *Supplmt.* 46.

(c) " The clerk (or scholar) with his Latin, the courtier with his Anglo-Norman, and the people with their good old English " : Wright, *Political Songs*; Camd. Soc. ix.

(d) St. Lect. XI and II, 229, 21; Hallam, *Mid. Ages*, ii, 306 (or 605-6).

(e) They would question, be questioned and find in English : Horwood, Y. B. 1302-3, xxv.

(f) Of " precedents " made about 1340 for some " imaginary courts " Maitland says : " They are partly in Latin, partly in French, the matter which is to be enrolled is in Latin the matter which is merely to be spoken is in French "; *the Court Baron*, 4 Seld. Soc. 15, probably even when an ecclesiastic presided.

tongue was also adopted in the Circuit of the justices in this reign and new forms of pleading and trial were introduced in the Assize, the names of which were French and which have been handed down to the present day. . . . In the . . . reign of Richard I the Crusade contributed materially to extend the use of French amongst the upper classes of England " (*g*). This, perhaps, describes the process of the forensic language of the upper classes, of which the fusion must have been gradual, as precisely as we are likely to find, but it must not be forgotten that the French were at the same time learning English. Whether the official language was Latin or French, when it was sought to interest the populace, English was used. When in 1291 some friars were anxious to assert their right to bury a man against the competing monks of Worcester, they made a pompous procession through the city " exhibiting their privilege to the townsfolk *materna lingua*," and when Edward I wanted in 1299 to reassure his subjects of the forest liberties of England he, too, made proclamation in that city " in their mother tongue " (*h*). There is, positive evidence (*i*) that about 1280 the *narratores* used French (*romana verba*) in court and that written exceptions were always in French.

There is authority, too, for the lesser courts, whither we have supposed the pleader was slower in penetrating.

" It is difficult for us (*k*) to believe that in the local

(*g*) Twiss, 1 *Black Book of Admiralty*, liii : Rolls.

(*h*) *Annals of Worcester*, 4 *Ann. Mon.* 504, 541 (Worc.) : Rolls; no doubt the same expedient was adopted elsewhere. Cf. Wright, 1 *Chron. de P. de Langtoft*, xxviii-ix; Rolls : During the 13th century " the Anglo-Norman had been breaking up in the mouths of a people who were adopting a different language. At the end of the 13th century it was sinking into that strange medley which has been since known as the French of the law courts."

(*i*) 2 Holdsworth, p. 325 : from Hengham's (?) *Modus Componendi* and *Exceptiones*.

(*k*) 1 P. & M., B. I, c. 3, p. 62, citing *Court Baron*, 4 Seld. Soc. 38, 41 : ed. Maitland, quoted above.

courts the suitors who were for the more part peasants, pleaded their causes and rendered their judgments in French; still from the 13th century we get books of precedents for pleadings in manorial courts which are written in French while we look in vain for any similar books written in English. We may suspect that if the villagers themselves did not use French when they assailed each other in the village courts, their pleaders used it for them and before the end of the 13th century the professional pleader might already be found practising before a petty tribunal and speaking the language of Westminster Hall."

It certainly is striking to find in a (French) report of a case in a village court about, apparently, the middle of the 13th century: " How will thou acquit thyself?" " Sir," saith his pleader, " he will give the lord a half mark that this may be earnestly inquired of by the best folk of the vill &c." Again, " Sir " (asketh [the plaintiff]) " do thou ask whether Walter [defendant] will avow what his pleader hath said on his behalf. And Walter answereth, Yea "; then judgment is given on a pure point of pleading.

Freeman, too, points out that French only established itself officially very gradually (l); " throughout the twelfth century " bilingualism was, at any rate, not rare. When French became [for a time] the public language it was one sign that " the fusion of Normans and English was now complete," and Acts of Parliament under Edward I, " never written in English," but commonly in French, are palmary instances of the official tongue.

That King himself used to speak (m) French and " used the French language " in the first statute of Westminster (1275)—the first in that language in the Statutes of the

---

(l) 5 N. C. 528, 527, 530; no laws or deeds in N.-F. earlier than H. III and first Eng.-Fr. document under John: St. Cf. the bilingualism of even lower class Belgians.

(m) David Jenkins, *Eight Centuries* (1661), itself written in Latin and French; for the superstitious respect for Latin and pleading at that date, see *ib*. 270.

Realm, unless that of the Exchequer (1 *St. R.* 197) be of 51 Henry III : the only French Charter of Liberty being of 1297 (*ib.* 37) : " and, what is more to the purpose, the petitions to Parliament " under E. I " are for the most part in French " (*n*).

What practically happened seems to have been that the numerically few English of the upper classes in " fusing " with the Normans learned French and used their knowledge tc get English adopted in the courts. Mr. Horwood acutely says (*o*) of (about) 1300 : " That the Norman-French was not the mother tongue of the pleaders will (it is thought) be the conclusion of the reader. An examination of their phrases seems to show that they thought in English and clothed English ideas and sentences with foreign words." It is less surprising that French had the monopoly as long as it had than that English got in at all. *Non nostrum* to discuss why English and not French became the national language, but we may summarise the conclusions of the historians.

William Rufus promotes the " upper hand " of the English over the other (non-French) " elements " in Northern Britain, and by the end of Henry I's reign [1135]

(*n*) Twiss (above), lv. Some scholars think that the Great Charter was drawn in French and that at the Oxford Parliament of 1258 all the Orders spoke French : *ib.*

(*o*) Cited p. 346*e*. Mr. Bolland makes the same point which confirms his theory about his " bills," some of which are still earlier : 30 Seld. Soc. xxx; *Year Books* 10. Maitland in a passage (17 Seld. Soc. xxxv), remarkable even for him, gives instances : " The law was not expressible properly in English until the ' lange du paiis ' [from St. of 1362] had appropriated to itself scores of French words; we may go near to saying that it had to borrow a word corresponding to almost every legal concept that had as yet been fashioned. Time was when the Englishman who in his English talk used such a word as ' ancestor ' or ' heir,' such a word as ' descent,' ' revert ' or ' remain ' must have felt that he was levying an enforced loan. For a while, the charge of speaking a barbarous jargon would fall rather upon those who were making countless English words by the simple method of stealing than upon those whose French, though it might be of a colonial type, had taken next to nothing from the vulgar tongue."

the distinctions between " conquerors " and " conquered " of its beginning, had disappeared and Normans born on English soil were " Englishmen "; later in the 12th century the highest social class was almost wholly Norman, the lowest almost wholly " old English," the intermediate " the smaller . . . landowners, the inhabitants of the towns " mixed (*p*). It is well to remember that as the common law, whatever its root and sources, was always administered by the upper classes, its expression would vary as their dialect varied. At any rate, it took two hundred years after the conventional date of fusion for the law formally to disclaim French (*q*).

" If," says Freeman (*r*), " we ask for a particular date for the victory of English we may take the year " 1362(3) " when English displaced French as the language of pleadings in the higher courts of law."

The statute, 36 E. III, st. 1, c. 15 (1362) (*s*) probably only declared what at that time had become frequent, for the City as early as 1356, and probably earlier, had decreed that plaintiffs—which does not necessarily negative defendants—in the City courts might plead in English. The statute runs :—

" Because it is often shewed to the King by the Prelates, Dukes, Earls, Barons and all the Commonalty of the great mischiefs which have happened to divers of the realm because the Laws, Customs and Statutes of this realm be

---

(*p*) " Jam cohabitantibus Anglicis et Normannis et alternatim uxores ducentibus vel nubentibus, sic permixte sunt nationes ut vix decerni possit hodie [c. 1160], de liberis loquor, quis Anglicus, quis Normannus sit genere." *Dialogus de Scaccario* : I, x, B : " the most distinct of all witnesses to the thorough fusion," Freeman, 4 *N. C.* 327; 5 *N. C.* 536, 825, 881; 2 *William Rufus*, 4, 455; Holdsworth, 2 *Hist.* 479.

(*q*) At Oxford statutes had to be made (in the 13th cent.?) that boys should construe in English and French " lest the latter should be wholly forgotten " : 1 *Mun. Acad. Oxon.* lxx : Rolls, v. 2, p. 438. For the University Courts about 1300, see p. 161*c*.

(*r*) 5 *N. C.* 536.

(*s*) 1 *St. Realm*, p. 375; French translated : it is founded on minutes 38, 39, 2 *Rot. Parl.* 273 b (1362).

not commonly [holden and kept] in the same realm for that they be pleaded and shewed and judged in the French tongue which is much unknown in the said realm; so that the people which do implead or be impleaded in the King's court and in the courts of other, have no knowledge nor understanding of that which is said for them or against them by their Serjeants and other Pleaders; and that reasonably the said laws and customs [the rather shall be perceived] and known and better understood in the tongue used in the said realm and by so much every man of the said realm may the better govern himself without offending of the law and the better keep save and defend his heritage and possessions and in divers regions and countries where the King the Nobles and other of the said realm have been, good governance and full right is done to every person because that their laws and customs be learned and used in the tongue of the country, the King . . . hath ordained, . . . by the Assent aforesaid that all Pleas which shall be pleaded in [any] Courts whatsoever before any of his justices whatsoever or in his other places or before any of his other Ministers whatsoever, or in the Courts and Places of any other Lords whatsoever within the realm, shall be pleaded, shewed, defended, answered, debated and judged in the English tongue and that they be entered and inrolled in Latin : and that the laws and customs of the same realm, terms and processes be holden and kept as they be and have been before this time; and that by the ancient terms and forms of [the Declarations : or Pleaders = *de counter*] no man be prejudiced so that the matter of the action be fully shewed in the declaration and in the Writ . . ."

John Capgrave, who was born thirty years after this Act passed, said of it : " And this yere was ordeyned that alle plees at the barre schuld be in Englisch tunge and in no othir tunge " (*t*). Fabyan writing about 1500 copies

---

(*t*) *Chronicles*, 222 : Rolls : So William of Worcester *Annales*, Pt. 2, v. 2, 749 : Rolls (*in lingua materna*).

Capgrave but makes a notable addition (*u*) : " And aboute thys tyme was an ordenaunce and statute made that sergaunts and prentyses of the law shulde plede theyr plees in theyr mother tonge. But that stode but a shorte whyle " (*x*)—the last words correcting a common error. Blackstone attributes (*y*) this statute—drawn in French—to the natural objection of a conqueror of France to use that language (presumably, he means officially) and he points out that Edward III had the precedents of his own great-grandfather, Alfonso X of Castile, about 1250 and of the German Emperor in 1286. But he is aware that " the practisers " as they needs must continue to think in French took their notes in French (and so wrote their reports in it) or, as Stubbs (2 *Hist.* 450) more generally puts it, " practice was in this instance much more powerful than statute and French continued to be the legal language for some centuries " (*z*). Modern historians (*a*), observers of " tendencies," note that 1362-3 was within " the period of experiments in economic and anti-clerical legislation," to verify which we have only to look at the preamble.

The net result is, in Maitland's words (*b*) :

" The Act of 1362 . . . was tardily obeyed and indeed it attempted the impossible. How tardy the obedience was we cannot precisely tell, for the history of this matter is involved with the insufficiently explored history of written pleadings. Apparently French remained the language of ' pleadings ' properly so-called, while English became the

---

(*u*) 7th part of Chronicle, CIX a.

(*x*) So it was a mark of fusion—Greek with Roman—when " Cumanis eo anno [180 B.C.] petentibus permissum ut publice Latine loquerentur et praconibus Latine vendendi jus esset " : Livy, XL, 42.

(*y*) 3 *Comm.* 318, where the subsequent history may be conveniently followed.

(*z*) The Chancellor's speech on opening Parliament was in English in 1363 but not always thereafter : *ib.* It is too strong to say " The Statute . . . was a dead letter " : Studer, *Oak Book of Southampton*, Supplement 10, n. (2).

(*a*) Tout (above), p. 380.

(*b*) 17 Seld. Soc. xxxiv.

language of that 'argument' which was slowly differentiated from out of the mixed process of arguing and pleading which is represented to us by the Year Books."

Thus for three hundred years " the bar " had heard little but French (and Englishmen had heard a great deal since the days of Edward the Confessor).

What we have called " French " is variously called Norman, Anglo-Norman, Anglo-French and law-French. The facts (c) seem to be that though the Normans brought a literary language with them, it was one of the varieties of existing French, not, for instance, that of Paris. That in this country the two native languages influenced one another is a commonplace but that French had become common among the lower English classes and, indeed, had maintained a " comparative purity," till the first years of Henry III so that in Southampton about 1300 though " the French dialect commonly used " there " had begun to show unmistakable signs of English influence—here and there, an expression . . . savours of home-bred Saxon— [yet] the syntax and vocabulary remained thoroughly French and the [latter] is substantially the same as that used in continental French " is perhaps not so generally known. But meanwhile Parisian French had been " coming on " to the hegemony which it has ever since held, whereas, from the French point of view, it had been decaying here—from, say, 1210 to 1250,—and hence, finally, the antipodes, Paris—Stratford-atte-Bowe. For this decline the lawyers are not responsible, though, no doubt, they increased a tendency which had affected them. In the end but " very gradually, the relation between the two languages was reversed." But it was not till English had

---

(c) These conclusions are borrowed from Prof. Studer's *Oak Book of Southampton* (about 1300) (*Supplement*, 1911; or his *Study of Anglo-Norman* : 1920 : Clarendon Press) who, however, " Frenchises " so to say, too much, and from Maitland and his authorities in 17 Seld. Soc. For Grammar, Phonology, etc., see both writers.

C.H.

finally beaten French (*d*) that the latter became in the lawyers' diction that " jargon " over which so many sober jurists (*e*) have made merry.

But if we are not entitled to dwell on the philology of law-French we are bound to note its concrete results on the profession. Whether the English of 1150—1300 would have " thrown up " a technical law language need not be solved for it never had the chance. Maitland, who practically discovered this learning, must be consulted first-hand by the special student, but two of his brilliant conclusions must be stated in his own words (*f*) : " during the later middle age English lawyers enjoyed the inestimable advantage of being able to make a technical language. And a highly technical language they made. . . . Precise ideas are . . . expressed in precise terms, every one of which is French (*g*); the geometer or the chemist could hardly wish for terms that are more exact or less liable to have their edges worn away by the vulgar."

Finally, he sums up :

" At the time of which we speak the English lawyer was a man of three languages. No one can have hoped for success at the bar without Latin as well as French.

(*d*) " Anglo-Norman was a dead language by the middle of the 14th century " : Studer (1920 : p. 12), as in last note.

(*e*) *E.g.*, Sir Frederick Pollock, *First Book of Jurisprudence*, 279-84 (1896). It would be natural to compare it to modern " Yiddish " or the Levantine *lingua franca*, were these not languages of the illiterate, which law-French never was.

(*f*) 17 Seld. Soc. xxxvi, lxxx.

(*g*) This is singularly borne out by what Fortescue says—with authority—of his own day—writing, by the way, in France after some years' residence there : " A certain statute first restrained pleading in French to some extent but French has not yet wholly disappeared, partly on account of certain terms which pleaders express more appropriately in French than English and partly because declarations on original writs [Latin] are learned and used in that language as more consonant to the matter [*naturam*] of those writs [than English]. . . . The Year Books, too, are in French and many statutes " : *de laud.*, c. 48; thus law-French in England is stereotyped—not vulgarly corrupted, as is French in France generally, because in England it is more written than spoken.

The statutes, the records, the private instruments that the English lawyer would have to expound were written in Latin and a false concord (*h*) in a writ was in his eyes a serious matter. . . . Let it be that the Latin and French were not of a very high order; still we see at Westminster a cluster of men which deserves more attention than it receives from our unsympathetic, because legally uneducated, historians. No, the clergy were not the only learned men in England, the only cultivated men, the only men of ideas. Vigorous intellectual effort was to be found outside the monasteries and the universities. These lawyers are wordly men, not men of the sterile caste; they marry and found families, some of which become as noble as any in the land; but they are in their way learned cultivated men, linguists, logicians, tenacious disputants, true lovers of the nice case and the moot point. They are gregarious, clubable men, grouping themselves in hospices, which become schools of law, multiplying manuscripts, arguing, learning and teaching, the great mediators between life and logic, a reasoning, reasonable element in the English nation."

Costume.

Certain information on this subject emerges very slowly after the Conquest. The evolution of English legal uniform has never been systematically attempted (nor, apparently, that of any other country). But it is possible to get a hint here and there. There is no suggestion that the profession ever deliberately invented a garb for itself and all the evidence (*i*) points, as we should expect *a priori*, to the

---

(*h*) Cf. *Crone's* case (1690), Macaulay, *History*, c. 15, or *Grahme's*, 12 *St. Tr.* 816 (1691).

(*i*) The authorities are not easy to harmonize even for a specialist. All statements of sartorial facts above are taken from one or more of these, the chief of which are Marriott, *Vestiarium Christianum* (1868); Prof. E. C. Clark, 50 *Archaeological Journal* (1893); Moroni, *Diz.*: *Avvocati* and *Vesti*; Druitt, *Costume on Brasses* (1906), and

adoption (or persistence) of ecclesiastical and scholastic modes.

The *toga*, the ordinary civil dress of the Roman, was the pleader's uniform (*k*); thus, the gown of to-day, descends from even pre-Ciceronian days. The mediaeval secular *avvocati concistoriali* of the Papal courts, and all lawyers of the Roman *Sapienza* wore long modest mantles at all public, even not sacred, functions. A *fortiori* reverend advocates in ecclesiastical or secular courts, for the Church had in all ages insisted on its officers normally wearing sober garments, chief among which it had inherited the simple *toga*. But this was also the common garment of the bulk of respectable people (except presumably manual labourers) in Christendom and hence, we are told (*l*), that in the Middle Ages, as late as the fourteenth century, the clergy (other than the friars) and the laity dressed externally in much the same way. As the ecclesiastical profession expands, it naturally strives to differentiate itself from other avocations and hence, by degrees, a great profusion of sacerdotal *ornamenta*. Sumptuary ecclesiastical enactments in the fourteenth century aim at repressing these extravagances (*m*), at any rate, in the inferior clergy, while in the same spirit, secular ordinances attempt to do the same for the population generally, and both, perhaps, aim at keeping the professions distinct. Thus the "long robe" (*n*) though, no doubt, it came

---

the popular volumes of Fairholt (1885) and Planché have also been consulted. For a special case, see p. 54.

(*k*) Moroni, *Vesti*, 177, cites Cassaneo [Cassianus or John of Marseille? *fl.* 430 A.D.]: *Clamys militem, purpura regem, stola sacerdotem, toga advocatum, cuculla* [sic] *monachum demonstrat.* Claudius is bidden to remember that advocacy is a career for commoners : cogitaret plebem quae toga enitesceret : Tac. *Ann.* XI, 7.

(*l*) Bonnard, 1 *Costumes historiques des 12°-15° siècles*, p. 63 : Paris, 1880; Mrs. Ashdown, *British Costumes*, p. 355 (1910).

(*m*) In 1342, according to Mrs. Ashdown, above, the Archbishop of Canterbury speaks of ecclesiastics being more like military men than clericals.

(*n*) The phrase occurs first, *semble*, in *De laudibus*, c. 51 : see p. 368.

into our courts, on the back of priests, came at the same time, on the back of laymen who had business there. And hence, at any rate, in the case of the latter it was not always, perhaps not commonly, black, for one writer states that he could not find in the time of Edward II that clerics or lawyers wore black gowns (*o*). We shall see that our first actual pictures of the lawyers bear out this statement. Probably, too, the same writer is correct in saying that while about 1340 there was a reaction against the prevalent lengthy garment in favour of the short and tight tunic or surcoat, all ranks of lawyers (but not their inferior officers) adhered to their gowns and cloaks and thus were distinguished from other laymen as " of the long robe." The facts seem to square not only with other facts but with the universal conservatism of the profession.

Probably by the time that lay lawyers had the monopoly of the secular courts and began to think consciously or corporately of robes, the chief survival from the ecclesiastical *régime* was a sense of gravity translated into attire; the laicisation of bench and bar, fairly coincident, was not a short sharp act. The early judges were prelates and the early pleaders clerics, occasionally monks, all for long centuries, men of uniform and—what is equally to the point — the pleaders were frequently, perhaps, in the " heavy " cases always *magistri* from the universities (*p*). There, we know, *more academiarum*, the doctrine of robes flourished and it is quite likely that the gay gowns of Oxford and Cambridge to-day are as much due to the taste of Bologna and Paris as are, as we know, the practice of uniform and many another university canon, to their

---

(*o*) Planché : *Hure: sed quaere.* The early Chancery clerks were " clerici " in both senses : hence the sartorial restrictions, p. 442, were no doubt a survival but their two heads, the clerks of the Crown are expressly excepted.

(*p*) There could have been little talk about costume in the days of William of Drogheda, for he says nothing about the robes of *advocati* : but he does mention the judge's *cingulum* (p. 572).

discipline. It seems, therefore, reasonable to suppose that the first lay pleaders who found themselves in the midst of clerics or doctors of laws were either themselves the latter or assimilated their habit to that of the former—though, perhaps, this required little effort as for long only inferior clergy had appeared (for poor persons) in secular courts. To aid this tendency, it happened, as we have seen, that the universities were beginning to make their influence felt just when a lay bar was coming into existence. The bench, too, which was slower than the bar to lose all its clerical members, exhibited continuity of uniform, sacred or profane, and thus encouraged legal attire—incidentally, perhaps founding the modern rule that when the bench robes the bar robes.

Thus, along two loop lines, both starting from one original main, the influence of dress made itself felt—through the Church and through the Schools. It is generally assumed that the latter form was taken from the simplest of other monastic institutions, the Benedictine, which prescribed also a close cope and a hood—all of which have descended in some guise to the bar. Thus, in one way, or another, it has borrowed from the Church the modest robe, the hood, the coif, and the bands—but not, of course, the tonsure.

Of these, the coif was, for long, almost the emblem of the profession. As it was merely a close hood for the head, made of white lawn or silk, it was of general utility and was worn by both sexes, *inter alios*, by prelates : " the earliest pictures, which we have of the mitre date from the 11th Century; they have the shape of a round bonnet (*bonnet*) . . . : under this bonnet we see sometimes a white *coiffe* whose borders overlap the bottom of the mitre " (*q*).

(*q*) Racinet, 3 *Le Costume historique* : Moyen Âge D. J. : Paris, 1888. Marriott, above, p. 112, cites Alcuin (10th or 11th cent.) : " pileos, id est, cuphias, gestant in capite . . ." If a guess may be hazarded, it was a substitute for the coarser hood.

It seems to have ministered to the comfort of the wearer for the Church, though forbidding its use generally to the clergy, allowed it when they were travelling (r). It was forbidden because it concealed the tonsure (s). This certainly was not, as has sometimes been supposed why lawyers wore it; there is no instance known of a serjeant who had taken orders (t). In 1259 one William de Bussey, *senescallus et principalis consiliarius* (u) *W. de Valentia fratris regis uterini* was arrested and tried on many charges : defence being useless, he was about to untie the strings of his coif (*ligamenta suae coifae*) to show that he had the clerical tonsure but was not allowed to do so (x). Obviously the coif covered the tonsure, but there is nothing in this incident nor in the description *consiliarius* (y) to suggest that de Bussey was a lawyer, indeed what the annalist says of him shows that he was the unscrupulous Valentia's unscrupulous land agent; no lawyer would speak as he did.

(r) *Const.* 5, *Othobon* in 1268, repeated *Const.* 21, *Peckham* in 1281 (Lyndwood (1679) : *Const. Leg.* 88 : *Const. Prov.* 32) : O. Reichel, 1 *Canon Law* (1896), 264 : " infulas suas (vulgo coyphas vocant ").

(s) Cf. " Le inception del wearing del coifes p le seruients al ley] fuit quia in initio fueront fryers et p ceo fuit a couer leur bald pates vid Sir Henry Spillman. The coyf is in similitud of a salet or headpiec, signifies that a saluted soldier ought to be bold in warr. So ought they in their clients causes. It signifies allso an honour. The uncovering of the head being a badge of servise. Spell. Gloss. voce coifa vid Wakes musae regnantes Harl. MSS. [f. 2 otherwise 5 a : see *Catalogue* 980]." R. R. Pearce's *Guide to the Inns of Court*, 2nd edn. (1855), p. 437, n., citing a MS. of T. Gibbons (about 1600). The reference to Spelman is in *Justitiarius* 335 : Wake's book cited is apparently not otherwise known. L. Campbell C.J. said " the present black patch represents what was worn to conceal the tonsure " relying on 1 *Bl. Comm.* 24 n. : *Bennett* v. *Hale* (1850), 15 Q. B. 175.

(t) Hervey de Staunton is in Pulling's list, but there is no evidence that he ever was a serjeant.

(u) Like Laurence, p. 134.

(x) 5 *Mat. Paris*, 738, Rolls : 984 Wats : the curious remark that he was seized " non per coifae ligamina " but by his throat, seems to imply that care was taken not to loosen the coif.

(y) Immediately before Walter de Scotinny, who was certainly not a lawyer, is called " principalissimus et specialissimus consiliarius com. Glov. et senescallus " : he is otherwise unknown.

Another incident has been misinterpreted. In 1305 one William de Brewes was sentenced by the King in Council for a contempt of court to go, *discinctus in corpore capite nudo et tena* (coif) *deposita* (z), from the King's Bench to the Exchequer where the offence was committed and purge himself. We know that William was a party in the suit in which he lost his temper, if he had been a *serviens ad legem*, the fact would certainly have been mentioned, and, again, it is inconceivable that a lawyer should have acted as he did. At any rate, it is not suggested that he was tonsured.

The fact is that the serjeants wore coifs because they were commonly worn, as no doubt, did the *narratores* and their other predecessors. A lay man " of the coif " was easily distinguished from the clerical pleader who (not being a prelate) was expressly forbidden to wear it. Moreover, just as he disappeared the apprentice rose and thus the Serjeant's title soon came conveniently to mean, not a junior. Skelton, however, in 1522 seems to be (a) the first to write " Serjeants of the coif."

The earliest connection of the thing with the law is in a Political Song (b) attributed by Mr. Wright to the time of Edward I, " A Satyre on the Consistory Courts."

" Furst ther sit an old cherl in a blake hure.

. . . .

An heme (hem) in an herygoud (cloak) with honginde (hanging) sleven."

(z) *Abb. Plac.* 256-7 : So in 1268 de Coleville to purge a contempt : p. 178. Britton says exactly the same of felons on trial : " dechaucez et deceyntz sauntz coyfe et a teste descoverte " : I 16, 2 : 1 Nicols 35 : *discinctus* = without the *cingulum* (which the judges also wore).

(a) N. E. D.

(b) Camden Soc. (1839) 156. The French advocate in court about 1250-70 was enjoined by Durand " to take off your cap or hood " [*bireto sive caputio*] : in Y. B. 32-3 E. I, XXVII, XXVIII, ed. Horwood; Dugd. *O. J.* 110 seems to infer that J. de Lyle was a serjeant about 1275 because his sepulchral effigy had a " coyf."

Hure is probably a coif (*c*). A black *hure* or *tena(e)* was part of an academic costume (*d*) so that the President of the court here satirised may be robed as a doctor of laws. If the caricatures which Riley conjectured to be of countors are contemporaneous (1305) then their *hures* are the earliest actual pictures of such headgear.

The thing is more closely connected with the word in 1391 if it be true that the following entry appears in the ward-robe rolls (*e*) of Richard II " 21 linen coifs for counterfeiting men of the law in the King's play at Christmas." This may well imply a distinctive badge but if the coif was common wear, the lawyers, too, would want them. However, the same doubt is not possible about a line (III, 320) in *Richard the Redeles* (*f*) which according to Skeat was written by the author of *Piers Plowman* in 1399.

" They cared for no coyffes that men of court usyn,"
where the context shows that the sense is technical for it is a denunciation of intruders into the law-courts who ostentatiously " wore headpieces instead of coifs [*houe*]" (Skeat).

Here the coif is identified with a hood but it is not the only or the most conspicuous legal hood.

From early times the hood was an utilitarian detachable addition to the gown or long outer garment, to protect the head in bad weather and in some form or other of the *cap(p)a* was universally worn in the Middle ages :.monks especially affected the hood from their earliest days (*g*). The *cappa* itself had a long ecclesiastical descent and in

---

(*c*) Planché, Clark : " a cap," 2 Fairholt, 258.
(*d*) Clark, p. 143.
(*e*) So stated, 2 Fairholt, 341, *Quoif*, but no authority is cited.
(*f*) Early Eng. Text Soc., ed. Skeat, pp. 497, 518; otherwise *Deposition of Richard II* : Camden Soc. (1838), p. 25; 1 *Polit. Poems* (Rolls), 409—both ed. Wright.
(*g*) So Richard Rolle of Hampole (d. 1349) to make himself look like a hermit " capuciavit se pluviali capucio superdueto " *Officium et Legenda*, etc., ed. Can. Perry, p. xvii (1866); Early Eng. Text Soc. probably contemporary.

time came to be worn by the Papal *avvocati* " benchè laici" (*h*), at any rate, on great occasions. It still survives at the Universities whither undoubtedly the monks brought it—even if it was not there before them : by that and the parallel route of the Church it probably reached the bar.

At any rate, it was there in 1293 when there was an instructive little scene in court, *viz.*, the Common Bench. The defendant's attorney comes to " his serjeant " Symond Est and whispers to him (presumably) that he has discovered collusion between the plaintiff and a vouchee, to the defendant's detriment, and begged him to tell the court, " No," says Symond, no doubt equally under breath, " by my hood (*i*) (*pur mun chaperun*) I will not say a word about it, now is not the time, wait, all in good time " (*k*), *i.e.*, that is better tactics. But " hood " hardly does justice to the serjeant's emphasis for *Chaperun* is not only the hood but the gown, too. In any case the point is that the chattel is characteristic.

This occurred about the time, as we have seen, of the consolidation of the profession and we shall not be surprised at the increasing attention to uniform. There is a reference to the legal hood, perhaps to both hoods in *Winner and Waster* (*l*) dated by the learned editor 1352-3. It contains a polemic against Scharshull J. (*fl.* about 1333) and other lawyers. We read, 149 :

(*h*) Moroni, *Cappa*. Durand (d. 1296) insists that to show respect to the judge " whether he be bishop, King or *Comes* or higher, the *advocatus* must take off his *biretum* or *caputium* ": *Speculum*, I, Pt. IV, c. 5, § 1.

(*i*) P. 220.

(*k*) Y. B. 21-2 E. I, 211, xi : ed. Horwood. This little passage is an excellent instance of Year Book style; it is jotted down by a learner, alive to human touches—in French till he gravely backs up counsel's retort, which, no doubt, he overheard, in Latin : " quod verum est " a legal tag; no judge is mentioned.

(*l*) Ed. Gollancz, 1920 : modernised text.

"A second [banner] is upborne with a bend of green
With three heads white-haired with hoods aloft
Curled full craftily combed in the neck.
These are the liegemen of this land that our laws shall guard."

"The bend of green" we are told, is a reference to "the green wax" [an early Exchequer term] (m) and the "three heads" to coifed serjeants. Again, 314 :

"And these barons on the bench with houes (n) [hoods] aloft,
That are known and acclaimed as clerks the best
. . . .
Would they were all shamed and Sharshull among them."

There is another important passage from the school of anti-lawyers, 1350-80. In *Piers Plowman* (about 1377) are the lines (o) :

"Conscience and the King into the court wenten,
Where hovede [hovered] an hondred in houes of silke.
Seriauntes they seemed that serve at bar
To plead, for pence and pounds, the law
And [do] not for love of our lord unloose their lips."

"Thou mightest better" (Skeat's paraphrase continues) "measure the mist on Malvern Hills than get a *mum* out of their mouth, until money be exhibited to them." Again (p)

"Shal no sergeant for that service were a silk hood
Nor pelour [fur] is his paueylon [coif : v. l. *cloke*] for pleading at bar."

The writer refers more than once to the courts at Westminster and clearly recognises a settled forensic

---

(m) *E.g., Cal. Just. Rolls Irel.* 64 in 1295 or *Cal. Docts. Irel.* 1293—1301, p. 381.

(n) Editor conjectures *biggins* (=coifs) for the sake of alliteration.

(o) Pas. i, 159 (Part III) or Prologue (Part II) 210-15 : both Early Eng. Text. Soc.

(p) *Ib.*, Pas. iv, 451.

system, the silk of which he is the first to mention. To-day, indeed it is in that material that almost the only trace of the lawyer's hood survives, for in " stuff " it has dwindled to an unrecognisable excrescence (*q*). That originally it was popularly regarded as as much the sign of the lawyer generally as the coif of the serjeant may (perhaps) be gathered from Stow (*r*) who no doubt, was copying an older authority. Of the commons' rising in 1381 he says they " tooke in hand to behead all men of Law, as well Apprentises as Utter-baristers and old justices, with all the jurers of the countrey . . . they spared none whom they thought to be learned especially if they found any to have pen and inke, they pulled off his hoode . . ."

The frail bands are elusive. The specialists are not clear on the point but it seems likely that these appendages developed from the overlapping borders of the mitre (*s*) and being tied under the chin, and called *infulae* or *tenae*, the latter word, really " strings," came to be identified with the whole coif. " They are still worn by lawyers and by clergymen always but often by parish clerks and ought to be by all graduates at least in the universities. Formerly undergraduate members also wore them, as do the scholars of some colleges still " (*t*). They are still part of some full dress at the universities and of certain officials there. Of those of the Christ's Hospital boys Rashdall says (*u*): they are " of course merely a clerical

---

(*q*) Exactly as in the cope it is now (it is said) represented by a mere ornamental half circle on the back.

(*r*) *Chronicle*, ed. Howes (1631), fo. 284.

(*s*) " They were adopted from the clerical costume by the early lawyers and by the clergy had been copied from the Jewish priests who wore them, *as representations of the two tables of the law* " : Pearce, *Guide to the Inns of Court* (1855), p. 436. No authority is or could be given for the words underlined.

(*t*) The Rev. J. Jebb cited without date or source 1 Fairholt (1885), 330; so, too, Hook's *Church Dictionary*, and cf. *The Reliquary*, v. 3, 145 (1862-3), by L. L. Jewitt.

(*u*) 2 *Universities*, Pt. 2, c. 14, p. 638.

collar . . . a survival from a time when all students were supposed to be clerks." Of the modern upstart wig this is not the place to speak.

We turn to the physical evidence. The earliest known pictures of serjeants-at-law are on brasses (*x*). That of John Rede S.L. in 1401 is as Checkendon, Oxon : he died in 1404 and is described there " serviens domini regis ad legem "; he wears the cassock-like gown and has a hood, etc., but no coif.

Nichol Rolond at Cople, Beds. may be S.L. about 1410 : he has a hood, tippet and coif. Thomas Rolf was S.L. in 1415 (Dugdale) died in 1440 and was buried at Gosfield, Essex. His brass has a cassock-like gown, tabard (*y*), tippet, hood, bands and coif and the legend " inter juristas : quasi flos enituit iste." This costume is supposed to be that of a Master of Arts (*z*) *plus* coif and bands; the latter being two loops or lappets hanging from the coif and appearing below the hood. His epitaph (*a*) says of him :—*legi p'fessus*. Of these and similar essays we must conclude that individual artists cultivated realism unequally.

As the material is so scanty perhaps we may interpolate what Thomas Gascoigne said (*b*) about 1440-50 : " Then [before his day] the judges of England wore in their official hoods of lambskin and not of miniver : for only bishops, doctors and masters in the Universities and lords of parliament at that time wore miniver and ermine and grey fur, as I have been told by eye witnesses and then only doctors in theology wore round hats when they preached to the clergy or the people."

(*x*) See Druitt, above, here copied.
(*y*) Supposed to be academic : " over the long robe."
(*z*) Or Scholar of Theology : Clark, see p. 368; for *pellura* in University dress, see 1 *Mun. Acad. Ox.* 301 : Rolls : 1432.
(*a*) 2 Morant's *Essex* (1768), 287, 380, 381, citing *Rot. feod. milit. ad Honor. de Clare spectan* : *Essex* (N. W.), Royal Comm. Hist. Mons.. (Eng.) (1916), p. 103.
(*b*) See p. 505; p. 202 there cited.

The next evidence in point of time (c) is the four famous illuminations already quoted (d) and dated about 1450.

In the Court of Chancery are two judges in scarlet robes trimmed with white badger or lambskin, one uncovered and tonsured, the other with a sort of brown cap; as the latter may be untonsured he is possibly the only lay Chancellor of that time, Neville, Earl of Salisbury, 1454. On each side of the judges are two persons in yellow or mustard-coloured robes, Masters in Chancery who are tonsured. Other officials are represented.

"At the bar stand three serjeants with coifs and wearing party-coloured gowns of blue and green and blue and brown; there are also two apprentices of the law . . . clad in party-coloured gowns of blue and light brown and green and light blue. All these party-coloured gowns are striped or rayed, some vertically and others diagonally, the division of the respective colours being separated straight down the front and back. In a row behind the last-mentioned figures are two other apprentices of the law . . . and three solicitors or clerks in court. . . . Each of these five is in a dress of a single colour."

In the King's Bench "may be seen five presiding judges, all of whom wear coifs; and all are attired in scarlet robes, trimmed and lined with white. . . . Below

---

(c) But see the sumptuary regulations of 1406 : p. 468. Chaucer perhaps was thinking of the lawyers' parti-coloured apparel and "the superfluitee in lengthe of the gounes"—a very early reference to the "long robe"—in the Parson's Tale, § 27, but the latter was too polite, in a lawyer's presence, to attack his special extravagance.

Jacke Upland says to the Friars : "Why use ye all one colour more than other christian men doe?" : 2 *Poltl. Songs*, etc., p. 19 : 5 : Rolls (1401).

(d) Mr. Corner's remarks are here copied or summarised. Some of the learned writer's identifications must be conjectural; he was not a lawyer. There is an excellent account of these works of art in *The King's Peace*, London (1895), by Mr. Inderwick K.C., pp. 120-4, with two woodcuts. The obscurity of the facts about counsel's robes is shown by the silence of this learned writer on the subject.

them sit the King's Coroner and Attorney (*e*), and the Masters of the Court, as at present. They all wear party-coloured dresses of blue (rayed) and white, or murrey and green. On each side of the prisoner [at the bar] stands a serjeant (*f*) in his coif: both the serjeants wear party-coloured gowns of green (*g*) and (rayed) blue."

In the Common Pleas there are seven judges (as was the case 1451-4 and 1455) "the prothonotaries and other officers of the court . . . are in party-coloured dresses of blue and light brown, rayed with blue stripes and green and similarly rayed light brown." On the right of the defendant " is a serjeant in a blue and green gown striped with white. Two other serjeants similarly habited (*h*) stand at the extreme right, while on the left are two other serjeants " [one of whom has the blue and the green in reverse order of that of the other four]. The judges are clothed in scarlet trimmed and lined with white budge and all wear coifs.

In the Exchequer, a judge—the Lord High Treasurer—presides wearing scarlet robes and a scarlet hat (" really the lofty turban-like hoods (*i*) which were worn by persons of importance and especially by judges in the 14th and 15th centuries, over a close-fitting professional law cap or coif "). Two others [barons?] sit on each side of him in mustard-coloured robes with similar hats, two with them off and two with them on, the two without them are not apparently coiffed. (They were not regarded as common law judges and Coke (Pt. x, *Introd.* xlii) remarks " I have known Barons of the Exchequer that were not of the coife

---

(*e*) An office held by the writer's brother.
(*f*) Not apparently defending him.
(*g*) Cf. the order of James II of Scotland about 1455 that " advocates who pleaded for money in the Parliament should have habits of green of the fashion of a tunekil with open sleeves " : Strutt, 2 *Eng. Dress*, 232.
(*h*) It is possible that these costumes are " Liveries," see p. 465.
(*i*) Cf. " hoods aloft," p. 363.

(*de gradu de la coife* (ut loquimur) and yet had judicial places and voices) remain in the houses of court whereof they were fellows and wore the habit (*ex more*) of apprentices of the law.") " In front are three serjeants and counsel in party-coloured and rayed robes of various colours and other persons." The entire absence of the hood is remarkable. It is not impossible that one of the common law judges in these pictures was Sir John Fortescue. He, too, writing about 1468-70 has left some account (*k*) of legal uniform. " As a sign that all common law judges have graduated [as Serjeants] each wears while he sits in the King's Bench a white silk coif (*birreto*) which is the first and chief badge of office with which serjeants at law on their creation are decorated. And that coif he shall never take off, neither as Serjeant or Judge, even in the King's presence, aye, if he be talking with His Majesty." Fortescue assumes that the common law judges were created from the serjeants and goes on : " on his appointment he changes his habit in certain particulars but not in all his badges. While as a Serjeant he wears a long robe (*l*) like a priest's (*m*) with a furred cape about his shoulders and an hood over it with two labels or tippets (*m*) like those of the doctors of laws in some universities, and a coif (*birreto*) as above described. But when he is made a judge instead of the hood (*collobii*) he puts on a mantle (*clamys*) fastened on his left shoulder but keeps the other *insignia* of a serjeant except the rayed or two-coloured garment (*stragulata veste aut coloris bipertiti*) and his cape (*capicium*) is furred with minever whereas the

---

(*k*) De *Laudibus*, cc. 50-1.
(*l*) *longa roba* : apparently the earliest mention.
(*m*) Grigor's translation of *cum capicio penulato circum humeros eius et desuper collobio cum duobus labelulis*, see p. 365 : *cap. pen.* =our " tippet " : *coll.* here=hood but it ought really to=" tabard " : *clamys* is a rather late form of hood; " in 1415 it was very like our present hood worn somewhat scarf-wise and buttoned on the right shoulder " as in the brass of Sir Hugh de Holes J. (K. B.) at Watford : Clark citing Haines, i, xc.

serjeant's has white lambskin. I beg you, sir, [H. VI's son] when you have the power to improve this (*n*) uniform to the dignity of the legal profession (*status legis*) and the honour of your realm." Fortescue was made a serjeant about 1429-30 and he speaks on his order with authority but as he did not write till about forty years later and in exile, the *minutiae* of costume may have altered in the interval. But in 1552 the new serjeants go in procession to Westminster Hall " in ther gownes and hodes of morrey and russet and ther servants in the same colers " : Machyn's *Diary* : Camd. Soc. (no. 42) p. 26; in 1559 they wear " skarlette hodes abowt ther nekes and whyt [hoods on] ther hedes and no capes [caps]" : *ib.* p. 195. It is not quite clear whether they got or gave " gownes of ii collers, morreys and mustars "; their sponsors, the old serjeants, wore " skarlett."

The incidental allusions to judges' robes serve to show which they discarded on their elevation, and in a general way illustrate the growing sense of professionalism which is always aiming at regulation. Probably the earliest pictures of judges are those in Dugdale (*o*) *O. J.* p. 100—all wearing the coif : one from a seal is of Grimbaud (*p*), *temp.* H. II : one of W. Howard, *fl.* 1293, from a window in the church of Long Melford, Suffolk, which was erected nearly 200 years after his death, but those of Richard Pycot and John Haugh in the glass seem to be contemporary, *i.e.*, of E. IV or H. VII. It would seem that accuracy of detail was aimed at in the stone effigy of Judge Gascoigne (born about 1350, K. S. 1397, C. J. of K. B. 1400 died 1419) engraved in " Sepulchral Monuments of

---

(*n*) Of judges or serjeants or both?

(*o*) His lists (*ib.*, c. 38) of materials for robes granted to judges (see now 2 Abbrev. Rot. Orig. 192, and 3 Foss, 358, 44) in 1347 (*not* 1292) might help an expert to interpret the Illuminations (above).

(*p*) But see 1 Foss, 254.

Great Britain " (*q*); is it intended to represent him in his daily habit or is he idealised? " He appears in a robe or mantle with long puffed sleeves edged with ermine and under them strait sleeves buttoned to the wrist over a tunic girt with a belt studded with roses whereat hangs his *anlace* or dagger and under his left elbow his purse. On his head and shoulders is a coif covering his ears which appear[s : *sic* (*r*)] through and falling in a flap at the sides of his face, his hair just seen under it "; in another passage what is here called a coif is called a hood but luckily both are delineated. The chief badge, then, of the serjeant he wore all through his legal career (*s*).

Of apprentices in all these pictures we have only heard once and that in a necessarily conjectural explanation (*t*). This negative evidence probably corresponds to the facts—there was little to say about them and still less to paint. Druitt (*u*) has no instance till " 1437. Robert Skerñ,

---

(*q*) At Harewood Church, Yorks : Gough, v. 1, Pt. i, clx, and v. 2, Pt. ii, p. 37.

(*r*) Clearly the singular is a misprint (not repeated at p. 37) as the picture shows.

(*s*) In " the Effect of " a speech by Coke at " the installing of " eleven serjeants in the Inner Temple Hall, 1614, printed 2 Inderwick's *Cal. I. T. Records*, 346, and 2 Malcolm's *Londinium Redivivum*, 191 (1803), when the speaker " improved the occasion " *more suo*, with much allegory and learning there are some details of interest to sartorial specialists :—The Serjeants have seven *insignia* [apparently]. 1. The Coyfe : white. 2. The Hood : the sergeants' is " borne in parte upon the shoulder and laying likewise in part upon the Brest." 3. Robes : the substance—Wool " the staple commodity of this realm." 4. [out of order] Robes—the Colour : " Parte of them are Murrye . . . Parte Blewe or Assure . . . parte Violett. . . . And for your Scarlett it is knowne to all men to be a judiciall colour. Your Blacke betokneth gravitie and patience, yett I wish not the use of an austeere or Stoicall gravitye." 5 Robes—the fashion . . . " wyde and easie." " Your gownes be losse before to admonish you of Secrecye in your Clyents Cause." 6. " Two Tongues " " not that you should be *bilingues*, double-tongued — (God fforbidd)." 7. " The four corners of your caps "=Science, Experience, Observation, Recordation "; cf. p. 472.

Some details on this subject are in Serjt. Chauncy's *Hertfordshire* (1700), pp. 76-8, 526-7, but for this period no fresh authorities are given.

(*t*) It does not appear why the artist should put them only in the Court of Chancery; but perhaps they are also in the other courts.

(*u*) *Costume in Brasses*, 232. In Plate 1, 3 Strutt's *Engl. Manners*

Kingston - upon - Thames . . . lege peritus : in civilian tunic " and then nothing till 1461 when John Edward of Rodmarton, Glos. is described as " famosus apprenticius in lege peritus "; he has a civilian tunic but a " curious high cap of velvet or some soft material with an edging of fur." Other references give *legis peritus* or *apprenticius* but show no special uniform. The inference—otherwise certain—is that about 1400 the junior bar is beginning to have a *status* of its own; the Serjeants are now well established and their titular successors are beginning to come into public notice and are accorded a place in society.

Perhaps of all marks of their emergence the account the sumptuary regulations of 1406 take of them for the first time, as has already been mentioned, is the most valuable historically. Apparently between 1363 and 1406 the *apprenticii* had been dressing beyond their means. It was natural that their professional *canon* should be a sober habit. Probably that is all that Coke meant by *ex more apprenticiorum*. A generation later Hale would pleasantly " admonish them if he saw anything amiss in them; particularly if they went too fine in their clothes, he would tell them, it *did not become their Profession*. He was not pleased to see Students wear long Perriwigs or Attorneys go with Swords; so that such young men as would not be perswaded to part with those vanities, when they went to him, laid them aside and went as plain as they could . . . " (*x*).

Nevertheless, the junior bar has always been well dressed.

Remuneration.

It would appear that this subject has not been touched by any modern writer and considering the scantiness of

---

the figures (3 and 4) of a counsellor and a serjeant are exhibited *temp.* H. VII.

(*x*) Burnet, *Life* (1862), 108. Hitherto they had worn " their natural long locks ": Campbell 1 *Lives* C.J. 585 n. †.

material, this is not surprising. It is, however, possible to collect some facts.

Whether Selden meant that " the practising lawyers " who lived in monasteries, monks, in fact, were in the habit of " getting money " by their practice in 1090, does not appear but probably all he means, by way of enforcing their secularity, is that they could generally, earn money. Indeed it may well be that as the ecclesiastics and the monks gave up the teaching (*y*) and practice of law, their lay successors were the first normally to demand a fee for their services; this would explain the piteous appeals to the judges for legal aid by penniless folk; in earlier days they would have gone to the *padres*.

Among the costs which Richard de Anesty reckons, about 1160, in his great lawsuit some went to the lawyers, *placitatores* (as well as to *clerici*), which he calls *dona*, and, as he records carefully every item of his expenses—which, by the way, throw much light on the details of law costs at that time—it may be that the sums of money paid to individuals were not fees given at the moment of the work being done, but gifts in gratitude when the case was won; in fact only lump sums are mentioned as being distributed to the pleaders and *clerici*.

This case is mentioned by the contemporary John of Salisbury and from his writings it is possible to get some information on this topic. John knew as well as any one living the practice of the Church courts and, as he was an Englishman, of the lay English courts, and indeed, of those of Christendom; we have seen him declining to take a case in an English court. At the date at which he was writing, there can be little doubt that in his criticisms and suggestions of reform, those, *e.g.*, to be found in App. VIII, he was thinking primarily of ecclesiastical practitioners —" apud curiales omnia . . . venalia "—but keeping an

---

(*y*) Selden deals with this point in the ch. (7, § 7) cited, p. 48.

eye, as it were, on " the *proconsules* who are popularly called itinerant judges " and on the sheriffs' courts. He distinctly says that the *causidici*, indeed lawyers " from top to bottom," make money out of the suits and he seems to have known (or suspected) cases where it was paid for the pleader's holding his tongue (*z*), that is, for betraying someone. But he does recognise—and considering his austerity and his object, this is important—the legitimate fee of the advocate.

That, he says, and certain other expenses *de juris indulgentia* may be properly paid by the *cliens* but though the *patronus causae* may be entitled to *merces ex causa honorarii* (*a*) he must take nothing like a pecuniary interest in the suit (champerty); it is quite fair for the advocate to sell his support (*patrocinium justum*) or the jurisconsult his opinion (*consilium*) (but by no means so for a judge to sell judgment) (*b*).

Now, John was well aware that lawyers' fees had been matter of statutory regulation by the early Empire and probably earlier still (*c*), and that the ecclesiastical courts had taken over and carried on this tradition from the secular courts. We have had an instance of payment of such fees in the Pope's own Court and of what a suitor lost by not being able to pay them, in the case of Thomas of Marlborough about 1205. But John mentions no sum as the limit of a forensic fee and when he speaks of *juris indulgentia* he either means generally that the severity of the old Republican law, which forbade any, had been mitigated later or that in his day if an immoderate fee were paid, the church courts would help the client to get restitution.

But he assuredly did not mean to discourage the

(*z*) Cf. Bromyard, p. 155.
(*a*) This is, perhaps, the earliest use of the word by an English writer.
(*b*) See App. VIII.   (*c*) Tac. *Ann.* XI, 5—8.

gratuitous representation of poor persons for when he suggests that the judge should assign the advocates fairly (*pari distributione partibus exaequabit,* sive eos petierint sive non, *ut aequo Marte possit causa procedere*) he can only be referring to litigants who come into court without legal aid. His contemporary Peter of Blois (*d*), another Englishman, who also was in a good position to know, enjoins this assistance in so many words, but explicitly recognises the ordinary right of a reasonable fee (*salarium*).

We have had some definite fees mentioned : in 1176 an Italian lawyer, stipulated for a mark in the Battel Abbey case. In doing so, he was within the Continental and especially the Italian tradition and perhaps we may say that the lawyer's fee in England was borrowed from foreign countries (*e*). William of Drogheda practically settled the principles of payment about 1240.

In 1289 the Priory of Dunstable (*f*) paid in respect of a named suit " specially per year 20 *solidi* to Roger of Hecham " [Higham Ferrers] : " and the same similarly to Henry Spigurnel and Walter of Aylesbury according to their agreements."

There are few instances of attornies' fees. About 1300 we had the City's disbursements to their attornies. In 1308 at Oxford there is an account (*g*) " Attorney's fee 6/8 " and for once we get a ready comparison for there, too, in 1309 we have " *Narrator's* salary 13/4." Probably " 20/- to James of Grantchester ' *pro placito sequelae* ' "

(*d*) App. IX, and p. 120.

(*e*) *E.g.*, *Avignon*, p. 77 (*r*).

(*f*) 3 *Ann. Mon.* (Rolls), p. 358 : " ita quod sint intendentes nostris negotiis, sicut in eorum cautionibus " : *cautio* = a bond with conditions. As Spigurnel is a well-known lawyer (though hitherto nothing was known of him " at the bar ") no doubt Roger and Walter were also lawyers, but they are otherwise unknown. Spigurnel also got a manor from the monks; clearly he was the leader. Note that the fees are paid in advance and—" specially "—annually.

(*g*) From Th. Roger's *Hist. Agric. & Prices in England* (1259— 1400) : 1866 : v. I, pp. 126, 283; v. II, pp. 578, 614, but " salary " above (*salarium*) probably = fee (not as T. R. " retainer "); the

REMUNERATION. 375

1344 and " Item [apparently 3/6¾] to Wm. de Lavenham for the plea " 1345, in a Gamlingay bailiff's accounts (g), refer to attornies.

About 1300, too, we had the City's retaining fees to counsel. In 1321 the King was paying le Scrop for attending him throughout a progress of three months " for his expenses in so staying 13l. 6s. 8d." Some years earlier we had some figures of the payments to Irish lawyers.

Presumably cash transactions in the secular courts were introduced gradually, at any rate, among poorer suitors. This would account for what Mr. Bolland says (h) about the remuneration of attorneys. " It seems to have been partly in cash and partly in kind. In [1331] . . . the complainant says that she paid her negligent attorney ten shillings in money and gave him, in addition, butter and cheese to the value of six(teen?) shillings. Considering the value of money in " 1331 " this seems a very generous fee for managing a case in a local court especially when it is considered that the complainant assesses her damages through her attorney's default at no higher than five pounds. . . . Adam de la Rue [in 1278] . . . received only five shillings for managing cases against several defendants in the county court of Shrewsbury. Piers of Quarndon in " 1331 " seeks recovery of a fee of six shillings and eightpence which was promised to him by Sir Roger of Oakover in a plea of trespass." The Court finds for

---

" Advocate's fee defending a will, 6/8 " (ib. ii, 576) in 1268 was almost certainly in an ecclesiastical court. It is noteworthy that this scholar in " Mediaeval Justice and Courts " (ib. c. vi) mentions no counsel's fee, though " the accounts . . . before me are those " of the JJ. in eyre, trailbaston, coroners' and manor courts.

This work by a specialist suggests that great research would be required to get within a given period a *calculus* of law prices and still greater to equate them with other expenses; compare, for instance, the figures above with, *e.g.*, the prices of live stock in the same years, in this book. There seems to be no clue to the degrees of economic estimates of forensic ability or the commercial differentiation of legal services—except, perhaps, in the fiscal assessment, p. 464.

(h) 30 Seld. Soc. xlvi.

Piers, who forgoes his claim for damages. Hugh Donvile agreed to act as Sir Walter Hopton's attorney for five years in the King's and county court for half a mark *per annum* : in 1292 ten years had elapsed but Hugh had not been paid and he complained in Eyre; Sir Walter paid twenty shillings into court which Hugh took, forgiving the balance, which included a robe, as a fee from Sir Walter's wife.

In the accounts of the Knights Hospitallers in England (*i*) we read in 1338

In banco regis { Et Thome de Thorp, attornato Prioris in eadem curia pro negociis domus prosequendis et defendendis   xls.

Sunt etiam quidam narratores in curiis predictis pro placitis in eisdem curiis placitandis narrandis et declarandis secundum leges et consuctudines Anglie qui capiunt feoda de Thesauraria predicta per annum, videlicet

Narratores in Curiis Regis. {
Robertus Parnyng (*k*) per annum   xls.
Et robam de secta (*l*) armigerorum Prioris cum furrura prout decet

Ricardus de la Pole, unam robam de secta armigerorum et   xls.
Henricus Poer unam robam et   xls.
Hugo de Loughteburgh attornatus Prioris in communi banco predicto   xxs.
Et j robam de secta armigerorum (*m*).
}

(*i*) P. 187 (*h*), at p. 204.

(*k*) A serjeant. The other names, though of " narratores," seem to be quite unknown.

(*l*) " *r. d. s.*," etc., presumably means a garment such or of the same value as that given to the Priors men-at-arms, a livery, in fact— just as (*ib.* 203) a *clericus* gets xls. and a robe *de secta clericorum Prioris cum furrura de Bogeto.*

(*m*) In 1381 in a Bursar's Roll of University College, Oxford, " our

Kemble (p. xlii) rightly calls these "retaining fees."
"Refreshers" have been already (*n*) mentioned.

In 1369 the Goldsmiths' Company (*o*) " paid to men of law and other counsel at Guildhall and to their counsel *de ley Cristyene* (*p*) for the suit against Thomas Berch 43s. 4d."

It seems from some of the suits mentioned in this chapter that there was no rule that lawyers could not sue for their fees; we saw (*q*) another instance in 1275 and conversely.

---

att. in Com. Banc." gets 6/8d. and one "copia placiti" 3d. : 2 *Mun. Acad. Ox.* 794 (Rolls).

We have a similar account to that in the text but nearly sixty years later and in the provinces of the legal expenses of the very litigious Abbey of Meaux, where in 1393-4 the "Fees for lawyers retained by the year" were £9 4s. (Rolls, v. 3, lxiv : or £9 11s. 8d. *'b.* lxvii) and the list of legal advisers is as follows :

    Johannes de Redenesse, seneschallus [is he legal?] xls.

    Robertus Tyrwhytt [a well known serjeant] xxvjs. viijd.

    Johannes de Burtona [perhaps a Master of the Rolls : he might "still advise" the House, *pace* the editor] xxs."

then follow a list of unknown persons at xiiis. viiid., xiis. ivd., xxvis. viiid., v.s. [n.b.] vis. and viiid.—(all in the whole list seem to come from the locality)—and then

    "Rogerus de Wele, attornatus placitorum et prosecutor brevium (quite untechnical language) xiiis. ivd.

    Magister Willelmus de Feriby, magister Alanus de Newerk, advocati et Magister Nicolaus Brown de Esyngwald, *procurator* in curia Christianitatis Eboraci xvs."

Before 1388 John de Lokton, afterwards J. had got "some fee from us yearly *pro consilio et auxilio suo* " : *ib.*, v. III, p. 211, and xxviii.

Here the provincial monk ignores *serjeant* and *narrator* and prefers the nomenclature of the ecclesiastical court, as he does in the great cause, certainly civil, p. 270, where the only lawyers are *attornati*.

On the litigiousness of the religious houses, see *ib.*, v. iii, p. xlix; the learned editor remarks (p. xlv) : "Where a person of small means and influence was threatened with a lawsuit for his property, he was easily tempted to make it over to the convent, which, more than the most powerful individual, knew how to defend its rights, and to support a weak title."

Bromyard, 1380-90, see p. 91*x*, mentions 40 *Solidi* by way of illustration as a fee to *adv.* : 35A, 36B; and a gift to a juror : 401B.

(*n*) P. 77; App. VIII.

(*o*) *Memorials* : ed. Prideaux.

(*p*) " of Ecclesiastical Law " : Ed.

(*q*) P. 263.

Thomas le Coffer in 1300 could perhaps have brought an action against counsel for professional misconduct (*r*), but preferred to be defendant.

It would seem that originally there was very little system in the remuneration of counsel, as in the case (*s*) in 1389. In 1424-6 in an information against Walter Aslak, drawn almost certainly by Serjeant W. Paston, it is recited (*t*) that " William Paston by assignement and commaundement of the Duke of Norfolk . . . was the Styward of the seyd Duc. . . . [And over that as sergeaunt of lawe, thow he be unworthy, withholdyn with the seyd Duc all the tyme that he was sergeaunt. . . . And all be it that the fees and the wages of the seyd William for hys seyd service unpayed draweth a gret some to hys pouere degree . . ." he will be content, etc.] In both these incidents we note a seeming indifference to fees and great deference to powerful clients. The stewardship, expressly confined to the two (local) counties, combined with local practice as a serjeant, is an interesting provincial sidelight. In fact, Paston had a general retainer for the duke.

On the other hand, by 1453 there seems to have been a scale, for Moyle, Serjt. arguing (*u*) then says : " If no certain sum of money be promised to him [counsel] then he shall have so much of common right, *i.e.*, to a serjeant forty pence and to an attorney twenty pence from him who retained him." By that time the practice of retaining counsel had developed. Not only magnates but monasteries kept lawyers in their pay (*x*).

The Crown, too, had found it necessary to begin the

(*r*) P. 240.
(*s*) P. 260.
(*t*) Gairdner, 1 *Past. L.* 16, the words in brackets were cancelled (perhaps long after they were written) but they are significant of their day; they are clearly an interpolation in a technical document.
(*u*) Y. B. 31 H. VI, 9.
(*x*) Plummer, p. 466*n*.

practice which has only gone to its extreme limit in our own day : in 1426 it was ordered " that no man be of the King's Council but such as be barely of his Council and attending to no one else's affairs " ; and in 1437 " that none of them take any fee of any other person than of the King " (*y*).

It is not impossible that the gift of robes to lawyers (*z*) as part of their pay was a survival from days when currency was rare and debts were discharged in kind, and not, as has sometimes been supposed, designed to provide costumes for wear in court. As these would not require to be renewed yearly they might be perquisites (which could be sold) and perhaps later (*a*) were commuted for increased pay. Did Chaucer mean us to think that his Serjeant, who
" Of fees and robes hadde he many oon "
kept an accumulation of garments? (*b*).

About this time we get some notices of the sums paid to the lawyers of Winchester College; the " advocatus " got 13s. 4d. yearly apparently, and so did the notary, but the " attorney in the Common Bench " only got " 6s. 8d. in 1398-9 and 13s. 4d. later," with an " extra reward of 3s. 4d. in 1406-7." So the attorneys in the Exchequer and in the Common Bench only got 6s. 8d.; the *jurisperitus* got 13s. 4d. in 1403-4, in which year W. Stokes " counsel " got the same, but when he became steward of the College manors, 26s. 8d.; J. Champflour counsel and " squyer " got 20s. in 1405-6, etc. John Hals himself got as " ser-

---

(*y*) *P. P. C.*, iii, 219; vi, 315.

(*z*) Foss, II, 190, citing *Hengham Magna*, 5 (ed. Selden, 1737), says that 1267 is the earliest entry of judges' robes being supplied from the royal wardrobe, but that the practice was then not new; perhaps before the grant was annual it was only intended to replace robes worn out, " quamdiu steterint [justiciarii] in officio d. r."

(*a*) When they were undoubtedly annual : 2 *Abbrev. Rot. Orig.* 192 (1347); 3 Foss, 44, 258. So in 1418 the City voted a gown yearly to a chaplain : Riley, *Memorials*, 660.

(*b*) But he may mean that he was retained by many magnates, each of whom would give a livery.

geaunt " 13s. 4d. in 1413-4, " with extra reward of 6s. 8d. in 1411-2."

Gratuitous legal aid was by no means unknown. In 1423 the Clerk of the Council was sworn " that everyday that the Counseil sitteth on eny Billes betwyx partie and partie, he shal, as ferr as he can, aspye which is the porest Suyturs Bille and that first to be redd and answered, and the King's Sergeant to be sworin (c) trewly and plainly, to yeve the poor Man that for suche is accept to the Counsail [*i.e.*, *in forma pauperis*] assistense and have trewe counsaill in his mater so to be suyd, wyth oute eny good [reward] takyng of hym, on peyne of discharge of their offices " (d). The word *their* seems to show that all the Serjeants were included in this compassionate purview. No detailed lawyers' bills seem to have come down to us before those ranging from 1460 to 1509 from the Goldsmiths' accounts (e). In 1472 we have a memo. of some expenses (f) of Thomas Stonor in " various suits : for the Original writ...ixd.; for suing a *capias* thereupon...xd.; for an attorney's fee...xxd. [twice]; for sealing exemplifications...1d.; for a writ of *latitat*...xiiid. Total 6s. 1d."

As time goes on observers more and more remark that the law is a money-making avocation (g) and the frequent early central and civic regulations to prevent the lawyer getting more than his fair share of the proceeds of litigation suggest strongly that his remuneration was haphazard, that is, as a rule, that he got as much as he could.

The impossibility of evaluating money of a date before, say, 1450, with that of to-day deprives us of some clue to

---

(c) Cf. the oath, p. 517.
(d) 4 *Rot. Parl.* 201; 3 *P. P. C.* xix, 150, 217.
(e) Herbert, 2 *Hist. 12 Livery Coys.* 185 (1836); for Sjt. Yaxley's retainer at Assizes in 1501 (part in cash), see Manning, *Serviens*, p. 182, or *Plumpton Corresp.* p. 152 : Camd. Soc.
(f) 2 *Stonor Papers*, 186 : Camd., 3rd ser., v. 30 (1919).
(g) Cf. p. 91, and especially Bromyard.

the grades of social position. But a little later we do get such a hint.

In 1460 (*h*) " Payed for counsell ayenst ye abbot of Woburne, iijs. iiijd."; 1469 " in the Chauncerie "

" For boat-hire to Westminster and home again &c. &c. 6d."

" For a breakfast at Westminster, spent on our counsel, 1s. 6d. To Mr. Catesby serjeant at law [and Recorder] to plead for the same [suit], 3s. 4d. To the keeper of the Chancery door, 2d.," and several other entries for breakfast and boat-hire. Four counsel, Fairfax, Catesby, Waters and Coytmore, " to understand the authorities of our charters &c." and refreshments at " the Cardinal's cap " cost £1 15s. 0d., and twice again the four (Burgoyne *vice* Fairfax) earn 40s. *between them*. In 1475 " Reynolds our attorney " in Chancery gets 20d., Recorder Catesby 3s. 4d., and Mr. Fairfax " at barr " 3s. 4d. (three times). As late as 1505 " Mr. Wood serjeant at law for his fee by the year " only gets 10s., and " Greene common serjeant for his advice in the book of ordinances, 3s. 4d."

Another Bill of Costs in 1471 is found in the Paston MSS. (*i*), " pro " Richard Calle, the Pastons' bailiff, " deff' versus W. H. q. in placito trans'." in K. B. The items are almost all for copies of records, but Hosey gets 3s. 4d. " for to enparle to the bill "; he and others named were probably counsel, for they are with " Mr. Fayrefax," doubtless the same person as the Goldsmiths' counsel. More than once, too, " wyne and perys [perry] at tavern ij tymes " are allowed " 14d. and 6d, 8d.," and that, too, at the " Cardenalls Hatte " (in Southwark). Three counsel get xs. " for the seying of the paper and comeynyng (?) of

---

(*h*) 2 Herbert, 185, where it is mentioned that in 1446 Robt. Blounte " was received into the freedom of the . . . mystery [Goldsmiths'] and was retained to be of counsel for the aforesaid mystery."

(*i*) No. 682, ed. Gairdner, 1875 : v. 3, p. 25.

the issewe," and two get (each?) vis. viiid. " for puttyng yn of the replicacyon."

As Hallam (k) says " What would a modern lawyer say to the following entry in the churchwarden's accounts of St. Margaret's, Westminster, for 1476? ' Also paid to Roger Fylpott learned in the law for his counsel giving 3s. 8d. with fourpence for his dinner.' Though fifteen times the fee might not seem altogether inadequate at present [1818], five shillings would hardly furnish the table of a barrister even if the fastidiousness of our manners would admit of his accepting such a dole."

Before taking up the chronological thread of development, we may glance at that of some civilised states abroad, chiefly to emphasize our own independence of theirs, by a consideration of the respective dates, and incidentally to suggest that the English forensic movement of—broadly—the reign of Henry III may have influenced that of the Continent.

Foreign Countries.

To preserve probable chronological order we begin with the most distant (what little is known about secular courts in Italy having been mentioned *apropos* of the *avv. concistoriali*).

French legal historians have not perhaps adequately explained a problem which arises somewhat earlier than the movement under St. Louis (*l*) (nor, indeed, anyone else), that is—whence came *Les Assises de Jérusalem* (*m*), which include an *ordo judiciarius*. In his *History of the Crusades* (*n*) Michaud says that when Godfrey de Bouillon took Jerusalem in 1099 he convoked a gathering of " learned and pious men . . . . charged to draw up a code of laws for

---

(k) *Middle Ages*, Pt. 2, c. 9, citing Nicholls's *Illustrations*, p. 2.
(l) Born. 1215 : r. 1226-70.
(m) Ed. Comte Beugnot : Paris, 1841-3 : 2 vols. folio.
(n) Paris, 1857 : v. I, B. 5, pp. 282, 466.

the new Kingdom. The conditions imposed on the possession of land, the military service of the fiefs, the reciprocal obligations of the King and the lords, of the greater and the lesser vassals—all that was settled according to the customs of France. What Godfrey's subjects were asking for above all was judges to put an end to differences and to protect the rights of each man. Two courts (*o*) of justice were instituted; the one, presided over by the King and composed of the nobles, was to deal with the litigation of the great vassals; the other, where the viscount (*vicomte*) of Jerusalem presided, was formed by the ' notables ' of each town and had to regulate the interests and the rights of the *bourgeoisie* on the communes. . . . The laws thus given to the city of David were, no doubt, a new spectacle for Asia; they became, too, a source of instruction for Europe itself, which was astonished to find overseas its own institutions modified by the manners of the East and by the character and spirit (*esprit*) of the Holy War. This legislation of Godfrey's, the least imperfect hitherto seen among the Franks and which grew or was improved in following reigns, was deposited with great pomp in the Church of the Resurrection and got the name of *Assizes of Jerusalem* or *the Letters of the Holy Sepulchre.*" It is only in these, " the works of the overseas jurists," that the real feudal procedure can be studied (*p*).

We have had one example of the possible effect of military feudalism on the growth of a lawyer class in our own country. The recurrence of the same main conditions elsewhere within half a century warrants our considering their corresponding effects. Michaud, again (*q*), says: " The most curious monument of feudal jurisprudence during the Middle Ages is . . . the Assizes of Jerusalem.

(*o*) Note by M. " *The Assises*, as we know them, are not entirely the work of Godfrey : but we can assert that he founded the two Courts . . ."

(*p*) Beugnot, I, p. xlii.

(*q*) Crusades, p. 466.

It is these assizes, the expression of the needs of a military kingdom, which we must study for the veritable character of feudalism in its native institution, such as had made it the ideas and the position of the barbarous races after the conquest of Gaul. For, indeed, the knights and the barons of the Christian kingdom of Asia found themselves in the same situation as the followers of Clovis when the kingdom of the Franks was founded; they had a population, sometimes hostile, to restrain, powerful enemies to beat back; the possession of the land was necessarily bound with its defence; feudalism, military services, therefore, could not but be established with this warrior hierarchy, which was the foundation of all the social institutions of the peoples of the North."

This eloquent picture of the facts diverts attention from the conclusions of the first paragraph. That the Christian States of the East had about 1100 some organised judicatures is certain, but were they in fact lessons to Europe? How did they suddenly spring into such a homogeneous work of art? Is it conceivable that there was " a bar " in Jerusalem in 1100? These are difficulties with which, apparently, no historian has grappled. Moreover, almost in the lifetime of the men who are supposed to have created or recreated this great code, France, the home or, at any rate, the *metropolis* of some of them, did in fact learn their lesson and, as we shall see, start its law afresh.

Now it may be a mere guess from symmetry, but the isolated development of the *Assises de Jérusalem* at the phase which we know is satisfactorily explained by Beugnot (r) thus : " One institution special to the feudal courts of the East, one which threw lustre on their trials was that of the *conseils* or defenders. Every *plaideur* had the right to ask one of his peers to lend him the aid of his ability (*lumières*) and to come to the tribunal, not to plead

---

(r) I, p. xliii.

(*plaider*) for him, for that was the province of the advocates or *avantparliers*, but to direct in his interest the course of procedure, to make the necessary [formal] requisitions, pronounce the ordinary *formulae*; in short, to act for him on all the occasions when the *assise* would require the intervention of a *conseil* (*s*). The lord, perpetually exposed to the snares of the parties himself, would choose a *conseil* who would speak in the name of the court." In short, the original Syrian representative was unprofessional, non-technical, friendly—just as we saw in Anglo-Saxon times.

It would seem that the earliest book (as opposed to fragments imbedded in later texts) of the *Assises* is that of the *Cour des Bourgeois* " by the most ancient jurist who wrote in the East," dated by Beugnot (*t*) between 1173-80, that is, before Saladin took Jerusalem (1187). In its present form it has probably been " touched up " by different hands (*t*), but it is, at any rate, " le monument le plus ancien du droit dans le royaume de Jérusalem," and probably it made use (*u*) of the codes known as the *Lettres du Sépulcre* which (included a code for the *Bourgeois* and) perished in 1187. Thus though we can never be certain that the Book of the High Court may not preserve something older on our subject, broadly, the system of the French Christians seems to have been that the court would assign *conseill* (*consilium*) to any suitor—Beugnot cites a

---

(*s*) The word is sometimes used by the Oriental jurists=a deliberation of the court: *ib*. II, 238a. So rarely *conseiller*=a jurist who fills the functions of *Conseils de cour*: *ib*. Glossary: see p. 583.

(*t*) II, p. xxxvii. *L'Abrégé* of this work he (*ib*. lix) dates about 1350—too late for our purpose, though valuable as explaining the two *Livres*, esp. Pt. I, c. 12 (II Beug. 245); Pt. II, c. 4 (*ib*. 351); in c. 13 of Pt. II (*ib*. p. 309) *avantps*. are mentioned as seen and heard in *C. des Bs.*; of some technical point, " many learned pleaders thought it a strange thing."

(*u*) The *Histoire littéraire de la France*, Vol. 21, p. 465 (1847), says roundly: " This Book which reproduced the Letters of the Sepulchre did not perish like the *Assises* of the H. C. but was transported to Cyprus probably at the time when a *Cour des Bourgeois* was set up at Nicosia."

case about 1205 (I, 496, n.)—but that he could choose his *avantparlier* for himself or be his own *plaideor, i.e.,* appear in person. It was later—in the time of *L'Abrégé* (*ib.* II, 240, n.) that the same man was *conseil* and *avocat.* Now, although some Roman Law was known (superficially (*x*)) to the author(s) it is noteworthy that the nomenclature of this book is French and not Latin—*avantparlier, conseil, plaideor: avocas,* which only became French in the twelfth century, is rarely used, and *cliens* (*y*), *actor, reus* not (apparently) at all.

The word *avantparlier* (*amparlier*) seems to have been invented in this school (and perhaps this is the reason— because it was novel—why Philip of Novara does not use it). It is not a translation of *pro-* or *praelocutor*, for at that date the word was rarely used (*z*), but it may be of *antiloquus* (=antel.), for Du Cange says: " Hinc avantparliers " (*a*), but that is an even rarer word. There is no difficulty in supposing that the inventers of a " bar " found a name for it. It must be remembered that about 1170-80 even in France there was no need for such a word; Luchaire (*b*), in his account of the " Organization of the King's Court," 1100-80, barely mentions a forensic lawyer (or, indeed, any); a *jurisperitus*, Mainier, " légiste de profession " takes a part in a judicial trial in 1166, but Luchaire is inclined to think that the presence of

---

(*x*) 2 Beugn. p. 31, n. (*b*).

(*y*) It is inconceivable that Philip and Jean did not know this word, yet throughout they use the clumsy phrase " he whose quarrel it is " probably because they were glad to incorporate *any* survival—there are other similar circumlocutions—from the " Letters of the Sepulchre."

(*z*) Du C. cites Pliny (viii, 21) for its forensic use and then a charter of 1160. French sources are singularly silent on this philology. B. I, 33 n., says " at *this* epoch the *avps.* were also called " *advouez* " : 1250?

(*a*) Adding " non quod ante judicium loquerentur . . . sed quod primas in loquendo partes obtinerent."

(*b*) 1 *Histoire des Institutions monarchiques* (987—1180), B. 3, c. 3, p. 325. See further, p. 403.

" légistes "—note the term—in the court goes back to an earlier date.

The *locus classicus* (c) in the *Assises* is : " Les jurés (d) en nul plait ne doivent estre avocas, ce est a dire avant-parliers et juges . . . " for " the law forbids—ut in una cademque causa nullus esse debeat advocatus et judex," or, " . . . l'avocat ce est l'avantparlier," if he wants to be " procuratour en cort de la chose [cause] d'aucun home " (e) he must show the court the authority of his principal (f).

The biography which we possess (in Beugnot (g), etc.) of Philip, hitherto called " of Navarre " must be rewritten in the light of M. Gaston Paris's (h) discovery.

He was not of Navarre, but of Novara (or *Novaria*, O. Fr. *Novaire*) in Italy; not a Frenchman, but an Italian from Lombardy; he calls himself a Lombard; his French style is good, and his rare Italianisms were probably

---

(c) *C. de Bourg.* c. 8 : II B., p. 24; from *Cod.* II, vi, 3 (and *Cod. Theod.* II, x, 2, but though the sense is implied, the words do not occur there).

(d) We are not specially concerned with the *jurés*, but here and in England and elsewhere they seem to have been a kind of " notables " called in from time to time to assist judicial and other enquiries and either sworn or liable to take the oath : see pp. 450, 451r. Here (c. VII, p. 24) they are solemnly enjoined by religion and honour to give the best advice and law they can to all men and women who seek to them. Beugnot, who cites *jurati* in Jerusalem in 1163 (I, 23 n.) and in Amiens in 1190 (II, 24 n.), thinks they were rather expert legists than popular magistrates (*ib.*) : in both countries " la loi . . . transformait la profession d'avocat en un devoir d'honneur et de conscience." The *jurés* could not be technical *conseils*; for later law, see the *Abrégé*, c. 8, *ib.*, p. 241. Cf. Stubbs, 1 *Hist.* 448, and 1 P. & M., B. I, c. 5, p. 123; *juratores* must be distinguished from *recognitores*, despite Spelman. Cf. " Lord Mansfield's special jurymen," in the City.

(e) *Cour des B.*, c. 20 : Vol. I, p. 31.

(f) The *Abrégé* of the *Livre des B.*, c. 12 (Vol. II, 245), calls the *avps.* " le compliment des officiaus " : *ib.*, for " *avps.*" Canciani, II, 545, " li quali sonno chiamati prolocutori."

(g) Vol. I, p. 475 : there and p. 536 Beugnot prints " (le livre de forme de plait que Sire) Felippe de Novaire " but always calls him " de Navarre," whence he says expressly, he came.

(h) *Romania*, 19th Year : Paris, 1890 : *Mélanges*, pp. 99—102 : Novara, he says, was in the " comté de Blandrate."

current in the Christian East. Here, then, we have a clue. It was not a young Frenchman from a country where in 1190 there was little law or procedure, but an Italian from the neighbourhood of Bologna (who may have taken that city on his way to the East). His interest in jurisprudence is easy to understand. His book and Jean d'Ibelin's are an integral part of the *Assises* (Vol. I). He was writing about 1240-50, having gone to the Holy Land as a Crusader (*i*) and no doubt met Louis IX there, or in Cyprus in 1248; both died in 1270. Beugnot (*k*) exclaims : " How can we suppose that Glanville (who took the Cross and died in the Holy Land in 1190) during his stay in Syria did not communicate to the *Seigneurs* of the East so passionately attached to feudal law, exact ideas on the state of this science in Europe? " and (much as Michaud above) " we ought to regard Philip as only an instrument which French feudalism used to set the feudal customs and manners of the East on the path which it was itself going."

Jean d'Ibelin, in whom the system is most developed (*ib.* v. I, p. 1, etc.), completes Philip's work which is " melted down " in his; he, too, was a Crusader, and jurist, pupil and successor of Philip. He is supposed to have been born about 1200, to have written about 1250 and died about 1266. Du Cange (*l*) said roundly of his book that it was nothing else than the laws and customs of France.

It seems then that Philip knew a system under which the feudal lord (*m*) was autocrat and supreme judge and was bound in religion and honour to protect his " men "; these vassals owed him a general duty of support, of counsel, if need be, and *inter se* they were similarly bound

---

(*i*) " I was at the first siege of Danietta " [1218] : v. I, c. 49, p. 525. He might then be 20—25, *Hist. Litt. de la Fr.* v. 21, p. 444 : 1847.

(*k*) *Ib.*, pp. xxxvi-vii.

(*l*) *Ib.*, p. lxxviii; from Du C.'s edn. of the *Établissements* : 1668.

(*m*) In the Book of the *Bourgeois*, there is, naturally, little feudalism.

to aid one another in all honourable ways and so before the tribunals. When Philip says that he had been a " pleader " all his life he means that he had taken part in composing differences between *seigneurs* at variance or between them and their vassals or between contending subjects, and he had learned by experience how these quarrels were sometimes conducted. Hence his frequent denunciation of *chicane* and the science of *soutillances*. But he by no means thinks (*n*) that every " pleader " was a professional man in our sense; in his time the *avantparliers* must have been few. He does not use the word " client " or " attorney." *Avocat* apparently does not appear at all in the Book of the High Court (*o*).

That the *consilium* (*p*) should grow into a profession was as inevitable anywhere else as it was in England. Beugnot neatly says (*q*) that the difference between the *avantparlier* and the *conseil* was that one carried on a profession and the other fulfilled a duty. The frequent references to the perils of the poor or feeble suitor in the feudal courts from the exactions of the powerful are, no doubt, stimulated by the recognition that the Church courts purported to protect the defenceless and imply the theory that feudality accepted the sacred duty. This legislation, by the way, has for the jurist the advantage that it is not

---

(*n*) Though perhaps Beugnot—who is altogether too precise on these terms—does, for *Glossary* (v. II, *Plaideor*) has : " ce mot était pris d'abord dans le sens générique de légiste, d'homme de loi; puis privativement dans celui de conseil de cour, jurisconsulte qui conseillait et dirigeait une partie dans la conduite d'un procès. . . . Quelquefois le *plaideor* portait lui-meme la parole. . . . Le plus souvent le soin de porter la parole était remis a un *avantparlier*. *Plaideor* et *conseill de court* sont donc des expressions synonymes." The Italian translators, sometimes correctly, translate by *litiganti*.

(*o*) But Beugnot (Index, v. I, *Conseil*) assumes it.

(*p*) There is no analogy between the functions of the *conseil* in the feudal courts and those of the Roman or modern *avocats*; *le conseil* was delegated by the *seigneur* and not by the party, and in doing his work he discharged a duty imposed by his fief and his homage : *Ib.* 39 n.

(*q*) *Ib.* II, 541.

dominated by the Church; its work in Syria was on a *tabula rasa*, though it treats the Church quite respectfully.

Has anything in these books come down to us from the contemporaries of Godfrey de Bouillon? It is generally believed that when Saladin retook Jerusalem in 1187 their *corpus* of law perished and what is now extant (*r*) was gradually constructed or reconstructed by the Christian jurists for the government of the now restricted Christian dominions.

Take, for instance, the proposition (*s*) that when a man has an *essoine* (*t*) for not coming to court he may get another day from the court " par un home de la loi de Rome " *if there be one there*; if not, he may do it by another man of [*sc.* under] any Christian law whatever; and if there is no Christian, it is said (*l'on dit*) that he may do it by a Saracen. And why? " Because an essoiner is a mere messenger. d'Ibelin correspondingly says " par deus homes de la lei de Rome who are not of those who have no voice or reply in court "; or if the party is suddenly " held up " he may do it through one or if he has no Roman handy by any Christian or failing that " any Jew or Saracen he finds " who (like any other essoiner) may swear " according to their law." It is hardly possible to believe that this provision dated from the time of Godfrey de Bouillon when even a Roman lawyer " if there be one there " would hardly have privilege and it is easy to suggest that these various adjuncts *ad hoc* had gradually, by Philip's time come into existence (and into the text)— and developed, by Jean's—and in due course were regulated. No doubt some of the old material " won

---

(*r*) Stephen (*Pleading*, 368 (6th ed.) : 1860) is not entitled to call it " fully recognised as an authentic compilation from the laws of France made towards the close of the 11th century "; his citation from de Mably appears, p. 408.

(*s*) B. I, p. 499, c. 26; *ib.* pp. 96-9, c. 59—both rare (if not the only) *direct* references to Roman lawyers.

(*t*) Cf. *Livre de Jean*, c. 18, 1 B. p. 43.

through "—this is the most we can say. But that the organized and developed advocacy of the present texts dates from 1100—when no code of the sort existed in any other part of the world—is incredible. That something of the sort must gradually have sprung from the ultra-feudal conditions is our thesis not only here, but in *pari materia*. The very archaic (*u*) French of these documents has not, it seems, been minutely analysed by a philologist or grammarian, essaying to date varying *strata* (*x*); we must be content to say that ultimately this school derives from France. Whether the France of 1200 owes anything jural to England remains to be seen (*y*).

But even if it should turn out that it does not, the study of the advocate on this large scale, the most systematic and the earliest after William of Drogheda's treatise, edited by men who might easily have read that book (and cannot have been wholly ignorant of Bolognianism) deserves a little space, and would deserve more if it could be shown that it had any reaction on this country (as it certainly did on France).

The gist of the code of advocacy—taken as representative of European conceptions of 1250—will be stated, more detail being relegated to an Appendix (XIII).

Perhaps the most famous passage of d'Ibelin is his " ideal counsel " (*z*) : " It becomes the good and clever pleader (*litigante*) to have wisdom, common sense (*senno natural*) which must be on the alert, and a subtle mind and he must not be timid or frightened nor shamefaced nor excited nor ignorant of his cause and his mind must be

---

(*u*) Sometimes corrupt, when only the *general* meaning is clear; the Italian translators, when they exist, seem to have felt the same difficulty.

(*x*) As the Higher Criticism has done for the Hexateuch.

(*y*) P. 407.

(*z*) Beugnot, I, p. 50 : c. 26 : Canciani, *Barb. Leges*, v. V, 162 (Venice, 1792)—translation here followed (except where the text is more intelligible).

fixed on it when he argues and he must be on his guard not to get angry or be discouraged in his pleading, for they are things which mislead and take away sense and knowledge (*a*). And the good pleader should speak freely and intelligently and be careful to use words so that his adversary cannot catch him (*prendre à point*) whereby he might lose his case or the cause be deferred, if he is plaintiff (*requereor*) or despatched if he is defendant; he must note well and cleverly all the phrases of his opponent, seizing on each one separately so as to know how to reply what is necessary [for his argument] and to find reasons to defeat all the other has said and to catch him if he can. And if he sees that his opponent has made a mistake, let him not show it lest the other is made aware of it and amend his error—but let him do so quite simply without any show of catching him and if possible without asking anyone's [*sc.* the adverse party's : so *Ital.* (*b*)] admission : however if he must ask him and his wife (if they are joint parties) let him do it with as little appearance (*contenance*) as he can [as shortly as : *Ital.*] of taking to task, so that they do not perceive the mistake and amend it at once. And when the party has adopted what has been said for him the good pleader will say to the Court ' You have heard so-and-so say so-and-so,' specifying what, ' and so-and-so has adopted it,' and then he should fully tell them what he objects to. But if he sees the other man speaking so well that he thinks that he will lose his case, or his argument be weakened, let him cast about and use his wit to get out of that *impasse* as he best can, either by challenging

---

(*a*) " Il covient à celui qui est bon plaideor et soutil qu'il soit sage de senz naturel et que il ait prest sens et soutil engin et qu'il ne seit doutif, ne esbay, ne hontous, ne nonchaillant de son plait et qu'il n'ait s'entente ni sa pencée aillors, tant come il plaidée ; et qu'il se garde de soi trop corroucier ne airier ne esmoveir en plaideant, que ces choses font tost tressaillir home en desraison et li tolent senz et conoissance."

(*b*) When there is no advocate against him? " Party " always = celui de qui la carrelle est.

his terms (*c*) or seeking subterfuges (*d*) or by showing various reasons for discrediting his speech or making [him] change it or by beating (*atainer*) him in argument courteously or by pretending that he is attacking him for what he has said wrongly in asking admission from the party, or making a great show of asking to have [from the other side] authority for the speech which his *avantparlier* [*advocato*] has spoken well in order that he may pick this speech to pieces, to see whether he can make his *conseill* [*el suo consultore*] give up this well made speech, according as he thinks that it is likely to injure him more to make this pretence than perhaps it would to have that speech given up—which might have greater force—and say other things by such *conseill* [*per consiglio*] as he may have. And the good pleader knows when to carry his case to a finish (? *bien ataindre plait* : *ben concluder la causa*) and when to run away (*e*) (*foyr* : *et ben fugire*) according to circumstances : and when to assume proof to himself and when to give it to the other side; and how to prove the negative when it suits him—and there are many other *semblances de plais* which the good pleader ought to know, to transcribe which here would take too long (*f*) and be too unseemly (*rioutouses*). . . . But the better and the more knowing the good pleader is than the other [against him?] the more of them he will contrive (*f*).

. . . . The more of them he knows the better pleader he is. And whatever people say—I hold him for the worst pleader who loses his soul for his pleas : I pray and beseech all pleaders that above all things they lose not their souls (*g*) for their pleas—for such a plea would be too ill and too dearly bought."

(*c*) ? lui traverser d'aucunes paroles : traversarlo d'alcune parole.
(*d*) ? par eschampes querre : per dimandar termine.
(*e*) Perhaps with reference to *fuiant*=defendant.
(*f*) So, too, C. 33.
(*g*) N.B. The *oath* of the *avps*. (*ib*. ii, 245; Abrégé) is much later; for the important mediaeval oath of Frederic II about 1230, see

The diction is not always clear (*h*) (and expresses a procedure which is not so clear to us as it was to the first readers) but the tone and the goal are clear.

The picture of the conduct of a case in court is so valuable—apart from its intrinsic merit—that another sketch by d'Ibelin may be translated (c. 22) " Who pleads in the High Court . . . should do so [a] wisely [b] loyally (*leiaument*) and [c] courteously : [a] wisely in that before he begins he should furnish himself with the wisest *conseill* [=person or *consilium*] he can, and should have his speech (*i*) spoken by his *conseill* or someone else, according as he judges best [at the moment] : let him be careful to say nothing in court which can prejudice him or admit anything which his opponent calls upon him to, except by the advice of his *conseill* (*le conseill de son conseill*) (*k*) and let him not undertake in court to prove something which he cannot prove if his opponent denies it; and let him not do anything to adjourn a case he ought to win or to bring on one he ought to lose : if he is plaintiff let him be as brief as possible for short talk (*clamor*) has two advantages—the Court retains and remembers the short better than the long and in case of the other side joining issue (*née*) it is easier to prove the short than the long; [b] loyally : let him not knowingly advance anything contrary to law or plead falsely by false warranties or

---

Canciani, I, 330 : *Const. Regni Siculi* : The appeal to a religious sanction may be easily parallelled in many Canonists, etc., and notably in William of Drogheda. There is a general resemblance between the forms on pp. 26, 517-8, and Frederic's.

(*h*) Partly perhaps because fragments from different occasions have been uncritically pieced together (as happened with other ancient documents which did not entirely survive); here it looks as if the same point slightly altered has been repeated twice or thrice.

(*i*) *Parole*, either a specific formula or *all* that he has to say.

(*k*) Cf. Delachenal, *Hist. des Avocats* (1885), c. 14 : In les *Assises* " un seul mot, celui de *conseil* sert à désigner ceux qui parlent pour autrui et ceux qui sont simplement appelés à prêter aux plaideurs le concours de leurs !umières." The phrase is repeated, *La Clef.* V. (II B., 579), see App. XIII.

otherwise and let him not purposely deprive his opponent
of his rights by [mere] points of pleading; [c] courteously :
he must neither use nor make others use insulting,
excessive or derisive words to the *seigneur,* the court, the
opponent or—his own counsel [!] but he must speak as
finely and as politely as possible to the best of his knowledge omitting nothing which his case demands." All this
is very modern.

This and much else is an expansion of what Philip had
written (Beug., I, p. 563 : c. 91) for " him who wants to
be a clever pleader and clever conductor of court affairs
and clever servant of territorial lords : he ought to have
five *manieres.* 1. Natural common sense of [? a natural
gift for] clever knowledge (*l*) and an acute mind : this is
the foundation. . . . 2. The will to be a good pleader
and the practice thereof for [mere] cleverness (*scutilance*)
will not further him much if he does not like his " job "
and does not practice it. 3. He must be strong in his own
resources or in other people's but the former is by far the
better, for control and management of a difficulty (*de
l'estrange*) may fail in many ways, for a feeble pleader
has not the courage to speak up and attack and sometimes
does not dare lay down the law correctly against his
opponent, if the latter is a powerful man. 4. This is the
most perilous for it endangers the soul—" for it often
happens that a pleader in order to be thought clever, or
from fear or love of a lord or friend or for pay or vanity
(*bobans*) or hate or to get a great place argues or lays
down the law (*juge*) or procures judgment falsely and
so loses his soul. 5. He must not take it amiss whatever
anyone says of him and sometimes he must make a show
of not having heard what is said or of not caring, let
everyone say what he likes, while he goes on with his own
case and performs his duty. This is very unpleasant for
all pleaders and more dangerous to the poor ones than to

(*l*) Naturel sens de soutil coneissance.

the rich and powerful for they will dare to call a poor man disloyal or treacherous (? tricky : *trechiere*) or a hireling, who would not dare to say so to a powerful one. And worse, for harm and damage can be wrought on such a pleader and on his folk, though it may not be there and then or avowedly for his speech. Many a time it has happened that for fear of such consequence some weak men have not done their best:—though it may happen, too, that it is right for a pleader however cleverly he has argued and cited law (*juger*) to lose."

Even if Philip had not in terms referred to his experience it would be obvious that these observations are " first hand." They are driven home (*ib.* p. 564 : c. 92) by an essay on the loyalty of the clever pleader, " to rich and poor who come to him " (*m*)—the theme of every mediaeval legal historian. On the other hand if he sees that he is to be called on to wage an unequal battle with overpowerful opponents, let him get out of court as quickly as he can but, if needs must, still he must do his work *cortoisement et loiaument.* And if the dispute leads to insulting language let him stop it as soon as he can (? *eschiver . . . d'estre avant plus*). . . . If a powerful lord or friend of his tries to induce him to do anything wrong (sc. *chicane*) he ought privately to dissociate himself and not to cease to object to such wrong doing; otherwise he must make some decent excuse (*covenable essoine*) for absence and get rid of the offence (*n*) for if he remains he must needs oppose his lord to his own hurt, and if he complies he may lose honour and soul.

But a rich and powerful man (*o*) does well and charit-

(*m*) The phrase here " if by any chance he finds himself in court and be assigned as *conseill* " is explained by B.'s note, p. 389*p*; this is *consilium* not *advocatus*.

(*n*) " le fort " a misprint for " le tort "?

(*o*) In the *Assises d'Antioche* by Sempad (d. 1276) " ce Joinville des Arméniens " Venice (1876), p. 50, orphans can get a *juré* to represent them but no other representative is mentioned.

ably if he goes voluntarily to the court for it is known that he has no desire to be a pleader [? = take sides] and he can do much good if he gives advice in good faith to those who have it not and are poor and if he sits in judgment others, who are not powerful, sit there too and are more forward to pronounce boldly with him (*o lui*).

The influence of the impartial rich is much insisted on. " It is of much importance that rich men should learn letters . . . those who have the means and the opportunity ought at least to learn to read and write " (*p*). On this note the book ends, after a few lines on the great authority of the *plaideor* : " by means of the able (*soutil*) pleader a man may save and keep in court his honour, his (feudal) rights and the heritage of himself and friends and by the pleader's mistake he may lose them all." Nothing shows more clearly than Philip's peroration that he did not mean by pleader a professional man, but someone who would speak in the High Court, for he enumerates, *in piam memoriam*, a list which includes kings and princes; many an one was *soutil de science* " in court and out " (*q*) and much loved *sapience et science* : "messire Hernois [Arnaud] de Giblet qui fu remembrant et esploitant et bon plaideor " while " messire Gille visconte . . . fu plus soutil positor de plait que tous les autres vavasours de son tens."

The system of legal representation collated from Philip and d'Ibelin seems to have been as follows. The High Court begins by granting a *consilium*, whom the party instructs : suitors are recommended to bring as many friends to court as possible, for without friends a man may not understand what is going on and numbers may influence the court, for any vassal of the *seigneur* could take part in the deliberations. Philip gives the pleader (who is not easily distinguished from the *consilium*)

(*p*) " car lor segré [affairs] en devra estre meaus celé [hidden] " : p. 565.

(*q*) A constant expression, cf. c. 49, p. 525, with this c.

technical " tips " how to gain time (*r*)—amongst others always to plead the *retenail* (= " saving all just exceptions "). To Jean the *plaideur* is an institution with an art, but beyond him there is the professional *avantparlier*. Thus the judges of the High Court must listen attentively to the points which the *pleaders* make and to the words— which they must remember, too—that the *avantparliers* (*s*) speak in Court. But from the attention paid by both these jurists to the *plaideor* it would seem that it was common for óne vassal to appear for another; the younger writer reproduces the exhortations of the elder. Those of both religious, moral, homiletical are in the tone of William of Drogheda and of his ascendants and descendants whose procedure as well as their ethics is *essentially* the same as that of the overseas Frenchmen.

That they drew from a common source is likely enough. That the Syrian *corpus* had any direct influence in English institutions is antecedently improbable and is almost certainly disproved by their respective dates. No historian, it seems, has suggested any such effect.

We must turn to

France

partly for its specific results and partly because this country may have counted for something in its forensic history, as it has been already suggested that in Norman times the current was rather thither than hither.

One English writer goes so far as to say (*t*) " From

(*r*) *Ib.* p. 478, c. 3. After some " fraudes dilatoires " (B.) it ends : " this way much time may be gained : one [delay] for the lord, one for the court, another for the essoin : whoever is in the wrong should come to terms or fly "—an instance of the " parole qui se cuevre de semblant de raizon " : *ib*.

(*s*) B. I, c. IX, p. 32. Is this almost verbal repetition within a few lines a doublet, *avantp.* being = *pl.* or are they here really two classes?

(*t*) R. Jones, *History of the French Bar*, 112 : London, 1855. For a sketch of the earlier period see Gaudry, *Histoire du barreau de Paris*, v. I : Paris, 1864, or *Avocat* in Larousse's *Grand Dictionnaire* (1866).

Charlemagne to St. Louis the Bar is lost in the obscurity which envelopes this period of French history." But this statement is exaggerated.

M. Delachenal has dealt with the question more carefully (*u*). " There were *avocats* as long as the use of the old [Gallo-Roman] procedure lasted, in which their function and attributes had been clearly defined. They were given different names, preferably that of *advocati* which their successors resumed in the 12th and in the 13th century, for we shall see soon that it was not borne without interruption. Must we take it that the victory of Germanic ideas was fatal to the *avocats* and that they disappeared in the anarchy caused by the rapid decline of the Merovingian dynasty? This question may be understood and answered in two different ways. It must certainly receive an answer in the affirmative, if corporations of *avocats* are meant, subject to regulations in every way like those which the last monuments of Roman legislation, which had the force of law in Gaul, reveal to us. Indeed it would be odd if the *avocats* alone had been spared when everything was conspiring to the ruin of judicial institutions, to whose fate their existence was straitly bound.

But the question may be put in more general terms— whether at any time litigants (*les plaideurs*) have been reduced to defend their own cause in person, for want of finding someone to take charge of it—to this question the answer will not be the same. It is true that for long years we absolutely lose trace of the *advocati* of Roman law and that we must wait for the *renaissance juridique* of the twelfth century (*x*) to see them reappear. But put your-

---

(*u*) *Histoire des Avocats au Parlement de Paris* (1300—1600). Paris : 1885. *Introduction*, pp. ii, ix, etc.

(*x*) A phrase which M. A. Tardif says is used " trop pompeusement " and which is " only strictly exact for Italy." *Hist. Sources Dr. fr.* p. 23-4. But he himself uses it of the 12th century : *Hist. Sources Canon.* p. 173. The 12th century *renaissance* directly affects our subject, see Tout (*Political*) *Hist. Engl.* 1216—1377 (1905), p. 88.

self at what period you will you meet the reference to men of law whose business it was to assist litigants, to represent them before the tribunals and to speak in their name. The collections of *formulae* used in the Frankish empire give many examples of mandates which could only be trusted to practitioners whose attributes, ill defined, must have been much like those of either the *avocats* or the *procureurs* . . ." After a passing reference to the legislation of Charlemagne and other early Germanic and feudal influences (*y*) (of which period he correctly observes, that the intermediaries to whom litigants in France were forced to resort are given names " between which it would be difficult to establish quite precise distinctions and which at the end of the 13th century were all replaced by one word, at once older and younger—*advocatus*, avocat ") M. Delachenal assumes what the authorities have said about the *avantparliers* and those on the same plane calling them " these precursors of our old *avocats*, whose memory will be lost from the middle of the 14th century but who have left their mark on the most ancient rules of the Order. Thus we may now lay it down that if the *avocats*—in the narrow sense of the word—were not perpetuated in France in regular and uninterrupted succession, feudal procedure re-established them under another name. This only applies to secular jurisdictions on which Germanic law had exercised a stronger and more lasting force. Ecclesiastical procedure, indeed, suddenly took the turn (*avait abouti tout de suite*) without going roundabout, of restoring the *avocats*."

Another authority (*z*) summarises this process at a point convenient for our purpose. " At the beginning of the 14th century . . . a large number of *avocats*, of *procureurs* and of other *gens de chicane* (*a*) were already living round

---

(*y*) See App. VI.
(*z*) E. Lavisse, *Histoire de France*, v. 3, pt. 2, B. III, c. 1, § 3, p. 330; ed. Ch. Langlois : Paris, 1901.
(*a*) *Either* from a Persian word originally=a crooked stick used in polo and " applied in Languedoc to a form of golf : golfers will readily

about the Palais de la Cité, the jurisdiction of the 'parlements'; the oldest Orders on the *avocat's* profession are of the time of Philip III [about 1270] and of Philippe le Bel [ab. 1285]. They exhort to virtue : we must suppose that there were then *avocats* who lied, who insulted their opponents, who abused dilatory processes, who exploited their clients, who took up dirty causes—for in 1274 and 1291 all these practices were formally forbidden." It cannot be said that between the limits covered by these two scholars, the information is very precise.

Some facts in chronological order begun at p. 386 may help towards a conclusion.

Thierry (*b*) makes a claim for an early "bar" at Amiens. A charter of 1091 replacing the Carolingian *échevins* (*Scabinat*) " whose very name had disappeared," by the feudal court of the *comte*, ordains that the judge (*vicomte*) shall give permission to an accused to " consulter, et après avoir pris conseil," he shall answer. After a revolution in 1117 in which the *comte* made, Thierry thinks, the concessions now minutely recorded in the charter of 1190 in that year King Philippe-Auguste, now *comte d'Amiens*, gave the city that great instrument. Only § 33 concerns us : " In omni causa et accusator et accusatus et testis (*c*) per advocatum loquentur si voluerint " (*d*). Of which Thierry, justly (to some extent) remarks that it " déroge sans doute à l'ancienne coutume "—a remark which has itself been doubted (*e*). This municipal charter

---

understand how the sense of taking advantage of petty accidents may have been evolved." Skeat, Weekley; *or* from L. *ciccum* = small, petty : Sk.

(*b*) *Essai sur l'histoire* . . . *du tiers état*, pp. 320, 327, 338, 357, 364 : Paris, 1864.

(*c*) This extraordinary provision has naturally been seized on as unique; it is a question of French not English history but it may be observed that to this day there is no "law of evidence" in France.

(*d*) By analogy with other municipal rules § 37 may aim at pleaders : si quis prepositum regis in placito vel extra placitum turpibus et inhonestis verbis provocaverit—he shall be in mercy, etc.

(*e*) By M. Hecquet de Roquemont, *Revue critique de Législation*, etc., Paris, 1871-2 : New Ser. v. I, p. 539, n. (2).

is certainly one of the oldest, if not the oldest, in France. But, if as it seems, a secular lawyer is here referred to, the instance at that time is isolated : it could only obtain in a local court. As the gradualness of his emergence in France, though it illustrates our thesis, is only ancillary to it, we confine ourselves here (almost entirely) to definite references to French authorities.

1100, about. *Brachylogus juris civilis* or *corpus legum.* Mainly an abridgement of Roman law (*f*); said not to date before the 10th century because " in a gloss which seems to be contemporary Normandy is mentioned—a name which cannot go higher than 912 when that province was ceded to the Normans," Caillemer (*g*) says that it was composed " in the schools of our country during the long interval which separates the fall of the Roman Empire from the foundation of the School of Bologna." Tardif inclines to Orléans as its home (though formerly it was attributed to the School of Ravenna); it has been thought, he says, to influence the *Sachsenspiegel* and the *Schwabenspiegel.* v. Bethmann-Hollweg (*h*) suggests a Lombard author about 1100 belonging to the rise of the Bolognian School, perhaps the founder himself : " Its excellence greatly exceeded that of earlier works and hence it opens the new epoch."

In 1153 was heard the Bishop of Langres v. the Duke of Burgundy in the court of Louis le Jeune. The Bishop says (*i*) : " I cited the Duke into my court : he did not

---

(*f*) A. Tardif, *Histoire, des sources du droit français—origines romaines*, 209 : Paris, 1890.

(*g*) *Le droit civil dans les Provinces Anglo-Normandes au XIIe siècle* 5 : Paris, 1883.

(*h*) 5 *Civilprozesz*, 323.

(*i*) *Textes rélatifs* . . . *Parlement*, no. XI, p. 20; by Ch. Langlois : Paris, 1888. It is curious that in this collection of early documents from France we only get all the titles of lawyers in a letter from an Englishman to an Englishman (and that in 1279)—Thomas of Sandwich, seneschal of Pontieu, to the King : after speaking of the King

come himself but sent *nuntios* for me to address (*responderem*) ... I declined ..." The Duke : " In the bishop's court neither my ancestors nor I have ever appeared (*placitaverunt*) except *per nuntios* and the practice always was to deal with (*respondere*) them." The Bishop says that his predecessors and he had only recognised the *nuntii* when the dukes were present and that the duke himself several times " *placitavit* in my house." " That was out of regard for you " was the reply. " No " was the retort " not only, but out of respect for your dominus and homage."

1160—1170-80 or 90. O. J. *Incerti Auctoris* (*k*). Perhaps by a Canonist writer who had relations with Lombardy and an Italian university but who wrote in France and perhaps in Paris (*l*). Tardif (*m*) who puts the author in the category of men like John of Salisbury " who were writing in France or in England about this time," thinks that the book is important for procedure in France at the time.

The *advocatus in causa* is taken as the normal case of *postulatio* : there are the usual prohibitions; he is very stern with the *adv*. appointed by the judge to take up a case, who refuses without good cause, especially from a mean motive (*ambitione*) or fear of the defendant—he may never again plead professionally—*illis judex perpetuum indicit silentium*. They must never be abusive " out of reason " (*ultra modum*). There is a curious passage *de*

---

and Queen " faire atourné en demandant et en defendant " in a certain matter " by open letters " he goes on to recommend a Frenchman who will be " bon vostre atourné " and your " procureur " (named) but it is advisable that " there (or he) should be *advocas* with your other *consel* " therein. This seems to be the only passage in the volume where " atourné " is used.

(*k*) Ed. Dr. Carl. Grosz, from a Göttweig MS., Innsbruck 1870 : dates 1170-80, so Caillemer. See Wahrmund *Ric. Anglicus*, p. xx, n. (2), and Grosz's text, Pt. I, iv, p. 94 and p. 115, xii : Pt. II, xii, p. 242.

(*l*) v. B.-H. 6 C. P. 94, 99 : dates 1170-90.

(*m*) *Dr. Can.* 268.

testibus; there is a *t. juris* and a *t. facti* : *testis est juris ille qui ostendit quid juris sit in facto*, quod proprie ad advocatos spectat (*n*). *Sed in eadem causa nunquam idem potest esse testis juris et facti.* To illustrate the difference between hiring a thing or services, *advv.* in causes are not bound to return their fees (*honoraria*) (*o*) if, *through no fault of their own*, they did not appear.

1170, about : *Summae legum Parisienses* perhaps from the diocese of Sens (*p*); nothing on *advv.*

1160-80 : at any rate, before 1190 : *Rhetorica Ecclesiastica*, purely ecclesiastical : almost total omission of *adv.* (except pp. 88, 90 : none allowed in criminal cases).

1164-71. *Summa Rufini*; Paris : of no importance for us (*q*). His pupil Étienne, Bishop of Tournai, born in 1128 (1135?) d. 1203, wrote a *Summa* (*r*).

1180, after : ? 1200. *Epitome juris Florentina* perhaps French (*s*) (Italian?).

1192. Placentinus dies : at Montpellier : (from Mantua and Bologna).

1197. Longchamp dies.

1208. Innocent III writes to the Bishop of Bayeux : " *cum in jure peritus existas et copiam habeas peritorum*, why do you consult me? " (*t*).

1213. First official mention of a Law Faculty at the University of Paris; but canon and civil law was taught there earlier : suspended by Honorius III in 1219; Gregory IX declared that the study of law was not prohibited to clerks who only had a simple cure of souls (*u*).

1226. St. Louis ascends.

(*n*) Does this throw light on § 33, p. 401.
(*o*) As old as Trajan in this sense.
(*p*) Pt. II of Grosz's edn.; Tard. *Dr. can.* 252, 259; Caill. pp. 15-6
(*q*) Tard. *ib.* 367; Caill. *ib.*
(*r*) Tard. *ib.* 367; Caill. *ib.* 15.
(*s*) Tard. *ib.* 257.
(*t*) Caill. p. 41.
(*u*) Tard. *Dr. fr.* 285.

1235-40. *O. J.* " Scientiam " (*x*). Attributed to France.

C. XII on " those who may act for others " has the usual list, including " *orphanotrophus* pro mis. personis." But *advv.* are not mentioned there. However when (C. XVI) he deals with objections to a cause being tried, he remarks that " a good *adv.* will, on consideration of the facts of each case, be able to find points. For instance, *causa feodalis est unde non debet hie tractari sed remitti ad dominum feodi.*" But to this there may be a *replicatio* (C. XVII) : " True but the ecclesiastical court has jurisdiction because of the legate['s authority] " etc., etc. In c. XXII he asks whether a *clericus* must take the oath *de calumpnia* in spiritual causes? A Decretal expressly lays it down that " this duty is to be delegated to competent *advocati.*" The context makes it doubtful whether secular *advv.* as well as clerical are here contemplated in spiritual courts. The same point arises in appeals — clearly to ecclesiastical courts (C. XXV) : " *Advv.* used to take oath that they would in good faith defend the cause of their *clientuli* " but—as, with the judges, it seems, the practice had ceased.

Three days are allowed for correcting the mistake of an *adv.* (C. XXVII, p. 48); it is not so bad for him to make a mistake as for the party about his own affairs. Thus in this treatise the *adv.* is very inconspicuous.

1236. Council of Trent decides that " *advocati* and *officiales* may not exercise their functions unless they have studied law, the former for three years, the latter for five " : The Law School at Angers [province of Tours] was already famous in the 11th century (*y*).

1250-4. *Summa Minorum* (*z*) : supposed to be by Magister Arnulphus, a canon of Paris, closely connected

---

(*x*) See p. 99*h* : W.'s *Introduction* : v. B.-H. 6 *C. P.* 80.
(*y*) Tard. *Dr. fr.* 295.
(*z*) And v. B.-H. 6 *C. P.* 141.

with the University. *Advv.* are not mentioned but c. 50 *de Procuratorio* contains a precedent of appointment for all causes ecclesiastical or secular before all judges whatsoever.

1251. An *Ordonnance* of Charles d'Anjou fixes a tariff of fees according to time without regard to the importance of the suit : " 5 sous par vacation [=time taken] " : followed by one of Jean I of Bretagne (*a*).

1251-70. *Curialis* : supposed to be by a French cleric. In cc. 79-80 *advocati* are mentioned in rubrics (with other *coadjutores*), but not in the text. C. 81 is a precedent of a request to a *decretista* to defend the writer because *inter alia* the *causidicus* against him is learned and very clever.

1257. Guy Foueard (b. about 1200) Bishop of Puy : becomes Clement IV, 1265-8 : studied law at Paris : described by his contemporaries, *lumen juris ob raram utriusque juris scientiam, jurisconsultorum peritissimus totius Galliae sine contentione primarius in curia regis causas integerrime agens* (*b*) : he had practised at the bar (*plaidé au Parlement*) before he took orders (*c*).

1270. St. Louis dies.

1270, about. Guillaume Durand publishes *Speculum Juris* : a Bolognian : born 1230 in Provence and " one of the founders of the French bar " (*d*) of which, about 1250-70, his book gives an account—reproduced by Horwood in Y. B. 32-3 Ed. I, pp. xxv-xxx (Rolls : 1864) (*e*).

1274 or earlier. First Ordonnance about *avocats* (*f*).

(*a*) Du Coudray, *Les Origines du Parlement de Paris aux 13° et 14° Siècles* (1902), p. 205.

(*b*) Platina (d. 1481) in *Mémoires de Loisel*, 466, 689 : Paris, 1652.

(*c*) Tard. *ib.* 286; cf. 16-7 : " l'avocat exemple du barreau . . . sur le trône pontifical " : *Gaudry*, 1 *Hist. du bar. de Paris*, c. 8, Paris, 1864.

(*d*) Tard. *ib.* 109, 110.

(*e*) When many fewer works of D.'s predecessors were accessible than now; yet H. acutely thought that a gloss referred to William of Drogheda (*ib.* p. xxviin.); see also H.'s Y. B. 30-1 Ed. I, p. xviii (1863).

(*f*) Ducoudray, p. 199.

1296. Beaumanoir (b. about 1247 : wrote about 1280) and Durand die.

A little known *O. J.* with a contemporary Gloss : ed. Warnkönig : Ghent 1835, about this time : a mere copyist but neat : touches shortly on *procc.* and *advv.*

1314, perhaps earlier. For an instance of the early development of the French bar, as shown by its terminology, see *La Commune d'Oleron*, p. 421*q.*

We have dealt at some length with French lawyers because we desire to suggest that the English school, especially William of Drogheda, had a decisive effect on the French school, and possibly indirectly on that of Palestine. A glance at the dates in the French development and another at the English—even assigning Ivo de Chartres and the Norman writers to the former—will show that Bologna had much more direct influence, at any rate, on this country than on France. Indeed, though Bologna radiated in all directions, it almost seems to have skipped France—the only great name on her soil is Placentinus. And however that may be, if Philip of Novara left his country about 1190-1200, where did he get his system which he worked out in the Jerusalem *Assises*? We now know that he did not start from France, but if he had done so, there was very little but pure Roman law and a little Canon law that he could take with him and his forensic legislation is certainly not borrowed from either.

French historians (*g*) generally trace their *legal* revival to increasing interest in the study of law after the discovery of the *Pandects* in 1137. " There is nothing," says Tout (*h*), " in history more remarkable than the wonderful growth of the French state under Philip Augustus " (1179-1223), but it is difficult to put one's finger on a critical turning-point in France before 1239, when William of

---

(*g*) Gaudry, v. I, c. VII, p. 83.
(*h*) *France and England in the Middle Ages*, p. 81 (1922); cf. pp. 63, 82.

Drogheda was writing. French writers have not faced the difficulty; de Mably says (*i*) : " We still have a precious work, well designed to shed light on the epochs of the origin of our customs : it is the *Assises de Jérusalem*. Godfrey of Bouillon and the *seigneurs* who drew them up had gone to Palestine towards the end of the eleventh century. Is it not reasonable to suppose that the customs on which they agreed amongst themselves were in France when they left it and that those of our usages of which they say nothing were then unknown? " But assuredly there was no " bar "—even if there were a few *advocati*— in France when the Crusaders departed in 1099; but in Philip's day there was a full-blown one. Michaud, too, may be correct that much " was settled according to the customs of France," but he (like many other authorities) was not thinking of " the bar." There is, however, good French evidence of English influence on the Oriental legislation. In the West, says the *Histoire littéraire de la France* (*k*) different authors had written on feudal customs : " Hence those compilations known by the name of *Consuetudines feudorum: Vetus auctor de beneficiis* : the treatise on the laws and Customs of England by Glanville, grand justiciar under Henry II : the *ancienne coutume* of Normandy : and, above all, the code of laws promulgated by Henry I, called Beau Clerc because of his learning. . . . The precedent of these works must naturally have had some influence on the lawyers of Syria and Cyprus whom the Crusades were keeping incessantly in touch with the West." Beugnot, we saw, suggested that Glanville in person inspired the Syrian jurists (*l*).

(*i*) *Observations sur l'histoire de France* [1765] vol. 2, p. 277 (Paris, 1823 : ed. Guizot).

(*k*) Vol. 21, p. 441 : Paris, 1847.

(*l*) It is curious that Beaumanoir visited England and Scotland (after 1265) and wrote on his return *Jehan de Dammartin et Blonde d'Oxford*, about 1274, but, owing to his youth, his English experiences are not reflected in his great work (c. 1285) *Coutumes de Beauvoisis* :

If Glanville in 1190, why not William of Drogheda in 1240? Apart from the *va-et-vient*, the considerable intercourse between the two countries, Louis (" Cœur de Lion "), afterwards VIII, had spent more than a year (1216-7) in this country as " King of England." Everyone knows that the great moment in French Law is at hand. There is no difficulty in understanding reciprocity of effect between the two (and still less between England and Normandy)—if there was any evidence of a movement from across Channel hither—and we may legitimately suppose that what culture France had, including legal lore, she passed on, with or without the help of the Crusades, to her colonies in the East. Nothing had come from Bologna so far of the magnitude, weight or minuteness of the *Summa Aurea* (m) and whether it travelled *via* Normandy or France —whither assuredly it arrived by its own merit—or went straight out to Syria, it must have been a godsend to Philip just setting up his own " bar," or remodelling an old one.

A systematic comparison of the details of the *Summa Aurea* and of the *Assises de Jérusalem* would, no doubt, reveal much specific legislation that was the same (whether because it was taken from the same source or not) and that experiment on a small scale, *e.g.*, on the functions, rights of the advocate in each of those works, does certainly not discourage the idea that Philip had read William's book. The constant appeals to religion and

---

Collection de Textes . . . Paris, 1899, ed. Am. Salmon : he calls York " Evoluic "; this visit seems not to have been known to Beugnot who edited the work (2 vols. : Paris, 1842); the *Notice* therein does not mention the French Bar, 1250-80. In his edition of *Les Olim* (Paris, 1839), on *audita advocatione* in a document of 1267 he says (I, 1047) : " In the *Olim* the intervention of *avocats* in the King's court is not mentioned—only *procuratores* who are only *fondés de pouvoir*. Nevertheless it is not open to doubt that parties came to the court *entourés de conseils*, amparliers ou *avocats* : this is the meaning of *auditis etiam hinc inde propositis*; yet the Editor of the *Olim* does not give us the name of one."

(m) " Scientiam," p. 405, is not comparable.

honour appear in both, and Philip (*n*) is in as much anxiety about the honest pleader's soul (*arme*) as William. Beugnot (I, lxviii) is at pains to show the absence of the least trace of religious ideas in the *Assises*, but he means papal or canonical, not pious. The theological tone is, of course, not a logical objection to the concomitant *chicane*.

The great legal upheaval in France proper is by common consent later than Philip's great effort (if not than d'Ibelin's). It is highly probable that, for our theme, at any rate, the authors of the *Établissements* did not neglect it. If that be so, the case is analogous to the classic reaction of Ionian and other colonies on the mother Hellas—especially manifested in codification and publication of the laws (*o*).

A real " epoch " is reached with the *Établissements* of St. Louis, no longer regarded as his own creation, but accepted as " a *coutumier* compiled before 1273 by a practitioner without a commission, who added to the exposition of principles of law, civil and feudal, observed in the Orléanais Anjou and Maine the text of certain royal ordinances " (*p*).

" The Order of Avocats," says Beugnot (*q*), who speaks with great authority, " was really founded in France " by the Ordinance of Philip III in 1274, which imposed on them and others the oath of office.

For the purposes of comparison with English views of the bar about 1250 a passage from the *Établissements* is set out in App. XIV.

(*n*) See pp. 395, and App. XIII.

(*o*) Art. *Colonia* : *Dict. Gk. & R. Antiq.* (1890) : " We look to America now to solve many of the political and social problems which are beginning to be sorely felt. . . . Without going so far as Roscher in asserting that in every branch of higher art and science Hellas proper was indebted for her first stimulus to her colonies yet they did react. . . "

(*p*) Lavisse, 3 *Hist. de Fr.* Pt. 2 e 3, p. 78, from P. Viollet.

(*q*) *Ass. de J.* I, 24n. So Warnkönig, *Französ. Staats u. Rechtsges.* v. III, p. 481 (1846), " zuerst also förmlicher Stand anerkannt."

Normandy.

What has been said about the " Chauvinism " of French writers and the traditional assumptions of German with reference to the *attornatus* is peculiarly relevant here. The authorities in question have confused Norman institutions with institutions which came into existence in " Norman times."

To the few legal books which can in any sense be called Norman (and which were rather due to England than affecting it) we must add " The Grand Custumier of Normandy " (r) which " is generally held to contain much of the old law and custom of England which our early Norman Kings extended to Normandy and made effective there." The latest edition (1881), not mentioned by Maitland, prints Latin and French parallel and is by W. L. de Gruchy (s), a judge of the royal court of Jersey. The Latin version is supposed to be the older and to have been made about 1275 and before 1280. It is certain, therefore that it reproduces some of the English thought of its period.

C. 63 (p. 151) is *De Placitatoribus* or *De Plédeurs*, *i.e.*, parties, not representatives.

C. 64 is *De Prolocntoribus*, *De Conteurs*.

C. 65 is *De Attornato*, *De Attourné*.

(r) Maitland, 30 Seld. Soc. xv, and so in art. cited p. 130 : also (*ib.*) *Summa de legibus consuetudinum Normanniae* or *S. d. l. in curia laicali*; carefully to be distinguished from *Le Très Ancien Coutumier de N.*: ed. J. Tardif, which=*Statuta et Consuetudines N.* or *Établissements et Coutumes de N.* (M.) : See 1 P. & M. 42, and Haskins, *Norm. Inst.* 4. Cf. Camus (1740—1805) *Lettres sur la profession d'avocat* : 4 th letter : p. 70 : Paris, 1818 (4th ed.) : " la Normandie a été assez longtemps occupée par les Anglais : ils y apportèrent plusieurs de leurs usages qui ont ensuite passé dans la coutume de cette province. Ils y prirent aussi et ils conservaient ensuite dans leurs pays d'ancions usages* soit de la Normandie soit même des autres provinces de la France." *Sc.* non-legal.

(s) Whose Preface says : " qui [the *Cout.*] renferme les sources originelles de notre Droit et dont le contenu sous certaines restrictions évidentes fait a ce titre même encore aujourd'hui autorité légale dans cette île."

The legal literature of England for the past half century has here borne fruit. It has had some effect but only gives a hint of the consolidation of the profession since William of Drogheda wrote, and that not in England. These three chapters are set out as an instance of English practice transplanted to Normandy.

De Placitatoribus. Those are called *placitatores* who carry on a cause in court, whether by plaint or response.

De Prolocutoribus. The *prolocutor* (*conteur*) is he whom anyone sets up to speak for him; his words ought to have the same weight as if they fell from the lips of his principal (*attornantis*); nor when once he has been appointed may that principal contradict what the former has said on his behalf, so long as the appointment exists, but he can displace him and appoint another, when he likes; for he cannot have two *prolocutores* at the same time. If the appointment of the *prolocutor* is made in these terms " This man is to speak for me against —— pray (*t*) hear him : if he propounds for me what I have instructed (*injunxi*) him, I will warrant him "; the judge ought to gave him audience and having done so ask his principal whether what he [*prol.*] has said he has said for him [*client*: sc. whether he adopts the speech]. If he warrants it, he may not " reprobate " it but should he allege that some of his statements were not authorised and decline to warrant them, the *prolocutor* shall amend and the proceeding will be limited to what is warranted. However a prudent principal will appoint in this form, for no prudent man will warrant beforehand what *is to be* said but only, if he thinks fit, what has in fact been said.

De Attornato. Attornatus is one who is commissioned (*attornatus*) by someone to prosecute or defend his right before a judge, in the exchequer or an assize, having a record and he ought to be accepted in the suit as in the

---

(*t*) Audiatis : pl. = either the judges or a polite singular.

same legal position as his principal (*qui attornat*) and *the former ought not to be heard if the latter is present* and, at any rate, he can only be heard in a case in which he is *attornatus*. There is a habit of constituting *attornati* in the absence of opponents but this may not be done of right, except when the king is sitting, for only his sole attestation makes a record. For as the court must show itself impartial it cannot alter the *status* of one party in the absence of the other. For in a court of record an *attornatio* made in the absence of the other side may unjustly prejudice it for if it obtains a record against the *attornatus* it will not know [who he is] nor can it demand a copy (*copiam, record*) of his appointment, through not being present and not knowing before whom the *attornatus* was appointed. By letters patent from the King read in an assize court of record when the other side is present, an *attornatus* is properly made, for of such *attornatio* there may be a good record.

Finally as showing what the compiler thought that the function of the *attornatus* was in Normandy (or, indeed, approximately in England) in 1280—practically, a conduit-pipe, without initiative, a bare " substitute " (*u*), we may see in c. 127.

One misses at once mention of *narrator* and *serviens* and notices the disproportionate emphasis on the " record " of

---

* * So the French, and possibly the Latin is corrupt but it may be intended that if the party appeared the *att.* (unlike the *prol.*) could not be heard; their function was different.

(*u*) Still a technical French legal term. In c. 127 : Attornati etiam attornantium conditiones non possunt immutare sed querelas accipiunt terminandas per judicium in eo statu et processu et circumstantiis in quibus eas attornantes habebant quando pro eis fuerunt attornati. Et sic attornati querelam possunt deducere placitando; nec tamen attornatus aliquid potest componere vel pacificare qui videlicet attornatus sit solummodo ad deductionem querelae terminandam. In componendo, pacificando vel alio modo quam placitando querelam non debet audiri nisi ad hoc specialiter fuerit attornatus.

In c. 126 : " Ego . . . praepositus attornatus tibi praecipi ut in curia . . . interesses . . . responsurus," *p. att.=prévost attourné= substitut.*"

the *attornatus* and, judging from this topic only, it looks as if the compiler were dealing with English institutions adapted to local or colonial use. Probably every positive rule here could be found in an English writer within the previous half century, but there is no attempt to synthesize English forensic practice in 1280.

In law, then, Normandy was anglicised rather than England normanised; at any rate, Normandy had (about 1250) a superiority in the study of law, which it acquired and long kept over all the other provinces of France—" a superiority attested by the number and fame of the Anglo-Norman lawyers " (*x*).

Germany.

The insignificance of Germany for jurisprudence till the reign of Charles IV (1347-78) is attested by the silence of many historians and the positive evidence of at least one. In these circumstances, the concise statement of an encyclopaedia (*y*) may be quoted : " The course of procedure may be gathered directly from the history of Roman law. In the place of the *patronus* of the earliest period, that is, of the protector taken from the ruling families, whose presence itself recommended the smaller citizen to the tribunal, appear later on in weighty matters the *Advocatus* that is one 'called in' at will, a respectable law-expert, who by his presence declares that the client is carrying on (*instruirt*) the case according to his advice, and the *Orator*, a ready speaker, a counsel but not always a legally trained one, who according to his materials of evidence defends the cause of his party in a speech covering the whole ground and seeks to work on the judges. . . . [Later] paid Agents (*patroni* in a new sense) gave their services to the parties before the tribunal and combined

---

(*x*) Beugnot, *Les Olim*, v. I, p. lxxvii : Paris, 1839. He recognises that long before this *recueil* the judges and *advocats* of the Norman *échiquier* had collected its *arrêts* but he tells us nothing of the *avocats*.

(*y*) *Conversations-Lexikon* : Leipzig ; Brockhaus, 1864 : *Advocat*.

the activity of the *advocatus* with that of the *orator* and made a business out of this employment. These Agents soon came under a kind of discipline and at length took rank as public servants, who when they had shown qualification, were permanently attached to definite courts.

The institution took a similar course in Germany. Here, too, in the earliest period only the unfree and the ' little man ' wanted a lord (*Herrn*) or protector to represent him in court. The citizen proper, on the other hand, stood up for his simple rights and the collective body saw to it that judgment did not swerve from the generally known tradition. Then, however, came representatives (*Stellvertreter*) and ' Fürsprecher ' (*Prolocutores*); but these required no special knowledge of law and anyone of good reputation could be invoked as a Fürsprecher. Their co-operation, however, was by no means compulsory, except when there was a question of appearing for ' poor persons ' or the local law required it. After ' the Reception ' of the Justinianian Code " generally associated with Charles IV " this system broadly came into force.

The right to appear with the parties before the court and to represent their interest by word of mouth, or in writing now became the business of a specific rank of *Anwalt* in which membership could only be obtained by legists of good reputation after formal recognition by boards of judges (*Immatriculation*). No doubt non-advocates might appear in court as authorised agents *instead* of the parties but not *with* them and if they drew up documents to be used in court for which technical knowledge was required, for other people, or otherwise exercised an *Anwalt's* profession they were liable to penalties for bungling or ' hedge ' law (*Winkelschriftstellerei*)."

A few lines may be added from H. Brunner and J. Kohler (*z*). " In trials the principles of the strictest

---

(z) In *Holtzendorff's Ency. der Rechtswissenschaft*, I, 127 : III, 296 (1915).

word-interpretation applied. A mistake in speech, on the fundamental principle ' A Man, a Word ' could not be amended by the party. Hence people put up *Vorsprecher* (a) to speak for them, whose words the party was permitted in certain circumstances to disavow and to amend (Right of *Erholung u. Wandelung*). But in such a case the *Vorsprecher* paid a fine for having spoken without the authority of his *Herr* [*dominus*] and only in his own, without the right to do so. Only gradually was it understood that this rigidity of form defeated the ends of justice and sooner or later in one place or another this difficulty was got rid of or diminished.

While verbal (*im Worte*) representation was permitted, representation in a lawsuit, the conduct of a trial through a plenipotentiary (*Gewalthaber*), a plaintiff, an *apparitor* (*Klagbote*), counsel (*Anwalt*), one with power of attorney (*Machtmann*), *procurator* or *mandatarius*, was in general denied at this period even to independent (*selbstmündig ? sui juris*) persons. . . . Only very sporadically do municipal laws of the 13th century allow in certain circumstances the appointment of a representative and the handing over to another of the accusation."

" These *Sprech-Anwälte* stood (like the *advocati*) in antithesis to the *procuratores*, the representatives of absent parties and thus the *procuratores* made a *status* for themselves and the *advocati* for themselves " : the English and French distinction between two classes did not endure in Germany.

(a) Other early titles were "vorisprecho, fürsprech, redner, redesmann, spruchsman, sagibaco, asega, eosago, praelocutor " : Magnus, *die Rechtsanwaltschaft* 4 : the German Barristers' *Verein* : Berlin, 1925. According to A. Weiszler *Geschichte der Rechtsanwaltschaft* : Leipzig : 1905, p. 27, " *Vors.*" is correct not " *Fürsp*," *prae*locutor like *avant*parlier is a better translation; the speaker primarily speaks (*formulae*, etc.) *before* the party, *not in his favour*. It was the old fundamental German principle that the *Vorsprecher* was not the representative of the party : *ib*. p. 50.

A recent authority (*b*) says : " From the numerous notices of the 13th century, which may be regarded as substantially fixing [the date of] old Customary Law, the course of development which *Vorsprechertum* had taken in Austria as early as the 12th century may be approximately settled. As sources of law the *Sachsenspriegel* (*c*) (composed about 1260) and especially the *Schwabenspiegel* (1275) must be considered, the extraordinary diffusion of which in Austria points to their provisions being consonant with actual usage. Further the Austrian *Landrecht* (1236-7) the oldest Austrian legal record of private law mentions the *Vorsprecher* (§ 62) . . .

However, German law created two safety valves, which made it possible for the unpractised *Vorsprech* [originally not " learned "] to act without too great danger to himself or his party, *viz*., the institutions which in mediaeval diction were known as ' Holung and Wandel ' [calling in and changing] and ' Run u. Rat ' [Whispering and Counsel]." The former was the right to call in a *Vorsprecher* but to disclaim beforehand the adoption of everything he might say. The latter was the right asked of the court by the *Vorsprecher* to consult, if necessary, a third person out of court [*consilium*]; he would be a public consultant in law called, in Austria *Weiser* or *Steurer*. Other German names were " Rauner [whisperer; cf. *souffleur*] Ratgeber, Warner, Anweiser, Lauscher [listener], Horcher, Hörer, Währer, Bewahrer."

" Mediators " says Jannsen (*d*) of the period before the close of the Middle Ages " were allowed and accusers and accused were invited to have recourse to them. Any

---

(*b*) Fr. Kübl, *Geschichte der öster. Advokatur*, 22-4 : Graz, 1925.
(*c*) In which the *Vorsprecher* is always honorary, never professional and appointed *ad hoc* : Weiszler, above, p. 58.
(*d*) *Hist. of the German people at the close of the Middle Ages* : Eng. transln., London, 1896, v. II, p. 141. " This simple state of law procedure survived until about 1460 and preserved up to that time its thoroughly German character " : *ib*. p. 140.

irreproachable freeman had the right to present the case of his client to a judge but always in the presence of the client or his representative. Middlemen who in the absence of the interested parties furnished written accusations or proofs were unknown in those days. Nor was there yet any body of professional advocates who made their living out of law suits and whose interest it, therefore, was to stir them up. On this point the author of " Welschgattung " says : ' With us commentations on the law are unknown. There are no ambiguities in justice ; the poor man's protector is the law which God gave him. We tolerate no advocate. Neither money nor favour obtains a verdict : justice is not bought.' "

We may safely assume therefore, that Germany had no influence on the forensic movement in this country at any time. The only German in Wahrmund's list is Eilbert of Bremen (*e*), of whom the German scholars (*e*) think lightly (*f*).

Spain.

The earliest mention (*g*) of *abogados* is said to occur in regulations concerning them in the *Fuero de Cuenca* granted by Alfonso VIII when he took that city in 1177. They are expressly said to be " defenders—of whom there were many in the 12th century." This must refer to the clerical

---

(*e*) Savigny, *Geschich.* V. 168, by an odd mistake translates " Wolfkero Patavino Episcopo " to whom Eilbert dedicated his rhyme as Bp. of " Padua "; v. B.-H. 6 C. P. 109, has " Passau "; Du C. *Suppl. Gloss. Lat. Germ.* " Patauia (ciu. in bauaria) passaw."

(*f*) Possibly there was a traditional antipathy to lawyers in Germany. The curious story in Florus (Epitome, IV, 12, or II, 30) that when Arminius defeated Varus's army in 10 A.D. the soldiery wreaked their vengeance *praecipue . . . in causarum patronos* in the Roman ranks, is explained (Mommsen *Hist. Prov. of the Empire*, B. 8, c. 1, Eng. trans., pp. 35, 48) by " the barbarians' " hatred of the administration of the Roman law through Latin, which had been forced upon them by bands of legal officials. The parallel with Jack Cade's mob is obvious.

(*g*) *Dicc. Hisp., Amer.*, Barcelona, 1887 : *Abogado* and *Fuero* (from *forum*).

advocati with whom we are familiar in Christendom. According to the same authority (*h*) *El Fuero Real* is the first Spanish code in which there is a Title organizing and regulating the profession (*abogacia*) (*i*); about 1255-65, that is, soon after the *Especulo* (for judges) which, in its turn, derived from *el Fuero viejo de Castilla* (where the old defending *abogados* were mentioned). In Aragon and Valencia, there was a more rapid development (somewhat hostile to the lawyer) than elsewhere—attributed to their more intimate connection with Italy, whence undoubtedly both the lay and the clerical impulse came. These thirteenth century movements were all unified by Ferdinand III or his son Alfonso X.

Mariana ends c. 8 of the 13th book (*k*) of his *History* thus " Dishonesty (*calumnia*) gradually increasing and the number of law suits (*l*), it became necessary to establish a new *forum*, whereas formerly the cities were satisfied with their local courts or, at any rate, would, to get a decision in law, summon only tribunals of neighbours (*m*), and thought it indecorous and unreasonable to invoke royal support. Power, too, was given to the great men to make a code of [new, Sp. trans.] laws (*legum condendarum*), but always with the injunction that they should collect [the old ones; Sp. trans.] those vulgarly known as *Partitas* [*sic*]—a work of immense labour which was finally com-

---

(*h*) And R. St. Hilaire *Hist. d'Espagne*, B. 12, c. 2.

(*i*) The proem to Tit. VI of the 3rd *Partida* (see below) accounts naïvely for the origin of advocates; the old sages who made the laws knew that business (*pleytos* = placita, often = law suits) was better done and the judges better informed and they decided better when parties, plaintiffs or defendants, who through ignorance or fear or inability to deal with technicalities might easily lose their rights in the courts, were allowed to be represented by *abogados*.

In law XIV the same sages found by experience that when advocates had a stake in the property in issue, they stuck at nothing to win and so they ordained a fixed but reasonable fee, under severe sanctions.

(*k*) Latin, The Hague, 1733 : vol. 2, p. 99; Spanish, Madrid, 1669 : p. 512.

(*l*) " por la malicia del tiempo."

(*m*) " con apelar a las audiencias de su distrito."

pleted in the reign of Alfonso X," his father (St.) Ferdinand III who died in 1252, having designed it. As Ferdinand succeeded in 1230, his reign was well within the juridical renascence which began in Italy.

The *Siete Partidas* was begun in 1256 : the jurists commissioned used Justinian's Institutes and Pandects together with the Decretals as the *substratum* of their work, into which, in order to conciliate established usages they admitted extracts from the *fueros* (without acknowledgment) and the Gothic code (*n*).

The third *Partida*, Title VI, deals with *los abogados* (*o*). On this M. St. Hilaire (*p*) says : " Roman legislation introduced into Castile by Alonzo X soon brought *chicane* in its train : the legists who filled the chairs at the universities promoted with the zeal of interest the knowledge of Roman law : monks, clerks, laics, everybody devoted himself to this lucrative profession; these improvised counsel, pitchforking themselves (*s'entremettant*) into all suits, wore out the parties and the judges with their subtleties and their delays. In 1258 Alonzo X himself was forced by the repeated complaints of the *concejos* [Councils] to forbid parties to have more than one advocate. He, in arguing, was to stand up, in a respectful (*convenable*) posture and was not to insult the judges or the other side. The presence, however, of an advocate at the trial was not obligatory, except for the poor, to whom the alcalde assigned one officially. Soon the ever growing number of these ' processspinners " forced the author of the *Partidas* to constitute the *avogacia* a regular profession and the law fixed the conditions required for exercising it : 1° Examination and election by the judges and magistrates of the *commune* : 2° An oath taken by the elect faithfully to fulfil the duties

---

(*n*) Rosseeuw St. Hilaire *Hist. d'Espagne*, v. 4, B. 12, c. 2, p. 228, Paris, 1884, used in the text above.

(*o*) Title v deals with non-professional representatives who cannot or do not wish to be present in court—practically, the *procuratores*.

(*p*) *Ib*. p. 246.

of his profession : 3° inscription of name in a public register. Despite these wise provisions, the number of advocates went on increasing without stop and popular prejudice was everywhere aroused against them : a large number of the *concejos* refused to admit them and Alonzo X was obliged to allow the objecting *communes* to do without them and to try a case in the old-fashioned way."

The Title on Advocates (*q*) contains much the same

(*q*) Law 1 : *Bozero* (or *vozero* or *vocero* from vox) es ome que razone pleyto de otro juicio . . . : *razonar*, normally = to argue. This root in a forensic sense certainly comes from the *customary* Maritime Law of the Mediterranean, preferably from Italy rather than Spain (where it is not, as elsewhere, confined to maritime customs). If, as is generally believed, the Ordinances of Trani (4 *Black Book of the Admiralty*, 522 : Rolls, ed. Twiss) date from 1063 (*ib.* xvi, cxxxi) they contain the earliest instance, *viz.*, *rasone* = " magistrate " (p. 536 : *piu in arbitrio de la dicta rasone*)—rather " judgment [*ratio*] of the magistrate," as it comes after *andare dricto ala rasone de signoria* (p. 534). The instances of *raison* (*ib.* Index) in cc. 43-9 of the " Maritime Assises . . . of Jerusalem (set out *ib.* 499—519) part of the *Livre* . . . de la *Cour des Bourgeois*, v. 2, pp. 42-7, ed. Beugnot, seem to mean rather *rights* or *right* than *law* (which Twiss suggests : (*ib.* Index, p. 499), for that *Livre* uses also " lei " " droit " " assise." It is true that Beugnot (Glossary : vol. II) has " Raison—droit, prérogative " (but no instance from the maritime cc.). In *La Commune d'Oleron* (2 Black Book 255) dated by Twiss about 1314 (*ib.* xxv, xxxiv-v : possibly earlier, Vol. IV, p. cxxviii) we read : c. xlvi (II, p. 316) : " Si hom parlet en cort por autre, cil por qui il parlet ou sis [*his*] autres conseil, puet corriger ou revoquer ce que sis *raisoneres* aura dit, seil veit que il ne die son profiet, mas ce que la plainte [plaintiff] ou li citez* [= defendant] dit de sa propre boche, deit tenir fermete et estre estable. Si seret ol [= il] ausi ce qui li *raisonayres* dit si li clientons** aveit dil, ge tienc pòr dit ceu que il dira. Mas si aiosteit [adjusts a question] sans lou [= le] commandement de me ou de mon conseil, adonques li clientons ou sis conseilz poent amander au *raysouneor* desique les parties se commandent juger. *Raisouneor** apelon plaideor qui parlet por autre. Clienton* apelon celuy por cuy hom parlet por autre en cort."

The procedure, these terms and the fact that *client* has to be defined, to say nothing of the dialect, point to a great antiquity. In c. 20, p. 284, *ib.* the attorney is recognised but not *by name*. Oleron was part of the patrimony of Eleanor of Guienne, wife of Henry II : she died in 1204 and had much to do with the original grant of a charter to Oleron. Thus English influence may have affected local maritime law; though Twiss (II, IX) seems to think that it was " the merchants and mariners of Spain and of France who frequented British ports " that " brought with them many traditions of maritime law." At any

material as we have seen in the various *Ordines Judiciarii*. The code (l. 3) is very emphatic in disqualifying any woman "however (wise or) learned" (*sabidora*) from practising, "for two reasons; it is not decent for a woman to compete publicly with men, in arguing for another : then because the sages in the past prohibited it after their experience of Calfurnia." This story seems to have had a fascination for Latin jurists (*r*).

Among those disqualified is the *paid* fighter with wild animals "for it is certain" that such a man would not scruple to commit fraud or do wrong "in the pleas" for money : *aliter*, if he does it from courage and gratuitously (law 4). Treachery to a client might be a capital offence (l. 15) (*s*).

M. St. Hilaire is (at any rate) justified in saying that Title VI of this Part (III) is borrowed almost entirely from the Digest, sometimes from the *fueros*. Almost every line in it could be cited from the Bolognian jurists (say, William of Drogheda, possibly known in Spain by 1255) we have mentioned. Exactly as in our own and other countries we gather from the legislation the mischiefs aimed at in professional life : the Spanish jurists either copied the

---

rate, the word (*r*.) never established itself in England. The same code (*ib*. 377-8) has : "Ne hom qui est plaideeres en cele meisme cause ne puet estre garanz a celuy por cuy il plaideet, car tan gent sunt soupeconos a porter garantage par la partie que il sostenent; mas li plaideor sunt ben recegu en garantage contre laverse partie." (*Ib*. p. 341. "Home qui vait a conseil dautre en son plait ne puet mie apres porter garentie avers laverse partie"—very difficult to understand; the translation throws no light.)

(*r*) Dig. III, i, § 5 : feminas prohibet [praetor] pro aliis postulare et ratio quidem prohibendi ne contra pudicitiam sexui congruentem alienis causis se immisceant ne virilibus officiis fungantur mulieres : origo vero introducta est a Carfania improbissima femina quae inverecunde postulans et magistratum inquietans causam dedit edicto.

Valerius Maximus has a chapter (VIII, 3) *de mulieribus quae causas apud magistratus egerunt*, where *Carfania* is called *Afrania*; the other two he praises. *Calphurnia's* story is repeated *O. J. incert. auct.* Grosz, p. 95, Pt. I, c. 4, § 2 : p. 403.

(*s*) See also *Part*. III, Tit. 16, § 20; V. 8, § 9; VII, 6, § 7; 7, § 1.

specific sanctions or learned the same lessons from experience as their brethren elsewhere.

i. Students.

The history of education in London has yet to be written. But in all cities where there was a church, at any rate a conventual church there was a school. That of St. Paul's is first mentioned (*t*) in (about) 1112. The Church has always guarded its schools jealously and a charter of 1134-41, which Mr. Round has unearthed (*u*) from Henry of Blois, Bishop of Winchester, Stephen's brother, to the Chapter of St. Paul's is typical of its vigilance : they are to pronounce sentence of anathema on any one who without the licence of " Henry Master of the Schools " presumes in the whole city of London to read (*legere* = teach school : Macdonnell) except the masters of St. Mary-le-Bow and St. Martin le Grand.

That Henry III, therefore, in 1235 should deal with these schools is not surprising but the contents of one Order (*x*) have never been satisfactorily explained : " The Mayor and Sheriffs of London are enjoined to proclaim stringently throughout the City that no master (*regens*) of a law school in that City should for the future " teach law (*leges*) : and if any one there is keeping that sort of school they must stop him at once. Selden was convinced that this decree did not include *English* law : other studies, he shows, had long flourished in London especially at St. Paul's (and incidentally he has no doubt that *advocati* who were clerics versed in " Caesarean," " Pontifical "

(*t*) Harl. MSS. 6956 : *History of St. Paul's School* (1909) 1 : by M. F. J. Macdonnell.
(*u*) *Commune of London*, p. 117 ; and see Macdonnell, p. 2.
(*x*) *De scola legum in civitate Lond*' : *Rot. Claus* : 19 H. III, p. 26, m. 22 (1808) ; *Cal. Close R.* (1234-7) ; 1 Bl. *Comm.* 24 ; Selden *ad Fletam*, c. 8, 2 where the title is " de scolis [? *scolas*] regentibus de leg. etc." and there is a slight variation in the text of *Close R.* : 1 P. & M., I, c. IV, p. 102.

and " Anglican " law practised in secular courts—*forum omnimodum*). But Coke (*y*) seems to think that it did refer to home law; " this Writ," he says, " took no better effect than it deserved." Blackstone agrees with Coke and thinks its " intention is . . . by preventing private teachers within the walls of the city, to collect all the common lawyers into the one public university, which was newly instituted in the suburbs " (*sic*): whereas, " if the civil law only is prohibited . . . it is then a retaliation upon the clergy who had excluded the common law from *their* seats of learning " (!).

Stubbs (*z*) agrees with Selden and Prynne, who " pointed out that " Coke's view " was inconceivable and that doubtless the Laws were the Civil and Canon laws. I think that under the term *Leges* both civil and canon law were intended, but certainly at the moment the danger from the canon law was greater. In 1230 Gregory IX had approved of the five books of the Decretals codified by Raymund of Pennafort. . . . In 1236 [is] the beginning of the Codex receptus of Canon Law in England in spite of the Council of Merton and the closing of the law schools of London."

Pollock and Maitland hesitate between two views, one that the writ was part of a movement in favour of ecclesiastical reform, the London schools being " primarily

---

(*y*) 2 *Inst.* Proeme : to *Magna Carta* and the *Carta de Foresta*. Of Waterhous's explanation (*Commentary on Fortescue*, p. 523 (1663), on c. 48 : by " Glanvil " he can only mean Bart. de Glanvil : 2 Foss, 354), it suffices to say that no one else has even hinted at any such " influence " : " When by the influence of the renowned judges Vere, Glanvil, Lucy and others, Gentlemen of great families and interest in the Nation, the scholes of Canon and Civil before and in that time publiquely kept in London and elsewhere were put down . . . about . . . 1234 . . . then I conceive these *publica studia* of the Law took root and sprouted more in a few yeares then before they had done."

(*z*) *Seventeen Lectures* (1900), c. 13, p. 353. It is difficult to understand *ib.* the King's " order which stands in close parallelism with the banishment of Vacarius." Was he banished from Oxford? Prof. de Zulueta in the *Life*, 44 Seld. Soc., does not mention it.

theological," the other, that "Henry is protecting the
Oxford law school against competition"; the King, by the
way, had been in Oxford in 1233 and had been generous to
it (*a*). About this time he founded a *Domus Conversorum*
there and in Chancery Lane. At any rate, these authorities scout the idea that the *leges* were "English—we shall
hear nothing of English law being taught for a very long
time to come."

Blackstone's bold statement that there was in 1234 " a
public university . . . newly instituted in the suburbs "
of the City—to say nothing of Waterhous's " few yeares "
—harmonises well with another (*b*) of his, which is also
misleading,—that the effect of John's (and Henry III's (*c*))
fixing the Common Pleas at Westminster was to bring
together " the professors of municipal laws who before were
dispersed about the Kingdom and formed them into an
aggregate body whereby a society of persons was established," to wit, of lawyers.

" . . . In consequence of this lucky assemblage they
naturally fell into a kind of collegiate order and * being
excluded from Oxford and Cambridge * found it necessary
to establish a new university of their own." Now the
concentration at Westminster of 1215 no doubt gradually
encouraged lawyers there and in London generally, but to
call them an " university " at that date or a provision in
1234 a deliberate effort to promote it, is to make too
symmetrical a picture of what was a process, to which,
indeed, possibly, but by no means certainly, the event of
1234 contributed. But so far as we know, the mandate
at the time attracted no attention.

But if we could take Blackstone's account literally it
would be very consonant with the ascertained facts fifty

(*a*) Stow, *Annales*, ed. Howes (1631), p. 183.
(*b*) 1 *Comm.* 23.
(*c*) 1 *St. R.* 22 (1224-5).
* * Unless this is a rhetorical statement that common law was
not taught there, it is difficult to know what it means.

years later. The disbanded learners were not schoolboys, who would not study law, and at any rate, would not be the objects of a royal decree. That instrument implies some importance in its scope; the technical words *scolas regens* are used twice, and it is reasonable to suppose that the numbers of the law students were not insignificant, as indeed we should expect of the City in 1234. If their ambition was to learn municipal law with a view to becoming practitioners, probably (though it cannot be said certainly) they could have found teachers within their own walls, but as yet we do not hear of apprentices—at this time they are silently growing up. But it is very improbable that they were young common lawyers (for interfering with whom there would be no motive), and it has been generally assumed that they were pursuing the traditional courses and that if they wished to continue therein they were perforce driven outside the City where the mandate was not in force, but as near to it as possible. This happy guess is expressed by Waterhous (*d*) thus : " It is probable at first men that studied the Common Laws dwelt and lodged in diffusion, where being far from the Courts of Westminster and uncertain to be found by those that desired their skill and advice, they to avoid that trouble to themselves and their clyents did associate and joyn their studies and lodgings each to other, which in time came to be accounted *studium publicum;* all of the Profession resorting to the common residence, and so making one publick presence of Law and Lawyers. After as they encreased, men of name withdrawing themselves for convenience of more room and better air, as their Clyents followed them, so also young Students, admirers of them, joyned themselves to them, till at last by time and agreement they grew into some proportion of a body, which had

---

(*d*) As above, p. 522. He complains that his "friends of the Long Robe" gave him no assistance : he was a "cock-brain'd man" (A. Wood in *D. N. B.*), and not a lawyer.

so much of Head and members, Lawes and Servants, as are necessary to a subsistence of Honour, and a perpetuation of Being."

If there was a migration *en masse*, no place was more convenient than the well-watered country round Holborn, as Stow (in 1603) speaks (*e*) of it in his day, quoting and adopting Fitz Stephen [in H. II's reign] " . . . Amongst which (wells), Holywell, Clarkes wel and Clements well are most famous and frequented by Scholars and youthes of the Citie in summer evenings when they walke forth to take the aire." We know that in 1375 about one of these spots (Clement's) Ficket's field was the playground of London (*f*). And if in 1234 law students already waited on the lawyers in the Parvise of St. Paul's they would not have far to go.

At any rate, we do in fact find about 1300 little colonies of practisers or readers of law settled between the City and Westminster, some of which ground is still " Law land."

Thus there is a gap between 1234 and 1275, when " apprentices " are perhaps referred to in a statute and (soon after, at latest) certainly mentioned by Fleta. That interval witnessed the development of the *narrator*, the *serviens* and the *attornatus* (to say nothing of the improvements in the administration of justice); the simultaneous growth of " a fringe " was inevitable. But, as so often happens, we must reckon back from the known to the probable. " By stages," says Maitland (*g*), " that are exceedingly obscure, the inns of court and inns of Chancery were growing." But are the stages more obscure than those of other ancient universities?

(*e*) Ff. 15, 424: vol. 1, p. 15 and v. 2, p. 70: Kingsford's edn. (1908).
(*f*) *Cal. Clôse R.* 1375, p. 210, m. 40 d.
(*g*) 2 *Coll. Papers*, 482, from *Social England* (1893).

ii. Clerici.

Another historical line converges to the same point. The " New Temple " (*h*), now " the Temple," London, had been used as a depository for treasures including Records since about 1200 and the Temple Church for some chattels even earlier (*i*); " . . . during the second half of the 13th century . . . the departmental activity of the Chancery is seen to be transferred to a new centre, the later Chapel of the Rolls, which may thus be regarded as superseding the old official establishment of the King's chapel at Westminster or elsewhere. The nature of this change is involved in the greatest obscurity, but it is perhaps possible to connect it with the financial operations of the Crown associated with the Temple and the strategical importance of the Tower during the civil wars of the period "; there was a " settlement of Chancery clerks in the houses adjacent to the *Domus Conversorum* " in Chancery Lane. In view of Selden's remark (*k*), Mr. Hall's note helps us. " There was also in the 13th century a close connexion between the King's clerks and the Church of St. Paul's." His text goes on : " It is certainly curious that the later judicial overflows both of

---

(*h*) 1119, Hugh de Payens establishes the first English house of the Templars in Holborn; 1185, it is transferred to the New Temple; 1312, the Pope dissolves the Order. The earliest (?) English form, " Temple Barre," is in 1381 by the contemporary Walseingham, 1 *Hist.* 457; or *Chron. Angliae*, 289 (both Rolls). In the will of Edmund Paston (1449), 1 Gairdner, *P. L.* 79, W. Mayes is called " Magister Novi Templi." " The Bar of the New Temple " occurs in 1338 : *Cal. Plea and Memor. Rolls*, 189, ed. Thomas; and " Chauncelereslane," *ib.* 188, both Latin documents; and, *ib.* 109, in 1339 " dwelling in the Rents of St. John of Clerkenwell within the Bar of the New Temple," described as a sort of " Alsatia." " Novum Templum " occurs 1 *Rot. Litt. Claus.* 128 d, in 1212; 2 *Rot. L. C.* 107, in 1226; in 1440 it is " templum jurisperitorum " : Will. of Worcester, *Annales*, 762; 22 Rolls, v. 3; in 1459, *ib.* 772, Roger Nevyle is " legis peritus de Templo."

(*i*) Hubert Hall, *Eng. Off. Hist. Docts.* 18ff. : Cambridge, 1908
(*k*) P. 423.

clerks and Records were in the same direction. In both cases probably the neighbourhood of Chancery Lane was the site most readily available for this purpose."

At what precise moment *clericus* = clerk in holy orders and *clericus* = merely scribe, were distinguished it is not worth inquiring, but the *dégringolade* is interesting to historians (*l*). Bracton, speaking of vitiated writs, supposes (*m*) the peccant falsification to have been made in the Chancery or " by another person such as the clerk of the sheriff " (*cler. vic.*); and elsewhere (*m*) of the forgetfulness of the *clerici de banco* and a " clerical " error in the rolls : human fallibility is not confined to Chancery clerks.

Fleta, of course, copies Bracton and (II, 13 *de Cancellaria*) says : " The Chancellorship ought to be committed to a prudent and grave man such as a Bishop or Clerk (*clerico*) of great standing, with charge of the Great Seal of the Kingdom, whose substitutes are all the chancellors (*n*) in England, Ireland, Wales and Scotland, and all keepers of King's seals everywhere, besides the keeper of the private seal; with him should be associated respectable and responsible *clerici*, sworn servants of the King with more knowledge of the laws and customs of England then other people [the *legaliter expertos* of § 14], whose business it is to hear complaints and examine petitions and to provide by royal writs a remedy for the alleged damage. . . . Mistakes [*or, perhaps*, erasures only] in writs may arise through a ' clerical ' error (*o*) due to the

---

(*l*) See Du Cange on the word : Selden on *Fleta*, c. 9, p. 541, ed. 1647.

(*m*) *De Ass. Nov. Dis.* c. xx, 3; p. 208, 3 Rolls, f. 188a; 2 *N. B.* 315; 3 *N. B.* 457.

(*n*) For the plural see p. 168.

(*o*) *E.g.*, in 1374 there were long proceedings to amend " concanonicus " where the writ had " comonachus," and " Ralph " had been written for " Robert " : *Cal. Close Rolls*, 9; 2 *Rot. Parl.* 461. About the same time Bromyard was writing (*Adv.* 38A) : habens in banco causam si advocatus deficiet in uno vocabulo quod non est ad rei

Chancellor's *clericus,* who really has authority, or to the audacity of a judge's or sheriff's clerk who has been ' got at ' by one of the parties, in which case all active or passive accomplices are to be punished as forgers. . . . In that office (*officio,* sc. Chancery) the King has his six clerks —*praenotarios*—who are like the others above mentioned part of the King's family (*familiares Reg.*) especially in living and dress (*pro victu et vestitu*) who are so called [*clerici* prae*notarii*] because they have to frame the writs according to nature of the litigation and all of them ought to be fairly found for livelihood and attire from the fees of the Seal, to whosesoever use the writs have issued (*p*). There are, too, youthful *clerici* of inferior rank (*pedites*) who issue the ' cursory ' writs, but always after calling in (*advocatione*) the superior clerks who adopt the formers' writs at their own peril . . . and lest the former should try to get a surreptitious (*superflua*) profit for their drafts the rule is that judges' clerks as well as those of the Chancery must not get more then one *denarius* for each writ they make " (*q*).

We notice in the transit from Bracton to Fleta that the supposed failing of the clerks has changed from mere clerical error to fabrication, which, in that interval, we had occasion to notice elsewhere.

Now, in 1232 Henry III founded and built the *Domus Conversorum* in (or near) what is now Chancery Lane in London. In 1290 Edward I " directs his Chancellor to

---

notificationem nec ad majorem rei justiciam habendam seu ab eis usitatum sicut . . . in narrando nominet tempus et annum regis si non addat " quem deus salvet," breve perditur et quidquid circa illud expendit.

(*p*) The grammar is obscure : quia ad brevia scribenda secundum diversitates querelarum sunt intitulati; et qui omnes pro victu et vestitu de proficuo sigilli in cujuscunque usus provenerint, debent honeste inveniri. Is the point of *intitulati* that *prae*(not) means special responsibility? for all the *clerici* wrote *brevia sec. div.*, etc. What is the subject of *provenerint*? Does *inveniri*=provided with?

(*q*) II, 36, *de clericis* deals with judges' clerks (much as above); perhaps *de hospitio* there includes *clerici* as in II, 14 : p. 219.

provide " a proper keeper. " This is noteworthy; there is a mysterious connection between the office of Master of the Rolls and the office of Keeper . . . for some time before the formal union of those offices in " 1377 " and I think this direction of Edward I may explain it " (r). The Master of the Rolls was one of the Chancellor's principal officers. In 1377 William de Burstall Keeper was made M.R.; " there was evidently a connection between the offices long before their formal union "; 1300 would, perhaps, not be too early. It must be admitted that the evidence is meagre, but Mr. Hall's conclusion (ib.) is: " From the end of the 13th century, then, we find the Chancery Records in current use preserved in the vicinity of the Inns of Court where the Chancery masters and clerks had their habitation. Owing to the departmental character of the business of this Court, the custody of writs and returns, petitions and pleadings, was naturally assumed by particular clerks or groups of clerks. Probably the line which divided the King's clerks from a college of notaries and the latter in turn from a corporation of cursitors was not very sharply drawn in the 14th century. . . . Now the Chapel of the *Domus Conversorum* . . . served this purpose [a readily accessible repository] admirably. From the year 1307 we can date the long succession of Chancery clerks who were at once keepers of the *Domus Conversorum* and of the Rolls of Chancery." Mr. Williams quotes (s) an instance of a man coming " into Chancery . . . in the chapel of the House of Converts " in 1299.

Thus we are led to the suggestion that between 1234 and (say) 1310 the two colonies, of law students from the

---

(r) *A History of the Rolls House and Chapel*, by W. J. Hardy, p. 11 (1896), reprinted from *Midsx. and Hertford N. & Q.*

(s) *Staple Inn*, p. 59 (1906), citing *Close Rolls*, 22 E. I, m. 11 d. [p. 384]. But when, *ib.* p. 60, it is stated "The Calendars of Patent Rolls for the 13th and 14th centuries contain scores of references to the Chancery being held in the neighbourhood of Holborn," search does not at all bear out this assertion for the 13th century.

City, and law clerks from Westminster, met and mingled in the intermediate ground about Holborn and lived in houses which before or since have been known as Inns.

That this was so in 1375 is vouched by a " touch of nature," *viz.* : " *Memorandum* (*t*) that lately a loud complaint as well of the Clerks of Chancery and the apprentices of the King's Court as of others of the people of the City of London being made before the Council that one Roger Leget has privily put and hidden engines of iron called ' caltrappes ' upon a dike by him newly raised in Fikettsfeld by the Bishop of Cicestre's Inn where the said clerks apprentices and others used to have their common sport . . . knowing that every day the said clerks apprentices and others came forth to play their common games there." In other words, Roger " queered the pitch "—now almost the site of the Bankruptcy Court—of Chancery *v*. Common Law; both sides were young, they lived within a stone's throw of one another and they played together.

If further indications are wanted of the existence of communities of youths in the neighbourhood, it is to be found in the " Town and Gowns." In 1338 four named Chancery clerks of the King were found by a jury (*u*) to have committed several crimes including housebreaking in Holborn. The " row " was no doubt of the same nature as the " great fray " in 1459 (by no means the last) between the City of London and " men of Cowrte which were drevyn with the Archeres of the Cite from the

---

(*t*) *Cal. Close Rolls*, 1375, p. 210. Mr. G. J. Turner, in 42 Seld. Soc., xl, states that here *appr.* perhaps=member of an Inn of Chancery; but the record over and over again distinctly opposes the " clerks " (the only " Chancery " men mentioned) to the *appr.*

(*u*) *Cal. Plea and Mem. Rolls*, ed. Thomas, p. 183. A similar entry, *ib.* p. 213, in 1344 : " certain apprentices of the King's Bench," *viz.*, two named Irishmen and John de Worcester, " were common evildoers who lay in wait at night and robbed passers by of their belts and purses."

Standarde in Flete Strete to ther innes ... some were slayne and some were taken " (*x*).

As early as 1180 the Chancellor was employing *clerici*, as we know from the *Dialogus de Scaccario*. No doubt their numbers grew as the business increased and they, too, became a hierarchy (*y*). As time went on there were grades of civil servants (*z*). Foss (*a*) regards the " Chancellors' Deputies authenticating Charters " as " simply clerks in the Chancery "; from 1199 for some years they are always archdeacons. In 1200 Hugh de Wells and John de Brancestre " two archdeacons were subordinate officers, a little perhaps above the clerks of the wax "; in 1206 Adam de Essex, a chaplain of the King was (perhaps) *clericus* or *magister scriptorii* or *scriptor rotuli cancellariae*. Even the lower posts were worth having. In 1243 Henry III writes (*b*) from France to his Chancellor, Walter, archbishop of York : " It was never the King's intention to revoke his grace to G. de Wulward and his fellows, clerks of the chancery, or to others to whom he had once granted a provision to be made, and he again commands him to provide for them, as soon as he can, in the form in which he has written for several of the same clerks, only giving preference over them to Nicholas Lungespe." In 1264 at Lewes, a few days before the battle, there is (*c*) an

---

(*x*) *A Short Engl. Chron.* 71, Camden Soc. N. S. no. 28, probably written under E. IV.

(*y*) In Normandy under Richard le bon it was always " a gentleman, the clerk, who drives the pen in Chancery " : Palgrave, 3 *Normandy*, 38 (1864).

(*z*) " The highest in rank among them we might fairly call ' under secretaries of state '. . . . The almost mechanical work of penning these ordinary writs was confided to clerks who stood low in the official hierarchy, to cursitors (*cursarii*) . . . ": 1 P. & M. pp. 172, 174, B. I, c. 6. In Banco, says Fleta, II, 36, " sunt clerici praenotarii et cursarii qui placita irrotulant et brevia faciunt judicialia necnon cyrographarii." (*a*) *Judges*, ii, 14, 23.

(*b*) *Cal. Pat. R.* 1232-47, p. 378 (English).

(*c*) *Ib.* 1258-66, p. 317 (" K. King of Almain " is a misprint for

acquittance to Louis King of France, expressed to be *per ipsum Regem Alemanniae* [Richard, Earl of Cornwall and King of the Romans], Edward [afterwards E. I], Henry son of the King of Alemannia [Germany], etc., etc., and " others of the King's Council." *Magister* " Arnulf, Chancellor of the King of Almain, dictated and wrote with his own hands the above letter without the counsel and assent of any clerk of the Chancery. . . ."

In 1265 (d) there is dated March 26 a " Grant to Thomas de Cantilupe elected to be chancellor of the realm by the King and the magnates of the council, of 500 marks a year for the maintenance of himself and the clerks of the chancery . . . the King with his own hand folded this writ." From 1261 there is mention (e) by name of serjeants of the rolls of the Chancery," *i.e.*, they required a custodian.

That some of the clerks began " at the bottom of the ladder " is shown by one incident in 1253. Henry in an angry speech (f) to his prelates says : " Do not forget that I raised Boniface here, Archbishop of Canterbury, to his present post and you William of Salisbury I promoted from the bottom, you, who were a scribbler of my writs and as a hireling justicier took part in many a dangerous judgment (g). And you Sylvester of Caerleon [Carlisle] who after long beslavering the chancery of my clerks became a

---

" R."); *Foedera* (Rymer, 1704), v. I, p. 789; edn. 1816, v. I, p. 440 : both Latin.

(d) *Cal. Pat. R.* 1258-66, p. 416.

(e) *Ib.* 195, etc. But " the King's serjeants in the Chancery " (*Cal. Close R.* 39) in 1374 may be lawyers.

(f) The sentiment is his though the words may be the historian's.

(g) M. Paris, *Chron. Maj.* v. 5, 374; ed. Wats. 866; cited 1 P. & M., B. I, c. vi, n. (p. 184 or 205) : " qui meorum brevium scriptitor extitisti et multis judiciis periculosis tanquam justitiarius et conductitiis interfuisti." What is the print of *periculosis*? It is not explained by P. & M. or D. N. B. (*William of York*) or 2 Foss, 525; apparently it = risky, doubtful, or even corrupt.

pettifogging *clericus* yourself (h), I raised to a bishopric." Others became judges. "These clerical lawyers," says Maitland (i), "are memorable, for the very rapid development of English law in the first seventy years of the 13th century was in great measure due to the fact that the *causidici* were also *clerici*, men whose education had been liberal and catholic and who were not ashamed to learn from all quarters. From that time onward the quality of the English lawyer's intellect became steadily worse and for two centuries after Bracton's death [c. 1268] not a law-book was written worthy to be kept in the same room as Bracton's book." And of the great ancient the great modern further said (k): "he may well have got his law, as some of his greatest contemporaries got theirs, namely as a clerk in the King's court and the King's chancery. To suppose that he made his fame by 'practising at the bar' would probably be an anachronism." That there could be no more likely nursery for the bar as we know it from 1250 to 1400 than the offices of the Chancery is almost self-evident. Perhaps the importance and opportunities of the officials is indicated by a false charge brought against one in 1313 that he " took gifts from the men of London for proroguing and hindering the King's rights " (l). By 1318, at any rate, the Holeburn Chancery is in full swing. On June 18 Edward II delivered the great seal to John de Hothum, Bishop of Ely, the Chancellor " who opened it in his inn of Holeburn on the Monday following . . . in the presence of the clerks of the chancery and sealed writs with it " (m). Holborn still

---

(h) " diu lambens cancellariam clericorum meorum ciericulus extitisti."
(i) *Pleas of the Crown* (Glos.) 1221, p. xii : 1884.
(k) 1 Br. *N. B.* 18.
(l) *Cal. Close Rolls,* 563.
(m) 2 *Close Rolls,* 11 E. II, m. 3 d., p. 619. So in 1340 Robert of Stratford at an Inn, "probably but by no means certainly" Lincoln's Inn: G. J. Turner, *Lincoln's Inn,* 15 (1903).

attests its connection with the diocese by Ely Place (*n*) and with another by " Chichester Rents " (*o*).

We see these officials " in real life " in a mandate of 1329 addressed to the Mayor of London, who had shut up a passage to the river through the New Temple, but who is bidden to open it " for the judges and *clericis nostris* and others, who are about their business in Westminster whither they desire to take water," and in another of 1330 with the same purpose *clericis de cancellaria nostra et aliis ministris nostris* (*p*).

Another mark of natural and healthy growth is the increasing notice of the social standing of these civil servants. Without taking Henry III's rude allocution to the bishops at its " face value," it is clear that a law clerk, who was a mere scribe, was, in his early days, a very humble personage. By Fleta's time, as we have seen, his emoluments and living have become a matter for the authorities; he is expected to keep up a certain style and must be provided for accordingly, unless he is a mere copyist, *de cursu*; there were, as to-day, " first class clerks " in the office, for example Hoccleve.

Thus in 1312 the Chancellor is enjoined (*q*) to keep

(*n*) William of Longchamp, Chancellor 1189-97, was also Bishop of Ely and " owner of the Fair held at the Bar of the Old Temple in Holborn " : Williams, *Staple Inn*, 1906. His successor Eustace was also Bishop of Ely.

(*o*) Henry III gave a house there to " Ralph *de nova villa* Chancellour of England and Bp. of Chichester and he built there a faire house for him "[self] : Sir G. Buc.

(*p*) Rymer, 4 *Foedera*, 406, 464, edn. 1707 : *Close R.* 4 E. III, m. 7.

(*q*) *Rot. Claus.* 5 E. II, m. 21; 2 E. III, m. 23; thereafter payment is often ordered to him for such expenses. In 1317, *Pat.* 10 E. II, pt. 2, m. 10; Madox, 1 *Exch.* 76, the " epicurism " (Campbell, I *Chanc.* 195, c. 12) of the Chancellor was provided for by order to buy poultry, but it was *pro sustentatione ipsius* . . . *et clericorum r. de eadem cancell.*; and so perhaps the grants of 1350 : *Cal. Close R.* 173, 444. In 1325, *Rot. Claus.* 19 E. II, m. 29 d., p. 503, the Earl of Chester (afterwards E. III) being at Dover was lodged in the " Maison Dieu," where " by ancient custom when the chancery was there " was the Ch.'s and his clerks' hotel; this the Earl did not know; when he found it out he put it on record that his stay was not to be a precedent. Foss *ib.* states that the clerks were called *magister* because they were

hospicium pro clericis. Foss (III, 191) gives some interesting instances tending to show that the superior officials live " like gentlemen "—" *pro victu et vestitu* "— habits continued to this day.

The seal, so to say, is put on this class when Parliament recognises them.

The 2nd Statute of Westminster, 13 E. I, 1285, c. 24, which invented the famous writ *in consimili casu*, goes on : " And whensoever from henceforth it shall fortune in the Chancery that in one Case a writ is found and in like Case falling under like Law and requiring like Remedy none is found, the clerks of the Chancery shall agree in making the Writ (*concordent clici de Cancellaria*) . . ."; if they fail to agree, *juris periti* shall be called in; the clerks are not yet authorities.

This clause presupposes the ordinary duties of the clerks of the Chancery. The most important of all was, of course, the framing and issuing of writs.

About a hundred years later we know that such legal training as there was out of court consisted in the science of writs and thus it came about that the clerks in chancery were the first *class* of elementary law teachers. Now, " the last years of Henry III's day we may regard as the golden age of the forms " (*r*). In Henry II's time (*s*), " As yet the King is no mere vendor, he is a manufacturer and can make goods to order; the day has not yet come when the invention of new writs will be hampered by the claims of a parliament; but still in Glanvill's day the *officina justitiae* has already a considerable store of ready-made wares and English law is already taking the form of

---

in orders; hence later " master in chy.," earliest in 1325 " mestres et le compaignouns de la ch." *Rot. Parl.* I, 418, F. III, 334, cites 2 *Rot. Parl.* 41 (1331), where clerks are called *méstres de la ch.* and other clerks are of the Exch. and the two benches; certain livings are the perquisites of (all) these clerks *only*. Their robes are provided : *Foedera* [1825] v. iii, p. 2, 196 (1357); superior clerks were perhaps limited to twelve in 1376; see 3 Foss, Index.

(*r*) 2 P. & M. p. 562; II, ix, § i.   (*s*) *Ib.* I, c. 5, p. 130.

a commentary upon writs." Again (*t*) " it was rather by decisions of the courts and by writs penned in the chancery that English law was being constructed . . . a new form of action might be easily created. A few words said by the chancellor to his clerks—' Such writs as this are for the future to be issued as of course '—would be as effectual as the most solemn legislation. As yet there would be no jealousy between the justices and the chancellor nor would they easily be induced to quash his writs." Hence we need not distinguish between common law and Equity writs. " The chancery had not yet fallen so far apart from the courts of law that the justices could not get new writs made if they wanted them " (*u*). " In its final form almost every message order or mandate, whether it concerned the greatest matter or the smallest . . . was a document settled in the chancery " (*x*). Moreover there was not much legislation to distract the learner.

The legislative oath (*y*) of 1344 or 1346 shows a development consistent with other progress. The writ is still " the thing," everything in fact : the enormous importance of the clerks as Keepers of the Seal to the Crown is recognised and they are straitly enjoined to do their duty—incidentally to the people, as well. The lowest grade, too, *de cursu*— must swear to permit no irregularity. Their detailed duties seem to be almost mechanical—they have nothing like the discretion of the superior grade who in case of doubt are bidden to consult the Chancellor, whereas the former are subject to several named officials. Especially it seems the second class clerks had to do with parties who came into the office ; apparently, a particular evil they had to guard against was the application by *attornati* for writs on behalf of parties from whom they had not authority.

(*t*) *Ib*. I, 149 ; B. I, c. 5.
(*u*) *Ib*. p. 175 ; B. I, c. 6.
(*x*) *Ib*. p. 173.
(*y*) 1 *St. R*. 306. *Book of Oaths*, 6 ; mentioned in § 22 of the *Renovacio*.

The institution has waxed to this day. In 1374 Knyvet, Chancellor, gets an order (z) for " the arrears of his fee of wine which he takes of the King for the expenses of the inn of Chancery "—where this phrase occurs for the first time. These few sumptuary details, which could be multiplied, point to the social standing of the *clerici* which was ultimately to make intermixture or clubbing together with the nascent " bar " easy and fertile of results. Indeed, it was the domestic arrangements of the clerks of the Chancery which were the germs of the modern system.

That system is known as the Inns of Court; it is rudimentary in 1300 and established in 1400, as we shall see. The known facts about the clerks of the Chancery account for their professional and social organization being earlier than that of the mere law students, and when the latter came into the neighbourhood, they have no other model for a collective home but that of those clerks, who were, indeed, sometimes their hosts; if there was to be fraternity, what other model was possible?

Now we possess in a document (a) of 1388-9 a picture of what such a college had become by that date. It is an Order of the Chancery and purports to be agreed between the Chancellor, Thomas de Arundel (Bishop of Ely) and " the twelve *clerici de prima forma ad robas in Cancellaria* " and to deal with their number and conduct; evidently the office was so supremely important that it had to be regulated minutely. It shows an easy and natural development from the isolated and widespread facts with

---

(z) *Cal. Close R.* 9; no doubt one particular inn is meant.

(a) Printed only in *Orders in Chancery*, v. I, p. 1; ed. G. W. Sanders, 1845; it is evidently a revised edition, accumulated out of earlier Orders. A later edition or " Renovacio " between 1413-22, *ib.* p. 7b, does not add much to our information. The language of the former, partly owing to this conflation, is not always clear (and perhaps has sometimes been misunderstood above); it is only cited here on the point of internal organisation; for its substance see *The Household of the Chancery* by Prof. Tout in *Essays . . . presented to R. L. Poole*, Oxf. 1927.

which we have just been dealing and clearly points to accumulated stages of growth; indeed it expressly preserved ancient usage at several points; notably it provides for (and uses the phrases of) the oath attributed to 1344-6. At whatever moment groups outside the chancery wanted a precedent for a common life they could find it there. The first legal " Inn " was certainly the Inn of the Chancery.

The Chancery had now reached a point, in a course with which other legal societies had been running parallel, for some sixty or seventy years and this document happens to be the best available evidence—by analogy—for the internal life of those societies.

The sumptuary regulations suggest a definite social standing, indeed, more than one, just as long ago Fleta (*b*) had done. The " big " twelve are " to live in their own *hospitia* or those hired by them in common or individually and not among others of a lower grade or *status*, in view of the dignity of their office and rank under pain of expulsion from the Court (*curia*). And the *clerici de secunda forma* shall " similarly " live together and not " beneath them," *i.e.*, decently according to their means (*propter honestatem gradus*) and under the same penalty, at any rate, the majority (*c*) who are not in the *hospicium* of the Custos Rotulorum or that of any first class clerk [*i.e.*, in attendance].

Second class clerks with certain exceptions are " to sit outside the bar of the Chancery while writs are being sealed or pleas held, in their allotted places *as of old* and strangers [non-officials?] too, unless they are called in."

Clerks of both classes must always preserve the order of precedence, as it is on the roll, when lodgings are

---

(*b*) P. 436.

(*c*) Or perhaps it is meant that *none* are in the *hosp.* of the Custos, etc. Note that *honor* and *status* are used only of the first class men; *gradus* of the second.

assigned for Parliaments and Councils and at the table
" below the Court or in court," " whether at Westminster
or elsewhere." Not only there but in ceremonial courtesies
everyone must be allowed his proper place according to his
formal election or promotion (*d*) *as of old*. Apparently
questions of precedence had arisen in the office.

No clerk of either class is to sit in the hanaper of the
Chancery nor in that of the Common Bench to read (*i.e.*,
check) writs or deliver them to plaintiffs; it is beneath
the dignity of their class and of the Court.

Then comes a clause specially valuable for our purpose.
" *Cursistae* (*e*) and all other clerks who wish to be in the
Chancery to learn or copy (*sc.* writs, *propter doctrinam et
scripturam adherere voluerint*), those [at any rate (*f*)] who
do not live in the *hospicium* of the Custos or in that of any
first or second class clerk, must abide in one or various
becoming (*honesta*) *hospitia* from time to time, and not
with *apprenticii legis, attornati,* or other non-officials
(*extranei*), nor may they have living with them attornies (*g*), clerks of other courts (*placearum*) or any one
else whomsoever having nothing to do with the business
(*formam modum et actum*) of the Chancery on pain of
expulsion, &c." Here apparently the original Order ended,
the clauses immediately following being added later. They
run :—And the principals (*principales*) of these hospicia
when they take office (*h*) shall swear in the Chancery that

(*d*) ? juxta formam eleccionis et prefeccionis.

(*e*) Clerks who actually wrote out the writs—practically a third
class; they are only to be appointed after *debita et sufficiens examinacio*
" as was the old practice," and their work is strictly controlled by
examinatores, taken from the superior clerks, because the want of
that control has led to many " frauds."

(*f*) See n. (*c*), p. 440.

(*g*) N. B. *appr. l.* are not in this group, perhaps because though they
are excluded from living in the same *hosp.* yet they might be entertained here (unlike the *att.*); it is intercourse with the *att.* that these
Orders chiefly aim at regulating.

(*h*) " in prima condicione eorundem in Canc.," perhaps = of the first
class men. For the oath see p. 438.

they will faithfully obey this Order thoroughly. The *principales* must not be married (*i*) and must have reached the grade of those who may sign [documents] in their own name. Two or more first class men are to be assigned (elected?) twice a year or oftener to supervise these regulations.

The sudden appearance of this domestic Head (and his assistants) suggests that experience had shown that he was necessary to the government of the inn and his place in the text, that he was not in the first edition.

Again, no one (except the two *clerici* of highest grade) in the Chancery is for the future to wear clothes cut (*k*) . . . or others of divers colours in Court. Then, all Chancery clerks are expected to behave as gentlemen—they must have nothing to do with the " dirty work " of parties (*l*) or anything which might bring discredit on the Court nor take money improperly for showing favour in the court : " if they want any favour to do a friend a good turn, or to take a fee for their work, let them openly tell the facts to the Chancellor or the Custos or the *preceptores* [a later superior clerk], who will deal generously with them in matters of this sort, considering their rank and profit "; *i.e.*, within limits the authorities will not scrutinise too closely their colleagues' nepotism or anything they can make out of their position; each grade and all grades together were to be " a happy family " or hierarchy with *esprit de corps*, which is, in other words, a code of honour. In the early organization of the office " the pickings " of individual clerks must have been considerable. " It was not " says (*m*) Prof. Tout " in wages and allowances so

---

(*i*) For the frequent prohibition of marriage in this Order see Tout as below, or *The Great Seal* (1926), p. 2, etc., by Maxwell-Lyte.

(*k*) Vestibus . . . scissis (slashed?); *i.e.*, sober; unfortunate blank in MS.

(*l*) Nulli . . . in partibus ad quas declinant negocia inhonesta assumant.

(*m*) *The Household*, etc., p. 55.

much as in fees, perquisites, opportunities for promotion in church and state, pensions for old age, and above all facilities for acting as counsel, attorneys, agents and usurers that the Chancery clerk's career had its claim to be considered lucrative as well as dignified." He is a man with prospects, very often well-to-do and he attracts to his society his connections and friends probably also well-to-do, whom without any trouble to himself, he can help on in a legal career; he forms a very nest for the bar.

It is probably the excesses of this tendency, downright venality, disclosure of official secrets or corruption (*n*), at which the Ordinance is specially aimed : for instance " No one, in the Chancery may intrude (*o*) into the King's *hospicium* or that of the Chancellor or that of the Custos of the Privy Seal to increase the business of the court or giving interested advice there, or giving " inside information (*p*) or getting " bills or letters in any way from the privy seal." Now, this clause is obviously aimed at backstairs influence which was inevitable in the primitive chancery where the Chancellor actually lived with a clerk or two : through them anyone, especially a *seigneur*, might easily " get at " the Chancellor and so at the sovereign. While that ministry was growing no doubt there was a good deal of running to and fro between the Chancellor's private house and the *hospitia* and the tradition must have survived; a designing *clericus* might easily turn the communication to his personal advantage or even tell tales of his fellows. The corporation feels that the time has come to regulate their trade union : early orders of court, too, teem with prohibitions of unauthorised persons. The point for the moment is that a rule of this sort implies a *sodalitas*

(*n*) In addition to the distinct mention (above) of systematic frauds the Ordinance is full of precautions against officials' abuses, *e.g.*, the improper sealing of writs.

(*o*) declinare = sneak in.

(*p*) pro negociis Curie cumulandis aut iniquis conciliis ibidem dandis seu secretis Cancellarie detegendis . . .

or confraternity and, as in a modern club, a man might be expelled for "conduct unworthy of a gentleman." It represents a social stage; the "upper ten" of the office try to repress the marked tendency of "the fringes" of the law—practically those who are not serjeants, to "hang together," to work together and to mess together—the authorities want their men to be the pick.

For lower grade clerks, who had opportunities of their own, if not the temptations of their superiors, there is another discipline : " No *cursista* nor any one else writing to the seal shall be attorney between party and party in any *placita, querelae, causae* or matters pending or to be moved in any court outside Chancery [*a fortiori*, in it] nor in any way take part in (*se intromittat*) *attornamenta* of this sort, unless he is a *generalis attornatus* under the King's letters patent : penalty, amotion." As the business of the Chancery clerks was almost solely with *attornati* (*q*) —this Ordinance is full of directions to all grades for dealing with them—it clearly could not be allowed that any of them—it is not hinted at, of the first and second class men—should appear professionally for the client—except in, what was no doubt, the rare case of the special appointment of one as *generalis attornatus* by the King—in which case the department was powerless. This is at the bottom of the attempt (above) to discourage social intercourse between this class of clerks and the actual lawyers—the very proper anxiety that no man should double a legal part. Incidentally, this edict clearly implies, what we know *aliunde*, the attorney's definite status.

No one is to be admitted to the first or second class except by the due election and seniority (*maturitatem*) of

---

(*q*) It is expressly stipulated that only the first and second classes shall deal with applications to appoint or act as *attornati*—" recipiant attornamenta "—in or out of court " as of old " [when leave to so act had to be got] and the second class may only endorse the resulting writs with the express sanction of a first class clerk who alone can deal with *generale attornamentum*—a very serious matter.

the first class men present [*i.e.*, seniority is to have a preference in election] and on the advice of the majority of the elder men the Chancellor shall appoint to a benefice (*r*).

The later edition regulates other internal details of the office and bears witness to more definite relations between the office and counsel and attorneys (*s*).

The details of these two documents are of great importance for the history of procedure. For our purpose we need but note that it is only the lowest grades in the chancery who are warned off too great intimacy with *apprenticii legis* and *attornati* : it was naturally not a mischief against which the higher grades needed to be cautioned; the undesirables are not fullgrown lawyers, *servientes*, who are not even mentioned. Perhaps we may infer that the exclusiveness begins to show itself at a time when law students were a heterogeneous number of youths of no great social standing, pressing on a settlement of some antiquity with considerable amenities of intercourse and great opportunities of professional and intellectual profit. The glimpse we get of internal organization of the chancery men's *hospitia* reminds us of that of the colleges of the day. At the date of this Ordinance some were springing up almost at the doors of those *hospitia*. Their earliest beginnings, it would seem, are a sort of coming to terms with the authorities of the august writ-factory without whose favour the history of the English bar would have run a different course.

(*r*) This seems to be the meaning of—de eorum majori et seniori consilio procedat Cancellarius de persona facienda : apparently=the senior men advise him.

The clause adds a rhetorical appeal to " duty to King and Country " (as in the Oath)—*i.e.*, not to stay away from the office without good reason, evidently the result of experience.

(*s*) On a "Summons for directions" (*causas dirigere*) ". . . ad peticionem consiliariorum vel partis seu, ejus attornati altera parte vel ejus attornato presente, . . . " the Masters have power to decide *exceptis excipiendis*.

iii. Inmates of the Inns.

A claim, not without probability has been put forward for Staple Inn (*t*), Holborn, as an early seat of law. A Staple is, no doubt, an early institution in every commercial town but the following extract (*u*) only purports to be a suggestion : " In such an important emporium as London the Corrector or Meter of the Staple would require, no doubt, a large staff of assistants with legal knowledge and, no doubt, disputants would be glad to make use of experts in law merchant to argue their case before him; and inasmuch as no school of law nor Inn of Apprentices of the law was permitted within the walls of the City, but only in what was then known as the suburbs, we can well imagine that Staple Inn was already a nucleus of the legal profession and was used at times as a piepowder court." The writer assumes that the Order of 1234 was operative for a long time. His theory is likely but not proven.

From about, broadly, 1300-20, these conventicles multiply, if they do not grow apace. It would not assist our object to treat them *seriatim* here but for convenience they are set out in Appendix XV.

The earliest (fairly) certain fact in the *synoikismos* of lawyers is that soon after 1311 (February, sometimes said to be 1310) there was such a party occupying part of what is now Lincoln's Inn. Sir George Buc, who died in 1623, wrote (*x*) about 1612 in " The Third Universitie of England," dedicated to Coke, that soon after the death of " Sir Henry Lacy, Earle of Lincoln [1310-11] . . . as it seems and is most probable the Benchers of this Colledge, tooke an Estate of long time by lease . . . by which estate they held this house untill their purchase from Sir Edward

---

(*t*) App. XV, no. 16 : " whereof so named I am ignorant." Stow, 2 Kingsford's edn. 40, 363 : f. 393 (1598).

(*u*) *Staple Inn*, 17, 61 : E. Williams, 1906.

(*x*) Appended to Howes's edn. (1631) of Stow's *Annales*, p. 1073.

Suliard " (*y*) (temp. Elizabeth). The Earl, " the closest counsellor of Edward I " (*z*) was a very able man and had had judicial experience, so that there is nothing improbable in Dugdale's relation in 1666 : Of him " is the tradition, still current amongst the Antients here [L. I.] that he about 1307, being a person well affected to the knowledge of the Lawes, first brought in the professors of that honourable and necessary study, to settle in this place : but direct proof thereof from good Authority I have not as yet seen any " (*a*). That the name was derived from the owner's or occupier's, as were those of many neighbouring Inns, is certain.

Now, surveying the dates in App. XV, we find that the earliest is 1310-11 (Lincoln's Inn) (*b*)—for a story about the Earl of Lancaster's tenants before 1322 see *ib*. no. 11—and the latest about 1550 (or allowing Thavies I. more antiquity) about 1500. Between those two years, colleges were springing up, exactly as they did at Oxford and Cambridge and elsewhere, but in an even smaller area —because the pioneers, whoever they were, were successful ;

" . . . alterius sic.
" Altera poscit opem res et conjurat amice."

What is certain is that, between 1300 and 1400, lodgings were required for persons connected with the law as practitioners, students or clerks, in and at both ends of Chancery Lane, and that between 1400 and 1500 still more were required. The process is familiar and as England and London were on the whole, " going ahead " in those periods, so was the law as a code and a profession. At the

---

(*y*) *Ib*. 1072 : *ex relatione* Sir James Lea L.C.J. (Ir.) " an auncient fellow " and " an excellent antiquary."

(*z*) St. 2 *Cons. Hist*. 346, § 249.

(*a*) *Orig. Jud*. ed. 1680 : p. 231, c. 64. Foss doubts about " the tradition " (IV, 257) but the date 1310-1 is accepted by Mr. Kingsford in D. N. B.

(*b*) Or Gray's Inn if anyone accepts the date in Harl. MS., no. 7 in App. Even Mr. Williams does not claim St. I as an abode of *appr*. in 1310.

"modern" end we see this clearly. The earliest *recorded* dates claimed for the now existing Societies, as such, are: Gray's Inn, 1391 (*c*); Inner Temple, 1440 (*d*); Lincoln's Inn, 1422 (*e*); Middle Temple, 1404 (*f*).

When therefore, Buc says (*g*) "Of all the Innes of Court without controversie the Temples . . . bee the most ancient," he must mean—literally, as Inns of Court, and even then may not strictly be accurate.

With the record of the unsevered Temple in 1381 we will deal. It must always be remembered that at these dates the Society is a going concern.

In later years the small Inns, are found attached respectively to one of "the big four." This was an obviously convenient system both for purposes of education and economy of "overhead" expenses and is analogous to the absorption of Halls at Oxford by neighbouring colleges in our day or to that of smaller by larger banks or railways or the amalgamation of richer and poorer coal-mines. Or we may compare the "feeding" of individual public schools by those known as "prep."

(*c*) *The Pension Book of G. I* (1901) by the Rev. R. J. Fletcher: p. xvii (or possibly 1355); in 1454 a Serjeant is quoted *ib*. p. xx, as saying " in Grays In wer I was a felaw " [=*socius*, an inmate]: *Paston Lett.* v. I, p. 297; ed. Gairdner, 1872.

(*d*) Inderwick *Cal. I. T. Rec.* (1896), p. xv, from *Paston Let.* [I, 41, No. 2] [edn. as above]: "qwan your leysyr is resorte ageyn on to your college the Inner Temple," to John Paston, who *ib*. p. 48 (No. 36), is " dwellyng " there in 1443: so *ib*. vol. 2, p. 66, no. 423, before 1460; the earliest record preserved is of 1505: Inderwick, *ib*. p. 1. For " Inner Inn " see n. (*f*) below.

(*e*) J. Douglas Walker, 1 *Black Books of L. I.* (1897), pp. ii, 1, 2 : " Liber Hospicii de Lincolsin " is the title of the MS.; in 1427 occurs " Lyncolnesyn." In v. I of *Rec. L. I. Admissions* (1896), pp. 1, 3, vi, it is made clear that there were admissions in 1420 and most probably in 1408.

(*f*) The existing records begin in 1501: Ingpen, *M. T. Bench Book* (1912), p. 17. In 1451 " Styward of the Mydill Inne and . . . of the Inner Inne " is in 1 *Past. Lett.* 186 (no. 140 : ed. Gairdner). So Ingpen, above, p. 53, of both in 1463 (Y. B. 3 E. IV Mich.), but, *ib*. fifteen years later both are " Temples." See further p. 591 and App. XV.

(*g*) P. 1069b : see p. 446.

The Temple alone among these units, owing to its inveterate tradition, was not called by the name of some owner or founder, indeed, so universal was the nomenclature of the Hostels that even after the fissure of the two Temples took place, a record (not a speech) has " Middle Inn " (h).

There was till 1851 a remarkable monument of the original autonomy of the smaller societies. Pearce (i) found " in the common-place book of T. Gibbons [about 1600] Harl. MSS. (f. 300 [otherwise f. 154 b, Catalogue] 980) : ' Upon Clifford's Inn Hall window is a coat of arms Asure 3 Fesse Or, betuin 8 Golden Keyes, 3, 2, 2, 1 with this inscription :—*Will. Screen, electus et vocatus ad statū et gradū servientis ad legem extra hospitiū istud* (k) *et non aliude, vixit temp. R. II, Hen. IV et Hen. V* ' " [1377—1422] (l).

The words " elected and called to be a *serviens* outside this Hostel and not otherwhence " are, however inelegant, clearly meant to express that Skreen was elected from Clifford's Inn to become one of the Serjeants and not from any other, *i.e.*, not, as you might expect, from one of the greater bodies, especially the four greatest. The unusual emphasis on the fact that he did not owe his origin to them certainly implies " a deviation from . . . practice " as Mr. Pearce points out but whether " that practice " was in 1415, the date of the promotion (m), so " cut and dried " as it was later, that only past " Readers " " in [one of] the four houses " were made serjeants, as Mr. Pearce

---

(h) Apparently the only instance (but cf. " Templars Inne " : p. 495) and probably soon after the severance. In 1426 a writer addresses from Bruges a letter in French to " les courtesans (=men of court) demorans en l'ostel du Templebar en la cite de Londres " denouncing Serjeant Paston. 1 *Past. Lett.* 23 : No. 6, ed. Gairdner. The writer, who seems to have been a foreigner, perhaps did not know of the severance nor to what *individual* to address the letter.

(i) *Guide*, p. 261.

(k) Mediaeval for *hoc*.

(l) The arms were still there in 1851 but not the inscription : 4 *Foss*, 141.

(m) Wynne's *Serjeant at Law* (1765), 31.

states, may be doubted. This unique evidence rather goes to show that about 1400 the relations of the Inns *inter se* had not yet solidified—as we should antecedently expect.

One other piece of contemporary evidence is weighty. Thomas Walsingham (*n*), our chief authority for Wat Tyler's doings in 1381, says: " The rioters began to kill every lawyer (*juris terrae peritos*), *apprenticii* as well as old judges and all the nation's *juratores* (*patriae*) whom they could catch (*nn*), without quarter or respect of person, declaring that there could be no real liberty till they were dead . . . so they burned all the rolls of the Courts " hoping to get rid of all the deeds. Next " they demolished the place called Temple Bar where sojourned the better class of *apprenticii* (*in quo appr. juris morabantur nobiliores*) and destroyed the muniments which the *juridici* kept in St. John's Hospital," at Clerkenwell. Wat himself " wanted above all to behead all the *juridicos* including the *escaetores* and everyone who was learned in the law or, by reason of his office, had anything to do with it. For his design was, when he had killed the lawyers, to determine all matters by *plébiscite,* no law was in future to be passed or, if it was, he was to make it at his will." The author insists upon the ringleader's belief that to get any social reform the whole of the legal machinery (*o*) must be " scrapped "

(*n*) Died 1422? D. N. B. 1 *Historia Anglicana*, 455 (Rolls). W. was a monk, hence his interest in the attack on law and lawyers shows how serious it was.

So Dick in 2 Henry VI (Act iv, sc. 2) " let's kill all the lawyers." Shakespeare, admittedly the author of the Cade episode transferred Tyler's scheme in 1381 to 1450; see 141 *L. Q. R.* 89—90, Jan. 1920.

(*nn*) Cf. the story from Florus, p. 418*f*, and the treatment of Cressingham by the Scots in 1296 : 3 Foss, 83.

(*o*) " Mors furit in foribus, mors pulsat ad ostia juris " : Gower, *Vox Clamantis* (1173), B. I, c. xv.

The comment of Thomas Fuller, *Church History*, B. IV, § 20, who had been a preacher in the Inns of Court is interesting as representing the conservative view of 1655 (and no doubt, earlier) and perhaps preserving a tradition : " as [the rabble's] spight was the keenest at, so the spoil the greatest on the Law; *well knowing* that while the banks thereof stood fully in force, the deluge of their

for (*ib*. II, 2) he describes how the malcontents in the eastern counties " like their London brethren sacked the houses and the lands of the great men, the lawyers (*jurisperitorum*) killed the *apprenticii* and John Cavendish the King's chief Justiciar " (*p*) the latter at Bury St. Edmunds. They killed, says a (perhaps) contemporary chronicle " manye questmongers, jurours, men of lawe, Flemynges and other aliens."

Another contemporary writer (*q*) (who either copied from or was copied by Walsingham) on the rising, in repeating these details, adds that the rioters broke open " the chests in the Temple church and in the apprentices' chambers and destroyed all books, muniments, deeds in their chests, whether ecclesiastical or lay. . . . They pulled down the houses of the *jurati* (*r*) in the city (*civitate*) into which even their old men almost decrepit climbed, wonderful to relate, with as much speed as if they were rats or impelled by some [bad] spirit . . . as indeed they were. . . . And they killed all the *juratos civitatis* and the common lawyers (*juris regni apprenticios*) they could find, out of hand."

---

intended Anarchy could not freely overflow. They ransacked the Temple, not onely destroying many present Pleas, written between party and party (as if it would accord Plaintife and Defendant to send them both joyntly to the fire) but also abolished many ancient Records to the loss of learning and irrevocable prejudice of posterity."

(*p*) In 1377 Y. B. 50 E. III, p. 6, pl. 12 (4 Foss, 45), " Candish (J.) " pressed to examine a lady about her age, said : " There is no man in England who can judge rightly whether she is of age or not, for every woman of thirty wishes to appear eighteen."

(*q*) (The Continuator of) Knyghton, 2 Rolls, 135. Twysden, 2636.

(*r*) For *juratores* (or *-ati*) see pp. 451*r*. The uses of either word were innumerable : Du Cange. Fabyan abt. 1500 translates " questmongers " (7th Pt., p. cxlii b : ed. 1533); Holinshed (d. 1580) " jurors " (*Chronicles*, p. 1027 : ed. 1577), *ib*. 1028 " other which by any office had anything to do with the law "; this seems correct and would include the *clerici*. Stow's diction, about 1600, measures a change : " men of Law, apprentises, Utter-barristers, old Justices, the Jurers of the countrey "; *Annales*, 284, ed. 1631. If, as we have suggested, they were " the notables " of a town the hostility of the rioters is explained.

The single word *nobiliores* in Walsingham's account, meaning, of good social standing, is a confirmation of our view that the numbers of legal practitioners and students—for *apprenticii* were the most numerous of, and include, those " which by any office had anything to do with the law "—the *servientes* would certainly not be spared by the mob—had grown to such an extent in and about the Temple by 1381 that we should expect (as with our modern colleges) to find social distinctions or *coteries* and as " it is not the worst fruits that the birds peck at," it is easy to understand that the richest loot and the longest title-deeds were to be found in the same *hospitia*, *viz.*, those of the well-to-do about Temple Bar. And perhaps we may assume that if the two great Inns hard by had had their present names then these would have been mentioned in the narratives. The trail of rapine was from the Temple to Clerkenwell, in which way lay many a small Inn but none is mentioned and no doubt the insignificance of many protected them.

Moreover, if the inmates of these hostelries were not mere scriveners of writs or *pauperes* students, like those of Oxford—if Temple Bar was not a mere *Quartier latin*—then we can see in these " better-class youths " the pioneers of the universal culture which we know had its seat there at the latest, a hundred years afterwards—and probably earlier. It is inconceivable that generations of young Englishmen could have been living together without pursuing the avocations, the pastimes and the tastes of gentlefolk. No doubt the enlightened fathers of that day as readily accepted residence at the Inns as a " liberal education " as they do to-day a degree in Jurisprudence. In a short time " study " there was accepted, as in a modern university, as a social " cachet."

Thomas Hoccleve (s) " (1370?—1450?) " is an object

(s) See Dr. Furnivall in *D. N. B.* and the *Works of H.*: Early Eng. Text Soc.

lesson for his time. About 1411-2 he was living at
"Chesters" Inn by the Strand (App. XV, 2). He was and
had been since 1387 (?) (t) a clerk of the Privy Seal and
it is quite likely that Chester Inn was then, as it certainly
was later, an overflow from the Middle Temple, just then
emerging into fame and that Thomas was a member. It
certainly seems that it was then a centre of good fellowship,
including, a Temple dinner-club, as Dr. Furnivall puts it,
going on " A few days before May 1, 1410, if I read the
lines aright, Hoccleve writes a chirpy poem to Somer—then
Sir Henry Somer, Chancellor of the Exchequer—from their
Temple Club ' the Court of Good Company.' "

The lines, to which the editor refers, he thus partly
paraphrases in the margin " You tell us that our Club
in the Temple was founded to spend a lot of money."
The actual text runs :—

> Rehercynge . . . , in the place of honour
> The Temple / for solace / and for gladnesse.
>
> . . . . .
>
> Yee allegge eek how a rule hath be kept
> Or this/which was good/as yee haue herd seyn :
> But it now late / cessid hath and slept :
> Which good yow thynkith / were up take ageyn :
> And but if it so be / our Court certeyn
> Nat likely any whyle is to endure;
> As hath in mowthe, many a creature.

Sir Henry had evidently endeavoured to recall the
cercle to the pristine temperance of the hostels. Thomas
was an avowed *bon vivant*. But he is a good contemporary witness. Thus he bears out—pathetically—in his
own person, the difficulty the lawyers had in getting their
pay from the Treasury. And he throws some light from
within on the constant complaints against the clerks in

(t) Furn., I, p. xi; the grant, *Pat. Roll* 1 H. IV pt. 2 m. 21, calls
him " *dilectus* serviens *noster*." Such a clerkship was created or
confirmed in 1311 by *Ordinance* 5 E. II, c. 14.

the offices—for those of the privy seal were no doubt very much like those of the chancery. They were not always free agents; powerful favourites might be influencing the office or the clerks themselves might be victims. His complaint of the bad treatment they suffered does not make the procedure of the cheat very clear but his verses (*u*) are thus paraphrased : " When anyone brings a Cause to the Privy Seal some Lord's man'll take all the Clerk's dues— and if they appeal to the King—they daren't accuse their robber, lest he should get them punisht :—The Lord knows nothing of his man's tricks—and the Clerks daren't tell him —Then this Cheater of the Privy Seal clerks declares he has paid em; and thus swindles the suitor and the Clerks, too " :—

" fful many swychë pursuours there ben " (l. 1534).

Perhaps, in plain English, the clerks' exactions had to be shared with outsite peculators. That there was much lawlessness abroad at this time is a commonplace. Hoccleve deplores (*x*) that " armed folk take the law into their own hands; they won't go to the Judges," or in his own—a lawyer's—words :

Hem deyneth naght an accioun attame [begin]
At comun lawe.

He marks then, the foundation of the legal houses, which, emerging as centres of organization—say in 1381 when the insurgents recognise them as such—are an epoch in the history of the bar.

But while it is true that the brethren were dwelling in unity, they were hardly strong enough for corporate action. The lawlessness of the times (*y*), 1350-1450, especially the

---

(*u*) *De regimine principum*, pp. 54-6, v. 3.

(*x*) *Ib.* p. 101.

(*y*) An extraordinary instance is the story—entirely one-sided, however—of Robert Tirwhit J. about 1412, when he had been on the bench three or four years, who, having a law-suit with a lord, assembled 500 armed men to lie in wait " there hym to harme and dishonure." The dispute was about rights of common. It does not appear that the

open oppression of a powerful politician or baron, might seriously hamper the independence of the bar or the attorney, especially in places remote from the capital. This is attested by the life and teaching of Paston J. who was born in 1378. We have seen (z) that he was in personal danger through his professional work, and after he was on the bench, he advises (a) someone not to go to law, " fer if thou do, thou shalt have the worse, be thy case never so true, for he is feid [feed?] with my Lord of Northfolk and much he is of his counsel; and also thou caunst no man of law in Northfolk or Southfolk to be with thee against him and forsooth no more might I when I had a plea against him and therefore my counsel is that thou make an end whatsoever the pay for he shall else undo thee and bring thee to nought."

On the other side, after the judge's death the Chancellor is petitioned (b) " to assigne and most streytly to comaund John Heydon [a lawyer, recorder of Norwich] Thomas Lyttylton [afterwards judge] &c., to be of counsell with [the] besecher," who had an action against the judge's widow, " for as meche as your said besecher can gete no

---

lord was in fact touched. Parliament appointed arbitrators who drew up an apology which Tirwhit made, saying, *inter alia*, " I am well aware that you, my lord, had you chosen, could have brought a much greater force to the spot in dispute, but you ' had consideration to your degree.' What I did was because I had information that I was personally in danger. ' Zet for as *myche I am a Justice* [and a Justice of the Peace *for the County*, the complaint had added] *that more than an other comun man scholde have had me more discretly and peesfully*,' " and he was to offer 100 marks, 2 tuns of Gascony wine, 2 oxen and 12 sheep to be spent on a dinner at the spot, but the lord was to take nothing but the materials for the dinner : 3 *Rot. Parl.* 650. The whole story has evidently been exaggerated; it recalls the heading by a modern judge of a party in a Sussex village, which stormed a disputed way, for which he was summoned. If the complainant had not been a magnate, nothing would have been heard of it; the (only) penalty, too, is quasi-comic. But *n.b.* the common-place in italics, above.

(z) See generally Bennett's *The Pastons and their England*, 1922, p. 171.

(a) *Paston Letters*, ed. Gairdner, I, 42, No. 28.

(b) *Ibid.* 60, No. 47 (1444-9).

counsell of men of court to be with him by cause " that the property concerned the late judge and " John P." his heir, " also a man of court." Note the assumption that the Chancellor had such jurisdiction over counsel; there is little doubt that in fact he had the power the petitioner invoked. In 1451 Prisot J., the younger Paston being plaintiff at Norwich, " wolde suffre no man that was lerned to speke for the pleyntyfs but took it as a venom and took them by the nose at every thred woord " (c). In 1455 the Earl of Devonshire and Lord Bonville being at variance, the former's son with sixty armed men attacked and fired the house in Devonshire of " Radford . . . whiche was of counseil with my Lord " B. and assassinated him (d). Again it is reported to the Chancellor. Thus redress is sought from another " great " man, not from a central " trade union " in London. Still even in these blemishes the bar is distinctly a profession alongside the great one which had hitherto held the field—indeed the second, though, no doubt, " a bad second." The best witness is Literature; others are Law and Legislation.

Legislation.

The remark of Stubbs (e) " the dislike of having practising lawyers in parliament appears as early as the reign of Edward III," is a very convenient starting point, for it assumes the existence both of the Legislature and of the profession.

Taking a comprehensive view of facts with which we

(c) *Paston Letters*, ed. Gairdner, I, 212, No. 158.

(d) *Ib.* 350, No. 257.

(e) 2 *Con. Hist.* c. xv, § 194, p. 208, n. 2; n.b. " practising," for in 1300-1 Oxford was commanded to send four or five good *jurisperiti* and Cambridge two or three : *ib.* p. 163; 1 *Parl. Writs*, 91. It seems that the Crown thought that civil lawyers would be useful for its purpose; thus in 1387 on a grave constitutional issue the King and Lords called in " the judges and sergeants and other *sages du ley de roialm* and also the *sages de la ley civill* " : 3 *Rot. Parl.* 236—an early instance of consultation between common and civil lawyers.

have dealt piecemeal, the same authority says (*f*) " The lawyers and the merchants occasionally seem as likely to form an estate of the realm as the clergy or the knights. Under a King with the strong legal instincts of Edward I, surrounded by a council of lawyers, the patron of great jurists and the near kinsman of three great legislators, the practice and study of law bid fair for a great constitutional position " which both classes got and still have.

The steps connecting or disconnecting the men who made the law with those who practised it seem to be as follows.

1330 (*g*). A writ (*h*) to the sheriff of Lancaster recites that there have been many oppressions by various persons of authority—" our ministers in divers offices . . . our counsellors among others . . . some of the knights (*Chivalers*) who have come to Parliament for the counties have been *gens de coveigne* [" legal malpractices " St.] and maintainers of false suits (*quereles*) "—and bids him get elected " two of the most loyal and fit (*suffisans*) knights or serjeants of the county who are no wise suspected of legal malpractice nor common maintainers of litigants (*parties*)." It has been supposed quite wrongly that *serjauntz* here means lawyers. Prynne (*i*) translates " Esquires " and Mr. A. E. Randall (*k*) " tenants by serjeanty " (and, perhaps, they are both right). The statute founded on the facts recited, 4 E. III c. 11, does not name either knight or serjeant (*l*).

(*f*) *Ib*. p. 206.

(*g*) The famous writ of 1275, 2 St. c. xv, § 214, p. 243, n. 5, is not to the point; two " de discretioribus et legalioribus militibus comitatus " are to go to Westminster; *legalis* and its comparative (merely " of dignity ") had long been = not in any way disqualified, *e.g.*, in the Assize of Clarendon (1166); = " not *exlex* " : Du C., for whose account of *m. legalis* see p. 150*u*.

(*h*) 2 *Rot. Parl.* 443; Prynne, 2 *Parl. Wr.* 85-6; 2 Rymer, 800.

(*i*) *Ib*.

(*k*) 143 *L. Q. R.* 284, n. 7.

(*l*) In 1324 Lincolnshire returned one " Chyvaler " and one " Serjaunt " : *Parly. Writs* (ed. Palgrave, 1830), v. II, div. 2, p. lxxvi.

1350. The King orders the Sheriff of Kent to have two fit persons elected " who must not be *placitatores* (*m*), maintainers of causes or persons living by that sort of trade " (*querelarum manutentores aut ex hujusmodi questu viventes*). Here is the earliest murmur of " too many lawyers " in the House of Commons.

The truth seems to be that in the infancy of that House, its constituents (if that word be not an anachronism) with their infant franchise—at first, no doubt, the more vigilant of them—took fright at the rapid growth of the lawyers' houses—roughly from 1330 to 1400—and the consequent consolidation of the profession. Both avocations no doubt had the respective failings of beginners. It is not open to doubt that the great grievance of the Commons of the time was the oppression and exaction of potentates and authorities and that among the malpractisers were lawyers who were not only extortioners like laymen but turned the very artificial screws of legal chicane. But the large and persistent class of " maintainers of suits " was an evil against which earlier reformers had protested long before " lawyers " were thought of as a body by representatives or represented, or anybody else, and, although when they do appear in public life, they might be like the Sheriffs very convenient instruments for the abuse of legal or constitutional forms, yet they could not but be a mere handful of men in comparison with the bulk of the clients who suborned them. It would seem that this early repressive legislation while aiming at a real mischief confounded

---

(*m*) So App. I, Pt. 1 (1829), to Lords' *Report on Dignity of a Peer*: v. III, p. 590, citing " Rot. Claus. p. 2 in dorso m. 3 " which Prynne, II, 92, quoting, reads *placitorum aut quer.* etc., which would not necessarily imply professional lawyers as *placitatores* does : this St. (*Hist*. III, 431) translates " pleaders," explaining " it was impossible to secure the election of belted knights but honest and peaceful country gentlemen might be hoped for . . . *accordingly*," pleaders, etc., are to be excluded. The difference of reading here is unimportant for undoubtedly the legislators meant to identify the forensic mischief-makers with persons connected in some way or other with law and public affairs.

through ignorance, not unmixed with jealousy, the opportunities for oppressing the weak, inevitable in a feudal society, with the special development of them, coincident with that legislation itself and due to the florescence of law at any given moment. In the mass of actual reports of the day which have come down to us in the Year Books, there are no traces of even legal venality (to say nothing of corruption) and the tone of public judicial utterances is high. There was not sufficient *esprit de corps* in the " men of law " who wrote these works to induce them to extenuate general moral failings.

The writ of 1350 was to circulate throughout the counties. It is, therefore, not improbable that there were lawyers living and practising in the provinces. Indeed a statute (*n*) of 1384 seems to show that there were, for it prohibits any " man of law to be justice of Assize or of the common deliverance of gaols in his own country (*patria*) "; the mischief aimed at is clear, even if the statute was disregarded.

At any rate, many cities other than Westminster must have been familiar with *servientes* and cognate learned persons who attended, even if they were not members of the Parliaments which sat within their precincts—*e.g.*, York, Northampton, Lincoln, Winchester, Bury St. Edmunds, Leicester, even Coventry, Reading, Salisbury, Gloucester, Carlisle, Nottingham, Cambridge, Shrewsbury (*o*)—mostly between 1298—1398 but as late as 1467 (Reading). We have to wait till 1649 to hear the able answer of Bulstrode Whitelock in the House (*p*) itself, or for Prynne's (*q*) in 1660, to the general objection.

In 1372 popular feeling animated a statute. " Among the petitions of this parliament one only was turned into

---

(*n*) 8 Ric. II, c. 2 : reversed in 1393-4, p. 267.
(*o*) All examples from 3 Stubbs, c. 20, § 414, pp. 417-8.
(*p*) *Apologia*, 3 *Memorials*, 118.
(*q*) 2 *Parl. Writs*, 125.

a statute and it betrays somewhat of the same jealousy towards the lawyers as had been shown in 1371 towards the clergy " (r). The statute runs : " Whereas Men (*Gentz*) of the Law who follow divers Businesses in the King's Courts on behalf of private Persons with whom they are [? engaged] do procure and cause to be brought into Parliament many Petitions in the Name of the Commons, which in no wise relate to them, but only the private Persons with whom they are engaged (*demorez*); Also Sheriffs who are common Officers of the People and ought to be abiding in their Office, for the doing Right to Everyone, are named and have heretofore been and returned to Parliament Knights of the Shires by the same Sheriffs; It is accorded and assented in this Parliament that hereafter no Man of the Law following Business in the King's Court nor any Sheriff for the Time that he is Sheriff be returned nor accepted Knights of the Shires; nor that they who are Men of the Law and Sheriffs now returned to Parliament have any wages; But the King willeth that Knights and Serjeants of the most worthy of the County be hereafter returned Knights in Parliament; and that they be elected in full county."

These provisions smack of modernism: we are acquainted with the local men of influence, practitioners of the law *inter alios*, who are elected or appointed to public posts with or without emolument and with or without indirect gains, such as patronage, matrimonial prospects, etc., etc., and we know how specially useful, for instance, in a case of public utility or private grievance, a lawyer in the House of Commons may be, if only by reason of his ready handling of statute-law and training in stating a case. The recognition of this state of things five and a half centuries ago is a reminder that it is inherent in our Parliamentary system, an inference which is driven

---

(r) St. v. 2, p. 461 : c. 16, § 261 : Statute in *St. Realm*, 394 : Petition, 2 *Rot. Parl.* 310 : the wording is practically identical.

home by the deliberate and avowed, but obviously unsuccessful, attempts to arrest an inevitable movement. One phrase in the instrument simulates such precision that it is a little puzzling. There could be no question whether a man was in office as Sheriff or not, but how could any authority know whether a *serviens*, a *narrator*, an *apprenticius* or an *attornatus* was " following business in the King's court " or not? What criterion was there in 1372 of a " practising " lawyer (other than a *serviens*)? Was it membership of an Inn? Perhaps at that date reputation would be decisive and certification would be easy; but the whole theory was so short lived that it is not worth while pursuing it further.

Stubbs (*s*) says on the whole matter : " It is difficult to draw any definite conclusions from the variations which occur in the writ of Edward III; they seem, however, to imply a mistrust of the influences supposed to be at work in the county courts and to have a general intention of urging the election of men of knightly rank and education, to the exclusion of professional lawyers and the maintainers of private suits. The mischief of faction and the danger of sacrificing public interest to private emolument were sufficient reasons for the restrictions inserted . . . the number of variations implies some power of resistance; the lawyers were not excluded and belted knights were not always chosen."

Moreover, " On any theory the conclusion is inevitable that the right of electing was not duly valued, that the duty of representation was in ordinary times viewed as a burden and not as a privilege, and that there was much difficulty in finding duly qualified members and that the only people who coveted the office were the lawyers who

---

(*s*) *Ib*. III, c. xx, § 419, pp. 434, 440; Longman, 1 *Edward III* (1869), p. 438 n. (who makes the mistake of the " serjeaunt " in 1330 being a lawyer), gives the following *crescendo* of anti-lawyer dates : 1330, -39, -49, -51, -55, -56, -72 : 1404.

saw the advantage of combining the transaction of their clients' business in London with the right of receiving wages as knights of the shire at the same time." But did they get those wages if they lived in London?

The first definite absence, whether it was a " lock out " or a " strike," took place in 1397 (if the probably contemporary chronicler is not confusing (*t*) with 1404). In a parliament at Westminster " they proceeded not according to the law of England but the civil law (*jura civilia*). Nor did any English lawyers (*legis periti Angliae*) present themselves there (*se intromittebant*=intruded themselves?)." The simple monk does not see that the first sentence is the effect of the second. Probably he intended to suggest, in view of his famous statement (below) that the lawyers kept away—were not yet formally banned.

In 1404, the first recorded year of the Middle Temple, came the real *experimentum crucis*; the Unlearned Parliament (*u*) met—expressly perhaps to get away from the law courts (*x*)—at Coventry and apparently gots its name there.

The contemporary Walsingham (or the author of *Annales Henrici Quarti* (*y*)) tells us that it was summoned under the new style writ by which " neither knights nor burgesses (*cives*) who had any tinge of law (*qui gustassent aliquid de jure regni*) should be elected—only illiterates "

(*t*) The Continuator of *Eulogium Historiarum*, v. 3, p. 373 : Rolls : see v. I, p. iv. This passage seems to have been overlooked. The writer is perhaps Thomas, a monk of Malmesbury.

(*u*) " By reason whereof [*sc*. the writ] this Parliament was fruitlesse and never a good law made thereat. . . . And seeing these Writs were against law, Lawyers ever since (for the great and good service of the Commonwealth) have been eligible . . . " 4 *Inst*. 48. There is perhaps an echo of the prejudice in 1430, 8 H. VI, c. 7; 2 *St. R.* 243. It would seem that much of the early legislation about Parliament was a dead letter. St. 3 *Hist*. p. 277, c. 18, § 368.

(*x*) St. *ib*. c. 18, § 311, p. 49.

(*y*) Rolls edn., p. 391.

(*omnino illiterati*). Even more emphatic is Walsingham's statement (*z*) that the King ordered the Sheriffs that on no account should they return (*eligerent*) anyone who was learned or even an apprentice in the law (*jure regni*), but only those known to be ignorant of any course of law (*cuiusque juris methodum*), " and so it was done." We know that this was accurate from the writ to the Sheriff of Kent (*a*). The Continuator puts it thus (*b*) : the King in 1404 commanded that no *juris peritus* should come to the Parliament, telling the sheriffs who the *milites* and *procuratores* of the counties (*c*) were whom he wished to be sent thither.

"*Procurator*," the earliest synonym of "M.P.," implies a contemporary view of the representative as the " man of business " of his employers, especially in money matters, *e.g.*, taxation.

The effect of this edict may be gathered from the fact that the next year Scrope, Archbishop of York, inveighing against the King's policy, demanded that the wicked counsellors about him should be removed and that " men learned in the law should come to Parliament and in their wisdom give advice " (and that the members should be *elected* and not " assigned " by the King, and that Parliament should be fixed in London (*d*)).

Among the lawyers two classes are clearly recognised—seniors and juniors—perhaps identified with the teachers and the pupils in the Inns; the third class assuredly did not in 1400 seek " Parliamentary honours."

For, as early as 1379 there is a record of this class.

(*z*) *Hist. Ang.* v. 2, pp. 264-5, under 1404.
(*a*) 5 H. IV, *Rot. Claus.* p. 2 in dorso m. 4 : printed 4 *Dignity of a Peer*, 792 : " We will that neither you or any other Sheriff or *apprenticius* or any man of law be in any way (*aliqualiter*) elected."
(*b*) Rolls ed., v. 3, p. 402.
(*c*) *or* cities (*communitatum* : v.l.).
(*d*) *Ib.* p. 406.

Parliament in that year imposed a graduated poll-tax (*e*). That on the legal profession is thus expressed :—

Item chescun Justice si bn̄ de l'vn Bank come de l'autre & ceux q'ont este justices de mesmes les Bankes & le Chief Baron de l'Escheqier chescun	Cs.
Item chescun Sergeant (*f*) & grant Apprentice du Loy	XLs.
Item autres Apprentices qi pursuent la Loy, chescun	XXs.
Item touz les autres Apprentices de meindre estat & Attournez, chescun	VIs. VIIId.

. . . . .

Item touz les Advocatz, Notairs, & Procuratours (*g*) mariez (*h*) paient, come Sergeantz de Loy, Apprentices du Loy, & Attournez chescun selonc son estat (*h*)	XLs. XXs. ou dī marc.

The meshes of the tax-gatherer are minute so that they are here a measure of the developed organization of the profession. And it is a luminous contemporary sidelight that the Chronicler of St. Alban's (*i*), in reporting this " new unheard of impost," states that the Government deliberately intended to spare " the commons " and tax " the rich," and as he then proceeds to summarise the full list from the original Record, referring to the *Justiciarius* (only—as the

---

(*e*) 3 *Rot. Parl.* 58.

(*f*) The meaning now entirely depends on its context, for in the same instrument, "chescun sergeant et frankelein du pays" are assessed as small folk (6s. 8d.).

(*g*) These are ecclesiastical officials : the analogy to lay lawyers is fairly accurate. (*h*) *I.e.*, not in orders.

(*i*) *Chron. Ang.* pp. 223-4 : Rolls : copied by the Monk of Evesham, *Ric. II*, p. 11 (ed. Hearne, 1729), and Walsingham 1 *Hist. Angl.* 392 : Rolls.

LEGISLATION.

first in the legal world, as above), he obviously intends to include in 1379 the lawyers among the well-to-do classes. So in 1403 among the rich people circularised by the King for loans to carry on war, " R. Hull [Hill] s̄geant de ley " is asked for 100 *librae* (*ii*) : so are nine other serjeants (*j*) not so called. Probably it was convenient to collect the apprentices' tax in the Inns.

But what is above all noticeable is the three classes below the *servientes* : there is a symmetry about them which only a Treasury for its own purposes could descry : (i) " the great " juniors, ready to replace their leaders and therefore of equal fiscal dignity (*k*); (ii) the smaller " juniors " who were doing " some business "; (iii) the rest who " also ran " and " came in with the crowd," including the attorneys—who, apparently, are here for the first time collectively spoken of as a profession, ancillary to the bar and like its humblest members, assessed most leniently of all practitioners—but all without exception conceived as " gentlefolk." The juxtaposition of these two classes is a sign that they both dwelt promiscuously in the Inns, as we know they did for a long time after this date. The only visible difference would be in the day's work.

Another subject of legislation is the clothes they wore and those they gave others to wear. In 1377, by 1 R. II, c. 6, " Counsellors, Procurers, Maintainers and Abettors " are aimed at. Liveries to promote maintenance are said to be given by people too " small " to afford it, even by esquires (*l*). In 1389 the evil of " Livery of Company," *i.e.*, of incorporating, by means of uniforms, favours or badges, retainers into a miniature army to prosecute private civil wars or suits, was severely restricted; the statute,

---

(*ii*) I P. P. C. xlvii, 202; 4 Foss, 326.
(*j*) 4 Foss, 139.
(*k*) Hence the ordinance of 1381, p. 318.
(*l*) 3 Rot. P. 23.

13 R. II, c. 3, does not mention lawyers unless they are (as they probably are) included in " Esquire or other of less estate " among those who may not give them or " Knight or Esquire " who may not receive them. " The evil of maintenance," says Stubbs (*m*), " was apparently too strong for the statutes: the very judges of the land condescended to accept fees and robes from the great lords. . . ." The great compliment of wearing a great friend's livery is best known to us from the City magnates donning that of the Lord Mayor, but the practice is well authenticated in the most exalted circles. Ten years later, the lawyers, presumably the serjeants, are " hit " by 1 H. IV, c. 7, enacted " to eschew Maintenance and to nourish Love, Peace and Quietness of all Parts through the Realm." *Inter alia*, spiritual and temporal potentates are permitted (exceptionally) to give " Livery of cloth to . . . his menial Servants and Officers or to them that be of his Council, as well Spiritual as Temporal, learned in the one Law or the other "—the last touch (*n*) is too precise not to be taken from life. That statute is recited 7 H. IV, c. 14, and extended.

Then, in 1429, both are recited in 8 H. VI, c. 4, *viz*., that no knight or anyone of less estate should bestow livery on anyone but his menials and " Men learned in the one Law or the other " (*o*), and though the mischief is still attacked yet the statute is not to extend " as for the Execution of examination (*p*) to the Mayor

---

(*m*) 2 *Hist*. 662, c. xvii; see also 3 *Hist*. 573-9, c. xxi. In 1346, by 20 E. III, c. 1, " our Justices . . . shall not . . . as long as they shall be in [that] Office take Fee nor Robe of any Man but of Ourself," and are strictly forbidden to take the smallest gift from *any one* before them, " except meat and drink and that of small value."

(*n*) The regular formula: so of the King's " Conseil apris de l'un Ley ou de l'autre " : 3 *Rot. P.* 478a, of livery. Plummer, *The Governance of England*, p. 309 (1885), suggests that they were exempt because they were retained generally.

(*o*) The statute is founded on a petition of 1427 : 4 *Rot. P.* 329-30.

(*p*) But apparently the privileged persons named are exempt altogether from the statute, not only from this " Examination."

and Sheriffs of London for the Time that they shall be Officers, Serjeants of the Law at the Time that they take the same Estate upon them and them that do commence in the Universities ... nor to them which for the Time aforesaid shall take any such Liveries of them [*sc.*, the givers]." The context seems to show that the Serjeants are here permitted to *give* liveries, like the Mayor during his term of office (as we know he did), but as the Serjeant was created at a definite moment for an indefinite period, his ability begins when he " commences." It is possible to understand this passage as meaning that these lawyers might accept these uniforms from great lords, etc.; this would allow the Mayor the same liberty—of which we have no other evidence. Otherwise the Act equally forbids persons giving and persons *getting* them.

These legislators obviously associated liveries, sumptuary excess, *vendette* or quarrels between nobles or disputes between neighbours, which they called " maintenance "—a word which had long (*q*) had a special

---

(*q*) This state of things is illustrated by a case as late as 1453, tried by Fortescue C.J. (Y. B. 31 H. VI, f. 8b.: translated Ld. Clermont's ed. of The *Works*, v. I, p. 17, App.). Action for maintenance by C. T. against J.: J. pleaded that he " prayed and retained one Moyle, apprentice in the law to be of counsel " for his servant and he was; this is the maintenance complained of. This must have been before 1443 when Moyle became a serjeant (Foss); at a later stage in " error," as serjeant, he quotes his own retainer. Danby *contra* said that J. gave two named persons £10 " to be distributed at their discretion amongst the men of the county . . . for the purpose of aiding the servant." Moyle argues that if these persons were " men learned in the law," it was legal. Fortescue C.J.: " It is to be seen whether for this master to give money to the counsel of his servant, be legal or not. And, Sir, I say that it is not; for a man cannot do more for his servant in such case than pray the justice that his servant's business may be quickly disposed of according to law. And so, he can pray a man of law to be of counsel with his servant, as the law allows. . . . [But] I will show that the deliverance of the money is maintenance, for by the money the matter on the servant's side can be so strengthened that it may be understood that the other party is the longer time delayed in his suit or barred or that recovery may be had against him thereby; so it is illegal maintenance." Moyle then (taking

address to lawyers. While the profession was slowly growing up and its exact functions were not defined, there was a popular confusion between the conduct of litigation and the instigation of it—no doubt warranted at times. This was inevitable in small societies, where the lawyer knew well, not only his client, but the client's adversary and probably as the avocation became more profitable, the zeal of the friend prompted the promoter to more and more adventurous activities, till the latter were formally regulated.

There is direct development of the sumptuary code. In 1406 the Commons petitioned (r) (though they did not then apparently pass an Act) against extravagance in dress. No clerk, they propose, should wear big *chaperons* unless he be (*inter alios*) " a Master of the King's Chancery, Chancellor or Baron of the Exchequer or other great Officer [or] clerk (*clercs*), being in his office in the courts of the King. Provided always that the Justices of either bench or the King's Serjeants may use their hoods as they think fit for the honour of the King and their own estate . . . and no Esquire Apprentice of the Law (*Esquier app. d. l.*) no Clerk of the Chancellery or Exchequer or of other posts (*places*) of court or in the King's *tinel* [where the retinue of barons were entertained] or living with other lords of the realm without office (*nient avancez*) should use furs or jewels or gold ornaments, etc." Perhaps, too, the prohibition of " loud " gowns was to apply to lawyers, as " no man of whatever rank (*condition*) he be " was to wear such. Yet neither in the sumptuary legislation of 1336-7

---

a purely technical point, incidentally) observes that there cannot be a retainer [of counsel] " except by gift of money." He then goes into the fees [see p. 378]. Fortescue later says : " It is forbidden for any to interpose between party and party . . . if a stranger give money to a juror who is empanelled to give his verdict for one side, although he may never be a juror, it is clear maintenance prohibited by the Statute." It was long before the law was settled (if it is settled).

(r) 3 *Rot. Parl.* 593.

nor of 1363 (*s*) is there any hint of a legal rank, though, in the latter " Esquires and all Manner of Gentlemen under the Estate of a Knight" are dealt with. It would certainly seem from this and other indications that in the latter half of the fourteenth century the bar was dressing " better " than before.

Who was the " Esquier Apprentice du Loy " ? or as Kemble (*t*) put it in 1857 : " I should like to know where and when arose the time-honoured privilege of barristers of being esquires of the law." The answer seems to be that it arose about 1350 and was a purely popular effort, almost a " tag." Since the Conquest at least people were familiar with the military *miles* in the service of the King, with his inseparable associate, the *scutifer* or *armiger*: now they were becoming accustomed to another *serviens*, often himself a *miles* or noble by birth, and they transferred to his professional fellow the title of the latter's analogue. About 1290 in the *South English Legendary* (*u*) we find : " Of Eorles and of barones and manie knihts, him to (came) : Of seriaunz and of squiers." The earliest use of " esquire " in English seems to be by Fortescue in 1460. Once attaching to the " grant Apprentice du Loy," as no doubt it first did, it soon ran through all the grades of the Apprentices and has been their " addition " ever since, in default of a better. The great Sir Thomas Smith, about

---

(*s*) 11 E. III, c. 4; 37 E. III, cc. 8-14, founded on petitions, etc., in 2 *Rot. Parl.* 278, 281; the latter Act seems to have been repealed the next year (perhaps this is why the Petition of 1406 did not mature into an Act). In the great sumptuary Act of 1463, 3 E. IV, c. 5, though " Judges, the Master or Guardian of the Rolls, masters of the King's Chancery, Barons and Chancellor of the Exchequer" are expressly excepted from its provisions, the bar is not mentioned; it is included in the " Esquires and Gentlemen under the rank of a Knight," *i.e.*, it is recognised as a normal social grade. *A fortiori*, in the similar Act of 1482-3 no lawyers are mentioned.

In 1392-3 the Commons say " menuez Gentz come Esquiers et Vadletz q'ont poy [peu] de vivre " : 3 *Rot. Parl.* 307.

(*t*) *The Knights Hospitallers in England*, 1338 : Camd. Soc. No. 65, p. lxvi.

(*u*) N. E. D.

1562-3, wrote (*x*) : " as for Gentlemen they be made good cheap in England. For whosoever studieth the laws of the Realme, who studieth in the Universities, who professeth liberall sciences : and, to bee short, who can live idlely and without manuall labour and will beare the Port, charge and countenance of a Gentleman, hee shall be called Master, for that is the Title which men give to Esquires and other Gentlemen and shall be taken for a Gentleman " (*y*).

A few years later, a specialist in heraldry bears even stronger testimony to the gentility of the primitive *hospitia*. Sir John Ferne entered the Inner Temple in 1576 and in 1586 published *The Blazon of Gentrie* in which he says (p. 24) : " it was not for nought that our auncient Gouernors in this land did with a speciall foresight and wisedome prouide that none should be admitted into the houses of Court beeing seminaries (sending foorth men, apt to the government of justice) except he were a Gentleman of blood : And that this may seeme a truth I my selfe have seene a Kalender of all those which were together, in the societie of one of the same houses, about the last yeere of King Henry the fifth [1422], with the Armes of theyr house and familie, marshalled by theyr names : and I assure you the selfesame monument doth both approoue them all to be Gentlemen of perfect discents and also the number of them, much lesse then now it is, beeing at that time in one (*z*) house Scarcely threescore whereas now pitie to see, the

---

(*x*) *The Commonwealth of England*, p. 27, B. I, c. 20 : 1621 : first ed. in 1583, posthumous. Mr. G. J. Turner, *Lincoln's Inn* (1903), p. 23, seems to suggest that it first became usual to call a barrister " esquire," *i.e.*, *armiger* in legal documents, *temp.* Elizabeth; he prints (App. 24) a document of 1581, where, too, an *attornatus regine* is called *armiger*.

(*y*) William of Worcester, about 1460-70, in a long list of names (probably official) calls the commoners either *clericus* or *miles* or *armiger* or " gentilman " : *Annales*, 778-9 (of 1461) : *Wars of English*, etc., v. 2, pt. II : Rolls.

(*z*) Probably if this had been the Inner T. he would have mentioned it.

same places, through the malignities of times and the negligence of those which shoulde have had care to the same beene altered quite from theyr first institution. But thys was the regarde of our wise Elders towards noblenesse with vertue, that they deemed those most fitte for the handling of the Lawes of theyr Countrey ... that did excell in bloud...." Sir G. Buc (*a*), about 1615, writes: "because by aunciept custome and by old orders of the houses ... all those which were admitted ... were and ought to be Gentlemen, and that of three discents at least, as Master Gerard Leigh affirmeth (*b*), therefore they which are now admitted are Registered by the stile and name of Gentlemen. But yet notwithstanding this if they be not Gentlemen, it is an error to thinke that the sonnes of Graziers, Farmers, Merchants, Tradesmen and Artificers can be made Gentlemen by their admittance or Matriculation in the Buttrie Role ... for no man can bee made a Gentleman but by his father.... [Even] the King cannot make a Gentleman for Gentilitie is a matter of race...."

Ferne makes his knight say (p. 10): "What store of families have beene in this land areared to the state of Gentrie (and some also to the degree of Baronadie) which had their firste beginnings either from the study of a Pleader or the shop of a chapman." A Herald agrees: "very many there be now and those most worthy and noble houses whose first ancesters were Lawyers, a Science nay rather a profession."

The foundation of a family by a plebeian lawyer was thus early matter of comment. A good instance is that

---

(*a*) As in App. XV, at 1068b.

(*b*) *Accidence of Armorie*, 1562, fol. 156: " the seventh [class] is a gentleman spirituall. This if he be chorles sonne and is adavunced to any dignitie he is then a gentleman but not of bloud. But if he be a Doctour of civill lawe he is a gentleman of bloud and his cote is perfect at the first bearing."

of the Pastons. Clement Paston (c) was " a good plain husband " [man] living on his own land at Paston (about 1350) which, he, being a villein *adscriptus glebae* held by a servile tenure; he married a " bondwoman " (*i.e.*, *adscripta g.*) the sister of Geoffrey of Somerton—" he was bond also " and " he was both a pardoner (d) and an attorney " to his lord. " Clement had a son William which that he set to school and often he borrowed money to find him to school; and after that he yede [went] to court (e) with the help of Geoffrey Somerton and there begat he much good; and then he was made a serjeant and afterwards made a justice and a right cunning man in the law." William, while a prosperous " junior," married an heiress of good family and became the ancestor of an aristocratic line. By the time William was made a serjeant, 1421, Assizes were becoming periodically social centres—relatively far more important *as such* than they are to-day—so that in 1420 a trusty official writes (f) to Henry V " upon Wedynsdaye next sall zour Justice sitte at Zorke upon the deliverance of the Gaole there and a cession of the Pees also, at which tyme I suppose to speke with many of the gentyls there."

Coke follows Sir Thomas Smith but does not refer to the bar. But it certainly appears from the " Effect " of

---

(c) *Letters*, ed. Gairdner, 1872, v. I, xxi; v. II, xxx, 227. The contemporary (and therefore probably mainly true) account " by an unfriendly hand " is supposed to be Sir W. Yelverton's (J.'s, 1443) just after Paston J.'s death.

(d) Apparently = the lord's man of business for certain purposes, including selling indulgences.

(e) Either (1) to London to push his fortune—the common and early sense, but here highly improbable, or (2) to an Inn of Court—but such abbreviation is unique. Still less likely does it mean to the courts of law as a student. He might get on in either sense but, in either, before he could be made a serjeant, he must have some legal education : hence especially from a judge (2) is preferable.

(f) Ellis's *Letters*, 1st Ser., v. I, p. 7 (1828). The writer would not expect all the " gentyls " to be lawyers.

his speech (*g*) to the Serjeants in 1614 that he would have maintained their right to be " gentlemen." " If the dignity of a baron or of a serjeant be questioned they shall be tried by the record which is the writ whereby they are called." Malcolm, just before (*h*) printing this speech remarks: " If serjeants be made knights, they do not precede or take place of any other serjeants who are not knights, being their antients. . . . Serjeants are, without controversy, above all esquires and are never called or written *esquire* because that place is drowned in the state of serjeant because more worthy; whereof it follows that serjeants being above all that are the knights inferiors they stand in equality with knights and therefore between them and knights standing; in terms of equality there is no other reason of precedency but seniority as it is between knights among themselves."

Sir Henry Spelman in an ardent passage (*i*) bemoans the horde of *soi-disant armigeri*—" the grand old name . . . soiled by all ignoble use "—but admits the night to it of law-students (*k*). " In the last century, at any rate," he says " the most distinguished lawyers, no longer young men, even filling public posts and with ample means were content with the title of gentleman (*generoso*), perhaps because then that civil name suited better the *gens togata* than the other martial one [*miles*]." Thus no fountain of honour or authority of chivalry has ever solemnly conferred this " addition " on members of the Inns, as might be inferred from the silence of these great scholars,

---

(*g*) 2 *Inst.* 666—" every Esquire is a Gentleman and every Gentleman is *arma gerens*," 1628 : cf. p. 370*s*.

(*h*) 2 *Lond. Rediv.* (1803), 191, from " a MS. case on precedency at the coronation of one of our Kings."

(*i*) Glossary : *Armiger* ; 1626.

(*k*) " Nec tantum juris candidati quam primum ad *barras* (ut loquuntur) venerint digni et emeriti [the title *armiger*], sed ipsos inter (classis dedecus) inertes saepe et contra morem veterem exima nonnunquam plebe . . . ' ; *candidati* seems to = students rather than actual practitioners.

the earliest of whom admits that a " King of Heralds " has authority, in a fitting case, to grant " armes . . . which being done, I thinke he may be called a Squire."

Its forensic attribution thus being popular, it does not appear what authority there is for the statement (*l*) : " Esquires may be divided into five classes :— . . . (4) by creation or office . . . judges . . . justices of the peace, barristers-at-law. . . . All these can *legally* use the title." Moreover " the correctness of this enumeration is greatly disputed " (*m*). Thus again we are reminded of the inconspicuous origins of the bar.

The latest legislation on lawyers we have referred to is of 1429 ; the earliest was of 1275. The intermediate dates on which they engaged the attention of Parliament are few and are all in a period in which the foundations of our " constitution " were—if not laid—often relaid or affirmed. The influence of " the Bar " on early domestic politics is an interesting theme but would be out of place here. Perhaps the suggestion may be hazarded that it is just at the end of our period, about the middle of the 15th century, that it begins to have a corporate influence. That this was largely due to the corporations, whose emergence is the gist of our legal history from 1300 to 1400, cannot be doubted. But a theory about society which is not reflected in or attested by Literature is artificial.

Literature.

A literary *leguleius*—if not an *apprenticius*—whom we have met in the Temple, Thomas Hoccleve, introduces our best witnesses " into his *De Regimine Principum*, a lament for Gower and Chaucer and calls Gower his master " (*o*).

This association of these three poets is not their only

(*l*) *Encyc. Brit.* 1878.
(*m*) *N. E. D., Esquire* (1897). In 1859 the Q. B. saw no objection to an ironmonger so describing himself : *Perrins* v. *Marine Soc.*, 2 El. & El. 321-3.
(*o*) Sir S. Lee in D. N. B. : *Gower*.

bond; they were all, if they were not technically lawyers, " in and out " the hostels, either as members or as guests, and knew what was going on in Law-land. So no doubt did John Lydgate who " knew London life well " (*p*). Thus they reflect the social, if not the professional, life of the Inns and add a harmonious stroke to our picture.

John Gower, 1325?—1408 (*o*), cannot be claimed for the law *optimo jure* (*q*). As Mr. Macaulay points out he would hardly speak of the profession as he does, if he was a " lawyer "; his tone, he says, rather suggests the litigant. But he thinks (*r*) that he may have been " bred to the law, though he may not have practised it for a living " and he acutely calls attention to *Mirour de d'omme*. l. 21772 &c. (written about 1376),

> Je ne suy pas clers [*clericus*],
> Vestu de sanguin ne de pers,
> Ainz [though] ai vestu la raye manc[h]e,
> Poy sai latin, poy sai romance . . .

This may well mean—I am not a priest and only technically a lawyer : of the three languages, the latter must know (*s*), I know little.

Gower's burden is " the utter degeneration of everything " (as, in the words of Queen Victoria, Carlyle's was). The advantage for us of his comprehensiveness is

---

(*p*) *Idem, ib.: Lydgate.*

(*q*) Leland's " coluit forum et patrias leges, lucri causa; praeter cetera tamen humaniores literas : multumque in poesi sudavit " (*Comm.* 414, edn. 1709; about 1545) is supposed by Mr. Macaulay (*Works*, 4 vols., Oxf., 1899-1902—Leland died 1552) to be a mistake and perhaps a confusion with Gower mentioned Y. B. 30 E. III [pp. 18, 20, 25] (but *not* " apparently a serjeant-at-law "); there is nothing improbable in Gower's " appearing " in 1357; Lee, too, rejects his " entering the Inner Temple " (which Inn *Leland* does not mention, and rejects Bale's notice which is however not in the edn. of 1548). Leland is certainly wrong in saying under Chaucer (*ib.* 420) " illis temporibus inter forenses clarissimus erat J. Joverus "; there is nothing intrinsically improbable in a youth going to the bar " lucri causa " and turning to letters for the love of them.

(*r*) Lat. works, xxvi, n.

(*s*) See p. 354.

what we learn incidentally about the contemporary state of the law, for he dealt very roundly with the profession. " Of all the secular estates that of the law seems to him to be the worst (*t*) and he condemns both advocates and judges in a more unqualified manner than the members of any other calling " (*u*). Even in a passing simile we get a glimpse of a court at work.

6217.   quant Richesee vient pledant
            Poverte vait sanz defendant :
            Richesce donne et l'autre prie
            Richesce attrait en son guarant
            Le jugge questour et sergant
            Par queux sa cause justefie :

Of course, he makes play with " the tricks of the trade."

l. 24205.   Si la querelle false soit
            Et ly plaidour ce sciet et voit
            Qant doit pleder pour son client
            Lors met engin comment porroit
            Son tort aider at l'autry droit
            Abatre, dont soubtilement
            Procure le deslayement [adjournment] :
            Et entre ce, ne say comment
            De la cautele se pourvoit
            Q'il ad au fin le juggement
            Pour soy. O dieus omnipotent
            Vei la pledour de male endroit [kind].

Apparently this *pledour* had learned William of Drogheda's *cautelae* (*x*). Then, pleaders are mercenary, want pay :

(*t*) He says so categorically : *Mirour*, 24805.

(*u*) Macaulay : *Mirour de l'omme*, lxii; ll. 24181—25176 are the substantive part.

(*x*) Cf. l. 24799 : " Mais ils la loy ont destourné / En cautele et soubtilité," and l. 24920. Cf. *Vox Clamantis*, B. VI, 27.

        Nunc cum causidicus adverse jus fore partis
        Scit, tunc cautelas provocat ipse suas :
        Quod nequit ex lege, cautelis derogat ipse,
        Cum nequeat causam vincere, vexat eam, etc.

they juggle with "tort" and "fort"; they will not appear against one another (*y*). This is a very early instance of "the professional bias" which in respect of the lawyers occasionally crops up about this time. It is difficult to conceive them as a *class* of litigants except in matters growing out of their dealings with their clients: we know that later the Serjeants thought it worth while to claim that they could only be sued in their own court. Gower, at any rate, implies, the "solidarity" of the bar in 1375: there was an *esprit de corps*.

There is a curious tribute to the "democracy" of the hostels. There is something wrong, he says, when cobblers send their sons to learn "what he can't understand for neither his nature nor his strain is seasoned with justice (*z*). A boor (*vilain*) does not want to understand law (*droit*): but if he is to make money (*lucre*) he holds justice cheap." Gower is too extreme to be trusted on such a point: possibly he knew an isolated case. He goes on

"Anyone who can get himself up so as to wear a pleader's cloak (*mantell*) in the court of Westminster, is certain of advancement, for there cannot be in his part of the world (*en son paiis*) a dispute among poor folk of which he will not be a partaker (*parçonier*) by taking one side—thus he earns bread and clothing: cursed be such a hireling." The insinuation of "maintenance" and "champerty" is commonplace but the express reference to a legal uniform at this time is rare and rarer still that to the provincial practitioner coming up to town (*a*).

That he was deliberately exaggerating legal abuses we may gather from his categorical statement (24288-311) (*b*) that surgeons delayed their patients' recovery to swell their fees and that the lawyers did exactly the same in

---

(*y*) So l. 241: *Vox Clam*.
(*z*) So Macaulay, l. 24272. *Translations* of archaic French, above, are tentative merely.
(*a*) Perhaps "en son paiis" is unemphatic and only = within his knowledge.   (*b*) Repeated *Vox Clam*. 121.

their turn. The former indictment is as false as the latter. But it is probably true that Gower in his day had seen the scale of lawyers' fees go up considerably: he had certainly heard of, if he had not lived in the days when such emolument was nominal or small: " solidarity " again had led to a higher standard, and the poet turned the fact to literary account. In our own day old practitioners noted with astonishment the enhanced *rates* of pay.

Perhaps the same criticism may be made of his charge that the lawyers evaded taxation (*gabelle — taillage — tollage*). No doubt people did evade taxation and it is probable that the " gens du loy " knew how to claim " exempcioun " better than " Count or Baron " but, as we have seen, the Schedules of 1379 caught them close—perhaps an effect of this diatribe. At any rate, Gower suggests expressly that " plaidours et advocatz " should be made by law to disgorge. He seems to mean by taxation (*c*).

Coming more to details he reveals " the custom at Westminster." There the money-making stage is appearance in court—*conter*. But there are degrees. First, (*au commencer*) the *apprentis* are " blooded " (*encharné*) by pleading at the assizes (*assises*): they are all right as long as they get their " quarry " (*quirée*) *De l'argent que leur est donné* day by day but they are liable to a " false scent," *viz.*, a rich fee from the other side.

" But when the apprentice has completed a certain time "—unfortunately we do not know how long at this date—" enough to be a pleader then he wants the coif settled on his head and the title of *Sergant* for his honour " (*pris*—a play on *prix*). Each rank grows hungrier for what feeds on. And then we get a touch which shows " inside " knowledge on the writer's part. " Now they have a custom that when the apprentice is promoted to

---

(*c*) And hence Mr. Macaulay, p. lxii, thinks that he was not a practitioner.

the grade of a serjeant he must give a little (*pitance*) gold
—a thing of great significance, for this bit of gold means
that for the rest of his life he may get back gold for his
profit. But this is a good deal—to get the whole loaf for
a crumb—this is hardly holding the balance equally." It
is barely possible that the reference is to the distribution
of gold rings by the serjeants on their institution, which
was a very ancient custom, but, on the whole, it probably
means that the elect novice had to pay fees to the Inn,
officials, etc.—as not long afterwards, we know he had.
Thus he casts his bread on the waters: whereas private
douceurs would not procure the rank which was to repay
his outlay.

For the rest, there are always the traditional jibes.
" The serjeants don't care whether the *bargain* be *gentil*
or *vilain*, they will take it up if they are only paid—
enough. They are worse than usurers [who at least have
a fixed rate] for if they plead and win the value of a penny
they get any amount of gold for it, and with the cash in
their pockets know how to get out of it, though the client
is out of pocket."

One would certainly gather from these accumulated
denunciations that the lawyers were a rich and very greedy
body. The wealth, imputed to them is not otherwise
attested but the couplets (*d*) which suggest the rapid rise
of " profiteers " are likely enough to have truth—in any
avocation. Those which contain the literary device of
" the biter bit " are a good conceit.

O tu pledeur, qant a ce cas [at the last judgment]
Scies tu le plee? Je croy que nay.
A celle assisse, tout perdras
Et les damages (*e*) restorras
Dont t'alme [soul] estuet (must) paier le pay.

(*d*) Ll. 24529-40.
(*e*) Perhaps the earliest use in a legal sense. It is possible that
briefs, l. 24512, is a legal reminiscence though there the lawyer " sends
his *brief* " to a client.

However, he is good enough to conclude :—
> La loy de soy est juste et pure
> Et liberal de sa nature.

It is its professors of whom he complains :—
> Mais cils qui sont la loy gardant
> La pervertont, et font obscure
> Si la vendant a demesure . . .

From that day to this the costliness of English law cannot be denied, but, as regards deliberate obscurification during the same period, nothing has made the layman see that the element of uncertainty is chiefly supplied by the words and deeds—in both senses—of the ignorant or careless public.

Of those professors the peccant members are not only those at the bar, but " la justicerie " is as bad and a good deal of space is given to their shortcomings. Incidentally he implies that suitors brought letters to the judges from " grans seignours " recommending their suits—a practice well known *aliunde* and reminding us of Hoccleve's complaint of the great lord's " man " interfering in his office. For the rest, he protests too much about the bench : no body of men could ever be so shameless as he suggests.

And so, to sum up—
> Le pledeur ove le president
> Et l' apprentis et l' attourné (*f*)
> Le noun [name] portont improprement
> Du loy;

Next the inferior officers of the law, " Viscontes [Sheriffs] Baillifs, et Questours [Juratores]." The sheriffs, of course, can pack juries (*g*).

> le viscomte . . .
> Qui le panell ordeinera
> Des fals jurours a l'avantage
> De luy q'ad tort.

and gets something out of both parties.

(*f*) Only here apparently. The *procurator* he does not seem to know, but he has *procurour* (non-legal).   (*g*) Ll. 24177-5177.

There is a valuable passage on the *juratores* (*h*) : " he tells us " says Mr. Macaulay " of a regularly established class of men whose occupation it is to arrange for the due packing and bribing of jurors. He asserts that of the corrupt jurors there are certain captains who are called ' tracers ' (*traciers*) because they draw (*treront*) the others to their will. If they say that white is black the others will say ' quite so ' and swear it too. . . . Those persons who at assizes desire to have corrupt jurymen to try their cases must speak with these ' tracers,' for all who are willing to sell themselves in this manner are hand in glove with them and so the matter is arranged. The existence of a definite name for this class of undertakers seems to indicate that it was really an established institution."

That may be so, but this definite organization is not otherwise known and probably refers to some local knot of men like Oates and Dangerfield or Tammany. But the practising on juries in Gower's day is well borne out—notably, as we have seen, by Bromyard (*i*). Possibly it was made easier because the gradual change from the accusing and testifying (*k*) jury, the steps of which have never been traced, to the judicial jury (*l*) was just then taking place. Thus " juror " to Gower does not mean

(*h*) Ll. 25033— : Macaulay, 'p. lxvii. So *Vox Cl.* B. VI, c. 6 : ll. 427-44.

(*i*) P. 154. Cf. 11 H. VI, c. 4 : 1433 : " the usual perjury of jurors impanelled upon Inquests . . . for the great gifts that such jurors take of the parties in pleas."

(*k*) Ll. 25105-16 may refer to such a jury but probably a witness who deliberately stays away is meant.

(*l*) L. 25169 : " le visconte ove (with) la douszeine "=some kind of jury. Probably the purely judicial jury began about this time for in 1402 certain friars " enditid before the justices " at Westminster, of treason, though the judge said " I counsel you to put you in the Kyngis grace," replied, " We put us on the cuntre," " And neither men of London, ne of Holborne wolde dampne thaym : and thanne thay hadde an enquest of Yseldon and thay saide ' Gilti ' " : *Engl. Chron.* 25-26; Camd. Soc. (1856); perhaps the earliest instance of a jury (or two) disagreeing. Britton, B. II, c. 21, amply provides for such juries in his day.

quite the same thing as it does now. We have endeavoured (*m*) to show that the *jurator* was generally the well-to-do citizen who would be called on when any sworn *inquest* was taken : hence *questour*.

The poet ends this *tirade* by emphasizing that what he has said is true—they are *all* in the same case—and regretting it.

Book VI of the *Vox Clamantis*—written soon after 1381 when the revolting peasants made a " dead set " at the lawyers—is devoted to the same theme and expressed to the same effect as the stretch of the French poem we have dealt with. There is therefore no need to recall it (*n*). But some lines may be singled out, *e.g.*,

    157 : Cum magis et numerum lex auget causidicorum.

This certainly implies that there was an official recognition of *causidici* and we know that the Crown created the Serjeants, one by one. In a satire of this nature the satirist might fairly include in his sweep the *attornati* who, we know, were beginning to swarm as he says (l. 289) " Absque tamen numero sunt legis in orbe (*o*) scolares." It may be doubted whether any more virulent lines have been penned than the following :—

225   Causidici nubes sunt ethera qui tenebrescunt,
        Lucem quo solis nemo videre potest;
        Obfuscant etenim legis clarissima jura
        Et sua nox tetra vendicat esse diem;
        Istis inque viris perdit sua lumina splendor,
        Verum mentitur, fraus negat esse fidem.
        Lex furit et pietas dormit sapiencia fallit
        Pax grauat et lites commoda queque ferunt.

Then we get an express recognition of the legal hierarchy, " rising," says the rubric, " from step to step, *causidici* and *juris advocati*, candidates for the bench."

(*m*) Thus Mr. Macaulay's " juror " for *questour* is misleading.

(*n*) Especially as there is an excellent analysis by Mr. Macaulay : *Latin* Works, pp. l—liii.

(*o*) Urbe? L. 430, " in urbe mea "=London. N.B. *Lex*=Law.

C. 4. 1. Est Apprenticius, Sergantus post et Adultus.
"If he has ambition at the first stage, much more he has it in the second, and the third degree is the most culpable of all." The refrain about lawyers being corrupted by gold is positively monotonous.

The references are not always easy to understand but one which apparently contemplates a lord's court is interesting. "With a full purse, I can escape the law: or (*p*), if a magnate's court is friendly to me, I don't want other help. I speak for myself"—which seems to mean, I appear in person. The next chapter is devoted to the venal bench (*q*), in terms which to-day would be colossal contempt of court.

C. vi corresponds to the French passage, p. 480. The rubric is "de errore . . . in assisis juratorum," where, and in the text, *assisis* may refer to the Eyres as distinct from Westminster, and not improbably does so, as in l. 547 the High Court (*curia major*) is also mentioned.

He certainly intended to paint from life—and he was not alone—when he wrote (*r*):

"And for him [a poor Roman Knight] lacketh of despence
Ther was with him non advocat
To make ple for his astat [state, case]."

He says to Julius, the Emperor-Judge:
' Behold mi conseil is withdrawne
For lacke of gold : . . .
Help that I hadde conseil hiere
Upon the trouthe of mi matiere.'
And Julius with that anon
Assigned him a worthi on."

(*p*) 305. Aut si magnatis michi curia sit specialis / Nil opus est legum viribus, ipse loquor.

(*q*) It is possible that the luxurious *vestes* (l. 391) refers to their official robes.

(*r*) *Confessio Amantis* : B. 7, l. 2066, p. 289, ed. Macaulay.

The two uses (*s*) of the same word in these lines shows that *consilium* was now beginning to be used of the person, the first English instance, being, perhaps, this.

The same theme—no money, no counsel—inspires John Lydgate's " London Lackpeny "—" a perfect picture of London " (*t*), *temp.* H. VI. At any rate, it shows us Westminster Hall at work about 1400.

> " To London once my steppes I bent
> Where trouth in no wyse should be faynt;
> To Westminster-ward I forthwith went
> To a man of law, to complaynt;
> I sayd for Maries love (that holy saynt)
> Pyty the poore that wold proceede;
> But for lacke of money, I cold not spede."

The last line is the refrain. The narrator " kneels " to the judge in the King's Bench—in vain : " a great rout " of clerks sat writing and calling out the names of the parties—the spectator suggests that those who could not find their fees " did not speed." Then he went to " the common place " [pleas]

> " Where sat one wyth a sylken hoode (*u*)
> I dyd him reverence (for I ought to do so)
> I told my case there, as well as I coude,
> Howe my goodes were defrarded me by falshood,
> I got not a move of his mouthe for my mede
> And for lacke &c. ."

Then he tries the Rolls and the " clarkes of the Chauncerye " : they think well of his " playnt " but are too busy " earnyng of pense " to attend to him. Back to Westminster Hall, where he supplicates " one which went in a long gowne of raye "—of course, in vain. After other

---

(*s*) But N. E. D. take the second also = a person and gives *conseil* from Chaucer in 1386 as = a person (*not* a lawyer).

(*t*) Strutt, 3 *Engl. Manners* &c. 59.

(*u*) Imitated from *Piers Plowman*, p. 363; Skeat, *Piers Pl.* pt. II, p. 22.

adventures, all threatening expense, he resolves " to medle no more " of the law and goes back to Kent, praying

" Save London and send trew lawyers there mede
For whoso wants money wyth them shall not spede."

Very much in the same vein is " the Childe of Bristow " (x), attributed to Lydgate. A wicked " squyer mykel of myght " having amassed great wealth, partly because " to lawe he went a gret while " (y) and thus robbed poor folk, naturally brings up his son to the law.

" When the child was xii yere and more
His fader put him unto lore
to lerne to be a clerke :
So long he lernyd in clergie,
till he was wise and wittye
and drad all dedis derke.
The fader seid to his sone dere
' to lawe thu shalt go a yere
and cost me xx marke;
for ever the better thu shalt be
ther shall no man be gile the (z)
neyther in worde ne werke.'
The child answerd w^t a soft sawe
' they fars [fare] ful well y^t lerne no lawe.' "

Perhaps we have here the earliest literary recognition of the combination of lore and law, the " learned " profession. At twelve the boy is " put to the university or a monastic school " (a) where he would be taught Latin. How long he stays there we do not know, but in order to become a practising lawyer, he is, it seems at a cost

---

(x) Camden Soc. 4 *Miscellany* 9 : no. 61; 1859.

(y) Apparently to study as in (z).

(z) So in 1445 Paston J.'s widow writes to her son in " Clyffords Inn " of " youre fadris counseyle to lerne the lawe for he seyde manie tymis that ho so ever schuld dwelle at Paston schulde have nede to conne defende hym selfe " : *Paston Let.* no. 46, ed. Gairdner : 1872.

(a) A. E. Randall : 143 *L. Q. R.* 283 n. : 1920.

of 20 marks *per annum*, to go to a *hospitium*, presumably in London, perhaps to one of the " minor " ones; if so, we have a hint what it costs to send a young law student (*b*)—he would be about fourteen or fifteen—up to town from the provinces about 1400. The " soft saw " is meant to convey popular satire, and the lad declines in so many words to go into such a soul-destroying profession.

If we could be sure that Lydgate was the writer, it would be almost certain that he was thinking of a young law-student going to an Inn of Court, for he was constantly making " topical " verses about London affairs, and herein, of lawyers. Another touch in this poem is " good law." The " childe's " father on his deathbed is very anxious about his " executor "; that word is used once (v. 19). Elsewhere he is called " my attorney." It is pretty clear that then as now the professional lawyer was called in to make a will and, very often, to execute it.

Enfin Malherbe vint. With Chaucer we have no longer to do with the recluse or the preacher or the *censor morum*, hardly with the critic, but with " a man of the world," whether it be that of affairs or that of idealism. His view of the lawyers represents the prevailing view of the English people.

His dates are 1340?—1400 (*c*). Leland (*d*) says that about the " last " years of Richard II he " flourished in France with great literary fame " which preceded him home to England; there " happy in his success he frequented the London *forum* and the hostels (*collegia leguleiorum*) who in those places (*ibidem*) study the laws

---

(*b*) Cf. p. 500, for the normal law student.

(*c*) Prof. Hales, in D. N. B., who does not mention the alleged connection with the law.

(*d*) P. 475*q*; *Comm.* 420 : " last " must be a mistake for " first "; *p'mos* (primos) has been read *postremos* : for Ch. certainly did not " frequent, etc.," shortly before his death. His last visits abroad (France, etc.) were about 1377-9 (D. N. B.), the earliest 1359-72. Speght translates L. without comment.

of their country, as *perhaps he had done before* he went to France (ante Galliam cognitam)."

Speght in (1598 or) 1602 confused the story further. " It seemeth that Chaucer was of the inner Temple; for not many years since Master Buckley did see a Record in the same house, where Geffrey Chaucer was fined two shillings for beating a Franciscane frier in Fleetstreet." Mr. Lounsbury remarks (*e*) that no one knows who Mr. Buckley was (and that none but he saw the paper), adding : " This like the meeting with Petrarch is a story which whether true or not, we all feel, ought to be true " (*f*).

Nevertheless it is quite likely that both Gower and Chaucer did in their youth frequent the legal abodes; the

---

(*e*) *Studies in Chaucer* (1892), v. 1, p. 172 : there may have been another G. C.

(*f*) Selden in 1653, *Judicium de X Scripp.*, 2 Works (1171-2), insists on Ch.'s acquaintance with law and lawyers and asserts that he was (as S. himself was) a member of the Inner Temple : but he gives no authority—perhaps merely follows Speght.

The point has been carefully argued in favour of Speght by Prof. J. M. Manly in *Some New Light on Chaucer*, pp. 11—14; New York, 1926 : relying upon Miss E. Rickert in " Manly Anniversary Studies." They assert that Mr. Buckley is " William Buckeley the late chief butler of the House [I. T.] in 1 Inderwick *Cal. I. T. R.* 265 in 1572 [and no doubt *ib.* 235 in 1564-5 " the elder Buckeley, the butler "] : very likely he " did see " such " a record," but their fallacy is in assuming that because the authorities fined someone he must have been " a member " : he may have been a guest or inmate —quite enough to found jurisdiction, for, if their order was not obeyed they could easily exclude the defaulter, certainly before 1400 (and probably now); probably the offender got in or out of a door or window of the Society's from or to Fleet St. Perhaps it was not the poet at all.

In 1926 in " Chaucer and the Rhetoricians " (British Acad. : Wharton Lect.), p. 6, the same scholar says : " The antient tradition that " Ch. " was educated in part at any rate in the law school of the Inner Temple has recently been shown to be possible, if not highly probable. The education given by the inns of court seems to have been remarkably liberal. What more likely than that the formal study of rhetoric not only was included in his academic curriculum as one of the seven arts, but also occupied much of his thought and reflection in maturer years? " There was certainly no public teaching of " Rhetoric."

literary critics we have cited, who deny their " entering " this or that Inn, perhaps attached too precise a sense to that activity. Leland never suggests that either practised, though he implies that Gower would have been glad to make money thereby if he could; perhaps it was because he could not that he " took to " literature like many others since. What Leland means is that these poets, like many other gentlefolk of their day, resorted freely to one of the two nurseries of culture in London. It was a centre of good fellowship and a fit youth might be free of it without being a registered " member."

Speght's story has, however, a slight value in showing that someone before his day believed that about (say) 1370 the Inns were exercising discipline over their inmates. Otherwise the earliest recorded instance (*g*) seems to be at Lincoln's Inn in 1465 when Kenelm Digas was " put out of the Society."

The internal evidence points to the same conclusion, *viz.*, that the poet was not a trained lawyer, but was conversant socially with legal circles.

There are few instances (*h*), it would seem, of technical law in his works, and those there are are such as any well read man might know. He was too great an artist to make his serjeant " talk shop " (*i*) when it came to his turn, or not to make the Host (try to) do so.

" Ye been submitted thurgh your free assent
To stonde in *this* cas at my jugement.
Acquiteth yow and holdeth your biheste
Than have ye doon your devoir atte leste."

(*g*) For drawing his dagger in Hall upon a " Fellow," *i.e.*, member. 1 *Black Books*, p. 40 : many other instances later.

(*h*) See 140 *L. Q. R.* 303, where the *Tale of Melibeus* is quoted : Dr. Furnivall suggested that perhaps it was originally meant for the lawyer; its " real author " was actually a lawyer : Skeat, v. 3, p. 406, and v. 5, p. 141.

(*i*) Which his commonplace in the Introduction cannot be called : " For swiche lawe as man yeveth another wight / He sholde himselven usen it by right."

The other poets whom we have cited have taken lawyers as a class for their theme; Chaucer is the first, whether he had any individual in his mind or not, to paint a definite man (k) and as it is the first finished picture of an English lawyer, we reproduce it.

> A Sergeant of the Lawe, war and wys
> That often hadde been at the parvys,
> Ther was also, ful riche of excellence.
> Discreet he was, and of greet reverence.
> He semed swich, his wordes weren so wyse.
> Justyce he was ful often in asseyse
> By patente and by pleyn commissioun :
> For his science and for his heigh renoun
> Of fees and robes hadde he many oon.
> So greet a purchasour was no wher noon.
> Al was fee simple to him in effect,
> His purchasing mighte not been infect.
> No-where so bisy a man as he ther nas,
> And yet he semed bisier than he was.
> In termes hadde he caas and domes alle
> That from the tyme of King William were falle.
> Therto he coulde endyte and make a thing,
> Ther coude no wight pinche at his wryting;
> And every statut coud he pleyn by rote.
> He rood but hoomly in a medlee cote
> Girt with a ceint of silk, with barres smale;
> Of his array telle I no longer tale (l).

(k) See p. 260u.
Apparently the only passage in which Chaucer speaks of the class, and that with the conventional blame, is :
  " She [Coveityse] maketh false pledoures
  That with hir termes and hir domes . . . "
ruin folk, is a translation from the French (*Romaunt of the Rose*, 1. 199) : Skeat, v. I, p. 101, who shows that this part of the *R. of the R.* is by Ch. The second of these two lines is purely English legal phraseology (repeated above : " In termes—alle ").

(l) Skeat's text (1894) and notes follow [when not bracketed] : parvys = church-porch or portico of St. Paul's. [But probably Westminster Hall is meant as Somner (d. 1699) in Glossary, *Triforium*,

490   A HISTORY OF THE BAR.

There are many significant points in this famous passage. That a writer about 1385-6 should take a serjeant as the type of a lawyer and that he was often a

to Twysden, *Decem, &c.* (1652), asserts; Whitelock, too, *Memorials of Engl. Affairs* under Nov. 1648 (p. 348 : ed. 1682), in a speech to the Serjeants, says that he found in a MS. [probably by Sir Roger Owen of L. I. (died 1617) and still in Harleian MSS. : Reeves, 1 *Hist. Eng. Law*, 8 (1787), thought little of it; see this speech and one immediately preceding] that the Serjeants " kept their Pillars at Pauls where their clients might find them "; " as if," adds Wh., " they did little better than *emendicare panem*. This was somewhat far from Westminster Hall and as far from truth, being grounded upon a mistake of one of their ceremonies of state where [when?] they went to Pauls to offer; "Pauls" seems to be due to W. Harrison's *Description of England* (1577), p. 181, prefixed to Holinshed's *Chronicle*, B. II, c. 9, p. 204, ed. Furnivall (1877) : " The time hath beene that our lawiers did sit in Pawles upon stooles against the pillers and walles to get clients . . ."; it was thus a legend in Harrison's day when the *parvys* was certainly at Westminster (as Somner says). In 1854 Sir Pat. Colquhoun said (? *Summary*, § 2009 : " even at the present time a pillar in the cathedral [St. P.] is assigned to a serjeant on his creation "). Whitelock is perhaps borne out by Machyn's *Diary*, 17 Oct. 1552 : Camd. Soc. No. 42, p. 26 : seven serjeants, on the day of their creation, go to Westminster Hall in the morning, and " after dener they whent unto Powlls and so whent up the stepes and so round the qwere—and ther dyd ther homage and so [came unto] the north syd of Powlles and stod a-pone the stepes until iiij old serjantes came together and feythchyd iiij [new] and broght them unto serten pelers and left them and then dyd feyched the resedue unto the pelers : and ther was an oration red unto them by the old sergants. . . ."
Much the same in 1559, *ib*. 195 : they go first to St. Thomas of Acres.

For Fortescue, see p. 497; *n.b.* he does not mention " Paul's."]

purchasour—fee—infect : Sk. cites Mr. W. H. H. Kelke, *Notes and Queries*, 5th s., vi, p. 487 : Dec. 16, 1876 : " purchasyng = conveyancing; *infect* = invalid. This was the very time when the wit of lawyers was exercised on methods newly contrived or adapted from the civil law, to circumvent the statutes *De Donis* and suchlike—methods which culminated in ' Taltarum's case ' and the elaborate fiction of common recoveries. The learned ' Sergeant ' was clever enough to untie any entail and pass the property as estate in fee simple. The whole context forbids any reference to criminal law." In termes : He was well acquainted with all the legal cases and decisions (or decrees) which had befallen since &c. : [perhaps it = knew them by their terms—as cases were always so dated : see p. 489k, where "t." = " legal jargon " (Sk. *Gloss.*). And so Selden, cited p. 487f : *temporibus statis seu diebus pro more fastis (quos Terms dicimus) distinctas causas habuit universas ac judicia* : he certainly thinks that there were reports as far back as William. But Sir F. Pollock, *First Book, &c.*, 278, doubts this and thinks the lines are " a poetic and humorous exaggera-

"Commissioner" of Assize is what we should expect, and we are glad to have authority that the fee system was already in full swing and that robes were part of the bar's *insignia* (*m*). And "by commissioun" we know to this day (*n*); "by patente," too, is strictly accurate. Britton, about 1290, says (*o*) expressly that in every county justices were to be assigned *par nos lettres patentes* " in causes of petty assises and other matters." But such work was exceptional; his ordinary business was conveyancing, the chief commercial or litigious interest being, of course, real property. Criminal courts are not mentioned, probably because counsel were seldom seen in them, and, at any rate, only for the Crown, though when he was " justice " he must try indictments. Nor is anything said about his best " barside " manner, though when he says (*p*) " I speke in prose," he means that that is what he is accustomed to in the courts; any play on his forensic mannerism would have destroyed the gravity of the picture; probably, too, there was little material therefor in the absence of cross-examination and speeches to juries or anything but technical argument. Yet Chaucer cannot refrain his humour from a sly hit at the busy man who seemed busier than he was—another trait which he has transmitted to his professional descendant. But he possessed what then constituted professional merit—great knowledge of statute and case-law—the latter still the distinction of many practitioners. Its mention, as suggesting the quotation of decided cases, either in opinions or public argument or both, shows that law reporting

---

tion," and no doubt the word " all " is : see p. 510.] endyte*: compose. thing : deed, document. pinche : blame. medlee, mixed stuff or colour. ceint : girdle. barres : *clavi*.

(*m*) See the suggestion, pp. 366*c*, 468.

(*n*) See Blackstone, 3 *Comm.* 60.

(*o*) I, i, § 10 : 1 Nich. p. 6. Bracton, *de actionibus*, 107b, calls it a " warrant " 2 Rolls, 180 : he distinctly says that such itinerants lost their jurisdiction as soon as their warrant was exhausted.

(*p*) Introdn. to his prologue, l. 96 : 3 Skeat, 406.

was now familiar. The reference to King William is probably not one to technical " legal memory," probably unknown at that date, but seems to imply, correctly, that the popular view was that the forensic system of the day practically began with the coming of the Normans and not earlier. The feat of memory, over about two centuries, is not so striking as would be the corresponding one of the modern lawyer (*q*), but it implies that there was no longer any hesitation what pronouncement of Parliament was law and what was not.

Finally, it has been pointed out by authority (*r*) that though our hero is represented as opulent yet he is plainly clad. In other words, in 1380 a prosperous lawyer is represented socially as belonging to the upper middle class, as are most of the immortal pilgrims.

But it is the negative implications of this scheme which are most valuable to the historian. The *narrator* entirely, and the *countor* almost entirely, have disappeared and the attorney is not as much as mentioned (*s*). Even if we could not expect a leading part for the latter, the law being so well represented, we should expect some reference to him somewhere, if, when Chaucer wrote, the individuality of his profession was prominent enough. We conclude then that it was not, though he was undoubtedly abroad in the land. The *countour* perhaps is not so totally ignored. The " Frankeleyn," the Squire or Country Gentleman

" A shirreve hadde he been and a countour "

" was no-wher such a worthy vavasour."

Even Skeat was doubtful what this meant, " perhaps . . .

(*q*) Coleridge, A.-G., told the House of Commons that Coke once said : if I am asked about the common law, I can answer it in bed, but if about statute law, I must get up and examine the statutes : *Hansard*, May 6 (1872), 280.

(*r*) 2 Strutt's *English Dress*, p. 280 (1799).

(*s*) If we may judge by Skeat's *Glossary*. The two instances in the *Suppl. Vol.* 1897 are not by Ch., but are contemporary.

auditor " (v. 5, p. 35); *i.e.*, accountant (or treasurer?);
at any rate, a county notable, as to-day, for
 " At sessiouns ther was he lord and sire,
 Ful ofte tyme he was Knight of the shire."
Thus the picture would be even more modern if we could
suppose that the M.P. and Chairman of 1370 had been
called " to the bar," but a *countour* means more than that
—it means an actual practitioner. But of this the poet
gives no hint and the combination in 1370 is most
improbable. Selden, perhaps, has preserved the poet's
real idea. Quoting (*t*) the couplet to explain *vavasour*, he
reads to rhyme with it *Coronour*, though he is well aware
of the ordinary reading. Despite his statement, " so some
copies have it," Skeat does not mention it (*u*). Selden
could hardly be mistaken that *coronour* was found and, as
he evidently preferred it, we may perhaps think that the
Squire was more likely to be a *coronator*—specifically a
county magistrate (*x*)—than a serjeant. Be that as it
may, Selden makes a point that Chaucer thought that a
vavasour was socially higher than a *serjeant* (or a
coronator) and no doubt in their early days he was.

But the most conspicuous absence is that of the
lawyers' Inns. For all that Chaucer says, his Serjeant

(*t*) *Titles of Honor*, 579; 3rd ed. 1672; Pt. 2, c. v, 4: *Complete Works*, 1726, v. 3, p. 661: at p. 1027 (" Additions, &c.") he only cites *countour* which he argues = serjeant. In this sense it and *coronour* are unique in Ch.

(*u*) Sk. cites " [l. 801. Or maynteyners of men with maistry]
 Or stewards, countours or pleadours "
(of the clergy in) *Plowman's Tale*, Pt. III (Suppl. vol. 172: or 1 *Polit. Poems* (Rolls), 328), which he shows (pp. xxxii, xxxiv) is not by Ch. and dates about 1394; he thinks *c.* = auditor here, too, but surely in this connection it means these people were mischief-makers—like the lawyers. So, " Now maynteneryers be made justys " (2 *Polit. Poems*, 235: Rolls, ed. Wright, dated about 1456) = the lawyers raised to the bench (in the ordinary way) are mere maintainers. See further p. 466.

(*x*) Who, being a " secular man," could be appointed by a friendly local lord as said in *Ordinances*, &c., p. 27, of the *Liber Niger Domus Regis E. IV*: Soc. of Antiq., 1790.

may never have seen one. If, in his days, the leaders of the bar had in those societies anything like the functions at which by a very logical process they arrived later, some allusion to such splendid literary material would not have escaped the sociable poet. The houses have not, in fact, escaped, but they are in the sphere of the Maunciple (*y*) and not of the Sergeant, and we infer from the want of " solidarity " between the two figures that they were unconnected in 1387.

" A gentil Maunciple was ther of a temple

. . . .

[It is wonderful]
That swich a lewed [not literate] mannes wit shal
    pace [(sur)pass]
The wisdom of an heep of learned men.
Of maistres hadde he mo than thryes ten
That were of lawe expert and curious;
Of which ther wer a doseyn in that hous
Worthy to been stiwardes of rente and lond
Of any lord that is in Engelond.

. . . .
. . . .

And able for to helpen al a shire
In any cas that mighte falle or happe; "

If the first line of this passage ended " *the* temple " the variant would have some importance, but as Skeat does not mention it, we may dismiss it (*z*). To what then did Chaucer refer? " *A temple*," says Skeat, " is here an ' inn of court ' (*a*); besides the Inner and Middle Temple[s] . . . there was also an Outer Temple." If this is a hint

---

(*y*) Purveyor to " a college, an inn of court, &c. (Still in use)." Sk., *e.g.*, at Queen's College, Oxford: from *mancipium*—a domestic servant, *e.g.*, App. XV, No. 11: Bownt perhaps was a grateful " maistre ": Robert may be the original of Ch.'s Sketch.

(*z*) Of 8 MSS. in the British Museum only one has " the ": 4 Foss, 28.

(*a*) An anachronism in 1387.

that the poet was thinking of three different adjoining buildings, whether so named in his day or not, we may accept the suggestion, for though, agreeably to his manner, we should not expect him to single out one Inn rather than another, yet if he only had two to choose from he would probably express that it was one of two. But as a matter of fact he had to distinguish from many others with the same name and origin, for the Order, says Stow (b), " had also other temples in Cambridge, Bristow, Canterbury, Dover, Warwick "—a fact with which Chaucer's readers would be familiar.

At any rate, there were three " Temples " next door to one another. As Dr. Bellot (c) justly observes " Inner " and " Outer " imply the existence of each other and " Middle " implies two others. Modern survivals do not contradict this relation. Of the Outer Temple Buc (c) tells us (p. 1069b) that originally " the Temples or the Templars Inne (for so I have seene them written in an old monument) . . . came to be divided into three several houses, yet they were at the first all but one house . . . (1070b) But the other third part called the Outward Temple, Doctor Stapleton Bishop of Exceter had gotten," *temp*. E. II, and it was long known as Exëter House. This seems to be the only authority for the early " Outer " Temple. As a building it never became the name of a legal society (d), though no doubt from time to time its homonymous neighbours acquired and absorbed part of its territory (e).

Next, is there another " Chaucerism " in the gullibility of the " heep of lerned men " ? Is it a reference to the conventional peculations or " pickings " of butler-like folk

---

(b) *Survey*, 402, citing Mat. Paris (p. 615, ed. 1640) : 2 Kingsford, p. 48.

(c) Cited App. XV, No. 11 and No. 8.

(d) Probably the outside site was of great commercial value.

(e) Thus in 1510 and 1517 the Inner Temple authorities dispose of a chamber : 1 *Cal. I. T. Rec.* 19, 40.

in general? or is it a characteristic hit at this particular one's employers? As they were titularly "lerned," it probably is, especially as they, we are immediately told, were expert lawyers. In other words, the steward "made a good thing" out of his masters, the commoners of the Inns. And he had more than thirty to look after. For that number is not chosen at haphazard—all the portraits of the Prologue are taken from life. And the figure is inherently probable, for Ferne tells us that thirty or (*f*) forty years later there were "scarcely threescore" in one of the Inns. These are the earliest statistics of the sort that we have.

The "doseyn" of promising lawyers in the society is no doubt a round number. They could hardly be the governors later known as benchers, for, apart from the probable anachronism, there would be an intolerable deal of sack to such a small amount of bread. Apparently what is meant is that in that group of expert and careful lawyers—for by this time opinion was distinguishing between the sound and the indifferent *causidicus*—about a third were specially capable of advising on real property —still the staple of litigation—or of administering it as we know William Paston did when he was at the bar. This is what we should expect if the societies were mainly recruited, as we have reason to believe, at this time from the landed families. Their youth would know about the land and their advice might be sought from their respective counties. Indeed, that about 1380 lawyers were advising "al a shire" is an interesting technical "item" and another indication that Chaucer was acquainted with the concerns of the Inns. For the unique English procedure by which "the men" of such a territorial unit were justiciable goes back at least to (about) 1100 (*g*) and probably earlier.

(*f*) According to the date of the Prologue : see 1 Sk. lxiii.
(*g*) " Si totus comitatus vel separatim hundreta super aliquibus

To Chaucer, then, these legal *sodalitia* were rather dwelling-places and houses of sojourn than seats of education—a theme which he does not touch. Perhaps, indeed, his silence confirms our belief that as yet there was no, certainly no developed, system of legal education. At any rate, for him the mature Serjeant represents the law; the prominent figure (*h*) from the *hospitia*—outside them, at any rate—is the Purveyor. Forty years later in the Paston correspondence various persons from the country seem still to frequent various of these Inns very much as to-day they do hotels. But it is easy to see in the poet's pictures the embryo of the society we know well.

John Fortescue.

There seems to be no doubt that he was born before Chaucer died in 1400. It was nearly seventy years later, we are told, when he wrote the book which chiefly concerns us. We shall have to ask, was he then writing about the days of his youth or of his age? If the former is true, he is describing therein the Temple which Chaucer knew; in any case the two works may fairly be called the obverse and the converse of the same picture, for assuredly the lawyer knew intimately what only interested the poet socially; but it is great literary luck to have both versions. Unfortunately there is little evidence about the interval, troublous times including the Wars of the Roses, 1450-71.

Fortescue was of good family and is said to have been at Exeter College, Oxford. There is no reason to doubt Dugdale's insertion of his name in a list (*i*) of the *Gubernatores* of Lincoln's Inn in 1425, 1426 and 1429.

---

inplacitentur etc." : *Leg. H. Pr.* § 48; 1 L. p. 571. In 1705 in *R.* v. *Inhabitants of Wiltshire*, Holt C.J. said: "An attachment may go against the inhabitants of the whole county and catch as many as one can of them " : 1 Salk. 389.

(*h*) Cf. p. 449*h*, the " courtesans " addressed corporately.

(*i*) *Orig. Judic.* 257, ed. 2, from " Registr. Hosp. Linc., v. 1, f. 9b and 17b " : he is called " junior " in 1425 and 1426.

Dugdale apparently did not know the entry in " Black Book no. 1 folios 1 to 7 " (*k*) of members admitted before 1420, among whom are " Fortescue Senr., Fortescue Junr.," the latter supposed to be John. His name frequently appears in the following years in the " Black Books " (*l*) of the Society, once as holding the important office of Pensioner and in 1444-5 as Chief Justice. He is mentioned as a counsel, apparently for the first time, in 1429-30 (*m*), and as he is not styled *Apprenticius* he was then probably a Serjeant. He was a judge (*i.e.*, Commissioner) of Assize in 1440 and 1441, Chief Justice in 1442. From 1463 to 1471 he was in exile in France till he returned to England, and is not heard of as alive after 1476. As he was writing, *inter alia*, his reminiscences in *de laudibus legum Angliae* about 1468-70, it is reasonable to suppose that he knew well the legal system which he had left behind only a few years before. In Lorraine, it is true, he would have few opportunities of getting points of practice from home, but, on the other hand, he had plenty of leisure after his return to revise his MSS., which were not published in his lifetime. Where his facts can be checked they are accurate, and there is no reason to doubt the soundness of his memory. We may believe therefore that his famous account of the Inns fairly represents them as he knew them, undoubtedly as an " apprentice " in his youth, and throughout his lifetime. It would not be an exaggeration to say that that account reveals exactly the sort of development we should expect *a priori* from what is known of their previous history.

Perhaps a fair criticism of that account is by Mr. Plummer, whose sketch of his Life, etc. (*n*), is by far the best, *viz.* : " It is tinged like the whole of the work

---

(*k*) *Lincoln's Inn Admission Register*, v. 1, p. 1 (1896).
(*l*) v. I, pp. 4, 15 (1897).
(*m*) Y. B. 8 H. VI, f. 8a.
(*n*) In his introduction, p. 41, to the *Governance of England*; Oxford, 1885.

from which it is taken with a very rosy colour." Fortescue would not have denied that he was an idealist, exhorting a future king to a noble polity, one of the bases of which was the existing fabric of the law and this, as a rule, he had no motive to garble. Thus, his first allusion (c. 8) is natural enough : " points of law (*l. sacramenta*) are left to your judges and advocates (*advocatis*) who in England are called Serjeants at law and to other skilled persons, commonly called [n.b.—it was not official] Apprentices." Incidentally the writer says that the skill in practice (*peritia*) necessary for judges is hardly acquired by the " lucubrationes " of twenty years (*o*)—which, in this context, fairly means that a man can hardly expect to get on to the bench before he has been twenty years at the bar, *i.e.*, presumably from entering an Inn.

We pass to the great chapters of this work, which might almost be called the charter of the profession.

C. 47. The Chancellor makes the Prince ask him : " Why are the laws of England not taught in the Universities as the Civil and Canon Laws are and why, there, are degrees of Bachelor and Doctor not usually conferred [on common lawyers] as in other faculties and Sciences?" The direct answer (c. 48) to this question is that studies at the Universities must be pursued in Latin while practice in the courts required a knowledge of French (*p*) and English as well—or, in modern language, theory is the business of the Universities, practice that of the lawyers in London, who are thus brought on the scene :

(*o*) Almost certainly a round number as in *De Natura legis naturae* pt. 1, v. I, c. 43; ed. Ld. Clermont) written about 1461-3 : see below, p. 511.

In c. 10 of that work (pt. 2, v. I, p. 124) he says of himself that " for *more than* 40 years he had studied and practised English law till now at length he filled the supreme judicial office," *i.e.*, he was (*quasi-*)Chancellor; he would hardly so describe the C.J. If so, he entered an Inn about 1415.

(*p*) For Fortescue's views on the origin of law-French, which are here interposed, see pp. 341*o*, 354*g*.

A* " Among French documents are reported the pleadings arguments, judgments in the courts which are reduced into book form for the instruction of those coming on." Thus the scheme of legal education is " let in " *ab imo*.

B " English law, then, is studied in a public school (*studio*) more convenient and handier (*proniore*) to that end than any university. For that school is situated near the *Curia Regis* where that law is pleaded and argued under which judgment is given by judges, old and sober men, who are experienced in that law and have a degree in it [=are serjeants] : thither, to those courts on every day that they sit the law-students flock, as to public schools (*scholis* sc. in the universities) and learn the law.

That School is situated between the seat of those courts and the City of London, which is the richest of all the cities and towns of England in its resources. And that School is not within that City where the turmoil of crowds might destroy quiet study but some distance apart, in a suburb of the City, nearer those courts which are thus easily accessible to the learners every day.

C C. 49. I will describe the school as best I can (*ut valeo*) (*q*). It contains ten — sometimes more — minor (*minora*) Inns, which are called Inns of Chancery. To any
D one of these belong, at least a hundred students (*studentes*) and to some, more, though, they are not all there at the same time. Most of them are young, learning the *Original Writs*, *i.e.*, the first elements of law : as they get on in course of time, they are taken into the major (*majora*) Inns of the School, the Inns of Court as they are called. Of these there are four and to the smallest of them belong in the sense before-mentioned (*r*) about two hundred. Now, in these major Inns no student can be kept for less

---

* Letters in the margin refer to pars. so marked below.
(*q*) Perhaps he means " from memory."
(*r*) *I.e.*, they are not all there together.

than 80 crowns (*scutorum*) (*s*) and if, as most do, he has a servant there, more. Hence it is only the sons of men of standing (*t*) who learn law there, for poor common folk cannot bear the expense and the merchants do not want to diminish their capital. Thus it happens that there is hardly a learned lawyer in the kingdom who is not noble or come of noble stock, and they cherish their rank, honour and repute more than other men of similar fortune (*status*). Both in the greater and the smaller houses, beside the school of law, there is, as it were, a Gymnasium of all culture which befits gentlemen. There they learn to sing and practise all kinds of music, to dance, and to enjoy every kind of amusement worthy of a gentleman, just as they do at court. On ordinary week-days the greater part of them betake themselves to the study of law, on feast days, after divine service, to Scripture and History. Thus there is to be found the training ground of the virtues, whence all vice is banished, so that on *this* ground knights, barons and other peers of the realm place their sons in these houses, though they do not want them to learn law nor live by it but on their patrimonies. There is hardly ever a disturbance there or quarrel or uproar and yet the only sanction they have is expulsion—which however, they dread more than any criminal does prison or chains. For a man once expelled from one of these societies is never received as a member (*socium*) into any other of them : thus peace ever reigns among them; the relation between them all is that of friendship. . . . Of the details of their study, I need only say that it is pleasant in itself and effective for its object. . . . In no French university, except Paris —though they come from all parts—are to be found so many students over age as here and yet here every one is of English origin.

A

(*s*) " £28 " Grigor; cf. p. 486.
(*t*) *Nobilium* = as the commentators say, the " lower " nobility and gentlemen; for the higher are brought up at court " gymnasium supremum nobilitatis," he had said, C. 45.

C. 50. [To return to the question of degrees] we have, I will not say a degree, but a rank (*status*) that is conferred there, *viz.*, that of a Serjeant at law, no less famous or formal than the degree of a Doctor. Thus—the Chief Justice of the Common Bench, with the advice and consent of all the judges, is accustomed, whenever it seems to him convenient, to select seven or eight of the elder men, who have distinguished themselves in the school of which I have spoken, especially in law and who are, in the judges' opinion, men of high character, and these names he gives in writing to the Chancellor of England who thereupon orders each one by royal writ (*u*) to be " before the King " on a given day " to take upon " himself " the estate and degree of a Serjeant at law " under a heavy penalty stated in the writ. On that day whoever appears is sworn on the Holy Gospels to be ready at an appointed day and place to receive that estate and degree and then to give gold [rings] according to established custom. I omit details of the ceremony, as too many for such a succinct work [*N.B.*] as this. . . . But I will add that on that day among other rites they keep a feast (*x*) like that at a coronation, which lasts seven days : none of the elect can escape for the ceremony of his creation, an expense of less than 1600 crowns so that eight altogether will exceed 3200 marks : part of this sum for each is the cost of a gold ring of the value at least of forty pounds of English money. Well I remember that when I took this degree, I paid for the rings I distributed fifty pounds (*i.e.*, 300 crowns)—for each new Serjeant must give a ring of the value of 26s. 8d.

(*u*) Cf. p. 339.

(*x*) " It was formerly usual for the new serjeants to walk two and two, arm in arm, to Westminster Hall from the place where the feast was intended; but that custom hath been discontinued as well as the words formerly spoke by the Judges upon the appearing of the serjeants upon the call, *i.e.*, " Methinks I see a Brother " : Hughson's *London*, v. 4, p. 130 n. (1807), no authority is given.

Many of the details in the text are illustrated by Machyn in his *Diary*, under 1552, 1555 and 1559 : Camd. Soc. (no. 42), pp. 26, 95, 195.

to every Prince or Duke or Archbishop then present and to
the Chancellor and the Treasurer : similarly to every earl
and bishop, to the Keeper of the Privy Seal, to each Chief
Justice, to the Chief Baron of the Exchequer one worth
20s. and one worth one mark to every Lord of Parliament,
Abbot and Prelate (*praelato*, probably=an ecclesiastic) of
high rank, or great [? official] Knight, to the Keeper of
the Rolls of the royal Chancery and to every judge, present :
rings of less price, but suitable to the rank, respectively,
of each Baron of the Exchequer, the *camerarii* (*y*), in short,
to officials and " notables " serving in the King's courts.
So that not the lowest clerk, especially in the Common
Bench, fails to get a ring proportionate with his grade.
Moreover, they give rings to other of their friends. Then,
too, they distribute largely a livery (*liberatam*) or uniform,
not only to their own serving folk but to others, personal
acquaintances who during the festivities will wait upon
them and look after them. [The Doctorate is not so
expensive] . . . [Thus] it is only in England that a special
degree is given to the law of the country nor does the
lawyer (*advocatus*) anywhere else in the world make so
much money in his profession as the Serjeant. Nor can E¹
anyone, however learned he be in English law, reach the
office and honour of a judge (*z*) in the Courts of Pleas
before the King himself or the Common Bench, which are
the ordinary supreme Courts of the realm, unless he has
first been created a Serjeant at law. And no one but such
a serjeant may appear in the latter Court, where all real
suits are tried. And so heretofore no one has been promoted to this rank who has not completed sixteen years
in the before-mentioned school of law.

(*y*) *Camerarii* Waterhous, *Comm.* 557, says, Receivers of the
Exchequer were originally so called.

(*z*) Two *ss. ad leges* are appointed judges with the usual fees by
the Privy Council in 1429 : 4 *P. P. C.* 4; see 340*l*.

Then follows some account of legal uniform (set out p. 868).

C. 51. When there is a vacancy on the bench (*a*) the King by the advice of his Council generally (*b*) appoints a serjeant . . .

The judges of England do not sit in the Courts more than three hours a day, *viz.*, 8—11 a.m. . . . Then parties go to the *Pervisum* and elsewhere (*c*) and consult with the Serjeants and their other counsellors.

Even in this fragmentary translation it is manifest that the writer speaks from personal knowledge of his subjects (*d*).

This great document is the gateway from the ancient forensic system to the modern as we know it. We must examine its positive and its negative conclusions.

Education. The emphatic distinction between the course at the Universities and that in the law does not imply that Oxford and Cambridge had no effect on the latter. They had about two centuries' start of the Inns which, when they organize consciously, have no other model but them: Fortescue's *studium* is a technical academic term. There is abundant evidence, too, that by his day the Universities were radiating the country, in kind, if not in degree as they are to-day. There was, of course, nothing like the flow there is to-day of undergraduates to the London *hospitia*—otherwise we should expect Fortescue and others to notice it—but there are many known instances

---

(*a*) " If a judge (dies) resigns or is superseded " *Grigor* for *aliter cessaverit*. There are generally, F. says, five judges in the Common Bench or six at most, and in the K. B. four or five. See Dugd. *O. J.* 39 b and p. 244.

(*b*) *eligere solet.*

(*c*) alibi . . . *aliis cons. suis.*

(*d*) Sjt. Pulling's suggestion, *Order*, &c., C. 5, that the cc. on the Inns are an interpolation about 1537, when *de L.* was first printed, cannot be accepted: see *Pension Book of Grays Inn*, p. xxii, and *Juridical Review* (Scot.), Vol. 34, no. 4, p. 314 : Dec. 1922.

of the combination (*e*). The Universities, too, looked much more to the Church than to the law for their future : what law they read was not Common Law.

Thomas Gascoigne (1403-58) tells us (*f*) that " before the great plague [1406? 1438?, or 1349 &c. to 1390?] there were few law suits (*querelae*) in England and few prosecutions (*implacitaciones*) and so there were few lawyers in England and few in Oxford, even when there were thirty thousand [*sic*] scholars there, as *I myself saw* in the rolls of the old Chancellors when I was Chancellor [1434 or 44]." Gascoigne is an intrepid critic of all institutions, not least of the law, but he speaks with authority about Oxford. Hence the link between that city and London is slender. One there must have been—the knowledge of Latin. This was only to be obtained from clerics or graduates and, in the absence of any express statement by Fortescue and writers on the same subject, we may assume that the youth of gentlefolk who entered the Inns learned their Latin at school, either at home or at Oxford or Cambridge. At any rate, it is not open to doubt that at all times to the present day some knowledge of Latin was universal at the bar and the further we go back—at any rate, 1400-50—the greater it was. Even the unpromoted students at their elements or " originalia "—to D which we shall return—must have had some Latin.

(*e*) See p. 485 and for (about) this period Bennett's *The Pastons &c.* (1922) c. 8 : the " literate laymen," p. 104, a new type, must have fed the bar; his somewhat irresponsible " semi-collegiate lodgings " at the universities probably well describes the indiscipline of the earliest *hospitia*.

(*f*) *Loci e libro*, etc., 1881 : ed. Rogers, p. 202; the large figures are perhaps due to the inclusion of " names on the books " : so perhaps Fortescue, p. 500, or to mistakes? " The number seems incredible " : Thorold Rogers, *Oxf. City Docts.* 146 (1891) : 18 Oxf. Hist. Soc. Gascoigne's " sentence is not clear and may refer only to the fact that there used to be fewer ' legists ' at Oxford which is the point G. is trying to prove. But anyhow the statement is hardly credible and the Middle Age was fond of large round numbers " : Boase, 1 *Reg. Oxf.* p. xv : 1884 : 1 Oxf. Hist. Soc.

Nearly all their books—MSS. with a limited circulation—were written in Latin (*g*): French would present no difficulty. We are not without a glimpse of what they were. In 1249 Muriella a Jewess of Oxford had in pawn certain " legales libros " (and perhaps others) but the original (*h*) does not name them. " One of the MSS. shows us what was probably a lawyer's library in the early thirteen hundreds. Besides the reports of cases it contains a number of statutes of Edward I and Edward II, Bracton's treatise, another treatise on quashing writs, another on the duties of justices, another on pleas of the crown, Mettingham's work on essoins, and Hengham's treatise called **Magnum and Parvum** [*sic*]. These works with Britton and the Register of Writs would be an ample legal library; and all these books could be tied together in one manuscript volume " (*i*). It would be a portly tome.

Roman and Canon Law flourished at the Universities and must have been known to some students in the Inns (*k*).

(*g*) In 1449 J. Paston " dwelling in the Inner Tempill " is asked by his wife to send to her brother at " Kawmbrege a *nominale* and a bok of sofystre." 1 *P. L.* 82 : no. 66, ed. Gairdner.

(*h*) From *Misc. Inq.* 3, 22 (Rec. Off.) : in Snappe's *Formulary*, 267 (1924), ed. Salter; 80 Oxf. Hist. Soc. : was a copy of William of Drogheda among them?

(*i*) Mr. Zane, 1 *Sel. Essays Ang.-Am. Leg. Hist.* 651. The MS. apparently includes a Year-Book.

(*k*) Hence it is worth noting that among the Duke of Gloucester's gifts to Oxford in 1443 is a " Johannes Faber ' In lectura super Instituta ' " : 1 *Epist. Acad. Ox.* 233 : 35 Oxf. Hist. Soc., ed. Anstey : or 2 *Munim. Acad. Ox.* 767 : Rolls, same edr., who at p. 768 includes from the same donor " Baldum super codicem . . . Baldum in lectura super tres libros Digesti " (called *libros ff.*, i.e., *Feudorum* in 35 *Oxf. Hist. Soc.* 234). *Ib.* 671, the will of Thomas Gascoigne leaves books to Oriel College but does not specify law-books. *Ib.* 582, among the goods of Master Ralph Dreff of Broadgate's Hall in 1448 is " Digest : infortiati* . . . Digest : vetus . . . Casuarius super Digest : vetere " : *ib.* 585, one of Dreff's books is " corpus juris civilis." So *ib.* 651, in 1452 the Archdeacon of Rochester bequeaths to D. C. " vetus

---

* " that is, the middle section of the Digest " : Maitland, 8 Seld. Soc. xxv, *q.v.*, for Bracton's books.

For 1400 the list of Coke, Preface to Pt. X, *R.*, to that date will serve; the *Mirror*, " Glanville," Bracton, Britton, Fleta, etc., and others now lost — hardly an advance on 1300-50 : many of them would at least put the reader on enquiry about Roman law, imperial and papal. The famous Sir William de Walworth who died 1385(6) left to his brother (*l*)—" also a book *Decretorum*, a book *Decretalium*, a book called *Sextus cum glosa*, a rosary, a *speculum judiciale*, a book *Hostiensis in Summam*, two books *Hostiensis in Lecturam*, a small volume a *Digestum vetus*, a *Codex*, an *Inforsiatum* and a book called *Compilacio super Codicem et Instituta*, upon condition that after his brother's death, he should cause all the books aforesaid to be distributed in alms for the testator's soul . . . or the value of them, *viz.*, 100*l*. at least : or if any of their kindred should study the laws, and want the books . . . then his brother should deliver them in such manner as he should think expedient for the testator's soul." The editor well observes that " the bequest of law books to his brother is highly interesting : his possession of so complete and valuable a collection implies a more than ordinary degree of proficiency in that study (*m*), while the value affixed to them affords a curious illustration of the high price of MSS. at that time and the consequent difficulties incident to the prosecution of the study of the law." In 1404 John Bownt (*n*) left " nova statuta mea " to John Beoff (*o*) " an apprentice of the court "—perhaps

---

corpus juris civilis videlicet *Digestum vetus* " and " codicem digestum novum digestum Fortiati pro usu studio suo " for 5 years and then the books are to be put " in cista mea Oxoniae in ecclesia S. Petri ad usum quem statui." Cf. *ib.* 515, the books found in the rooms of a *magister* of Brasenose Hall in 1438. Hence Anstey *ib.* v. 1, p. lxxiii, is justified in saying that in the study of the Principal of an Oxford Hall at this time we should find probably " a few books on law canon or civil." In 1373 there were many booksellers at Oxford : *ib.* 233.

(*l*) *Excerpta Historica* (1833), 137 : ed. S. Bentley.
(*m*) *Quaere* : he was not a lawyer. (*n*) See App. XV, no. 11.
(*o*) There is a Wil. Boeff admitted to L. I. in 1428, 1 *Rec. L. I.* 6 and *Gubernator*, 1434-5; 1 *Black Bk.* 5 and Index.

the " Boef " who sat as a judge of Assize with Fortescue (*p*) in 1459.

We happen to have a good commentary on these wills in another, that of Paston J. written in 1444 (*q*) : he makes provision for his son Edmund, who was then a law student at Clifford's Inn and about twenty : the judge we may note, was born in 1378 and was a man of culture; he speaks therefore with knowledge : " till he is twenty one, the boy is to have reasonable *victus, vestitus, apparatus* and *sustentatio*, according to the needs of his rank, but so that he behaves as a gentleman (*non superbiat*) and for [at least ?] half a year he is to have tuition (*sub sana tutela*) in philosophy (*artis dialecticae* = the higher learning), civil law (*jus civile*) for a year and English law afterwards to a proper extent (*ad sufficienciam*)—subject to his taking to the study and making progress." The old judge was an utilitarian educator, in the best sense of the words and he willed the same *general* course for all his sons (*r*). Note that books are not mentioned.

In the reign of Edward IV among the books of John

(*p*) Y. B. 37 H. VI, f. 5b, pl. 10.

(*q*) Gairdner, 3 *P. L.* 452, 453. In the case of the younger Clement who was not, perhaps, a law student, the trustees are to put him " tam ad scholas grammaticales quam alias et caeteras erudiciones prout praedicitur de predictis fratribus suis "—but the only brother (in our fragmentary will) is Edmund.

(*r*) Light is thrown back on this period from a little time ahead. In March 1479 (3 *Gairdner*, 245 : no. 829) Edmund Alyard, " that was my rewler at Oxforth " (says Walter Paston *ib.* p. 246 : in his will *ib.* 249-50, he is *magister*) writes to his (W.'s) mother, Walter's " labor and lernynge hathe be and is yn the Faculte of Art [with a view to the Church] and is well sped there yn, and may be Bacheler at soche tyme as shall lyke yow, and then to go to lawe . . . as I conceyve ther shal non have that exibeshyon [allowance, maintenance] to the Faculte of Lawe. . . If he shal go to law and be made Bacheler of Art before, and ye wolle have hym hom this yere, then may he be Bacheler at Mydsomor and be with you yn the vacacion and go to lawe at Mihelmas . . . : At Oxinforth "; cf. *ib.* pp. xlvii, lvii-iii. Note the wise Paston tradition of laying the foundation of a legal career in a liberal education. (Gairdner *ib.* remarks in 1875 : " At the universities, unfortunately, law is studied no longer and degrees in that faculty are now purely honorary " !)

Paston (almost certainly the Templar) are " a Boke off nyw Statuts ffrom Edward the iiij " (s). Statutes, of course, were an essential part of the apprentice's stock-in-trade and a " complete set " must have been a valuable legacy. We may guess that many a law library was started by a common fund, to secure the necessities of legal life.

Whether we may so call the Year-Books—of which c. 48 above contains the earliest mention—or whether they were luxuries we need not enquire. The theory that apprentices were largely occupied in the production of them " made by learners for learners " directly affects their normal studies and perhaps, may be said to hold the field (t). It chimes with what is, after all, the paramount element in their training—attendance in court. At any rate these " vernacular report[s] of an oral debate " (Maitland) must have passed from hand to hand in the hostels. Maitland tells us that it is not impossible that these volumes sprang from little books of precedents for pleaders, 1260-72, and that good pleading rather than positive law was what the earliest reporters sought. If so, the studious youth had all the more reason to read and write Year-Books.

What they would hear in court would be, in essence, B. no doubt what their successors would hear to-day. There would be more serjeants' voices than judges', and we must consider what the burden of the former was. But there was one kind of utterance from both ranks which must not be overlooked—tradition. We have had instances of

---

(s) So Gairdner, 3 *P. L.* 301 : no. 869, but Bennett, the *Pastons* 261, must be right in reading "Edward III." *Ib.* p. 111, Sir John Fastolf has in 1450 among his books at Caister " Instituts of Justien Emperor."

(t) See Maitland, 17 Seld. Soc. xi, viii, xiv : F. Pollock, *Essays in the Law*, 242 : Bolland, The Year-Books 35 — : 1921. They all reject Coke's theory of *official* reporters : 3 *R.*, Pref. iii, xxix : 4 *Inst.* 4. It would seem that some of the early reporters were aware of their shortcomings, *e.g.*, in 1367 " Mes icy *Quaere* un melior report de cel cas car touts mes copies variont " &c. *Reports del Cases en ley* : 40—50 E. III, p. 15.

reminiscence from the bench and the bar : Fortescue often indulges in it. Perhaps, after all, Chaucer's Serjeant remembered the leading cases back to William I. Primitive lore is often transmitted " by heart " in great masses (*u*).

We can only surmise how the " fellows " entered the Inns : by the way, they are not always youthful, just as to-day. We have suggested that in their origin they were casual social gatherings, like the early colleges at Oxford and Cambridge, such as they, too, soon became in constitution. For, by this time, those Colleges were organized and any unit in the law area could adopt that model at any moment it wished. Almost the earliest records of Lincoln's Inn are regulations for its good government and probably the same would be true of the other Inns if their records went back so far : or possibly conscious incorporation begot the records. That there was anything like " an entrance examination " for admission is very unlikely. Till the houses got a distinct stamp as schools of lawyers, no doubt there were some mere lodgers in their midst, inmates not unknown to other learned societies for centuries. But as soon as they began to " mean business " some knowledge of Latin must have been required, however informally, moreover, such a test would go far to keep out youth not of the well-to-do classes. Once started, a *hospitium* would naturally be recruited by friendly nomination. On these premisses it is easy to see how this kind or any kind of college blossomed into " a gymnasium of all culture."

B   Thus the title of *apprenticius* was popular : it never was conferred by authority, it was not a degree, as Serjeant was. Indeed, it would seem that originally the serjeants, as such, had little to do with the internal life of the Inns : the total silence of Fortescue dealing substan-

---

(*u*) So the advocates of Doctors Commons : Holdsworth, *Sources* &c. 89. The Talmud was " transmitted orally for centuries," 12 *Jew. Encyc.*

tively with him (and may we add of Chaucer?) seems to be conclusive. It is a mechanical throwback from later precise arrangements, which has suggested the systematic instruction of the juniors by the seniors. When Coke says (x) " the Apprentice at law is not sworne," whereas the serjeant is, he means that the latter is officially recognised—it is the only degree. And so did Fortescue, but he has perhaps been misunderstood on a matter here relevant. We have so far had no figures for the period of candidature for this degree. That the Serjeants were usually chosen from the distinguished juniors is certainly what he means and is certain. Now Fortescue had previously (1461-4) written incidentally in *De natura legis naturae* (y) : " why do they who study the laws of the Kingdom of England which are merely insular, and the knowledge of which these students scarcely so far acquire by twenty years' lucubrations, as to deserve to be selected for the lowest degree usually granted in these laws [do it] ? (while, what is more, upon taking that degree they have to pay for the ordinary expenses which the solemnity requires, not much less than 2000 crowns)." By " lowest degree " he must mean that (z) of serjeant : it could not cost " not much less than 2000 crowns " to become an apprentice. Moreover, in c. 50 above, where greater precision is required, he mentions 1600 crowns as his specific estimate for serjeantship : two thousand here, is a round number. And so is " the twenty years' lucrubrations " above, and in C. 8 ; the sixteen of C. 50 are formal. That it took sixteen years, at least, from " matriculation " to graduate *optimo jure* at the bar would not be unreason-

---

(x) 2 *Inst.* p. 214 : on the St. (c. 29) of 1275 : see p. 517 for the oath.

(y) Pt. I, c. 43 : p. 108. Ld. Clemont's ed. : 1869, and p. 240 transln.

(z) Not of apprentice as Mr. Plummer, *Governance* &c. p. 41 n., suggests : if this were so, it would have taken 20 years to become an apprentice !

Cf. p. 499, and note that the *de laud.* is the later.

able : some rule (*a*) on the period may well have existed in Fortescue's day, though, it is possible, that like other jurists, when laying down the law, he puts into a *lacuna* what he thinks ought to be there. He may well have meant sixteen years as a junior, and four as a senior before one is eligible for the bench.

Of the serjeant in court little remains to be said. His monument is the Year-Books, the genuine study of which is in its infancy. We can but copy the conclusions of those who have read some of them. Of these Coke, though sometimes uncritical, speaks with authority in his own time. He writes (*b*) " The ancient order of arguments by our Serjeants and apprentices of law at the bar is altogether altered. 1. They never cited any book, case, or authority in particular (*c*) as is holden in 40 E. III &c. (*d*) but [we find] *est tenus, ou agree in nr'e luivres, ou est tenus adjudges in termes* or such like, which order yet remains in moots at the bar in the Inner Temple to this day. 2. Then was the citing general but always true in the particular; and now the citing is particular, and the matter many times mistaken (*abs re*=not to the point) in general. 3. In those days few cases in law were cited but very pithy and pertinent to the purpose and those ever pinch most." It is difficult to reconcile the statements about books here (*e*) but it is clear that he thought that about 1360 very little " authority " was cited at the bar. And about this he has the support of Maitland (*f*) for half

---

(*a*) In 1614 Coke, p. 370*s*, said to the serjeants : " No profession but attaineth the highest degree sooner than the lawyer. But things of greatest weight and consequence move slowly . . . the youngest called of 28 years continuance, the eldest of 44 standing," *sc*. in his day.

(*b*) 10 *Inst*. Pref. xxi.

(*c*) " vix unquam librum vel authoritatem nominatim produxerunt " : apparently the original, the English being a translm.

(*d*) Passage not identified.

(*e*) Unless he means—they referred to " our books " without quoting them.

(*f*) Cited p. 509.

a century earlier: "for a very long time any explicit citation of cases by judges or counsel is so rare that we might easily be guilty of an anachronism if we thought that what was wanted was 'authority.'" He proceeds humourously to point out that what the readers wanted was not so much the law as (may we put it?) the controversy, how to conduct a "fight." Even the casual skimmer of a Year Book can see that it might be put together piecemeal by an immature reporter, by no means uninterested in his law but glad to find incident and much more interested in some points, according to his knowledge and taste at the moment, than in others and not always anxious to get to the bottom of a theme.

In the work out of court distinctions may be drawn. C. D. Here we meet the famous classification of the Inns—of Court and of Chancery. Fortescue's "asides" are often convincing, and when he says that the latter *hospitia* sometimes fluctuated in number, it is exactly what we should expect; some of the ventures in common house-keeping "caught on," some did not. That the minor were stepping stones to the major, who were later their suzerains, is attested by the well-known practice of succeeding centuries. It may well be that ten is a round number (*g*) and that each cannot now be certainly identified. There is little doubt about the great Four, even if the adjective be only understood of numbers.

Broadly we have suggested that the settlement of the Chancery officials and some law students by chance in the same neighbourhood, *viz.*, "Law-land," had very much encouraged intimacy between voluntary groups of youth who looked to the law for a livelihood. This harmonizes admirably with Fortescue's scheme. The beginner learns *Originalia* (*h*), *i.e.*, the writs on which all process is based.

(*g*) Cf. the enumeration, App. XV: at this date (about 1468) ten is not far out.

(*h*) *Originalia et quasi legis elementa*: c. 49; *brevia originalia et judicialia*: c. 48.

Where can he find a better teacher than the clerk who frames them or a better school than his house? The system grew gradually, but none simpler could have been devised given the vicinity of master and pupil and the needs forensic and physical of the latter. These are Fortescue's *hospitia cancellariae*, a conduit to his *hospitia curiae*. No doubt the Latin assonance was earlier than the English equivalents, but we meet in a translation with "inn of Chancery" in its ordinary sense (*i*) in 1374 and in 1437 we read that the Privy Council, fearing that the Duke of Burgundy would besiege Calais, ordered that "men of court in innes of courte be warned to be arraied" (*k*). This is the earliest known mention of "Inn of Court," and the title probably came gradually into use as an antithesis to "Inn of Chancery." The latter belonged to an earlier and more numerous class, generically called Inns of Chancery, before contradistinction was required; when the lesser ten were differentiated from the greater four, "Inn of Court" was not an inappropriate combination for the abode of men who appeared before the judges. So possibly "House of Lords" was coined as a set-off to "House of Commons" (*l*).

D   Fortescue's figures are at first surprising: 1000 inmates of the Inns of Chancery and at least 800 in those of Court, but he must mean that there were about 1800 "names on the books" (which would include many *attornati*), for, he adds pointedly, they are not all there at the same time; nor do we know whether he is speaking of his youth or of a later period. Trustworthy estimates are difficult to find. Ferne (*m*) believed that in 1422 one Inn of Court had barely threescore "gentlemen," in the heraldic sense; he ignores others. There seems to

---

(*i*) P. 439: original in Latin.
(*k*) P. P. C. v. V, 74: no doubt they meant both kinds of Inns.
(*l*) 68 *Sol. Jour.* 271: Jan. 12, 1924.
(*m*) P. 470.

be no reason to tax Fortescue with exaggeration, but
membership did not mean to him what it does to us.
When the government wanted recruits in 1437 they would
not have called up the lawyers as a class unless there had
been a considerable number of them (*n*). Mr. Inderwick
apparently accepting (*o*) Fortescue's figures—" the least
frequented Inn has 200 "—states that in 1574 " the least
frequented," *viz.*, " Lincoln's Inn, had 160 and the average
of the four Inns was 190. The whole number practising
at the Bar was . . . 177 " (*p*). There is a table of the
total yearly admissions to Gray's Inn from 1521 to 1674
from Harl. MSS., 1912, said to be (*q*) by Simon Segar, an
official of the House about 1660-70; there were 15 in 1557
and 200 in 1619. The statistics later than Fortescue do
not help us, for his, and probably Ferne's, are the more
correct.

E, E^1. The *cursus honorum*—junior, senior, judge—
noted by Fortescue, being natural, was common before his
day and has survived to this; no case seems to be known
in his time or long after of an apprentice being raised to
the bench. And the privileges of the Serjeants—exclusive
audience and succession to judicial vacancies in the
Common Pleas and the King's Bench, which he is the first
to mention (*r*), is a commonplace. Serjeant Manning
appositely translated (*s*) *Paston* v. *Genney, Serjt.* (no
doubt known to Fortescue) to illustrate those privileges in
1471. Choke J., agreeing with Bryant C.J., remarks:
" Serjeant at law is not bound to attend on this court

(*n*) Cf. p. 432 of 1459.

(*o*) 1 *Cal. I. T.* lxxviii.

(*p*) From *State Papers* " Domestic Elizabeth," v. 95, no. 91: in App. III, 1 *Cal. I. T.*

(*q*) Douthwaite, *Gray's Inn Hist. &c.* (1886) p. 23: the table is printed, Foster, *G. I. Admissions*, viii.

(*r*) Horwood *conjectured* (boldly) that about 1300 " in the Bench a litigant would not probably have been allowed to dispense with . . . the services of a serjeant ": 30-1 E. I, xxviii.

(*s*) *Serviens* &c., 230 from Y. B. 11 E. IV, fo. 2, pl. 4.

except at his will, for he is not sworn to attend upon this court [C. P.] as an attorney, but he is sworn that he will not delay the people, &c.; but if he will not be of counsel by our assignment we can *estrange* him from the bar (*t*), as to any plea, &c. And, Sir, I have seen here where an apprentice took challenge to the jury and gave evidence (*u*) (*evide̅ce*) in default of his serjeant, &c. . . ." Littleton J. : " If all the serjeants were dead we could hear the apprentices to plead here by necessity, in ease of the people, &c."—the hyperbole enforces the theory that audience of the serjeants was not of right but by favour of the judges. Incidentally Bryan remarks that an apprentice and a party in person will be heard anywhere but in the Common Pleas.

E[1]

He also draws a distinction between the serjeants who are members of the court, " who occupy here of record," and " ministers of the court who are the officers and attorneys for the members," *e.g.*, a sheriff. This fleeting distinction, made for the purpose of the moment and perhaps misunderstood, is like so many utterances in the Year Books, not heard of again, but it may point to an official recognition of the *status* of the attorney in court, side by side with that of the bar. Fortescue apparently does not mention the *attornatus* anywhere. This omission from *de laudibus* cannot be accidental, it may be due to his reiterated plan of compression, but it certainly suggests that about 1470 his scheme of a legal hierarchy did not include the attorney.

Or rather, he recognised it as a distinct branch and he was not dealing with it, for, probably, by this time, the mutual exclusiveness of the two was recognised. Thus Bryan Rocliff, not yet a Baron of the Exchequer, writes (*x*) about

---

(*t*) So Sjt. Genney relates of " my master Cheyne," C.J. 1424.

(*u*) = apparently read or put in documents.

(*x*) *The Plumpton Correspondence*, 2—3; Camd. Soc. 1839: cf. 5 Foss, 71. The words hardly mean " because I am an officer of the court (Exch.)," for then it would not be his duty to advise : he is

1459 to Sir William Plumpton : " I have gotten one that shall appear for you. . . . I have labored a felaw of mine to be your Atturney in the Court for I may nought be but of Counsell . . . ," *i.e.*, I may only appear as counsel. Hence in 1436 it is quite natural for the King's Council to point out (*y*) that certain persons could be " suyd be his attorney . . . with the assistance of his . . . sergeantes of law."

Two oaths of the incipient serjeants are mentioned, but like other details of the ceremony which are expressly omitted, the form of the important one is not given. In the *Governance of England* (c. 15) Fortescue expressly says that the oath of the King's Council (some of whom he thinks may be " counsellors of private persons ") was " in especial that they shall take no fee nor clothing [livery] nor no rewardes off any man except only off the Kynge; like as the Justices off the Kynges benche and off the Common place be sworne when thai take ther offices."

We are not, however, in much doubt about the Serjeant's oath. The prescribed oaths for justices and clerks of the Chancery, preserved, 18 or 20 E. III, 1344 or 1346, 1 *Stat. Realm*, 304-6, were, no doubt, models, to a certain extent. There is no reason to doubt the *Mirror's* statement (*z*) (1285-90) that " Every pleader is bound by oath that he will not knowingly maintain or defend wrong or falsehood, but will abandon his client immediately that he perceives his wrongdoing."

Coke, 2 *Inst.* 213, cites this and more (*a*), and gives two *résumés* of the oath. He obviously had before him the following two precedents in the *Book of Oaths* (1649 or 1689) of " the King's " Serjeant at Law : " Ye shall well

---

very anxious to oblige Sir W. P. Note *ib.* that at some of the proceedings " I nor my said felaw may nott attend."

(*y*) 35 Seld. Soc. 102.

(*z*) It seems to have no special relation to the City oaths, p. 250.

(*a*) It may be, as Coke thought, that the *Mirror* included sentences following the words above in the *oath* : not so, 7 Seld. Soc. 48.

and truly serve the King and his people as one of his Serjeants of the Law and truly counsel the King in his matters when ye shall be called and duly and truly administer the King's matters after the course of the law after your cunning; ye shall take no wages nor fee of any man for any matter where the King is party, against the King ye shall as duly and hastily speed such matters, as any man shall have to do against the King in the law, as ye may lawfully do, without delay or tarrying the party of his lawful process, in that that to you belongeth, ye shall be attendant to the Kings matters when ye shall be called thereunto. As God help you and his Saints."

Of " a Serjeant at Law " : " well and truly ye shall serve the Kings people as one of his Serjeants at law and ye shall truly counsel them, that ye shall be retained with after your cunning and ye shall not defer, tract nor delay their causes willingly for covetousness of mony, or other thing that may turn you to profit and ye shall give due attendance (b) according. As God you help and his Saints." This is almost word for word the latest modern form (c) and is, doubtless, the ordinary form.

The strong invitation in the former to act *against* the King raises the suspicion that the framer had some theory distinguishing " King's " Serjeants and was anxious to display the exceeding magnanimity of the King's special advocate; the legislation of 1344-6 encourages no trace of tenderness on the part of royal servants towards claims against the Crown (even on the most favourable reading of the clause about the clerks in chancery). The " King's " serjeant, later the Attorney-General, was certainly not expected to " speed " suits against his employer. Fortescue, who might have been expected to do so, does not mention a " King's serjeant."

(b) Quoted by Choke J. in 1471 : 11 E. IV, 3, p. 516.
(c) Manning, p. 31 (1840), "which is now taken . . . and is an immemorial form " : Pulling, p. 229 (1884).

The former's indifference to the bare attorney was explicable, but his ignoring an Attorney-General, if any such title existed, would not be, for the relation of royalty and law was his theme. We are driven to the conclusion that the name did not then exist.

Thus these famous chapters are not only valuable for our theme in what they give, but also in what they omit.

1450.

Fortescue was Chief Justice and his unique evidence about his profession covers this date. Other writers had not his reasons for interest in its organisation; some of them care only for the relation between Law and Justice, so that in their case we can only gather our gleanings through their view of the former. It is a gloomy picture. In 1450 Jack Cade's followers " had risen " (d), says Sir James Ramsay, " against the intolerable feebleness of the Government which gave free play to every kind of malversation and tyranny. No man could enter a court of justice with any hope of success unless he had interest at his back." We naturally ask whether a corrupt bar is included in this sweeping judgment. It is true that seventy years earlier professional censors of public morals, like Gower, are never tired of denouncing the mercenariness of lawyers, but it has been attempted to show that their indignation was largely due to the fact that the profession was crystallising, so to say, under their eyes, but that they observed nothing but fresh public burdens; they had seen something like a scale of fees grow up in their lifetime. This was their definite charge against the practitioners as a class—they are " profiteers," a new race; they do not allege corruption except in so far as they conceived the whole of contemporary society to be tainted by it, and no doubt the " bar " they knew reflected the prevailing vices.

(d) 2 *Lancaster & York*, c. ix, p. 126 (1892).

We might set off against this school of detractors not only the silence of Chaucer but his positive respect for the men of law, but his classical optimism would be urged in reply. But he and they are united in denouncing the paramount social evil of the times, the oppression of "the great," which, as the historian quoted above says, was vigorous nearly a century after their days; it was not diminished by the lawlessness of the Wars of the Roses. Of its immediate and crude action on the courts and their *personnel* we have had many instances. The bar was not yet, nor for a long time to come, a bulwark of the laws.

Legislation, too, seems to acquit of, or rather to cease to charge the once familiar forensic mischiefs. The tone of the Statute of 1275 is no longer heard; judges, serjeants, attorneys, all are regulated, but there is no longer the constant struggle with maintenance, champerty, collusion with the other side, betrayal of the client, to say nothing of the *étiquette* of demeanour in court. The improvement in that homely item is borne out by the Year Books, to which, indeed, we might appeal for support on the charge of corruption, were it not that the reputation at stake is that of their authors. But the legal associations which produced those men and those works are a conclusive argument that in 1450 the bar had purged itself of that gravest indictment, whether it had been true in greater or smaller measure, earlier or not, for it had obtained corporateness and unity in the Inns. It is impossible to conceive a concentrated and organised profession with a low sense of honour.

Despite the lack of literature we are not without witnesses at this time. Allowing for the improvement suggested, we are still a long way from even elementary modern standards. A layman can understand as well as a lawyer the legal conditions of the following picture (drawn by a servant, apparently ignorant of the law, hostile to the person defamed and perhaps misinformed of the facts) sent in 1450 to his master, John Paston, a member of the bar; for in our ignorance of the exact facts, the law is unintelligible, but the *social* relations of judges, lawyers, and litigants *inter se* which it reveals, are amazing.

" Heydon [an active anti-Pastonite lawyer] was with my Maister Yelverton [now J.] and desired hym to see the recordes of his endytementz and axed of hym if he were indited of felonye; and my Maister Yelverton told him it was. And thereto H. seide ' Sir ye wole recorde that I was never thef,' and he seid &c. [about one P.] . . . And my Maister Y. seid to hym he [H.] cowde not knowe the laborer of th' endytement and H. seid ageyn he knewe weel the laborer thereof; and my Maister Y. conceyte is H. ment yow [John P.]. Wherefor he advyseth yow that in onywyse ye make P. to take apell accordyng; for if he so do, thanne is H. barred of his conspirace, and also of his damages, though that he be nonnsewed therin, or though be afterward discontynued &c., and ellis are ye in jopardy of a conspirace, for H. hopeth to have the world [sheriffs, jurors, &c.?] better to his entent thanne it is nowe. For it is told me that rather thanne he should fayle of a shiref this yeer comyng for his entent, he wole spende m^1 *li*. [£1,000].

This communicacion be twene them was on Moneday last passed and on Tewisday last passed H. mette with Maister Markham [John the second J.], and he tolde H. his part how that he levid ungoodly in putting awey of his wyff and kept an other &c., and therwith he turned pale colour and seid he lyved not but as God was pleased with, ne dede no wrong to no person. And therupon Maister Markham reherced how he demeyned hym a geynst *men of Court* and named yow and Genneye . . ." (e).

(e) James Gresham to John Paston : 1 Gairdner, *P. L.* 157, no. 117. In the last sentence Markham must mean to tell H. how he (M.) dealt in his court with counsel generally, for Paston and W. Jenney,

Thomas Gascoigne (*f*) was writing about 1440-50; he is a great academic; his interest is in the church and he considers it part of his duty, therefore, to criticize other institutions. One of his grievances, he expressly says, is that property meant for sacred objects goes to the lawyers (*g*), owing to the increase of litigation; he sees a great multiplication of lawyers in his day; suits are long drawn out and expensive and only come to an end through interest, *i.e.*, the intervention of the rich (*h*), etc. He tells one or two stories which in a general way show the development of the fee system. " I heard," he says, " a

---

now governor of Lincoln's Inn, but not serjt. till 1463, were sure to be on opposite sides as they were hostile : 4 Foss, 488. For Heydon see No. 88.

(*f*) P. 505; pp. 109, 127-8 of work cited.

(*g*) His terminology at this date, is odd; he calls them *legistae, advocati, juristae, defensores* : his avoidance of the current popular titles almost looks as if he disclaimed attack on *servientes, apprenticii*, etc. *Defensores* may be a reminiscence of criminal law which was coming into prominence. However, only a fragment of his book is printed.

At Oxford in 1432 among representatives in the University Court are (perhaps the *Magister in ordinario* of either party), *advocatus assignatus, procurator constitutus* : titles which had survived locally. There may also be *arbitrator electus* : 1 *Mun. Acad. Ox.* 306, see p. 161c. " Arbitrator " is low Latin : 1284, in Du Cange. In 1431-2 the parties " have compromitted them either party to stand to the award and arbitrament of a squier and a man of counsell learned in the law . . . of all manner accions reall and personall &c." : if the two disagree there is to be " an Noumper " [=an Umpire] : *Plumpton Correspondence* Introdn. li ; Camd. Soc. 1839.

The absence of " barrister " in these pages may have been noted. The earliest date *N. E. D.* gives for it, is 1545, but in 1454-5, we have in Latin " Herbert and Sulyard are admitted " to a chamber in Lincoln's Inn " especially because they are two of the best " barrer' " of the Inn." 1 *Bl. Bks. L. I.* 26. As late as 1627 it was ruled that a " barrister . . . may not give advice albeit he had Letters-Patents to enable him as fully as if he had been called to the Bar " : Popham's *Reports*, 207; cf. in 1594, *ib.* 39, a " Case was very well argued by one Brock, a Puny utter Barrister of the Inner Temple. . . . And it was the first Demurrer that he argued in Court." Waterhous, therefore, in 1663, had some ground for saying of students anciently " Yea and who when they were called to the Barr (which they never or rarely importun'd) did forbear practice till they had ruminated well " its duties, etc., *Commentary*, 523.

(*h*) " magnorum finem suum habent."

baccalaureus legum say, ' I wish there were more malefactors (*i*) because then we practitioners (*legistae*) should make more money.' This is like the folk who bring false charges on which a man is arrested so that they can get ten marks out of him for bail." He gives the name of a *ballivus regis* at Pomfret in 1448 who bribed a man with a gift of wine to create a disturbance there. This was done, but the man suborned got so drunk that he broke the suborner's head. All this is not very serious, and there is no hint of corrupt lawyers, though there is of maintenance. Gascoigne no doubt felt that he was in the line of the old reforming divines from John of Salisbury; at any rate, their old traditional prejudice against paid advocacy was not and is not extinct.

It may then be claimed that between 1381 and 1450 (*k*), between the two popular risings, the law had grown in popular favour. Even Gower had admitted, just after the former, that some lawyers " laboured for true law and justice " (*l*), and we get the same concession in 1450. A proclamation made by Jack Cade, or rather a declaration by his followers (*m*), carries on the old polemic against law. " Item the law servyth of nowght ellys in thes days but for to do wrong, for nothyng is sped almost but false maters by coulour of the law for mede, drede and favor, and so no remedy is had in ye cowrt of conscience in eny wyse." The next paragraph contains perhaps the most deadly description of the State ever penned; a few lines

---

(*i*) Cf. the old popular toast on circuit, " Success to Crime " !

(*k*) Wycliffe died in 1383. Historians ignore any influence on the legal profession but Sir Charles Oman remarks among Wycliffe's grievances : " The higher clergy were statesmen, lawyers, diplomatists, administrators, politicians, anything rather than hard-working overseers and guardians of Christ's flock." *Political Hist. of England* (1377—1485), p. 69, c. 3. It might fairly be said that the gradual elimination of the ecclesiastical element among lawyers during the century 1350—1450, suggested in the text, was a form of protestantism.

(*l*) Mr. Macaulay's Analysis : *Latin Works*, p. 1.

(*m*) J. Gairdner, Preface, p. ix, to *Three 15th Century Chronicles,* Camd. Soc. (1880) N. S. no. 28 : see p. 96 for above.

lower : " Item we wyll that all men knowe we blame not all the lordys, ne all tho that is about ye kyngs person ne all jentyllmen ne yowmen, ne all men of lawe, ne all bysshopes, ne all prestys, but all suche as may be fownde gylty by just and trew enquery and by the law." It cannot be denied that this is a judicial utterance.

Like all popular declamations, this one is loud against " red tape," which is regarded as a cloak for exactions, the odium of which was often vented on the ministers of the law; we have had many a suggestion even in legislative circles that the clerks of the courts levied a toll on suitors or connived with attorneys and even judges (*n*). Hence we are not surprised to find another " item " in this list : " they desyre that all the extorsiners myght be leyd downe, that is to say, ye grene wexe (*o*) the which is falsly used to the perpetwall hurt and distructyon of the trew comyns of Kent; also the extorsiners of the Kynges Benche, the which is ryght chargeable to all the comyns with owten provysyon of owr sovereyn lord and his trew cowncell."

The complainants then demand a solemn inquiry into the present discontents, but

" Item to syt upon this enqwerye we refuse no juge except iij chefe juges, the which ben fals to beleve." Apparently they mean Fortescue, Prisot and Ardern.

The authors of this presentment, of course, laboured under the disabilities of all contemporary critics, but later historians, *sine ira et studio*, have, broadly, justified their catalogue. However difficult we may find it to exemplify their aspersions on the profession in detail, we must acquiesce in the general verdict of the experts. At any rate, we accept in one of the most outspoken documents

---

(*n*) Cf. in this manifesto : " hensforthe no man upon peyne of deth beyng abowt the kyngs person shall take no maner of brybe fer eny byll of petysyons or caws spedynge or lettynge."

(*o*) Cade : " 'tis the bee's wax " : 2 *Henry VI*, IV, ii.

ever published the admission in the last year of our period that it did not impugn the whole bar—" ne all men of lawe."

The last few words illustrate the difficulty under which these pages have laboured throughout. At any given moment we do not know enough of the actual facts; our inductions must necessarily be imperfect. We cannot even now reconstruct every step in or the course of an ordinary trial in 1450. *Desiderantur exempla.*

They must come from more intensive research; perhaps the unexplored recesses of the Year Books will yield something; it is an age which reads MSS. No doubt some surmises here submitted will be displaced; perhaps some will be justified. " Whatever record leaps to light," the history of the origins of the bar of England will never lose its quality of being inseparable from the History of England.

APPENDIX I.

Mr. Laughlin in *Anglo-Saxon Legal Procedure,* in *Essays in A.-S. Law,* Boston, U.S.A., 1876, p. 213, says that sometimes the defendant vouched to warranty. " By vouching to warranty the defendant did not aim at rebutting the claim of unwilling loss suffered by the plaintiff, but by introducing his *auctor* he was freed from the suit and the warrantor was substituted in his place. . . . In German law the defendant withdrew from the procedure, if his *auctor* accepted the obligation of warranty. The distinction is well expressed by the Lombard law : ' Langobardus semper dat auctorem et nunquam stat loco auctoris; Romanus semper stat loco auctoris et nunquam dat auctorem.' It is the purest German law, the established procedure of the *Sachsenspiegel* [about, perhaps before 1235] and later German jurisprudence as well as that of the Lex Salica, the earliest law extant. . . . [Defendant] produced his *auctor* not to prove the tradition of the goods as in our day, but that he might escape the charge and put it upon his *auctor* " (218-9).

APPENDIX II.

In the case of stolen property Mr. Laughlin (App. I) says that the first mention of it is in the laws of Hlothaere and Eadric, § 7 of which Th. (p. 13) translates : " If one man steal property from another and the owner afterwards lay claim to it, let him vouch to warranty at the King's hall, if he can, and let him bring thither the person who sold it him; if he cannot do that, let him give it up, and let the owner take possession of it." Laughlin, p. 219 and L. I. 10 agree substantially with this version.

We soon get the advantage of an early Latin translation : " Q.'s," see p. 4. In 688 Ine became King of the West Saxons and published laws (Lambarde (1568) : *Archaionomia* : Th. 45 ; L. I, 89, who dates them 688-95), preserved as an appendix to Alfred's laws. § 47 is : " If a man attach stolen cattle, the party may not vouch a ' theowman ' [an unfree man : L.] to the warranty of it."

Si aliquid furtivum intercietur, non debet advocari ad servum.

Here we meet for the first time the term *advocare*.

Between 880 and 889 King Alfred made a treaty with King Guthrum the Dane :

(L. I, 129). § 4. Et omnis homo sciat advocatum suum de hominibus et de equis et de bobus : Q. adv.= warrantor (Th.) Gewährsmann (L.).

Edward the Elder, 901-24 : " § 1. I will that every man have his warrantor (advocatum : Q.) and that no man buy out of port [= the town] but have the portreeve's witness or that of other unlying men whom one may believe. And if anyone, buy out of port then let him incur the King's ouerhyrnesse [fine for disobedience] and let the warranty (*advocatio* : Q.) nevertheless go forward, until it be known where it shall stop. Also we have ordained that he who should vouch to warranty (*qui advocare debet* : Q.) should have unlying witness to the effect that he rightfully vouched it (*recte advocat* : Q.) or should bring forward an oath which he might believe who made the claim " : Th. 68; L. I, 139. *Ib.* § 1, 5 : " vel sibi propriet aut advocet " : " either he must declare it as his own or call in a warrantor " : L.

By (about) 1000 A.D. the law on this subject was greatly developed. L. calls an appendix to the Laws of Ethelred " a fragment of a law," and dates it 930-1030 : probably 950-1000 : I, 224; Lambarde, 92; Th. 123.

§ 8. Q. translates : Si quis deprehendat quod amisit, advocet inde cum quo deprehenditur, unde venerit ei, et mittat in manum et det plegium quod adducet advocatum suum.

1. Si viventem warrantum vocet et sit in alia scira quem vocat, terminum habeat. . . .

2. Si advocet ultra unam sciram, habeat terminum unam ebdomadam; si advocet ultra duas scyras. . . .

§ 9. Aliquando fuit quod ter advocandum erat; ubi prius aliquid interciabatur et deinceps eundum [the claimant had to go after the assurer wherever the possessor told him : L.] cum advocante, quocumque advocaret.

Unde consuluerunt sapientes quod melius erat ut saltem advocaretur ubi deprehendebatur donec innotesceret in quo stare vellet ne forte impotens homo longius et diutius pro suo laboraret et ut vexetur magis qui inuste conquisitum habet in manibus et minus qui juste prosequitur.

After providing for the case of the *advocatus* being dead,

4. Etiam inter advocandum si quis hoc recipiat nec ultra advocet, si propriare sibi velit, non potest hoc ei jure denegari, si credibile testimonium locum ci faciat accedendi; quia propriatio propinquior semper est possidenti quam repetenti.

". . . this appendix is of importance generally for the course of law in seizure of stolen chattels and in warranty " : L. III, 155.

One of the oaths preserved in this process is—sic advoco sicut hoc mihi vendidit cui nunc in manu mitto. (Q.) : L. I, 397; dated 920-1050, *i.e.*, the collection in Anglo-Saxon was then made.

In the Second Laws of Canute (1027-34) we find (L. I, 327) :

Q.	Cons. Cnuti.
23. Et non sit quisquam alicuius advocationis dignus, nisi credibile testimonium habeat unde venerit ei quod cum eo deprehenditur.	Neque quisquam advocacione tutacionis dignus sit . . .
24, 1. If *not*, non liceat ei advocare—	—nulla sit advocacio tutacionis—(elsewhere *trahere ad tutelam*).
2. But if he has *testimonium*, tunc liceat inde ter advocari.	

The other paraphrase, *Instituta Cnuti* has *warantem* (=*advocatum*) *vocet*.

Add Laws of William [I], § 30 in French (dated St. *Lect.* 47, 1250-1300, but by L. 1090-1135) : bondmen must not seek new *avurie* : L. I, 513.

APPENDIX III.

Relevant passages from *Leges H. P.*

1. Advocatus.

In view of the importance of this work earlier texts which it incorporates are referred to under it rather than in the reverse order.

10, 3. Et omnibus ordinatis [men in orders] et alienigenis et pauperibus et abiectis debet esse rex pro cognacione [kinsman] et advocato, si penitus alium non habent.

Translated St. *Lec.* 154. (The same, 75, 7a, with *Francigenis* for *ordinatis*).

This is traced back through *Laws of Canute* (" II," L. : " Secular " Th. 161), § 40—about 1027-34 : =to § 12 *Laws of Edward and Guthrum* (so Th. 171 : " Edward's Law after the acquisition of Guthrum's territory " : L. I, 135, who dates 921-38) which is cited above, p. 2.

There is some doubt about the meaning of—

31, 8a. In Westsexa duo modi testium sunt; nominati et electi, electi et non nominati; judices : constituti, advocati. L. I, 564 : nominati etc.=oath-helpers, either half nominated by the opponent and half chosen by the oath-taker, or only chosen and none nominated [*sc.* by the opponent] : judgment finders—here, too, there are two kinds; permanent or called in by the parties.

Th. who reads " nominati et electi, electi et non nominati; judices : constituti, advocati " (232) says (270) " Compurgators named by the defendant were called *advocati.*"

43, 3. Qui sibi facit advocatum contra dominum suum per superbiam perdat quod de eo tenet.

" If any unfree man chooses defiantly a legal protector against his lord, he shall lose &c." L. here (and I, 513) citing *Doomsday* and Maitland (as above, p. 7), and adding *Doomsday*, I, 218b : " unde nec liberatorem nec advocatum invenit."

In these passages (except 31, 8a) and another L. translates, *adv.* " guardian, protector; defender in court: representative official (*Vogt*) " [=magistratus].

85. Quod quivis liberet [=represent, guarantees as surety] eum quem in malum duxerit. 1. Qui ad dampnum vel malum aliquem duxerit liberet eum advocacione vel emendacione vel participacione. 2. Non omnes cause omnibus [*sc.* ab omn. L.] suo possunt interventu suffragari; que vero possint vel non possint promtum est inveniri a causa, a persona.

2a. Capitales enim et criminales cause ita prelatis [=" big men "] et subditis et modis omnibus interdicte sunt ut non solum auctor ipse sceleris puniendus sit, set quicunque dando vel recipiendo vel defendendo vel casu conscius fuerit aut consilio aut consentaneus in aliquo, simili pene subjaceat; et nemo possit super hiis alterius inde warrantus esse.

(In view of the last words 82.6 may be inserted here : et in quibusdam potest dominus homini suo warantus esse, si precepto suo verberaverit vel alio modo constrictaverit aliquem qui pertineat vel non pertineat ad eum; in quibusdam vero non poterit.)

2. Consilium.

46, 4. In aliis [*i.e.*, than *felonia*] querat accusatus consilium et habeat ab amicis et parentibus suis—quod nulli jure debet defendi—maxime eorum quos secum adduxerit vel ad placitum suum rogaverit; et sic in consilio suo fiducialiter rerum veritatem fateatur ut de placito vel de pace (*a*) salubrius videatur.

46, 5. Bonum autem est ut cum aliciuus consilium in

(*a*) *I.e.*, that peace may be kept between the parties either by going into court (*placito*) or by avoiding self-help (*pace*) or private vengeance.

placito redditur cum emendacione (*b*) dicendum predicatur : ut, si forte perorator vel superadiecerit aliquid vel omiserit, emendare liceat ei.

6. Sepe (*c*) enim fit ut in sua causa quis minus videat quam in alterius et in ore alterius plerumque poterit emendari quod in suo non liceret.

" Now it is a good thing that when the conclusion to which the conference has come is reproduced at the trial [by the advocate : L.] that he should state it " with the right to amend : " so that if by chance the speaker has added or omitted aught the party may amend it. For it often happens that one sees [the point] less in one's own case than in that of another and it is often open to amend the oral mistake of another when it is not to amend one's own " (*d*).

59, 16. Omne autem bellum per emendacionem et respectum capi debet.

bellum = juridical duel (fight) : L. II, 585 : respectum = adjournment.

In the Middle Ages, especially in foreign countries, a capital distinction will be found between the representative who is the mere mouthpiece of the party and one who has the much fuller authority of the pleader or legal agent.

Emendacio &c. is here used in its classical sense of amendment, correction improvement. As it is important to know to what period this idea is due, we must look at § 22. De grithbreche et hamsocna : Sepe etiam ex i(nsc)icia platitancium cause transeunt in jus aliorum : [1] exaggeracione rerum—ut qui nominant et promittunt " grithbreche " vel hamsocnam vel eorum aliquid quod socnam et sacam eorum excedit, ipsa nocendi cupiditate prepositi dum ad witam castigacius posset inflecti— :

(*b*) = Verbal emendation, a change of form in the party's plea : L. II, 61; see below.

The vital importance of the form of pleas for many centuries (before and after Q.) is well known, see p. 14.

(*c*) L.'s note : Rarum ut sit idoneus rei suae quisque defensor : Quintilian, IV, 1, 46 (*Instit. Orat.*).

(*d*) L. cites Brunner, *Forschurgen*, 354; for the general rule 374 : see p. 136.

[2] difforciacione recti : [3] miscravacione : [4] presumptis accusationibus : [5] tarditate—ut qui in prefectura vel qualibet potestate constitutus sepe differt exigere dum licet, quod sepe cum labore frustraque prosequitur destitutus— : [6] transeunt etiam in mislocutione—miskenninge—que magis inhorruit in Londonia.

Note the number of Anglo-Saxon words and the half Anglo-Saxon " mislocutio " : " miscravacio " is only Latin in form.

The meaning seems (*e*) to be : Causes go over to other [new] jurisdictions when [1] Pleaders or plaintiffs frame their charges, *e.g.*, " peace-breach, too high—exaggerate their allegations to their own disadvantage because if they win they lost the fine, which goes to the Crown, whereas if they had framed their case less seriously, it would have gone to the owner of *socn* and *sacn*, *i.e.*, the (land)lord having this charter could get from the King's judge the fine imposed on an ox-stealer but if he chooses to allege *hamsocn*, an outrage with violence on the home, the King's judge awards the mulct to the Crown : [2] the Court declining to hear the case : [3] incorrect form of complaint : [4] other accusations having been previously made : [5] delay, as, for example, when a judicial officer puts off levying a sum on the goods of the defendant when he could do so—which the injured complainant often tries to do and loses his pains : [6] in bad pleading, too—*mislocutio*, *miskenninge*—which went to great lengths in London [where the practice of the judge getting fines for verbal inaccuracies became so rampant that it was finally abolished under Stephen : Th. Glossary : *miskenning* : so L. and under *Missesprechen*]. Some of this is obscure (and part, perhaps wrongly rendered) but the tone of the whole is that of an advanced procedure. We are only concerned with *miscravatio*, *mislocutio*, *miskenninge*. See pp. 15, 16, 206.

47. De causis criminalibus vel capitalibus. De furto et murdro et prodicione domini et robaria et utlagaria et

---

(*e*) According to L.'s notes (published and private).

husbreche et bernet el falsaria et causis criminalibus vel capitalibus nemo quaerat consilium quin inplacitatus statim perneget sine omni peticione consilii cujuscunque nacionis vel condicionis sit; vel ejus affirmacionem vel negacionem defensor (*f*) aut dominus prosequatur competenti termino comprobandam.

48. Quomodo possunt uti consilio. In aliis omnibus potest et debet quilibet uti consilio : in consulendo etiam consulte agere consilium est (*g*).

1a. Si quis enim a justicia regis inplacitatus ad consilium exierit et ad inculpacionem non responderit XX ma(n)ce [m. = $\frac{1}{8}$ of a pound] vel ouerseunesse [a fine] regis culpa sit.

1b. Quando itaque aliquid habetur in inplacitacionibus pretendendum, in inculpacionibus ostendatur; et ad consilium de implacitacione non exeat qui placitare non deliberat.

1c. Judicium enim est : qui sine contradicione vel preoccupacione super implacitacionem exit ad consilium intrat in placitum, et de quibus non responderit, concesserit.

§ 48 seems to mean (according to L. in Norman times)— if the accused has good ground for not yet taking part in the process, he must at once make that point good : leaving the court in order to take counsel implies submission to the jurisdiction. He is not bound to plead to every complaint nor to answer everyone then or there.

49. Quibus causis statim responderi debeat quibus non. 1. Quedam cause sunt de quibus statim respondere (tenetur) sicut dictum est, set non statim placitare neccesse est; quedam de quibus sine competenti summonicione non cogitur aliqius vel placitare vel respondere sine consilio vel in omni loco; quedam, de quibus respondere et placitare oportet; quedam in quibus nec respondere oportet tam in causis quam (in) causatoribus [*i.e.*, of whatever rank they may be].

2. Pro statu vero causarum et esse temporum et modo

(*f*) See *Defensor* below (4).
(*g*) L. thinks this jingle is merely for effect.

inplacitatorum vel inplacitancium unusquisque deliberet tam ex presentibus quam (ex) preteritis, an ei inpresentiarum sit, vel non sit placitandum. 2a. Melius autem aliquando erit, secundum amicorum vel inimicorum presenciam vel absenciam differre placitum et aliquando, cum placitare possit, dilatari. (Here out author speaks as the accused's adviser : L. II, 323.)

3a. In quibus vero expedit, debet ei, si pecierit, consilium dari.

3b. Et cum responderit, queratur, an amplius dicere velit? ne quis occasione [Chicane : L.] potius quam ratione placitare videatur . . . : a point against earlier formalism : L. II, 640.

52, 2. Clericus per consilium prelati sui vadium dare debet cum dederit (deciderit : conj. L.) in accusatione.

55, 3. Omnis homo fidem debet domino suo de vita et membris suis et terreno honore et observacione consilii sui, per honestum. . . .

One of the " passages which are the high-water marks of English vassalism " : 1 P. & M. 280; *n.b.* " English."

57, 8. Pensandum autem erit omni domino sive socnam et sacam habeat sive non habeat ut ita suum hominem ubique manuteneat ne dampnum pro defensione vel pro demissione dedecus incurrat juxta causarum modum et locum diffinitum. . . .

82, 4. Ad eundem modum consilio pariter et auxilio debet [dominus] et modis omnibus potest sine forisfacto homini suo in oportunitatibus subvenire.

This and some preceding passages are traced by L. (I, 599; II, 426; III, 60) to Alfred's Laws (I, 77) dated 870—900, where Q. translates § 42, 5 : Item diximus ut homini liceat pugnare [apparently=fight, literally] cum [=for] domino suo sine wita [=penalty] si quis assalliat ipsum dominum. Sic liceat domino pugnare cum homine suo. 42, 6. Ad eundem modum potest homo **pugnare** cum germano cognato suo. . . .

L. here cites Maitland, *Domesday*, 72; cf. § 85, above p. 532.

Some passages seem to fall both under

3. Advocatio and Consilium.

52. De proprio placito regis : " A man impleaded by the King, whoever may be his immediate lord, must give security at once or fall into the offence of contempt : his lord cannot intervene to save him from so much of responsibility." St. Lect. 159.

52, 1b. Si fuerat [sc. the defendant] inde submonitus legaliter, et dies emendacionis positus vel emundationis (h), ipsa die oportebit eum, si justicia cogat, respondere vel perdere si dominum suum (i) habeat sive non habeat.

61, 14. De omnibus et quibuscunque causis communibus [=not criminal] vel emendabilibus inplacitetur aliquis, si petierit, debet habere terminum requirendi et habendi dominum suum, ubicunque sit, ex competenti [=a moderate time] : modus enim in omnibus. 16. Si sine domino aut termino placitare cogatur aliquis, injustum est : et per judicium poterunt recapitulare placitum ejus et emendare.

17. Quando autem aliquis inplacitatur sine domino suo nisi de illis sit in quibus statim oportet responderi, ut de furto, de incendio, de murdro, de hamsoena et capitalibus—terminum quaerat et respectum [=adjournment] donec dominum suum habeat sceundum rectum; et interim, si opus est, vadium det et plegios mittat.

We may add (from L. I, 500), § 10, 2 of *Leis Willelme* (dated 1090—1135 by L. who says, III, 284, that Stubbs's date in *Lect*. 47 (1250—1300) is much too late : 1 P. & M. 80, not later than " the early years of the 12th century "); in coming to terms for wounding &c. " se sun quor (=coeur) lui purportast e s'un cunseil lui dunast [=donnât], prendreit de lui ceo que offert ad a lui," where the Latin translator (of probably 1170—1200, perhaps later, L. III, 286) has : *si hoc in animo sibi sederet et amici consulerent* (k).

(h) A gloss on *emendacionis*?
(i) For the benefit of his advice : L.
(k) Modern German version : wenn sein Herzes ihm eingäbe und wenn man [sein Verwandtenkreis] den Rath ihm gäbe.

4. Defensor.

§ 5. De causarum proprietatibus.

In causis omnibus ecclesiasticis et secularibus legaliter et ordine pertractandis alii sunt accusatores alii defensores alii testes alii judices in omni discussione probitatis ydonei nullaque simul exactione permisti [= in no way connected with the trial].

Here *defensores* must = defendants : " defenders " St. *Lect.* 161, whose remarks show that undoubtedly this passage gives a picture of a trial at law, apparently, only of the essential elements. The absence, therefore, of any reference to legal representatives is not so significant : p. 12. In § 7, 2, too, where there is a curious list of officials (St. 166) who might be expected to attend a court, there is no suggestion of advocates, but as the list is of the bench—*potestates*—they are more in the nature of *judices*.

These " are not judges ordinary but nominated or selected and liable to be refused by the person impleaded as suspect " (*ib*. 162) : possibly " persons qualified in the same way as the *judices* of the shiremoot, the *judices* and *juratores* of the county court; *i.e.*, the persons qualified to act as assessors with the bishop and [the] Sheriff " : possibly, but less probably, intruded here unintelligently from some canon using the word in the Roman sense. He never sits alone in England : L. II, 702 (5) *sub Urteilfinder* : (= doomsmen ?) citing *L. H. P.* 32, 1. See 1 P. & M., B. II, c. 3, § 1, p. 535; and cf. App. XII (c. 152).

59, 9. Pueri autem ante XV annos plenos nec causam prosequantur nec in judicio resideant. 9a. De rebus hereditatis suae interpellatus post XV annos defensorem habeat vel idem respondeat.

(See further, p. 28).

59, 9 has like some other passages an incidental importance as being (largely) borrowed from the *Lex Ribuaria* [beginning about 512 and going on to the 8th century] c. 81 (*Mon. H. Germ. Leg.* vol. 5, p. 264 : 1889). At 90, 4a, *L. H. P.*, it (*Lex R.*) is quoted by name. At

89, 1, *Lex Salica* or an addition thereto in 819 is quoted : *Mon. H. G. Leg. Sec.* **IV**, v. **I**, p. 293 : ed. Pertz, **I**, 113 ; from c. 5 of which 59, 9a above, is perhaps a reminiscence : L. See Pertz *ib.* 226.

59, 9a. L. infers from these words that it was only about the *hereditas* that the trial was put off till the majority of the heir : " in other civil process the guardian (*Vormund*) was his representative."

Defensor here = defender in court, advocate, *Vorsprech* : elsewhere = representative in court : L. **II**, 50 ; cf. Lass. p. 61 and see on 43 and 47 above.

It is distinguished by L. in

26, 1. Defensor aut dominus de furto pulsatorum ... (*pulsatores* = complainants to a tribunal : L. **II**, 178).

47 ... ejus [defendant] affirmacionem vel negacionem defensor aut dominus prosequatur. ... Here (L. **I**, 562, and **II**, 50) *defensor* = " Fiscalvogt [a magistrate or official] oder Herr unter dessen Gericht Verklagte stehen " : " not an English but a technical Frankish term."

78, 2b. Quia multi potentes volunt si possunt defendere homines suos modo pro servo modo pro libero sicut interim factu facilius sit : set legibus hoc interdictum est : *legibus* sc. of Canute. This is traced by L. **I**, 323, to the Second Part of the Laws of Canute : 1027-34 : § 20, 1, where he sets out three Latin translations thus :—

Q. (*l*).	INSTITUTA CNUTI (*m*).	CONSILIATIO CNUTI (*m*).
Multi strecman (id est potentes sive fortes) volunt, si possunt et audeant,	Multi fortes homines volunt cum ingenio defendere in placitis suos subjectos quo	Multus austerus homo uult (omne) si potest et sibi licet tueri suum

---

(*l*) We cannot call in aid Q.'s (Law of William " Wl Lad " : L. **I**, 484 : 1066-77) : Etsi untrum sit (id est, invalidus) et nolit bellum vel non possit, querat sibi legalem defensorem—because *leg. def.*—a champion for a duel.

(*m*) These two tracts are of the early years of the 12th century (about 1110-20 or 30 : L.). "In each case the translator tried to be more than a translator; he borrowed from other Anglo-Saxon documents, some of which have not come down to us and endeavoured to make his work a practicable law-book." 1 P. & M., **I**, iii, p. 79.

Q. (*l*).	INSTITUTA CNUTI (*m*).	CONSILIATIO CNUTI (*m*).
defendere homines suos, ad utrumlibet, sicut eis videbitur, quod tunc procedat, modo pro servo modo pro libero; sed nolumus hanc iniusticiam pati.	levius illis posse videtur, pro servis aut pro liberis sed nos huic iniusticie consentire nolumus.	hominem u t r o modo, siue p r o libero suie p r o servo quo facilius eum tueri poterit : sed nolumus illam injuriam pati.

L.'s translation shows that this means that people tried to defend their *homines* or *subjecti* in court sometimes as free sometimes as unfree men, whichever was the more convenient for the defence.

Again, II Canute § 27 (L. I, 331), the Latins have " qui in placito se ipsum vel hominem suum distortis compellationibus defendere presumpserit habeat totum hoc *forspecen* (cassatum) " : Q. : " vult defendere &c." : Inst. Cn. : " in placito defenderit contra calumpniis, totum illud sit perlocutum " : Cons. Cn. L. translates " And whoever defends himself or his underlings by countercharge(s ?) let him have said all this in vain and let him answer his opponent as to the Hundred Court shall seem good."

Placitator is dealt with more conveniently, p. 59.

5. Professional lawyers.

Q. in the *Dedicatio* to an unknown friend (L. I, 531) says, § 24 :

Vereor itaque futura de te judicia dum me talia [*supply* locutum : L.] professorum manus impure convenient. . . . L. (III, 177) has no doubt that the *professores* here and § 8, 7, below are technically learned lawyers.

27 : Inde sum, fateor, de rustico causidicus.

38 : Cuius te dispensationis [=undertaking, commission] hortatorem secutus judicem quoque statuo, veniam postulans ne prius haec patiaris grandia professorum debachationibus

---

(*l*) See note (*l*), p. 539.   (*m*) See note (*m*), p. 539.

[=attacks] occupari quam tuae nobilitatis . . . intuitu superflua reseces.

Here the sense of technical jurists is not certain : " prof." may=speaking " big."

L. H. P. § 6, 3a. Ipsorum etiam jura comitatuum per provincias [=shires] plerunque dissenciunt sicut videlicet cupiditas et maligna professorum detestanda studia graviora nocendi genera legalibus statibus adjecerunt.

Here perhaps " prof."—intriguers (as above). L. seems to think they are judicial officials whose greed prompted them.

St. (*Lect*. 152) translates " But in many things they differ, but in many they agree; and even in the several provinces the rules of law of the several counties often differ, according as the greediness and malignant researches of professors have added to the legal statutes* heavier kinds of offences, that is, as the ingenuity of lawyers has invented distinctions of crimes and penalties. [6, 4] For so great is the perversity of the world and the overflowing of evil that the definite truth of the law and the permanent providence of healing art can be rarely found out; but to the greater confusion of all, methods of impleading are sought out, new methods of injury are found, as if the old ones did not do mischief enough, and that man was to be judged of most value to society who had inflicted on it the greatest hurts " : L. (III, 315) says *statibus*=judicature (*not* statutes*).

6, 5. Illis tantum reverentiam et amorem stigia simulatione pollicemur quibus carere non possumus : quicquid nostre crudelitati pari congressione non respondet, nobis natum non reputamus. St. *Lect*. 152 says : " Our friend now becomes so bitter as to be unintelligible : ' nevertheless to those whom we cannot do without, we do, by a sort of infernal hypocrisy, profess love and reverence; whatever does not answer *pari passu* to our own crudelity (possibly credulity) *nobis natum* or non *reputamus*.' The reading is uncertain and the sense absolutely lost."

L.'s translation of *quibus* . . . *possumus* is : " we (Crown jurists) associate ourselves to the tyrannical harshness of the fiscal administration of justice of the Crown: so 63, 4 (below), and cf. 8, 7 (below).

8, 7. Et si quid professioni nostre congruum precedencium vel sequencium capitula docuerint. . . . See above *Dedic.* § 24.

9, 8. personarum distinctio est in condicione, in sexu, secundum professionem et ordinem . . . : *prof.* = any trade, profession : L.

63, 4. Set dum favorem et gratiam dominorum catervatim malitiosa semper cupiditate prepostera candida nigris, nigra candidis commutamus : unde consequenter et sane competenter evenit [ut] continuis miseriarum passionibus ac variis infortuniorum casibus nosmet ipsos evertamus.

Here and in § 6, 5 above L. thinks that " we " = high judicial officers [of the high court] and that the writer confesses that royal judges too often allow jurisdiction to the *domini* of inferior courts, to the injury of defendants.

Prolocutor.

See *Narratores*, p. 171q.

In the Laws of Edmund I (940-6), Lambarde (*Arch.* 59) translates § 7 : " De Inimicitiis. Inimicitias capitales prudentum est extinguere. Primo igitur . . . arbiter [*forspecan*] ad interfecti cognatos praemittitor eisque interfectorem compensaturum significato : tum praeterea arbitri in manus ac potestatem dator homicida ut pacate coram venire ac de capitis aestimatione solvenda spondere possit. . . ."

Thorpe, p. 107 : ' Of Faehthe ' [feud]. The ' witan ' shall appease ' faehthe.' First, according to ' folk right ' the slayer shall give pledge to his ' forespeca ' (n) and the ' forespeca ' to the kinsmen, that the slayer will make ' bōt ' to the kin. Then after that it is requisite that security be given to the slayer's ' forespeca ' that the slayer,

---

(n) Th.'s note is " The Anglo-Saxon ' forespeca ' is the Contour of the Norman law-books : the Advocatus rather than the Attornatus of the Latin documents." If this were correct it would very much simplify our subject.

may, in peace, near [*sic*], and himself give ' wed ' for the ' wĕr.'

Q. (in L. I, 189, who dates 943-6) is: Sapientum est sedare factionem: Inprimis juxta rectam populi lagam debet prolocutor (*o*) occisoris in manum dare cognationi quod rectum ei per omnia faciet. Deinde oportet ut prolocutori (*o*) detur in manu cur interfector audeat accedere cum pace et ipse weriam vadiare. L. understands *prol. occ.* that the slayer shall solemnly promise " his Fürsprech and this Fürsprech shall promise " the kinsmen compensation, etc., and that the aggrieved kinsmen shall assure the slayer's " Fürsprech " of the slayer's safety; but warns us (II, 637-8, 726; III, 128) that here " Vorsprech " does not mean surety or protector or counsel but an arbitrator or intercessor—a view quite incompatible with Thorpe's.

Coote (*The Romans of Britain*, 313 (1878)) is emphatic that there is no Roman reminiscence in this " savage intermediary who palavers in a blood-feud." But, at any rate, there is a customary intermediary.

(*o*) With the inevitable v. r. *praelocutor*.

APPENDIX IV.

Spence in the *Equitable Jurisdiction of the Court of Chancery* (1846), v. I, p. 280, points out that the clergy wrote the Anglo-Saxon and Danish codes : many, he says, of the customs of these conquerors " were accommodated to those of a corresponding nature which had prevailed amongst the Romans. . . . At first this connection [of ' Lord and Man, the parent of Lord and Vassal '] like that between the patron and the client was purely personal. In process of time, however the institution of lord and man may have originated, all the incidents of the relation of patron and client were transferred to it. . . ." In a note the learned author adds : " The more I consider the constitutional and legal history of these early times the more I am confirmed in the opinion that the basis of the Anglo-Saxon and Continental relation of lord or master and man was that of patron and client and patron and freedman, not of prince and *comes*."

For the specific duty of legal aid which the *patronus* owed to the *cliens* see any book on early Roman law or a Latin dictionary; for a good instance in a play see the *Menaechmi*, IV, ii, 6. Tacitus says of the Britons in fight " honestior [=of higher rank] auriga : clientes propugnant " : *Agricola*, 12 ; but *clientes* is merely literary. The only instance of *cliens* L. gives is *Cons. Cnut.* § 20a (I, 323) : sive paterfamilias sive cliens (sit, volumus) ut omnis sit in centenario et fidejussione positus et fidejussor eum servet et ad omnem rectitudinem perducat.

Nothing can be inferred from the use of the word. Some of the details in the relations between lord and man supposed by Q. in *Leges H. P.* are singularly like the details of Roman usage : see Marquardt and Mommsen's *Handbuch : Clienten* : v. III, pt. 1 : probably similar effects from similar causes. Forsyth appositely remarks,

Hortensius, c. iv : " The transition of the name from the patron who gave his client the benefit of his opinion and counsel in legal difficulties to the advocate who openly espoused the cause of another in a court of justice is too obvious to require proof." Cf. " with the single exception of the practice of clientship or commendation (that is, the custom for every freeman to be in the mund or protection of a lord) there is no resemblance between the feudal and Roman systems." St. *Lect.* 20 : cf. 264.

APPENDIX V.

According to Du Cange the earliest *Cancellarii* were ushers, officials of judges—" dicti potissimum qui ad *cancellos forenses* [" rails . . . which separated the *Secretum* from the rest of the court " : Bingham, *Christ. Antiq.* III, 11, § 6] seu judicum, stabant "; the *cancelli* being originally openings in walls through which people outside could be addressed. The *cancellarii* " supplicantes introducebant ad judicem . . . jussa eorumdem explebant . . . patet eosdem fuisse quodammodo ostiarios." In France " Notariorum munus obiere. Unde in Lege Ripuar . . . sunt ii qui testamenta et acta publica conscribunt "—which N.B. and the foll. paragraphs : *e.g.*, " Cancellariorum munus etiam Ecclesiasticum fuit . . . Cancellarii Ecclesiae Romanae quanta fuit in Romana Curia auctoritas docet S. Bernardus Epist. 31 " (*p*). Cf. the title in the Theodosian and Justinian's Codes : *de Adsessoribus domesticis et Cancellarius* : cited Bingham, above.

(*p*) Cf. under *Cancelli Forenses* " inde nostri *Barreau* forum litigantium vocant quod *Cancellis* pariter muniatur " : sed *quaere*.

APPENDIX VI.

A.

Monumenta Historica Germaniae, III; ed. Pertz, p. 567.

500 A.D. (about). Leges Burgundionum : Liber Legum Gundebati.

XXX. De testibus falsa referentibus et calumpniatoribus.

3. Etiam qui calumpniatori [plaintiff] consilium dederit ad dimicandum, si victus fuerit, similiter, ut superius statutum est, multa feriatur.

Does *consilium* mean in court or out? The word *calump.* suggests a fraudulent trial : Lass.

650 A.D. or end of 7th century. *M. H. G. Legum*, Sect. V [4º].

Marculfi formulae B. I.

21. De causas alterius receptas.

Fidelis, Deo propicio noster ille ad nostram veniens presentiam, suggessit nobis eo quod propter simplicitatem suam causas suas minime posset prosequire vel obmallare. Clemenciae regni nostri petiit ut inlustris vir illi omnes causas suas in vicem ipsius, tam in pago quam in palatio nostro ad mallandum vel prosequendum recipere deberit (*sic*) : quod [et] in presente per fistuca [*i.e.*, the symbol of a retainer] eas eidem visus est commendasse. . . .

746 A.D. *M. H. G. Legum*, vol. IV, p. 191 (Pertz).

(Regis) Ratchis Leges.

C. 11, vii. Si quis causam alterius agere aut causare presumpserit in presentia regi aut judici, excepto si rex aut judex licentiam dederit de vidua aut de orfano aut de tale hominem qui causam suam agere non potit conponat weregild suo medietatem regi et medietatem ei contra quem causaverit. Et si forte aliquis per simplicitatem causam suam agere nescit veniat ad palatio et si rex aut judex praeviderit, quod veritas sit, tunc ei dare debeat hominem qui causam ipsius agat (p. 184, *ib*. same King and date, a shorter version).

Lass. remarks that Lombard legislation is " after law the weightiest law in the Frankish age."

782-6 A.D. *M. H. G. Leg.* Sec. II; v. I, 192 ed. B. (4º) : Pertz, v. III, fol., *Legum* I, 43.

Pippini Italiae Regis Capitulare.

C. 6. ubicumque pontifex [=bishop] substantiam [? property] habuerit, advocatum habeat in ipso comitatu qui absque tarditate justitias faciat et suscipiat. Et talis sit ipse advocatus, liber homo et bonae opinionis, laicus aut clericus, qui sacramento (*v. l.* —tum) pro causa ecclesiae quam peregerit deducere possit [juxta qualitatem substantiae] sicut lex ipsorum est.

C. 5 is : Ut viduas et orfanos tutorem (*v. l.* auctorem) habeant juxta illorum legem qui illos defensent et adjuvent et per malorum hominum oppressiones suam justitiam non perdant. Etsi tutor (*v. l.*, actor) aliquis eorum esse noluerit, judex praevideat Deum timentem hominem juxta ut lex ipsorum est, qui per nostra praeceptione illorum peragere debeant causa (*sic*).

800 A.D. or before. *M. H. G. Leg.* Sec. II (I, 85 : ed. Boretius); P. v. 4, *Legum* : I, 181 813 A.D. ?

Cap. de Villis.

29. De clamatoribus ex hominibus nostris unusquisque judex praevideat ut non sit eis necesse venire ad nos proclamare. Clamator=plaintiff (Lass, following Du Cange : =litigator, actor, reus and, sometimes, causidicus).

803. (I, 113, B. : I, 113, P.).

Capitulare legibus additum.

C. 4. Si quis hominem in judicio injuste contra alio altercantem adjuvare per malum ingenium praesumpserit atque inde coram judicibus vel comite increpatus fuerit et nagare non potuerit, solidis XV culpabilis judicetur.

There is an obvious echo of this with increased costliness

in certain Capitularies (I, 295, B.; I, 227, P.) in or about 820 A.D.

C. 4. Si homini cuilibet causam suam in placito aut coram comite palatio [*quaerenti* : editors] aliis fuerit inpedimento, et causam ejus injuste disputando inpedierit, tunc volumus ut sive comes palatii seu comes ipse in comitatu suo jubeat eum exire foras; et si noluerit oboedire tunc solvet bannum dominicum id est LX solidos, et illi cui adversatus est donet wadium suum pro lege sua.

" Alius " here must = a representative (Lass).

802 (prob.). *M. H. G. Legum*, Sec. II, v. I, p. 93, ed. B.; 91, ed. Pertz.

C. 1. A grave warning by Charlemagne against injustice to ecclesiis Dei neque pauperibus nec viduis nec pupillis nullique homini christiano.

The editor's warning that this text is more or less corrupt and sometimes difficult to understand peculiarly applies to

C. 9. Ut nemo in placito pro alio rationare usum habeat defensionem alterius injuste, sive pro cupiditate aliqua, minus rationare valente (*q*) vel pro ingenio rationis suae justum judicium marrire [= impedire, perturbare, italice *smarrire* : Boretius] vel rationem suam minus valente (*q*) opprimendi studio. Sed unusquisque pro sua causa vel censum vel debito ratione reddat, nisi aliquis isti [sit?] infirmus aut rationes nescius, pro quibus missi vel priores qui in ipso placito sunt vel judex qui causa huius rationis sciat rationetur con placito; vel si necessitas sit talis personae largitur in rationem qui omnibus provabilis sit et qui in ipsa bene noverit causa. . . .

rationare = *loqui*, in court (Lass.); Spanish, *razonar*. Now, this code is in the commission expressly given (c. 1) to prelates, etc., and " laicos religiosos "; c. 9, therefore, undoubtedly refers to secular courts : its clerical counterpart is c. 13 where the great ecclesiastics are bidden— Advocatos adque vicedomini centenariosque legem scientes

---

(*q*) *minus valente*[*m*?] perhaps means the less powerful (*potens*) party; or there may be a reference to the coin *valens*, p. 27*d*; if so, the text is as corrupt as it is ungrammatical.

et justitiam diligentes pacificosque et mansuetus habeant
, . . quia nullatemus neque praepositos neque advocatos
damnosus et cupidus in monasteria habere volumus. . . .

No doubt the mischief of *cupidi* or *injusti advocati* is
here contemplated, but the high character demanded of
advocati equally in both sets of courts must have helped
to keep up the standard and popular esteem for the class.
See under 819.

M. H. G. I, *Leg*. Sec. II ed. 206 : B. 781-810 A.D.
I, 151 : P. : 806-10.
Karoli M. Capitulare Missorum Italicum.

C. 6. De pravis judicibus, advocatis, vicedominis,
vicariis, centenariis vel reliquis actoribus malivolis non
habendis.

End of 7th century (or 823 ?). Formulae Senonenses
recentiores; no. 10 : *M. H. G. Legum*, Sec. V, p. 216 :
Formulae : otherwise the 31st formula of Marculf.
Mandatum.

Legibus institutum est et consuetudine per tempora
conservatum ut, quicumque advocatum instruere velit,
mandato legaliter dato atque solemniter confirmato, eum
instruere debeat ut omnes causas quas adgredi vel
repellere debet prosequi et defendere inoffense valeat.
Igitur ego ille sanctae illae aecclesiae vocatus episcopus
inungo mando et per has litteras delego tibi illo fideli meo
de rebus sancti illius sitis in pago illo, in locis muncupatis,
cum adjacentiis vel aspicientibus ad eas locis aliis per
omni jure investigare inquirere prosequi et admallare debeas
per mallos, vicos, castella, oppida et civitates necnon etiam
si necessitas incubuerit in palatio, ante vicarios, comites,
missos dominicos, comites palatii sive ante omnes judices
quibus hoc officium delegatum est ut causationes et lites
definire et terminare juste et rationabiliter debeant; et
quicquid legibus cum justicia inde prosecutus fueris et
definieris, scito, apud me ratum et acceptum atque inconvulsum mansurum. Quod mandatum in te conlatum ut
firmum fixumque permaneat manu propria subterfirmari
et qui adfirmare deberent rogavi.

801 (806?) —810 A.D. *M. H. G. Leg.* Sec. II, v. I, 209, B.; P. I, 103 : 802 A.D.

Pippini Cap. Italicum.

C. 10. Ut vassi et austaldi nostri in nostris ministeriis sicut decet, honorem et plenam iustitiam habeant et si presentes esse non possunt suos advocatos habeant qui eorum res ante comitem defendere possint et quicquid eis queritur justitiam faciant.

11. Volumus ut advocati in presentia comitis eligantur non habentes malam famam sed tales eligantur quales lex jubet eligere.

805 A.D. *M. H. G. Leg.* Sec. II; I, 123, B.; I, 133, P. Capitulare [of Charlemagne]. Missorum in Theodonis villa (Thionville), &c.

C. 8. De clamatoribus vel causidicis qui nec juditium scabinorum adquiescere nec blasfemare (r) volunt antiqua consuetudo servetur—*i.e.*, they were kept *in libera custodia*; n.b. " antiqua consuetudo."

C. 12. De advocatis : id est ut pravi advocati, vicedomini vicarii et centenarii tollantur; et tales eligantur quales et sciant et velint juste causas discernere et terminare. Et si comes pravus inventus fuerit, nobis nuntietur.

Cf. Muratori, *Scriptores*, v. I, Pt. II, p. 96, who gives the formula of appointment of an *advocatus* by the *comes* at the request of the bishop—for purely ecclesiastical work—but (almost certainly) of a layman.

818-9 A.D. *M. H. G. Leg.* Sec. II, v. I; B. 281; P. I, 211 : 817 A.D.

Hludowici Pii Cap. legibus addita.

3. De viduis et pupillis et pauperibus. Ut quandocumque in mallum ante comitem venerint, primo eorum causa audiatur et definiatur. Et si testes per se ad causas suas quaerendas habere non potuerint vel legem nescierint comes illos vel illas adjuvet, dando eis talem hominem qui

---

(r) According to Du Cange=they do not formally object to the *judicium*, but perhaps *nec* simply=et.

rationem eorum teneat vel pro eis loquatur—an instance of a " Fürsprecher in Grafengericht " : Lass.

819 A.D. P. I, 228 : not in B. who (v. I, *Leg.* Sec. II), p. 460, n. 1, says that the following *cap.* is Canon 50 of the Council of Mainz in 813 : see p. 158.

Capit. Italica.

Omnibus igitur episcopis, abbatibus, cunctoque clero omnino praecipimus vicedominos praepositos advocatos sive defensores habere bonos non crudeles non periures non falsitatem amantes sed Deum timentes et in omnibus justitiam diligentes. See under 802.

813 A.D. Coleti's *Collection of the Councils* (Venice, 1729), v. IX, col. 339, gives Can. 50 (as here). Part of Can. 8 is : ut laici in eorum [the bishops'] ministerio obediant episcopis ad regendas ecclesias Dei viduas et orphanos defensandos . . . , where *laici* = advocati.

Can. 12 : ut monachi ad saecularia placita nullatenus veniant neque ipse abbas sine consilio episcopi sui . . . nequaquam tamen contentiones aut lites aliquas ibi movere praesumat sed quidquid quaerendum vel etiam respondendum sit per advocatos suos hoc faciat. Can. 40 : Praecipimus ut in ecclesia aut domibus ecclesiarum vel atriis placita saecularia minime fiant.

Presumed or accepted dates A.D. of these Laws are : Salic, 422 ; Burgundian, 502 ; Visigoth, 506 ; Ripuarian, 539 ; Lombard, 745. Sohm, *M. H. G. Legum*, Sec. V, p. 192, thinks the parts of the Ripuarian varied in origin from the first part of the 6th century to the beginning of the 8th.

Bataillard, *Les Origines, &c.*, c. 1, p. 33, cites le P. Thomassin, *La discipline de l'Eglise*, to the effect that under Charlemagne's successors the same *advocatus* was sometimes employed to defend a church against all wrongs " either at the bar and before the secular magistrates or against the lords and soldiers." See p. 27.

Benedict Levita : mid. of 9th cent. A.D. Collection of Capitularies in 1 Baluze (1677), col. 1059 ; B. vii, § 157 (in marg. : " Ivo. par. 16, c. 355 ").

Si advocatus in causa suscepta iniqua cupiditate fuerit repertus, a conventu honestorum et a judiciorum communione separetur, et videat ne judicis et assertoris personam accipiat.

B.

For a period later than A (above) see M. Thévenin's collection, *e.g.*, note *ib.* p. 218 (no. 150)—the manumitted *servus* who, in 1029-31, is expressly allowed to have any *advocatus* he likes : and *ib.* p. 109 (no. 80) in 845 Guinifred the *advocatus* of Rodbertus the *vicarius* (of the *comes*) who tries the case reports to his " senior " " in responsis," *i.e.*, he is a *judex*. So in 858 (p. 127, no. 93) an *advocatus* sits for a *vice-comes*.

APPENDIX VII.

1.

Willelmus, rex Anglorum, Lanfranco archiepiscopo, Roberto de Oilleio, et Rogero de Pistri, et omnibus fidelibus suis totius regni Angliae, salutem. Sciatis me concessisse Sanctae Mariae de Abbendonia, et Athellelmo abbati ejusdem loci, omnes consuetudines terrarum suarum, quaecunque jacent in ecclesia predicta, ubicumque eas habeat, in burgo vel extra burgum, secundum quod abbas iste Athellelmus poterit demonstrare, per breve vel cartam, ecclesiam Sanctae Mariae de Abbendona, et praedecessorem suum, eas consuetudines habuisse dono regis Eadwardi.

Quarum recitatio literarum in Berkescire comitatu prolata plurimum et ipsi abbati et ecclesiae commodi attulit. Siquidem regii officiales illis diebus hominibus in ecclesiae possessionibus diversis locorum manentibus multas inferebant injurias, nunc has, nunc vero illas consuetudines, eis pati satis graves, ingerentes. Sed exhibitis praedictis imperialibus mandatis, quibus rectitudines ecclesiae per cartam Eadwardi regis et attestatione comitatus in eodem comitatu tunc publice ventilatae, ipsi officiales repulsam sibi adversam, ecclesiae autem commodam, suscepere: id viriliter domno Athellelmo satagente. Cui plurimum auxilii ferebant duo ecclesiae hujus monachi, germani quidem fratres, quorum major natu Sacolus, junior vero Godricus vocabatur, cum quibus et Alfwinus presbyter, tunc ecclesiam regiae villae Suttune huic vicinae gubernans; quibus tanta secularium facundia et praeteritorum memoria eventorum inerat, ut caeteri circumquaque facile eorum sententiam ratam fuisse, quam edicerent, approbarent. Sed et alii plures de Anglis causidici per id tempus in abbatia ista habebantur quorum collationi nemo sapiens refragabatur. Quibus rem ecclesiae publican tuentibus, ejus oblocutores elingues fiebant.

2.

Post quartum annum adquisitionis regis Willelmi istius terre, consilio baronum suorum fecit submoniri per universos patrie comitatus Anglos nobiles, sapientes at lege sua eruditos ut eorum consuctudines ab ipsis audiret.

Electis igitur de singulis (s) totius patrie comitatibus duodecim, jurejurando inprimis coram eo sanxerunt, ut quoad possent, recto tramite incedentes legum suarum ac consuetudinum sancita edicerent, nil pretermittentes nil prevaricando commutantes.

(s) *I.e.*, $12 \times 32 = 384$: (" ! ") L. I, 627g, who doubts the whole story and suggests that the *sapientes* were supposed to be taken from the pre-Conquest Witan.

APPENDIX VIII.

Policraticus, B. 5, c. 10 : § 563.

Sed et ipsas syllabas et apices nisi eum [a court underling] tibe propitium feceris, sic distorquebit, tot tibi verborum ponet tendiculas, ut pro pace bellum pro quiete litigium, amici instrumento [under the guise of] videatur inscribere. . . . Tunc de singulis verbis in consilium itur, deliberationi praescribitur tempus et apices singuli ponuntur in statera. Nisi eum praemulseris, occurret tibi non fideliter rei gestae concepta series, aut stylus incultus oberit aut a publica forma notarii vel scrinarii divertens benignitas (*t*) aut negligentia juris et aliquis semper nodus pecunia vindice indiget . . . apud curiales omnia . . . venalia (564a).

Causidicorum siquidem est lingua damnifica, nisi eam, ut dici solet, funibus argenteis vincias . . . Hoc autem a maximis pertransit ad minimos qui nisi mulceantur obsequiis et reficiantur (*u*) muneribus sibi fieri injuriam suspicantur (564c).

In uno tamen piissimos esse miraberis, quod querelas libenter audiunt, fovent humiliorum causas, et eo usque patrocinantur afflictis dum exhauriant loculos pleniorum. Nam quocunque modo causa procedat hoc semper agitur ut loculi impleantur, etsi avaritia nequeat satiari (565c).

C. XI . . . quod judicem oportet habere juris et aequi notitiam . . . et in eo quidem tempore nihil miserabilius vidi quam judices scientiae legis ignaros, bonae voluntatis inanes, quod convincit amor munerum et retributionum [rewards] (568b).

C. 12. Sed ubi ad forum ventum est in quo inanis ostentatio ingenii conquiescit et seria dumtaxat agitantur,

---

(*t*) " or that the partiality of the notary or scribe has departed from the prescribed form " : Prof. Dickinson's transln.

(*u*) " refreshers," Webb (1909), *aptissime*.

sine periculo litigatorum aut judicis in sententiae calculo non erratur. Nec est, ut opinor, quidquam utilius quam periculum differri si omnino vitari non potest. Iniquissimum tamen est jurgia [recriminations, suits] protelari cum alterutrius litigantium periclitatur utilitas et rei difficultas moram non contrahit (572d).

Policrat, B. v, c. 13. J.'s ideal.

. . . litigatores ipsos personas videlicet principales non ante ad litem judex admittit quam ei praestito sacramento faciant fidem quod justitiae suae insistent et calumpniam omnem facient procul. Actor quidem juret non calumpniandi animo litem mouisse sed existimando bonam habere causam et quod nichil in tota lite faciet calumpniose ut nec probatio nec dilatio frustatoria exigatur sed id solum quod justitia videtur exigere. Reus autem jurabit quod putans se bona instantia uti pervenit ad reluctandum et quod in nullo totius litis articulo calumpniose versabitur, id solum a judice vel aduersario exigens quod pro veritate putat ex necessitate justitiae exhibendum. Uterque vero juramenti sui extrema clausula hoc complectetur ut jurent se nichil dedisse aut promisisse aut daturos esse vel per se vel per mediam personam sive judicibus sive aliis quibuscumque personis pro ca causa exceptis his quae advocatis et quibusdam aliis certis personis de juris indulgentia praestari licet. Quodsi actor sic jurare recusaverit exclusus a lite cadit ab actione tanquam improbus litigator. Reus vero detrectans subire juramentum habetur pro confesso et sententiam dampnationis expectat. Sed et ipsi patroni causarum quo fidelior possit esse examinatio ab ipsa contestatione litis, juramento artantur ad veritatem et fidem, jurantes quod cum omni virtute sua omnique ope quod justum et verum existimaverint clientibus suis inferre procumbunt, nichil studii relinquentes prout cuique possibile est et quod ex industria sua non protahent lites. Nam eas oportet a judicibus infra biennium vel triennium terminari. Ipsos quoque advocatos pari distributione partibus exaequabit sive eos petierint sive non ut aequo Marte possit causa procedere. Haec autem paritas et in virtutis merito et vivacitate ingenii, consilii profunditate, et opinione scientiae et nominis auctoritate consistit, ut haee omnia, si fieri possit, apud partes quadam aequitatis lance librentur. Quodsi unius prae ceteris est fama hilarior ex officio judicantis, prout poterit, parti adversariae compensabitur. Qui tamen alicujus litigatorum archana praenovit, non patrocinabitur adversario, nisi forte citra coniuentiam judicis separatim cum pluribus alter tractaverit, ut alteri paris defensionis copia subtrahatur. Nec est qui a judice monitus sine excusatione probabili possit cuicumque parti patrocinium denegare nisi forum sibi praecludi velit ut postmodum in causis agendis minime audiatur. Si vero praevaricatus fuerit advocatus in convictum oportet pro qualitate commissi penam gravissimam exerceri.

Munus siquidem patrocinii fidelissime implendum est et sine adversariorum injuria. Rationibus namque non probris contendendum est et ex edicto principis patitur opinionis dispendium [loss of fame] quisquis negotio derelicto procax in adversarii sui contumeliam aut palam pergit ant subdole. Sed licet patrono merces ex causa honorarii debeatur, concinnatorem [instigator] vel redemptorem (*x*) litium esse non licet ut certae partis emolumentum cum gravi damno litigatoris et quadam depraedatione paciscatur. Quicquid autem patronus allegaverit, praesente domino, perinde est habendum nisi ex continenti, id est infra proximum triduum contradixerit. Licet autem patronum vinci contigerit, in nullo leditur fama eius, si nichil omisit ex contingentibus et clientis sui justitiam fideliter fouit : non emim cogitur patrocinari mendacio. Si quid vero lesionis affert causa in litigantes cadit, sive civiliter sive criminaliter actum sit. Hoc autem, quicquid sit, sententia diffinitiva declarat, quae reos condemnat vel absolvit et interdum in ipsos auctores consultissime acerbitatis effundit aculeos . . . (573a—574b).

C. 15, 576c. Quae vero de praesidibus aliisque judicibus dicta sunt debent et apud proconsules, quos nostrates vulgariter dicunt justitias esse errantes, optinere (*y*).

(*x*) Cf. : Ideo constitutio imperialis ab officio *postulandi* semovit litium redemptores : Peter of Blois, Ep. 26 (App. IX).

(*y*) Cf. *Dial de Scacc.* : per comitatus communes assise a justitiis errantibus, quos nos deambulatorios vel perlustrantes iudices nominamus

576d. Plebiscito continetur ne quis praesidum munus donumve caperet nisi esculentum poculentumve (z) et id quidem intra dies proximos prodigatur ... Quod et ad alios ... magistratus transit ... Licet enim patrocinium justum possit vendere advocatus et peritus juris sanum consilium (a), judicium vendere omnino non licet (577a) (b).

C. XVI. Omnes cognitores [=*gens de justice* : Fr. trans.] et judices a pecuniis atque patrimoniis manus abstineant, neque alienum jurgium *des differens d'autruy*] putent suam praedam. Etenum privatarum litium cognitor, idemque mercator [*trafique du droit*] statutam legibus cogetur subire jacturam (578d); from Cod. IX, 27, 3 (Webb).

Sed et leges ipsae et consuetudines quibus nunc vivitur insidiae sunt et laquei calumpniantium. Verborum tendiculae proponuntur et aucupationes sillabarum : vae simplici qui sillabizare non novit (579a).

Nam de vicecomitibus et justitiis quae, ut vulgari nostro utar, recte dicuntur errantes, nichil tale auditur, eo quod diligunt munera et sequuntur retributiones ... (580a).

... : rex ... secuit regnum in VI partes ut eas electi judices, quos errantes vocamus, perlustrarent et jura destituta restituerent (I, viii, D. : II, ii, F. : pp. 95, 119, ed. Hughes).

(z) In 577d he gives an instance of a Bishop of Chartres who followed this rule " et hoc cum summa frugalitate." Cf. 582a of the prophet Samuel. The exception is significant of the times when entertainment was not to be had easily everywhere. Thus Fortescue, de *laudibus* C. 51, says that the judge shall abjure (literally) from any suitor *donum ... praeterquam esculenta et poculenta quae non magni erunt pretii* : cited 3 *Inst.* on Bribery of any man in " judiciall place " : 4 *Black Comm.* 140—embracery of a jury includes " entertainments." The importance of this exception is that it not improbably led to the special jury : a well-to-do suitor came attended by his friends and he entertained the jury after the trial with them, some of whom might be on the jury : for the custom see Pepys, Evelyn, Richardson's novels &c.

(a) N.B. the recognition of the difference between pleading and consultation.

(b) From *Decreti*, Pars II, Causa XI, Qu. 3, c. 71 : I *C. J. C.* 663 (Leipzig : 1879, ed. Friedberg). It is also quoted by William of Drogheda on *Fees*, p. 107.

APPENDIX IX.

Peter of Blois : Ep. 26 : Migne, v. 207, p. 91 : 1 Giles, p. 94 (contemporary of John of Salisbury : studied law at Bologna in 1160 and perhaps taught it).

Lex equidem saecularis gloriosa suppellectili verborum lepidaque orationis urbanitate lasciviens me vehementer allexerat et inebriaverat mentem meam. . . . Adhuc tamen quia nondum dilatavi gressus meos in lege domini, lectioni Codicis et Digestorum plerumque ad solatium non ad usum, tempus vacationis impendo. . . .

Res plena discriminis est in clericis usus legum, totum enim hominem adeo sibi vindicat ut eum rei familiaris providentia fraudet . . . suspendat a spiritualibus, a divinis avellat.

John Chrysostom, he goes on : " noluit tamen ad instantiam amicorum gerere officium advocati . . . Nemo simul potest precari et orare, petere et postulare, exercere Christi ministerium et officium advocati . . . "

But it is a good thing to know the laws—non ad quaestum non ad iniquum juris compendium—" but in case I have to sit as a judge aut judicis assessor " (p. 202). Then follows the sentence on p. 120 and that in App. VIII. He goes on : Debuerat advocatus quod gratis acceperat gratis dare, advocare pro pupillo et vidua pro utilitate reipublicae . . . Fructuosius esset ei salarium modicum et honestum quam sinum inexplebilis avaritiae per fas et nefas extendere in immensum : nam melius est modicum justo super divitias peccatorum multas.

APPENDIX X.

Essoins.

The word is apparently from an old Teutonic root, not from *excusatio*: it occurs in a Latin form several times in L. H. P. see 2 L. : *soinus*. The innumerable references to the subject in 13th century records and writers all over the British isles (Bracton, p. 141u; Britton, *the Mirror of Justices* : Bateson, 1 & 2 *Borough Customs* : 18, 21 Seld. Soc. : Gilbert, *Hist. and Munic. Docts. Ireland* : Rolls : Indexes) must be justified by its importance then. Much research would be required to speak with certainty but a Danish equivalent (forfal = essoin = a reasonable excuse, in Danish law : 1 *Rec. of Leicester*, 116, 120-1, 152-3 : about 1260 and 1277) rather points to the derivation from an even earlier and more rudimentary representative : " — let the pledges . . . if they wish, have on the day a *forfal* for him [defaulting defendant] instead of an essoin, as was formerly the custom . . ." If a conjecture may be hazarded, some such evolution may have produced the essoin as the embryo of the *attornatus*.

The law of essoins is mysterious—we seem to have lost the key to it. Bracton and Britton developed the doctrine which they found in " Glanvill " : perhaps the large space the former gives to it hardly corresponds to the facts of his day; he thought possibly that this glimmer of legal reprentation was going to develope.

" Habent," he says 5 Rolls edn. 156, " etiam essonia ordinem sicut et actiones."

On the whole, perhaps the simplest statement is that of *Hengham magna* (about 1270-90), C. VI : Essoniator autem, absente vel presente adversario suo, tantum potest facere quantum attornatus omni die nisi eo die quo oportuerit partes litigare. Litigare autem pro domino suo non potest essoniator. Sed si petens essoniatus fuerit vel compareat essoniator tenentis, bene potest capere diem versus eum adeo bene sicut dominus suus vel ejus atturnatus . . . Quando autem essoniator sequitur defaltam pro domino suo vel pro suo atturnato certum nomen ejus irrotulabitur in Rotulatione defaltae illius . . . Quando autem atturnatus sequitur defaltam pro domino suo, non sic fit : nisi dubitetur de fraude atturnati. C. VII. Post igitur essonium redditum potest reus apparere in Curia et facere atturnatos . . . nec cum reus fecerit atturnatum oportebit petentem se essoniare versus illum atturnatum, immo versus principalem, Attornatus autem si fuerit essoniandus, semper nomine suo essonietur et non in nomine principalis.

Hengham Parva, c. 1. There are five essonia : de (1) *ultra mare* (2) *terra Sancta* (3) *malo veniendi* . . . istud solum essonium et non aliud tam jacet attornato quam principali personae. Ita tamen quod si quis essoniaverit seipsum et non attornatum suum, non allocabitur [will be awarded] ei essonium suum. (4) *malo lecti* (5) *servicio d. regis.*

Hengham Magna, c. V : In judicando essonio semper respicienda sunt brevia originalia et status placitorum, ne forte per iterationem essonii nimis differatur petitio petentis seu per machinosam cautelam prosequentis aliquid hujusmodi essonium — sed si tale essonium irritum fuerit convertatur in *defaltam.*

APPENDIX XI.

Ric. Angl., C. XXVI. Qui a postulando prohibeatur
. . . Item [prohibentur] qui de certa parte litis pacti sunt. . . . Si qui advocatorum, aestimationi suae immensa atque illicita compendia praetulisse sub nomine honorariorum ex ipsis negotiis quae tuenda susceperint, emolumentum sibi certae partis cum gravi damno litigatoris et depraedatione poscentes, fuerint inventi, placuit ut omnes qui in huiusmodi severitate [scil. saevitate] permanserint, ab hac professione penitus arceantur. Salarium nuda sponsione constitutum petatur condictione ex lege. . . . Si autem nullum fuerit salarium constitutum agendum est judicis officio, ut constituatur pro facundia advocati.

C. XXVII. Ut advocati honorem judici exhibeant et sine probris certent.

Debent igitur advocati omnem honorem judici exhibere, alioquin removentur.—Caecum utrisque luminibus orbatum praetor repellit, videlicet quod insignia magistratus videre et revereri non possit.

Item sine atrocitate verborum suae petitionis aequitatem judici debent commendare.

Non probris sed ratione debent contendere : Si quis adeo procax fuerit ut non ratione sed probris putet esse certandum, opinionis suae imminutionem patietur. Nec enim conniventia [with one party] accommodanda est ut quisquam negotio derelicto in adversarii [the other party] contumeliam and palam pergat aut subdole.

Non moveant tumultum ant impetum committent aut clamoribus utentur—*owing to the sanctity of the building*—the offender, ultimo supplicio subjacebit. Agat advocatus quae causa desiderat, temperet ab injuria, quantumcumque voluerit peroret . . .

Here he copies word for word the famous censure on *advv.* who were mean and grasping about fees from *Codex*

Justin. II, 6 : Apud urbem Romam etiam honoratis qui hoc putaverint eligendum, eo usque liceat orare quousque maluerint, videlicet ut non ad turpe compendium stipemque deformem haec arripiatur occasio sed laudis per eam augmenta quaerantur. . . . Quisquis igitur, ex his quos agere permisimus, vult esse causidicus, eam solam quam sumit tempore agendi, sibi sciat esse personam, quousque causidicus est. Nec putet quisquam honori suo aliquid esse detractum cum ipse necessitatem standi elegerit et ipse contempserit jus sedendi.

Quae dixerit advocatus intelligantur quasi a cliente dicta. . . . Ea, quae advocati, praesentibus hiis quorum causae aguntur, allegant, perinde habenda sunt ac si ab ipsis dominis litium proferantur. Si tamen erraverit revocare potest dominus quando voluerit ante sententiam . . .

Judex autem patiens esse debet circa advocatos, . . . sed cum ingenio, ne contemptibilis videatur nec adeo dissimulare si quos causarum concinnatores vel redemptores deprehendat; eosque solos pati postulare quibus per edictum ejus postulare [as in Dig. I, 16, 9 § 2] permittitur.

Et si minus [*sc.* adv.] dixerit in jure ipse suppleat . . . Et excedentibus [advv.] formidabilem se faciat . . . Sed contemptum non patiatur judex.

Si quis vero strepitum fecerit ejiciatur. . . . Cultum suum justitia perdit, quando silentia judicii obstrepantium turba confundit. . . . Debet ergo quicquid aut confidentium consultationibus agitur aut ab accusantium parte proponitur, sic mitissima verborum prolatione proferri ut nec contentiosis vocibus sensus audientium turbent nec judicii rigorem de tumultu enervent. . . .

Whether the court be disturbed *tumultu aut contumeliis aut risibus*, the offender may be ejected *by divine* law and with every mark of infamy be sentenced to three days' excommunication.

C. 28. No *lis* is to be begun before the *disertissimi advv.* on both sides have *with* the parties (*principales personae*) taken the oath (*sc.* calumniae), *i.e.*, that the suit is *bona fide*, without collusion, not a cloak &c. The parties must swear that *causâ patrocinii* they have given and will give, absolutely nothing directly or indirectly to the judge or others — exceptis his quae propriis advocatis pro patrociniis praestant aliisque personis quibus nostrae [sc. Roman] leges dari disponunt [on the authority of a Novella].

Sometimes a *procurator* must take the oath.

C. 30 (end), *de testibus*. The producer of witnesses and his *adv*. must swear in certain cases that they have not tampered with the depositions or the witnesses.

C. 31, *De instrumentis* (Documents). At si notarius adsit prosit ejus testimonium.

C. 36. A judgment may be revoked, ratione corrupti advocati.

C. 38 is *de procuratore*. In c. 40 defensor civitatis = apparently, a municipal officer.

C. 35 includes a precedent for a judgment, the proem of which indicates ecclesiastical judges and the end of which deals judicially with Costs.

In nomine patris et filii et spiritus sancti, amen.

Domine de vultu tuo judicium meum prodeat, oculi tui videant aequitates.

(To be in writing): Anno ab incarnatione domini M° C° X. C° VI° [*v. l.* MCXX] ego R. cognitor causae, quae vertebatur inter Titium et Seium, auditis et cognitis et inspectis allegationibus utriusque partis, condempno Titium Seio in restitutionem fundi Corneliani cum fructibus perceptis a tempore litis contestatae quos percepit vel percipere potuit. Et nomine expensarum in praedicta causa factarum praedictum Titium praedicto Seio in X . . . [?] condempno quae praedictus Seius, me taxante, juravit se circa litem impendisse.

APPENDIX XII.

1. *Advocatus* IN WILLIAM OF DROGHEDA.

Forty-two chapters are devoted continuously (33-72) to the clerical *advocatus* in ecclesiastical courts; twelve (87-98) to hints, *cautelae*, for the defendant's *adv*. (which are sometimes shrewdly recommended to the plaintiffs). **Pref.** The reader of this book will become *optimus orator*, *advocatus tutissimus*, fit for political office, highly moral. His Oxford pupils are to be made *tutissimi legum oratores*.

Causes are : 1 civil, 2 spiritual, 3 criminal, 4 mixed. To be treated of in 6 Books :—

1. de praeparatoriis judiciorum et de judiciis et de arbitris, et de actore et de reo, de judice, de advocato, de assessore, et de hiis quae antecedunt litis contestationem.
2. de litis contestatione et de hiis quae antecedunt sententiam.
3. de sententia et de hiis quae sequuntur.
4. de appellatione per quam impeditur executio rei judicatae.
5. de causis matrim. et earum effectu.
6. de accusationibus et earum effectu et de electione et electi potestate et de postulatione.

Costs : c. 8. Before you go to law, consider the resources of the other side, for none of us are equal to the rich (*potentioribus*); compare your wealth with that of the other side and weigh the merits (*statum*) of your case; don't go to fruitless expense : therefore avoid unnecessary litigation. On the other hand, no man ought to be deterred from a just suit, by fear of expense.

Consider, too, whether you are a *jurisperitus* while your opponent is not; if you are, though he may be rich, you are better off, for you have " a legitimate treasure which you never can lose." On the other hand, if he has both

these " pulls," better not go to law with him : for by
Roman law a rash litigant may be condemned in travelling
expenses and the costs of the suit. There may be security
for costs. In one case—of the *contumax*—costs are
expressly called a " third penalty " (c. 28 : two MSS.) :
for the same offender it is expressly laid down that the
costs against him must be reasonable (c. 32, on the
authority of a Decretal which allowed one mark sterling
after taxation). One reason in certain cases why the *adv.*
should try to make the parties come to terms, is to avoid
costs at the end of the case (c. 65) : he ought to put in
his *libellus* that the client is willing to withdraw his suit,
if the opponent can make a good defence, so that if he
ultimately loses, his costs may be less : pleadings before
litis contest. always ask for costs (c. 69 ; so c. 169) :
pleadings cannot be amended to the detriment of the
defendant, *propter expensas et viatica et advocatorum
salaria* : costs " thrown away " must be repaid (c. 350).
In the case of an *excommunicatus* the maxim, from *Dig.*
XXXIX, c. 4, § 5, is cited : alterum enim utilitas
privatorum exigit, alterum vigor publicae disciplinae
postulat : accordingly excommunication is inflicted on
public, and costs on private grounds, for the plaintiff only
" gets his own " back (c. 467).

C. 33. *Advocatus.* The language is as often as
possible borrowed from Roman law. The traditional
definition (repeated c. 98) is : *Adv.* dici potest ille
qui quoquo studio causis agendis operatur : from *Dig.* L,
13, 1, § 11.

" I want to know why *advv.* were invented (*inventi*) ? "
The answer is that they might satisfy the scruples
(*instruerent religionem*) of the judges who wanted to know
how to proceed, *e.g.*, in the case of minors' &c. property :
the authority is *Dig.* XXVII, 9, 5, § 11, where the praetor
must " find " someone beyond suspicion or assign an *adv.*
to the minor.

Then comes the famous piece of rhetoric (almost
verbatim) from Codex II, 8, 14 (often copied by jurists,
e.g., Durand, *Speculum*, B. I, pt. 4, p. 253 : 1668).

Ad officium vero ejus pertinet lapsa erigere, fatigata reparare suae defensionis viribus, tam in publicis quam in privatis causis, quia non solum militant qui gladiis et thoracibus et clipeis nituntur sed etiam patroni causarum qui gloriosae vocis confisi munimine, laborantium spem vitamque defendunt. . . .

Unde militant sub inermi militia, alii autem militant sub armata militia. Ad officium ejus pertinet postulare. Next, c. 34, What is pleading in court (*postulare*)? It is (*Dig.* III, 1, 2) expounding the demand of oneself or friend to one who has legal power (*jurisdictioni*), by moving (*agendo*) or replying for him or by opposing the defendant's claim (*voluntati—contradicendo*).

C. 35. Who may plead? Anyone, except—heretics, women (except *pro se et pro conjunctis personis*); slaves (with one exception), the *infames* (but they may appear for themselves and " certain others " : *conj. personae*?), minors under 17 years (*v. l.*, 25), the excommunicated and infidels. " Nor may monks be *advv.* except for their monastery or regulars except by command of their Abbot . . . nor a soldier," nor (c. 46) the illegitimate.

This list of exclusions from the *ecclesiastical* courts must be taken as in force in William's day; it is made up from imperial or Papal authorities and is " common form " in many works.

What he says here of the Clergy is important. " *Clerici* may not be *advocati coram saeculari judice* whether they are in minor or major orders . . . hence not even *praelati*, especially if they are priests, nor bishops," but there is the usual saving for a *clericus*—he may appear in a secular court for himself, and those identified with him (*conjunctis*), the poor, or his monastery : so cc. 40-5, 469. Note that there is no suggestion of a monopoly of audience, and see c. 98, which may be called a second edition of c. 35.

C. 36. " The *adv.* must state (*proponere*) *instrumenta causae*, *i.e.*, especially the documents he relies upon." He must show due respect to the judge or he may be removed as *contumax*," but he should " open " as shortly as possible: still he must preface his case (c) [borrowing a fine passage from Gaius: *Dig.* I, 2, 1].

C. 37. Nay, more; there must be a compliment, *commendatio* (d) to the judges. The address to the Papal delegates (e) is a typical jumble of texts *adapted* from the Bible and the Digest, to bespeak the good will of the bench, exhibiting the " deference " of to-day. Of course the defendant's *advocatus* does the same, in his turn (c. 87), who, *inter alia* (f), remarks : " Your patience with the bar is well known and appreciated. . . . You will remember that my friend in opening commended to you his client's cause and character. As he has addressed (*respondet*) me courteously (*curialiter*) and temperately, I will meet him with the same tone, for what can be more natural than untying a thing with that with which you tied it up? . . . But had he been rude to me I certainly should have replied in the same tone, for a thing is cured by its contrary and I should call him ' a fool ' and say ' I don't understand you,' as once a great lawyer did " (g). Or he might say : " With all respect to him I advise him to retire from the case : his compliments (*blanditiae* (h)) are not to be trusted."

After more fulsome panegyric suggested to the plaintiff's counsel, he is reminded that all these compliments need not be used up in one day; " as the proverb [?] says: moderns love novelty." His opponent, too, is advised to ration the judges with " soft soap," according as his case requires.

(c) So Faraday used to say before an experiment, " Tell me what I am going to see."

(d) It begins : Vos, saeculi justi judices et vera mundi lumina. . . .

(e) " Vobis prae omnibus et super omnibus est oboediendum, missis a principe, hoc est, a papa praecellenti qui est ordinarius singulorum : C. II, q. 6, c. 6." " Any judge," he says, " delegated by the Pope is above the ordinary in any given suit . . . because the Pope has confided it to him *ex certa scientia*." See c. 152.

(f) *E.g., omnia jura habentes in scrinio pectoris vestri*—a reminiscence of Cod. VI, 23, 19, and the stock of one of our common law doctrines.

(g) *Dig.* 28, 1, 27.

(h) Or fallacies?

C. 38. The opener commends the *persona* of his client, *quia pia, quia justa, quia religiosa, quia pauperrima*—the last " to excuse security for costs if necessary." Then he ought (c. 39) to vouch after enquiry the good faith of his case and his own pure motives in taking it up—a point urged by every jurist—and go on to suggest that it is the other side's " game " to delay proceedings. He must point out that he has his witnesses there ready to prove (at least) the *intentio* (part of the statement of claim) and that he ought not to suffer pecuniarily through the other side not being ready; if there is urgency he should point it out, for " it is ever judge's duty to end litigation " (*i*).

Cc. 40-5 are a series of excuses for the *adv.*—presumably clerical—for appearing in a secular court, for no apology would be needed in an ecclesiastical; they are : (1) The party could find no other (and, it may be, the judge has called upon him); (2, 3) The resources of the opponent who has hired or silenced—a common mischief denounced by Bromyard—all other *advv.*, or merely the inequality of the two parties; or (4) The poverty of the client, so that the *adv.* is acting, *prece non pretio*, on purely philanthropic grounds, identified with religious doctrine; and so of (5) " I dare not remain silent though I am no speaker "; (6) Gratitude to the litigant or kinship or friendship, the orders of a bishop, or someone in authority. Then comes apparently (*k*) an excuse for declining to appear for the party—on the ground that the *adv.* of the other party (or *v. l.* that party himself) is an intimate friend or even benefactor of the proposed *adv.*, for the stronger bond dissolves the weaker.

C. 46. What an *advocatus* may not do.

He may not be rude of speech to the judge, on pain of punishment. Nor may he use any violent language, or attack party or judge except what his case demands. If he discovers in the course of his case that it is bad or trumped up, he must give it up.

(*i*) And *multa contra juris rigorem pro libertate sunt constituta* : *Dig.* 40, 5, 24, 10.

(*k*) " loqui non valeo," etc., here and in par. 1 seems out of place.

There must be no bickerings or " rows " on pain of expulsion. There must be no bargain with the other side (*pacta sive conventiones* (*l*)). He may take what (fees) litigants offer, but nothing unreasonable. He must not sit (while arguing). There must be no champerty, *i.e.*, no agreement for a definite (*m*) fraction of " the spoil," but there may be for a sum (at the moment) an uncertain fraction thereof. *Advocati* may not be *assessores*, nor act as judges, in causes in which they have advised (the parties? (*n*)), " for a natural affection for his own opinion would get him the reputation of being corrupt " : penalty (*o*)—a fine of ten pounds and name to be struck off the register, or a greater penalty.

" A man must not be an *advocatus* unless he has been *examinatus* and *probatus*, as Otho's Constitutions provide " (*p*).

C. 47. Penalties on *Advv.* for unprofessional conduct. They shall become *infames* and suffer *diminutionem opinionis* [like *dem. capitis* :] *i.e.*, presumably their formal opinion as *assessores* &c. shall not be taken (or by anyone?) : they may not argue in court ever or for a stated period : or " sometimes *advocatio* is forbidden them, sometimes the *forum* " (*q*), *i.e.*, total suspension or merely audience : in law they are to be deemed *praevaricatores*. So for the simoniacal, *i.e.*, those who have acted for pay [beyond the scale] or " have sinned against the duty of an *adv.*, they are to be " disbarred and " turned out of the forum " (*q*).

(*l*) Another common mischief.   (*m*) Cf. c. 54.

(*n*) Or, perhaps, the judges as *assessores*, as in *Cod.* I, 51, 14, here cited.

(*o*) Literally from *Cod.* I, 51, 14.

(*p*) *Cod.* II, 6, 8, and *Const.* p. 103, here cited make it clear that the test is religious not jural; in *Const.* the oath is before the diocesan. The test was real : when (1130-40) Nicholas Breakspear wanted to get into the Abbey of St. Alban's, being " arte clericali satis supinus," he was " examinatus " and found " insufficiens " by the Abbot, who said " Expecta, fili, et adhuc scolam exerce ut aptior habearis " : 1 *Gest. Abb.* (Rolls), 112. See on c. 98 below.

(*q*) As both passages are quotations from the *Dig.* probably the word does not imply clerics in the secular courts.

The *adv.* who refuses his services [gratuitously] when the judge asks for them, shall lose his right of audience (and perhaps, for ever) : where the old praetor used to say " if you have not an *adv.* I will give you one," to-day the formula is " if you have no money to buy *consilium* I will give it to you " : c. 162, and to the poor client he must give advice " intuitu dei " : *ib.* : see c. 162, p. 581.

C. 48. Litigants must not retain so many *advv.* that none are left for the other side [a mischief frequently regulated] nor reject one [assigned by the court] in favour of another, but if one has " thrown up " a case, another may take it.

C. 49. The duty of the Court and of others to *advv.* It is the business of judges to listen patiently to the arguments, provided that they are not too long (*ultra modum*) or put forward merely to earn a hireling fee (*r*) : else there is an appeal.

No personal feeling of the judge must induce him to refuse to hear an *adv.* nor may he lose his temper however ill he may think of the pleader (*s*). He must be easy of access and not averse from helping appeals to Rome or to the *sanctum* of the judges. Judges must salute the *advv.* and show them all courtesy (*honor*). When the *advv.* are not in a case they ought to sit next to (*juxta*) the judge but only then. " Provincial " offices and public duties ought not to be imposed on them [*i.e.*, to interfere with their practice (*t*), as in the original *Codex*]. In c. 162, p. 581, the judge or assessor who had to provide counsel for poor suitors is solemnly exhorted to be kind : he must not depreciate the help of a jurisconsult.

This c. and c. 50 suggest what the bar had occasionally to fear from the bench.

A judge who " molests " an *adv.* by insult or threat of punishment shall lose his girdle (*cingulum*) and be

---

(*r*) A verbal repetition (as much else on the *adv.*) of Ric. Anglicus, App. XI, c. 27, *i.e.*, taken from the same source.

(*s*) He must be—non acerbus, non contumeliosus, sed moderatus et cum efficacia benignus et cum instancia humanus; non asperus.

(*t*) Adapting *Cod.* II, 7, 3 : Quicquid enim adquisierint, id habeant quasi castrense peculium in proprio dominio ad exemplum militum.

further punished (*u*), severely. For lesser offences to the *adv.*, *e.g.*, imposing *prohibitio*, not returning his salutation or recognising his right to sit on the bench, he is to be fined and his officials, too, [if necessary]—just as conversely the *adv.* is punished.

Elsewhere (c. 405) he refers incidentally to an assault on the *adv.* conducting or in charge of a case—obviously an event not unknown : they, of course, have privilege as *ministri causae*. He seems (c. 358) to adopt the ground for adjournment of a case, that suggested in *Dig.* IV, 6, 15, 3 " the client has to find an inn or unpack his baggage or look for an *adv.*" as a good one in his day.

C. 51. Is the client bound by his *adv.*'s statements? Yes, if he is present and understood them [without objecting] : it is as if he had made them himself—the general mediaeval theory. But the reverse, if he was absent. Still there are *dicta* to the contrary and after quoting several texts he says " concludo "—as follows : if the *adv.* was chosen by a *laicus*, we must forgive his ignorance in not consulting more experienced people when he chose him; if he consulted no one we must distinguish whether he is a *rusticus* or not : if he is or he had to take the *adv.* the court gave him, we must be lenient : if not, he must put up with his counsel.

But a *clericus* who suffers through not being present, has only himself to blame; he ought to know a competent from an incompetent *adv.* : scienti et volenti non fit injuria [adopted from *Dig.* XLVII, 10, 15].

Surely this opinion is due to actual experience.

C. 52. Still, *advocati* do make mistakes. So the client, if he was present, has three days from the judgment—*revocare errorem* [a sort of interlocutory appeal]. A mere *laicus*, perhaps, has three days from his discovering the mistake. A *literatus* must act on the same day : the mistake is thus on the *facts*. If it be in a point of law (*scientia*) the mistake may be rectified any time before the

---

(*u*) Another and even severer sanction in c. 467 includes loss of the *cingulum*.

suit is concluded. The main point is that a *laicus* may have time to consult a lawyer.

C. 53. On supplying the defects of *advv.* : *sc.* in *law*. It is the judge's business to supply it—and so it is, of the facts, if they are " judicially " known.

CC. 54-7 : see p. 107.

Then some technical " tips " in statements of claim (*x*) (c. 58) : put all your grounds of action in one claim and (apparently) sue as many defendants as you can (c. 60) : if there are several causes of action, stick to the best by which you can get most, reserving, however, the right to any other; but you must make your election not later than the *contestatio litis* (cc. 62, 69).

Get rid of the old fashioned verbiage (*solempnitatem*) in pleading : " it is out of court to-day " : state your facts " pure and simple "—as a witness, too, ought to do; c. 61. If you have more than one action to recover something, choose that which will produce the most : if you are not sure which will, try others reserving the right to get what you can from any one : c. 62. If you claim a chattel claim damages, too; c. 63. In an action *injuriarum* (assault, trespass) consider under what statute you will proceed for the legal effects may differ : " satisfy yourself whether since cause of action your client has eaten or drunk with defendant or been friendly with him or come to terms about the case or has acted as if there had been no *injuria* " : c. 64.

The *adv.* ought to try to bring the parties to terms (not only to avoid costs, but) to avoid the *infamia* of a bogus action : and so ought the judge. The *adv.* ought not to have to blush (for not checking litigation), " as it is written, *non lusisse pudet sed non incidere ludum* (*y*). But if you go on with your *actio injuriarum* inflame your damages as much as you can : for the wound, for the place [*e.g.*, a church] for the class of spectators, for the nature or severity of the *injuria* : " but in England you must be

---

(*x*) *E.g.* Always plead possession if you can; for *possessor plus juris habet*.

(*y*) Hor. *Ep.* I, xiv, 36.

careful what you claim [on each head] lest a royal Writ of Prohibition issue against you " (see pp. 103*s*, 107) and you must decide whether to proceed civilly or criminally; c. 65. Here naturally comes the story of William's own smartness in piling up damages. " And what can be done in this *temporal* action can be done in others. And in an *actio injur.* a careful *adv.* might plead for an extension of time because a petition has gone to the *princeps* (Pope or King) and (apparently) a year is allowed for the answer." Probably we may apply here what Maitland (12 *E. H. R.* 653) says of another " hint " (c. 91) : " This looks sadly like the suggestion of a lie. The defendant's advocate is to gain time by professing that a compromise is on foot, while he is sending to Rome for revocatory letters."

The following cc. are full of hints how to frame a statement of claim : many no doubt are " taken from life."

C. 66. If you have a good case and your proofs ready, press it on from day to day, get rid of dilatory pleas at once, the more the other side hold back (*contumacia*). But if you have a bad case then try for an admission or suspension of the case (arising apparently from any flaw in the opponent's case) and come to terms.

C. 67 is on " How to evade royal prohibitions," as Maitland called it : see p. 105.

W. recommends the same caution in *famosae actiones* (slander or libel) against " big " influential people " to whom respect must be shown." (*Advv.* often shrank from arguing these actions : c. 59.)

C. 69. See p. 567. Always put in the general clause : *salvo jure addendi mutandi minuendi et novae editionis faciendae.*

C. 70 has a purely clerical scope—a difference between the plaintiff's judges and those of the defendant [an incident of eccl. courts] about jurisdiction : the pl.'s *adv.* must be quick to get judgment from *his* judges in favour of the jurisdiction and forestall the opponent by suspension and excommunication ! because *priores tempore potiores jure.*

C. 71. The minutes (*acta*) of the trial should be made up from day to day for memory is treacherous, *judges may* be unjust and falsify facts (sic), and for the perpetuation and easy proof of the testimony; there ought to be no interlineations or erasures or signatures (z) : and see that neither the pen nor the ink has been changed (*quae mutant veritatem negotii*) : a certified copy requires the judges' seals or if they be unobtainable those of the *assessores* or witnesses. Of course, the *acta* must be agreed by both sides and therefore should be settled in conference.

" But it is possible that one party in the absence of the other may get hold of the *acta* from a foolish judge and put in something which never took place at the trial "— again, a touch of experience, " I disapprove " says the author. So the *adv.* ought to make up true *acta* day by day (a) " putting in words helpful for his case," so that the judge next day may work on them and when he comes to judgment may have the complete series before him. " Yes " says William (in a " consilium ") " and he (*adv.*) must stick to his own minutes like flesh to bone—and not trouble about the flimsy suggestions of the challenging side trying to make little points (*apices*) of law " : c. 72.

In c. 87 begins the treatise on the defendant's *advocatus* : naturally it is " on the lines " of his opponent's, including the *commendatio* (above). One difference arises at once from mere defendantship. The *adv.* will do well to decline all admissions at the outset and had better keep it quiet that he is the party's *adv.*, and so had the party, and wait patiently till the *citationes* and other formalities have been duly proved.

Thus he will see first whether the judges are unfairly favourable to the other side or to him, and likely to acquit

---

(z) In the case of another document he adds to these tests *falsa grammatica* : cc. 90, 96; obviously *written* instructions were much commoner in the case of a *procurator*, and when he is dealt with substantively (cc. 121-2) false grammar and Latin and other *indicia* of forgery are treated more fully.

In c. 122 letters of procuration from the Pope are *presumed* to be in good Latin (because *per tot purgatoria transeunt*); the precautions taken to secure correctness are enumerated. In private letters the test is—is the sense clear?

(a) He insists strongly on this in c. 96, whence it appears that it might be a serious thing for a defendant not to have the *acta*.

or condemn (on the pleadings) : if the former, he need not appear; if the latter, let him make his client appear. The same before *assessores*—a course which may help him if he wants to take exception to the judges or to get the *assessores* removed : c. 89.

Pettifogging of this sort points to the existence of little hole and corner tribunals, alongside of the more august (*b*). In c. 90, next, we find out whether plaintiff appears in person or by *procurator*, *i.e.*, who put in the plea—which may be attacked (for grammar, tampering, &c.) as we saw (c. 71).

Then cc. 91-5 come " The Tricks recommended to the defendant's advocate " (Maitland). For utilitarian practicality William here touches " bedrock." " If he can trust the judges and has a good case, away with subterfuge and on with full speed to judgment. But if he has a bad case, adjournment and compromise are his line. If he cannot by negotiation get a compromise defendant should ask for an adjournment so that he may confer with his friends. Then he can send to the *curia* at Rome (as many agents as he can : c. 92; cf. d'Anesty's messengers) for suspensory (*or* prohibitory) letters, to get rid of the unfavourable judges, on some good legal ground(s), on the understanding that meanwhile the judges ignore (*cassare*) the *procuratio* and suspend the proceedings until the commissioner (*nuntius*) returns from Rome with a reply. Meanwhile he should get [from the Court] another day for negotiation with his opponent and " add this time that he really believes that terms will be arrived at." What Maitland thought of this appears above on c. 65.

The procedure is not quite clear but it is obviously *ex parte* and " at chambers," for if he cannot get time to go to Rome he is to try *dilationes et cavillationes et recusationes* " till he gets his job done."

C. 92. "If he cannot by any [other] means stay the business let him summon the plaintiff by other *litterae* before other judges on the points most harmful to his case,

---

(*b*) Cf. cc. 91-5 below.

that they may inhibit the judges unfavourable to him from proceeding on pain of suspension or excommunication; then he must cite the latter to assemble at a fixed time and place to discuss the question of jurisdiction—always remembering to put a clause in the *litterae* "anything to the contrary in certain *litterae* obtained in ignorance of these *litt.* notwithstanding"—because the other side too, may have got *litt.* secretly.

Another trick (for delay) suggested is getting a hearing fixed on a public holiday. But

C. 94 if, with all this, he cannot keep the suit back, "let him speak to the special friends of the judge to get the latter to absent himself &c., or to appoint a distant day." But he must be on his guard against expressly or tacitly accepting [given] judges or he may lose his appeal [against their sitting].

C. 93. Unless the judge insists "don't show your hand : *viz.* the *jura* on which you rely—this is only to give your opponent information : ' if you see the arrow coming you may avoid it.' "

C. 98. See c. 35. All sorts of people want *indifferenter* (c. 97) to plead—but may a " laicus vel idiota " be admitted to plead *against a *clericus** ?

Now, a *clericus* ought to be *litteratus* : *Pro*. ⁎⁎ [note his method or logic], a *laicus* who is not, ought not to be admitted, for he cannot plead to the point (*congruenter non respondet*) and does not know Latin : there is abundant authority that a pleader must know law (*jura*) (*e.g.*, interrogatio, stipulatio, respondere). Moreover the practitioner ought to have read law (*audire jura*) for five years (according to the *Dig.* Pref. *Omnium* § 5) : see p. 571.

Contra. Yes, he may : the language has nothing to do with it : p. 104. As for, learning a judge is not removed for ignorance of law : ⁎⁎ an *adv.* is not. From the very word—*ad vocatus*—called in, he is admitted.

Solutio. The upshot is—(a) a layman may appear for himself, if he is poor (unless the judge assigns him counsel).

⁎ * These words are not in all MSS., and are not implied in the text.

The judge (and not the *adv.* against him) is to explain the meaning of a speaker : the essential thing is that someone on each side should understand the other or his *adv.* through a good interpreter, if necessary. (b) But if he appears for anyone else, *distinguo* : if connected with him and *unable to pay*—yes : (c) if for strangers, *subdistinguo* : if he has any training (*notitiam exercitii causarum*), Yes : if not, no. " It were ridiculous that he should instruct others who does not know how to instruct himself." Now, the judge's *consiliarii* and *assessores* are taken from the *advv.* and so instruct (or correct) the *adv.* pleading : *** the latter must have some learning—especially in eccl. causes.

Probably the whole discussion is started in reminiscence of some such passage as that in *Rhetorica Eccles.* (p. 99*h*) : Laici ergo contra clericos et clerici contra laicos sicut in accusatione ita nec in testimonio sunt audiendi . . . (ed. Wahrmund, p. 72).

2. W. OF DROGHEDA ON *Procurator.*

C. 119. Why may a *proc.* who is *infamis* act as such while an *infamis adv.* may not? Because as the *adv.* gets the advantage of a fee (see pp. 108*h*, 133*oo*) so he must bear the burden (*gravatur*) of exclusion. The *proc.* gets nothing or not so much [hence to exclude him would be to release him from a burden]. Again " procurare est oneris " so he is not excluded, " advocare est honoris " [so *he* is]. Perhaps the real reason is (*ib.*) : *procurare est facti, advocare est juris* : or *advocare* praemii *est et juris* : . . . *procurator exponit factum advocatus autem exponit jus*— though both *postulant* (=appear in court).

This is a good specimen of W.'s ambling.

C. 90. If plaintiff appears per *proc.* the first thing is to enquire formally into his credentials.

See p. 576*z* and cc. 121-2.

C. 99. procurator est qui mandato domini spontaneus procurat ejus negotia.

CC. 121-2. Inventi fuerunt ideo procuratores ut qui suis rebus superesse vel nolunt vel non possunt hoc per alios possent. *Negotia* include *forensia n.*

C. 101. Non licet in dignitate constituto in propria persona litigare sed procuratorem constituere.

C. 102. Officium vero procuratoris est, agere ea, quae verus dominus faceret si esset praesens nisi prohibeatur a jure, ut transigere et compromittere, nisi ad hoc habeat speciale mandatum.

C. 135. Suppose a party absent from a trial through illness; must he appoint a *proc.*? Yes or an *excusator* [=essoin]. (He quotes (& c. 85 cites) II *Corp. Jur. Can.* : *Decret. Gregor.* IX, B. II, Tit. 14, c. 6 (ed. Friedberg, p. 294) by Innocent III [1198—1216] : sicut excusatorem ad nos direxerat, sic dirigere potuerat responsalem—" as he [a party] had not been ordered to come in person but might send *proc. idoneum,*" called a few lines later *sufficiens responsalis.*)

W. only mentions *responsalis* in this quotation and *attornatus* not at all. *Proc.* is evidently of higher standing than *excusator.*

C. 142. After the *adv.* and the *proc.* the *Defensor,* because he has his place in trials : he is defined as " one who without *mandatum* offers himself for the defence," *i.e.,* apparently, as bail for an absent defendant.

C. 144. Anyone may appear as *defensor* for any accused whatever in a criminal case for it is to the public interest that the absent should be defended.

C. 148. *Syndicus* is Greek for *defensor* and = the representative of a corporation (*universitas, collegium*) which may also be represented by *actores* and *yconomi* (c. 146 : *yconomos* is from Gk. *ycos = dispensator* and *comos = pauper* : c. 150).

The syndic ought to be a *clericus* for it is incogruous that a layman should be the deputy of a bishop and try (or argue with) *viros eccles.* c. 148 : nor ought he to be an arbitrator in spiritual matters.

C. 152. Of judges. Some are ordinary some delegated by (a) the Pope (b) judges subordinate to the Pope : some are *arbitri* (c).

(c) In c. 158 there is a precedent of reference to arbitrators, W. himself being umpire : *subrogabitur mr. W. de D.*

Ordinary are either **Major**, *e.g.*, the Pope *inter clericos*, the Emperor *inter laicos* : or, **Minor**, delegated by either of these potentates : these have the greater jurisdiction [*i.e.* the most familiar to the writer and his contemporaries].

Then follows a fine passage on the ideal judge.

C. 159. De assessoribus et juris peritis. They are appointed by the agreement of the parties and sit with the judges or the judge appoints. They must remember on the bench, they are not *now adv.*—a natural caution.

C. 160. Their business is to admit or reject *advv.* [generally or in a given cause?] with the law (*jus*), *interrogationes* [interrogatories or cross-examination?] in passing statements of claim.

C. 161. They may take a fee : c. 162, there are heavy penalties for misconduct : it seems to have been their business to find legal aid for poor suitors (see c. 47)—haec est misericordia dei.

C. 348. On the meaning of some terms in pleading. The *reus* is exhorted to search any document (*editio*) served on him for ambiguous words, " flaws " which may be good for adjournments : a great many examples are discussed but, as he says " Enough of *cavillationes*, if you want to impugn documents, come back here."

He still has incidental " tips " for the (ecclesiastical?) *adv.* : thus, when a judge excuses himself from taking a case, the cautions *adv.* must take care that there is no collusion behind it—*ambigua sunt fata causarum* : but there is always a presumption that everything is " straight."

The ordinary disqualification for being a judge, *viz.*, having been *adv.* or *assessor* in the cause is repeated, c. 437 and another is suggested, that a *clericus* of the judge ought not to appear for a party before him—as actually happened with the Dean of Oxford at St. Frideswide's (c. 442) : but where an ecclesiastical judge assigned " his own *clericus* against a monastery the Pope on appeal upheld the judgment," apparently because otherwise the party would have been no match for the other side : *ib.*

Finally, he asks (C. 469) : may the rector of a church or a priest be *adv.* or *proc.*?

This is a good instance how
"   Crimina rasis
    Librat in antithetis . . . "
Yes, he says, on the general grounds of benevolence :
No, because the Code (I, 3, 41 : de episcopis et clericis (*d*)) lays it down that " it is absurd and even degrading to *clerici* to wish to show skill in the wrangling of the courts and, if they do, they ought to be fined 60 gold pounds " : Cf. C. 35, p. 568. He decides finally that " these clerics are not to be admitted indifferently but as a concession—for their churches and poor people." This privilege is granted to them because they are permanently attached to their houses and so would not go about [like other *advv.*] to the neglect of their divine duties—and this " not only in old Rome but in this royal state and all over the world wherever Christianity is cultivated." And in a few more lines he ends (or ends as we have his book).

(*d*) Also quoted c. 409 for a classical difference between *clerici* and *laici* : it is headed *Imp. Justinus A. Archelao pp.* : but the sanction is *fifty* pounds. William cites from memory : pp. = praefecto praetorio.

APPENDIX XIII.

Les Assises de Jérusalem.
Livre de d'Ibelin.

C. X : I, B. 33.

Le plaideor doit estre loial et estable, que il doit bien et leaument conseillier toz ciaus et totes celes à qui conseill il est doné, et plaideer por eaus leaument le miaus qu'il saura contre totes genz, ne mais que [=except] contre soi ; ni ne deit laissier por amor que il eut à celui contre qui il plaidée, ne por haine qu'il ait à celui à qui conseill il est doné, ne por doute ne por paor qu'il ait d'avoir honte ne domage ne maugré ne por don ne promece que l'on li face, que il bien et leaument ne conseille celui, ou celle à cui conseill le seignor l'a doné ; que se il le faiseit autrement, il feroit que desloiau. Et doit celer les privautés que celui ou celle à qui conseill il est, li dira des choses de quoi il est à son conseill, ne ne doit dire en court ne dehors court chose de ce dont il est a son conceil qu'il cuide qui li griege [thinks that it will hurt him].

Moreover if *le conseill* hears another speaking for his side and saying something [wrong but] capable of amendment he must either rectify himself *or* mention it *privily* (*n.b.*) to the party or *the speaker before it is too late.*

Ib. c. XI, p. 34, I, B.

Qui viaut plaideer en la Haute Court dou reaume de Jerusalem, il doit demander au seignor à conseill de court le meillor plaideor de la court a son escient, se il est plaideor (*e*) on se il ne l'est ; porce que se il n'est plaideor, que son conseill li sache sa raison garder et sa carelle [quarrel, cause] desrainier [defend] de ce dont il est

---

(*e*) Apparently if the party himself have the right of audience (being a vassal) : it cannot mean that the professional *plaideor* was specially a litigant.

requerreor et defendre de ce dont il est defendeor. Et se il est plaideor (*e*), por ce qu'il ait plus de conseill; car il n'est nul ni sage plaideor qui ne puisse bien et souvent estre averti el [=en] plait de ce que bon li est par un autre plaideor o [=avec] lui; que deus plaideors sevent plus et veent plus cler el plait, et faillent meins que un; que se l'un faut, l'autre l'amende; et por ce que a ennuis [=hardly] plaideera l'on fà si bien por soi come por autre, que corous [anger] ou malle volonté tolt et amerme [diminishes and takes away] souvent conoissance d'ome et l'esmuet [turns it into] en ire qui desvoie sens d'ome plus tost et plus souvent por sa carelle que por celle d'autre. Et por ce doit encor le plaideor à (*f*) celui qui n'est plaideor demander conseill à droit; car qui dit sa parole en court, se il i faut ou mesprent, il n'i peut amender; et qui la fait dire a autre et celui à qui il la fait dire mesprent ou il i faut, il et son conseil i poent amender ainz [before] jugement, se il n'otroie [adopts] ce que celui qui est a son conseill a dit por lui.

It looks as if the client in person had not the right to argue a point of law, *viz.*, that of amendment.

It seems that the litigant may choose as *conseill* anyone composing the court except the *seigneur*, even one who is not a vassal of the *seigneur* (*g*) and, on demand, the *seigneur* may assign a second *conseill*, of his own choice [but this, perhaps, is only when he wants the first nominee, being *de ses homes*, for his own conseill. For] se le seignor retient a son conseill ou a sa parole garder (*h*) [as his mouthpiece, a sort of assessor], the first nominee who is to argue against the *seigneur* himself, he must assign the second best *conseill* to the party : see C. 18 below. If the suit was not against the *seigneur*, the plaintiff got his *conseill* as a matter of course, but the *defendant* (sic) (*il veut le plait foyr*) apparently, had to show good reason.

C. XIII. The requisites of a demand for legal aid were

(*e*) See note (*e*), p. 583.
(*f*) Read *et* with the Italian translator.
(*g*) Or, perhaps, even if the party be not his vassal.
(*h*) See *ib*. c. 19.

a personal application in court : " Sir, the plea not being against you, I ask for so-and-so : he is here in court and I am your man : against so-and-so and for such-and-such a cause . . . saving all just exceptions."

A great amount of space is devoted to the right to have the services of a given *conseill* or, alternatively, to that of his not being assigned to the opponent. Evidently it was of great practical importance.

C. XVI. The *seigneur* cannot assign *conseill* to one who without it has begun a plea or claim in court, *en forme de plait* : or has not put in an answer to an opponent's demand or claim or defence; in the last case " it was the practice " not to allow *conseill* (*i*). Again, highly technical.

C. XVIII (end) would be more in place in c. XII above. " If a second *conseill* is asked for, he ought to be assigned and be one who knows *covenablement plaideer selonc les autres homes de la court* : *i.e.*, an average man, " for the *seigneur* is not bound to give him the best *plaideor* of his court after his first choice, otherwise the opponent might be aggrieved, nor one of the least expert, lest *he* be aggrieved; for the *seigneur* ought to be in the court like a just balance; he must not put off the cause when he thinks the plaintiff has law on his side nor hurry it on when he thinks the defendant (*le fuiant* (*k*)) has . . . he should be more favourable to widows and orphans . . . than to other folk, &c., &c. . . . But let him act so that he transgress neither against God nor man nor woman."

The suggestion of a list of counsel in order of merit surely points to a " bar " of some standing.

The grievances of suitors here referred to point to incidents of actual experience.

Cc. XX-I deal in some detail with the *seigneur's* right to be represented by counsel in, so to say, " actions for or against the Crown."

(*i*) Because the defendant had made oath? as in the East sometimes now.

(*k*) Cf. ὁ φεύγων.

C. XXVII contains a number of technicalities (*l*), probably the commonest—which anyone who "undertakes," "holds himself out" to appear "ought to know"; if not, they will easily come to grief (*mischever*) and lose their clients' rights or their own; but to know these things means work.

Cc. XVIII-XIX. Disqualifications for audience are those common in the Middle Ages : a woman (except for a sick father), the blind, *infames*, convicts, bribers who buy off prosecutions; but anyone may appear for his family.

(*l*) Many more and even tricks are suggested in *La Clef des Assises de la Haute Court*, *ib* p. 579 : a *précis* of d'Ibelin's book : date not stated.

APPENDIX XIV.

M. Viollet's conclusions are :—
Vol. I.
The work is copied from two Ordinances of St. Louis, a *Coutume* of Touraine-Anjou and a *Coutume orléanaise*, and without any official character whatever. Avant-Propos ii. The anonymous jurist was probably Orléanais : *ib.* iii.
Introd. p. 1.
Opinion is divided whether it was promulgated by St. Louis. M. Viollet thinks not.
It was composed before June, 1273, and probably All Saints, 1272.
B. II, c. 15, is Orléanais by origin : Introd. p. 78.
The references to *avocats* in the ordinary sense are few, the chief being that of B. II, c. 15, but *conteor* is occasionally used (see IV, 349, 378) for *avocats* in judicial duels.
In 1251 an *ordonnance* of Charles d'Anjou regulated the *honoraria* of the *avocats* (I, 289).
Les Établissements de St. Louis : ed. Paul Viollet : Paris, 1881-6, 4 vols.
B. II : c. XV, vol. 2, p. 370.
Quant aucuns a bones deffanses et loiaus et porfitables, li avocaz ou li avantparliers doit metre avent et proposer en jugement ses deffanses et ses barres, et toutes les choses qu'il cuide que valoir li doient et puissent loiaument*; *Car ce que li avocaz dit, si est ansin bien estable come se les parties le deissent, quant il antendent que il dit, et il ne le contredient presentment, selonc droit escrit ou Code, De l'error des avocaz, en la premiere loi** : et toutes les raisons à destruire la demande de la partie adverse ; *et le doit dire cortoisement sans vilenie dire de sa bouche ne en*

---

* * See *Intr.* v. I, p. 4.

fez, ne en diz, el il ne doit faire nul marchié à celui por qui il plaide, plet pandant; et droiz le deffant ou Code, De postulando, lege, Quisquis vult esse causidicus Et ce apartient à loial avocat, Si come ladit loi le dit. Et doit dire et requerre à la joutise, en souploiant : " de mes barres et de mes deffanses que j'ai dites et proposées en jugement par devant vos, *qui me sunt porfitables si come je croi, ne me vueil je pas partir sanz droit et sanz loial jugement de vostre cort, car l'en puet metre et oster en sa demande jusqu'à jugement,* si fais je bien retenue de plus faire et de plus dire, en leu et en tans quant droiz m'i amenra, *si come de barres peremptoires qui ont leu jusqu'à jugement ou jusqu'à sentence, selonc droit escrit ou Code, Sententiam rescindi non posse, lege, Peremptorias exceptiones . . .* ; Si que je ne chiée mie en tort euvers le demandeor ne envers la joutise; dont je vous requier droit com a joutise, se vos le me devez faire ou non. . . ."

The italicised passages are excrescences, according to M. Viollet, on the original *usage d'Orlenois* which he has conjecturally reconstructed (vol. 1, p. 495 : § xiii, p. 502). That *usage* the learned editor thinks to be earlier than the *ordonnance* of St. Louis in 1254 prohibiting the judicial duel (*ib.* 80) and of course not later than 1273. Other elements of the *Établissements* were (*ib.* p. 85) a *Coutume de Touraine-Anjou*, restored by the editor (III, 3 -), drawn up in his opinion about 1246 (I, 24) and a Paris Police regulation founded on a royal *ordonnance* of 1260 (*ib.* 85).

APPENDIX XV.

Hospitia.

1. Barnard's Inn.—"Oldborne," "of Chancery," "*alias* Macworths " : not known till 1454 : Stow, *Survey* [1598], i, 77; ii, 39-40 (Kingsford's edn.) or f. 77 and f. 393 : Buc, p. 1075, adds nothing.

2. Chester or Strand I.—See p. 455 : Stow, *Survey*, i, 77; ii, 92, " of Chancery " : date unknown : pulled down *temp.* E. VI to make room for Somerset House.

3. Clement's I.—Stow, *ib.*, i, 15, 77; ii, 97, " of Chancery "; apparently the name does not occur till 1480 (*n*).

4. Clifford's I.—Stow, *ib.*, i, 77; ii, 41-2 : a record of 1345 says that the widow of Robert Clifford demised it [in that year " *apprenticiis de banco* pro X li. annuatim " : " now letten to the said Studentes for foure pound by the yeare " (Stow : 1598) : 2 *Cal. Inquis p. m.* 118.

5. Farringdon I.—" in Chancellors Lane " : first about 1400—known as *hospicium* J. *Skarle* : then, 1411, as F. Inn from R. F. *clericus d. r.* who is probably the *cuidam clerico cancellariae* to whom the *hosp.* J. *Skarle, conceditur* in 1407 : about 1414-6 it was demised (as " F. I.") to two *justiciarii* and one *apprenticius legis* : from about 1484 it is known as " Serjeants' I." Herbert, *Antiq. of the Inns* (1804), p. 351-2; authorities not stated. Buc, 1069a.

Fleet St. I.—One Serjeant's I. is sometimes so called.

6. Furnival's I.—Perhaps an abode of law-students before 1383, but not so called till 1408. Master Kniveton told Sir G. Buc " of his certaine knowledge " (1075a) that Lincoln's Inn bought it from the Earl of Shrewsbury at the

---

(*n*) Rastell, *Book of Entries* (1596), f. 108 : *Briefe* : Mich. 19 E. 4, rot. 61. *Misnomer* : . . . . " C. I. quod quidem hospicium est et tempore impetrationis brevis et diu antea fuit quoddam hospicium hominum curiae legis Temporalis necnon hominum consiliariorum ejusdem legis. . . ."

beginning of Elizabeth's reign, having previously rented it yearly : of Chancery.

7. Gray's I.—Buc (*ib*. 1073b), on the same authority, which he puts very high, says that it " was taken in the Raigne of K. E. III by the Gentlemen and professors of the common Law " : " a goodly house . . . by whome builded or first began I have not yet learned " : Stow, II, 87 : f. 440, as above. It is stated that the de Grey property in Portpool came by devise to R. de Chygwelle in 1280 : his son became King's Clerk in Chancery, Queen's (Philippa's) Chancellor, &c. : Williams, *Staple Inn*, p. 22-3. About 1300 it got back to the de Greys, first and second Lords of Wilton, both " justices " of a sort (*o*). But there is no extant record of its being a law hostelry till (at earliest 1506-7 or) 1515 : 3 Foss, 38 & v. 4, 273-5 : the case of " un Chapleyn de Greyes Inne " in 2 H. IV, Y. B. p. 8 (Nos. 40, 41), claimed by Pearce, *Guide*, 316, is by no means conclusive as evidence of the *legal* body : 4 Foss, 141. But that it was one of " the big four " " alluded to by Fortescue in 1460 . . . may without hesitation be admitted " : *ib*.

But all these dates would be belated if the MS. (*Harl*. 1094, f. 75) quoted by Mr. Douthwaite, the learned librarian and author of *Gray's Inn* (1886), p. 19, was trustworthy.

" Vincent's Visitation of Northamptonshire.

Thomas Andrewe of Carliel=Magdalena filia et haeres
| W^i Tokett filii et haeredis
| Rogeri Tokett militis.

Ralphe Andrew 2 Sonn
  was of Grayes Inne   =Mary &c.
  in Com. Midd. a
  bencher anno 1311.   "

As the Visitation was made and the MS. written in 1618-9 the title " bencher " is a manifest anachronism and the

---

(*o*) Hence Williams, *St. I.* p. 38, thinks it was a home of law " most probably " towards the end of E. I's reign !

INNS OF CHANCERY AND OF COURT. 591

mention of Gray's Inn in 1311 valueless. The earliest instance of " bencher " in this sense is from 1582 : *N. E. D.*

8. Inner Temple.—See Middle T. below.

Sir G. Buc (as above, p. 1070b) says : " certaine of the reverend, ancient professours of the Lawes, in the raigne of King *Edward* the third [1327-77] obtained a very large or (as I might say) a perpetual Lease of this [*viz.*, " the New "] Temple or (as it must bee understood) of two parts thereof, distinguished by the names of the middle temple and the Inner Temple, from the foresayd *Joannites* (then residing in their goodly house neere Smithfield called the Priory of Saint Johns of Jerusalem) to pay yeerely Ten pounds." Herbert (as above, p. 187) puts the date of the demise " soon after " 1348 " to certain students of the common law who are supposed to have removed from Thaive's Inn " : see No. 17 below.

Our Lady I.—See New I.

9. Lincoln's I.—See p. 446.

10. Lyon's I.—Of Chancery; purchased *temp.* H. VIII : Buc, 1076a. It existed *temp.* H. V. [1413-22] " how long before . . . it was an inn of chancery is uncertain." Herbert, *Antiq.* p. 276 : " situate between Holywell St. and Wych St." *ib.* (1804).

11. Middle Temple.—See Inner T. above. Before severance " If we may trust an ancient MS. formerly the property of Earl Somers and afterwards of Nicholls, the antiquary, certain lawyers ' made composition with the Earl of Lancaster [Thomas, d. 1322] for a lodging in the Temple and so came hither &c.' " : Dr. Bellot, 36 *Law Mag.*, 5th Ser., p. 274 (1911); authority not stated. The Earl, however, " was Lord of the Manor, of the New Temple including Ralph Neville's house in Chancery Lane on part of the modern Lincoln's Inn " : Kingsford, 2 Stow's *Survey*, 372. *Ib.* v. I, p. 85, in the Earl's Account-Book for the twelve month 1314-5 occurs : " For 129 dosen Parchment with Inke 4 li. 8s. 3d. ob " [olus=½d.]. This kind of expense has been supposed to be for legal documents. The exact date of the severance of the two Temples is not known : tradition assigns it to the early

years of H. VI [1422] : Inderwick, *Cal. I. T. Rec.* XIII (1896); Ingpen, *Mr. Worsley's Book*, Introdn., p. 13 (1910). The earliest known use of the name " Middle Temple " is in a will of 1404 discovered by Mr. Bolland, 24 *L. Q. R.* 401 (1908). It is also the oldest name-record of the four great Inns. The testator is John Bownt of Bristol and there is a bequest " Roberto mancipio medii Templi " and another of cash and " nova statuta mea " to John Beoff (see p. 507), " apprenticio curiae and my very good comrade." So Bownt was probably a lawyer. In 1450 a letter-writer says " Prentise is now in the Mydle Inne " : 1 *Paston L.* 159 : No. 117, ed. Gairdner.

12. New I.—" So called as latelier made ' Of a common hostery, and the signe of our Lady, an Inne of Chancery for Students . . . to wit, about " 1485 " and not so late as some have supposed " : Stow, *ib.* ii, 97, 38. Buc says *temp.* Ed. IV [1461-83] " in *Wych street*," Herbert (1804). Buc says (p. 1075-6a) that its inmates " students of the law " migrated thither from " St. George's Inne in the little Old Bailey—reputed to have beene the most auncient Inne of Chancery when it stood."

Outer Temple.—See p. 494.

13. St. George's I.—See New Inn; remains were still visible in 1804 : Herbert, 283.

14. Serjeant's Inns.—(1) In Fleet Street; purchased by lawyers *temp.* H. VIII (1509-47); Buc, 1069a : used by serjeants past and present, hence by the judges. He notes that " the most part of the " serjeants are " imployed in the circuits as judges and as justices itinerant in the times of the vacation, to determine causes and to give justice . . . in all the severall shires " [as Recorders?]. Herbert, 355, dates it earlier than Henry VI [1422-61], relying on a document of 1442 but the identification of site is uncertain.

(2) In Chancery Lane. See Farringdon I. and

15. Scrope's I.—" scituate against the Church of Saint Andrew in Oldborne " : Stow, ii, 35, who found the name first in a record of 1459 : owing to its proximity to Ely House the serjeants sometimes had their feasts there, the

INNS OF CHANCERY AND OF COURT. 593

first in 1464 : *ib.* : probably their own hall was too small. In 1494 it was " late called Sergeants Inne," *e.g.*, in 1483 : Herbert, p. 357 : " now [1804] Scrope's Court." Buc, 1068b, explains that formerly " Judges, Barons and Sergeants continued in those houses of Court whereof they were fellowes and wherein they . . . had studied and practised. . . . But afterward . . . left those auncient great houses of Court and tooke lesser houses for themselves onely (and as I take it) the first peculiar house which they had " was this until such time as they took " these other two houses (which now they possess)." He expressly includes the Judges in Sergeants.

16. Staple I.—See p. 446. Mentioned as in St. Andrew, Holborn, in 1333 : " St. Hall "=a wholesale storehouse : stated to have become an Inn of Chancery in 1413 : Kingsford, 2 Stow, 363, citing *Staple Inn* by E. Williams (1906) : it was " within the bar " : *ib.* 6 ; " though few are the facts upon which we may base our conclusions, all the inferences seem to justify the opinion that S. I. was the earliest of those Inns of Court and of Chancery " : *ib.* 63.

" In the reign of Henry V [1413-22] and probably before, it had become an inn of chancery, the society still [1804] possessing a manuscript of the orders and constitutions made at that period " : Herbert, p. 347.

Strand I.—See Chester I., called " Davye's Inne " in 1451 (4 *Cal. Inq. p. m.* 40, cited Kingsford) and a conveyance of 1548 : 4 *Rec. of L. I.* 287 (1902), Baildon.

17. Thavies I.—In 1551 it was granted to the benchers of Lincoln's Inn for the use of students of the law and was " soon afterwards " made an Inn of Chancery : Herbert, 323. So Stow (ab. 1600) calls it (i, 77; ii, 39, 363 : ed. Kingsford) " in Oldborne." It seems to be agreed that the eponymous owner died in 1348 : Coke, 10 *R. Proem*, xxxvii; Kingsford, ii, 363, above.

The theory started by Coke, *ib.*, that T. referred in his will to a " *hospicium* where law students were wont to live " is now exploded. The word *legis* does not occur after *apprenticii* in the MS. (Husting Rolls, 77, no. 242) Baildon, *ib.* : (*City*) *Letter Bk.* F 102 : later—1920—

inspecters : 36 *L. Q. R.* 274 : from the MS., *quo* necessary to the sense, is omitted, but Coke prints it; what is worse he twice prints *Armiger* for " armurer " (*sic*) which Baildon, repeating Buc, says that Thavie was. The truth seems to be that someone made an incorrect copy for Coke and that he never saw the MS., for Buc—who took a very special interest in the Inn, " for besides that at my first coming to London, I was admitted for probation into that good house I take it to bee the oldest Inne of Chancery at the least in holborne " (1074b)—relates that Coke showed him " the transcript " of the Hustings record : probably if Coke had seen the MS. itself he would not have put in the spurious words or the mistranslation. Dugdale (*Or. Jud.* 271) only copies Coke, not quite accurately, and, *ib.* 143, thinks that " Davies " or " Thavies " of his day (1666) may be a corruption of the " Travers " who owned land in that parish in 1340 : *Rot. Fin.* 11 E. III, p. 2, m. 14.

If, then, the *apprenticii* of T.'s will were not his own, it is idle to speculate whose they were. Yet so good an authority as Mr. Baildon " sees no reason to doubt " that these lodgers were lawyers. He refers to Y. B. 29 E. III, M. T., 1355, for " apprenticiis " alone = *appr. legis* [though the late Mr. A. E. Randell, the editor of L. Q. R., v. 36, p. 374, n., could not find the passage; still, as he says] no authority is required for this point—*in a law book.*

Apropos, could not *armiger* be correct? Even if an *armiger* could not keep a shop in 1348, the shops may have been let to another for his apprentices.

18. Buc has a chapter, p. 1070b : " Of the sixe Clerkes Inne or Kedermisters Inne."

". . . the Inne or common house of the learned Gentlemen, the Atturneis in the high Court of Chancery, commonly called the Office of the sixe Clerkes of the Chauncery. They are a Society of Gentlemen learned in the Lawes, and were at first Priestes, and thereupon called Clarkes. . . . These Clarkes live and lodge and common together in one house in Chauncery Lane, purchased and accommodated for them by Master *John Kedermister*

Esquier (*p*), one of this Society, and a most skilfull man in his profession and as faithfull a man to his friends and clients, as ever was in his place, as I can testifie by good proofe. . . . And it is right worthy to have the title of an Inne of Chauncery, because that onely chauncery men live and onely chauncery matters are handled and recorded in this house."

19. *Ib.* 1077a : " Of Bacons Inne or Corsiters Inne." Founded by Sir Nicholas Bacon (1509-79) : Their business " is to make all originall writs to bee served and sent into all parts " of England ; they numbered 24, but Buc admits his ignorance of the Inn which is attested by his ridiculing the name—derivation from *de cursu* [*sc.* writs]—preferring that of *Chorister* !

(*p*) He was the son of a City clothworker and about 1550 acquired the tenancy of Harfleet Inn on the site of the northern portion of the present Law Society; the Six Clerks subsequently got the freehold : *MS.* by Master Pretor Chandler.

(597)

INDEX.

Abingdon, law at, 46
    Writ, 554
Absent lawyers, 214
    party, 85, 413, 561, 573, 580
Abusive language in court, 231, 232, 234, 235w, 403, 551, 558, 563, 564, 569, 571, 572-3 : cf. 222
Accused, absent, may be defended, 580
    sometimes not allowed advice, 12, 278, 295p, 532, 535
acephali, 6m
Acta judicii, 107, 575
    publica, 167, 546
Action(s), " bogus," 304-5
    classified, 210 cf. 312
    forms of (about 1300), 312
    lawyers, against, 334-5
    on the case, 335
actor, 580
Addressing the Court, 197h
Adelard, 31
advocare, to warrant, 528-30
Advocata, 24q
Advocate of the Court of Arches, 109k
Advocates, College of, London, 109k
    Rome, 25
Advocatio, 2, 5, 131l
Advocatus, -i, 3, 5, 9, 11, 36, 400
    abuses by. See *Attorney, Lawyers*.
    acts as judge, 553, 581
    afraid to advise, 72 cf. 403
    See *Independence*.
    appointment of, by *comes*, 552
    assault on, 573
    assessores. [See]
    assigned. See *dativus* below.
    bargains with client, 237.
    See *Champerty*.
    Canonised, 221d

Advocatus, -i (continued)
    Canonists? 68
    character of, 548-50
    Cleric. See *Clerical*, &c.
    in lay courts, 423-4
    or layman, 2, 5a, 26, 27, 548
    ought not to be, 560
    Compurgator? 531
    Consiliarii of judges, 579
    contrasted with *j. peritus*, 559
    Court matches, 98f, 119, 374, 557 cf. 581
    dativus; cf. *Serjeant*, assigned, 34 cf. 98f, and 456, 551-2
    refusing, 405, 558, 572
    Spanish, 420
    ecclesiastical, 24, 71, 131l, 145h, 203?
    in a lay Court, 17, 18, 570?
    regulated, 159
    excommunicated, 101
    gratuitous, 560, 572
    " hireling," a, 71z
    ideal, 119, 557-8
    inferior judge, 26b, 34 cf. 63 and 581
    lay in lay Court, 26a
    many on one side, 74, 77, 82b cf. 558, 572
    none, 200
    not mentioned, 70
    oath of (1230), 393g cf. 557
    in France, 405
    pay of, 145h, 557, 560, 565
    personal effect of, 79
    professional, 36 cf. 2e
    prohibited. See *Placitatores*.
    punished, 198

598 INDEX.

Advocatus, -i (continued)
 Roman [See]
  defined, 567
Ægelric, 51
Affidavits, 83
Affray, City v. Inns, 432
agendo—defendendo, 225
Alderman, *ealdorman*, 7, 226
Alfonso X, 419
allegationes, 76, 78, 89, 100h, 565
Alwyn, 45
Ambrose, *Magister*, 67
Amendment in Court, 198, 203n, 288, 533, 583 cf. 584.
  See *emendatio*.
 of pleading, 208f, 567
  writ, 288
amicus, 71z, 108
 curiae, 220a, 314
Amiens (1091), 401
" Anglo-French," 341, 353
" Anglo-Norman," 353
Anglo-Saxon period, 1
 trials, 1-19, 538
Anti-clerical legislation, 352
antiloquus, 386
Anwalt, 33a, 35d, 130, 136a, 221d, 415-6
apocrisarii, 88
Appeal from King's Court, 56h, 68
  to Rome, 53a, 64, 68, 80, 572, 577
 of felony, 210
  pleading in, 204, 208
appellationes, 65p, 80, 566
Apprenticius, -i See *Students*, 155k, 189n, 306-322, 352
 (1234-75), 427
 =*appr. legis?* 594
 ad barros, 255
 and *attornatus*, 284
 aprentifs, 190q
 at " assises," 478
 attacked, 450-1
 audience of, 516
 " better," 318, 464-5, 501
 chambers of, 451
 cistae of, 451
 costume of, 468. See *dress* below.

Apprenticius,-i (continued)
 curiae, 592
 de banco, 589
 devilling, 516
 dress of, 371 cf. 317
 lege peritus, 371
 made Serjeants, 340
 =member of an Inn? 432t
 " M.P.," 316
  not to be, 463
 name, not official, 499, 510
 nobiliores, 450 cf. 281 and 318, 451. See " better " above.
 not known, 426
  to live with clerks of Chancery, 441
 sworn, 511
 of K. B., 432u
 " the Court," 507
 Ordinance (1292), on, 281
 pictures of, 366, 370
 practising, 522g
 Recorder (City), 244
 several to one sjt., 316
 social position of, 281, 371 cf. 355, 452, 469
Arbitration, 3
arbitrator, 522g, cf. 53, 543 and 580c
arbitri, 566, 580c cf. 53
Ardern J., 524
" Argument," 353
armiger, 470x, 473, 594
Ars Notariae, 100h, 167y
Articuli super Cartas, 182n, 191
assertor, 35, 202, 553
Assessores, 202f, 232, 560, 566. 571, 576, 577, 579, 581 cf. 584
assidens, 187g, 202
Assisa, 122k, 146p, 148, 224z, 483
assises, 478, 483
Assises d'Antioche, 396o
 de *Jérusalem*, 112, 382-98, 408
  Maritime, 421q
Assizes of Clarendon, 84, 121
 Northampton, 123
 provincial, 153, 558y
 serjeant, 218, 265, 302
 social value of, 472
atorne (-é), atourne, 133, 403i

INDEX. 599

atourner, 127
attestatio (evidence), 78-9, 83, 554
attornans, 412
attornare, 126, 127, 127b, 412-13
attornata, 126x, cf. 134
attornatio, 3, 73, 136a
attornatus, (-i, etc.) See *Attorney*,
127-43
 ad hoc, 183, 334
 addressing Court, 284
 admission of (E. II?) 298-9
  (H. VI), 306
 and *apprent.*, 284
  narrator [see], 195
   in same case,
   297
 authorisation by, 205
  of, 72, 127,
  135, 138,
  139m, 141u;
  cf. 136a :
  142, 209h,
  279 cf. 289,
  294k, 300,
  304, 336y,
  412, 438 cf.
  443
avowing *sjt.*, 297 cf. 303
 Brunner's theory of, 135-6;
 cf. 295p; cf. 411; cf.
 416a
 Chancery clerks not to associate with, 441
 City, in the, 228
 " clerk " originally, 201
 Continental theories on,
 411; cf. *Brunner* above
 = deputy *or gerens vices*,
 etc., 126, 294, 310
 earliest in a trial, 74
 = executor? 133p, 323
 facere, 138; cf. 225, 301
 first legislation on, 301
  mentioned, 286
   as a profession, 465
 generalis [See]
 " Glanville," in, 134-6
 in eccl. cases, 280z
 King's, the, 214, 330, 333
 more than one, 135, 137,
 271, 276, 293h, 328

avowing *sjt.* (continued)
 Norman, 412
 not = executor, 133p
 not mentioned, 70, 71, 75,
  83, 99,
  106 cf.
  580, 330
  in Chaucer,
  492
 not *narrator*, 127a, 175,
  194, 205
 not so-called, 127a
 numbers of, 336y
 paid? 134
 procurator [See]
 professional, 175i
  and non-profl.,
  a link between, 288
  (1280-1300), 331
 punished, 335. See *Prison*.
 regis, 269, 330, 332. See
  placitator.
 removal of. See *de attornatio*, and cf. 335, 412
 Rolls of. See *Attorney*.
 sequitur pro, 214
 specially concerned with
  writs, 175
 Stat. Westm. I (c. 33), in,
  194
 suable. See *Attorney*.
 sue for fees, 305
 unauthorised, 297-8
 women, 134
 writs special business of,
  331
Attorney(s) See *Attornatus*, 277,
 306, 322
 betraying client, 234; cf. 307
 clerks. [See]
 conceded to defendant, 302
 dearth of, 267
 examined, 303
 fees of, 374
 functions of (H. V) 267, 303
 -General, 286, 325 cf. 330,
  332, 518
  not in Fortescue,
  519
 " general " or " special,"
  278

600 INDEX.

Attorney(s) (*continued*)
  in Chancery, 594
  in itinere, 302
  King's, 214, 220z, 330, 332
  laches of, 253 cf. 307, 375
  livelihood of, 268
  making, 225
  more than cne. See *Attor natus*.
  non-professional, 195-8
  not in a capital case, 278
    to be countor, 232
    essoiner, 234
  oath of, 248
  " of counsel," 327
  of " Great Lords," powers of, 290
  officers of the Court, 516
  partnership (?) of, 282
  professional (distinctly), 305, 516
  punished, 335
  Rolls of, England, 218, 335
    Ireland, 276*h*
  serjeant, 128*f*; cf. 329
  servile, 239
  " special," 291*y*
  status of, assumed (1388), 444; cf. 516
  sued for negligence (1297), 276, 334
  sworn, 234*r*
  with serjeant, 517
aturne, 127, 128*f*, 307
auctor, 35, 527, 548
Audience, 215, 216, 310
  of party, 516
avantparlier, amparlier, 385, 398, 400, 409*n*, 587
Avignon, 77*r*
avocas, avocat(z), 386, 387*d*, 587
  abuses of, 401
  and *procureur*, 133*oo*
  first Ordinance on, 406
avoué, 24*q*, 26 cf. 386*z*
Avvocati concistoriali, 25, 26, 356, 362
Ayscoghe J., 340
Azo, 78

Bacon's Inn, 595
Bailiffs, 165. See *ballivus*.

Bailiffs (*continued*)
  abuses by, 304
  and attorney, 278
  = presiding official, 207, 233 cf. 304
ballivus (or *baillivus*, 150*u*), 127*a*, 129*f*, 142*z* cf. 150*u*, 323
  of Dublin, 276
  London, 228
  regis, 523
Bands, 364
Bar, *barra*, *barros*, etc., 181*m*, 197*h*, 232-3, 235*w*, 301, 320
  (1280), 232, 255
  of Chancery, 440
  = the profession, 256, 340
    solidarity of, 179, 337
Barnard's Inn, 589
Barnwell Book, 114*r*, 127*b*, 152
Baro, 17, 18*z*, 62*c*, 65 226
Barons' Articles, 123*l*
Barons of the Exchequer, 367
Barrators, 118, 290
Barrister, 522*g*; cf. 256*i*
  " esquire " ? 469, 470*x*
Bataillard cited, 37, 552
Bathe, H. de, J., 150*u*, 156*o*
Battle, trial by, 61*c*, 539*l* cf. 536
Beaumanoir, 407, 408*l*, cited 345*z*
beaupleder, 207-8, 534
Becket, Thomas à, and lawyers, 88
bellum = *lis*, 533. See *Battle*.
Bench, the, and early bar, 124
" Bencher," 590-1
Bennett v. *Hale* (1850), 326*p*, 359*s*
Bereford J., 190*r*, 215, 221, 313, 321, 329
Bernard, St., of Clairvaux, 120
  Morlaix, 145
Berwick, 207*z*, 230*m*
Bethmann-Hollweg, von, cited, 33*a*, 34*d*
Beugnot, le Comte, cited, 112, 117*z*, 145*h*, 384-5, 408, 410, 414*x*
Bigelow, Profr., cited, 42, 46*x*, 49*g*, 51*t*, 55*e*, 60*s*, 62*e*, 64*h*, 72*d*, *e*, 75*n*
biggins, 363*n*
Bilingualism, 344-6, 348 cf. 370*s*
billetta, 209*h*
Bills, 173, 225, 310*d*; cf. 443
  in English only? 345, 349*o*

INDEX. 601

Bills, instances of, 270, 306 (Eyre)
    of costs, 381
    promoted by *attornati*, 286q
    serjeants not suable by, 175k, 186b
Bolland's books, 173b, 306, 349o
    discovery, 592
Bologna, 50, 86, 93, 94-9
    secular law of, 167a
Bolognian jurists, 117
Book(s)
    in monasteries, 45, 65p
    of Entries, 186b
    law, early, 20i, 89, 158
        (1250-1450), 124o, 506-9, 592
        (1268-1468), 435
Bownt J., 507, 592 : *Addenda*
Brachylogus, 402
Bracton, 124o, 177, 191, 197h, 201, 435
    cited, 103s, 491o
    on *attornatus*, 141
Branches, two, both in same case, 297, 303
    distinct, 285f, 326p, 330, 331, 516
bref, 218
breve, (*-ia*) = writ, 66, 211q, 562 cf. 69
    perdere, 323h
Brevia Placitata, 93
Bribes to judges, 261a
Bricstan. See *Trials*.
"brief," 203n; cf. 479e
Bristol (-ow), 206, 207
    lawyers at, 185a, 268, 485
Britton cited, 189n, 191, 204, 238, 278, 481l, 491
Bromyard, 91x, 146m, 154, 213, 283l, 373z, 377m, 429o, 481
"Brother" (legal), 503x
Brunner cited, 3, 129, 135, 285, 301
Buc(k), Sir G., 446, 448, 471, 589-95
Buckley, W. (1572), 487
Bulgarus, 90s, 95
bundi, 140
Burnell, K., 235
bursarii, 90s
Business, fluctuation of, 243, 339

Cade. See *Jack*.
Caen, 95r
Caesar, Julius, cited, 17r
Calfurnia, Carfania, 422
"Call(ed) to the bar," 309 cf. 478k, 522g
Calumnia, &c., 97, 118, 140 cf. 240, 263f, 287, 293h, 419, 540, 557, 564
Calumpniatores, 547
Cambridge Assize, 153
    law at, 87t, 504
    lawyers at, 456e
Camus cited, 411r
Cancellarii, 31, 168, 256i, 546
Canciani, 391z, 584f
Candidatus = law student, 478k
Canon Law in England, 424
    Oxford, 506
Canonists, 94-5, 97
    and Civilians, 97
Canute (Cnut), laws of, 4l, 5, 32, 539
Capa, 361
Capgrave cited, 351
capitalis, 150a
Capitulum of 819...158, 552
Capucium, 361g, 362h, 368
Case Law, 41, 48, 86r, 103s, 489, 491, 510, 512
Causare, 547
causator = a party, 535
Causes, Kinds of, 57, 223, 566
Causidicus, -i, 35, 47, 59, 61, 63i, 88, 118, 167, 298, 343 (Juvenal), 482 (Gower), 554, 556, 564
Clerici, 124, 435
    = *attornatus*? 298
    = *serviens*? 229
cautela(*e*), 102, 106; cf. 476, 562, 566
cautio, 374f
Cavendish J., C.J., 451
cavillationes, 104u, 577, 581
ceorls, 6
"Chambers, at," 577
Champerty, 98f, 118, 190, 191, 229, 234, 237, 373, 477, 558, 563, 571
Chancellor, the, 31, 429
    first, 29
    gifts (fees?) to, 271, 272
    lay (1454), 366
    more than one, 168, 429

INDEX.

Chancery, the, 30, 236
    Court of, pictured, 366
    Lane, 428-9; cf. 589
chaperon, 319o, 362; cf. 220, 468
Charlemagne's laws, 36, 37, 549
Chaucer, 322, 486-97
    's Man of Law, 260u
    Parson's Tale, 366e
Chester Inn, 453, 589, 593
Chevaliers en lois, 150u
Cheyne C.J., 516t
chicane, 113, 389
    the word, 400a
Chichester House, 436
Chichester Inn, 432
chlamys, 368; cf. 356k
Choke J., 515, 518b
    Sjt., 194, 222
Christian Courts 154 cf. 155k, 160a
    cf. 272s, 377m
Christian on *Solicitors* cited, 235w, 268h
Christianity, effect of, 21-4
Church, the, 21-3
    and the Law, 88g, 155, 161c, 560
Churchmen and lawyers, 149-56, 236
Cicero cited, 16r : cf. 57 : 223, 231q 338b
cingulum, 357p, 360z, 572, 573u
citatio, 576
City, the, 223-62
    attorneys of, 290
    Charters, &c., of, 228
        1168 or 1170...139
        1189...224
        1259...228
        1268...228
        1356...85m, 235w
        1393-4...85m, 235w
        H. V...165
    common law in, 233u
    documents, language of, 231p
    education (legal) in, 313
    law students in, 423, 426 cf. 446
    Ordinances (1280), 230-4, 313
        (1356), 85m, 235w
    narratores in, 240

City, the v. Inns, 432-3
Civil lawyers, 456e
    procedure, 23, 56, 89k
    v. criminal, 558
    ecclesiastical [see]
Civilis = forensis [see]
clamator, 35, 548, 551
Classical lawyers, 2e
Clement's (Inn), 427, 589
clercs, les, 345z
clergy. See *Clericus* : cf. 544
Clerical " error," 429
    judge(s), 149-52
        in civil cases, 147, 423-4
        lawyers, 38, 59, 64, 75, 145, 151
        prohibited, 28, 33, 96, 149, 151x, 158; cf. 404
    usurping lay jurisdiction, 152; cf. 272s
Clericulus, 435h
Clericus, -i, 428-45
    and *laicus*, 582d
    as clerk, 30, 143
    causidici, 124; cf. 345z, 435
    defined, 96, 143
    forbidden to plead, &c., 28, 33, 404, 568
    ignorant of law, 73, 76p
    in secular causes, 96, 568
    not to be *adv.*, 560, 568
    regis, 58n, 589
Clerk called *serviens*, 453t
    = *clericus*, 292, 298; cf. 485
    intimidated, 454
    " lowest," 503
    Norman, 433y
Clerks *de cursu*, 433, 438
    of Chancery, 30, 58, 143c 484, 429-30, 524
        abuses by, 443 cf. 453-4
        advise, 327, 331, 443
        robes of, 437q
        social position of, 432 cf. 433y, 436, 439-44
        suable, where? 186b
    Courts, 43, 118, 163-4
        (in 1400), 484
    attornati, 331c

INDEX. 603

Clerks of Courts (*continued*)
    fees of, 197*h*
    trilingual, 200, 346
    King, 30
    judges, 118, 163, 239, 429-30
    attacked, 297, 429-30 cf. 443
    serviens? 240
    sheriffs, 165
    students were, 365
Cliens, 11, 19 cf. 92, 544
Client, access of, 326*p*
    confidence of, not to be revealed, 583
clientulus, 100*h*
Clifford's Inn, 317, 320, 449, 485*z*, 508, 589
Code for representative, first English, 85
codices publici, 167
cognatus, &c., 3
cognitor(es), 559, 565
Coif, 358-61, 363, 367
    =hood, 370
    origin of, 358
    pictures of, 240*h*, 365-70
Coke cited, 38, 142, 188, 194, 209*f*, 211, 367, 424, 462*u*, 492*q*, 511, 512, 517
    for list of books, 507
    on Thavies Inn, 593-4
    speech of, to Sjts., 185*b*, 194, 211, 370*s*, 473, 512*a*
College(s), early, 510
    of Advocates, 109*k*
Collett's Inn, 273*a*
Collobium, 368
Collusion of lawyers [see], 208
Colquhoun, Sir P., cited, 326*p* 490*l*
Combat. See *Duel*.
comes, -ites, Comtes, 26*b*, 37 cf. 57, 552
"Commendation," 7, 545
Commercialism, early, 107
    later, 334
Commissioner(s) of Assize, 267, 338, 491, 592
Common Clerk, 227
    Council, 227

Common law = *jus regni*, 451
    lex temporalis, 589*n*
    only province of lawyers, 338
    lawyers with civil, 456*e*
    Serjeant, the, 11*u*
    oath of, 250
    of the City, 225, 243. 251, 253-4
    or Common Pleader? 250*z*, 253
"Commune" of London, 224
communis advocatus, 202
    meaning of, 253
    serviens, 253
    narrator, 202
Compurgator, 8, 23, 531
Comtes, les. See *Comes*.
Conduct in Court. See *Demeanour*.
Conference. See *Consultation*
    in 1389...260
conseil, 483-4
conseill not allowed, 585
Conseils, les, 113 cf. 331, 384-98, 394*k*
Consiliarius(i), 76, 154, 155, 177, 304, 323, 379? 504*c*, 579
    legis, 589*n*
    principalis, 359
    specialis, 150*u*
Consilium, 5, 11, 13, 18, 28, 55*e*, 192, 195, 199, 215, 217*n*, 373, 385, 389 cf. 417
    business of *juris p.*, 559
    in L. H. P., 532-7
    instance of, 74
    = opinion, 576
    refused, 53, 532, 535
Constitutions of Clarendon, 84, 122, 144
    Otho, 103, 159, 169*i*, 571
    Salisbury, Bp. of, 159
    Papal, 97
Consultation, 316
    with other side. See *Imparl*.
Contempt of Court, 336, 564

604 INDEX.

Contestatio litis, 118, 557, 565, 566, 574
conteur, 175
Continent, the, and England, 21-4, 414, 421q cf. 65, 407-8
contradicere, 55, 56h cf. 70z
Coote on Roman influence, 20, 543
Copying by jurists, 99, 101k, 563, 567 cf. 579
Coronator, coronour, 123, 493
Corsiter's Inn, 595
Costliness of law. See *Litigation.*
Costs, 81, 83, 110, 153, 566-7
    recovery of, abuse of, 305
    to be taxed, 100h, 197h, 565
Costume, 355-71, 475, 477
Cotton, Bart., cited, 207z
Corruption. See *Venality.*
Councillor of the King, 248
counsaill = (a) counsel, 270
    (b) not technical, 327
Counsel retained by attorney, 326p
Counter (verb), 176, 356
Countour, Counter, 151, 170, 492
    caricatures, of, 240h, 361
    compulsory, *Addenda*
    not to be attorney, 232
    = serjeant, 230, 253
" Country " = jury, 154, 481l
    patria, 155, 181m, 202, 209
County, a legal unit, 496
    Court, the, 23, 61, 301
    elections in, 123, 457
    placitum in, 46, 50
    lawyers (J.P.), 223
Court(s), Anglo-Saxon, 18, 22-3; cf. 17
    Central, permanent, 150
    demeanour in, 220, 279
    hours of, 504
    inferior (baron, &c.), 208f, 304, 318, 347, 351, 375g, 542
    lawyers in, 348
    French, 405
    lords'. See *inferior* above.
    Westminster, at, 425, 478, 483-4
Cressingham, H., 450nn

" Crib," the, 321
Criminal causes [See *Accused, Civil*], 532, 580
Cross-examination, 211, 237. See *Interrogation.*
Crown, the, as defendant, 64
    litigant, 133, 214 cf. 585
    " briefing " many advv., 217n lawyers,
    no private practice of, 379
    privileges of, 289
    venality of, 209
Curia Regis, 54
    in the King's absence, 71
Curia Romana, 25z, 163h
Cursarius, -ii, Cursitor, *cursistae,* 433z, 441-4
" Cursory " writs, 430
Cursus honorum, 222, 340l, 515. See *Promotion.*

Damages, 83, 197h, 305, 574
    the word, 479
Damasus, 98
dampna = costs [see]
Danvers, R., J., 222o
dativus advocatus. See *adv. judex,* 33-4
Davye's (Davies) Inn, 593, 594
d'Amory, 122i
    miles regis, 271
d'Anesty, R., 66, 577
de Bek, Sir J., 217
de Brewes, 178c, 360
de Brok, L., 185
de Coleville, Sjt., 178, 360z
d'Ibelin, Jean, book of, 114, 388, 583-6
de Luci, R., 66, 69, 72, 167
de Monte or Torrigny, 87
de Vere, Aubrey, 63, 158, 183
Deadvocatio, 134, 198, 297u, 299, 300
    not of *serviens,* 329
Dearth of lawyers. See *Serjeant.*
    a public grievance, 341

INDEX. 605

Deattornatio, 278, 279, 291*y*, 299, 300*g*, 412
Declarations. See *libelli*.
Decretals, 101, 147, 420, 424, 567
Decretista(e), 97, 406
Decretum, 95, 96
dedimus potestatem, 295†
Defence, of prisoners, 211
    pleading, 204
defendant, 584
defendant may have *att.*, 302
defendere, 13
" Defending an action," 8
defensio, 8*q*, 9
Defensor(es), *Difensori*, 5, 9, 25, 36, 100*h*, 522*g*, 535, 580
    =defendant, 538
    civitatis, 565
    ecclesiae, 24
    legalis, 539*l*
    of children, 14, 538
    =official, magistrate, cf. 565, 538
    pauperum, 24
Delachenal cited, 394*k*
Delays, 84; cf. 557
Delegation of judges [See], 25*z*, 80, 98, 538
Demandant v. *Tenant*, 8, 119*a*, 561-2
Demeanour of *adv.*, 108, 119; cf. 220-2, 232, 279, 558, 563, 570-1
" democracy " of *hospitia*, 470, 473, 476
demur, 205
" devil," 241 (?)
Dialogus de Scaccario cited, 132*o*, 172*y*, 350*p*, 433, 558*y*
Digest, the, 88, 407, 420
di(s)rationare, -ocinare, 51*o*, 225
    (*desrainier*), 583
Disavowing. See *deadvocare*.
Disqualification for appearing. See *Placitatores*.
Division of the profession. See *Branches*.
Domesday Book, 7-8, 9, 532
domini judices, 73*g* cf. 55
dominus, 8*q*, 35, 137
    and *homo, subjectus*, 544
dominus litis, 119*a* cf. 35, 141*u*, 564

Domus Conversorum, 425, 428, 430, 431
dona=fees, 372
" doomsmen," 538
Doubt on point of law (1170), 86*r*
Drogheda, 207*z*. See *William of Drogheda*.
Du Coudray, 133*oo*, 167*y*, 406*a*
Dual system, 217, 263, 326
Dublin, 207
ductor patriae=foreman? 155*m* cf. 581
Duel, 14, 61, 539*l*, 588
Dugdale's pictures of judges, 369
duodenarii, 155*m*, 173*c*
Durand (d. 1296), 103*s*, 233*s*, 360*b*, 362*h*, 406
    (1776), 159

Eadmer, 49*g*
Earliest English laws, 1-2, 21, 527-30
Ecclesiastical
    authority *v.* civil, 37, 56*g*, 71, 74, 80, 144, 155, 272*s*, 286
    in Ireland, 273
    displaced by lay representatives, 143
    fear of secular law, 80-3
    judges. [See]
    lawyer, 236
        elimination of, 523*k*
    procedure [See *attornatus, civil proc.*], 22, 53, 400
    veto on secular Courts, 74, 151*x* cf. 149
Ecclesiastics and lawyers. See *Churchmen*.
    compose writs, 125, 434-5
échevins [See *scabinii*], 401 cf. 37, 168*g*
economus (*yc-*), 100*h*, 580
Education. See *Students*.
    in Inns, 501
    in monasteries, 45
    legal, 86-94, 312, 504
    liberal (1440), 508

606 INDEX.

Edward the Confessor, 29
    the laws of, 32
    Elder, 2, 528
Edward I,
    Acts of Parliament of, 348
    legal policy of, 235-6
Ely House, 435, 592
Embracery, 249, 481i, 559z
emendatio, 11, 16, 533. See *Amendment*.
Emo, 89
English. See *Earliest*.
    Chancellor's speech in (1363), 352z
    language displaces French, 350
        in courts, 341-55, 430
        of sheriffs, 234w
        restored, 343
Entertainment of judges, 559z
Error in judgment, 233
    on the records, 80a
errorem revocare, 573
" Esquire," 319, cf. 379, 457, 465-6, 469
    " apprentice," 468-9
Essoin, 8q, 85, 138, 235, 396, 398r, 561,
    instance of, 68, 138
Essoiner, 228, 232, 234, 235w, 258, 390
Établissements, les, 388l, 410, 587, 587-8
    et Coutumes de Normandie, 411r
Evidence. See *Attestatio, Testes*.
    jury give, 155m
    oral, 83
Examination, 510 cf. 421, cf. 578, 571
    of *apprenticii*, 283
        attornati, 303
        clerks in Chancery, 441e
        witnesses, etc., 211, 212x
        religious, 571p
Exchequer, officials, suable where, 186b
Exclusive audience, 215, 216 cf. 310, 321, 515r cf. 229
Excommunicated, not to be *adv.*, 568
Excommunication, 80, 81, 83 cf. 105a
    of *adv.* 101, 564, 568
    judge, 575
Excusator, 561, 580
Executor, 133p, 169 cf. 323 : cf. 60u, 81a
    as attorney, 486
Expulsion from Inns, 501

Fabyan cited, 182p, 351
facere attornatum, 138, 141u, 562
    legem, 141u, 294
Fact and Law, 78, 109, 573
Families founded by lawyers, 471
Farringdon Inn, 589
Feast of Serjeants, 339, 502
Fees [See *Remuneration*] allowed, 191-2, 557, 558, 571, 581
    =*dona*, 372
    earliest (?) English, 118
    for writs, 271
    French, 406
    go up, 478
    highest, 287d
    in court, 326p
    instances of, 73, 203, 235w. 262, 287d (?)
    Irish, 275
    none, 380
    of *advocatus*. [See]
        attorneys, 305, 374
        bacc. legum, 523
        City lawyers, 235, 241
        judges, 260-1, 262 cf. 557
        King's lawyers, 337
        Roman eccl. *advv.*, 27, 107
    principle of, 279, 563
    scale (?) of, 378
    statutory (1432), 333
    suing for, 264
    suitors cannot pay, 174-5
    theory of *Mirror of JJ*. about, 279
Fellow=*socius*. [See]
Felony, no advisers in, 12
Ferne cited, 470, 496, 514
Fet à saver, 93
Feudal system, effect of, 6-10, 383-4, 388, 400, 545

INDEX. 607

Ficket's field, 427, 432
Fines, *Addenda.*
firmarius, 59
First lay English lawyers (?) 47
FitzHervey, Osbert, 147, 156o
FitzStephen, W., 223, 427
Flambard, Randolf, 58, 60
Fleet St. Inn, 589
Fleta cited, 189n, 191s, 195, 307-8
 314, 429
Florus cited 418f, 450nn
Food and drink, 466m, 559
Foreign countries cited as models, 351
    languages in Court. See *Languages.*
"Foreigner," 259
forein = non-citizen, 249, 296; cf. 305
forensis = secular, 96, 144f
forespeca, 3 cf. 136, 542
forfal, 561
Formalism. See *Technicality.*
formulae, 136z, 193, 400
forspeaker, 176o
Fortescue J., 497-519, 524
    picture of, 368
    serjt. 316 (?), 339d (?), 369
    young? 266, 277
Foss, 156
Foucard, Bp. See *Pope.*
Four Inns, the. [See]
France, 398-410; cf. 145h
Francigenae, 51n
Frankpledge, 2, 9, 121, 317
Frank vassalage, 7
French, 353
    advocacy in, 104 [See *France, Language*], 162-3, 200, 499-500
    Bar, early, 37, 162, 162d, 382
    lawyers' titles, 402i
    record, first, 342
Friars, coming of, 123
Friends at a trial, 11y, 12, 18, 559z
Fueros, 418-9
furiosi, 28
Furnivall's Inn, 589
Fürsprecher [See *Vorsprecher*], 34d, 415, 543, 552

Galletti cited, 24, 33
Gascoigne J., 369
    Thomas cited, 365, 505, 522
Gautier de Coinsi, 162d
generale attornamentum, 444q
generalis attornatus, 291, 304u cf. 332g, 444
gentz de ley, 256, 460
German authorities cited [See *Brunner, Liebermann*], 135, 547-53
Germanic law, 15, 16, 20, 547-53
Germany, 414-8
Gesetze der Angelsachsen, 1b, 4, 528-43
Gilbert of Thornton, 153, 201, 287
Giselham, W. de, 201a, 330
Glanvil J., 424y
Giraldus Cambrensis, 90t
Glanville, R. de, 84-6, 408
    cited, 8q, 48a, 388
    in Palestine, 408
    justiciar, 72
Glendower O., 316
Godfrey de Bouillon, 382
Godric, 45
Godwin, Earl, 31
"going out." See *imparl.*
Gothic law, 420
Gower, 474-85, 519
    cited, 45o, 523
Gowns " raye," 484
    sober, 468
Grades of lawyers. See *Hierarchy.*
Grammar and pleading, 113r, 173, 204, 355
    false, a mark of forgery, 576
Grand Custumier de Normandie, 38r, 411
Grand Jury, 18, 336y
Gratian, 95, 96
Gratuitous legal aid, 380
Gray's Inn, 447, 515, 590
Green wax, 363, 524
Grimbaud, 369
Guardian represents ward, 191s
Guiot, 127c, 162d

INDEX.

Hale, Sir M., 371
Hals J., 222
   Serjt., 379-80
Hanmeare Sjt., 189
Harfleet Inn, 595*p*.
Harvest. See *Vacations*.
Haskins, Professor, cited, 41, 131
Head uncovered, 360; cf. 362*h*
Hengham J., 347*i*
   Magna, 93, 295*p*, 379*z*, 561
   Parva, 93, 137*c*, 562
Henry I, Charter of, to City, 206
   II, 143-4
   III, 423
Herle, 188, 287*d*, 315, 328
Herlwin, 41
Hierarchy of clerks, 433, 442
   professional, 155*k*, 314, 482-3, 516
Higden cited, 343
Hilary, Bishop, 67, 150
Hill. See *Hull*.
Hlothaere, laws of, 1, 528
Hoccleeve, 334, 436, 452, 474
Holborn, 150*z*, 427, 432
   Chancery, 435
   jury, 260, 481*l*
   Williams's work on, *Addenda*
Holkat, 163*f*, 341
Holung und Wandel, 417
homo curiae legis temporalis, 589*n*
   legis, 223*r*; cf. 322*e*
honorarium, 107*f*, 373, 404, 558, 563
Hood, Serjeant's, 257, 319*o*, 361-4, 468
   See *houe*, 361*ff*
Horn, Andrew, 320
hospitii serviens, 183*p*
hospitium (*-a*), 446-56, 589-95
   "democratic," 470, 473
   earliest, 219, 277, 476; cf. 486 (1429)
   seasons at, 266
Hostels, 320, 476, 486
houe = hood = coif, 361, 363
House of Commons, name of, 514
Hubert de Burgh, 134, 171
Hull (or Hill) Sjt., 465
Hundred Courts, 123, 191*s*, 346

hure, 357*o*, 360
Hustings, Court of, 228, 231, 234

Ibelin, Jean d', 114, 388, 583
Illuminations. See *Inner Temple*.
imparl, 199, 207 cf. 381
in camera, 55
in consimili casu, 437
in forma pauperis, 380
Independence
   of the bar, 72-3, 160, 403, 454-5.
   See *Intimidation*.
   judges, 454-5
Inderwick K.C. cited, 366*d*, 370*s*
India, parallel of, 44
Indictment, 125, 209; cf. 122
Ine, 528
infames, 234, 558, 564, 568 cf. 551, 552, 571
infula = coif, 259*s*, 364
Inn(s) [See *Hospitium*], 270, 308
   cf. 312 and 320, 446-56, 589-95
   discipline of, 488, 501 cf 505*e*, 510
   effect of, 520
   expulsion from, 501
   Four, the, 513
      dates of, 448 cf. 500
   Irish, 273*a*
   numbers in, 496, 500, 514
   of Chancery, 500, 513
      first mentioned, 439, 440
      oldest? 592
   Court, 494 cf. 432 and 472, 500, 514
      earliest mention of, 514
   origins of, 427
   small, 448
   system of, 439, 488
Inner Inn, 448*f*
   Temple, 448, 591
      Illuminations in, 256, 366
"Inquest," 144
Instructions to Counsel, 296, 325
instruere, 35, 550
instrumenta = documents, 96, 565, 568

INDEX. 609

Interlocutory proceedings, 68, 76
Interrogation by *attornatus*, 287
    judges, etc., 174,
        211-2, 581
Interrogatories, 98*f*, 100*h*, 581
Intimidation by judges, etc., 154,
    181
    of counsel. See *Independence*.
Ipswich Charter, 123*l*
Ireland, 272, 318*l*
    writs (precedents) in, 139, 276
Irishmen in England, 277, 432*u*
Irnerius, 50*h*, 93
Italy, early law in, 50, 93-4; cf. 382
Iter, the, 172-3
    (1221), 226
Itinerant Justices, 74, 122, 123, 144,
        156, 172, 174*d*,
        373, 559
        Irish, 272
        oath of, 248
        origin of, 558*y*
Ivo of Chartres, 37
    Cornwall, 73
    St. [See]

Jack Cade's rising, 418*f*, 450*n*, 519,
    523
" Jargon," legal, 349*o*, 354, 490*l*
Jersey, 411*s*
John, King, 224, 342
    of Cambridge, 311
    Salisbury, 72, 87, 116, 145,
        177*y*, 372-3
        cited, 556-9
J. P. lawyers, 222-3
Judge(s)
    accused openly, 190*r*
    advising clients, 261
    Anglo-Saxon, 144
    called Serjeant, 219*t*
    censured, 19*c*
        by Gower, 480
        John of Salisbury,
            556
    delegati, 25*z*, 80, 98, 167*a*, 538,
        580
    depositories of common law,
        569*f*
    duty of, to *adv*., 564, 572

Judge(s) (*continued*)
    ecclesiastical, 149-51
        abuses by, 104
        training of, 147
        cf. 157
    entertainment of, 559*z*
    fees of, 148; cf. 154, 466
    " getting at," 108, 163
    gifts to, 154, 557, 559 cf. 564-5
    itinerant. [See]
    =*proconsules*, 558
    jurisdiction of, bought, 108
    language of, 221
    lose by promotion, 340
    Mapes, W., on, 84*h*
    not to take case in which he
        has been *adv*., 581
    numbers of, 244, 504*a*
    ordinarii, 580
    pictures of, 366, 369
    previously in the case, 177, 571
    professional, 144, 149
    return to bar, 262
    robes of, 358, 365, 369
    training of, 157; cf. 147
    venality of, 163, 237*b*, 556
judgment, form of, 565
judices, wide use of, 35*d*, 98 cf. 531
Juniors, 241 (?), 288, 314, 316*y*,
    318, 329 cf. 339 and 360
" Jurat," 294
jurati electi et triati, 260*u*
jurator(es). Cf. *jurés*, 173*c*, 197*h*,
    450, 451, 480-2, 538
jurés, 387; cf. *jurator*
juris candidati, 256*i*
Juris consultus, 277
    peritus, 322
        consilium of, 559
        sitting as judges, 581
    professor, 150*u*
Jurists apt to moralise, 117
Jurors, Jurours, cf. *Jurator* (1085),
    122, 364, 451
    gifts to, 155*m*, 377*m*, 468*q*,
        480-1
Jury, the,
    agreement of, forced, 155*m* cf.
        173*c*
    Bromyard on, 155
    disagree, 481*l*
    give evidence, 155*m*

C.H.   39

Jury, the (continued)
  "got at," packed, 153, 155m
  imprisoned for ignoring, 173c
  origin of, 122
  packing, 249, 480-1
  special, 18
  trial by, 224
Justiciarius major, 173c
  minor, 173c
Justinian, 21, 88, 407, 420

Kedermister's Inn, 594
Keepers of the Peace, 223
Keleseye Sjt., 240, 334
Kemble cited, 187k, 376
Kent, laws of, 1, 528
King, the,
  attorney of, 201a, 337
  "presence" of, 141u, 200u
  Serjeants of. See "*King's*"
  servientes [See] of.
"King's Counsel," first, 64
"King's Serjeant," 180e, 201, 287d, 332g, 337, 338, 380, 518
Knights of the Shire, first, 457
  Hospitallers, 187h, 195, 324l, 376

Laga Eadwardi, 4l
laicus, i, 55
  choosing *adv.*, 573
  may plead? 578
  not *clericus*, 582d
"landless," the, 6, 7
Lanfranc, 41, 49, 97, 554
Langtoft, P. de, cited, 298y, 347h
Language(s), forensic, 43o, 104, 162-3, 170, 200, 341-55, 579
  Fortescue on, 499
Lambarde, *Arch.*, cited, 542
Lass, 33a, 35, 167, 547, 549
Lateran Council, 158
Latin. See *Language*.
  forensic, 345
    in 1661...348m
    indispensable, 578
  official, 43
  retained by statute, 351
  study of, 505, 510
Laurence (Hubert's), 134q, 171q

Law, Constitutional, 338
  costly, 67t, 480
  demoralising to students, 283l
  not a "liberal" study, 91x
    cf. 151a
  remunerative, 91, 93, 146, 151a, 401, 420, 503
  "student," 308, 423-7
    costs of, 486, 500
  study of, 86, 90, 123, 404
  "the one . . . or the other," 466
Law and fact, 77, 79, 109, 404, 579
Law Officers,
  School, 87-8, 90, 500
Laws of England " declared " in 1070...47-9, 122h, 555
Lawyer(s). See *Adv.*, *Attorney*.
  assigned by Chancellor? 456
  betraying clients [See], 208, 234, 422
  bills of, 380-1
  dearth of, 266-7; cf. 335
  dependence of, 160
  earliest date of (word), 322
  foreign, earliest called in, 65
  in 1200-1300...286
    Parliament, 461-2
  incapable, 238
  minor employments of, 222-3, 267
  oaths of, in City, 248
  practising (1372), 461
  punished. See *Prison*, and cf. 415
  social position of, 355, 371, 380-1, 492
  sue for fees, 263, 377
  sued. See *Attorney*.
  unknown [See], 184u cf. 223
  venality of, 164 (E. I), 479, 556
Laymen. See *laicus*.
  Chancellors, 366
  narratores are, 180
  none against clerics, 59
    cf. 104g
le Mareschal, T., 180, 201, 265
"leaders," 216m, 341; cf. 374f
Leading cases, 510
"learned friend,"; cf. 71z, 108
Legal aid, 19, 584
  expenses See *Costs*.
  gratuitous, 380

INDEX.

legalis, es, etc., 65, 281*e*, 457*g*
Leges Henricus Primi, 4, 32, 43, cf. 408, 531-42
Legislation, anti-lawyer, 456-74, 520
legislator, 322
legista(e), "legist," 91*x*, 94-5, 97; cf. 322*e* and 386-7; 522*g*
legum, -is, doctor, 150*u*
    homo, 322
    peritus, 462
Leicester, 200*s*, 253, 259*p*, 264, 294
Leland cited, 475*q*, 486, 488
lex = law, 65*p*, 482*o*
Lex Cincia, 2*e*
Lex Ribuaria, 538, 546, 552
Lex Salica, 15*o*, 36*h*, 527, 539, 552
libelli, 100*h*, 103*s*, 104, 105, 106, 109
Liber Albus, 226
    date of Pt. I of, 293*h*
    Custumarum, 230
    de Antiquis legibus, 207
    Niger domus regis E. IV, 493*x*
    Pauperum, 90
"Liberal" education, 89, 91, 508 (1440) cf. 124, 151*a*
Liebermann, Dr., cited, 1-19, 528-43, 561
    his scheme of *servientes*, 325*m*
Lincoln, 202, 207*z*, 265
Lincoln's Inn, 320 cf. 435*m*, 446, 448, 591
    excludes Irishmen, 277
Literate laymen, 505*e*
Litigant in person, 60, 81, 516
Litigation,
    abuses of, 193
    costly, 67*t*, 76, 77, 83, 118, 154*f*
    duration of, 84, 557
    fomented by lawyers, 146*l*, 305
Littleton J., 194
    Tenures of, 93
Liveries, 367*h*, 376*l*, 379*b*, 465, 503
Livy cited, 11*y*, 16*r*, 352*x*
Local names of representatives, 172*u*, 522*g*
"Locals," 202, 235*w*, 266; cf. 267
Lokton J., 187, 300, 377*m*
Lombard law, 552

London, 224
    Charters (1131), 60*u*
    (1268), 207
    "Commune," 123
"Long robe," 356, 366*c*, 368
Longchamp, W. de, 92, 404
Lord and man, 19, 544
    Court of, 405. See *Courts, inferior*.
    Steward, 183*p*
"Lords, my." See *domini*.
Louis VIII, 409
Louis, St. (IX), 404, 406, 410, 587
Louther, Hugh de, 186
Luchaire cited, 37, 386
lucrandum vel perdendum, 75*o*, 85*o*, 86, 135
Lucrativeness of law [See *Fees*] cf. 34*d*
Lydgate, 475, 484-6
    cited, 260
Lyon's Inn, 591

Macworth's Inn, 589
Magister, 87*a*, 89, 196, 197*h*, 202, 357, 434 (1438), 507*k*, 508
    = in orders? 436*q*
Magna Charta, 123, 349*n*
Magnus cited, 221*d*, 416*a*
Maine, Sir H., cited, 15, 17
mainpast, 10
"Maintenance," 9, 191, 465-8, 523
"Maintainors," 132*o*, 237*c*, 457-8, 461, 477, 493*u*
Maitland cited, 1, 7, 14*k*, 16*r*, 20, 28, 30, 101, 130, 204, 210, 212; *passim*
"make law," 141*u*, 294
Malberg Gloss, 15, 16
malpractices (1350), 458
"Man of (the) Law," 322, 460, 484
man-bot, 8, 542
Manciple, *mancipium*, 494, *Addenda*, 592
mandamus, 229*j*
mandatarius, 35, 35*d*, 416
mandatum, 136
Mapes, Walter, 73*h*, 84*h*, 163*h*
Marculf, *formulae* of, 547, 550
Maritime Assises de Jérusalem, 421*q*
    Mediterranean law, 421*q*

C.H.   39*

Markham C.J., 521
Master of the Rolls, 431
Masters
  in Chancery, 30
      earliest, 437*q*
      pictures of, 366
  of Courts, pictures of, 367
" Maunciple," 494, *Addenda*
" Meat and drink," 466*m*. See *Food*.
" Mediators," 417
" Men of (the) court," 432, 521
" Men of (the) law, 235*w*, 322*e* cf. 223*r*, 460
Menko, 89
Merton, Council of (1236), 424
      Statute of, 140
Middle Inn, 448*f*, 592
      Temple, 448, 591
miles (*-ites*) *legalis* [see], 150*u*, 295*p*
        literatus, (*-i*) [S e e d'Amory], 150*u*, cf. 51*n*, 122*i*, 184
milites, 149*s*
" Ministers " holding pleas, 351
ministri causae, 513
Minors, 14, 28, 225, 405, 538, 551
" Mirror of Justices," 134*t*, 151, 189, 193, 230, 278-9
  verses in, 319
miscravatio, 15, 534
misdemeanours, 211
miserabiles personae, 24*v*, 28, 158, 405, 547-8, 551, 572, 581
Miskenning, 52, 206-8 cf. 289 and 405, 534
mislocutio, 15, 16, 534
missi, 37, 122*i*, 549
Mistake of *adv.*, 405
      supernaturally explained, 14, 17
Modus levandi fines, *Addenda*
Monasteries,
  advv. of, 24*q*
  lawsuits of, 45. See *Trials*.
  lawyers in, 45, 48, 378
  litigious, 377*m*
Money, value of, early, 375*g*, 380
Monks, not to be *advv.*, 552, 568
      secular, 45*u*, 48
" Moot(s)," 312
      at Oxford, 90

Moroni cited, 25, 355*i*, 356*k*, 362*h*
Moyle, Sjt., 378, 467
mund, 23, 545
Murimuth cited, 150*u*
" My lords," 55, 73*g*; cf. 199
" Sire), 209 cf. 222

Narracio, 170*o*, 172*u* cf. 43*o*
Narrator(*es*), 169-82, 322 cf. 163*l*, 205
  called *servv.*, 179*e*
  communis, 242*o*
      in City, 252
  (1288-9), 240
  die out, 180*i*, 327
  disavowed, 198
  laymen, 180
  not mentioned, 176, 189, 216
  pro d. *rege*, 332*g*
New Inn, 592
      Temple, 591
Nigellus Wireker, 70*z*, 166
nobiles, nobiliores, 450, 501*t*
" noble and learned," 15*u*
Non - professional representatives [see]
Norman Conquest, effects of, 39, 112
Normandy, Normans, 29, 402, 411-4
      discourage English? 341
  English influence on, 38, 131, 414
  " Englishmen," 350
  French views of, 38*t*, 40
  Law School in, 95
North, Roger, cited, 327*
Northampton, Assize of, 123
Norwich, 235*w*, 252, 263
      Charter, 182*p* cf. 123*l*, 265
notaire, 133*oo*
notarius, -i, 37, 100*h*, 546, 556, 565
      prae-, 430. See *proto-*
Notary, the, 167-9
  forerunner of Solicitor, 100*h*
  in Chancery, 303 (1344) 132*o*
  London, at, 167*c*, 228
  Winchester, at, 379
Novae Narraciones, 93
Novum Templum, 428*h*. See *Temple*.
Numbers of *att.* [see]
      lawyers, 522

INDEX. 613

nuntius, 71, 142, 168, 172*u*, 403, 577
    specialis, 133*o*, 172*u*

Oath-helpers, 531
Oaths, 245-51; cf. 557
    Books of, 247*m*, 250*y*, 438*y*
    of *advocati*, 564; cf. 26-7
      apprenticii, none, 511
      attorneys, 234*v*
      avantparlier, 393*g*
      avocats, 410
      Chancery clerks (1344-6), 438, 440
      Continental *advv.* (1230), 393, 420
      Countors, 233, 250
      defendant, 557, 564
      narratores, 254
      plaintiff, 557, 564
      propter calumniam, 97, 557
      Recorder of City, 245
      Roman (eccl.) *adv.*, 26-7
      serjeants, 337, 380, 502, 517-8
occasio, 229, 536
occasionari, 207
Occleeve. See *Hoccleeve*.
" Official, the," 109*k*
officina brevium, 30
    justitiae, 437
Oleron, 421*q*
Olim, les, 409*n*, 414*x*
" Opening " the case, 568-9
Opinion(s) differing, 86*r*
    on case, 216
" Or other " [see]
Oral pleading, 204
Orator, 287 cf. 319 and 338*b*, 414, 566
Oratore, de, cited, 16*r*, 338*b*
Ordeal, 14, 23
    abolished, 123
Order in court, 189*n* cf. 221*e*, 231*q*
    of H. III, 423
    1388...303*s*, 304, 439
Ordericus Vitalis cited, 41, 49, 61, 342, 344
Orders, 143
    lawyers in, 151

Ordinance of City [see]
    1311...453*t*
    1356...85*m*, 235*w*
    1388...243*t*, 439
    E. IV, 493*z*
    royal (1292), 281, 284, 302, 314-5
Ordo Judiciarius, O. J., 94-101
Ordonnance of 1254...588
Organ, John, case of, 283, 306-11
" Original " writ, 102, 125, 144, 500, 513, 562, 595
orphanotrophus, 405
" Other," " Other Pleaders," 189, 195, 330*b*, 351
Otho, Card., 103, 571
Otto Papiniensis, 97
Our Lady Inn, 591
Outer Temple, 494-5
Oxford, 86, 88*e*, 89, 91*x*, 94, 101-2, 103*s*
    French at, 350*q*
    H. III favours, 425
    Irish at, 277*m*
    law books at, 506
    lawyers at, 24*r*, 65
      titles of, 161, 265, 456*e*
      (1430-40), 505, 522
    Provision of (1258), 202*n*, 208, 342, 349*n*
Owen, Sir R., 490*n*

Pandects, 407, 420
" panell," 481
Pan(n)ormia, 94
Papal *breve*, 103
    Courts, 76-9, 120 cf. 169
Paris, lawyers at, 92, 404
    University of, 92, 404, 501
Paris, Matthew, 170
Parliament asks lawyers' opinion, 336
    in provinces, 459
    lawyers in, 124, 220*z*, 316, 456-63
Party in person, 229, 324 (?), 328, 516
Parvise, 489, 504
Paston, Will., J., 261, 265
    Serjt., 378
    will of, 508

614 INDEX.

Pastons, the, 472
    Letters of, 268
patria = country [see], 450
    = county, 459
patrocinator, 36 cf. 373
Patron Saint, 221
patronus, p. causarum, 11, 18, 19, 27, 36, 146, 414, 418*f*, 557
    and client [see], 544
Paul's, St., 489*l*
pauperistae, 90*u*
Pearson, C. H., cited, 43
Penalties, 198*k*
Pennenden Heath, trial, 51
perorator, 11, 533
perplacitare, 324*k*
persequi, 134*r*, 286. See *sequitur*.
petens = plaintiff, 119*a*, 561
Peter of Blois, 120, 145, 374, 560
Petitions, E. I, 349
    1363...319*p*, 469*s*
    1364-5...266
    1372...459
    1402...319
    1406...319, 468
    1415...267
    1432...333
    1439...333*n*
    1451...333
    1453...(1) 304
        (2) 305
Philip of Novara, 112-3
Philip of Novara, 112, 387, 407
Piers Plowman, 363
Phraseology, forensic, 70*z*
Pillius, 95, 98
Pinchebek, W., 260 cf. 489
Placentinus, 97, 404, 407
Placitator(es), 59, and *p*
    and *att. reg.*, 269
    disqualified, 586
    not to be M.P., 458
    officer, 131*l*
    = party, 60*u*, 411-2
    prohibited, 140, 558
placito, sine, 64*l*
placitor, 60*s*, 131*l*
placitum, -a [See *Ordinance*], 11, 59, 60*u*
    aule, 183*p*
    not put in force, 284

placitum, -a (continued)
    regia, 57
Plautus cited, 544
" pleader " = party *or* advocate, 391
Pleading, abuse of, 395
    early, 52, 125, 203, 238
    regulated, 205
Pleadings, 66, 98*f*, 110, 247
    " coloured," 78
    language of, 346, 534
    nicety in, 14, 15, 16, 117, 181, 204, 328, 534 cf. 289 and 395
    written, 125, 205*t*, 211, 352
Pleas of the Crown, 123
" Pledge," 2, 7
pledour, 310
Plowman's Tale, 493*u*
Policraticus, 87*y*, 116, 155
Poll Tax (1379), 464
ponere loco, 86
    suo, 75*o* cf. 72, 73*q*, 127*a*
Poor persons, defence of, 175 cf. 221*d*, 247, 248
    suitors. See *mis. pers.*
Pope, the, as judge, 76, 102*p*, 117, 121 cf. 569*e*
    ex-practising lawyer, 406
positiones, 98*f*, 100*h*, 103*s*, 110
" Practising " in 1372...461
praelocutor, 172*u*, 386, 415*a*
praepositus, 60, 263
    hundredi, 191*s*
praevaricatus adv., 558, 571
Precedent books, 509
Preston, G. de, 156
primicerius defensor, 25, 33
principales of Inn of Chancery, 441
principalis = *dominus*, 562, 564
Prison, lawyers sent to, 209-10, 287; cf. 289, 335
Prisot J., 456, 524
Private practice of Crown lawyers, 379
Procedure. See *Civil, Eccl.*
    early, 18, 22, 39*y*, 51, 61
    English, origin of, 106
    of *curia regis*, 105
    technical, 14
Processions, lawyers in, 259-60, 369

INDEX.   615

proconsules = itinerant justices, 558
Proctors, 109*k*
Procurator, -*es*, 35, 36*f*, 59*q*, 109,
  132*o*; cf. 154*k*, 565; cf. 577,
  579-82
  abuses by, 104*u*
  advocati, 100*h*
  attornatus, 130*l*
  Brunner on, 136
  ecclesiastical, 36*f*, 76, 106. 132*o*,
    377*m*, 464
  et advocatus, 73, 132*o*
  excommunicated, 81
  French, 133*oo*, 406, 409*n*
  generalis, 132*o*, 187*k*
  German, 416
  lay, 150*u*
  legitimus, 81
       not, 81
  = M.P., 132*o*, 463
  oath of, 565
  Oxford at, 522*g*
  primarius, 59*q*, 63*i*
  regni, 84*h*
  = *responsalis*, 126, 132*o*
  retained, 132*o*
  saecularis, 132*o*
  Spanish, 420*o*
  sufficiens, 71
Procuratour, 278 cf. 387, 464
  = attorney, 132*o*, 133*o*, 169, 259*p*
Procuratrix = informer, 133*o*
procureur, 128*c*, 133*oo*, 400
" procurour," 128*c*, 480*f*
prodeshommes, 231
professio claustralis, 149*r*
Profession(s)
  each distinct, 232
       recognised (E. II), 257
  origin (alleged) of, 63
              in Spain, 420
Professional lawyers
  in L. H. P., 5, 540
  1162-70...88
  none before 1066...28, 43
Prohibition, royal, 107
              writ of, 80, 103*s*,
              575
Prolocutor, 5, 171*q*, 386, 411-2, 415,
  542

Promotion
  to bench (Continental), 26*b* cf. 34
  from bar, 157, 185, 220,
    222
  of " King's Attorney,"
    201*a*
prosecutor, 36, 377*m*
prosequi of laymen, 276*ff*
persequitur, 286
Protection by the lord, *protector*, 7,
  45-6, 415
Protonotator (notary), 168*c*, 211, 367
Provinces, the, 220, 262
  serjeants in, 302*q* cf. 348, 459
Proxy, letters of, 139
Prynne, 459
Pucelle, Gerard, 72, 73
pugna = *lis*, 34
pulchre placitando, 207
Pulling's *Attornies*, 326*p*
          Order of the Coif, 184
" puny utter barrister," 522*g*
pur son donant, 192 cf. 203

Q(*uadripartitus*), 4, 161
" questmongers," 451
              questour,   476,
              480-2
Qui sequitur, 180*e*, 183*p*, 215, 245
" Quibbles," 112
Quibbling, 206
Quisquis vult esse causidicus, 588

rationare, 549
Rayner of Perugia, 76*q*, 94*h*, 100*h*,
  167*y*
razonar, 421*q*, 549
" Readers," 449
" Reasoner," 421*q*
" Recognition," 123, 144 cf. 387*d*
Recorder(s)
  of the City, 244, 314
              salary of, 246
  Serjeants? 592
Records destroyed, 451*o*
Rede, Sjt., 365
redemptor litis, 558, 564
referendarii, 26
Refresher, 77, 377, 556
Regenbald, 29

616 INDEX.

regionarii, 25z, 26
Registrum Brevium, 93, or *Cancellariae*, 188
relatores, 163
Remuneration [See *Fees*], 371-82
  bad, 334, 453
  early legislation on, 98f, 107, 333
  gradual, 414-5
  in *Mirror of Justices*, 279
  of Serjeants, 231, 233, 333-4
renaissance juridique, 399x
Renovacio, 303s, 438y, 439a
Reporting, 490l, 491-2
Representation,
  advocatus's view of, 73g
  compulsory, 229j, 415
  first (?) authorised in England, 85
  ignored, 226, 227
  in Pleas of the Crown, 229-30
  origin of, 29, 192
  principle, theory of, 85, 136, 573
Representatives. See *Code*.
  authority of, varies, 533
  incapable, 231
  non-professional, 195-8, 199o, 229, 230 cf. 231, 232, 238, 258, 278-9, 310, 414, 418, 420o
  numbers of, on one side. See *Atts.*, *Serjt.*, and cf. 420
  various titles of, 35-6, 100h, 132o
    at Oxford (1300), 161e
    (1448), 132o, 522g
respondere, 126, 139m, 403
responsalis, 8q, 71, 88g, 126, 580
  early *attornatus*, 86, 126, 134
  in Bracton, 142
  sufficiens, 85o, 142y; cf. 291y, 580
Retainers, 132o, 146h, 153, 288p, 300, 323 cf. 347g, 377
  (1446), 381h
  (1453), 467q
  (1501), 380e
  by *att.*, 327
  general, earliest, 242
  in the City, 242, 246, 253
  of *att.*, 290
    consiliarius, 323
  of counsel by attorney, 326p

reus, 76q
" Rhetoric " in the Temples, 487f
Ricardus Anglicus, 99, 563-5
Richard I, 342, 347
  of St. Ives, 172u, 265
    the Redeles, 318, 361
Rings of sjts., 479, 502
Robert of Gloucester cited, 343
Robes not to att., 333
  of Judges, 54, 333o, 379
  Recorder of City, 247
  Serjeants, 333o, 379
Rogers, Thorold, cited, 77r, 277m, 374, 505f
Rolf Sjt., 319, 365
Rolle of Hampole, 331, 361g
Rolls, of *attornati*, 276h, 335
  tampering with, 218
  the, 484
Roman *advocati*, 76, 77r, 149t, 567
    disappear, 399
  influence, theories of, 20, 21m
  Law copied, 101k
    in England, 19, 21, 22, 65, 103 cf. 399
    Oxford, 506
  lawyers' style imitated, 88-9
Rome. See *Appeal*.
  Church of, 21
    courts of, 22
    prohibits a judgeship, 149
  Law School at, 94h
  mediaeval, 23
  republican, 29
Round cited, 29, 57, 182p, 245f, 423
Run und Rate, 417
Ruota, the, 25x, 27b

Sachsenspiegel, 402, 417, 527
Sacol, 45
Sages et apris de la leye, 223
  gents, 191
St. George's Inn, 592
  Ives, 263
  Ivonius (Yvo), 221d
  Louis, 404
  Paul's, 423, 489l
salarium, 107, 146, 374, 560, 563

INDEX. 617

Salic Law, 15*o*, 16, 36*h*, 527
sapientes (A.-Saxon), 555
sapienza, the, 356
scabinii [See *échevins*], 37, 168*g*, 401, 551
schöffe, 34*d*
scholas frequentare, 73, 87*b*
scholastici, 28, 36*h*
Schools of Law, 87, 91*x*, 94*h*, 95, 99*h*, 170*n*, 423
Schwabenspiegel, 402, 417
" Scientiam," 405
Scots lawyers, 367*g*
Screen, W., 449
scrinarius, 118, 556
Scrop(e), Geoffrey le, 183, 253*s*, 287, 329, 330, 375
   Harry le, J., 288
   's Inn, 339*g*, 592
secta, *sectatores*, 301
Secular. See *civil*.
Seal, Keepers of, 168*g*
Seat only for Bench, 96*x*, 232, 264, 271, 572
Selden on Abingdon lawyers, 47
   Chaucer, 487
   de laudibus, 341*o*
   Order of H. III, 423
senescallus, 72, 131*l*, 134*q*, 190*q*, 359
sequi, 138, 142, 286*t*
sequitur pro [See *persequi*, *qui s.*], 185, 201, 288; cf. 234*w*
   rege . . . coram rege, 329
Serfs, Anglo-Saxon, 6
sergeaunt de ley, 253
serjancius, 187*g*; cf. 217*n*
serjaunt not=lawyer, 457, 461*s*
Serjeant(s), *Sergantes*
   appointment of, compulsory.
   See " *King's*," *Serviens*; cf. 502
   assigned by court, 516
   attorney, 329 cf. 128*f*
   avowed by *att.*, 297
   betraying clients, 234 cf. 335 and 373
   =catchpole, 296
   Chancery, of? 434
   Commissioner. [See]
   compulsory for client, *Addenda*

Serjeant(s), *Sergantes* (continued)
   countour, 230, 253 cf. 493
   course of, professional, 511, 515
   dearth of, 218 cf. 335, 266, 338
   decline to advise, 337-8
   demeanour of, in court, 220, 232 cf. 401*d*, 408, 520
   distinguished from "advocates," 21
      attorneys, 21
   feasts of, 339, 502, 592
   Fortescue on, 499, 502
   gifts of, 479
   in Eyre, 302*q* cf. 592
   judges have been, 368, 503
   " King's." [See]
   " le Roy " [See " *King's* "], 217*m*, 319
   " leading," 216*m*, 341 cf. 374*f*
   litigant must have? 515*r*, *Addenda*
   not in Inns, 510
   oath of. [See]
   " of the county," 457 cf. 459
   " office " of, " at the bar," 340
   opinion of, collectively taken, 219-20
   originally had no special Inn, 593
   paid well, 503
   pictures of, 366
   precedence of, 473
   privileges of, 575
   retained, 378. See *Retainers*.
   servile, 239
   socii, 219
   suable. See *Servientes*.
   taxed, 464-5
   temporary judge, 233, 592
   unknown [See], 251*b*
   work of, 491
Serjeanties, 182*p*, 457 cf. 461*s*
Serjeants' Inns, 592
Serviens (-*tes*) [See *Serjeant*], 182-223, 322
   ad legem, Manning's, 182*p*
      first in 1310...188
   leges, 332, 335, 340*l*
   and *attornatus* [See], 329, 333
   appointment of, 188, 339
   called *narrator* [See], 180
      in City, 252

618 INDEX.

Serviens (*-tes*) (*continued*)
Communis. [See]
costume of, 355
duty of, out of court, 192x
fees of. [See]
hundredi, 123, 191s
in *curia regis*, 154
inferior officials, 182p, 185a, 285e, 300i
" King's." [See]
languages, know, 200
law, dealt with, by, 210 cf. 512
litigant must have? 515r, *Addenda*
more than one, 216-7 cf 288, 328
nostri, 335u
not a lawyer? 323
mentioned, 445
oath of. [See]
of the party, 241k
Ordinances, etc. [See], concerning
privilege of. See *suable* below.
provinces [See], in the
regis [See, and " *King's* "], 182 cf. 196
ad legem, first, 187
suable, 334
where, 186b, 477, 515
unwilling to be, 339-40
varieties of, 325m
writ appointing, 188, 502
Serviens regis [See *King* and " *King's* "], 54, 64, 123, 182
as official, 191s
not in City documents, 230
Sharshull J., 363
Sheriffs = *viscontes*, 480, 481l
in City, 212x
Courts of, 231, 234, 373
Court, 54, 57, 64
influence of, 521
Parliament, 460
Siete Partidas, 419-22
Silk, 363-4
" Simony," 571
" Sin " = offence, 336

sine peccato, 98f
placito. [See]
Sitting, right of. See *Seat*.
Six Clerks' Inn, 594
Smith, Sir T., cited, 469
Social relations of lawyers, 521
Socius, (*-i*) = fellow (of Inn), inmate, 448c, 501, 510
of judges, 122i, 128f, 158, 190r, 223r, 271
servientes, 179, 219
" locals," 235w
socn, soke, 9, 536
(hamsocn), 533, 537
soinus, 561
Solicitor, 133oo
-General, 332g
modern and Bar, 326p
name (1469), 332g
or attorney? 285; cf. 100h
Solidarity of the Bar, 219, 477
Southampton, English at, 345b, 353
Spain, 418-23
Special jury, 18, 559z
" Specials," early, 269
speculum juris, 406
" Squire " [See " *Esquire* "], 522g
Stand, adv. must, 96x, 232, 564, 571
Staple Inn, 446, 593
stare cum, 202, 241
" State Trials " (1289-93), 173c, 296r
Statements of claim, 109, 574, 575. See *libelli*.
Statuta et Consuetudines Normanniae, 411r
Statutes,
1224-5, Magna Carta, 425
1235-6, Merton, 140, 301
1267? Exchequer, 349
Marlborough, 208
1275, Westminster I, 189, 208e, 236, 239, 258o, 298, 336y, 348, 511x
cc. 27-8...332
29...301
33...289
1278, Gloucester, 302
1285, Westminster II, c. 1, *de Donis*, 490l
c. 10...291
c. 24...437

Statutes (*continued*)
  1290? *Modus levandi fines*, Addenda
  1292, *de Consp.*, 190
  [1292, Ordinance : see]
  1299, *Ord. de Libertat. perquir.*, 291*y*
  1322(?) *De Fin. et Att.*, 298
  1328, Northampton, 223*q*
  1331, c. 11...457
  1336-7...468
  1346...261, 466*m*
    Oath of Chancery Clerks, 438, 517
  1349, etc., of Labourers, 270
  1362-3...318, 349*o*, 350, 469
  1372...460,
  1377...465
  1384, c. 2...459
      c. 3...201
  1385...332*f*
  1389...465
  1393-4...267
  1399...466
  1402...283, 303
  1405...466
  1429...466
  1430...462
  1432...333*n*
  1433...481*c*
  1455...268
  1460...336*y*
  1463...469*s*
  1482-3...469*s*
Staunton, H. de, J., 151, 359
Stephen, King, and the City, 206
  J. F., cited, 14*i*
Stilus Curiae Parliamenti, 114*r*
Stolen property, 2, 528-30
Strand Inn, 589
Stubbs, Bishop,
  on Anglo-Saxon society, 6
    closing of the schools, 424
    early forensic procedure, 22, 51, 61
    Flambard, 58
    language in Courts, 43*o*
    legislation against lawyers, 461
    Norman Conquest, 39, 42
Students [See *Apprenticii*], 423-7
Studium generale, 86

Stulta responsio, 206*y*
Stulti loquium, 209*j*
Subjectus. See *dominus*.
Substitut, 413
Suffragari, 532
Summa Rufini, 404
    de legibus consuetudinum Normanniae, 411*r*
"Summons for directions," 303, 445*s*
Sumptuary laws, 465-9
  (1363), 319
  (1406), 319, 366*c*, 371, 468
  regulations (Chcy. Clerks), 440
Surety, 2, 7, 23
Suspension, 571
Syndici = defensores, 100*h*, 580

Tabard, 365, 368*m*
tabelliones (-atus), 167*y*, 169
Tacitus cited, 356*k*, 544
Tancred, 98
Taxation, 81, 100*h*, 197*h*
  of lawyers, 464-5, 478
Technicality,
  generally, 14, 15, 117-8, 125, 166, 204*p* cf. 419*i*, 524, 586
  verbal [See *Grammar*], 429*o*, 581
Templars Inn, 449*h*, 495
Temple, a, 494
  severance of the, 491-2, Addenda
  The "New," 428, 591
  "Old," 436*n*
  Bar, 320, 449*h*, 450
  Club, 453
tena(e), 360, 361, 364
"Tenant by serjeanty," 457
"Terms," 489, 490*l*
Testa de Nevill, 183*p*
Testes, 51*r*, 83*d*, 531, 565
Text book, first, 84
Textus Roffensis, 49*g*
Thavies Inn, 447, 591, 593
Theobald, Abp., 65
Theodosian Code, 22
Thierry cited, 401
Third parties intervene, 212

Thomas of **Marlborough**, 75, 373
Thomastown, 206
Tilton (Ty-), 186, 195
tippet, 368
Tirwhit J., 454*y*
toga, 356
togati, 36*h*
Tonsure, 358, 359
tornare, 128
Toud(th)eby, Sjt., 329
" Tracers," 481
Trent, Council of, 405
Très Ancien Coutumier (de Normandie), 42, 130, 411*r*
Trevisa cited, 343
Trial by jury, 346, 481*l*
Trials,
  Anglo-Saxon, 317
  at Rome, 33, 76-8
  counsel, with or without, 62-83
  friends of parties at, 12
  in London, 270
  mentioned :
    Abingdon, Abbot of *v.* Officers of the King (about 1087), 46
    Armagh, Abp. of *v.* Theo. de Verdoun (1302), 280
    Ballingham *v.* Burghill (1313), 214
    Battel Abbey cases (1150?-1176), 71
    Belisme, R. 's, case (1102), 55*e*
    Bennett *v.* Hale (1850), 326*p*, 359*s*
    Bricstan's case (about 1115), 61, 172*z*, 344
    Canterbury, Abp. of *v.* Abp. of York (abt. 1070), 50
      v. Bp. of Rochester (1253), 198, 200
      v. Odo of Bayeux (1071), 49-50
    Cantok, T. *v.* de Wyche, R. (1294), 196
    le Coffer, T. *v.* de la Rose, A. (1300), 240, 378
    d'Anesty, R. 's, case (1158-63), 372
    de Luci, G. *v.* Abbot Odo (bef. 1097), 52

Trials, mentioned (*continued*)
    Durham, Bp. of, case of (1088), 11, 52, 182, 183
    Ermenold *v.* Abb. Faritius (H. I), 60*s*
    Evesham, Abbey of *v.* Worcester, Bp. of (1202-5), 75
    Exeter, Bp. of, 's case (1278), 286
    Farfa, Abb. of *v.* St. Eustachio (998), 33
    Faritius, Abbot *v.* Nigel d'Oyly (abt. 1100), 11
    Flambard *v.* Anselm (1093), 60
    Lanfranc *v.* Odo (1071), 49-50
    Latimer, Ld., impeachment of (1377), 217
    Lutone Church, case of (1164), 71
    Meaux, Abbey of, cases of (1249-69), 62*c*, 79-85 (1358), 270, 377*m*
    Modbert *v.* Prior, etc., of Bath (1121), 62
    Odo *v.* Church of Canterbury (abt. 1090), 52
    Paston *v.* Genney Sjt. (1471), 515
    R. *v.* W. Borill (1313), 214
    Ramsey, Abbey of, case of (1165), 17
    St. Augustine's (Cant.), Abbot of *v.* Thanet (1198), 75
    St. Edmund's, Abbot of *v.* Bp. of Thetford (1076-9), 57
    St. Fountain's, Abbot of, case of (1313), 61*c*
    Somerton's Case (1433), 334
    Stephen, King, case of, 63
    Tavistock, Abbot of, case of (1096), 60
    Wheeler *v.* Huchynden (R. II), 270*p*
    Wykeham, W. of, impeachment of (1377), 217
  State [E. I]. [See]
Trilingual lawyers, 354, 475
  proclamation, 342
Trusts, 106

INDEX. 621

tuitio, 9
Turstan, 134, 138
tutor, 9, 14, 16, 548
Twelve Tables, the, 17

Ulpianus *de edendo*, 95
Umpire, 522*g*, 580
universitas, 226, 580
Universities, early influence of, 124, 504
Unknown lawyers, 184*u*, 202, 240*g*, 265, 269, 323, 374*f*, 376*k*
Unlearned Parliament, 462
Urse of Abetot, 54, 182
Unprofessional conduct, 568, 571
Ushers (*janitores*), 164 cf. 546
Utriusque juris, doctor, 98*d*
" Utter Barrister," 364, 451*r*, 522*g*

Vacarius, 64*l*, 65, 344
    banished? 424*z*
Vacations, 266
Vadlet, 251*f*
Variance [See *Pleading(s)*], 204
Vassalism, 536
Vavasores, 61
Venality of lawyers [See *Judges*], 36*z* cf. 459, 117, 118, 120
Verbalism [See *Grammar*,"*Word*,"], 416, 429*o*, 534 cf. 560
vicecomes, 60, 559
    adv. sits for, 553
vice dominus, 26
vicomte [See *Sheriff*]=judge, 401
victu et vestitu, 430
villani, 7
Violence to bar [See *Demeanour*], 455, 513 cf. 454*y*
Vocabulary, legal, 29, 354
Vormund, 4, 539
Vorsprech(er), 3*k*, 4, 136, 416, 417, 539, 543
Vouching to warranty, 2*c*, 5, 527
    instance of, 264

" Wage " law, 304
" Wages " of King's advisers, 337

Wahrmund, Prof., 99*h*, 418
Walter, Hubert, 84*h*, 149, 156*o*
    of Henley, 128*d*
Walworth, Sir W., books of, 507
Warrant, warrantor, -y [See *advocare*], 2, 5, 8, 10, 264, 527, 528-9
    not a pleader, 422*q*
Wat Tyler's rising, 364, 450
Waterford, 207
Waterhous on Fortescue, 424*y*
Waylond J., 157, 184
Weiszler, A., cited, 35*d*, 416*a*, 417*c*
Welsh, disabilities of, 269
wer-gild, 8, 543, 547
Westminster Hall (1400), 478, 484, 489*l*
Whitelocke, Bulstrode, cited, 185*b*, 188*i*, 459, 490*n*
Wigmore, Prof.'s, translation of Brunner, 3*k*
William I, synod of (1070), 555
    Rufus, 57-9
    of Drogheda, 79, 94, 101-12, 161
        effect of in France, 407
        on *advocatus*, 566-79
        fees, 374
        procurators, 579-82
        robes, 357*p*
    Exeter, 287-8
    Langley, 288
Winchester College, lawyers of, 222*o*, 379
Winner and Waster cited, 362
Witan, the, 555*s*
Witness(es). See *Testes*.
    action, 62*e*
    French (1190), 401
    in 1290 sworn and examined, 296*t*
    1300...211
Woman *advocata*, 249
    attorney, 134
    pleader, 422
Worcestershire, writ to, 62
" Word for word," 204*p* cf. 416
Words. See *Verbalism*.

Writ(s). See *Attornatus*.
   (1275) 457*g*
   Abingdon's, 554
   cost of, 430*o*
   framing of, 437
   mistakes in, 429
   multiply, 193 cf. 210
   " office " of, 30, 124
Writing, 16, 30 cf. 115
Written law, 16-7, 123
      absence of, 115
      pleadings, 125, 205*t*, 211, 352

Wycliffe, 523*k*

Year Books, 93, 210
      earliest mention of, 509
      printed, 186
      origin of, 312, 509
      reporter in, 293*i*
      tone of, 459, 362*k*
Yelverton J., 472*c*, 521
York, 207*z*